THE KOREAN WAVE:
A SOURCEBOOK

THE KOREAN WAVE: A SOURCEBOOK

EDITED BY
YUN MI HWANG
STEPHEN EPSTEIN

THE ACADEMY OF KOREAN STUDIES PRESS

The Korean Wave: A Sourcebook

Published in April 2016
Published by The Academy of Korean Studies Press
Edited by Yun Mi Hwang and Stephen Epstein
Translated by Jamie Chang, Chris Dykas, Amber Kim, Sora Kim-Russell, and
Eunji Mah

The Academy of Korean Studies Press
323 Haogae-ro, Bundang-gu, Seongnam-si, Gyeonggi-do, 13455, Korea
Phone: 82-31-708-5360
E-mail: akspress@aks.ac.kr
Homepage: book.aks.ac.kr

This work was supported by the Academy of Korean Studies Grant
(AKSR2013-H05)

ISBN 979-11-5866-049-9 93300

Printed in Korea

Contents

Preface

As I write this preface, CNN is reporting that PSY's "Gangnam Style" music video has surpassed two billion views on *YouTube* to claim a stellar global milestone. Across Asia, HB Entertainment's K-drama *My Love from the Star* is garnering top ratings and creating consumer stampedes for whatever luxury products the characters showcase, such as Jimmy Choo shoes. Kimchi has emerged as an eagerly sought superfood in global cuisine that is stocked in mainstream grocery stores such as Walmart in the United States. Park Chan-wook's *Oldboy* is a rite of passage for anyone who claims to be a true cinephile and a restorative tonic for those tired of Hollywood predictability. These are just some of the head-turning global manifestations of the *Hallyu* phenomenon.

We all have our own story of how we first encountered *Hallyu*; mine dates back to 1999. I was in Paris conducting dissertation research on Hong Kong action cinema and teaching at the University of Paris IV—Sorbonne and the American University of Paris. A half-page newspaper article in *The International Herald Tribune* announcing the arrival of South Korea's first Hollywood-style big-budget action film surprised me: Kang Je-gyu's *Shiri* was South Korea's most expensive film and set new box office records. A little while later, *The New York Times* also reported that while James Cameron's *Titanic* had conquered each and every national box office, the film failed to unseat *Shiri* from its top position in South Korea. These events made me realize that South Korea's cultural paradigm had undergone a dimensional shift of epic proportions.

Before *Shiri*, life as a diasporic Korean was rather odd; even Koreans found Korean culture wanting and difficult to explain to someone outside the Korean bloodline. While many non-Asians knew of China and Japan, only rarely would those I encountered know anything about Korea or be able to locate it on a map. South Korea's existence as a nation is due to the US military's intervention in the Korean War under a United Nations Command that involved combat forces from a total of 15 countries and humanitarian assistance from 5 more in a "police action." Without America's military leadership and might, North Korea's armed forces would have succeeded in unifying the Korean Peninsula by force. Given this history, there is an amnesia effect at play, with the Korean War becoming known as the "Forgotten War" where no one wanted to "die for a tie," and South Korea becoming the "Forgotten Nation." *Hallyu* reverses this disruption in remembrance by transforming South Korea from the "Forgotten Nation" into the "Unforgettable Nation."

We all also have our own stories of how this initial encounter with *Hallyu* had a ripple effect across media platforms and created new social relationships.

I viewed *Winter Sonata* in one sitting thanks to the DVD set, purchased a CD of the original soundtrack, wondered at the Yonsama craze in Japan, and embraced the popularization of a gentler side to Korean masculinity. I also became a big fan of Kim Gun-mo, purchasing his entire discography. His music video for "Swallow," as in the bird, is especially poignant, with Koreans dressed in Yi Dynasty clothing while singing and dancing to hip-hop. All of a sudden, the traumas of past military dictatorships, the rigidity of Neo-Confucianism, and the excesses of evangelical Christianity were displaced by a new assertion of revitalized freedom and individual expression.

Hallyu made non-Koreans take notice, and these *Hallyu* aficionados desired to become cultural Koreans. When I first taught Korean cinema at Illinois State University in 2001, I began with Im Kwon-taek's *Sopyonje*. I chose this film because it embodied a classical Korean perspective that contradicted the cultural norms of my American students. Nevertheless, my students connected with the film, and some went so far as to state with conviction that the film spoke to them in a manner that no previous Hollywood film had ever done. A few went even further to say that due to this cinematic encounter they felt more Korean than American. This was not an isolated phenomenon, but one that was increasingly reported all over the globe. Because of *Hallyu* there has been an uptick in non-Koreans learning Korean, traveling to Korea, taking romantic interest in Koreans, and even undertaking cosmetic surgery to look Korean.

How *Hallyu* manifested across different media platforms, countries, and phases is explained in this sourcebook. In it you will encounter the government white papers, case studies, media reports, and invisible synergies involved as *Hallyu* moved from its first phase to its current third phase. Dr. Yun Mi Hwang and Dr. Stephen Epstein have brought together key primary documents that grant both the neophyte and the dedicated *Hallyu* connoisseur access to behind-the-scenes events that will enhance their understanding of the forces that make *Hallyu* possible. These sources will serve the research needs of scholars, government officials, and cultural entrepreneurs as they analyze, extend, and replicate the *Hallyu* phenomenon.

Hallyu catapulted South Korea's super-hip culture to Asia's top soft-power force, which is studied, emulated, and at times even suppressed. While Bhutan made headlines with its assertion of Gross National Happiness, South Korea would be able to claim Asia's top spot in any Gross National Sizzle index via the dissemination and impact of *Hallyu* globally.

We all have our own thoughts as to how much emptier our lives would be should *Hallyu* come to an abrupt end, creating a post-*Hallyu* dystopia. I, for one, would prefer a future where *Hallyu* continues to flourish in its nth incarnation. More importantly, I embrace the new social connections that I am making with *Hallyu* as the magnetic force that draws Koreans and non-Koreans together. Most importantly, I envision a future where *Hallyu* serves as a template for other marginal national cultures to attain their own success in making global culture truly live up to its global aspirations.

Aaron Han Joon Magnan-Park, Ph.D.
University of Hong Kong
Hong Kong
June 1, 2014

Introduction

"Tokyo, Seoul, London, New York…" So begins "Mr. Taxi," a chart-topping 2011 single initially released in Japanese by K-pop superstars Girls' Generation. In the accompanying music video, the nine group members appear in checkered yellow and black faux-leather uniforms that recall the internationally ubiquitous yellow cabs. The leggy songstresses then dance in unison in front of an oversized world map framed by a bright color chart, boasting of their global access and the ease with which they travel. Korean words and English phrases sprinkled into the Japanese lyrics enhance the sense of cultural commingling. The song's video evinces playful awareness of the international spread of South Korean popular culture generally, and K-pop more specifically, in the last decade or so. With a wink, "Mr. Taxi" acknowledges the global aspirations of what has come to be called *Hallyu* or the Korean Wave. The song is thus part of *Hallyu* as well as about *Hallyu*.

Readers who have found their way here undoubtedly already possess at least a modicum of familiarity with *Hallyu*, the cultural phenomenon that is the focus of this sourcebook. At its core, *Hallyu* denotes the dramatic rise in the popularity of Korean culture throughout the world in recent years; pinning down precisely what elements of Korean culture deserve inclusion under the rubric of *Hallyu* can be a more difficult matter, however. Regardless of such ambiguities, journalistic and academic interest in *Hallyu* as a phenomenon and a framework for viewing and understanding contemporary South Korea has clearly surged both inside and outside the country. Scores of Korean-language books, theses, and articles bear the term in their title. Work on the topic appears in English and other languages. Conferences around the world investigate aspects of the Korean Wave; a "World Association of Hallyu Studies" has now been formed. Korean institutions, keen to piggyback on the trend, have established courses, degrees, and even graduate schools; in 2012, the Catholic University of Korea opened the Hallyu Graduate School, and by 2014, the Graduate School had launched *The Journal of Hallyu Business*. The South Korean government itself has also eagerly promoted *Hallyu*, organizing numerous academic and non-academic events under the auspices of the Ministry of Culture, Sports and Tourism, the Korea Foundation for International Culture Exchange, and other centrally funded bodies. Interest in *Hallyu* currently remains strong.

This volume itself is part of the Contemporary Korea Sourcebook Series conceived by the Academy of Korean Studies (AKS) as a way to grant international readers access to Korean-language primary sources. A total of 10 sourcebooks have been commissioned thus far, covering such topics as the education system, religion, and the Democratization Movement. The sourcebooks, each about 400 pages long, strive for historical and social contextualization of the given topic, with an emphasis on providing accurate, readable translations of original sources. Because of the global nature of *Hallyu* and because its *raison d'être* is to introduce new audiences to Korean culture, concern has arisen that many keen to learn more about the topic, both for general interest and academic research, do not have sufficient language skills to consult key primary sources in Korean. This sourcebook aims to at least partially address this lacuna.

Work on the sourcebook began in 2013. The editors sifted through a vast amount of Korean material published in connection with the Korean cultural industries and their recent international spread to identify documents that, taken together, effectively represent dominant topics, themes, and trends. Industry white papers and policy reports by the Korea Creative Content Agency and other ministries and councils served as important sources. National dailies, major magazines, and Internet sites offered further compelling material. Choi Seung-hwan and Lee Yu-ri, affiliated with the Hallyu Graduate School at the Catholic University of Korea, participated as research assistants and gave invaluable aid in trawling through and compiling material for inclusion. Jamie Chang, Chris Dykas, Amber Kim, Sora Kim-Russell, and Eunji Mah became part of the team and worked diligently to produce high-quality translations of the selected material.

A sourcebook on *Hallyu* brings its own special challenges. The recent nature of the phenomenon reduces critical distance and complicates the task of determining what is and will be most significant, reliable, and useful. Even while this sourcebook was being produced, trends evolved rapidly, such that by the time this work is published we recognize that its portrait of the Korean Wave will already seem dated. A further unique difficulty is that *Hallyu*, which involves the global spread of Korean culture, by definition occurs beyond the borders of South Korea itself. However, our brief was to select and translate only sources that originally appeared in Korean. Excluded almost entirely, therefore, are first-hand reports from international audiences about their experience of Korean culture, as well as foreign media accounts of the performance or presence of Korean content. If one is interested in examining the particularities of Korean drama viewership in Kuwait, Colombia, or Cambodia, local sources offer essential insights that supplement what appears here.

What this sourcebook provides, in particular, is a sense of the largely celebratory (and, to be fair, occasionally self-reflective and critical) discursive frameworks employed by the Korean media and government to promote and sustain *Hallyu*. The material here includes both descriptions of, and prescriptions for, how official interests, government and corporate, wish to see Korean cultural products disseminated elsewhere. Occasionally these interests are filtered back to us through members of the Korean diaspora (see Document 3.4.3, "New Year's Party for Those Who Make *Hallyu* Shine: A Mexican Fan Event").

This perspective serves as the sourcebook's key contribution and distinguishes it from much secondary research on *Hallyu*. From government strategy reports to blog posts, the language reverberates with wonder and delight at the discovery of the nation in a transnational context. The documents provide a window into how, for example, Koreans reported and reacted to the news that 5,000 Japanese fans had gathered to greet Bae Yong-joon at Narita Airport in 2005

(Document 2.4.1), or that 1,000 hopefuls came to SM Entertainment's talent search in Almaty, Kazakhstan in 2011 (Document 3.6.1). In this sense, readers should not be surprised by occasional displays of blind nationalism that border on jingoism. Some may raise an eyebrow at Document 1.1.2, "Hallyu Spearheads the Korea Premium," which uncritically praises the achievements of the Lee Myung-bak Administration. However, such texts are interesting precisely because official discourse provides an implicit exegesis on how top-down interests understand the Korean Wave and aspire to develop it. Clearly, what may have started out as an incidental and heterogeneous cultural movement has metamorphosed into an overt business strategy, with the government eager to impose policy.

As such, the documents presented here reveal much about contemporary South Korean national aspirations and anxieties. Nomenclature and statements associated with the international spread of Korean culture can be disconcerting. The term *Hallyu* itself, with its imagery of ebb and flow, betrays concerns that Korea's current success may someday wash away. Yet only rarely is the appropriateness of the wave imagery questioned. South Korea, a late capitalist society with a strong economy that has risen to global prominence, will naturally have its popular culture exposed to the rest of the world, and all the more when the government is at the global forefront of supporting cultural industries as a strategic growth area.

In the remainder of this introduction, we address issues in the study of *Hallyu* that come to the fore in this sourcebook. While debate may exist over the history of the term *Hallyu* as well as the parameters of what should be included within its reach, *Hallyu* has become an omnipresent neologism in Korea. The term regularly encompasses such diverse industries as music, television, film, animation, games, fashion trends, food, and tourism. As the texts here illustrate, the term can be deployed so freely that its usage almost loses meaning. The popular media often bandy about the term *Hallyu* with little restraint when the country engages with the world outside its borders. Thus, we encounter "*Hallyu* medicine," "*Hallyu* beauty," "*Hallyu* essay writing contests," and even wordplay like "Hallyuwood."

In surveying the situation in Southeast Asia, Document 3.3.1, "*Hallyu* Forever: Southeast Asia," lumps a Korean construction company's participation in the real estate boom in Singapore and the spread of K-pop in Myanmar under the single umbrella of the Korean Wave. One might raise questions about the English translation of Shin Kyung-sook's novel *Please Look after Mom*, cited three times in the sourcebook's documents as an example of *Hallyu* success: what inherent connection, other than ultimate Korean provenance, links Shin's book to PSY's "Gangnam Style"? As a result, source selection, categorization, and space constraints imposed difficult choices; the nature and breadth of the topic itself virtually guarantee that gaps are inevitable. We accept that each reader who comes to this sourcebook may question the inclusion of some items and the omission of others.

Given this situation, a working definition of *Hallyu* and the Korean Wave and their scope in this sourcebook is important for understanding the selection of material. According to Document 1.1.1, "The History of *Hallyu*," the term *Hallyu* (韓流) itself first appeared in Chinese-language media in 1997 in Taiwan as a play on the homonym "cold wave" (寒流), both rendered in Mandarin as *hanliu*; Korean media and academia, however, generally date the first use of the term in its current conception to a 1999 Chinese newspaper (p. 5). The origin of the English phrase "Korean Wave" is less certain, although it appeared as the title of a show on the Korean cable music channel M.net around the turn of the millennium. We may safely assume that the desire to reify the growing spread of Korean pop culture as a movement was inspired by similar designations elsewhere (e.g., the French New Wave). Both *Hallyu* and the Korean Wave have now acquired a status and circulation that are devoid of ironic undertones, and they can be used in a neutral and largely interchangeable manner. Inside the nation, even in English contexts, the word "*Hallyu*" has carried the day. Outside Korea, however, "Korean Wave" is often preferred, although as time passes and Korean culture becomes more embedded internationally, more and more non-Korean speakers themselves are becoming as familiar with the term *Hallyu* as they are with kimchi and soju, *hanbok* and *hangeul*. Both the Korean Wave and *Hallyu* carry associations of national pride and lucrative potential, a vernacular signal that Korea has arrived on the world stage. We use both terms in this sourcebook for the purpose of variation.

How far does the scope of *Hallyu* extend? Consider, for example, South Korea's gaming sector, the economic powerhouse of the nation's cultural content industry. As the table "Export of South Korea's Content Industry" on page 19 shows, gaming's export revenue is a remarkable six times larger than that of the music and broadcast industries combined. But do the thousands of fans of a multiplayer computer game like *Dungeon & Fighter*, set in a mythical world, enjoy the game because of its "Koreanness"? While documents included here regularly cite online games as a clear component of *Hallyu*, how should we understand the propagation of games in relationship to the Korean Wave? Does *Hallyu* require a cultural odor of "Koreanness," or is an export label that reads "Made in Korea" sufficient? Korean popular discourse often tends to the latter usage, lauding the success of all things Korean in the global market as a manifestation of Korean excellence, and thus the Korean Wave itself. The prominence of Korean dramas, K-pop, Korean films, and the stars of these genres in the global rise of Korean popular culture, however, leads us to make them the primary focus here. Gaming, food, inbound tourism, and other industries surfing the crest of *Hallyu* take a back seat, as does the Korean Wave's role in attracting marriage migrants and spurring a surge in the number of those studying Korean. In the interest of space, we have also selected texts that summarize legislation, rather than include items like the dense and lengthy 2011 Cultural Content Industry Promotion Law.

The documents contribute a view into the formation and circulation of popular discourse within Korea. They not only offer a lively and important window into the development of Korea's cultural industries in the 21ˢᵗ century, but also serve as a key case study for a more general understanding of global media flows in a rapidly changing world. It is our hope that the sourcebook can generate discussion and support research on contemporary Korean society within the global academy.

This volume consists of three main sections. Part 1, "Institutional Contexts," draws on documents that encapsulate the rationale and strategies behind the Korean government's promotion of *Hallyu*. The underlying assumption shared by the texts grouped here is that this phenomenon offers an opportunity to demonstrate the excellence and wide appeal of Korean culture in the international market. As such, from former president Lee Myung-bak's government's *National Administration White Paper* to the *Cultural Industry White Paper*, the documents focus on which Korean products have been successful and why. Subsection 1.1, "*Hallyu* Overview," succinctly demonstrates the *Hallyu* discourse produced and managed by the central government. This section theorizes the Korean Wave from industry and government perspectives by charting its history and predicting its future, while illustrating types of support deemed relevant through Korean Cultural Centers around the world. Subsection 1.2, "Cultural Content Industry," provides an overview of South Korea's cultural exports and market performance, backed up by detailed statistics, as a way to understand the economics of *Hallyu*. Reviewing the export market over the 10-year period from roughly 2003 to 2012, the texts here show how the language of growth and profit is closely linked with the Korean Wave. Expansion of Korean cultural industries overseas, backed up by numerical data, becomes the rationale for the government to take control of and advance *Hallyu*.

Part 2, "Industrial Operations," covers four sectors within *Hallyu* that have arguably drawn the most attention: television, film, music, and celebrity. Terms such as K-drama and K-pop, now common, highlight the importance of television and music in penetrating international markets for Korea. Although the film industry has yet to generate equivalent revenue, it continues to play a significant role in the Asian market and international film festivals in enhancing awareness of Korea's status as a "hot" producer of cultural content. Supporting these trends as a whole is the popularity of *Hallyu* stars, be it through films, dramas, or idol groups. The glamorous, personalized, and ever-consumable images of Bae Yong-joon, Rain, and Gianna Jun have made *Hallyu* celebrity an industry in itself, the popularity of their images looping back to the celebrity machine. Examples of costly, carefully planned film and drama projects relying on star power, product synergy, and secondary markets resound throughout the sourcebook. While Part 1 focuses on official government publications and industry data, Part 2 adds newspaper articles and interview pieces, thereby painting a more comprehensive picture of attitudes.

Part 3, "International Reception," treats the presence and peculiarities of *Hallyu* in seven regions around the world (China, Japan, Southeast Asia, the Americas, Europe, Central Asia, and the Middle East), as seen from a Korean perspective. Consumers themselves, rather than genres or industries, and regional and national reception become topics of research. The 2013 volume *Hallyu Forever: The World Is Hallyu Style*, published by the Korea Foundation for International Culture Exchange, forms the core of the excerpts in Part 3. Citizen reports and blog posts depicting Koreans' everyday experiences of the Korean Wave while traveling abroad also appear. These recollections of cross-cultural encounters intersect with and strain against official agendas, revealing a range of emotions from pride to perplexity. Part 3, and thus the whole volume, ends with a piece on the "Cosmetics Road" in Seoul, which brings our global *Hallyu* journey back to Korea and considers how the international popularity of Korean culture and its varied fans are having an impact on the landscape of central Seoul itself.

Some remarks on style are also in order: we have attempted to strike a balance between harmonizing the selections that follow to make the end result user-friendly and allowing the idiosyncrasies of the different texts, which range from dry policy documents to journalistic reporting, to shine through. As anyone who has translated Korean into English or edited a volume with numerous contributors well understands, achieving consistency is no simple task. We hope that we have achieved a modicum of success and take full responsibility as editors for any shortcomings.

To make the text more accessible and coherent, we have removed the original section and footnote numberings of the documents and started afresh with each piece. To assist those who wish to consult the original texts, however, we have been careful to provide enough information to allow location of original passages readily. Numerical data has been rounded to two places after a decimal point in the text to enhance readability; tables retain original figures. Some sources, such as Document 2.1.4, "2011 Content Industry Trends: Korean Drama in Japan," were written in bullet point style. To facilitate reading, such texts have largely been reformatted into paragraphs. Factual errors in the original text have been noted with [sic] and, when appropriate, explained in a footnote marked with the insertion [editors].

As *Hallyu* is a recent phenomenon and our sources dwell neither on the period before the division nor inter-Korean politics, North Korea appears rarely in what follows, though the question of South Korean popular culture's penetration in North Korea is itself an important one (albeit rather different from how *Hallyu* is to be understood more generally). Throughout this sourcebook, then, references to "Korea" should be understood as indicating South Korea. Likewise, unless otherwise noted, all dollar figures refer to United States currency.

For a variety of reasons, including not only the nature of *Hallyu* and its close ties to the contemporary South Korean government, but also the AKS's support that funded this project, we have found it appropriate to use the Revised Romanization system adopted in 2000 over the McCune-Reischauer system, though the latter is often preferred by Western scholars. Some technical terms in the text appear in conjunction with a Romanized form, which aids clarification. The Appendix includes the English and Korean names of government agencies, affiliates, and legislation featured in this volume. Key abbreviations that appear in what follows and which readers should be familiar with from the outset include: the Ministry of Culture, Sports and Tourism (MCST), the Korea Creative Content Agency (KOCCA), and the Korea Foundation for International Culture Exchange (KOFICE).

Finally, a number of acknowledgements are in order: the editors thank the AKS for offering generous funding for this sourcebook on the Korean Wave and their support throughout the project. Seong Woo-sun and Kim Chang-il from the Research Administration Office, Lee Chang-il from the Research Policy Office, and Park Seon-yeong and Na Hye-young from the Academy's publishing house have provided practical assistance along the way. We thank the translators, Jamie Chang, Chris Dykas, Amber Kim, Sora Kim-Russell, and Eunji Mah, for their spirit and commitment to the project and never missing a deadline. Choi Seung-hwan and Lee Yu-ri met the daunting task of searching through data on *Hallyu* and collating it under significant time pressure with grace and skill.

Many have contributed to this project in formal and informal ways, indicating important sources, offering useful suggestions, and boosting our morale during difficult periods of editing. We thank Aaron Magnan-Park of Hong Kong University for his belief in the project and writing the preface. Im Hak-soon from the Hallyu Graduate School at the Catholic University of Korea generously provided expert advice. Ko Jeong-min from the Department of Culture Arts Management at Hong-ik University shared his expertise as an industry analyst, helping greatly in planning the sourcebook's overall framework. Shin Hyunjoon at Sungkonghoe University provided useful pointers on K-pop and *Hallyu* star interviews. Ahn Soojeong at the Catholic University of Korea also shared her invaluable networks to aid the project, helping us secure research assistants. Seo Nam-su from the MCST aided us in obtaining permission to use materials published by the ministry and the government. Noh Jun-seok from KOCCA lent invaluable insight on technical terminology within the cultural content industry. Many others helped with language and cultural expertise in locating foreign sources and information: Seo Jin-seok answered a query on the recent status of *Hallyu* fan clubs in Lithuania, and Mohira Suyarkulova found the appropriate Uzbek translation of a Korean drama. Last, but most importantly, the co-editors extend thanks to each other's families for their kind hospitality at various stages during the project and to their own for support throughout.

Yun Mi Hwang
Stephen Epstein

Institutional Contexts

Part 1, "Institutional Contexts," looks at the Korean Wave through the lens of the Korean government. The sources gathered here attempt to define *Hallyu* from this top-down view and explore its impact on the cultural content industry and the government's contribution to expanding the Korean Wave. As has often been related, the watershed moment when Korea awoke to the potential of cultural industries occurred in 1994 when the Presidential Advisory Council on Science and Technology impressed upon President Kim Young-sam that the revenue from the film *Jurassic Park* was equivalent to the sale of 1.5 million Hyundai vehicles. From that point, the country's cultural sector received increased support, soon leading to its 1997 nomination as a core industry (*jureok saneop*) of the 21ˢᵗ century. The Kim Dae-jung government laid more concrete foundations by establishing the Framework Act on the Promotion of Cultural Industries in 1999 and allocating an unprecedented portion of the national budget to the cultural industry sectors. Subsequent governments have continued these investments. This national policy agenda was then bolstered by *Hallyu* success stories, which legitimized the government's efforts; the discourse on the cultural content industry's growth thus became inextricably linked with *Hallyu*. Accordingly, the consumption patterns and multiple levels of appreciation for Korean popular media in overseas locales by different groups of fans are often elided in official discourse in order to construct a linear, progressive, and even teleological spread of the Korean Wave.

During the course of preparing this sourcebook, the change of government from Lee Myung-bak to Park Geun-hye in early 2013 coincided with the aftermath of excitement over PSY's astonishing and unexpected success, augmenting fanfare over *Hallyu* and the Korean cultural industry. A confidence bordering on arrogance is palpable in numerous official documents. The sources gathered in Part 1 thus together give insight into policies through which the government supports the cultural content industry. Export data and figures illustrate how a cultural trend can become institutionalized and systematically appropriated to serve the rationale of various schemes. The efficacy of such schemes and their influence on business become even clearer in Part 2, "Industrial Operations," where a detailed discussion of major *Hallyu* industries is presented.

1.1.   *HALLYU* OVERVIEW

Probably the most comprehensive recent government publication about the Korean Wave is the 280-page *Hallyu White Paper* (2013). This volume, weighed down by neither undue statistical data nor the dry language one might expect of white papers, is a readable introduction to the Korean Wave, laden with colorful images and spiced up by interviews with *Hallyu* fans, industry figures, and *Hallyu* stars. The *White Paper* series, published annually by the MCST, features extensive data, arranged to present a yearly review of each cultural sector's achievements. Even though the format and content of the *Hallyu White Paper* differs from more solemn white papers, its inclusion within such a series makes governmental attention to *Hallyu* an emblematic phenomenon worthy of serious attention.

Document 1.1.1, "The History of *Hallyu*," excerpted from this *Hallyu White Paper*, attempts a periodization of trends. Charting the timeline of the Korean Wave has preoccupied many, not only because of the appeal of pointing to a goal-oriented progression, but also because a considered framing of history can serve as a speech act: projecting hopes and plans for the future can (ideally) will them into being. This document, reflecting the rising interest in Web 2.0 and the software updates that have become a regular part of contemporary life, adopts computer language to delineate the progress of the Korean Wave, breaking it into such stages as *Hallyu* 1.0 and 2.0. The terms also intersect with Korea's desired identity as a digitally savvy and technologically advanced nation.

The table on page 9 situates *Hallyu* 1.0 between 1997 and the mid-2000s—a period marked by the popularity of Korean dramas in Asia. *Hallyu* 2.0, led by K-pop, made a strong impact in wider regions through the early 2010s. With a grandiose flourish, the document heralds the arrival of *Hallyu* 3.0: K-culture. This phase, which ideally should have achieved a foothold in the early 2010s, aims at broad exposure of Korean culture around the world, and, notably, emphasizes the inclusion of traditional arts that serve as icons of Korean identity. That the launch of the Hallyu Culture Promotion Taskforce in January 2012 was intended to signal the dawn of *Hallyu* 3.0 underscores the policy-driven nature of this phase. Other views on the periodization of *Hallyu*, however, are readily found: Document 2.3.1, "K-Pop Drives Resurgence of the Korean Wave," employs the term "neo-*Hallyu*" (*shinhallyu*) to similarly herald a new era.

Such chronologies derived from the language of digital culture reveal the government's desire to refashion the Korean Wave within an essentialized vision of Korea, reigning in the chaotic and organic spread of "Korea" that has arisen through embracement of items like "Gangnam Style" and Samsung smartphones. The authors of the document appear aware of this tension in defending the government against the charge of aggressive meddling:

> This is not to say that the government is intervening (*gaeip*) in the successful forms of cultural production that make up *Hallyu*; rather, the government has determined to involve itself in a new *Hallyu* to promote forms of Korean culture with global appeal. (Page 7)

President Lee Myung-bak's government published 12 volumes in a series called *National Administration White Papers* to illustrate its achievements. *Korea:*

A Cultural Stronghold, from which Document 1.1.2, "*Hallyu* Spearheads the Korea Premium," is excerpted, mentions *Hallyu* most frequently. Many eminent government officials, including the Secretary to the Minister of Culture, Sports and Tourism, were involved in the publication of the volume. Although *Hallyu* accelerated its global spread during the Lee Administration and the Korean Wave features prominently in this document, the extent of the government's role in the success of Korean dramas like *Jewel in the Palace* in the Middle East is unclear. The feasibility of its vision of *Hallyu* 3.0 is even murkier. The mention of SM Town's 2011 French concert and the appearance of *Jumong* on Uzbekistan television both in this piece and in Document 1.1.1 suggest which success stories are deemed worthy of recycling by the central government. The appearance of multiple fields stamped with the letter K for Korea ("K-culture" in Document 1.1.1; "K-arts" in Document 1.1.2) draws attention to the eagerness to brand the nation with slogans associated with *Hallyu*: "special K," one might call it.

Document 1.1.2 also seeks to explain the rise of *Hallyu*, but runs headlong into questionable generalizations. For instance, the piece argues that:

> South Korea's unique acceptance of, and harmonious coexistence with, other cultures plays an important role in the country's cultural strategy; for this reason, people of different historical backgrounds and experiences can accept *Hallyu* without a sense that it carries cultural imperialism. (Page 18)

This statement partially contradicts other texts (e.g., Documents 2.1.2 and 3.3.1) that lament the protectionist measures taken by the Chinese and Vietnamese governments in restricting Korean content on their national television channels. Most intriguing here is the detailed description of schemes highlighting the desire to develop the Korean Wave as a platform to promote and market Korean products. Echoing Document 1.1.1, Document 1.1.2 gives a more concrete example of what *Hallyu* 3.0 might entail. An exhibition of traditional artwork in London and aspiring Korean pianists winning prestigious awards at international competitions are reported under "*Hallyu* to Continue through K-Arts."

As of 2015, 28 Korean Cultural Centers, overseen by the Korean Culture and Information Service, under the jurisdiction of the MCST, operate around the world and serve as official venues for cultural promotion and exchange. The 2012 budget for the Korean Cultural Centers was ₩27.8 billion, nearly a fivefold increase from 2005. Their numbers are still rising and their services becoming more comprehensive. Document 1.1.3, "Korean Cultural Centers: Expanding Korean Cultural Exchange Overseas," describes the successes of these cultural centers and future plans to develop them. Here, one can see how *Hallyu* has inspired interest and investment in cultural diplomacy and sense why so many Korean cultural festivals abroad are compelled to promote traditional music and arts, alongside K-pop and *Hallyu* star events.

Page 32 in Document 1.1.3 provides insight into the sort of interministry competition that President Lee himself warned against. Korean Education Centers, under the Ministry of Education, Science and Technology, have traditionally offered Korean language courses to non-resident Koreans. With the expansion of Korean Cultural Centers primarily catering to non-Korean locals, the Lee Administration moved to consolidate language education under the Korean Cultural

Centers, much to the evident chagrin of the Ministry of Education, Science and Technology. At present, both Korean Cultural Centers and Korean Education Centers remain in operation, indicating that full agreement on a centralized Korean language teaching system has not been reached. The issue of "scattered" *Hallyu* management is also mentioned in Document 1.1.2 and, especially, in Document 2.1.3, "2009 Broadcast Video Content: Strategies and Policies for Propagation" (p. 113). Different ministries have been trying to tap into the attractive opportunities created by *Hallyu*, creating a struggle for territory, as also noted in the *Korea Times* article "*Hallyu* Boom Triggers Bureaucratic Turf War" (March 12, 2012). Despite the government's celebratory Korean Wave discourse, rival maneuvers to gain an upper hand at an institutional level occasion significant debate.

1.1.1.   The History of *Hallyu*

Reference: *Hallyu White Paper*, MCST, May 2013, pp. 14–25.

Despite having only entered our lexicon a decade ago, the neologism *Hallyu*, or the Korean Wave, has become quite familiar. From dramas to music, Korean popular culture has transcended Asia and is now branching out around the globe. Most recently, PSY's "Gangnam Style" took the world by storm. From its beginning in the late 1990s, the Korean Wave has been breaking new ground in 21st-century Korean popular culture. Given its continuous shifts and evolution, the concept of the Korean Wave is subject to misunderstanding and misinterpretation. Here, we take a concise look at the development of *Hallyu*.

A.   The birth of the Korean wave: Hallyu 1.0

Many consider *Hallyu* to have originated with the 1997 broadcast of the drama *What Is Love?* on Chinese Central Television (CCTV), which received a viewership rating of 4.2%. Despite the popularity in Japan of singers such as Jo Yong-pil and Gye Eun-sook during the 1980s, *What Is Love?* can be regarded as launching the Korean Wave because, first and foremost, it aired in China during a period when the country was not active in popular culture exchange. As such, South Korea was able to pioneer uncharted territory. Secondly, unlike the transient nature of popular music, *What Is Love?*, through its serial format, enjoyed sustained popularity. Some 39 million people eagerly tuned in each Sunday morning when the series aired. Third, following *What Is Love?*, Korean dramas saw a clear increase in popularity, as did Korean music; *Hallyu* content in general grew more diverse. The popularity of Korean dramas continued with such titles as *Star in My Heart*, *Medical Brothers*, and *Men of the Bathhouse*, and Korean music also enjoyed a boost.

Beginning in 1997, Korean music—in particular dance music, introduced on the Beijing-based radio show "Seoul Music Studio"—became widely popular among the youth. The definitive outbreak of a craze for Korean pop culture in China occurred in February 2000 when Korean idol group H.O.T. performed at Beijing's Workers Stadium. Around the time of this performance, the term *Hallyu* first appeared in Korean media, which indicates that Koreans began to recognize the phenomenon that had been mentioned in *Beijing Youth Weekly* in November 1999:

"Sometimes East Winds Blow East"
At a time in which both Eastern and Western culture are popular, it seems any trend can boom. Some "Korean Wave" fanatics, once so passionate about the group Clon that the duo seemed to have become an ironclad dragon, now clutch posters for H.O.T...

– Beijing Youth Weekly, November 19, 1999

Beijing Youth Weekly refers here to Chinese teenagers' fascination with Korean pop songs, television series, films, clothing styles, and the like as "*Hallyu*," or the Korean Wave. This was the first time "*Hallyu*" was used from a foreign perspective to describe an important social phenomenon, although the term had been employed in 1997 in Taiwan's *China Times* in reference to Korean industry and consumer goods. Once groups such as Clon and H.O.T. began to achieve fame in the Chinese-speaking world, the term came to refer to the influx of Korean popular culture.

Hallyu gained its initial momentum during the late 1990s and early 2000s in East Asian locales such as China, Taiwan, and Vietnam. Family, the human condition, and true love (*sunaebo*) were the stuff of dramas that touched the region's viewers, and lively dance music impassioned Asia's youth. That Korean popular culture gained such popularity abroad relied intrinsically on its qualitative and quantitative development. Also contributing to this growth were such external factors as the development of cable TV and satellite broadcast media, as well as cultural proximity.

After a short lull for *Hallyu* in 2002 and 2003, dramas such as *Winter Sonata* and *Jewel in the Palace* achieved broad success and entered new territory. In 2004, *Winter Sonata* was broadcast in Japan and received wide acclaim from middle-aged women, propelling lead actor Bae Yong-joon ("Yonsama" to his Japanese fans) to stardom. That year, the Hyundai Economic Research Institute estimated Bae's economic influence at ₩3 trillion. Before this point our tendency, whether consciously or not, was to imitate Japanese popular culture, and for this reason the success of Korean dramas in Japan represents a progression of *Hallyu* to the next level.

Jewel in the Palace met with great popularity in Taiwan in 2004 and Hong Kong in 2005. The drama set a record in the latter, when the final episode of the series, broadcast on Hong Kong's TVB, was watched by 47% of the total viewership. The popularity of *Jewel in the Palace* did not stop there, but spread to Southeast Asia, the Middle East, Africa, and Eastern Europe.

This stage of progress for the Korean Wave, which began in China and then moved into the wider world from Japan, can be described as "*Hallyu* 1.0." During this period, between the late 1990s and mid-2000s, the primary platform for the Korean Wave was television drama, followed by popular music and film. Though Asia served as the epicenter of this popularity, *Hallyu*'s reach spread outward.

B. *K-pop and Hallyu 2.0*

Between the mid-2000s and early 2010s, the character of *Hallyu* changed, and K-pop came to have the most prominence. Clon's popularity originated in

Taiwan in 1998 and then spread to China. After H.O.T.'s 2000 Beijing performance, Korean music took the lead as *Hallyu* became a household term. Even
in the early 2000s, Korean music, with idols at center stage, made repeated
attempts to stake a claim abroad and found wide recognition in China, Japan,
and Southeast Asia. Artists such as BoA, Rain, and Wonder Girls moved
beyond Asia and launched careers in the heart of the popular music business,
the United States.

The use of "K-pop" as a term specifically describing the dance music of idol
singers and groups began with an SM Town concert held at Le Zénith de Paris in
France in June 2011. K-pop fans from France and beyond poured into the concert
hall, making the event a smashing success. Though France is known for cultural
conservatism, this K-pop concert managed a great triumph in Paris, the nation's
capital of culture and art. Prominent journalists from around the world detailed
the happening. *Le Figaro* on June 9, 2011, told of how the "Korean Wave Takes
Zénith by Storm," and *Le Monde* published an article describing the event as a
"Korean foreign diplomacy delegation" (June 16, 2011). *The New York Times*
published a review of an SM Town concert in New York that same year under
the title "Korean Pop Machine, Running on Innocence and Hair Gel" (October
24, 2011).

Such interest in Korean culture from European and American media was
a first. This once unimaginable phenomenon drove not only foreigners but also
Koreans to rethink the Korean Wave. In 2011 the term *"shinhallyu"* (New Korean
Wave) appeared, marking a shift away from the existing geographies and genres
of *Hallyu*. People began to look at this new K-pop-centered *Hallyu* as having
transcended Asia to take on a globalized form.

The success of K-pop not only in France but also around the globe can be
explained in terms of both intrinsic elements of the content and extrinsic social
conditions. The intrinsic aspects of K-pop can be epitomized as novelty, openness, moderation, and familiarity.[1] Compared to mainstream anglophone and
J-pop artists, Korean idol groups, with their lively choreography, held novelty for
Europeans. At the same time, thanks to the infusion of Western elements, these
audiences found K-pop readily accessible. The absence of violence and gratu-
itous profanity in K-pop, along with its lyrical content and choreography, makes
the genre light and airy. K-pop idols also make themselves available to audiences
on TV and at their concerts. Such qualities may have been present in Korean
popular music before K-pop became the phenomenon it is today, but from 2011,
they came to be expressed in a more refined form.

The most crucial condition allowing for the global rise of K-pop has been the
prevalence of social networking sites and *YouTube*. Since the late 2000s *YouTube*
has become the primary forum through which K-pop is exposed to the world.
On June 9, 2009, the music video for Girls' Generation's "Gee" was released;
by March 2012 it had reached over 69 million views. Social media sites like
Facebook and *Twitter* enabled word of mouth about K-pop to spread quickly, and
ignited a desire in K-pop fans to see their favorite artists with their own eyes. If
the media that made *Hallyu* 1.0 possible were cable TV, satellite broadcasting,

[1] Son S., "Europe's Korean Wave and K-Pop Fandom: Its Origins and Meaning," 2011 Korean Society
for Journalism and Communication Studies Conference, pp. 86–88.

and the Internet, then *YouTube* and social networking sites enabled K-pop to go global.

This era, in which we may truly recognize a K-pop craze, can rightfully be labeled *Hallyu* 2.0. Still, *Hallyu* 2.0 cannot be treated as encompassing K-pop alone. Although K-pop undoubtedly lies at its core, other cultural content, such as dramas, films, and games, has been released abroad. Marked success has been seen in arts and culture as well.

Jewel in the Palace opened the floodgates for Korean dramas to flow out beyond East Asia. Its influence was observed again in October 2011, when the program was broadcast during prime time on Jordanian national television. In addition, ratings for the drama in Iran stood at 86% in 2007. Similarly, ratings for *Jumong* reached 85% in 2009. What is more, as of 2011, *Jumong* had been broadcast in Uzbekistan five times. The process by which *Jewel in the Palace* branched out from Taiwan and Hong Kong across the globe can itself be viewed as reflecting the evolution from *Hallyu* 1.0 to 2.0.

The success of *Jewel in the Palace* differs from that of *Winter Sonata* in two ways: first, the drama takes traditional Korean culture as its source material, and second, its popularity has not been confined to Asia. In general, period dramas have difficulty finding success abroad, given historical and cultural differences. However, the combination of historical charm, rich displays of traditional food and clothing, and a universal story line enabled *Jewel in the Palace* to surmount these obstacles, leading it to move beyond the confines of Asia.

In arts and literature, the most representative success is Shin Kyung-sook's *Please Look after Mom*, which was released in the United States in April 2011 and reached #14 on *The New York Times* bestseller list for hardcover fiction. This performance demonstrated that *Hallyu*, although focused on popular culture, had the potential to expand and that other Korean artistic forms could circulate even in the United States, the heart of global capital and culture. Around this time, terms such as "culinary *Hallyu*," "fashion *Hallyu*," and "tourism *Hallyu*" appeared.

Thus, it can be said that the era of *Hallyu* 2.0 was that in which Korean popular culture, led by K-pop, branched out globally beyond Asia, opening up possibilities in the arts and sparking a broader interest in Korean culture. Nonetheless, an issue equally important to these external phenomena is the fundamental question of how Koreans are to understand foreigners' conception of *Hallyu*.

C. K-culture: Hallyu 3.0

The *Hallyu* 3.0 era was initiated with a search for answers to questions such as that posed immediately above. The Hallyu Culture Promotion Taskforce, established on January 30, 2012, unveiled a plan to link *Hallyu*, including K-pop, with Korean culture in general, which they designated "K-culture." This is not to say that the government is intervening in the successful forms of cultural production that make up *Hallyu*; rather, the government has determined to involve itself in a new *Hallyu* to promote forms of Korean culture with global appeal.

The *Hallyu* 3.0 era is centered on K-culture, which encompasses traditional culture, the arts, and popular culture. If *Hallyu* currently incorporates only the latter two, with special focus on popular culture, K-culture represents the addition of traditional culture and an organic link between all three constituent parts.

As such, K-culture moves beyond the sphere of culture per se. Although traditional culture, the arts, and popular culture make up its foundation, this core serves as a launchpad for a mission to introduce the world to all that represents Korea. Much as *Hallyu* 2.0 came to include Korean food and medicine, *Hallyu* 3.0 is now a cultural and post-cultural phenomenon. The government will play a role through the MCST and interagency initiatives.

In order to bring this mission to fruition, two courses of action are necessary. The first involves systematic support for the sustained development of the existing forms of *Hallyu*. The second involves fostering universal appreciation for all things Korean, not just the nation's popular culture.

To describe this initiative as a mere proclamation of government policy is inadequate; rather, the initiative reflects a general societal desire. On March 22, 2012, for example, the *Maeil Business Newspaper* held its 19th Citizens' Report Competition under the theme "Hallyu's True Colors," and on May 16 and 17 the *Seoul Economic Daily* held its 2012 Seoul Forum, "Hallyu: Encompassing the Global Economy." Academia has also seen an intensification of Korean Wave research, including the foundation of graduate schools of *Hallyu*. In the spring and fall semesters of 2012, respectively, the Graduate School of Hallyu Cultural Industries at Pai Chai University and Catholic University's Hallyu Graduate School opened. This is the extent to which *Hallyu* represents one of Korea's hottest topics in 2012 and serves as an example of collaboration between the government and the civil sector.

Just as the geographies and audiences of *Hallyu* are evolving, the *Hallyu* of today has set its sights on reaching beyond Asia to the rest of the globe and transcending its niche audience to reach the citizens of the world. In the latter half of 2012, the rise of PSY's "Gangnam Style" served as a watershed moment. If the 2011 K-pop explosion took place in Europe, the "Gangnam Style" craze took place on the world stage, even penetrating the stronghold of popular music, the US. The song remained at Billboard's #2 position for seven consecutive weeks, and was iTunes' most downloaded song for over two months. "Gangnam Style" also holds the world record for *YouTube* views, and reached the top of the charts in more than 20 countries. *Hallyu* 3.0 represents the globalization of the target market for Korean cultural content, turning the trend into "a Korean Wave for all the world to share." The wave that began in the mid-1990s is moving forward, evolving into a globally shared K-culture and representative of Korean style, "K-style."

D. Evolving Hallyu

Hallyu's constant evolution means that its spheres of influence and target audiences are fluid. Accordingly, the Korean Wave is understood as having different versions with unique areas of expansion and stages of development.

Depending on whom one asks, the foci and elements that accompany labels such as *Hallyu* 1.0, *Hallyu* 2.0, and *Hallyu* 3.0 differ. What is constant, however, is the understanding that in this progression, *Hallyu* moved from dramas to K-pop, from K-pop to the arts, and then on to a broadening awareness of Korean culture overall.

Table 1–1.   Characteristics of *Hallyu* 1.0, 2.0, and 3.0

	Hallyu 1.0	*Hallyu* 2.0	*Hallyu* 3.0
Period	1997-mid 2000s	mid 2000s-early 2010s	early 2010s onward
Characteristics	birth, centered on video content	growth, centered on K-pop idols/stars	diversification
Primary Genres	Dramas	K-pop	K-culture
Genres	dramas, film, Korean popular music	popular culture, the arts	traditional culture, arts, mainstream popular culture
Primary Target Destinations	Asia	Asia, parts of Europe, Africa, the Middle East, Central and South America, parts of the US	the entire world
Consumer Base	a small number of fans	teens and those in early 20s	citizens of the world
Primary Media Distribution	cable TV, satellite TV, Internet	*YouTube*, social networking services	all media

Treating the names for the different versions as deriving from the content emphasizes the economics of the industry. In 2005, the Samsung Economic Research Institute categorized *Hallyu* as growing in the following stages: popular music garners fans → merchandising of related goods → merchandising of Korean goods in general → preference for Korean brands. In July 2011, the Korea Trade-Investment Promotion Agency (KOTRA) released a market analysis that categorized *Hallyu*'s expansion into various countries by the levels of residents' awareness and purchase of Korean products. A division into pre-entry, entry, brand recognition, growth, and maturity phases indicated that *Hallyu* needs to progress into the mainstream, translating into the sale of goods that piggyback off of *Hallyu* in the maturity phase.

However, rather than focus on the regions into which *Hallyu* and the sale of Korean goods are expanding, we will be better off examining the composition of *Hallyu* content, the periods in which it rose, its typical consumers, and areas of expansion. The characteristics of *Hallyu* 1.0, 2.0, and 3.0 are summarized in the table above.

The *Hallyu* of 2012 is based on K-culture, in which people the world over share an affinity for three aspects of Korea: traditional culture, the arts, and popular culture. Although this arises from a variety of cultural aspects, the end result converges on K-style, represented by a broader concept of culture and all things Korean. *Hallyu* is not merely a series of "waves (流)" defined by a narrow scope of content that achieves popularity in a particular time and place; rather, the process of bringing K-culture and people around the world together—a process that creates an ecosystem of traditional culture, the arts, and popular culture content—lies at the heart of *Hallyu*.

1.1.2.   *Hallyu* Spearheads the Korea Premium

Reference: *Korea: A Cultural Stronghold*, 10ᵗʰ Volume from *National Administration White Paper of President Lee Myung-bak's Government* (2008–2013), MCST, February 2013, pp. 158–168, 171–177.

(pp. 158–168)

A.   *The global expansion of Hallyu and its trajectory*

The spread of *Hallyu* and its routes

Hallyu is expanding beyond Asian consumer markets to Europe, Latin America, and the rest of the world with the help of social networking services (SNS) and other digital media. Major developed nations recognized for their own advanced cultural content industries are also turning their attention towards *Hallyu*. Dramas and films, largely responsible for *Hallyu* in its initial stages, have been joined by popular music. Since the mid-2000s, *Hallyu* has gone through a metamorphosis, with idol groups such as KARA, Girls' Generation, Big Bang, and B2ST moving to the forefront. Teenagers and those in their twenties, quick to adapt to digital media, have established fan communities. Reborn with the Japanese craze for Korean girl groups, the Korean Wave has now spread beyond Asia into Europe, South America, and other parts of the world. At the same time, the level and speed of penetration of Korean cultural products differs from country to country.

According to a document published by KOTRA in July 2011, the penetration can be divided into five phases that distinguish recognition from the general public and the development of the country's *Hallyu*-related industries: pre-entry, entry, brand recognition, growth, and maturity. Let us move in reverse order: the maturity phase indicates the highest level of *Hallyu* penetration. This phase describes countries in which Korean content is well known to the general public, and sales of subsidiary products are strong. Examples include Japan, China, Thailand, Taiwan, Vietnam, and Singapore.

Prior to maturity comes a growth phase where *Hallyu* is popular among the general public, but sales of *Hallyu*-related products are in an incipient state. Malaysia, the Philippines, Myanmar, Cambodia, Hungary, and Uzbekistan may be regarded as examples of countries in the growth phase.

In the brand recognition phase, *Hallyu* has an established fan base and the general public is aware of Korean content. Countries in this phase include the US, the UK, France, New Zealand, Peru, Brazil, and Argentina.

In the entry phase, *Hallyu* has a small fan base but is not yet recognized by the general public. Examples of such countries are Sri Lanka, India, Greece, and the Czech Republic. Countries in which the Korean Wave has yet to arrive are in the pre-entry phase.

If we consider these phases as a whole, we find that the growth and maturation of *Hallyu* has been concentrated in Asia, while countries in Europe and the Americas remain in the entry and brand recognition phases. These regions also differ in their methods of consumption. Television is the main distribution media for Korean content in Asia (e.g., China, Japan, and Taiwan), while the Internet is the general medium for accessing Korean content in Europe and the Americas (e.g., the UK, Brazil, and Russia).

Table 1–2.   Phases of *Hallyu* penetration

Phase	Description	Countries
Maturity	Korean cultural products are popular among the general public; *Hallyu* subsidiary products are widely sold	Japan, China, Thailand, Taiwan, Vietnam, Singapore, Hong Kong, Kazakhstan
Growth	Korean cultural products are popular among the general public; sales of subsidiary products are in an incipient stage.	Malaysia, the Philippines, Myanmar, Cambodia, Hungary, Uzbekistan
Brand Recognition	Korean cultural products have a fan base, and the general public is aware of Korean content.	US, UK, France, New Zealand, Peru, Brazil, Argentina, Egypt
Entry	Korean cultural products have a fan base.	Sri Lanka, India, Greece, Czech Republic
Pre-entry	*Hallyu* has not been introduced.	Bangladesh, Switzerland, Oman

K-drama Consumption Route

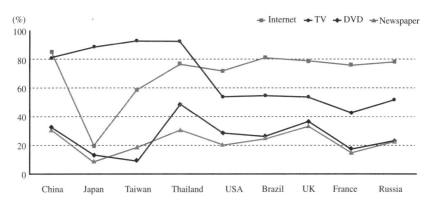

Figure 1–1.   K-drama consumption route

K-pop as the force behind *Hallyu*

K-pop's role in propagating the Korean Wave can largely be attributed to the development of the Internet. The growth of *Hallyu* has now reached noteworthy levels, and studies and reports with statistics and objective indicators have shown the extent of *Hallyu* expansion. *YouTube*, the world's largest video-sharing website, transcends national borders and allows people to access content of their choice from all over the globe. *YouTube* view counts are a key index of interest.

K-pop videos were viewed 2.3 billion times on *YouTube* in 2011, a 191% increase from the roughly 800 million views in 2010. In this period, K-pop views

K-pop Consumption Route

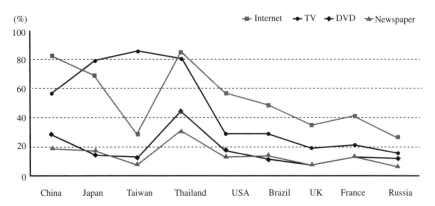

Figure 1–2.   K-pop consumption route

on *YouTube* increased 155% in the US, 168% in France, and 258% in Germany. Only two countries reported zero views, a fact that shows the extent of global interest in K-pop.

Numbers show that *Hallyu* is no longer limited to Asia. Its influence has reached Europe, as evidenced by German and French reportage on the phenomenon. On June 9, 2011, the culture section of *Le Monde*, a major French daily, printed an article titled "The Korean Pop Wave Reaches Europe" in anticipation of the SM Town concert. This in-depth article on K-pop covered how SM Entertainment, one of South Korea's largest talent agencies, develops idol groups, from conception to training to production.

With the growing interest in K-pop, South Korean artists represented by large agencies are increasing their mainstream presence and holding concerts in major cities around the world. On March 12, 2011, South Korean idol group Big Bang reached #7 on Billboard's Heatseekers Albums chart, which ranks "new or developing acts" by album sales, and #3 on the magazine's World Albums chart. A single released by the Wonder Girls in May 2010, *2 Different Tears*, reached #21 on the Heatseekers Albums chart. In September, the "SM Town Live 10 World Tour," featuring artists such as Girls' Generation, Super Junior, and BoA, was held at the Staples Center in Los Angeles. The multiethnic audience of 15,000 included Koreans, other Asians, and Hispanics. A record-breaking 8,000 tickets were sold within 4 hours of going on sale.

The greatest sensation among Korean artists has been PSY, whose "Gangnam Style" swept the world. On August 3, 2012, CNN USA reported on the "Gangnam Style" craze, and on September 14 PSY performed live in Manhattan for *The Today Show* on NBC. Fans started gathering at 3 a.m. for PSY's performance. By 6 a.m., Rockefeller Plaza was so packed that people could barely move. During the performance, resident Koreans, exchange students from Korea, native New Yorkers, and foreign tourists mingled, singing along to "Gangnam Style" and performing the "horse dance" en masse. A Korean in Canada wrote in his blog that although non-English songs rarely appear on

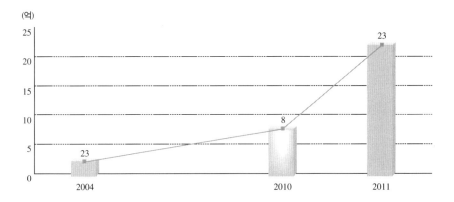

(억)

Figure 1–3. K-Pop Views on *YouTube* (100 million)

Canadian radio, local stations were playing "Gangnam Style," and Toronto's City TV was introducing the song. Britney Spears, Tom Cruise, Katy Perry, Nobel Laureate economist Paul Krugman, and many other celebrities around the world mentioned PSY. He was discussed in such venues as CNN International, *The Wall Street Journal*, *Financial Times*, *Harvard Business Review*, and the global politics magazine *Foreign Policy*. This coverage proves that PSY is no longer a mere online sensation but has become a true global celebrity. In November 2012, the video for "Gangnam Style" reached 800 million views on *YouTube* and became the world's most viewed video of all time, surpassing "Baby" by Justin Bieber.

K-pop fever soon reached the Middle East. On October 21, 2012, the second K-Pop Talent Show was held at the Maadi Public Library in Cairo. Before the start of the event, "Gangnam Style" was played and the participants, students and professionals alike, performed the song's horse dance together on stage, heightening the festive mood. The 400 people that filled the auditorium danced along, shouting "*Sana-ee!*" and "*Oppan* Gangnam Style!"

In a K-pop competition held in Chile, employees of the Korean Embassy performed the dance with *Hallyu* fans, and on September 16, 2012, some 300 *Hallyu* aficionados organized a "Gangnam Style" flash mob in Mexico City's Zócalo. A similar event occurred in Brazil the next day. On November 5, about 20,000 people gathered in Paris to see PSY perform, and sang and danced passionately to "Gangnam Style."

A Wikipedia entry was created for "Gangnam Style," further establishing the song's status as a global phenomenon. The lengthy page introduces the song in detail, with references for its chart performance in various countries, cultural impact, academic responses to the song and arguments for its success, and the role of social media in its rise to fame. Scholars from the world's top business schools, including Harvard and Wharton, have analyzed the popularity of "Gangnam Style" and its ripple effects from various angles. They point to the song's catchy beat and PSY's humorous dance and animated performance as factors that allowed the song to overcome language barriers, and attribute the song's success to social media.

Table 1–3.   "Gangnam Style" timeline

2012	July 15	"Gangnam Style" released.
	July 16	"Gangnam Style" ranks at the top of real-time music charts on Korean music streaming sites, including *MelOn, MNet, Bugs*, and *Olleh Music*.
	July 30	American singer and film actor T-Pain praises "Gangnam Style" on *Twitter*.
	August 2	"Gangnam Style" music video reaches 10 million hits on *YouTube*. Huffington Post reports the milestone.
	August 3	CNN USA reports on the "Gangnam Style" craze.
	August 8	*7:45 PM*, a news program on French TV channel M6, features "Gangnam Style."
	August 9	"Gangnam Style" reaches 20 million views on *YouTube*.
	August 21	"Gangnam Style" tops the iTunes music video chart in the US and reaches 40 million views on *YouTube*. PSY showcases the "Gangnam Style" horse dance on the "Dance Cam" at a Los Angeles Dodgers game.
	September 2	"Gangnam Style" reaches 88.3 million views on *YouTube*, breaking the record for a Korean artist, previously held by Girls' Generation for "Gee."
	September 14	PSY performs "Gangnam Style" in Rockefeller Plaza in New York City for *The Today Show* on NBC.
	September 18	"Gangnam Style" reaches 200 million views on *YouTube*.
	October 1	"Gangnam Style" tops the UK Singles Chart.
	October 21	"Gangnam Style" reaches 500 million views on *YouTube*.
	December 22	"Gangnam Style" reaches one billion views on *YouTube*.

Hallyu to continue through K-arts

Expanding on the interest in Korea inspired by K-pop, the South Korean government is preparing to promote K-arts, a term coined for Korean cultural content that encompasses a variety of fields.

The performance of the Korean National University of Arts (KNUA or K'Arts) has been remarkable. The university was founded with the purpose of nurturing the nation's finest artists, and it offers programs in music, dance, traditional arts, film, and various other cultural fields. Its students have consistently performed well in competitions at home and abroad, upholding KNUA's reputation as one of Korea's best arts universities. In the 2012 Boston International Ballet Competition, several KNUA students and an alumnus of its School of Dance won awards, including two gold medals. In the XIV International Tchaikovsky Competition, Park Jong-min and Seo Seon-young won top prize in the male and female vocal categories, respectively. Son Yeol-eum won second prize in piano, and Lee Ji-hye won third prize in violin. Hong Hae-ran was awarded first prize in the vocal category in the 2011 Queen Elisabeth Competition. Han

Seung-woo won second place in the 39th Prix de Lausanne, an international ballet competition in Switzerland, while Kim Ki-min won the Grand Prix in the 12th Youth America Grand Prix in 2011. These superb performances in international competitions are a good reason to anticipate that the expansion of *Hallyu* will encompass diverse genres, including classical music and dance, rather than centering on K-pop alone.

The government is continuing to increase efforts to support K-arts as part of *Hallyu*. In one such effort, a K-art exhibition was opened at the end of April 2012 to boost *Hallyu*, increase understanding of Korean art, and seek a new paradigm for its development in the era of globalization. The exhibition showcased about 80 works of art with the underlying theme "Dynamic Power," a characteristic of Korean contemporary art. The exhibition featured 13 artists who will play a pivotal role in enhancing Korea's status in the global art market.

In June 2012, the South Korean Cultural Centre UK in London celebrated the London Olympics by hosting a "100-Day Festival of Korean Culture." Various programs of the festival, titled "All Eyes on Korea," showcased the past and present of Korean culture, with exhibitions of Korean art in various parts of London. Examples of traditional Korean art, including wooden figurines carved in various shapes, demonstrated the excellence of Korean traditions and piqued audience interest.

During the Olympics, a special exhibition featuring contemporary Korean art was held with sports as its theme. Sports art is a new field that includes works of art thematically related to sports, regardless of medium. Because of recent trends in the diversification of art, it is reasonable to categorize art thematically, rather than by medium, such as photography, oil painting, or sculpture. As the supervisor of the exhibition explained, "People who work in new genres, such as character design, illustrations, and designer toys, are coming to be perceived as artists, a perception that in turn has widened the realm of sports art."

Popular culture has contributed much to *Hallyu* today. However, general agreement exists that for *Hallyu* to persist and mature, it must encompass Korean culture widely, including such areas as traditional arts, fine arts, and literature. The government plans to continue its promotion of *Hallyu* in various artistic fields as well as in popular culture, and to increase exchanges with foreign countries, realizing that insisting on a unilateral flow can create misunderstanding and resistance.

B. Expansion and evolution of Hallyu

Backdrop to the expansion of Hallyu

New media
Many factors led to the initial spread of Korean content, but the three main ones were the appearance of new media, the development of mass communication, and the regionalization of culture. When *Hallyu* began in the late 1990s, new media platforms such as cable TV and satellite broadcasting had appeared in Asia, increasing demand for more diverse programming. Existing terrestrial broadcasting was based on single-channel transmission, but cable, satellite, and the Internet allowed multi-channel communication. Cable and satellite broadcasters typically operated over a hundred channels.

At first, cable TV merely retransmitted terrestrial programming, but it eventually developed comprehensive programming with multiple specialized channels. Beginning with Japan and Hong Kong, many countries introduced satellite TV. These developments caused demand for programming to skyrocket, but supply remained insufficient. Countries in Southeast Asia, unable to meet domestic demand, began to import content from elsewhere, including Japan and South Korea.

Development of mass communication
The development of mass communication created a convenient environment for the public to access information about the entertainment industry and helped spread Korean content in East Asia. In the past, sources of entertainment news were limited, and people depended on print media such as magazines and terrestrial broadcasts for information about overseas entertainers. With the development of the Internet, the proliferation of broadcast media, and an increase in overseas travel, sources of information became more open and diverse. The appearance of such new media as cable TV and satellite broadcasting led to the growth of specialized channels that introduced entertainers and provided music charts, spurring the diffusion of Korean content. Entertainment websites and fan communities allowed users to form clubs and share information about artists and programs. As two-way communication systems developed, companies selling Korean content created websites to upload material, opened homepages for celebrities, and marketed their wares on other popular websites. Active online communication helped spread content, trends, and entertainment news by word of mouth, increasing the speed at which information was disseminated.

Cultural regionalization
"Cultural regionalization" refers to the phenomenon of greater regional popularity of content that expresses a particular culture and sentiments. For example, *telenovelas* depicting love and adventure stories are popular throughout Latin America, where they have a larger following than soap operas from the US. They are exported to more than a hundred countries around the world.
      Cultural regionalization can be found among East Asian countries such as China, Taiwan, South Korea, and Japan. In the 1980s, movies from Hong Kong became popular in the region; Japanese animation, manga, dramas, and console games spread from the 1970s onward. Films and dramas from India depicting its religions and history have become popular throughout South Asia. The global cultural industry has been diversified by such regionalization of culture, shifting the global cultural market from a US-dominated structure to one of regional blocs. Cultural regionalization derives from the kinship consumers feel for culturally proximate content. The Latin American popularity of *telenovelas* can be attributed to a sense of cultural proximity among Hispanic countries. Similarities in language, religion, fashion, music, nonverbal communication, humor, and ethnicity cause people to feel commonality. The shared culture of Confucianism, use of Chinese characters, and similarity in phenotype contribute to feelings of kinship among East Asians. *Hallyu* was initially fostered by such cultural proximity, which led to cultural regionalization.

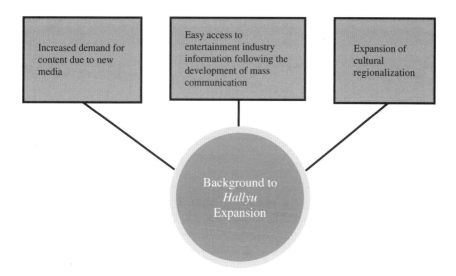

Figure 1–4.   Background to *Hallyu* expansion

Characteristics of Koreans and *Hallyu*

Openness

The prime driving force of *Hallyu* is the openness of the Korean people, who throughout history have embraced the notion of a universal civilization. Beginning in the Bronze Age, Koreans accepted Chinese script, Buddhism, and Confucianism from the north; in more modern times, they have taken in Western culture. Historically, the Korean Peninsula, as a terminus for the Silk Road, which stretched across land and sea, was a region where diverse traditions came into contact with one another. Since ancient times, Korea has welcomed advanced cultures. This openness kept Korea from lagging behind and allowed the nation to remain in step with global trends despite its geopolitical limitations as a peninsula. Korean content is sought for the originality of Korean culture (such as traditional culture and drama), as well as for its universal appeal. This is a manifestation of Korean openness.

Originality (goyuseong)

Koreans tend to preserve the essence of the cultures they adopt, while at the same time advancing them creatively, rather than merely reproducing the original. Although Korea has preserved earlier forms of Confucianism and Buddhism, Koreans have also, as exemplified by the invention of *hangeul*, demonstrated excellence in creating new cultural paradigms and refining the practices of advanced civilizations.

A key factor in the warm reception of *Hallyu* is that South Korea has presented its culture in a readily communicable form and has not acted as a mere end-user or transmitter of Western culture. As a result, the dramas *Jewel in the Palace* and *Winter Sonata*, spread in the early stages of *Hallyu*, and the novel *Please Look after Mom* by Shin Kyung-sook, have been well received. The driving force behind *Hallyu* is the revelation of the essence of Korean culture in a refined style.

Compatibility (gongjonseong)
Koreans embrace and internalize foreign cultures. Different cultures can coexist and evolve peacefully within the nation, increasing local diversity. South Korea is one of the few countries in which the presence of multiple major religions with many devotees has not caused internal conflicts. South Korea is also rare in that Western lifestyles, shamanistic practices, Confucian values, and Christian and Buddhist views of life and death coexist. South Korea's unique acceptance of, and harmonious coexistence with, other cultures plays an important role in the country's cultural strategy; for this reason, people of different historical backgrounds and experiences can accept *Hallyu* without feeling that it carries cultural imperialism. *Jewel in the Palace* and the musical *The Last Empress* depict uniquely Korean historical and cultural characteristics, while K-pop and performances of *Nanta* do not betray a clear national origin. The situation described above explains the coexistence of diverse content, from which one can anticipate further expansion of *Hallyu*.

(pp. 171–177)

C.   Key impacts of Hallyu policies

Impact of *Hallyu* on South Korea's economy

After the initial tide, *Hallyu* seemed to lose its force for a period, but as K-pop gained popularity and many South Korean idol groups became active in the Japanese market, fervor for Korean cultural products returned with even greater intensity. Rather than remaining concentrated in Asia as it had initially, *Hallyu* reached various regions of Europe, and a K-pop concert was held in France with great success. *Hallyu* spread with few geographic limitations to Latin America, Africa, and beyond.

The first wave of *Hallyu* was led by dramas such as *Winter Sonata* and *Jewel in the Palace*, and their lead actors, including Bae Yong-joon, Choi Ji-woo, and Lee Young-ae, commanded attention. With the Japanese craze for Korean girl groups, however, K-pop emerged as the new driving force of *Hallyu*. This shift from drama to popular music laid the foundation for the diversification of *Hallyu* content.

Hallyu products like dramas and popular music have had an enormous impact on Korean content industry exports overall. The resurgence of *Hallyu* has contributed greatly to the recovery of these exports, which had slowed due to the global financial crisis.

South Korea's national brand value, enhanced through *Hallyu*, has elevated the credibility and perceived quality of Korean products overseas, increasing their consumption. In particular, the fashion industry, which is closely associated with *Hallyu* stars, is enjoying increased demand, especially in China, Southeast Asia, and other regions heavily influenced by *Hallyu*. Admiration for *Hallyu* stars' good looks has also heightened demand for plastic surgery. Well-known plastic surgeons in Korea have responded to this increased demand by training coordinators for foreigners and developing service packages that include shopping

Table 1–4. Export of South Korea's content industry (Unit: $1,000,000)

Category	2008	2009	2010	2011	Yearly increase (%) (2010–2011)	Average annual increase (%) (2008–2011)
Publishing	260.0	250.8	357.9	283.4	−20.8	2.90
Manhwa	4.1	4.2	8.2	17.2	111.1	60.9
Music	16.5	31.3	83.3	196.1	135.5	128.4
Games	1,093.9	1,240.9	1,606.1	2,378.1	48.1	29.5
Motion Pictures	21.0	14.1	13.6	15.8	16.5	-9.0
Animation	80.6	89.7	96.8	115.9	19.7	12.9
Broadcasting	171.3	184.6	184.7	222.4	20.4	9.1
Advertisements	14.2	93.2	75.6	102.2	35.3	93.0
Character Design	228.3	236.5	276.3	392.3	42.0	19.8
Knowledge and Information	339.9	348.9	368.2	432.3	17.4	8.3
Content Solutions	107.7	114.7	118.5	146.3	23.4	10.7
Total	2,337.6	2,608.7	3,189.1	4,302.0	34.9	22.5

trips and tours. Also, the cosmetics industry has successfully entered overseas markets, focusing on regions where *Hallyu* has had a strong impact. Indeed, the beauty, plastic surgery, and cosmetics industries are all directly influenced by *Hallyu*.

Research shows that the expansion of *Hallyu* has spurred growth within related service and manufacturing sectors and elevated the brand value of Korean electronics, motor vehicles, and IT. Inbound tourism has also enjoyed a boom thanks to *Hallyu*'s enhancement of South Korea's national image and its appeal as a travel destination.

One analysis estimated the direct economic effect of PSY's "Gangnam Style" at ₩10 billion as of September 2012. Sungshin Women's University professor Seo Gyeong-deok, an expert on Korea's public relations, claimed that "the economic impact of 'Gangnam Style' on the K-pop market is easily over ₩1 trillion," a figure Seo derived from the flow-on effects of PSY's previous campaigns, including a billboard advertisement in Times Square and full-page ads in *The Wall Street Journal*. As *Hallyu* spreads, more research is being conducted on its economic effects, and results have confirmed a direct relationship between the expansion of *Hallyu* and its financial impact.

One such study, "Analysis of the Impact of *Hallyu* on South Korea's Exports and Measures for FTA Utilization, with a Focus on China and Vietnam" (Dec. 2011), was conducted by the Korean Association of Trade and Industry Studies. In order to analyze the impact of *Hallyu*, the study surveyed university students in China and Vietnam and gathered information on their levels of consumption and contact with *Hallyu* and its subsidiary products, and their willingness to

---

"Gangnam Style" Economic Impact Estimated at ₩1 Trillion after 100 Million *YouTube* Views

On the 4th day of this month, PSY's music video became the first by a Korean artist to surpass 100 million views on *YouTube*. This figure was reached only 52 days after upload, a feat previously achieved by only a select few pop stars, including Justin Bieber, Lady Gaga, and Jennifer Lopez. The unprecedented success of this video of less than four minutes came at no cost in promotion fees. Some experts project that the economic impact of "Gangnam Style" will reach as high as ₩1 trillion.

Seo Gyeong-deok, professor at Sungshin Women's University and an expert on Korean public relations, claimed, "The economic impact of 'Gangnam Style' on the K-pop market is easily over ₩1 trillion." Seo derived this figure from the flow-on effects of his placing of a billboard advertisement in New York's Times Square and full-page ads in *The Wall Street Journal*.

Profits from domestic sales of PSY's sixth album, released in July, are expected to reach ₩760 million. With the addition of an estimated ₩3 billion in concert revenues and royalty payments, the total comes to over ₩4 billion. Additional profits of ₩4–5 billion are expected from 9–10 product endorsement deals. Profits from PSY's music video, which has been viewed over 100 million times on *YouTube* and ranks high on iTunes, are growing. In addition to his existing product endorsements with a mobile communications company and a sound equipment company, PSY is negotiating deals for a dozen more. PSY's income from endorsements is expected to reach ₩3–5 billion. "Gangnam Style" also caused a stir in the stock market. Because of the "PSY effect," YG Entertainment, his management company, has seen its stock price jump from ₩46,000 per share to ₩64,800, as of today.

—Park Myoung-gee, Reporter, The Korea Economic Daily (Sept. 5, 2012)

---

purchase Korean consumer goods. The results showed that contact with and consumption of *Hallyu* content boosted preference for Korean products in both countries. It was found that 76.58% of respondents in China and 74.93% of respondents in Vietnam who had been in contact with *Hallyu* content showed increased preference for Korean products. In addition, 76.58% of Chinese students and 89.46% of Vietnamese students answered that contact with *Hallyu* significantly improved their perception of South Korea. The responses of Chinese students revealed that popular music, TV dramas, fashion, advertisements, and *Hallyu* stars had a meaningful positive effect on South Korea's national image. The responses of Vietnamese students suggested that all *Hallyu* genres (popular music, films, TV dramas, fashion, performances, advertisements, and *Hallyu* stars) except animation had a meaningful positive effect on South Korea's national image.

One of *Hallyu*'s major contributions has been boosting foreign tourism. Je Sang-won, manager of the Hallyu Division of the Korea Tourism Organization, said, "The number of foreign visitors to South Korea in 2011 was 9.7 million, an 11.3% increase from the previous year, which can be partly attributed to the power of *Hallyu.*" He added, "Tourists from Malaysia increased 38%, and those from Hong Kong increased by 23%. The popularity of Korean content certainly helped."

In March, the Korea Chamber of Commerce and Industry published the results of the "Survey on the Economic Effects of *Hallyu* and its Applications in South Korean Companies." Of the 300 major companies in the service and manufacturing industries surveyed, 82.8% responded that the expansion of *Hallyu* enhanced the image of South Korea and its products, and 51.9% responded that *Hallyu* stimulated sales, confirming the Korean Wave's practical role in increasing corporate revenue.

Reorganizing the promotion system for sustained expansion of *Hallyu*

Official launch of the Hallyu culture promotion taskforce
At a New Year's meeting on January 2, 2012, the Minister of Culture, Sports and Tourism stated that the focus of *Hallyu* must be extended from popular culture to K-culture, which encompasses all aspects of Korean culture, in order to benefit South Korean industries. On January 30, the Ministry launched the Hallyu Culture Promotion Taskforce for the sustained expansion of *Hallyu*. The Taskforce was designed to provide comprehensive and systematic support for the promotion of *Hallyu* and thereby redirect the fervor for K-pop to K-culture, which encompasses all areas of Korean culture. The Taskforce has established long-term strategies for promoting *Hallyu* and elicited cooperation from related government offices and private enterprises.

The First Vice-Minister of Culture, Sports and Tourism was appointed as director; the Policy Planning General was appointed as deputy director; and the Director General of the Culture and Arts Bureau was appointed as executive administrator of the Hallyu Promotion Taskforce. Other members include the Heads of the Popular Culture Industry Division; Regional & National Culture Division; International Culture Division; Performing Arts & Traditional Arts

Table 1–5. Perceived impact of *Hallyu* on sales by industry (Unit: %)

Industry	Impact perceived	No impact perceived
All	51.9	48.1
Culture	86.7	13.3
Tourism	85.7	14.3
Distribution	75.0	25.0
Food	45.2	54.8
Electronics	43.3	56.7
Cosmetics	35.5	64.5
Automobiles	28.1	71.9
Apparel	23.3	76.7

(Source: Korea Chamber of Commerce and Industry, "Survey on the Economic Effects of *Hallyu* and its Applications in South Korean Companies.")

Division; International Tourism Division; International Sports Division; Broadcasting & Advertising Division; and Culture City Policy Division.

Following the launch of the Taskforce, the Ministry announced its three-part plan to promote *Hallyu*. The Taskforce announced "creative strategies for the revitalization of traditional culture" on January 30; "strategies for the advancement of South Korea's arts and their global enjoyment" on February 28; and "measures to increase the global competitiveness of South Korean cultural content" on April 17.

First, the vision of "creating a sophisticated, cultured nation through the promotion of traditional culture (K-arts)" was presented, with the declared goal of sustaining the newly opened "*Hallyu* 3.0 era." The Taskforce set up 10 projects under 5 promotion strategies for traditional culture: (1) to expand the base of traditional culture; (2) to facilitate harmony between traditional and contemporary cultures; (3) to increase overseas exposure of traditional Korean culture; (4) to create a basis for the promotion of traditional culture; and (5) to increase opportunities to enjoy traditional culture. Based on these strategies, the Taskforce plans to work towards penetrating the global market. It aims to: disseminate and popularize traditional culture, starting in the public sector; form favorable conditions for creative applications of traditional culture; and enter overseas markets through strategic cultural exchanges.

Second, with the goal of developing "global enjoyment of South Korean art (K-arts)" and the vision of "creating a nation of advanced art and culture," the Taskforce set up 10 core projects under 4 promotion strategies for the arts: (1) to strategically foster core cultural content; (2) to nurture a specialized workforce to promote art and culture; (3) to create "smart" art and culture; and (4) to exchange art and culture as a way to expand *Hallyu*. The Taskforce has carried out additional projects for the promotion of Korean literature, fine arts, performing arts, traditional arts, and crafts.

Third, under the vision of "a powerful nation with globally competitive content that communicates with the world," the Taskforce set up 15 projects under 5 promotion strategies for cultural content: (1) to increase content competitiveness; (2) to create a healthy ecosystem for cultural content; (3) to support entry into global markets; (4) to maximize ripple effects; and (5) to increase reciprocal exchanges. These strategies aim to promote sustainable development of industries that produce key *Hallyu* content, including K-pop and dramas, and to maximize the effects of *Hallyu* expansion.

The advisory committee for the promotion of Hallyu

On April 3, 2012, the Advisory Committee for the Promotion of *Hallyu* was formed to discuss the sustained expansion and promotion of *Hallyu*, as well as policy directions. Experts in art and culture came together to beat a new path for Korean culture in the *Hallyu* 3.0 era. The Committee is comprised of 19 experts from various fields, including traditional culture, fine arts, cultural content, tourism, and economics. The Committee was formed to discuss ways to expand the focus of *Hallyu* from popular culture to K-culture, which encompasses all aspects of Korean culture, thereby benefiting those industries in this age of *Hallyu* 3.0.

At the first three meetings, the Committee had in-depth discussions on the strategic areas set forth by the MCST (revitalization of traditional culture;

advancement of South Korea's arts and their global enjoyment) and measures to link *Hallyu* to industrial development. Through the Committee, the Ministry will continue to hear from various fields related to *Hallyu*, review the opinions of committee members constructively, and apply those opinions to policies and projects in various fields.

Foundation of the Hallyu support council and international culture communications forum
On April 27, 2012, the MCST helped inaugurate the Hallyu Support Council, led by the Federation of Korean Industries. The Hallyu Support Council is comprised of major economic organizations, industry groups, content industry experts, and entertainment agencies. Taking advantage of *Hallyu*, the Council aims to enhance the image of South Korea and its enterprises, and to sustain the development and expansion of *Hallyu*. The Council is expected to contribute to the formation of a virtuous cycle involving *Hallyu* and the development of related industries.

In June, the International Culture Communications Forum was held to promote reciprocal cultural exchanges in response to the expansion of *Hallyu*. The Forum is operated by 12 members on a planning and steering committee and roughly 10 staff in each of 4 divisions: art and culture, media relations, academia, and cooperation. With the overarching goal of "globalization of Korean culture," the Forum plans to meet monthly to discuss the current status of cultural exchange, as well as future tasks, visions and strategies, and measures for action.

Discovering talent and fostering a creative workforce
In April 2012, the MCST established the K-Arts Academy to help content creators understand the value of traditional arts in contemporary society. The Academy was opened to creative individuals in the cultural production industries, including broadcasting, film, and digital content, and produced its first 134 graduates in May. The K-Arts Academy has expanded under its current name of Hallyu Academy.

The programs were designed as part of efforts to create a "*Hallyu* of traditional arts" that will help Korean culture embed itself in international mainstream cultures, rather than subside like a fad. The Hallyu Academy provides hands-on experience in traditional arts with instruction from celebrated masters. In addition, lectures on traditional arts are organized for public diplomacy employees to enhance their knowledge of Korean culture and increase understanding of *Hallyu* content.

Efforts have been made to increase the spread of Korean literature and art. Featured authors, such as Im Cheol-woo and Jung Yu-jeong, have been selected for overseas promotion as representatives of Korean literature, and samples of their works have been translated to elicit response in foreign markets and seek connections with literary agencies. Programs for the overseas promotion of up-and-coming visual artists have also been organized, and various other efforts have been made to introduce Korean artists at an international level.

The above programs endeavor to nurture talent with humanistic value, promote the international exchange of art and culture, and increase opportunities for Korean artists to enter overseas markets. These meaningful efforts are laying a firm foundation for South Korea's cultural content in the long term.

Future tasks

The unbalanced concentration of *Hallyu* in select regions and the limitations of the profit model are two of the greatest challenges facing further promotion. Although the genres within *Hallyu* have diversified in recent years, popular culture still comprises its bulk. Conformity of content that focuses on celebrities is a growing concern. Of the 1,200 foreigners who participated in a survey conducted by KOFICE in February of this year, 62% responded that *Hallyu* will subside within five years. The overwhelming concentration of *Hallyu* exports within Asia also must be addressed. China, Japan, and Southeast Asia account for 70% of all *Hallyu* exports. A study by *Maeil Business Newspaper*, titled "True Colors of *Hallyu*" (April 2011), showed that Japan accounted for 80.8% of overseas K-pop consumption. Southeast Asia and China accounted for 13.6% and 4.4%, respectively. These figures show that the spread of K-pop is skewed. In order to overcome this imbalance, restructuring and diversification of profit models will be necessary.

Opposition to and antagonism of the Korean Wave pose further challenges that must not be overlooked if *Hallyu* is to be sustained. In Korea, overemphasis on profitability might arouse negative responses, and opposition to *Hallyu* might arise abroad among those who want to protect their own culture and industries. In some areas, malicious, disparaging rumors have caused the formation of anti-*Hallyu* forces. A case in point is the dissemination by Japanese anti-*Hallyu* groups of manga belittling Korean celebrities. In order to curb the popularity of South Korean dramas in China, broadcast of imported content was banned during prime time, from 19:00–22:00.

Finally, organic integration is lacking in promotional efforts for *Hallyu*. Scattered government departments and affiliated organizations currently oversee *Hallyu*-related policies, making it difficult to set a unified direction, share plans, and cooperate on projects.

1.1.3.   Korean Cultural Centers: Expanding Korean Cultural Exchange Overseas

Reference: *Korea: A Cultural Stronghold*, 10th Volume from *National Administration White Paper of President Lee Myung-bak's Government* (2008–2013), MCST, February 2013, pp. 195–203.

A.   Building Korean cultural centers: Bases for international cultural exchange

Establishing cultural centers to spread Korean culture

Following measures to strengthen cultural cooperation and encourage exchange, Culture Promotion Centers (*hongbowon*) were built in Russia, Germany, China, and Osaka, on top of existing centers in Paris, New York, Los Angeles, and Tokyo; these Culture Promotion Centers were renamed Korean Cultural Centers (*munhwawon*) in 2006, with additional centers built in the UK, Shanghai, Vietnam, and Argentina between 2006 and 2008. These additional centers brought the total to 12 by the end of 2008.

In 2008, in order to diversify and expand ties with such regions as the Middle East, Central Asia, Africa, and Eastern Europe, as well as to support diplomatic efforts in energy resource cooperation, centers were built in Kazakhstan, Nigeria, and Poland. Culture and Information Officers were dispatched to these three nations in September of that year to oversee cultural promotion activities. A review was then conducted of the conditions and procedures involved in building these new centers; remodeling began in 2009. The Korean Cultural Centers in Poland and Kazakhstan were completed in December 2009; day-to-day operations began soon thereafter. Opening ceremonies were held in early 2010. In March 2010, renovation efforts were also completed at the Korean Cultural Center in Nigeria, and it opened in May. Korus House, which had been a de facto cultural center under the Government Information Agency, was converted into a Korean Cultural Center to serve Washington, D.C.

The Korean Cultural Center in Poland has functioned as a base to introduce Korean culture to Central and Eastern Europe and to expand cultural ties with Eastern Europe on the whole. The Korean Cultural Center in Kazakhstan also responds actively to Central Asia's passion for *Hallyu*, while grafting Korea's image as a cutting-edge IT superpower to that of a cultural powerhouse and offering a harmonious presentation of Korea's contemporary and traditional cultures. The Korean Cultural Center in Nigeria will help strengthen Korea's ties with West Africa and introduce Korean culture to more Africans, which will in turn support energy diplomacy.

In 2009, plans were drawn up to establish centers in Indonesia, the Philippines, Australia, and Spain to strengthen and expand cultural exchange with Southeast Asia, Oceania, and Western Europe. A review of the conditions and procedures surrounding the establishment of these centers was conducted, then buildings were secured in 2010 and renovation started that same year. The centers opened in the first half of 2011. Since then, further centers have opened in Turkey, Hungary, and Mexico, and in December 2012, a 24th center opened its doors in India. In order to expand cultural exchange and strengthen Korea's cultural promotion activities, the government will continue to build centers, focusing on locations where Culture and Information Officers have been sent.

Strengthening operations for Korean cultural centers

Accomplishments of Korean cultural centers

Operations have been improved and reinforced at the 24 centers so that their programs can be carried out more efficiently. A major project in 2011 focused on strengthening the centers' role as hubs for the spread of *Hallyu* and localizing, specializing, and branding their promotional activities. Center operations have been made more systematic.

Accomplishments resulting from these efforts are fivefold. First, the explosion in *Hallyu* fans worldwide has contributed to the expansion of the scope of Korean culture. Fan activities have been encouraged in the countries where cultural centers are located, and other events have been organized, such as K-pop contests and Korean culture festivals held by local clubs. Second, students enrolling in classes at the centers and the number of classes offered have surged. The Korean Cultural Centers in Russia and Kazakhstan saw an enormous jump in enrolments. To meet demand, the centers had to find additional classroom space

Table 1–6.   Current Status of Overseas Korean Cultural Centers (2011)

Location	Visitors	Korean Language Classes (Number of Classes/Persons)	Culture Classes (Number of Classes/Persons)	Movie Screenings (Number of Screenings/Persons)	Exhibitions (Number of Exhibitions/Persons)	Performances (Number of Performances/Persons)	Website Traffic (Persons)	Miscellaneous (Field Trips, etc./Persons)
Tokyo	66,729	493/7,267	201/2,291	19/6,150	29/10,520	62/21,665	1,151,346	18,836
Osaka	49,371	1,781/24,183	413/4,572	24/310	7/2,613	28/11,360	333,465	6,333
Beijing	73,168	519/13,078	149/3,186	51/2,307	13/1,647	34/7,113	255,742	47,637
Shanghai	46,019	174/12,462	74/1,478	1/152	10/991	25/57,388	82,240	11,159
Vietnam	28,860	628/18,109	130/2,903	28/98	8/1,047	36/2,790	113,428	3,913
France	31,712	654/10,604	124/1,028	16/486	19/24,981	65/4,738	190,081	7,928
Germany	16,763	250/2,783	329/3,005	12/173	14/905	38/3,023	89,661	6,790
Russia	31,712	654/10,604	124/1,028	16/486	19/24,981	65/4,738	190,081	7,928
UK	22,420	209/2,174	8/782	35/2,226	9/540	53/105,117	162,304	2,220
New York	15,440	–	–	22/2,700	9/7,630	14/52,030	263,000	4,470
Los Angeles	98,284	47/9,368	15/1,044	41/2,315	12/9,450	23/6,664	367,928	69,443
Argentina	46,368	39/1,749	–	48/897	7/30,449	–	83,398	103
Kazakhstan	18,027	959/9,923	264/2,284	49/1,455	6/19,418	2/3,600	27,503	4,679
Poland	10,442	1,112/2,410	245/1,796	11/257	5/850	33/1,757	31,581	3,372
Nigeria	14,434	168/1,661	272/3,329	45/807	2/900	22/3,370	8,211	3,819
Washington, D.C.	27,414	74/4,350	57/4,680	16/2,100	11/2,030	26/12,260	1,041,116	2,034
Sydney	44,792	32/1,324	87/836	25/930	1/177	24/25,689	44,562	12,676
Spain	4,129	22/304	51/389	5/157	4/654	2/140	32,055	3,362
Indonesia	13,520	378/3,425	3/80	12/335	17/1,732	23/2,846	38,131	5,102
Philippines	19,182	316/4,926	192/2,463	6/410	62/5,349	24/2,442	44,662	3,592

(Source: MCST)

and affiliate with local universities to offer year-round classes. Third, overseas Cultural Center programs have been localized, specialized, and branded. The centers offer several unique programs under the "One Center, One Trademark Program" policy. They also offer "Korean Culture at Your Doorstep" programs where classes are taught at local community venues so that people do not have to travel. Items of everyday culture, including Korean food, beauty practices, fashion, and other lifestyle activities, are also introduced. Fourth, centers have developed more specific operating systems, with more training offered by Culture and Information Officers, who have begun to be dispatched with greater frequency. Increased attention is being paid to spreading awareness of the centers' corporate logo. Other accomplishments followed to strengthen the brand image of centers and establish accounting systems that enhance transparency. Fifth, performance evaluations of Culture and Information Officers were conducted. Along with achievements made in cultural promotion activities and center operations, bookkeeping systems were set in place.

Specialization and branding of center operations
Promotional activities are customized to respective cultural centers by reflecting on local needs and reception of Korean culture. "Korean Culture Week" activities unique to each center are held, and select programs are chosen as each center's distinct face. Furthermore, programs are taken directly to communities so that they can better resonate with locals. Classes that meet local needs are also provided to support the spread of *Hallyu*.

Events specific to different centers, such as the Korea-Japan Festival (Tokyo) or Korean Cultural Day (Los Angeles), are branded under the "One Center, One Trademark Program" policy, and activities are put in place to encourage experiences of Korean culture, contribute to local society by inviting the underprivileged, and bring events directly to communities under the "Korean Culture at Your Doorstep" initiative. Language courses are offered to marriage migrants and workers going to Korea. Other targeted classes support the spread of *Hallyu*. Spaces are created to allow participants to experience elements of Korean culture (food, beauty, fashion, etc.), and special courses are established for dedicated fans of Korea. Contests are held to select the best schemes offered by centers, through which the most creative and exemplary activities are discovered. Center directors with winning programs receive incentives from the government. Each year the best program is chosen and the winning center receives a prize.

Specialized Programs of Overseas Korean Cultural Centers in 2011

Asia, Oceania (8)

Korean Cultural Center, Tokyo

– Nationwide speech competition, "Talk Korean"
– K-pop concert in support of recovery from the Tohoku Earthquake
– K-pop contest
– Korean Culture Tourism Week
– Korean Cultural Exchange Night
– "Korean Film Week" at the Tokyo International Film Festival, etc.

Korean Cultural Center, Osaka

- Korean traditional art performances (in four regions, including Hiroshima and Tokushima)
- *"Hanmadang"* benefit for victims of the Tohoku Earthquake
- Korean speech contest
- K-pop contest
- Instructors dispatched to teach taekwondo
- 2011 Korean Film Week in Osaka, etc.

Korean Cultural Center, Beijing

- *"Hahoe* God Mask Game" at Pingyao International Photography Festival
- K-pop contest
- Korean costume exhibition
- Culture classes taught in local communities
- Korean movie screenings
- "2011 Korean Culture Festival: Beautiful Clothes, Delicious Food"
- 2011 Korea-China Taekwondo Festival
- Film festival featuring director Lee Jun-ik, etc.

Korean Cultural Center, Shanghai

- National Dance Company of Korea tour
- Korean Culture Tourism Festival, etc.

Korean Cultural Center, Vietnam

- New7 Wonders Jeju-do and Halong Bay Promotion
- K-pop contest
- Korea-Vietnam children's traditional storybook publication, etc.

Korean Cultural Center, Sydney

- Performances commemorating the 50th anniversary of diplomatic ties between South Korea and Australia
- Opening ceremony for the Korean Cultural Center in Sydney
- Research on Korean national image
- "Korean Art Today" special exhibition for the 50th anniversary of diplomatic ties between South Korea and Australia
- "Cinema on the Park" film screenings, etc.

Korean Cultural Center, the Philippines

- Opening ceremony for the Korean Cultural Center
- "Pinoy K-Pop Star" competition, Korean film screenings (*Apartment, Daytime Drinking*)
- *Hangeul* Day events
- Korea-Philippines cultural exchange events
- Promotional booths at film festival, etc.

Korean Cultural Center, Indonesia

- Drum Cat performances
- Exhibitions of Korean literary paintings

– Korean culture globalization events
– Korean food tasting, etc.

North and South America (4)

Korean Cultural Center, Washington, D.C.

– Art exhibitions (*Miindo,* exhibitions of four artists, Buddhist art, "Light and Wind Exhibition," works featuring local artists, etc.)
– Performing arts concerts (recitals by violinist Park Ji-hye and singer Park Ji-yun; performances by the Bibimbap Backpackers; opening ceremony for the American University Korea Garden, etc.)
– Korean film screenings (regular screenings, screenings featuring invited special correspondents), etc.

Korean Cultural Center, New York

– Korean culture classes in NYC public schools
– Staging of the Acom Company musical *Hero* at the Lincoln Center
– Support for the Sejong Soloist Gala Concert
– New York-London Exchange Exhibition
– "2011 Taste of Korea"
– Korean traditional dress fashion show
– *Hanbok* fashion events at the Metropolitan Museum of Art
– Funding for costumes and instruments for traditional music performances, etc.

Korean Cultural Center, Los Angeles

– Korean history and culture workshops (for police officers, educators, law enforcement officials, etc.)
– Spring seminar on Korean history and culture
– Korean performing arts showcase
– K-pop contest
– AFM (American Film Market) Night of Korean Cinema
– The 7th Dari Awards
– Production support for TV cooking show promoting Korean food
– Participation in LA Times Food Festival

Korean Cultural Center, Argentina

– K-pop contest for Latin America
– Support for Korean cellist to perform at the Ushuaia International Festival
– 2011 International Book Fair, etc.

Europe, Africa, and Commonwealth of Independent States (7)

Korean Cultural Center, UK

– Introduction of Korean culture at the Thames Festival
– K-pop contest
– "Monologue" special exhibition for artists at the creative studio of the Museum of Modern Art
– Launch of London Korea Film Festival, etc.

Korean Cultural Center, France

- Korea special at the "Made in Asia" Festival, Toulouse
- "Korea Week Special" at the Aquitaine Museum in Bordeaux
- Korean movie screenings at the 12th Tours Asian Film Festival
- National Chorus of Korea tour of Europe
- "Korea Connection" Korean Cultural Festival
- "Night of Korean Video Art" at Centre Pompidou
- Korea-France Exhibition on Culture & Arts Exchange
- "Korea Special" at the Villefavard Festival
- Korean booth at the Avignon Festival
- K-pop contest
- The 6th Korea-France Film Festival

Korean Cultural Center, Germany

- "Korean Culture at Your Doorstep" program
- National Chorus of Korea performance in Berlin
- Korean Food Week at the Free University of Berlin (inclusion of Korean items on university cafeteria menu)
- K-pop concerts and support for K-pop fan clubs
- National Gugak Center performance

Korean Cultural Center, Russia

- *Andong Hahoe* mask dance performance
- Performance by Theater MulKyul
- Namsadang Baudeogi performance
- K-Pop Cover Dance Festival
- *Hanbok* fashion show
- B-boy performance
- Festival of Korean Short Films

Korean Cultural Center, Kazakhstan

- The 1st Almaty K-Pop Contest
- Opening ceremony and commemorative performances for "Korea Year in Kazakhstan"
- Kukkiwon World Taekwondo Headquarters demonstration
- Korea Film Festival
- Publication of *Introduction to Korea* booklets

Korean Cultural Center, Spain

- Performance for the opening of "Beautiful Mind"
- Preliminary competition for European K-Pop Cover Dance Festival
- Support for Taekwondo "Tal" performance
- The 1st Art Exhibition of Korean Women Artists in Spain

Korean Cultural Center, Nigeria

- The 2nd Korea-Nigeria Drawing Contest
- Support for performances by K-pop cover groups
- The 2nd Korea Film Festival

Creation and Introduction of centers' logo
The rise of *Hallyu* has occasioned surging demand for Korean culture and a corresponding increase in Korean Cultural Centers overseas. In light of these developments, the need for a unified image to represent all overseas Korean Cultural Centers has grown. Countries such as the UK, Germany, France, and Italy either have developed or are working to develop a corporate logo for their respective cultural centers as well. Korea's Cultural Centers can be grouped together under a single logo and emerge as a branded base of operations for promoting Korean culture. This logo can be used on the centers' plates, signage, PR materials, newsletters, banners, and souvenirs.

Establishment of an accounting system
An accounting system has been in place since January 2012. The existing computer accounting program for the centers and their Culture and Information Officers was transferred to an online platform so that headquarters can access information on how the centers and officers are executing their budgets. This change has systematized budget management and made the process more transparent.

Compilation of data on Hallyu fan clubs
The network of Korean Cultural Centers has identified Korean fan clubs in 20 regions globally. Of the 20 regions where Korea has a center as of 2011, 182 fan clubs are active, with an estimated 3.3 million members. Club locations include Shanghai (11 clubs, 1.05 million members), Beijing (14 clubs, 730,000 members), New York (6 clubs, 500,000 members), Russia (23 clubs, 260,000 members), and Turkey (17 clubs, 170,000 members). The clubs can be further categorized by their orientation, that is, whether they are dedicated specifically to musicians, actors, movies, or television dramas, or oriented more generally. A feature of the phenomenon has been that the more widespread *Hallyu* is in a given locality, the greater the variety in fan clubs. Many clubs, for example, are dedicated to an individual singer or actor.

K-pop world festival
From 2011 to 2012, every center hosted a K-pop contest, with winners invited to Korea to compete in a final round. This event was intended to spread awareness of *Hallyu*. The "K-Pop World Festival" jointly involves the K-pop contest and performances by *Hallyu* stars, and has since established itself as a yearly festival.

The two World Festivals so far were held in Changwon, South Gyeongsang Province. In 2011, 21 winning teams composed of 40 contestants from 17 regions in 16 countries competed, and in 2012, 43 contestants from 15 countries went head to head in a fierce competition. Participants were given the opportunity to stay at a traditional *hanok* house, tour Gyeongbok Palace, and enjoy Korean culture.

Expanding Korean centers: "One-stop shops" for Korean culture

The MCST has been promoting Korean Centers as a new concept to meet demands for Korean culture together with the Korean Cultural Centers. The Ministry is working to establish a network of organizations to introduce more people to traditional and folk cultures, promote the cultural industry, encourage the creation of new tourism content, enhance competitiveness, and build a support system for making effective inroads into other countries. To that end, the Ministry plans to expand and reorganize the Korean Cultural Centers and locate the overseas offices of KOCCA and other relevant organizations in the same building. These buildings, known as Korean Centers, can provide one-stop services relating to Korean culture and art, the cultural industry, and tourism. Planning for the building and operation of Korean Centers has been pursued in earnest since 2006.

Construction on the Tokyo Korean Center began in June 2007 and was completed in April 2009; it opened in June 2009. This overseas Korean Center is located on a main street in Shinjuku and has a performance hall with 300 seats, a ulti-purpose exhibition space, a library, a reception room, and a traditional garden. The center is expected to spread *Hallyu* in Japan as well as play a defining role in encouraging exchanges of culture and the arts, tourism, cultural content, and sports.

In November 2008, the MCST purchased an empty lot in midtown Manhattan to build the New York Korean Center and inaugurated a design competition in October 2009 to select a winning architect in December. The New York Korean Center will function as a multi-purpose venue for cultural activities and will consist of seven floors and a basement, with a performance hall, exhibition rooms, *Hallyu* experience booths, lecture rooms, and a production studio for creative arts. These will serve as excellent spaces for performances, exhibitions, classes, and so on. This center is slated to open in 2014.

Thus far, Korean Centers are operating in four locations: Los Angeles (opened September 2006), Beijing (March 2007), Shanghai (July 2007), and Tokyo (June 2009). While their basic mandate involves paving the way for the continued spread of *Hallyu,* they also help globalize Korean traditional and folk culture, introduce "Han Style" to overseas audiences, and strengthen online information services. They are expected to improve cultural and tourism services oriented towards users in a way that goes beyond the existing cultural centers. The MCST is planning site expansions and other ways to support the Korean Centers' operations.

Integrating Korean cultural centers and Korean education centers

The spread of *Hallyu* has sharply increased demand for Korean language and culture education. This process has led to the belief that synergy can be acquired by integrating cultural services with educational offerings. Discussions began in 2011 with center directors overseeing programs for providing language lessons, which were offered to Koreans living overseas and local residents, at the Korean Cultural Centers. Upon receiving the MCST's plans for the upcoming year on December 29, 2011, President Lee Myung-bak remarked, "It is appropriate to integrate cultural centers and education centers. We should consider this issue from the perspective of users, and the ministries should not compete for credit. I'd like the matter settled as soon as possible." Discussion accelerated after he ordered plans for integration to be drawn up as soon as possible.

Debates on the particulars of the plan occurred during meetings organized by the Prime Minister's Office for relevant ministries. Initial discussions planned for the centers to be united and named Cultural Centers. However, when the Ministry of Education, Science and Technology requested that the word "education" be included in the centers' name, the Prime Minister's Office commissioned a consulting firm from February 20 to March 5, 2012, to come up with an appropriate name. After analyzing examples from 15 countries and conducting in-depth interviews, it was found that "Korean Cultural Center" received high marks for matching international trends, global recognition, and images of accessibility. After settling on that name, the Vice Minister of Culture, Vice Minister of Education, and Vice Minister of Foreign Affairs and Trade signed a memorandum of understanding (MOU) on April 12, with the Prime Minister's Office presiding, which declared that the integrated centers would henceforth be designated "Korean Cultural Centers," and included provisions for clauses referring to "education centers" to be removed from the Act on Education Support, etc., for Overseas Koreans. The MOU further stipulated that "education centers" be added to the functions listed in the organization plan of the Ministry of Foreign Affairs and Trade. At the meeting, participants decided on guiding principles for the new centers, including procedures for reviewing their operational structure.

After opinions were gathered from April 18 to 24, 2012, on the best way to integrate duties at the eight locations that had both a Korean Cultural Center and a Korean Education Center (Tokyo, Osaka, New York, Washington, Argentina, the UK, France, and Sydney), guidelines were drawn up for the integration (March 2012) and coordination (July 2012) of center operations.

Since June 2012, the centers have created synergy by exchanging information, conducting marketing efforts, and planning cultural programs that make use of the education centers' networks. The centers have also organized training sessions for Korean language instructors and workshops featuring Korean language experts. Korean language education programs will be offered at King Sejong Institutes in the Korean Cultural Centers.

The Act on Education Support, etc., for Overseas Koreans was accordingly amended by deleting all mention of education centers, and the cultural centers assumed all duties of the education centers. After the required period set aside for notification of this proposed regulation had passed, the revision was brought before the Cabinet on July 10 and submitted to the National Assembly on July 20, completing the legislative procedure.

As a result, the cultural centers, which were formerly responsible for international cultural exchange and overseas promotion of Korean culture, were integrated into new Korean Cultural Centers that also provide Korean language education to Koreans overseas. Korean Cultural Centers can not only provide enhanced benefits by delivering educational and cultural offerings together, but can also respond to growing demand for Korean language classes and information on Korean culture.

Locations hosting Korean Education Centers are now renamed Korean Cultural Centers or branches of such centers. The sites will be expanded to locations including the Commonwealth of Independent States (CIS). The challenges for medium- to long-term growth are balancing out overemphasis on certain countries to achieve more even global distribution of centers, and ensuring that educational and cultural services are offered effectively in these locations.

1.2. CULTURAL CONTENT INDUSTRY

The documents in this subsection provide a diachronic overview of South Korea's cultural export and market performance as a way to explain the economics of *Hallyu*. Together they demonstrate how the Korean Wave has become enmeshed in a discourse of growth and profit. The "cultural content industry" (*munhwa kontencheu saneop*), sometimes referred to simply as the "content industry," is the regular term for the set of enterprises across the nation that produce and sell creative goods. The term "culture content" first became widespread in the early 2000s, thanks to its high-tech overtones. While as late as 2008 the MCST published white papers on the "cultural industry," by the following year the favored term became "cultural content industry." These industries are overseen by an institution under the Ministry's umbrella, KOCCA, which consolidated the Korean Game Industry Agency and Korea Broadcasting Institute in May 2009 to form a larger governmental body whose annual budget reached ₩280 billion in 2012. Many documents in this sourcebook have some association with KOCCA, given its core responsibility of conducting research on cultural industries and publishing white papers. Because each white paper reaches a gargantuan 600 pages, we have excerpted judiciously.

Document 1.2.1, "Cultural Content Industry: Prospects and Projects," summarizes the status and prospects of nine cultural sectors as of 2012: *manhwa*, music, gaming, film, animation, advertising, licensed characters, knowledge and information, live performances, newspapers, broadcasting, and publishing. While the document distinguishes between "Content Industry" and "Media Industry," cultural sectors that receive official attention and designation change over time. In 2009, for instance, the *Content Industry White Paper* featured a brief on the "crafts industry," and in 2011, it included "fashion culture." What is crucial here is not the categories themselves but the increasing implication of multiple industries within *Hallyu* discourse, with aspirational and potentially disciplining effects.

Document 1.2.1 also treats the challenging issue of copyright. As seen elsewhere in this sourcebook (e.g., Document 2.3.1, "K-Pop Drives Resurgence of the Korean Wave," and various excerpts from *Hallyu Forever*), piracy and copyright infringement, together with anti-*Hallyu* movements, are regularly viewed as significant obstacles to the propagation of the Korean Wave. While the document does not offer concrete solutions for tackling misdemeanors, it provides mission statements on copyright, giving a window into how the government hopes to protect *Hallyu* content. Currently, in fact, four Copyright Commission Offices operate around the world (Beijing, Bangkok, Manila, and Hanoi), monitoring the situation in the most challenging locations.

Document 1.2.2, "2006 Cultural Industry White Paper: Imports and Exports," presents key export data from 2003 to 2005, which coincides with the end of the so-called "*Hallyu* 1.0" era. Document 1.2.3, "2011 Cultural Content Industry White Paper: Imports and Exports," reports similar data for the 2008 to 2011 period. Readers may use the two sources together to observe, with the support of statistics, the development of Korea's export market over that time frame. For example, Table 1–8 (p. 49) reveals that during the 2003–2005 period, gaming, broadcasting, and film exports had a strong presence, but the music industry had yet to make a substantial impact outside Korea. However, a shadow loomed over the broadcast industry despite its healthy 19.6% growth in 2005, and the data presented here links well with the situation illustrated in Document 2.1.2, "Initiatives to Overcome the 2007 Broadcast Export Crisis."

A definition of original equipment manufacturing (OEM), a term that appears several times in what follows, may help readers. As Table 1–9 on page 51 shows, overseas product sales are sub-divided into OEM and finished goods. OEM is similar to contract manufacturing, that is, the supply of services and products to another company in the form of outsourcing. OEM has been the main means by which Korean animation is sold overseas. In 2005, OEM accounted for 71.7% of all exports in this sector, largely because of Korean animation studios' connections to American television. Perhaps the most well-known example is AKOM Production's lengthy partnership with *The Simpsons*, a subcontract business relationship infamously parodied by Banksy in a 2010 intro sequence for the show.

Document 1.2.3, "2011 Cultural Content Industry White Paper: Imports and Exports," presents more sophisticated and comprehensive data on cultural exports. For instance, an improvement over the 2006 document is the inclusion of information on industry imports and exports by region (p. 67). A comparison of Tables 1–24 and 1–25, in particular, reveals the striking trade imbalance in Korea's favor with the main *Hallyu* destinations—China, Japan, and Southeast Asia—in music and broadcast content. This imbalance is a primary reason for the rise of anti-*Hallyu* sentiment in major Asian markets, as seen in Document 2.1.3, "2009 Broadcast Video Content: Strategies and Policies for Propagation."

"Knowledge and Information" (*jisik jeongbo*) and "Content Solutions" appear as new industry categories in page 65. The business components of the knowledge and information industry include a hodgepodge of digital materials that rely on software development, such as e-learning materials, database construction and management, Internet portal sites, and even indoor golf simulators. The content solutions industry is primarily concerned with mobile devices and platforms, with multimedia message services and mobile payment systems forming the core of the sector. The difference between "Broadcasting" and "Independent Broadcasting Productions," also featured in Table 1–23, is explained in the introduction to Section 2.1, "Television," on page 91.

This segment on the cultural content industry ends with a short article from a weekly magazine on the Korean gaming industry, "Korea Conquers Gaming World," which makes the striking claim that "the Korean Wave is more dominant in the gaming industry than in any other (p. 86)," an often accepted statement in Korean media. For this sourcebook, however, as discussed in the Introduction, we have not allocated a full section to the gaming industry because its products do not draw attention specifically back to Korea in the way dramas and K-pop do. To put it succinctly, gaming may boost the Korean economy, but it appears to do little to boost Korea's soft power. This article may then suffice as a demonstration of the pride invested in this sector. It is worth noting in passing here that the export sales data presented in this document do not match the figures in Document 1.2.2, "2006 Cultural Industry White Paper," (p. 56–59), apparently because the two respective organizations, KOCCA and the Korea Entertainment System Industry Association (KESA), used different methods to collect data.

1.2.1.   Cultural Content Industry: Prospects and Projects

Reference: *Korea: A Cultural Stronghold*, 10ᵗʰ Volume from *National Administration White Paper of President Lee Myung-bak's Government* (2008–2013), MCST, February 2013, pp. 580–591.

A.   *Prospects of the cultural content industry*

Despite forecasts of overall economic contraction, South Korea's content industry is expected to continue to grow due to increases in content exports, competitiveness of Korean content, domestic demand, and export destinations. The growth rate of the content industry is projected to exceed twice that of the nation's economy as a whole. Despite increasing uncertainty, sales in the content industry for 2012 are projected to reach ₩88 trillion, a 7.7% increase from the previous year. The content consumption paradigm is also expected to change. With the increase in smartphone users, thrift within the "smart" environment is expected to grow, as consumers use group coupons and discounts through websites and specialized applications such as WeMakePrice, Ticket Monster, Groupon, and Coupang. Due to the double blow of recession and inflation, frugal consumer behavior is expected to persist.

Manhwa

Although sales figures for printed books will likely continue to wane, the webtoon industry is expected to fare relatively well. Changes leading to increased profitability are projected, such as the introduction of advertisements. Making open markets more vital and expanding home shopping will enhance *manhwa* market distribution. Capitalizing on webtoons' success in South Korea, the *manhwa* industry is expected to increase Korea's presence in foreign markets, increasing exports to Japan and elsewhere in Asia. It is also anticipated that the industry will build upon its recent emergence in Latin America and enter the United States, in part through the publication of well-known educational *manhwa* in English.

Music

With increasing awareness of K-pop in South Korea and abroad, the music industry is expected to show relatively high growth, with large Korean talent management agencies at the center. The propagation of smart devices and music-related apps will help spread digital audio and increase the market's size. However, the growth of the industry will be directly related to the progress it makes in pricing audio sources. Expansion of talent searches, auditions, and related programs on terrestrial and cable channels will lead to an increase in related audio content. Music industry exports are expected to rise as performers affiliated with large domestic agencies reach beyond Asia into the diverse markets of Europe and the Americas.

Gaming

Despite concerns over increased regulation of the domestic gaming industry, intensifying global competition, and recession in the domestic market, gaming sales are expected to grow due to the propagation of smart devices and the expansion of online and mobile cross-platforms. Diverse game models based on mobile technologies such as augmented reality and location-based services are anticipated. However, the influx of Chinese funding and other massive forms of capital into the domestic market through such methods as mergers and acquisitions is expected to have a negative impact on local enterprises' sales. Continued export growth is projected, centering on China and other emerging markets. The focus will shift from online games to those targeting smart devices. Proactive marketing by larger game developers as well as mobile game developers is expected to contribute to increased exports.

Film

The keys for film industry growth include a steady stream of box office hits by domestic production companies and measures to increase exports. Stable growth is expected for theatrical releases as long as imported blockbusters and domestic films continue to become hits. Increased demand for Internet Protocol Television (IPTV) and similar services as a result of the popularity of smart devices will lead to the emergence of additional markets.

Continuing the trend from 2011, exports to Asia and other select areas are expected to grow. Although the industry will be hard-pressed to escape the effects of overall recession, the export of films with sophisticated storylines, the success of well-known South Korean producers abroad, and the broad link to K-pop and *Hallyu* are expected to mitigate such issues.

Animation

Sales are expected to grow in the animation industry, centered on creative production and increased government and private sector investment. Anticipation of new demand and the growth of IPTV as a result of smart devices are leading to expansion of the children's animation market. An increase in broadcasters, following the launch of new comprehensive programming channels, is expected to diversify distribution, boosting demand for animation. However, the slow recovery of the global economy, particularly in the US, Japan, and other major destinations, will have an adverse effect on foreign subcontractors.

Exports have grown overall since 2006 as a result of increased awareness of South Korean animation. Russia will be a new export destination. The active participation of Korean enterprises in overseas exhibitions and the development of subsidiary products are expected to increase sales for local animators. Market globalization will increase demand for joint productions, especially with Chinese companies with growing market potential, and companies in the US and Japan, which have robust animation markets.

Advertising

The advertising market is expected to expand following a paradigm shift towards smart advertisements and the introduction of media representatives. Success overseas will play a determinant role in sales growth for major advertising companies affiliated with large export corporations. As a result of the rise of smart devices, technology convergence in the broadcast and communications industries, and the concomitant appearance of smart advertisements, market growth is anticipated.

In addition to traditional distribution via terrestrial networks, the advertising industry will utilize the Internet, mobile, and SNS platforms. Decreased advertising expenditure from corporations concerned about global recession will have an adverse effect on market expansion.

Licensed Characters

Although continued recession is projected in Korea and abroad, if exchange rates and commodity prices stabilize, the character market has potential for expansion. Joint ventures for the development of characters in Korea have increased, as well as applications utilizing characters. The market share of characters targeting women and children is expected to grow. Despite decreasing demand, reasonable exchange rates will reduce the cost of capital goods and increase profits for character developers. However, an unbalanced focus on specific character products, issues of piracy brought to light with the conclusion of the South Korea-US fair trade agreement, and the enactment of related laws and regulations are likely to impede market expansion.

Character industry exports will grow not only in major existing markets in the US and Europe but through entry into emerging markets, including China and India. Exports to Europe will grow slowly due to the aftereffects of the financial crisis. Success in emerging markets with high projected growth rates, including China, will determine overall export growth.

Knowledge and Information

The knowledge and information industry projects an expansion of its domestic market for edutainment and e-learning services that use smart technology. Despite South Korea's economic slowdown, demand for online advertising and the number of smartphone users are rising. Services using online and mobile technologies, such as cloud and nScreen services, are expected to show relatively high growth. Market growth resulting from the propagation of smart devices will be prominent, especially in children's textbooks and other edutainment and e-learning fields, on which an economic slowdown has a smaller impact. The involvement of platform businesses such as communications companies in the e-learning market will determine the overall increase in demand.

Diversification of export destinations is expected. While exports are currently concentrated in Vietnam and other emerging markets, increasing trade between Korea and China will facilitate the entry of edutainment content into China, and the development of original content and solutions will allow for the expansion of Korea's market share in the Americas.

Live Performances

The market for live performances is expected to expand as a result of the continuous production of small- and medium-scale original musicals and growing demand from the K-pop concert craze. The export of successful domestic musicals is expected to flourish and cover more destinations, including China and other emerging markets as well as developed markets such as the US and Japan.

B. Policy strategy and challenges for the content industry

In 2011, the MCST announced the "First Master Plan for the Promotion of the Content Industry (2011–2013)," in which the Ministry presented its overarching goals of setting a national agenda for the industry, leading the nation to a per capita income of $30,000, improving quality of life, and building a globally competitive industry through an enhanced national brand. To this end, the Ministry established the "2012 Enforcement Plan for the Promotion of the Content Industry," followed by the "2013 Enforcement Plan" (Nov. 21, 2012).

Under this vision, titled "Smart Content Korea," the 2013 policy direction for the content industry includes increasing sales from an estimated ₩88 trillion in 2012 to ₩100 trillion, and increasing exports from an estimated $4.5 billion to $5.2 billion. The plan also includes a target of 620,000 workers in the content industry through the creation of 20,000 new jobs. The Ministry has thus set up 15 core projects grouped under 5 implementation strategies: 1) preparing a national system to foster the content industry; 2) creating jobs for young workers through the promotion of creativity; 3) increasing global market share; 4) forming an ecosystem of shared growth; and 5) strengthening core infrastructure for production, distribution, and technology development. Through these core projects, the Ministry plans to prepare for the "creative economy era" and promote the content industry as an engine for growth. The working budget for the implementation of the five major strategies set forth in the 2013 Enforcement Plan is ₩396.1 billion. From 2011 to 2012, ₩724 billion was invested in the content industry (₩327.9 billion in 2011 and ₩396.1 billion in 2012). The Ministry's total investment in the industry is projected to reach ₩1.115 trillion by the end of 2013.

C. Prospects and direction of copyright policies

Prospects

As a society evolves from a manufacturing-based industrial economy to one based on knowledge and creative industries, the importance of intellectual property grows. With living conditions improving around the world, and platforms and media for the enjoyment of content becoming more diverse, demand for popular content is growing, which in turn is increasing awareness of the significance and value of copyrights. With growing emphasis on the economic and industrial aspects of creative work, the share of copyright-related industries in world trade is growing steadily. The need to develop copyright policies that balance protection and utilization of copyrights is greater than ever.

First, preparing a framework for a system through which copyright holders and content users can communicate and coexist is the most urgent task. Policies must prevent an increase in conflicts and disputes that arise from content users' lack of copyright awareness and one-sided claims to rights. In addition, cultural norms must be encouraged to evolve through the establishment of national policies regarding public works and the promotion of a copyright sharing (*nanum*) culture. This will allow for the distribution and use of high-quality content.

Second, copyright policies are vital for tackling new methods of duplicating content, which result from an increase in media types, diversification of distribution platforms, and the integration of SNS in daily life. Preventing illegal

Table 1–7.

Five Implementation Strategies	Core Projects
Prepare a national system to foster the content industry	Build an integrated implementation system for research on, and development of, cultural technology. Increase investment and support funding for the content industry. Develop government-wide content and create new markets.
Create jobs for young workers through the promotion of creativity	Nurture specialized, site-specific workforces. Support employment and job creation in content fields desired by young consumers. Strengthen creative competencies of content producers.
Increase global market share	Expand the Korean content industry and enhance its resilience through the creation of new markets. Secure opportunities for entry into overseas markets through international promotion and networking. Determine globally competitive companies and support customized content production.
Form an ecosystem of shared growth	Improve copyright protection to meet increased content consumption and export. Continue efforts to create an environment for fair market competition. Amass creative resources through the discovery and distribution of public domain content.
Strengthen core infrastructure for production, distribution, and technology development	Invigorate convergence services based on smart technologies. Support mobile games' entry into the global market. Expand development and standardization of innovative technologies.

duplication online will be a major issue in protecting content from copyright violation. As Korean content is attracting attention worldwide, new protection policies are necessary. Measures must be taken to safeguard the rights of the entertainment and sports industries and improve their business conditions.

Third, copyright policies must allow for new, diverse industries and businesses based on copyrights to flourish. The World Intellectual Property Organization categorizes core copyright industries into: publishing and literature; music, theatrical productions, and opera; motion pictures and video; radio and television; photography; software and databases; visual and graphic arts; advertising services; and copyright collecting societies. South Korea's core copyright industries constitute 3.53% of the national economy, second to, but far lower than, the US, where such industries constitute 6.4%. Korea must seek balanced growth in platforms, content, and services. It is urgent to establish support strategies to foster competitive content and software. The government must act quickly to improve the copyright system in order to stabilize the market for digital content like electronic publications and e-learning services.

Fourth, increased educational and promotional efforts are necessary to improve understanding of copyright, which will lead to changes in behavior and development of a culture of lawful use of copyrighted material. These efforts must guide users to agree and sympathize with stronger copyright protection, rather than feeling increasingly inconvenienced in their use of copyrighted work.

Major policy challenges

The following are specific policy tasks regarding copyright:

The first task is establishing a communicative and flexible copyright system. Organizations such as a cooperative copyright council should be formed to open avenues of communication, and such issues as orphan works with unknown copyright holders must be addressed proactively to promote the proper use of copyrighted materials. The current system, which is based on automatic protection and exclusive rights, is limited in its ability to satisfy the demand for ubiquitous services utilizing all-inclusive databases of creative works in certain fields. In order to solve the problem of orphan works, as often found on *Google Books*, Korea should consider introducing the Extended Collective Licensing System, which was developed in Scandinavia.

Policymakers should examine the publicity rights of industries that depend heavily on the celebrity of artists and athletes. Publicity rights are already widely accepted in the industry, and their existence and parameters can be confirmed through judicial precedent. However, a lack of legislation is deterring lively exchange and leading to unnecessary conflicts, burdening society with high costs. Thus, a consensus is forming on the necessity of statutory rights of publicity.

A second challenge is building a foolproof copyright protection network by reinforcing online and offline regulations in response to changes in the digital environment. Most importantly, follow-up measures must be taken to enforce the registration system for special classes of online services, following the Telecommunications Business Act. In order for the registration system to work properly, the evaluation and certification processes for the application of technical protection measures such as filtering must be refurbished, and the system's enforcement should be monitored. A balloon effect from enforcing this system is expected to redirect mainstream copyright violations from platforms like online hard drives to those that are more difficult to regulate, such as torrent services. To address this problem, the Korea Communications Commission and other relevant departments must cooperate to seek solutions like blocking access in accordance with the Information and Communications Network Act.

Crackdowns should remain in force for businesses prone to illegal offline duplication and distribution, such as vendors at highway service stations and copy centers near universities, especially at the beginning of semesters. Persistent policing is necessary to curb violations; measures such as creating senior citizen watchdog groups could provide extra support.

While the eBook market has yet to mature, policies should ensure that published books are not distributed illegally in the form of scanned images and other file formats. It is also necessary to respond actively to copyright violations abroad. The government should set up a system in which a civil-governmental consulting body can provide services customized to corporate needs. As in the Philippines, the Korean government should open Copyright Commission Offices in areas where the Korean Wave is spreading, including India and the Middle East. The government should provide targeted protection services while cooperating actively with local authorities and institutions. It is necessary to integrate organizations and cooperate with cultural centers as well as branch offices of KOCCA. Rather than focusing solely on protection of South Korean content overseas, it is advisable to support local copyright holders and policymakers in strengthening their capacity. As part of such efforts, the South Korean government is disseminating the Illegal Copyrights Obstruction Program to overseas governments and organizations.

A third challenge is integrating smart technologies with the use and distribution of creative content. New systems should be built to accommodate increased demand for content through active acquisition and distribution of public domain content. Some works that fall in the public domain, as a result of copyright expiration or other reasons, remain underutilized because of a lack of publicity, low accessibility, and so on. To satisfy popular demand, policies should support the discovery of such works and increase their online accessibility. In order to also increase access to content copyrighted by the government or public organizations, guidelines should be disseminated and consultation provided for public organizations as needed.

The fourth challenge is shifting the focus of copyright education and promotion from punishing violations to encouraging appropriate use. Policy promotion should focus on increasing popular awareness, utilizing promotional efforts and data collected from campaigns for legal usage of copyright in everyday life. Copyright education and promotion should guide people to use creative content appropriately rather than ban illegal reproduction. The general reactions to copyright enforcement are irritation and fear. These reactions are thought to result from copyright holders responding aggressively to violations without providing inexpensive, convenient alternatives for accessing content. In collaboration with the Ministry of Education, Science and Technology, proper etiquette for using copyrighted content should become part of school curricula.

Promotion of copyrights should appeal to the sensibilities of users and arouse their sympathy so that proper use of copyrighted material can be seen positively. An economic effect analysis based on data will be necessary to garner information on the advantages of a healthy intellectual property industry as well as the negative effects of illegal reproduction.

With the development of technology and the resulting changes in the distribution of copyrighted materials, the rules of the game for copyright holders, distributors, and users must also change. However, delays are to be expected in arriving at a consensus on new guidelines and means of implementation. Much time and effort will be necessary for industries and the general public to adapt to these rules in business and daily life.

In general, such delays are more pronounced when technology is new and the resulting rules are novel. Frustration is likely to spread if delays are too lengthy. Current negativity regarding copyrights among copyright holders and content users can be understood as the result of such delays and could hinder the advancement of an effective system for intellectual property management. Policymakers must be sensitive to changes and react promptly to keep problems from persisting or repeating.

D. Prospects and policy tasks of the media industry

Newspapers

According to the 2010 "Fact-finding Survey of the Newspaper Industry" by the Korea Press Foundation, newspaper sales totaled ₩3.73 trillion (₩3.32 trillion from printed newspapers and ₩402.3 billion from online news) in 2010, a 6% increase from 2009. In the same year, the industry reported 34,680 employees, 19,750 of whom were reporters. Revenue includes earnings from advertisements and adjunct businesses, sales of print newspapers, online content, and resale of content. Of the industry's sales in 2010, earnings from advertisements accounted for 63%, or ₩2.35 trillion; earnings from adjunct businesses had the second largest share at 20% (₩743.6 billion); sales revenue from print newspapers was ₩566.7 billion (15.2%); and online content drew ₩51.3 billion (1.4%).

Due to rapid changes in the digital media environment and the introduction of media representatives, advertising is undergoing restructuring, heralding difficult times for the management of print media such as newspapers and magazines, which depend heavily on advertising income. Moreover, as distribution and consumption of news shift towards smart technologies, readership and subscription rates for print newspapers and magazines are expected to drop steadily. Changes in the media environment will likely result in new business models (i.e., paid online news content).

Over the past five years, the government has implemented policies to strengthen industry competitiveness by modifying media-related laws and institutions. Amendments to the Newspaper Act and the Act on Press Arbitration have been necessary to prevent delayed regulation from hindering industrial development and to reconcile the law with the changing media environment. As such, understanding of changes must be accompanied by constant interest as well as research on the roles of the government, the rights and duties of enterprises, and protection of the rights and interests of consumers. Despite their important societal roles, traditional media industries, including newspapers, are facing a deepening crisis. The government, the industries themselves, and academia must work together to foster the recovery of competitiveness and regain customer trust. Ultimately, the media industries will require a more refined promotional system to develop. To this end, consideration of the roles and statuses of institutes involved in promotion, understanding of the methods of promotion, and necessary funds are imperative. Policymakers should devise short-term plans as well as roadmaps for medium- to long-term development, while taking into account existing policies.

Broadcasting

In 2010, the broadcast industry reported 926 businesses operating and ₩11.2 trillion in sales. In the same year, its exports were US$184.7 million, while imports were US$104.9 million. Exports increased steadily from 2008, with an average annual growth rate of 9.4%. Increasing export of broadcast media products is very significant as it introduces Korean culture and leads to the export of other goods. The world's broadcast market is valued at around US$400 billion, larger than the markets for semiconductors, electronics, and mobile phones, in all of which Korea has a competitive edge. However, the global share of Korean products in broadcasting is only 1.13%. For the advancement and globalization of

Korea's broadcast media industry, the movement of funds invested in production must become transparent, thereby increasing fair trade and further investment in production. Market leaders and policymakers must also concern themselves with fostering globally competitive media groups.

Policies promoting the broadcast media industry will enhance Korea's national image through content export and indirectly support the export of related goods. Moreover, to foster the broadcast media industry is to enhance the most popular channel for culture and leisure. Policies that support the broadcast media industry not only seek to secure industrial competitiveness, but also to enrich culture and improve the welfare of South Korea.

Publishing

Sales in the publishing industry, excluding newspapers and magazines, showed a mild decline from ₩3.99 trillion in 2007 to ₩3.89 trillion in 2010. More specifically, between 2007 and 2010 the book industry declined by -2.7%, although the educational publishing industry grew by 16.8%. Printing businesses showed growth of 13.8%, with sales rising from ₩3.63 trillion in 2007 to ₩4.13 trillion in 2010.

A total of 19.5 million books constituting 44,000 new titles were published in 2011, an average of 2,500 volumes per title. The average list price of a book was ₩13,100. The number of new titles increased by 9.3% from the previous year, and the total volume increased by 3%.

As a result of the development of large brick-and-mortar chain bookstores, the growth of online vendors, and the appearance of discount open markets, small- and medium-sized bookstores are becoming less competitive. Large bookstores are growing while smaller ones are disappearing rapidly. Industry statistics show that sales by book and magazine retail businesses valued under ₩1 billion are decreasing. Revenue for small bookstores, valued at under ₩100 million, is decreasing at an annual rate of 29%. Online bookstores, however, have been growing rapidly: online sales of books surpassed ₩1 trillion in 2009 and totaled ₩1.3 trillion in 2011.

Online bookstores are now estimated to constitute more than 30% of the publication and distribution market. A global research institute estimated South Korea's book market at $1.59 billion in 2010. It is expected to grow at an average annual rate of 0.8% and reach $1.65 billion in 2015. As of 2010, Korea's eBook market was valued at $255 million, a figure that is expected to grow annually at 7.8% and reach $400 million in 2015. The educational eBook market is projected to grow at an average annual rate of 67.9% until 2015.

In order to respond to changes in the market environment, it is important to reinforce strategic medium- to long-term plans for the promotion of the publishing industry, and to establish a robust, balanced structure for publication and distribution. To cultivate a sound market for electronic publishing, policymakers must establish a virtuous cycle of production, distribution, and consumption by securing quality eBook content. They must also make improvements such as adopting a list price system. Other urgent matters include improving distribution and after-sales management for books published overseas, enhancing the global competitiveness of Korea's publishing industry, and increasing the export of copyrights through the international publishing trade.

"Development of the content industry is crucial for Korea to become a digital technology powerhouse. The digital network, which makes crossing national boundaries possible in real-time, is both a space of infinite competition and a territory of the imagination. Individuals and nations cannot occupy an inch of this territory without original content. The Korean government will concentrate the country's competencies on the content industry so that it can become a core growth engine leading our economy. Intellectual property is emerging as a source of industrial and national competitiveness. The National Assembly of Korea passed the Framework Act on Intellectual Property in April, and the Presidential Council on Intellectual Property was inaugurated in July, combining the forces of the private and public sectors. These events have laid the foundation for Korea's transformation into an advanced country with a knowledge-based economy. With these instruments in place, the government plans to present a detailed blueprint to turn Korea into an intellectual property powerhouse. Despite the global financial crisis, Korea's research and development budget has risen from ₩11.1 trillion in 2008 to ₩14.9 trillion this year, at an average annual growth rate of 11%. This investment aims to make South Korea a knowledge-based, advanced country. The government will continue to increase the research and development budget."

(President Lee Myung-bak, October 10, 2011. Policy speech at the submission of the 2012 Proposals for Budget and Fund Management.)

1.2.2. 2006 Cultural Industry White Paper: Imports and Exports

Reference: *2006 Cultural Industry White Paper*, Ministry of Culture and Tourism, 2006, pp. 5–7, 29–31, 198–200, 228–229, 240, 256–258, 276–277, 280–281, 299–300, 335, 375–376.

(pp. 5–7)

A. Hallyu growth and strengthening of overseas marketing

Despite the rise in exports of cultural content and related commodities and the continued growth of interest in Korea and *Hallyu*, an "anti-*Hallyu*" sentiment exists in Asia, and the illegal reproduction of Korean cultural goods continues. Moreover, there is currently a lack of expertise in overseas marketing and legal services. Accordingly, in 2006, in order to foster Korea's brand power through the "globalization of *Hallyu*," to increase Korea's global market share through strategic marketing, and to strengthen overseas expansion through trade partnerships and international cooperation, the following policies were implemented.

Increasing Korea's brand power through the globalization of *Hallyu*

Reforms in Hallyu support policies
i.   Use of overseas cultural centers and offices of the Korea Tourism Organization for *Hallyu* growth and marketing.

- Proposals for and connections with Korea Centers to combine promotion of culture and tourism; strengthening overseas marketing networks for Korean cultural content.
ii. Promoting the reshuffling and expansion of private sector efforts to support *Hallyu*.
    - Maintenance of cultural exchange and domestic/international networks related to *Hallyu*; strengthening the functions of organizations responsible for collecting information in multiple spheres.
    - Korea Foundation for Asian Culture Exchange renamed Korea Foundation for International Culture Exchange.
iii. Foundation and operation of information infrastructure and services dealing with market trends and systems in *Hallyu* regions, where Korean cultural products have become popular.
    - Provision of information in *Hallyu* regions online via the Content Export Information System (CEIS).
    - Operation of local correspondence in *Hallyu* regions (over 20 countries), cultural industry market surveys, creation of databases on cultural industries in *Hallyu* regions, implementation of webzines and portal sites, services for news mailings, etc.

Development of policies to relieve anti-Hallyu sentiment
i. Strengthening the image of *Hallyu*; avoidance of having *Hallyu* appear as a unidirectional flow.
    - Efforts to improve Korea's image through spreading *Hallyu* as the leader of an "Asian Wave" and to celebrate the rich cultures and traditions of Asian nations and Korea's status as their Asian cultural partner.
ii. Alleviating animosity and promoting trust through expanded bilateral cultural exchange.
    - Import of outstanding examples of Asian cinema and broadcast media from China, Southeast Asia, and other *Hallyu* regions.
    - Overseas television and press association visits to Korea and efforts to create more *Hallyu* reports (7 visits, involving more than 70 individuals).
    - Opening the Global Culture Industry Forum with the participation of world leaders in cultural industries.
    - Hosting the "Asia Song Festival" and building a distinctively Asian music festival.
iii. Creating mutual, long-term cultural and economic benefits through increased personnel exchange.
    - Programs: Korean Film Academy Association Asian Scholarship Program (two recipients, one-year duration); Asian Film Academy (over 30 recipients); Asian Film Talent Internships (two to three recipients, six-month duration).
    - Korea-Japan and Korea-China exchanges between broadcasters (over 50 individuals, KOFICE).

Increasing global market share through strategic promotion

Advancement into emerging economies (e.g., BRIC countries) and efforts to capture overseas markets

i.   Proactive marketing efforts in the large, latent cultural industry markets of Brazil, Russia, India, and China (BRIC countries).
  –   Conducting local analysis in countries such as Brazil and India for the release of cultural content into new markets.
  –   Implementation of cooperative relationships with the Indian film industry (Bollywood); joint participation in film festivals, exchanges, etc.
  –   China's cultural industry market is slated to surpass Japan's in 2008; the annual audience for film screenings in India reaches 3.1 billion admissions, the largest in the world; Russia's film industry is demonstrating high growth (18.3%); Brazil's entertainment industry is worth $10 billion, the largest in South America.
ii. Promotion of gaming in emerging economies and opening of import/export consultation for foreign investment.
  –   East Asia Investment/Export Consultation Fair (April 2006; Taiwan, Thailand); Japan Investment/Export Consultation Fair (September 2006); Export Gaming Publisher Invitational Consultation Fair (June–November 2006).
iii. Diversification of capital procurement through revitalization of foreign film collaborations and overseas distribution.
  –   Support for Korea-France and Korea-Canada film collaboration; increase in Korea-China broadcasting collaboration; support for international co-productions through competition for new film projects.
iv. Refinement and systematization of information within the CEIS.
  –   Statistics on cultural industries; linkage to directory of domestic companies and increase in entries (from 35,000 to 40,000 items).
  –   Information on domestic products, overseas marketing, and analyses of information related to purchasers, suppliers, and export consultation.

Strengthening overseas marketing through international events

i.   Offering broad marketing opportunities for domestic corporations by supporting large-scale international events.
  –   68th Union Internationale du Cinéma non-professionnel (UNICA) general assembly and film festival support (August 2006, Daegu, over 40 countries in attendance); UNICA is the world's premier non-profit video/film festival.
  –   Concentrated support for leading international film festivals including Busan International Film Festival and Bucheon International Fantastic Film Festival.
  –   G-Star (November 2006); established itself as the world's foremost online gaming expo.
  –   International Content Conference DICON 2006 (September 2006); Seoul Character & Licensing Fair.

ii. Attendance at leading international events; holding overseas events; support for effective, cooperative public relations.
   – Support for attendance at international film festivals, gaming expos (Electronic Entertainment Expo), music trade shows (Marché International du Disque et de l'Edition Musicale), and animation content market (MipTV); "Korean Cinema Promotional Booth" at leading film markets such as Cannes and Berlin.
   – Setting up the Korean Center for Cooperation at the world's leading trade fair for animation, characters, *manhwa*, music, and edutainment; offering support for businesses to attend.

Minimizing losses of Hallyu marketing by strengthening overseas copyright protection
i. Establishment of Beijing office of KOCCA and other Copyright Commission Offices.
   – Establishment of export support entities, employment of copyright experts, market analysts, and legal counsel, etc.
   – Investigation of copyright infringement in such locales as China, Hong Kong, and Vietnam, and publishing of annual reports.
   – Cooperation with overseas governmental entities such as the Chinese Copyright Market to conduct market analyses of copyright in general and co-sponsor two seminars.
ii. Construction and maintenance of a website for reporting copyright infringement in Korean, Chinese, and Japanese.
   – Cultural industries' exporters operate at such a small scale that information on copyright infringement and proposals to confront it are limited for them; a site for reporting infringement will enable systematization of information and establishment of response measures.
   – Cooperation with overseas government entities, export support entities, and cooperative sites to maintain an Overseas Copyright Protection Commission and Overseas Copyright Promotion Center.
   – Support for overseas copyright law consulting and lawsuits in countries where infringement occurs.
   – Assessment of current copyright infringement and establishment of joint seminars with foreign governments.
   – Proposing joint plans with Chinese organizations for effective policing of pirated Korean materials in China.

(pp. 29–31)
B. *Overseas market expansion*

Summary of domestic cultural industries' imports/exports

A detailed look at cultural industry imports and exports for 2005 reveals that total exports ($1.23 billion) increased substantially (31.6%) over 2004. The leading export industries were gaming (growth of 45.6%), film (30.4%), broadcasting (73.2%), animation (27.0%), and *manhwa* (71.2%).

   Overseas cultural industries' exports nearly doubled between 2003 and 2005, from $630 million to $1.23 billion, achieving a high average annual increase of

Table 1-8.   Cultural industries' imports/exports (Units: $1,000,000, %)

Industry	Exports					Imports				
	2003	2004	2005	% of sector total	2003–5 annual growth %	2003	2004	2005	% of CI	2003–5 annual growth %
Publishing	149.7	182.2	191.3	15.5	13	214.7	227.1	231.7	7.8	3.9
Manhwa	4.1	1.9	3.3	0.3	−10.3	5.2	0.4	0.9	0.0	−58.4
Music	13.3	34.2	22.3	1.8	29.5	16.0	20.6	8.3	0.3	−28.0
Gaming	181.6	387.7	564.7	45.7	76.3	166.4	205.1	232.9	7.8	18.3
Film	31.0	58.3	76.0	6.1	56.6	60.4	66.2	46.8	1.6	−12.0
Animation	75.7	61.8	78.4	6.3	1.8	2.0	8.0	5.5	0.2	65.8
Broadcasting	42.1	70.3	121.8	9.9	70.1	28.1	58.6	43.2	1.4	24.0
Advertising	–	20.8	9.3	0.8	−55.3	–	918.7	2,292.8	76.8	58.0
Licensed Characters	116.3	117.3	163.7	13.2	18.6	99.4	129.4	123.4	4.1	11.4
Digital Education and Information	16.9	4.9	5.2	0.4	−44.5	8.3	0.4	0.4	0.0	−78.0
Total	630.7	939.4	1,236.0	100.0	40.0	600.5	1,634.5	2,985.9	100.0	123.0

(Source: Ministry of Culture and Tourism and KOCCA, "2004 Cultural Industries Statistics," "2005 Cultural Industries Statistics," and "2006 Cultural Industries Statistics")

40.3%. Showing particular growth in line with the influence of *Hallyu*, broadcast programming exports increased by 70.1% and film by 56.6%. Despite ample growth in Southeast Asia, exports by the music industry decreased as a result of sluggish exports to Japan and the US, among others. In 2005, exports of games exceeded imports by more than twofold; notably, online gaming accounted for a substantial 45.7% of the total. The shift from the OEM of the past to production of original animated works meant that exports fell in 2004 by 18.4% from the previous year, but increased again in 2005 by 26.9%.

In contrast, cultural industry imports increased 82.7% over 2004 to $2.98 billion, even though all sectors apart from *manhwa*, gaming, and advertising experienced a drop. Imports exceeded exports by more than $1.755 billion. As import/export numbers in the advertising industry are aggregated by country within the scope of overseas activity in the service sector, import rates are inflated due to domestic sales by foreign-owned advertising agencies.

From the overall publishing, *manhwa*, music, film, animation, characters, and digital education and information industries, types of export products include the following: finished goods (34.6%), licenses (29.8%), OEM (25.7%), IT services (8.5%), and other activities such as foreign investment in joint productions (1.4%). A closer look at each industry suggests that publishing and music led finished goods exports, *manhwa* and films topped licensed products, animation led OEM, and digital education and information were first in IT services.

Turning to channels for expansion into foreign markets, one sees that indirect export via domestic and overseas agents accounted for 45.4% of the total, while direct export through avenues such as overseas expositions, event attendance, and overseas distributors made up 44.9%. A closer look at the channels through which expansion occurred suggests that domestic agency activity accounted for 25.3%, implementation of foreign distributors for 23.1%, and foreign agents for 20.1%. In comparison to the previous year, growth occurred in overseas exposition and event attendance (8.6% → 12.1%), domestic agency implementation (23.7% → 25.3%), and percentage of sale by foreign agencies (14.7% → 20.1%). A breakdown by industry reveals that the licensed character goods industry accounted for 22.2% of overseas exposition and event participation; film accounted for 40.3% of overseas distribution; digital education and information accounted for 4.1% of online overseas commerce; publishing made up 16.3% of overseas corporate activity; *manhwa* accounted for 55.5% of domestic agent activity; and music made up 36.1% of foreign activity.

(pp. 198–200)

Types of overseas expansion for Korean cultural content enterprises

Business expansion into foreign markets takes varying forms, including product sales, licensing, franchising, and foreign direct investment (FDI; which itself includes overseas joint ventures or wholly owned subsidiaries). The Korean culture content industry has mainly been using product sales and licensing to enter foreign markets.

A survey of 305 enterprises in 7 sectors of the cultural content industry (publishing, *manhwa*, music, film, animation, characters, and digital education and information) conducted in 2005 revealed that slightly less than 50% and nearly 30% of enterprises entered overseas markets via product sales and licensing, respectively (Table 1–9).

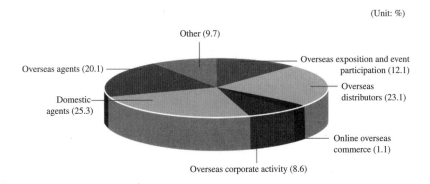

Figure 1–5.   Channels of overseas cultural industry expansion
(Source: Ministry of Culture and Tourism and KOCCA (2007), "2006 Cultural Industries Statistics")

Table 1–9. Expansion into foreign markets by sector (Units: Number, %)

Genre	Year	# of Companies	Product Sales OEM*	Finished Goods	IT Licensing	Services	Other
Publishing	2004	22	27.3	59.1	13.6	0.0	0.0
	2005	85	22.3	58.3	18.6	0.0	0.8
Manhwa	2004	27	7.0	15.4	76.9	0.0	0.7
	2005	38	7.9	26.3	63.2	0.0	2.6
Music	2004	–	–	–	–	–	–
	2005	36	11.1	52.8	25.0	8.3	2.8
Film	2004	35	17.0	36.4	45.7	0.9	0.0
	2005	42	10.2	39.1	47.1	2.2	1.4
Animation	2004	33	63.0	21.4	14.8	0.0	0.8
	2005	36	71.7	25.8	0.0	2.5	
Characters	2004	–	–	–	–	–	–
	2005	48	37.2	31.8	28.7	2.3	0.0
Digital Education and Information	2004	17	20.3	20.9	10.6	48.2	0.0
	2005	20	19.3	21.1	12.8	46.8	0.0
Total	2004	134	26.9	30.6	32.3	9.8	0.3
	2005	305	25.7	34.6	29.8	8.5	1.4

* Original equipment manufacturing.
(Source: Ministry of Culture and Tourism (2006 & 2007), "2005 Cultural Industries Statistics" and "2006 Cultural Industries Statistics")

The status quo for product sales consists mainly of finished goods manufactured in the country of origin and sold in foreign markets. As this process relies on producing the goods, business costs incurred abroad are low; however, because trends in the countries of sale are in constant flux, maintaining export strategies is difficult.

Numerous Korean companies are expanding into overseas markets via product sales; however, Korean products are less familiar than other global cultural content due to limited direct overseas business dealings, caused by Korean companies' lack of international experience. As a result, many companies expanded routes into international markets through steady efforts at prominent expos, thereby increasing visibility and transactions for products manufactured in Korea. Fortunately, as of 2000, and hand-in-hand with the growth of *Hallyu*, Korea has produced more successful cultural works, leading to marked growth in awareness of the Korean content industry and its products. As a result, just as with animation, genres that possess significant capital have seen success either in foreign investment, co-productions (and the like), or selling international distribution rights prior to production.

After product sales, the next most utilized strategy for expansion into foreign markets is licensing. As licensing involves the sale not of goods but intellectual property rights (trademarks, copyright, etc.) to overseas companies, various products are released in the target market. For example, the famous 1983 Korean character Dooly the Dinosaur was released through licensing agreements in Europe, the Americas, China, and elsewhere in Asia, with the logo appearing on a range of products including stationery, clothing, and shoes. In a licensing contract, the seller of the rights to use the content (the licensor) concludes an agreement with the purchaser (the licensee). Once the licensor sells these rights, business in the target market is up to the licensee. As such, although the licensor cannot directly participate in business in the target country, companies without experience in that market can avoid the uncertainties of direct activity.

Unlike with product sales and licensing, direct activity in target markets is possible through subsidiaries, either via FDI, which involves joint investment with a local company (in the form of capital, marketing, etc.), or establishing a fully owned subsidiary with a 100% capital investment in the target market. FDI carries more risk than other channels proportional to the amount of investment; however, in the event of success, higher profits can be gained than through product sales and licensing. Accordingly, many manufacturers choose FDI over the latter two, utilizing low-wage labor in target countries (efficiency advantage) and resources (resource advantage), capturing a large portion of the target market (local market advantage), and purchasing strategic assets (capital advantage). Although overseas expansion in the Korean cultural content industry first took root in product sales and licensing, as seen in Table 1–10, business activity in target markets is increasingly occurring through FDI.

As seen above, the majority of Korean enterprises have entered overseas markets via the less globalized channels of product sales and licensing. This phenomenon can be understood as stemming from their recent establishment, and subsequent limits, of the Korean cultural content industry. In general, as these businesses accumulate international experience, they can expand their overseas reach, thereby coming to take on the greater risk and investment necessary for

Table 1–10.   Methods of entry into overseas markets (Unit: %)

Method of Overseas Expansion		2004	2005	Change
Product Sales	OEM export	26.9	25.7	–4%
	Export of finished goods	30.6	34.6	13%
Licensing	Product licensing	32.3	29.8	–7%
	IT services	9.8	8.5	–13%
FDI	Overseas investment in co-productions	0.1	1.4	366%
Other	Other	0.2		

(Source: Ministry of Culture and Tourism (2006 & 2007), "2005 Cultural Industries Statistics" and "2006 Cultural Industries Statistics")

FDI. However, the majority of Korean enterprises, mostly established after 2000 and thus having limited overseas experience, operate on a relatively small scale, making the burden of direct operations in target markets large.

C. *Cultural content industry sectors*

Film Industry

(pp. 228–229)

In 2005, Korean films were screened and favorably received at an array of festivals, and a variety of Korean films were introduced around the world via themed screenings and director retrospectives. A total of 172 feature-length films were shown in 487 screenings at 130 film festivals internationally. Of these, 27 films received 40 awards at 29 festivals, which means that in addition to these films' box office revenues in Korea, their quality and artistry provided an opportunity to advertise Korean directors' prowess to the world.

According to statistics for 2005, 202 Korean films were exported around the world for $76 million, a 30% increase from the previous year. After 2001, when the $10 million mark was first broken, export showed steep growth, and the number of films exported increased steadily as well. Several noteworthy phenomena were behind this recent international expansion. First, one may observe segmentation in the films exported by region. Whereas in Asia, with Japan at the forefront, star power has led to an increase in the commercial scale of releases and sales, the pathways for distribution of art films in Europe, France and Germany in particular, have meant films by such directors as Kim Ki-duk, Hong Sang-soo, and Park Chan-wook have been consumed. Second, export has primarily focused on Asia, which makes it easy to recognize the deep connection to current *Hallyu* trends. Third, in comparison to 2004, the method of overseas export has been changing from mere sales after the Korean release to pre-sales during post-production and investment while the screenplay is being shopped around. This remarkable development resulted from an increase in awareness of both Korean cinema in general and of star directors and actors.

A close look at exports by country reveals that Japan accounted for 79.4% of the total ($60.32 million), the United States for 2.7% ($2.01 million), Thailand for 2.0% ($1.52 million), and France for 2.0% ($1.5 million). The year 2003 saw a reduction in the concentration on Asia, but in 2004, after a brief increase in the

Table 1–11.   **Export of Korean films by year (Units: Number of films, $)**

	2001	2002	2003	2004	2005
Number of Films	102	133	164	193	202
Export Revenue	11,249,573	14,952,089	30,970,000	58,284,600	75,994,580
Rate of Increase	59%	33%	107%	88%	30%
Average Cost Per Film	110,289	112,422	188,896	301,993	376,208

(Source: Korean Film Council (KOFIC) (2006), *2006 Korean Film Almanac*)

Table 1–12.   Export of Korean films by country (Units: $, %)

	2002		2003		2004		2005	
	Revenue	Market Share	Revenue	Market Share	Revenue	Market Share	Revenue	Market Share
Japan	6,582,103	44.0	13,893,000	44.8	40,401,000	69.3	60,322,686	79.4
US	862,000	5.8	4,486,000	14.5	2,361,000	4.0	2,014,500	2.7
France	732,415	4.9	709,000	2.3	2,084,000	3.6	1,504,820	2.0
Thailand	823,217	5.5	1,448,500	4.7	1,771,500	3.0	1,520,000	2.0
Germany	461,770	3.1	1,908,500	6.2	1,558,000	2.7	1,237,250	1.6
Taiwan	179,254	1.2	906,500	2.9	1,069,000	1.8	997,000	1.3
China	379,000	2.5	805,500	2.6	206,000	0.4	530,500	0.7
Hong Kong	1,483,000	9.9	834,500	2.7	702,000	1.2	1,145,500	1.5
Other	3,449,330	23.1	5,987,500	19.3	8,132,100	14.0	6,722,324	8.8
Total	14,952,089	100.0	30,979,000	100.0	58,284,600	100.0	75,994,580	100.0

(Source: KOFIC (2006), *2006 Korean Film Almanac*)

proportion of American and European sales, the export focus on Asia, and in particular Japan, returned in conjunction with the Korean Wave and the wide release in Japan of films such as *Silmido*, *Taegukgi*, and *Untold Scandal*. The rise in export of Korean films to Oceania and South America demonstrates incremental expansion into these regions.

Animation Industry

(p. 240)

In 2005 total exports for the animation industry stood at $78.43 million, with imports at $5.46 million. By regional category, the largest amount ($44.62 million) was exported to North America, followed by Japan ($24.7 million), then miscellaneous others, including Latin America ($4.7 million), Europe ($3.52 million), China ($470,000), and Southeast Asia ($390,000).

Music Industry

(pp. 256–258)

In 2004, exports for the music industry grew markedly to $34.22 million, but then decreased in 2005 to $22.28 million. Imports also grew in 2004 to $20.58 million before contracting sharply to $8.31 million in 2005. Although many feared that opening up to the Japanese music market would inundate the domestic market with Japanese product, technology, and business activity, or provide a shock from an influx of choices or low-quality, violent material, in fact no significant influence appeared. This was as a result of the overall decline of the domestic music market, negative sentiment towards Japan, and sanctions on radio play of Japanese music.

Table 1–13. Animation industry imports/exports (Unit: $1,000)

	Exports		Imports	
China	194	471	0	0
Japan	16,245	24,705	7,883	4,867
Southeast Asia	114	392	0	0
North America	36,101	44,626	0	573
Europe	3,408	3,529	0	18
Other	1,603	4,706	0	0
Uncategorized	4,073	–	120	–
Total	61,765	78,429	8,003	5,458

(Source: Ministry of Culture and Tourism (2007), "2006 Cultural Industry Statistics")

Table 1–14. Trends in music industry imports/exports (Unit: $1,000)

	2003	2004	2005
Exports	13,312	34,218	22,278
Imports	16,035	20,580	8,306

(Source: Ministry of Culture and Tourism (2007), "2006 Cultural Industries Statistics")

Due to stagnation in the domestic album market, 2005 saw a paradigm shift in overseas expansion and related industries, as witnessed in remarkable trends involving trade with Southeast Asia. Particularly noteworthy has been export to Indonesia, a country that has overtaken Japan to become the number one export market for Korean music. In 2005, album exports to Southeast Asia (with the exception of the Sinophone region) totaled $3.5 million, or nearly 44% of the total. At first glance, this figure may appear to have resulted from the successful revitalization of *Hallyu*; however, if one takes into consideration the economic and cultural realities of Southeast Asia, the trend appears more transitory, with a sharp decrease likely in 2006, followed by more gradual growth. Japan follows Southeast Asia in album exports, accounting for 40% of the market ($3,262,000). Although this figure marks an unfortunate 7% decrease from the previous year, given the accelerated expansion of Korean artists into Japan, licensing activities will likely increase, and Korean artists should have more work in Japan. However, exports of finished goods are predicted to remain roughly the same. In addition, export to the Sinophone region (China, Taiwan, and Hong Kong), reached $555,000, a 131% increase over the previous year's $240,000.

Overall, as to be expected, 2005 revealed the strength of Asian music markets influenced by *Hallyu*. In contrast, export to regions such as the US and Europe accounted for a meager 8.5% of the total.

Table 1–16 shows imports by country. Korea imports the most music from Germany, with a total of $2.32 million in 2005, a 12.7% increase

Table 1–15.   Exports by country (2004–2005) (Unit: $1,000)

	2004		2005		Change from Previous Year
	Amount ($)	Number	Amount ($)	Number	
Japan	3,513	8,495,180	3,262	5,063,053	–7%
Chinese-speaking Region	240	28,455	555	40,047	131%
Southeast Asia	282	33,874	3,506	11,045	1,143%
US	640	82,934	438	52,383	–32%
UK	2	516	9	2,825	305%
France	14	10,000	8	3,031	–43%
Germany	52	127,251	26	7,134	–50%

(Source: KOCCA (2006), "Music Industry White Paper 2006," Financial Supervisory Service Data Analysis, Retrieval and Transfer System)

over the previous year and 28% of the total album import market. Following Germany is the United States, the world's largest album market, which recorded $2.06 million in imports, similar to the previous year. Next come Japan ($933,000), England ($814,000), France ($57,000), and the Chinese-speaking region ($118,000). Import volume from Southeast Asia, in contrast to export, stood at a mere $8,000. Conversely, whereas exports to Europe and the US were low, album imports accounted for a great majority of the market (73%) and demonstrated a stark imbalance.

Foreign albums are either distributed through labels with domestic licenses or through direct import agencies. In the past, contractual agreements between direct distributors and domestic production companies were common; however, albums are now supplied through either branch offices of direct distributors or collaborating companies.

Currently there are four major players in domestic album production: Warner Music Korea, EMI, Sony BMG Music, and Universal Music Korea, all of which operate in Korea using direct distribution. Generally, they supply overseas pop tracks; however, recently a number of direct distributors, keen to a striking drop in sales, are struggling for alternatives and expanding activities to include searches for local talent and the production of albums in Korea.

Gaming Industry

(pp. 276–277)

In 2005 export of domestic games totaled $564.66 million, an increase of 45.6% over 2004, while imports increased by 13.6% to $232.92 million, continuing the post-2003 dominance of exports. In fact, in 2005 the export level doubled that of imports. Notable in 2005 was the ongoing prominence of online games among exports and video games among imports. Whereas arcade game exports increased slightly from the previous year, fueled by strong export of components and used consoles, the struggling PC game market declined sharply. The

Table 1–16.   Import trends by country (2004–2005) (Unit: $1,000)

	2004			2005			Change from Previous Year
	Amount ($)	Weight	Number	Amount ($)	Weight	Number	
Japan	1,140	20,176	189,747	933	31,853	198,021	−18.16%
Chinese-speaking Region	96	15,089	402,469	118	15,235	277,362	22.92%
Southeast Asia	31	1,744	41,716	8	613	5,706	−74.19%
US	2,031	133,142	679,470	2,064	105,351	588,014	1.62%
UK	852	46,861	206,831	814	38,896	205,379	−4.46%
France	521	13,425	99,700	570	11,436	89,147	9.40%
Germany	2,060	65,938	563,959	2,321	79,921	593,942	12.67%

(Source: KOCCA (2006), *2006 Music Industry White Paper*)

Table 1–17.   Import/export trends and prospects for the domestic game market (Unit: $1,000)

	2001	2002	2003	2004	2005	2006 (Est.)	2007 (Est.)
Exports	130,470	140,796	172,743	387,692	564,660	677,592	779,231
Imports	65,340	160,962	166,454	205,108	232,923	279,507	321,433

(Source: Korean Game Industry Development Institute (2006), *2006 Gaming Industry White Paper*)

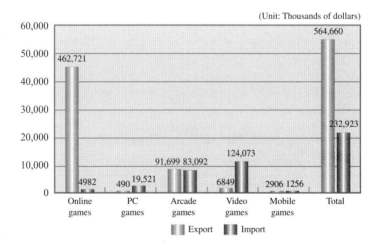

Figure 1–6.   2005 Domestic game imports/exports by platform
(Source: Korean Game Industry Development Institute (2006), *2006 Gaming Industry White Paper*)

main thrust behind export growth was the approximate 60% rise in online game exports. Imports increased for arcade and video games.

Comparison of exports between 2005 and 2004 reveals a 60% increase for online games. Although the percentage claimed by online game platforms increased from 74.9% to 81.9%, exports for all other platforms declined.

Imports fluctuated by no more than 2% in each platform. Video games decreased by just under that figure, and arcade games grew by that amount. Stagnation in PC gaming affected overseas imports in this area as well, with an approximate 2% decrease from 2004.

The main regions for overseas export of domestic games in 2005 were Japan (42.6%), China (20.8%), the US (15.7%), Taiwan (9.5%), Southeast Asia (5.8%), and Europe (5.0%). Other regions accounted for 0.8%. Export to Japan has continued to increase steadily. The share of online game exports to Japan, approximately 80% of total domestic exports, increased in proportion to decreased exports to China, a result of the country's protectionist policies.

In contrast to this steady increase in exports to Japan (25.7% in 2004 to 43.4% in 2005), the relative portion of exports to China decreased 18.7%, from 43.3% in 2004 to 21.6% [sic] the following year. Although exports to the United States and Europe increased, exports to Asian countries other than Japan decreased.

Korean game industry's international economic competitiveness

(pp. 280–281)

A look at the domestic game industry in relation to the global market reveals that online PC games hold the largest share, with 31.9% among all platforms, after which come arcade games with 14.2%, mobile games (i.e., played on mobile phones) with 12.1%, and PC and video games, each with 1%. Video games, which occupy the highest market share globally after arcade games, have tended to play an insignificant role in the domestic market; Korea's video game global market share was the lowest among domestic market share rates. Korea's share of arcade games in the global market came out 10% higher than

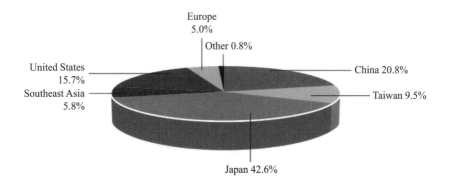

Figure 1–7.   2005 Domestic game overseas exports by country
(Source: Korean Game Industry Development Institute (2006), *2006 Gaming Industry White Paper*)

previous years, while online and mobile games were approximately 7% and 3% higher, respectively.

In 2005, Korea's gaming industry accounted for 10.2% of the global market, but fell to 8.5% in 2006. After further falling to 7.5% in 2007, it is expected to recover to 8% in 2008.

The Korean industry's $1.46 billion stake in online gaming ranks first globally and third ($189 million) in mobile gaming after Japan ($449 million) and the US ($252 million). Korea ranks 15th globally in the video game and PC gaming industries and 5th in arcade games.

Table 1–18. 2005 Domestic gaming market global market share
(Unit: $100 million)

	Arcade Games*	PC Games	Online Games**	Video Games	Mobile Games	Total
Global Market	326.52	36.39	44.06	214.95	15.67	637.59
Domestic Market	46.51	0.37	14.06	2.13	1.89	64.96
Market Share	14.2	1.0	31.9	1.0	12.1	10.2

* Figures for arcade games include arcade sales (consumer sales for casinos excluded).
** Estimates for online games are based on network subscriptions for PC, both individual and for Internet cafes (with the exception of game users' usage rates at Internet cafes, online game-related connection fees, package fees, video network, advertising revenue, etc.).
(Source: Korean Game Industry Development Institute (2006), *2006 Gaming Industry White Paper*)

Table 1–19.   Korean gaming industry's global market share (2005)
(Unit: $1,000,000)

	Online Games Sales	Rank	Mobile Games Sales	Rank	PC Games Sales	Rank	Video Games Sales	Rank	Arcade Games Sales	Rank
Japan	289	4	449	1	203	–	4,501	2	7,750	2
United States	907	2	252	2	1,132	1	9,018	1	9,790	1
Europe	996	–	520	–	1,543	–	6,539	–	10,455	–
China	403	3	118	–	54	–	92	–	–	–
Taiwan	278	5	60	–	18	–	248	–	–	–
Korea	1,406	1	189	3	37	15 (est.)	213	15 (est.)	4,650	5 (est.)

Online gaming market size based on network game subscriptions for PC (individual and Internet cafes). Excluded are usage rates at Internet cafes, online game-related connection fees, package fees, video network and advertising revenue, etc. Since PC-based online games and console-based games are included in the same network in US online gaming, these figures exclude network gaming market share (8.7%, according to DFC 2004). As "mobile gaming" includes both mobile phones and PDA devices, these figures are based on content producers' and mobile communications providers' revenue.
(Sources: DFC Intelligence, 2002–2005; Informa Media Group, 2002–2005; In-Stat/MDR, 2005; NPD Group, 2005; Screendigest, 2004–2006; Cnet Research, 2005; CESA, 2004, 2005; Jamma, 2005–2006; IDC, 2004–2005; FGH, 2006

Manhwa

(pp. 299–300)

Exports for the leading corporations in the *manhwa* industry rose nearly 71% from $1.9 million to $3.26 million. Imports for the leading corporations in the *manhwa* industry more than doubled from the previous year's $444,000 to $900,000, although it should be noted that import figures for 2004–2005 have been aggregated with licensing fees. Export regions include North America as a whole, at 43.7%, followed by Europe, Southeast Asia, and Japan. Domestic agents accounted for 55.5% of export, followed by sales at expos (16.7%) and overseas agents (14.1%). Major means of expansion overseas include licensing (66.1%), followed by finished goods (26.2%), OEM (6.7%), and other (1%).

Licensed Character Industry

(p. 335)

In 2005, exports for the character industry stood at $163.66 million, a 39.5% increase over 2004. Of this figure, exports to China totaled $60.09 million (36.7%), followed by Europe at $41.17 million (25.2%), miscellaneous countries at $20.98 million (12.8%), and North America at $18.65 million (11.4%).

Imports for the character industry totaled $123.43 million, a 4.6% decline from 2004. China accounted for $55.12 million, or 44.7% of total imports, followed by Japan with $33.06 million (26.8%), North America with $12.70 million (10.3%), and other countries with $9.65 million (7.8%).

Table 1–20.   *Manhwa* industry exports by region (Unit: $10,000)

China	Japan	Southeast Asia	North America	Europe	Other	Total
29.0	33.9	46.2	142.7	41.3	33.7	326.8

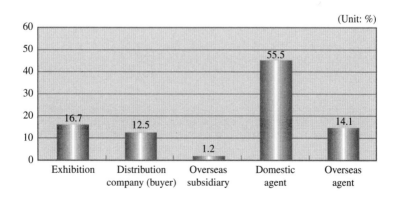

Figure 1–8.   *Manhwa* industry means of overseas export

Table 1–21.   Character industry exports (Unit: $1,000,000)

	2003	2004	2005	%
China	116,313	117,336	60.094	36.7
Japan			13.837	8.5
Southeast Asia			8.918	5.4
North America			18.656	11.4
Europe			41.178	25.2
Other			20.983	12.8
Uncategorized			–	–
Total	116,313	117,336	163.666	100.00

Table 1–22.   Character industry imports (Unit: $1,000,000)

	2003	2004	2005	%
China	99,381	129,402	55.123	44.7
Japan			33.061	26.8
Southeast Asia			6.725	5.4
North America			12.700	10.3
Europe			6.172	5.0
Other			9.653	7.8
Uncategorized			–	–
Total	99,381	129,402	123.434	100.00

Broadcasting

(pp. 375–376)

According to the Korea Broadcast Industry Promotional Agency, broadcast programming enjoyed a record-breaking surplus of more than $100 million in 2006, a year in which total exports increased $24.25 million over 2005, hitting a record-breaking $147.74 million. Meanwhile, total imports stood at $31.66 million, a $5.32 million decrease from 2005. For five years following 2002 there were surpluses, nearly quadrupling over this time to $116.09 million, marking strong success.

In particular, a large increase in exports to new markets such as Central and Latin America made this 19.6% growth possible, as well as the establishment of the first Korean-language channel in Taiwan. Major sources of momentum for growth in 2006 were Taiwan, which recorded $20.18 million ($12.54 million the preceding year), and other regions such as Central/North America, which recorded $17.50 million ($2.64 million in 2005).

Concerns remain in the face of this remarkable shift. First of all, the 2006 rise in the export of domestic films and broadcast materials represented a 19.6%

increase over 2005's $123.50 million, the lowest level of growth after 2001 and only slightly more than one quarter of the highest recorded growth (2005, 72.8%). This slowing stemmed from a drop in the average price per program episode ($4,378, down $543 from the previous year), a decline in the number of programs (19,617, down 1,034 from the previous year), and decreased demand in the major broadcast *Hallyu* markets, China and Japan.

Secondly, the main export genre, drama, declined significantly. During 2004 and 2005, dramas accounted for more than 90% of exports; however, given the 2006 decrease in total exports ($15.73 million less than the previous year) and the number of programs, the proportion occupied by drama experienced a sharp drop of 77%. Dramas once stood at the epicenter of broadcast *Hallyu* and served as its driving force, but this decrease may point to a bleak future for the Korean Wave's broadcast content. Still, increase in the proportion of programs other than dramas from 8% in 2005 to 23% in 2006 has led to a diversification of export genres, which can function as inspiration. For instance, noteworthy increases in total sales and programs distributed were exhibited by documentaries, variety shows, and other programming, whose sales increased by factors of approximately 3.6, 2.4, and 5.1, respectively.

A third concern is stagnation of the two major markets for broadcast *Hallyu*, namely China and Japan. With Japan's $17.20 million decrease to $49.17 million and China's $3.43 million decrease to $7.53 million, the market has seen a significant contraction. The number of units exported decreased in Japan by 3,154 from the previous year to 5,315, while in China they decreased by 167 to 4,159. Leading factors in this overall decline, in the case of Japan, have been recycled ideas, an absence of "killer content," and weakened price competitiveness. Government policies in China have also led to the stagnation of the overall market for *Hallyu* broadcast content.

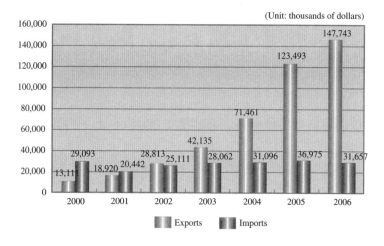

Figure 1–9.   Trends in broadcast programming imports/exports
Note: Data include revenue from broadcasts directed at Koreans overseas and video sales
(Source: Ministry of Culture and Tourism and Korea Broadcast Industry Promotional
Agency, "Current State of Broadcast Programming Imports/Exports.")

Nonetheless, this year we have begun to see an easing of anti-*Hallyu* sentiment in China and, as the market opens up (including to dramas featuring *Hallyu* stars), *Hallyu* may experience a resurgence if Korea can maintain the quality of its programming and receive appropriate exposure in target countries.

1.2.3.   2011 Cultural Content Industry White Paper: Imports and Exports

Reference: *2011 Cultural Content Industry White Paper*, MCST, September 2012, pp. 70–79, 294, 306–308, 313–314, 324–325, 351–352, 360–364, 388–389, 402–405, 486–487.

A.   Cultural content industry imports/exports

(pp. 70–79)

Overview

The content industry's import and export figures for 2011 show that exports increased 33.3% over the previous year, reaching a total of $4.3 billion. The gaming industry surpassed other sectors, accounting for 53.6% of total exports ($2.3 billion). Other export areas include film with $29.06 million (0.7%), animation with $135.8 million (3.2%), music with $184.11 million (4.3%), character goods with $383.17 million (8.9%), *manhwa* with $16.35 million (0.4%), publishing with $322.43 million (7.5%), broadcasting with $246.06 million (5.7%), independent broadcast productions with $18.38 million (0.4%), advertising with $108.57 million (2.5%), knowledge and information with $421 million (9.8%), and content solutions with $148.19 million (3.4%).

Imports for 2010 stood at $1.70 billion, a 4.1% decrease from 2009. Advertising made up the largest share with 43.4% ($737.16 million), followed by publishing with $339.81 million (20.0%), and gaming with $242.53 million (14.3%). A breakdown of the remaining sectors is as follows: film with $53.37 million (3.1%), animation with $6.95 million (0.4%), music with $10.33 million (0.6%), characters with $190.45 million (11.2%), *manhwa* with $5.28 million (0.3%), broadcasting with $110.49 million (6.5%), independent broadcast productions with $8.19 million (0.5%), knowledge and information with $440,000 (0.03%), and content solutions with $350,000 (0.02%).

Content exports in all sectors but publishing increased over the previous year. Most notably, music industry exports rose by 121.1% on the back of the K-pop phenomenon. Furthermore, gaming, which accounted for 53.6% of all exports and essentially drove content industry exports, recorded high growth (43.5%). Film industry exports, which have been decreasing consistently since 2007, also picked up once more this year, increasing by 114%.

On the other hand, imports for 2010 fell in almost all sectors, excluding advertising and knowledge and information. Independent broadcast productions saw an 86.6% decline in imports vis-à-vis 2009, and a concomitant decline for the broadcast industry that reached 39.6%. The publishing and gaming industries fell 2.4% and 27.0%, respectively, occupying 20.0% and 14.3% of total imports, respectively. The drop in imports has been marked.

The 2010 figures for all 11 sectors of the content industry show that exports ($3.23 billion) exceeded imports ($1.70 billion) by $1.53 billion, creating a trade surplus. Exports have grown consistently since 2007, whereas imports have decreased, leading to a surplus every year. If this trend can be buttressed by policies that facilitate participation in international fairs and support the efforts of domestic agencies to make inroads into overseas markets, this situation will likely continue. The following sections offer a breakdown of specific categories in 2010.

Regional imports/exports

Japan made up the largest share of 2010 content industry exports with $800.23 million (26.2%), followed by China with $747.66 million (24.5%), Southeast Asia with $671.9 million (22.0%), North America with $403.93 million (13.2%), Europe with $267.68 million (8.8%), and other areas totaling $157.55 million (5.2%).

Exports to China grew 29% over the previous year and 35% on average per year between 2007 and 2010. The figures for Japan, Southeast Asia, North America, and Europe respectively were 21% and 21.5%; 46.6% and 13.5%; 4.2% and -4.3%; and 23.1% and 15%. Exports to all remaining regions grew 24.7% over the previous year and increased 5.8% on average.

In the case of content imports, North America constituted the largest share with $275.92 million (38.9%), followed by China with $136 million (19.2%), Japan with $103.8 million (15.6%), Europe with 86.39 million (12.2%), and Southeast Asia with $64.76 million (9.1%). Other areas totaled $35.57 million.

In 2010, imports from China grew 2.9% over the previous year and 0.1% on average per year from 2007 to 2010. The figures for Japan, Southeast Asia, North America, and Europe were 3.8% and -8.5%; 2.3% and -0.5%; -17.6% and -0.9%; and -7.8% and -7.1%, respectively. Imports from all other regions grew 2.9% over the previous year and increased 1.8% on average.

Market entry mode

Research into how seven different industries (publishing, *manhwa*, music, animation, character goods, knowledge and information, and content solutions) accessed overseas markets showed that entry was made via licensing (45.2%), finished product sales (39.9%), OEM sales (12.7%), technology services (1.9%), and other miscellaneous means (0.3%).

Typically, content was exported under licensing contracts or as finished products. Since 2007, product licensing has increased, whereas OEM exports have been losing ground, which suggests an increase in the export of content created in Korea rather than subcontracted material.

Market entry routes

Examination of the entry routes of the seven industries shows that establishing contact with an overseas distributor was the favored option, at 26.4%, followed

Table 1-23. Korean content industry imports/exports

Industry	2007	2008	2009	2010	Share (2010)	Increase and Decrease (YOY*) 2009–2010	2011 Projection	Share (2011)	Increase and Decrease (YOY) 2010–2011	Annual Average Increase and Decrease (2007–2011)
Film	24,396	21,037	14,122	13,583	0.4%	−3.8%	29,065	0.7%	114.0%	4.5%
Animation	72,770	80,583	89,651	96,827	3.0%	8.0%	135,802	3.2%	40.3%	16.9%
Music	13,885	16,468	31,269	83,262	2.6%	166.3%	184,113	4.3%	121.1%	90.8%
Gaming	781,004	1,093,865	1,240,856	1,606,102	49.8%	29.4%	2,305,508	53.6%	43.5%	31.1%
Characters	202,898	228,250	236,521	276,328	8.6%	16.8%	383,173	8.9%	38.7%	17.2%
Manhwa	3,986	4,315	4,209	8,153	0.3%	93.7%	16,350	0.4%	100.5%	42.3%
Publishing	213,100	260,010	250,764	357,881	11.1%	42.7%	322,437	7.5%	−9.9%	10.9%
Broadcasting	150,953	171,348	184,577	228,633	7.1%	23.9%	246,061	5.7%	7.6%	13.0%
Independent Broadcast Productions	–	11,228	14,349	13,691	0.4%	−4.6%	18,381	0.4%	34.3%	–
Advertising	93,859	14,212	93,152	75,554	2.3%	−18.9%	108,577	2.5%	43.7%	3.7%
Knowledge and Information	275,111	339,949	345,693	363,282	11.3%	5.1%	420,990	9.8%	15.9%	11.2%
Content Solutions	112,678	107,746	113,418	116,487	3.6%	2.7%	148,195	3.4%	27.2%	7.1%
Total	1,944,631	2,337,603	2,604,232	3,226,092	100.0%	23.9%	4,300,271	100.0%	33.3%	21.9%

Exports

(Continued)

Table 1–23. (*Continued*).

Industry		2007	2008	2009	2010	Share (2010)	Increase and Decrease (YOY) 2009–2010
	Film	67,527	78,775	73,646	53,374	3.1%	–27.5%
	Animation	8,148	6,132	7,397	6,951	0.4%	–6.0%
	Music	9,831	11,484	11,936	10,337	0.6%	–13.4%
	Gaming	389,549	386,920	332,250	242,532	14.3%	–27.0%
	Characters	225,257	198,679	196,367	190,456	11.2%	–3.0%
Imports	*Manhwa*	5,901	5,937	5,492	5,281	0.3%	–3.8%
	Publishing	354,404	368,536	348,336	339,819	20.0%	–2.4%
	Broadcasting	64,939	149,396	183,011	110,495	6.5%	–39.6%
	Independent Broadcast Productions	–	71,153	61,277	8,1931	0.5%	–86.6%
	Advertising	2,225,807	780,696	610,277	737,167	43.4%	20.8%
	Knowledge and Information	398	415	432	442	0.03%	2.3%
	Content Solutions	–	–	387	352	0.02%	–9.0%
	Total	3,351,761	1,986,970	1,769,531	1,697,206	100.0%	–4.1%

* Year-on-year

Table 1–24. Content industry exports by region (2010)

Industry	China (incl. HK)	Japan	Southeast Asia	North America	Europe	Others	Total
Film	966.0	2,258.0	3,488.0	1,421.0	4,518.0	932.0	13,583.0
Animation	1,577.0	18,810.0	1,151.0	52,463.0	19,527.0	3,299.0	96,827.0
Music	3,627.0	67,267.0	11,321.0	432.0	396.0	219.0	83,262.0
Gaming	595,864.0	435,254.0	242,521.0	147,761.0	138,125.0	46,577.0	1,606,102.0
Characters	49,368.0	16,457.0	27,226.0	85,327.0	59,668.0	38,282.0	276,328.0
Manhwa	568.0	1,527.0	2,004.0	1,723.0	2,258.0	73.0	8,153.0
Publishing	23,790.0	30,204.0	149,984.0	88,009.0	20,976.0	44,918.0	357,881.0
Broadcasting (excluding independent productions)	20,954.8	49,712.8	49,554.8	2,814.8	2,317.6	1,702.1	127,074.9
Knowledge and Information	33,621.0	141,332.0	168,063.0	8,611.0	3,398.0	8,267.0	363,282.0
Content Solutions	17,331.0	37,426.0	16,593.0	15,376.0	16,497.0	13,264.0	116,487.0
Total	747,666.8	800,237.8	671,905.8	403,937.8	267,680.6	157,551.1	3,048,979.9
Percentage (%)	24.5%	26.2%	22.0%	13.2%	8.8%	5.2%	100.0%

Table 1–25.   Content industry imports by region (2010)

Industry	China (incl. HK)	Japan	Southeast Asia	North America	Europe	Others	Total
Film	1,754.0	1,229.0	78.0	42,085.0	5,038.0	3,190.0	53,374.0
Animation	11.0	6,905.0	–	35.0	–	–	6,951.0
Music	93.0	2,135.0	52.0	2,166.0	5,455.0	436.0	10,337.0
Characters	81,569.0	20,342.0	40,337.0	21,692.0	3,528.0	22,988.0	190,456.0
Manhwa	85.0	4,862.0	–	263.0	71.0	–	5,281.0
Publishing	51,452.0	69,137.0	24,171.0	120,197.0	66,653.0	8,209.0	339,819.0
Broadcasting (excluding independent productions)	1,036.5	5,777.5	128.6	88,833.8	5,595.6	664.2	102,036.2
Knowledge and Information	–	–	–	301.0	57.0	84.0	442.0
Content Solutions	–	–	–	352.0	–	–	352.0
Total	136,000.5	110,387.5	64,766,6	275,924.8	86,397.6	35,571.2	709,048.2
Percentage (%)	19.2%	15.6%	9.1%	38.9%	12.2%	5.0%	100.0%

Table 1–26. Market entry modes for content exports

Entry Mode	2006	2007	2008	2009	2010	Growth Year on Year
Licensing	26.7	27.7	31.5	44.4	45.2	0.8%
Finished Product Sales	42.2.	44.7	45.9	37.2	39.9	2.7%
OEM Exports	24.1	21.9	19.7	15.3	12.7	−2.6%
Technology Services	6.4	4.4	2.8	2.5	1.9	−0.6%
Other	0.6	1.3	0.1	0.6	0.3	−0.3%
Total	100	100	100	100	100	–

(Source: MCST and KOCCA (2012), *2011 Content Industry Statistics*)

Table 1–27. Market entry routes for content exports

Export Mode	Export Route	2006	2007	2008	2009	2010	Growth Year on Year
Direct Export	Overseas Expos and Fairs	15.2	14.7	18.0	20.0	19.6	−0.4%
	Overseas Distributors	27.0	26.7	25.5	24.3	26.4	2.1%
	Online Sales	1.1	2.6	2.8	2.7	3.1	0.4%
	Overseas Affiliates	9.4	8.6	8.0	7.1	6.6	−0.5%
Indirect Export	Domestic Agents	22.0	25.2	25.6	23.0	21.7	−1.3%
	Foreign Agents	13.0	16.0	16.0	19.9	20.1	0.2%
Other		12.3	6.2	4.1	3.0	2.5	−0.5%
Total		100	100	100	100	100	–

(Source: MCST and KOCCA (2012), *2011 Content Industry Statistics*)

by use of Korean domestic agents (21.7%), use of foreign agents (20.1%), participation in international exhibitions and events (19.6%), use of overseas affiliates (6.6%), online sales (3.1%), and miscellaneous other means (2.5%).

An examination of the data for 2009 reveals that direct exports accounted for 54.1% of total exports, a figure that increased slightly in 2010 to 55.7%. Direct exports stood at 52.7% in 2006, approximately 5% higher than indirect exports and other modes (47.3%), but in 2010, the gap increased by over 10%. Most notably, participation in overseas exhibitions and events jumped from 15.2% in 2005 to 19.6% in 2010.

Among export routes, working with overseas distributors increased over the previous year (2.1%), as did online sales (0.4%) and use of foreign agents (0.2%). Percentages for other routes fell. The biggest drop was in the use of domestic agents, which tumbled 1.3% from 2009. Use of overseas affiliates and foreign agents both fell 0.5%, while participation in international expos and fairs fell 0.4%.

B.   Industry sectors

Films

Export growth

(p. 294)

The total value of Korean film exports in 2011 reached $15.83 million, a 16.5% increase from 2010 and a turnaround after six years of decline. This figure encompasses 366 films, the highest number ever. Exports to Japan and China boosted the figure for Asia, which accounted for 56.9% of total exports. In particular, exports to China increased 94.8% from the previous year. Exports in the postproduction and service sectors, including visual effects (VFX), digital intermediate (DI), 3D conversion, special effects, martial arts, and sound mixing, fell 58.7% from $28.634 million in 2010 to $11.82 million in 2011. The 3D conversion sector reported a particularly sharp decline. Although export dwindled in these technology services, the overall growth for film is encouraging.

Film exports and overseas entry

(pp. 306–308)

The year 2011 was a meaningful one for the Korean film industry, with a boom in the domestic market and a recovery of foreign sales after a lengthy downturn. Total exports, although not comparable to the mid-2000s when Korean cinema boomed abroad, increased by 16.5% from 2010, a positive sign after the recession of recent years. In 2011, revenue for Korean films totaled $15.83 million overseas, up 16.5% from $13.58 million in 2010. A total of 366 films were exported, the highest number in the new millennium, topping the previous record of 361 in 2008. Meanwhile, average export price, calculated by dividing the sum of all contracts by the number of films exported, stood at $4.48 million, which was lower than previous years due to sudden increases in contract price and the number of films exported.

Asia was the largest market in 2011, accounting for 56.9% of total overseas sales at $9.01 million, up 34.3% from 2010. Reliance on exports to Asia grew from the previous year, caused by increased export to Japan and China. Export to Europe was valued at $3.52 million, a 22.0% decline from 2010. In contrast to soaring demand in Asia, the share of exports to Europe declined by approximately 11%, presumably because export sales prices dropped as a result of the recession in Europe and because Korean directors popular in Europe made fewer new films. In other regions, export figures did not differ greatly from previous years.

The biggest buyer of Korean films in 2011 was Japan, which spent $3.66 million, constituting 23.1% of total sales and representing a 62.3% increase from $2.26 million in 2010. Given that exports to Japan had been decreasing by an annual rate of 40%, bottoming out in 2010 at 16.6% of the market, sales there appear to be finally turning around.

Notably, exports to China almost doubled from 2010 (a 94.8% increase), recording $1,000,000 and making China the fourth largest market for Korean films. If Hong Kong ($623,950) is added, China becomes third after Japan and the US. This growth was led by China's massive purchase of online rights to

Table 1–28. Exports of South Korean films by year (Unit: $)

Year	2004	2005	2006	2007	2008	2009	2010	2011
Foreign Sales	58,284,600	75,994,580	24,514,728	24,396,215	21,036,540	14,122,143	13,582,850	15,828,662
Contract Fees (minimum guarantee+flat+other)	58,284,600	75,994,580	24,514,728	12,283,339	20,541,212	13,930,262	13,166,280	14,815,146
Overage (Extra profit)	–	–	–	12,112,876	495,328	191,881	416,570	1,013,516
Change from Previous Year	88.14%	30.39%	–67.74%	–0.48%	–13.77%	–32.87%	–3.82%	16.53%
Films Exported*	194	202	208	321	361	251	276	366
Average Sales Price**	300,436	376,211	117,859	38,266	56,901	55,499	47,704	40,479

* Overage films are not included in the figures for film exports.
** Average sales price = Sum of contracts/number of films exported.
(Source: KOFIC (2012), *2011 Report on the South Korean Film Industry*)

Table 1–29.   2010–2011 exports of South Korean films by region

Region	Export Amount ($) 2010	Share	2011	Share	% Change
Asia	6,712,061	49.42%	9,012,061	56.94%	34.27%
Europe	4,518,034	33.26%	3,522,333	22.23%	−22.04%
North America	1,421,297	10.46%	1,672,677	10.56%	17.69%
Oceania	207,038	1.52%	309,891	1.96%	49.68%
Latin America	157,500	1.16%	147,000	0.93%	−6.67%
Middle East	193,600	1.43%	132,000	0.83%	−31.82%
Africa	3,000	0.02%	53,000	0.33%	1666.67%
Other	370,320	2.73%	979,700	6.18%	164.55%
Total	13,582,850	100.00%	15,828,662	100.00%	16.64%

(Source: KOFIC (2012), *2011 Report on the South Korean Film Industry*)

Table 1–30. Korean film exports to 10 major destinations in 2010 and 2011

Destination	2010 Exports ($)	Share	2011 Exports ($)	Share	% Change
Japan	2,257,517	16.6%	3,663,437	23.1%	62.3%
US	1,421,297	10.5%	1,652,594	10.4%	16.3%
Germany	876,518	6.5%	1,490,930	9.4%	70.1%
China	515,500	3.8%	1,004,000	6.3%	94.8%
France	1,781,860	13.1%	940,980	5.9%	−47.2%
Taiwan	1,297,900	9.6%	931,000	5.9%	−28.3%
Singapore	612,264	4.5%	799,600	5.1%	30.6%
UK	582,500	4.3%	780,000	4.9%	33.9%
Thailand	943,500	6.9%	715,000	4.5%	−24.2%
Hong Kong	451,000	3.3%	623,950	3.9%	38.3%
Other	2,842,994	20.9%	3,227,171	20.4%	–
Total	13,582,850	100.0%	15,828,662	100.0%	–

(Source: KOFIC (2012), *2011 Report on the South Korean Film Industry*)

Korean films, from hit movies of the past to the latest releases. Considering that Korean films screened in China are enjoying success and the online market has tremendous potential for growth, China's share is expected to expand further.

A total of 56 contracts were signed in the film production service sector in 2011, and the value of orders reached $19.04 million. VFX/DI accounted for 85.6% of orders received ($10.13 million). The 3D/3D conversion and special effects and makeup sectors accounted for around 5% of orders received ($664,300

Table 1–31. 2010–2011 foreign contracts by film production service sectors

Service Sectors	2010		2011	
	Exports ($)	Share	Exports ($)	Share
VFX/DI	4,400,750	15.36%	10,125,071	85.64%
3D/3D Conversion	21,750,000	75.94%	664,300	5.72%
Special Effects and Makeup	1,877,756	6.56%	624,880	5.29%
Martial Arts and Stunt Work	522,000	1.83%	261,703	2.22%
Sound Mixing	87,000	0.31%	145,891	1.23%
Subtotal	28,637,506	100%	11,821,845	100%
Foreign Media On-Location Shooting*			7,219,318	37.91%**
Total	28,637,506	100%	19,041,163	100%

* This amount is the total expenditure in Korea by foreign media productions while shooting on location.
** This share is from the total of $19,041,163.
(Source: KOFIC (2012), *2011 Report on the South Korean Film Industry*)

and $624,880, respectively). Although the newly surveyed sector of on-location shooting of foreign media products was excluded from the above breakdown, earnings from such projects totaled $7.22 million, equal to 37.9% of the amount earned in all other sectors combined.

The 3D movie boom is weakening, and this had a significant impact on companies involved in 3D/3D conversion, leading to an overall decline in orders received. As this situation resulted not simply from the end of a boom but a global economic downturn, recovery may be slow. Conversely, the reputation of South Korean VFX and DI companies in Asia is rising, evidenced by their growth rates. Surveys suggest that supply is evenly distributed among companies. Therefore, stable growth is projected for the VFX and DI sectors.

Globalization of South Korean films and the rise in international co-productions

(pp. 313–314)

The biggest change in globalization policies involved a shift from export-centered policies to the introduction of, and growing interest in, inbound projects, including incentives for on-location shooting of foreign media products in Korea. Countries around the world are increasing governmental support for their film industries, offering tax deductions for production expenses and adopting inducement strategies for on-location shooting. However, Korea lacks a framework for a comprehensive scheme to attract foreign film productions, with inadequate government systems and policies, and a shortage of international networking and marketing. Using New Zealand's Large Budget Screen Production Grant as a benchmark, Korea has introduced an incentive program to bring on-location shoots to the country.

Under this program, foreign movies or TV dramas shooting in Korea are eligible for up to a 25% rebate for production expenses incurred in Korea. The scheme is being actively promoted along with cash incentives offered by 10 regional film commissions. As of the end of 2011, the program had attracted four projects, including *The Way: Man of the White Porcelain* and *Bhikkuni: Buddhist Nuns.*

Using local offices as bases for international co-productions
The International Co-production Support Taskforce was created in September of 2010, but the group remained largely inactive because of a lack of full-time staff and financial resources. The government and the Korean Film Council (KOFIC) established a strategic plan for international co-production for each

Table 1–32. Co-production strategies and support measures by region

Country/ Region	Co-production Strategy	Support Measures
US	The co-production model, whereby Korean companies are responsible for activities from planning, development, and preproduction to primary production of a joint venture project, is growing. In this situation, adequate profit sharing models are important so that domestic companies can secure sufficient investment to carry out a significant part of production.	– Improvement of investment conditions to shift focus from sale of remake rights and encourage domestic companies to enter co-production from the planning and development stages – Invitation of influential Hollywood figures to business meetings – Provision of legal advice
Europe/ Canada	Through government support, the share of Korean companies should be increased to enable them to enter co-production with French and Canadian companies under equal terms.	– Continuation of meetings organized by KO-PRODUCTION (a company that supports international meetings for pitching new projects) – Focus on introducing well-known Korean directors
Japan	Japan is showing new interest in overseas co-production. Strategic formation of a consortium with Japanese media, distribution, and merchandising companies could increase opportunities for successful entry into the North American and European markets.	– Thorough preparation for an increase in post-production orders – Selection of high-quality products to be introduced at KO-PRODUCTION meetings – Employment of local mentors for practical assistance
China/ Southeast Asia	Despite inherent obstacles in China and Southeast Asia such as low-quality film productions and unstable management, emerging markets have a high potential for growth. Therefore, South Korean companies should form strategic co-production networks in the region.	– Formation of co-production agreements between states – Establishment of local networks in China – Provision of legal advice and translation services

(Source: KOFIC (2011), *Medium–term Plan to Increase International Projects*)

region, considering countries favored by Korean companies based on surveys of needs analysis, entry barriers, and level of cooperation with overseas agencies and governments.

Based on the strategies for each region, support for overseas offices was reinforced through increased staffing, granting of authority to facilitate their roles as key bases for entry into foreign markets, promotion of international co-productions, and promotion of on-location shoots in Korea. Growing interest in China meant that as of December 2011, 81 co-production projects were in development by South Korean and Chinese firms. The importance of Chinese offices as bases for co-productions has increased, but many challenges remain, including strict import quotas and censorship. Accordingly, demand is growing for a Korea-China memorandum on co-production and business matching for independent projects.

Efforts to fulfill these demands continue in the key projects of 2012. With the goal of establishing a South Korea-China agreement on co-productions by the end of 2012, the Korean government and KOFIC are continuing networking efforts with the Chinese government and operating "China Business Centers" to aid Korean film professionals in their co-production activities in China.

Pioneering new markets
The US, Japan, China, and Europe have been the primary export destinations for Korean movies. Popular demand has risen for Korean content with *Hallyu*, however, paving the way for Korean movies to pioneer new markets in the Middle East and Latin America.

In terms of overseas entry of Korean movies, 2011 saw 10 co-production business matches, 672 trainees for entry into the Chinese market, 4 global projects completed with location incentives, a 24% increase over 2010 in businesses receiving international film market support, and a 117% increase in support for entries in international film festivals over 2010.

Table 1–33.   New market entry strategies by region

Middle East	Latin America
– Rising content consumption	– Dubbing into Spanish is essential
– High demand for Hollywood blockbusters	– Special screenings of Korean films → showcasing → broadcasting
– Networking with top officials is necessary	– Link to K-pop
Russia	India
– Utilize theaters in high-end museums	– India is the largest producer of films in the world, and the audience prefers local movies
– Target the DVD market	– Unauthorized remakes are common
– Promote scheduling of Korean films on TV movie channels	– Target local cable TV

Table 1–34.   Animation industry imports/exports (Unit: $1,000)

Industry	Exports 2008	2009	2010	Change from Previous Year (%)	Average Annual Growth (%)
Animation	80,583	89,651	96,827	8.0	9.6

Industry	Imports 2008	2009	2010	Change from Previous Year (%)	Average Annual Growth (%)
Animation	6,132	7,397	6,951	−6.0	6.5

(Source: MCST (2011), *2011 Animation Industry White Paper*)

Table 1–35.   Sales of original and subcontracted products in the animation industry (Unit: $1,000)

Type	Original and Subcontracted Product Sales 2008	2009	2010	Change from Previous Year (%)	Average Annual Growth (%)
Original Products	43,837	50,602	60,575	19.7	17.6
Subcontracted Products	36,746	39,049	36,252	−7.2	−0.7
Total	80,583	89,651	96,827	8.0	9.6

(Source: MCST (2011), *2011 Animation Industry White Paper*)

Animation

(pp. 324–325)

Animation industry exports in 2010 were $96.82 million, an 8.0% increase from the previous year. Annual growth had a 9.6% three-year average. Industry imports totaled $6.95 million, a decrease of 6.0% from the previous year, but annual growth over the years remained positive, at 6.5%. Original animation sales accounted for $60.57 million, an increase of 19.7% from $50.6 million in 2009. On the other hand, the figure for subcontract sales was $36.25 million, a decrease of 7.2% from $39.04 million in 2009. Export of original domestic animations thus increased, while export of subcontracted works decreased.

Music

(pp. 351–352)

Music industry exports reached $83.26 million, up 166.3% from the previous year. The average annual growth rate of exports between 2008 and 2010 was 124.9%. Imports were $10.33 million, registering a 13.4% decrease from the

Table 1–36.   Imports/exports in the music industry in 2010 (Unit: $1,000)

Type	Imports and Exports			Change from Previous Year (%)	Average Annual Growth (%)
	2008	2009	2010		
Imports	16,468	31,269	83,262	166.3	124.9
Exports	11,484	11,936	10,337	−13.4	−5.1

(Source: MCST (2011), *2011 Content Industry Statistics*)

previous year and an average annual growth rate of -5.1%. Exports increased fivefold in the span of two years: from $16.46 million in 2008 to $31.26 million in 2009, and then to $83.26 million in 2010. Music industry imports were $11.48 million in 2008, $11.93 million in 2009, and $10.33 million in 2010.

Music industry exports have been increasing substantially each year. In the past, significant time and effort were required to export a few idol groups to Japan and Southeast Asia, but the emergence of *YouTube*, *Twitter*, and other SNS has simplified marketing around the world, presenting the Korean music industry with useful opportunities.

Exports include not only idol groups but also a notable proportion of globally competitive genres, such as original musicals, which are recognized for their sophisticated production. Due to the large scale and long runs of these productions, musical theater is expected to boost music industry exports greatly. Therefore, policy support is warranted for increased export of not only idol groups but also musical theater and similarly competitive genres.

Gaming

(pp. 360–364)

Imports and exports
In 2010, game industry exports increased 29.4% from the previous year to $1.6 billion.[2] This rate is slightly higher than the average annual growth since 2006. Surpassing the $1.6 billion mark is a noteworthy export milestone. Industry imports totaled $242.53 million (₩280.4 billion), a 27.0% decrease from the previous year. Imports decreased in 2009 and 2010 because many foreign companies in the video game market, which account for the majority of imports, either did not launch innovative products or postponed distribution of new models in the Korean market.

The most salient trend in 2010 imports/exports is the disproportionate increase in online game exports. While the market share of online games dropped slightly from 97.6% in 2009 to 96.2% in 2010, total exports in fact increased by over $300 million, surpassing $1.5 billion. In particular, Neowiz Games Corp. saw an increase of ₩149.5 billion in exports from 2008 to 2010, amounting to 37.7% of total sales. These high figures may be attributed to the steady popularity of *Crossfire* in the Chinese market. Nexon Co. Ltd. has also made a major

---

[2] Equivalent to ₩1,857 billion. Conversion based on the 2010 annual average exchange rate of ₩1,156 to the US dollar, set by the Korea Exchange Bank.

contribution to game industry exports, with an increase of ₩163.8 billion in two years, from ₩102.6 billion in 2008 to ₩266.4 billion in 2010.

In 2011, game industry exports are projected to grow and remain above 2010 levels, a trend that will become more obvious as overseas market entry of new online games, game server relocation, and export contracts all become more common. Moreover, with an expansion of export destinations arising from diversification efforts, exports in 2011 are expected to grow 34.8% from the previous year and reach an estimated $2.2 billion. In contrast to the drop in video game imports in 2010 resulting from a lack of innovative games and a delay in the distribution of new products in Korea, a 10% growth is projected for imports in 2011, given the expectation of the launch of the Nintendo 3DS in Korea and a rise in demand for older models after a reduction in price.

Online games remained at the forefront of game exports for South Korea, accounting for 96.2% (97.6% in 2009) of the total ($1.54 billion). Online games accounted for 15.7% of total game imports ($37.97 million), down 11.6% from the previous year. Video games led South Korea's game imports. The share of video games was 75.5% of the total (81.2% in 2009) and amounted to $183 million. Video game imports dropped 32.2% from the previous year, their share of total game imports also decreasing slightly. Video game exports totaled $3.96 million, just 0.3% of total game exports.

Mobile game exports reached $8.48 million (0.5% of the total); imports were $2.54 million (1.0%). Arcade game exports were $48.74 million (3.0%); imports were $7.33 million (3.0%). These figures suggest that arcade game makers are seeking alternative markets overseas due to negative perceptions and strict regulations in South Korea. PC games recorded $65,000 (less than 0.01%) in exports and $11.69 million in imports (4.8%).

Breakdown of exports by destination
In 2010, China was the largest export market for South Korean games, accounting for 37.1% of all game exports. Japan was the second largest market, with 27.1% of all game exports, followed by Southeast Asia (15.1%), North America (9.2%), Europe (8.6%), and others (2.9%).

China surpassed Japan in 2008 to become the top export destination for South Korean games. Following an increase in 2009, China's share of Korean game exports rose a further 2.2% in 2010. Japan's share increased by an annual rate of 0.6%. China and Japan continue to loom large as the major export destinations for Korean games.

In 2010 South Korea's exports to China and Japan rose to over 64% of all game exports, while exports to the US and other countries declined. The share of exports to the US dropped from 16.9% of the total in 2008 to 12.3% in 2009. Game exports to all of North America in 2010 made up only 9.2%, implying numerous challenges in marketing Korean games in the region. Challenges in exporting games to North America and the concentration of exports to Asia suggest that diversification strategies will be necessary in the long term. Exports to Europe rose 0.4% annually, indicating that opportunities to diversify export markets remain.

Online game exports were also concentrated in China and Japan, reflecting the overall trend. By contrast, online game exports to the US declined 3.1%

Table 1-37. Game industry imports/exports and prospects (Unit: $1,000)

Category		2003	2004	2005	2006	2007	2008	2009	2010	2011 (Est.)
Exports	Amount	172,743	387,692	564,660	671,994	781,004	1,093,865	1,240,856	1,606,102	2,164,970
	Growth	22.7%	124.4%	45.6%	19.0%	16.2%	40.1%	13.4%	29.4%	34.8%
Imports	Amount	166,454	205,108	232,923	207,556	389,549	386,920	332,250	242,532	266,785
	Growth	3.4%	23.2%	13.6%	10.9%	87.7%	−0.67%	−14.1%	−27.0%	10.0%

(Source: MCST and KOCCA, *2011 Gaming Industry White Paper*)

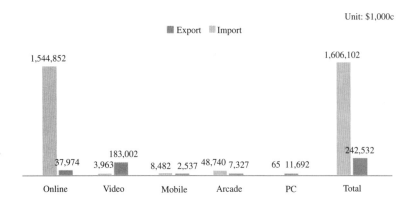

Figure 1–10.   **Changes in game imports and exports by platform**
(Source: MCST and KOCCA, *2011 Gaming Industry White Paper*)

Unit: %

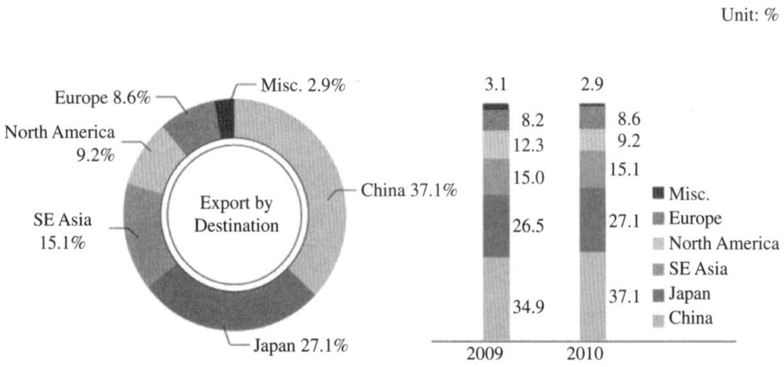

Figure 1–11.   **Breakdown of Korea's game exports in 2010 by destination**
(Source: MCST and KOCCA, *2011 Gaming Industry White Paper*)

annually. Mobile games occupied the largest share of exports to the US, account-ing for 57.2% of the total. Japan followed, receiving 28.7% of all mobile game exports. Europe's share of the mobile game export market is also on the rise, increasing from 6.4% in 2008 to 9.4% and 9.7% in 2009 and 2010, respectively.

Global market share for South Korean games
Korean games occupied a 5.8% share of the global market in 2010, with sales amounting to $4.9 billion of the $84.82 billion total. This figure is 2.7% higher than the 3.1% of 2009, and shows that Korea's game industry grew at a faster pace than the overall game market. The Korean market benefited from global fluctuations, especially dramatic shifts in the video game market. Considering the trends in the Korean and global game markets, the global share of Korean games is expected to grow steadily. Current projections suggest 6.8% in 2011, 8.3% in 2012, and 9.7% in 2013.

Table 1–38. Global market share of South Korean games in 2010 (based on sales) (Unit: $1,000,000)

Market	Online Games	Video Games	Mobile Games	PC Games	Arcade Games	Total
Domestic Market	15,913	33,788	8,569	3,068	23,481	84,818
Global Market	4,123	369	274	10	128	4,905
Share	25.9%	1.1%	3.2%	0.3%	0.5%	5.8%

Arcade market size is calculated by combining sales of arcade machines and revenue from operation of arcade game rooms. Sales of vending machines that are included in the US arcade market were excluded due to the situation of Korea's arcade market. PC games include only boxed games. For online games, membership fees, in-game item sales, and revenue from advertising are included in the global calculation, but in-game item sales and revenue from PC gaming rooms are not included when calculating the Korean market size. The mobile categories include only games for mobile devices such as cellular phones and PDAs. The video game market combines sales from console and portable games. From this year, Eastern Europe is included in European market size. The statistics provided by the International Data Corporation (IDC) revealed a year-on-year increase of over 50% in video game market size. The figures shown reflect this adjustment and have thus changed significantly from those in the *2010 Gaming Industry White Paper*. This report reflects cases in which figures had been altered by statistics providers, such as PricewaterhouseCooper (PwC) and DFC Intelligence. Standard exchange rate: USD/KRW = 1156.26, USD/RMB = 0.1478, USD/JPY = 114.23.
Sources: DFC 2011; Enterbrain 2011; IDC 2011; Informa 2005–2007; in-Stat 2006; iResearch 2011; JAMMA 2007–2010; JOGA 2011.
(Source: MCST and KOCCA, *2011 Gaming Industry White Paper*)

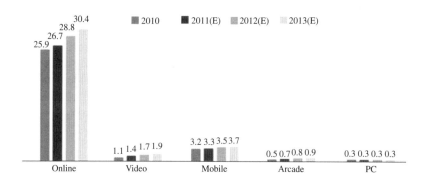

Figure 1–12.   Projected global market sales of Korean games (2010–2013) (Unit: %)
(Source: MCST and KOCCA, *2011 Gaming Industry White Paper*)

Korea accounted for 25.9% of the global online gaming market, second only to China's 30.4% share, proving once again its strength in this area. Korea, having once dominated the global online game market, was pushed to second place in 2008 by China's explosive growth. These figures, however, which represent a 2.9% annual increase for Korea, but a 0.9% decrease for China, show that Korea has resumed its pursuit of China.

One challenge for Korea has been its low global market share of platforms other than online games. Although video and arcade games still represent a large proportion of the global market, Korea's share in these platforms is only around 1.0%. The total market share for Korean video games also rose slightly to 1.1%, reflecting a shift in the global game market. The global share for Korea's mobile games rose by a small margin, from 2.8% in 2009 to 3.2% in 2010, an increase believed to have resulted from rising smart device penetration and diversification of distribution routes.

Licensed characters

(pp. 388–389)

In 2010, North America was the largest export destination for South Korea's character goods industry, constituting an estimated 30.9% of all character exports ($85.33 million). Exports to Europe accounted for 21.6% ($59.67 million), and those to China 17.9% ($49.37 million). Exports to miscellaneous other regions accounted for 13.9% ($38.3 million) and those to Southeast Asia for 9.8% ($27.23 million). The smallest share of the regions in the breakdown went to Japan, which purchased 6.0% of overall exports ($16.46 million).

Exports to Japan increased from $12.78 million in 2008 to $14.63 million in 2009, and to $16.46 million in 2010. The 2010 figure represents a 12.5% increase from the previous year and an overall average annual increase of 13.5%. Exports to China increased from $38.35 million in 2008 to $43.59 million in 2009, and to $49.37 million in 2010. The 2010 figure represents a 13.2% increase from the previous year, and also a significant overall average annual increase of 13.5%.

Exports to Southeast Asia totaled $20.77 million in 2008, $21.33 million in 2009, and $27.23 million in 2010, showing a 27.6% increase from 2009 to 2010, and a 14.5% average annual increase. Exports to North America totaled $74.41 million in 2008, $74.51 million in 2009, and $85.33 million in 2010, an increase of 14.5% from 2009 to 2010, and an average annual increase of 7.1%. Exports to Europe also showed consistent growth, climbing from $50.44 million in 2008 to $51.34 million in 2009, and $59.67 million in 2010. Exports to

Table 1–39.   Character industry exports (Unit: $1,000)

	2008	2009	2010	Share	Change from Previous Year (%) (2010)	Average Annual Increase (%)
China	38,346	43,593	49,368	17.9	13.2	13.5
Japan	12,782	14,631	16,457	6.0	12.5	13.5
Southeast Asia	20,771	21,332	27,226	9.9	27.6	14.5
North America	74,410	74,513	85,327	30.9	14.5	7.1
Europe	50,443	51,338	59,668	21.6	16.2	8.8
Other	31,498	31,114	38,282	13.9	23.0	10.2
Total	228,250	236,521	276,328	100.0	16.8	10.0

(Source: MCST (2011), *2011 Character Goods Industry White Paper*)

all areas increased in 2010. Exports to miscellaneous other areas increased 23% between 2009 and 2010, with an average annual increase of 10.2%. The total dropped slightly from $31.5 million in 2008 to $31.11 million in 2009, but rose again to $38.28 million in 2010.

Character goods industry exports are increasing in North America and Europe as well as China, Japan, Southeast Asia, and elsewhere, which shows the competitiveness of Korean character goods and their appeal to consumers from different cultural backgrounds. Increased smart device penetration offers opportunities for export of Korean characters, as Korean companies can develop and distribute apps as a new method for entry overseas. A variety of factors give character industry exports a very bright outlook.

Manhwa

(pp. 402–405)

In 2010, the Korean *manhwa* industry recorded $8.15 million in exports and $5.28 million in imports. While exports soared by 93.7% from the previous year, imports declined by 3.8%, continuing a trend that began in 2008. Although the domestic *manhwa* market has been stagnant, exports have risen steadily, with Korean *manhwa* receiving favorable reviews abroad.

The lion's share of exports went to Europe ($2.26 million; 27.7%), followed in order by Southeast Asia, North America, Japan, and China. In particular, the popularity of educational *manhwa* for children led to a jump in exports to Southeast Asia from $5.25 million in 2009 to $20.04 million in 2010, a 281.7% increase from 2009. Japan accounted for over 90% of the industry's imports, totaling $4.86 million. North America was the second largest source, followed by China and Europe.

Domestic agents remained the most important avenue for export sales in 2010, accounting for 54.6% of overall *manhwa* exports. Exports via fairs and expo participation increased 1.6% from 2009 to 41.2%.

Looking at *manhwa* industry exports by format, sale of licensed products increased 6.8% from the previous year to 73.7% of overall exports. Finished goods sales had the second largest share, at 26.3%.

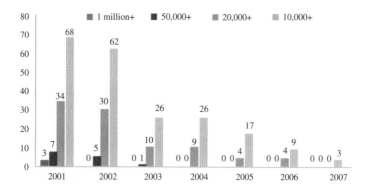

Figure 1–13.   Imports and exports in the *Manhwa* industry
(Source: MCST (2011), *2011 Manhwa Industry White Paper*)

Table 1–40.   *Manhwa* industry exports by destination (Unit: $1,000)

Destination	Exports 2008	2009	2010	Share (%)	Change from Previous Year (%) (2010)	Average Annual Increase (%)
China	421	432	568	7.0	31.5	16.2
Japan	616	597	1,527	18.7	155.8	57.4
Southeast Asia	507	525	2,004	24.6	281.7	98.8
North America	936	943	1,723	21.1	82.7	35.7
Europe	1,623	1,667	2,258	27.7	35.5	18.0
Other	32	45	73	0.9	62.2	51.0
Total	4,135	4,209	8,153	100.0	93.7	40.4

(Source: MCST (2011), *2011 Manhwa Industry White Paper*)

Table 1–41.   *Manhwa* industry imports by region (Unit: $1,000)

Source	Imports 2008	2009	2010	Share (%)	Change from Previous Year (%) (2010)	Average Annual Increase (%)
China	109	97	85	1.6	−12.4	−11.7
Japan	5,432	5,041	4,862	92.1	−3.6	−5.4
Southeast Asia	–	–	–	–	–	–
North America	297	278	263	5.0	−5.4	−5.9
Europe	99	76	71	1.3	−6.6	−15.3
Other	–	–	–	–	–	–
Total	5,937	5,492	5,281	100.0	−3.8	−5.7

(Source: MCST (2011), *2011 Manhwa Industry White Paper*)

Table 1–42.   *Manhwa* exports by channel (Unit: %)

Type	Entry Path	2008 Survey	2009 Survey	2010 Survey	% Change from Previous Year
Direct Exports	Overseas expo and fair participation	36.3	39.6	41.2	1.6
	Direct contact with overseas distributors	3.2	2.3	2.1	−0.2
	Overseas online sales	–	–	–	–
	Use of overseas affiliates	–	–	–	–
Indirect Exports	Use of domestic agents	55.6	55.9	54.6	−1.3
	Use of overseas agents	4.1	2.2	2.1	−0.1
Other		0.8	–	–	–
Total		100.0	100.0	100.0	–

(Source: MCST (2011), *2011 Manhwa Industry White Paper*)

Table 1–43. *Manhwa* industry exports by format (Unit: %)

Export Format	2008 Standard Survey	2009 Standard Survey	2010 Standard Survey	2008–2010 YOY Change (%)
Finished Goods	49.3	31.7	26.3	−5.4
Licensing	50.1	66.9	73.7	6.8
OEM	–	–	–	–
Technical Services	–	–	–	–
Other	0.6	1.4	0	−1.4
Total	100	100	100	−1.4

(Source: MCST (2011), *2011 Manhwa Industry White Paper*)

Table 1–44. Broadcast industry exports by medium (Unit: $1,000)

Medium	2008	2009	2010	Share	Change from Previous Year (%)	Average Annual Growth 2008–2010 (%)
KBS	34,315	33,926	41,848	18.3	23.4	10.4
MBC	22,268	31,298	33,522	14.7	7.1	22.7
EBS	223	822	517	0.2	−37.1	52.3
SBS	34,125	35,310	45,784	20.0	29.7	15.8
Other Regional Broadcasters	200	23	98	0.04	326.1	−30.0
Program Providers	2,789	2,867	6,043	2.6	110.8	47.2
Broadcast Services for Overseas Koreans	15,306	24,513	44,970	19.7	83.5	71.4
Sale of Videos and DVDs	33,362	20,900	15,301	6.7	−26.8	−32.3
Sale of Time Blocks and Formats	17,533	20,569	26,859	11.7	30.6	23.8
Independent Production Companies	11,228	14,349	13,691	6.0	−4.6	10.4
Total	171,349	184,577	228,633	100.0	23.9	15.5

(Source: MCST (2011), *2011 Content Industry Statistics*)

Broadcasting

(pp. 486–487)

In 2010, broadcast industry exports totaled $228.63 million, a 23.9% increase from 2009, with an average annual growth of 15.5% from 2008 to 2010. The increase in exports from 2008 to 2009 was slight, but the popularity of TV dramas led to significant growth in 2010.

Table 1–45.   Broadcast industry imports by medium (Unit: $1,000)

Medium	2008	2009	2010	Share	Change from Previous Year (%)	Average Annual Growth 2008–2010 (%)
KBS	1,414	1,605	1,791	1.6	11.6	12.5
MBC	270	267	477	0.4	78.7	32.9
EBS	2,145	1,287	1,982	1.8	54.0	–3.9
SBS	1,089	171	–	–	–	–
Other Regional Broadcasts	702	282	109	0.1	–61.3	–60.6
Program Providers	72,641	118,039	97,677	88.4	–17.3	16.0
Sale of Time Blocks and Formats	–	83	266	0.2	220.5	–
Independent Broadcast Producers	71,135	61,277	8,193	7.4	–86.6	–66.1
Total	149,396	183,011	110,495	100.0	–39.6	–14.0

(Source: MCST (2011), *2010 Content Industry Statistics*)

Imports amounted to $110.49 million, down 39.6% from the previous year but showing an average annual increase of 14.0%. Broadcast industry imports rose from $149.39 million in 2008 to $183.01 million in 2009, but fell back below the 2008 level in 2010 to $110.49 million.

1.2.4.   Korea Conquers Gaming World

Reference: "Korea Conquers Gaming World," *Weekly Chosun*, Baek Gang-nyeong, March 11, 2004, Issue No. 1794, p. 35.

South Korea dominates online games in Asia, including China, Taiwan, and Thailand. Game exports in 2003 record ₩294.8 billion.

After capturing the Greater China Region, South Korea's online game companies have now won over gaming communities in Thailand and the rest of Asia. It is no exaggeration to say that the Korean Wave is more dominant in the gaming industry than in any other.

WEBZEN's online game *Mu* has had as many as 300,000 simultaneous players in the Chinese market. *Mu* is competing for first place in China against *The Legend of Mir 2*, a game created by another Korean company, WeMade Entertainment.

The number of simultaneous *Mu* players in Japan has also exceeded 300,000. After success in Taiwan and Japan, *Mu* entered the Thai market. Recruitment for beta testers for a restricted trial service in Thailand resulted in 70% of all the country's Internet cafes joining. The game astonished local media by attracting some 100,000 players within just 20 days. The official homepage of *Mu* (www. muonline.in.th) became the seventh most visited website in all of Thailand.

NCSOFT, the world's largest online game firm, earned ₩28.1 billion from foreign royalties last year. The company's projection for overseas sales this year stands at ₩47 billion. Most of the company's revenue comes from within Asia.

Japan has been known to prefer console games to online options. However, one week after the open trial of *Lineage II* was launched there on February 11, the game had attracted 170,000 total registered players, with up to 30,000 simultaneous players.

South Korea's domestic market is effectively saturated. Over 200 online game companies are showcasing one new product after another. These companies have no choice but to look abroad. Export to Asia has been particularly successful. It is fair to say that South Korea's online games are Asia's online games.

According to the "2003 Game Industry Annual Report," published at the end of last year by KESA, game exports more than doubled in the past three years, reaching ₩97.7 billion in 1999, ₩84.6 billion in 2000, ₩109 billion in 2001, and ₩221.7 billion in 2002. KESA projects that Korea's game exports will reach ₩294.8 billion in 2003, ₩179.2 billion of which is projected to come from online games.

Industrial Operations

Part 2, "Industrial Operations," presents sources that explore the origins and development, strengths and weaknesses, and challenges and future of four major *Hallyu* industries. As mentioned in the Introduction, Korean dramas, Korean films, K-pop, and *Hallyu* stars, in addition to generating significant revenue, are the *Hallyu* sectors that receive the most international publicity; hence, they have been prioritized in this sourcebook. The diverse array of primary sources here contextualizes stories of the successes and failures of *Hallyu* products. As indicated in Part 1, while the Korean Wave is a de facto cultural movement, within Korea its contribution to the national economy as an industry is emphasized. Concerns thus focus on viable market strategies and financial rewards.

Subsection 2.1, "Television," expresses this concern in its discussion of how to tackle the slump after the first K-drama boom of *Winter Sonata* and *Jewel in the Palace* in Asia. Consisting of strategy reports commissioned by the MCST and KOCCA, this subsection addresses the challenges of anti-*Hallyu* sentiments in key Asian markets and provides information on how to streamline drama productions and exports, as well as urging branching into new drama markets in Latin America. Subsection 2.2, "Film," delves into similar issues: the status of Korean movie exports around the world and methods of sales promotion. In general, Korean cinema is consumed in Asia as mainstream entertainment, with hits and misses at the box office. In other locations, especially in the US and European markets, internationally recognized Korean directors' works are celebrated at film festivals and art cinemas, with little expectation of financial returns. The documents analyze this situation using industry data. Subsection 2.3, "Music," likewise offers an industry perspective, analyzing how the rise of K-pop heralded the arrival of neo-*Hallyu* in the late 2000s, opening up new business opportunities for its performers, especially in Asia. It also explores aspects of idol production and management. In particular, Document 2.3.4, "The World of Idols: Jumping through Endless Hoops," exposes the harsh realities of maintaining idol status, nicely paving the way for Subsection 2.4, "Celebrity," which echoes concerns expressed elsewhere about *Hallyu*'s reliance on star power. From Bae Yong-joon and Jang Nara to the Wonder Girls and PSY, Korean stars face a number of issues when entering the global arena, from negotiating their political stances to the feasibility of breaking into a foreign market to, in the case of PSY, accounting for their surprise international success. Overall, the sources here present case studies on Korean cultural content's performance in the international market, and underscore the confluence of national pride and economic incentives driving the supply of *Hallyu*.

2.1.   TELEVISION

Much primary material is available on the topic of television and *Hallyu*, but the documents here will focus on drama exports. A set of biennial snapshots from 2007 to 2013 allows an understanding of how the contours of *Hallyu* in television have changed over time, with a glimpse into the peaks and troughs. Discussion of the initial drama boom in Asia in the first half of the 2000s, in particular *Winter Sonata* and *Jewel in the Palace*, can be found elsewhere in the sourcebook, most notably Document 2.4.1, "Yonsama Madness Unveiled," which considers the phenomenal popularity of Bae Yong-joon in Japan, and the multiple excerpts from *Hallyu Forever*.

Document 2.1.1, "2012 Broadcast Industry White Paper: Imports and Exports," presents important technical terms used in Korea regarding television operation that deserve highlighting. First, one should note that public service broadcasters KBS1 and KBS2, as well as the privately owned MBC, SBS, and other regional stations, are all considered part of terrestrial broadcasting or broadcast television, in contrast to cable and satellite television. In addition, by supplying content to cable television system operators, "program providers" together manage about 200 channels. These providers offer more specialized and niche channels, such as FoodTV (food), MNet (music), OCN (film), OnGameNet (gaming), Tooniverse (animation), and shopping channels. Terrestrial broadcasters dominate the content export market, selling 10 times more product than program providers (p. 93). Whereas most popular *Hallyu* dramas come from terrestrial broadcasters, cable and satellite television providers are also attempting entry into foreign markets with such programs as *Byeolsungeom,* an investigative crime drama series set in the Joseon Dynasty that was sold to Japan, Vietnam, and the Middle East (p. 358).

Document 2.1.1 categorizes foreign sales into the following types: broadcast content, time block, video and DVD, broadcast material for overseas Koreans, and format. "Time block" and "format" call for further explanation. "Time block," also termed "channel rental," occurs when a Korean broadcaster secures a slot on foreign television to show Korean programming; revenue can then be generated by selling advertising spots to Korean corporations. In 2007, for example, MBC Game struck a deal with Vietnam's VTC Media Corporation, acquiring a three-hour time block from channel VTC-5. The term "format" refers to the sale of a program's concept rather than episodes made in Korea. *X Factor,* a talent search show that originated in the UK before being sold to several other nations, is an example. The format of KBS2's popular reality show *1 Night 2 Days* was sold to Sichuan Satellite TV in 2013, and the first season of the Chinese version aired shortly thereafter.

The policy report found in Document 2.1.2, "Initiatives to Overcome the 2007 Broadcast *Hallyu* Crisis," assesses the status of Korean dramas after their initial explosion in Asia in the early 2000s. This short piece, written under the auspices of the defunct Korea Broadcasting Institute, provides a frank account of the market at the time and suggests action strategies for the government and the industry. Between 2001 and 2005, Korean broadcast content saw remarkable export growth. About 77% of export content consisted of dramas in 2006, underscoring the crucial role they played in driving the Korean Wave during that period (p. 97). However, 2006 witnessed a sudden drop in foreign sales. This report explores in detail the three main Korean drama international markets—China,

Japan, and Taiwan—and concludes that while anti-*Hallyu* sentiments and restrictive measures by the Chinese government put up roadblocks for Korean content, the situation was far less politically charged in Japan, where what rendered Korean products less attractive was largely market forces.

An excerpt from the 300-page government-funded research report *2009 Broadcast Video Content* builds upon issues covered in Document 2.1.1 and proposes strategies to support *Hallyu* in the broadcast sector. The document delves into production issues, which warrants contextualization: in 1990, in order to diversify broadcast production methods and challenge the vertically integrated operations of major terrestrial broadcasters, an "independent production" (*woeju jaejak*) policy was introduced. Currently, major broadcasters like SBS must commission roughly 35% of their programming from independent production companies rather than in-house production teams. In fact, *Winter Sonata*, a noteworthy *Hallyu* drama, was created by the independent company Pan Entertainment and sold to KBS for broadcast in 2002.

Concern exists, however, that the explosion of Korean drama in Asia and government intervention have resulted in cutthroat competition among independent producers. According to an MCST report, the number of independent companies reached a remarkable 1,500 in December 2010, with small companies vying to strike gold. Nonetheless, success stories, like HB Entertainment's recent *My Love from the Stars*, are rare, and many businesses collapse under the pressure of production costs and steep star and writer fees. The reference to "last-minute scripts" (*jjokdaebon*) in this document reflects ad hoc production methods, whereby scripts are rewritten at the last minute in accordance with audience reaction to the previous episode. This practice puts production teams under immense pressure to complete shooting and editing before air time. In addition to exploring issues surrounding production, Document 2.1.3 details the support available for those interested in selling broadcast content abroad. Funding for "reformatting" is available for companies that need dubbing, subtitles, additional editing, and music effects before their work can enter foreign markets.

Document 2.1.4, "2011 Content Industry Trends: Korean Dramas in Japan," surveys the operational context for Korean dramas in Japan in 2011, providing information on their performance post-*Winter Sonata*. Interesting points include changes in fan demographics, from Yonsama fandom spurred on by women "in their fifties and sixties (p. 117)" to younger K-pop fans, who follow the likes of Jang Keun-suk of *You're Beautiful* fame. Document 2.1.5, "Korean Dramas' Entry into the Latin American Market," moves beyond Asia to perform a similar task for Latin America and considers how Korean dramas compete and interact with the dominant local form, *telenovelas*.

2.1.1.   2012 Broadcast Industry White Paper: Imports and Exports

Reference: *2012 Broadcast Industry White Paper*, KOCCA, 2012, pp. 89–93.

A.   *Broadcasting: Exports and imports*

According to the *2011 Fact-finding Survey on Broadcasting Communications* by the Korea Communications Commission, exports of broadcast media content by terrestrial broadcasters and program providers totaled $203.35 million in 2011, while imports totaled $127.92 million. Exports increased 18.9% from the previous year, while imports increased by 25%. Imports had decreased 16% from 2009 to 2010. The dramatic increase in 2011 imports is attributed to the purchase of a large amount of foreign media content in order to ensure competitiveness following intensified industry competition.

Total exports from terrestrial broadcasters in 2011 reached $189.86 million. Of this figure, sales of broadcast content accounted for $158.07 million (83.2%). Time block sales had the next largest share, accounting for $17.71 million (9.3%), followed by video and DVD sales at $11 million (5.8%). The share of broadcast materials for non-resident Koreans and sales of show formats was insignificant. Exports continued to be concentrated in Asia, with Japan as the most notable destination (59.9%), followed by Taiwan (13.0%) and China (10.8%). These three countries accounted for 83.7% of total exports, an increase over 2010. Exports to the US amounted to $2.56 million, only 1.6% of the total.

Total exports from terrestrial broadcasters decreased approximately $19.03 million from the $208.89 million of 2010. Compared to 2010, when broadcast content made up 58.3% of all exports, its share rose significantly in 2011. On the other hand, revenue from broadcasting to overseas Koreans, which had accounted for 21.5% of all exports in 2010, fell dramatically to 1.1% in 2011. Time block and video/DVD sales dropped from 2010, as did their share of total exports.

Total imports by terrestrial broadcasters in 2011 reached $4.25 million, all from acquisition of overseas broadcast programs. This figure reflects a slight decrease from 2010, when it stood at approximately $4.36 million. Imports came primarily from the US (44.5%) and the UK (35.2%). The concentration of imports from these two countries was greater than in 2010.

On the other hand, total exports from program providers in 2011 totaled $13.5 million. Of this figure, exports of broadcast programs accounted for $10.87 million (80.6% of the total). Video and DVD sales made up 16.1% of the total, at $2.18 million. Revenue from broadcasting to overseas Koreans was $441,000 (3.3%). Japan was the largest export destination (67.4%), followed by the US (8.9%). Exports were heavily concentrated in Asia.

Exports increased significantly in 2011, up $7.45 million from $6.04 million in 2010. Format sales dropped from $590,000 in 2010 to zero in 2011. Video and DVD sales rose dramatically, from about $40,000 (0.6%) to $2.18 million in this period.

In 2011, imports by program providers, which totaled $123.67 million, were higher than those by terrestrial broadcasters. This figure shows an increase of roughly $26 million from $97.68 million in 2010. The majority of imports by program providers consisted of shows for broadcast, including $2,400 (12 programs) in format imports. Imports of broadcast media content from the US exceeded $100 million (89.3% of all imports), which reveals the serious imbalance in source countries.

B.   Import and export status by broadcast program genre

Below, imports and exports of broadcast programs by terrestrial broadcasters are examined by genre. Of the 55,436 program episodes exported, 86.5% (47,951)

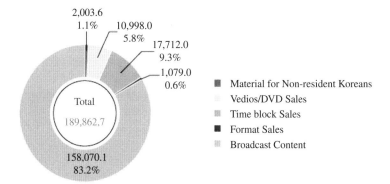

Figure 2–1.   Total exports from terrestrial broadcasters in 2011 (Unit: $1,000)
(Source: Korea Communications Commission, "2012 Fact Finding Research on Broadcast Industry")

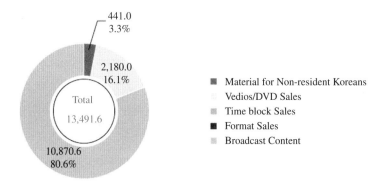

Figure 2–2.   Total exports from program providers in 2011 (Unit: $1,000)
(Source: Korea Communications Commission, "2012 Fact Finding Research on Broadcast Industry")

were dramas. Revenue for drama exports by terrestrial broadcasters amounted to $150 million. A greater number of dramas were sold overseas for a higher total in 2011, compared to 37,260 episodes for $116.09 million in the previous year. The share of dramas among overall broadcasting exports dropped slightly from 88.8%, but the heavy reliance upon them remained unchanged. A total of 4,878 variety show episodes were exported for $6.03 million; 916 animation episodes were exported for about $120,000; and 604 documentaries were exported for $1.3 million. In 2010, 2,449 variety shows were sold for $2.07 million and 278 documentaries for approximately $3.04 million.

On the other hand, 1,849 broadcast programs were imported by terrestrial broadcasters. The largest share (43.7%) was made up by 808 animated programs, followed by 673 documentaries (36.4%), 196 drama episodes (10.6%), 86 films (4.7%), and 85 educational programs (4.6%). Documentaries topped all other genres in scale of import, however, totaling $2.26 million, followed by $760,000 for films, $740,000 for dramas, and $390,000 for animated programs. A total of 2,000 shows and episodes were imported in 2010, in similar ratios, with animation again having the largest share (1,001; 50.0%), followed by documentaries (704; 35.2%), dramas (88; 4.4%), and films (87; 4.4%). Imports in 2011 were marked by a drop in the share of animation and a rise in the share of dramas and documentaries, with an especially prominent increase in drama imports.

Program providers exported 5,504 units of broadcast programs across all genres, a 45.7% increase from 3,777 in 2010. Unlike exports by terrestrial broadcasters, in which dramas dominated, variety shows made up the majority of program provider exports. A total of 2,022 episodes (37.6%) were exported, followed by dramas (1,122; 20.6%). While the number of variety shows exported was nearly double that of dramas, revenue from drama exports was greater (roughly $4.61 vs. $4.37 million). The average sales price of a drama episode thus approximately doubled that of a variety show. After variety shows, dramas were followed in number by 700 music programs (12.9%; $890,000), 663 educational programs (12.2%; $55,000), 430 miscellaneous programs (8.0%; $740,000), and 364 sports programs (6.7%; $40,000). While terrestrial broadcasters mainly exported dramas, variety shows, and documentaries, program providers sold almost all common genres. In 2010, providers exported variety shows above all (2,564; 67.9%), followed by dramas (582; 15.4%), documentaries (295; 7.8%), and music (219; 5.8%). Compared to 2010, the export of drama and music programs increased greatly in 2011.

Imports by program providers reached their highest level ever in 2011, with 23,266 program units being imported, at a cost of $123.67 million. Dramas held the largest share, with 5,870 episodes (25.2%), followed by 5,242 animated programs (22.5%), 5,004 films (21.5%), 3,362 documentaries (14.5%), and 2,516 variety shows (10.8%). The list ordering changes, however, if arranged by expenditure: most expensive were films ($84.98 million), followed by dramas ($19.34 million), animations ($6.61 million), variety shows ($6.21 million), and documentaries ($5.54 million). While animations and documentaries made

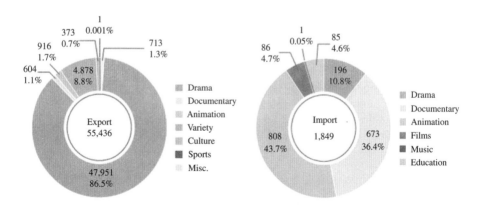

Figure 2–3.   Imports and exports by terrestrial broadcasters
(Source: Korea Communications Commission, "2012 Fact Finding Research on Broadcast Industry")

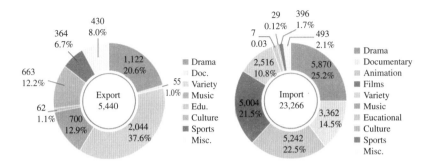

Figure 2–4.   Imports and exports by program providers
(Source: Korea Communications Commission, "2012 Fact Finding Research on Broadcast Industry")

up the majority of imports by terrestrial broadcasters, imports by program providers were more varied and included dramas, animations, motion pictures, and documentaries. In 2010, program providers bought 21,134 programs. Imports were led by 7,132 drama episodes (33.7%), followed by animations (5,975; 28.3%), variety shows (2,593; 12.3%), educational programs (1,714; 8.1%), and documentaries (1,252; 5.9%). From 2010, imports of dramas and documentaries decreased in both number of programs and share of imports, while films soared from 940 (a 4.4% share) in 2010 to 5,004 (21.5%) in 2011.

2.1.2.   Initiatives to overcome the 2007 broadcast *Hallyu* crisis

Reference: *Initiatives to Overcome the 2007 Broadcast Hallyu Crisis*, Yun Jae-sik, KBI Focus 07–01, No. 21, Korean Broadcasting Institute, January 2, 2007, pp. 2–21.

A.   *Summary*

In 2006, broadcast content exports increased 19.1% to $147.74 million from $123.5 million in 2005, and imports shrank by 14.6% to $31.66 million. Although the rate has slowed, export growth is still on the rise, while program imports are steadily declining. Dramas continue to be the most exported genre; however, their share of total export volume is decreasing. Examination of exports by destination shows that Japan, which accounted for 60% of exports at its peak, has dropped to 44%. As the Korean Wave in East Asia has encountered a rise in anti-*Hallyu* sentiment and resistance to Korean products, both the Chinese and Taiwanese governments have instituted regulatory measures. Whereas China has put off making decisions on the import of Korean dramas, Taiwan has introduced such protectionist actions as tariffs. As a result, it seems necessary to respond wisely and proactively to government actions in regions experiencing anti-*Hallyu* sentiment and, in the long term, engage with the Chinese and Taiwanese markets with a view toward cultural exchange. In Japan, copyright infringement occurs due to lack of awareness about intellectual property. Because Japan is the only country in Asia with a well-established secondary circulation market, there is a need to protect ancillary business by strengthening production and distribution companies' understanding of copyright. Attention should be paid to copyright within the production process itself, and more effort should be put into supporting secondary businesses through merchandising. Today *Hallyu* is seeking to move beyond the markets of Asia and expand into the Arab world, Eastern Europe, and the CIS. It is recommended that areas within these regions be targeted as bridges for the implementation of expansion strategies. Rather than focus on short-term profits when entering new markets, it is necessary to take a long-term perspective and implement aggressive, early investments in a systematic strategy that includes free content, program sales, co-productions, joint investments, and channel launches. Finally, in order to counteract hostility and resistance towards *Hallyu* in Asia, it is necessary to expand cultural exchange and urgently establish a network of human capital to further such exchange.

B.　Broadcast and Hallyu: 2006

With average production budgets only a tenth of Hollywood movies and less than a sixth of Japanese television dramas, the seemingly small capital of Korean cultural products has managed to capture attention in Asia under the guise of the Korean Wave, and this popularity is being used as a springboard to move into the Middle East, South America, and Eastern Europe. According to the media, *Hallyu* was worth more than ₩2.5 trillion in 2005. However, as of 2006, there are signs that the Korean Wave is in crisis.

In 2006, broadcast programming exports increased 19.6% over the previous year, while imports decreased 14.6%. Total sales in 2006 stood at $147.74 million, a 19.6% increase over the previous year's $123.49 million. More specifically, exports of terrestrial broadcasts increased 15.3% from $113.43 million to $131.11 million, while cable TV and independent production company exports increased 70.4% from the previous year's $9.75 million to $16.62 million. Broadcast imports declined 14.6% to $31.65 million, within which terrestrial broadcasts decreased 17.6% to $10.42 million. Cable and independent production companies' imports shrank 12.7% to $21.23 million. As the rate of broadcast programming exports slowed, so too did the sharp growth that *Hallyu* had been experiencing.

Table 2–1.　2006 Broadcast programming imports/exports (Unit: $1,000)

	Exports			Imports		
	2005	2006	Growth	2005	2006	Growth
Total	123,493	147,743	19.6%	36,975	31,657	–14.6%
Terrestrial Broadcasters	113,736	131,116	15.3%	12,657	10,426	–17.6%
Cable TV, Independent Production Companies, etc.	9,757	16,627	70.4%	24,318	21,231	–12.7%

Table 2-2. 2006 Broadcast programming exports by genre (Unit: $1,000)

Genre	Total	Terrestrial	Cable	Proportion (%)
Drama	85,891	85,131	760	76.99
Documentary	1,260	301	959	1.13
Animation	2,803	116	2,687	2.51
Film	0	–	–	0.00
Variety Show	5,581	1,912	3,669	5.00
Music	0	–	–	0.00
Others	16,031	8,081	7,950	14.37
Total	111,566	95,541	16,025	100.00

Table 2-3. Comparison of broadcast programming exports by genre for 2005–2006 (Unit: $1,000)

	Drama	Documentary	Animation	Film	Variety Show	Music	Other
2005	101,620	354	2,937	–	2,346	–	3,170
2006	85,891	1,260	2,803	–	5,581	–	16,031

2006 Broadcast programming imports/exports by genre

Exports by genre

Although dramas accounted for a still dominant 77% of 2006 broadcast content exports, a notable decrease from the previous year's level (92%) can be seen. The decrease in total export volume of dramas, the driving force behind broadcast *Hallyu*, seems to have derived from current resistance and antagonism towards *Hallyu* in Asia. In China, although the recommended programming import quota in 2005 was 32 units (one unit = 20 hours), as of November 2006 only 11 units of Korean programming have received import permission. With estimates for December at four units, a 54% decrease is expected from 2005. With the exception of animation, the sales price for program episodes decreased from the previous year. Specifically, a lack of bargaining power resulting from 2005's sharp increase in the sales price of dramas meant a drop in 2006 (average unit sales price: $4,046 in 2004; $4,921 in 2005; and $4,378 in 2006).

Imports by genre

Film maintained a steadily high share (56.7%) of imports, followed by dramas (24%). Based on rates from 2005, imports of genres such as film, drama, and documentary are expected to increase.

Current imports/exports by country

The skewed concentration of exports to Asia seems to be easing (2005, 90.1%; 2006, 83.61%). Major countries of export and the related figures are as follows:

Table 2–4.   2006 Comparison of average unit sales price by genre (Unit: $1,000)

	Terrestrial	Cable TV, Independent Production Companies	Average
Drama	4,375 (4,880)	4,810 (6,968)	4,378 (4,921)
Documentary	1,056 (2,721)	2,465 (1,150)	1,869 (1,648)
Animation	460 (218)	16,912 (1,997)	6,820 (1,668)
Total	–	–	4,319 (4,349)

The numbers in parentheses indicate the 2005 average unit sales price.

Table 2–5.   2006 Broadcast programming imports by genre (Unit: $1,000)

Genre	Total	Terrestrial	Cable	Total (%)
Drama	7,599	1,064	6,535	24.00
Documentary	2,635	1,007	1,628	8.32
Animation	723	506	217	2.29
Film	17,907	7,574	10,333	56.57
Variety	1,246	41	1,205	3.93
Music	0	–	–	0
Other	1,547	234	1,313	4.89
Total	31,657	10,426	21,231	100

Table 2–6.   2006 Comparison of import unit price by genre (Unit: $1,000)

	Terrestrial	Cable TV/Independent Production Companies	Average
Dramas	4,708 (2,227)	2,116 (1,519)	2,293 (1,857)
Documentaries	1,648 (2,845)	1,213 (898)	1,349 (1,493)
Animation	1,675 (1,001)	624 (1,288)	1,112 (1,254)
Total	–	–	3,344 (2,750)

The figures in parentheses indicate the 2005 average unit import price.

Japan (2005, 60.1%; 2006, 44.1%), Taiwan (2005, 11.4%; 2006, 18.1%), China (2005, 9.9%; 2006, 6.7%), Thailand (3.4%), etc. Exports to Japan totaled $66.37 million in 2005, but shrank to $49.17 million in 2006, in accordance with Japanese consumers' diminishing interest in Korean dramas and the subsequent decrease in sales of broadcast media. Without a prominent drama such as *Winter Sonata* or *Jewel in the Palace*, exports will continue to shrink.

In contrast to the drop in exports to Japan, sales to Taiwan grew (2005, $12.54 million; 2006, $20.18 million). Although export of broadcast media to Taiwan has risen continually, overall figures are expected to decrease given the

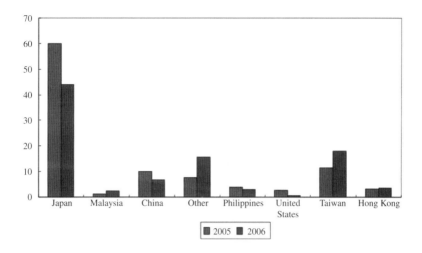

Figure 2–5.   Exports by country (Unit: %)

soaring prices of Korean dramas and Taiwanese government policies to strengthen and promote the local broadcast and digital content industries.

While export to Asian markets has declined, new markets are emerging, ranging from South America (Mexico and Brazil) to the Middle East (Turkey and Jordan) and India.

Korea imports broadcast content mainly from the US (25.1%), the UK (3.4%), China (2.5%), Japan (1.6%), and Hong Kong (1.2%). The primary import genres are film and drama. Whereas the proportion of imports from the US in 2006 decreased sharply from the previous year (62.5%; 25.1%), overall imports from North America, if Canada is included, and from countries in Europe, such as the UK and Germany, decreased only slightly.

In the case of Asia, imports from Japan decreased by a sharp 17.8% as a result of declining interest in Japanese broadcast media among Korea's domestic consumers. Imports from China showed little change from the previous year (2005, $741,000; 2006, $776,000).

Trends in broadcast programming imports/exports, 1998–2006

An examination of import and export trends for broadcast media reveals marked increases for both beginning in 2004. The strong increase in the 2004 export market can be attributed to an intensification of broadcast material exports to Japan after *Hallyu* took the country by storm after the 2003 success of *Winter Sonata*.

The proportion of domestic terrestrial broadcast programming exported to Japan accounted for 20.4% of the total in 2003, increasing to 47.1% in 2004 and 60.1% in 2005. This trend is concerning: more than half of domestic terrestrial broadcast programming exports were consumed in Japan. However, as broadcast exports to Japan in 2006 decreased to $49.17 million, the total proportion decreased to 44.1%.

Table 2–7.   2006 Import/export figures by country

	Total				Terrestrial Broadcasters				Independent Productions, etc.			
	Export	%	Import	%	Export	%	Import	%	Export	%	Import	%
Total	111,566 (25,830)	100	31,657 (9,468)	100	95,541 (22,299)	100	10,426 (1,620)	100	16,025 (3,531)	100	21,231 (7,848)	100
Japan	49,167 (5,315)	44.1	495 (323)	1.6	49,004 (4,411)	51.2	83 (32)	0.8	163 (904)	1.0	412 (291)	1.9
China	7,528 (4,159)	6.7	776 (1,628)	2.5	7,514 (4,074)	7.9	169 (5)	1.6	14 (85)	0.1	607 (1,623)	2.9
Hong Kong	3,985 (1,551)	3.6	369 (367)	1.2	3,985 (1,551)	4.2	156 (5)	1.5	–	0.0	213 (362)	1.0
Singapore	2,029 (1,435)	1.8	–	–	1,997 (1,400)	2.1	–	–	32 (35)	0.2	–	–
Taiwan	20,178 (3,471)	18.1	–	–	19,777 (3,445)	20.7	–	–	401 (26)	2.5	–	–
Vietnam	762 (680)	0.7	–	–	762 (680)	0.8	–	–	–	–	–	–
Malaysia	2,540 (1,032)	2.3	–	–	2,540 (1,032)	2.7	–	–	–	–	–	–
Indonesia	29 (76)	0.0	–	–	29 (76)	0.1	–	–	–	–	–	–
Thailand	3,751 (1,441)	3.4	–	–	3,666 (1,415)	3.8	–	–	85 (26)	0.5	–	–
Philippines	3,260 (1,034)	2.9	–	–	3,221 (1,008)	3.4	–	–	39 (26)	0.2	–	–
United States	579 (219)	0.5	7,939 (1,548)	25.0	477 (174)	0.5	5,964 (413)	57.2	102 (45)	0.6	1,975 (1,135)	9.3
Canada	45 (19)	0.0	153 (142)	0.5	–	–	113 (120)	1.1	45 (19)	0.3	40 (22)	0.2
France	80 (16)	0.1	124 (170)	0.4	20 (16)	0.0	124 (170)	1.2	60	0.4	–	–
United Kingdom	117 (105)	0.1	1,064 (740)	3.3	117 (105)	0.1	746 (462)	7.2	–	–	318 (278)	1.5
Germany	10 (1)	0.0	114 (154)	0.4	10 (1)	0.0	101 (151)	1.0	–	–	13 (3)	0.1
Australia	3 (1)	0.0	133 (90)	0.4	3 (1)	0.0	44 (32)	0.0	–	–	89 (58)	0.4
Other[1]	17,503 (5,275)	15.7	20,490 (4,306)	64.7	2,419 (2,910)	2.5	2,926 (230)	28.1	15,084 (2,365)	94.2	17,564 (4,076)	82.7

[1] "Other" includes countries in Europe (Hungary, Sweden, Finland, Italy, etc.) and South America (Brazil).

Table 2–8.   Trends in broadcast programming imports/exports, 1998–2006
(Unit: $1,000)

		Terrestrial Broadcasters		Cable TV/Independent Production Companies		Total	
		Amount	Annual Growth	Amount	Annual Growth	Amount	Annual Growth
Export	1998	7,756	11.3%	2,261	67.4%	10,017	20.4%
	1999	10,836	39.7%	1,900	−16.0%	12,736	27.1%
	2000	11,664	7.6%	1,447	−23.8%	13,111	2.9%
	2001	17,147	47.0%	1,773	22.5%	18,920	44.3%
	2002	26,187	52.7%	2,626	48.1%	28,813	52.3%
	2003	36,889	40.9%	5,246	99.8%	42,135	46.2%
	2004	63,638	72.5%	7,823	49.1%	71,461	69.6%
	2005	113,736	78.7%	9,757	24.7%	123,493	72.8%
	2006	131,116	15.3%	16,627	70.4%	147,743	19.6%
	Total	418,969	–	49,460	–	468,429	–
Import	1998	15,386	−60.4%	11,650	−36.6%	27,036	−52.8%
	1999	20,094	30.6%	8,639	−25.8%	28,733	6.2%
	2000	26,743	33%	2,350	−72.8%	29,093	1.3%
	2001	18,032	−32.5%	2,410	2.6%	20,442	−29.7%
	2002	18,768	4.1%	6,343	163.2%	25,111	22.8%
	2003	18,344	−2.3%	9,718	53.2%	28,062	11.8%
	2004	14,298	−22.1%	16,798	72.9%	31,096	10.8%
	2005	12,657	−11.5%	24,318	44.8%	36,975	18.9%
	2006	10,426	−17.6%	21,231	−12.7%	31,657	−14.6%
	Total	154,748	–	103,458	–	258,206	–

As seen above, in recent years, exports to Japan, China, and Hong Kong, the main markets for *Hallyu*, have markedly decreased, leading to increasing awareness of a crisis for the Korean Wave.

Multiple factors have created aversion and resentment towards Korean broadcast media. These include adverse reactions to the steep increase in unit sales price; unidirectional trade resulting from the popularity of Korean broadcast media; awareness in export destinations that the lack of domestic competitiveness has led to oversupply of Korean material; and growing concerns that the import of Korean broadcast media will hurt local broadcast production infrastructure.

In particular, the Chinese government has demonstrated clear irritation at Korean intentions to sell programming without purchasing much from China, a stance that has intensified Chinese embarrassment over the rapid expansion of Korean programming. As a result, China's State Administration of Radio,

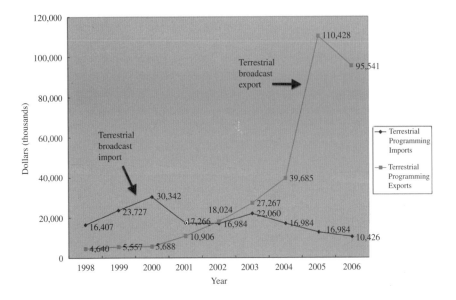

Figure 2–6.   Trends in terrestrial programming imports/exports

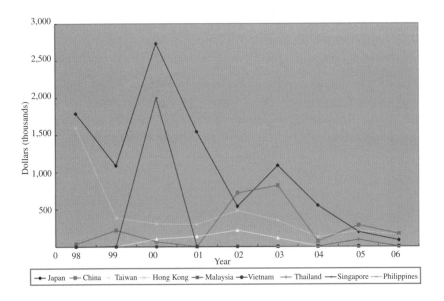

Figure 2–7.   Trends in terrestrial programming imports by year and country

Film, and Television (SARFT), which reviews imports of all video broadcast programming, instituted a blanket deferral of acceptance for Korean dramas from January to June of 2006, demonstrating a defensive policy toward penetration of foreign content. Through diverse means (e.g., contacting production companies, the media, etc.) the Chinese government has worked towards curtailing rampant circulation of Korean cultural products and unidirectional growth in exchange;

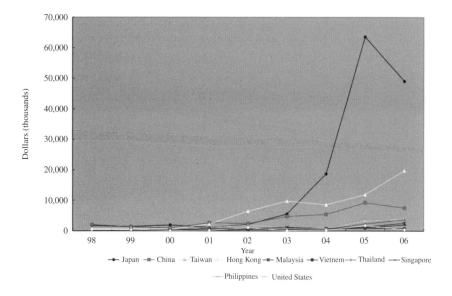

Figure 2–8.   Trends in terrestrial programming exports by year and country

appropriate response on the part of Korea, however, has been insufficient. Chinese production companies have complained to their government about the deterioration in China's production infrastructure and difficulties in managing Korean imports. Broadcast corporations have also indicated there is an issue in the imbalanced trade relationship, as sales of Chinese content in Korea are not matching purchases of Korean broadcast content.

On March 24, 2006, China's *Guangming Daily* reported the following:

"China's passion for Korean dramas brings us to another problem. Although purchasing Korean dramas brings high revenue, over the past five years Korea has imported only five or six Chinese dramas, and not for broadcast on television at that, but rather as direct-to-video material. Why don't Koreans import our contents? Is Korea reluctant to hurt its own market? China is more broad-minded in this regard."

On June 29, the *Chongqing Daily* stated that "China's 2006 import policy for foreign dramas will show real change," quoting an anonymous representative of SARFT who concluded that "this shift amounts to the end of Korean drama in China."

The sharply increasing sales price of programs and a glut of monotonous, trendy dramas have meant that buyers in Japan, the main importer of Korean broadcast content in 2005, are losing interest in Korean material. No top-tier productions have followed the dramas at the core of *Hallyu* in Japan, *Winter Sonata* and *Jewel in the Palace*. Nevertheless, as the price of programs increases and is further bumped up by broadcasters and production companies seeking diverse sales routes, the market position of Korean dramas in Japan is weakening. Although the average price per episode of Korean dramas in Japan stands at

$20,000–30,000 for terrestrial television, some shows exceed this figure, such as *Super Rookie* ($110,000 per episode) and *Princess Hours* (total ₩1.5 billion), etc. Furthermore, some Korean stars' management agencies demand high fees for promotion and the like in Japan, and this excessive focus on profit is drawing criticism from the Japanese media.

When copyright for specific elements used in dramas, such as the soundtrack and video clips, is not properly settled, lawsuits frequently arise after sale. As no single agency manages the rights to Korean broadcast content, domestic broadcast and overseas sales rights are often separate. For example, soundtrack and DVD rights are held by separate bodies, making buyer access difficult.

C.   Outlook for broadcast Hallyu and areas for improvement by country

Lately, export of domestic programming to Asia, once the epicenter of *Hallyu*, seems to have peaked. As a result, the steep growth in broadcast programming exports will slow. Through efforts to open new markets from the Middle East to Eastern Europe and the CIS, expansion of Korean broadcast media exports may be possible.

China

Central government policies to undermine Korean wave broadcast content
The Chinese government is concerned over the influence of Korean dramas. Based on its judgment that the monodirectional flow of broadcast material from Korea to China will continue, the government has initiated policies to counteract this flow via an ad hoc deferral of review of Korean cultural products.

The rise of a new market
With CCTV taking a leading role, television corporations and major local stations are following new avenues to enhance their own competitiveness.[1] Broadcasters in each provincial center have been pushing forward local coalition strategies to foster growth. As cable television reaches saturation in cities, demand for content that appeals in rural areas is increasing. In order to meet this demand, Hebei Television launched a channel for those in the countryside in May 2005. In addition, China's broadcasters have dived into development of animated programs as they have grown in popularity among the nation's "little emperors." Also, new digital broadcast services such as IPTV, mobile TV, and network TV have blossomed, and demand for digital content that can be purchased is increasing.

Unification of policy on broadcast exchange with China
In contrast to the position of China's SARFT as a superordinate organ for broadcast regulation, Korea's Ministry of Culture and Tourism and the Korea Communications Commission constitute separate avenues for exchange policy. Korea must therefore unify the two to improve overall efficacy.

---

[1] *Jewel in the Palace*, for example, saw success when broadcast via Hunan Province satellite television.

Pushing forward concrete, multi-phased, detailed strategies
The Chinese government's regulations may ease with the upcoming 2008 Beijing Olympics. As such, the Korean government must take prudent and proactive measures. Given anti-*Hallyu* sentiment in China, establishing contacts in each province is necessary. Adequate content supply strategies for each must be established, taking into account distinct features and needs. By connecting such contacts to strategic alliances with behemoth media groups in China like SMEG, we may continue to advance into China's provinces through co-productions and joint ventures. We must establish cooperative partnerships through sustainable networks and explore the viability of a Korean-Chinese joint channel in the middle to long term.

Japan

Status and prospects
Not only is Japan the largest export market for broadcast content, its subsidiary businesses are the most developed. Although Japan's share of total broadcast export dropped from above 60% in 2005 to 44% in 2006, it continues to show enormous strength. In particular, as the only country in Asia with an established secondary market for broadcasting, ancillary business is possible in the form of sales of OSTs (original soundtracks), DVDs, etc. Unlike China and Taiwan, where anti-*Hallyu* movements are taking place, aversion to *Hallyu* in Japan has had minimal commercial impact. Even institutional obstacles put up by the government are negligible. Nonetheless, market forces have naturally pushed Korean products away from the central position.

Problems and recommendations
Sharply rising sales prices and unresolved copyright issues, as well as diverging paths to rights acquisition, make purchase of Korean broadcast content difficult. On average, in terrestrial broadcasting a drama series costs $20,000–30,000 per episode, though some content can cost far more.[2] Issues with music and video clips used in dramas remain in cases where copyright has not been secured. Different agents hold domestic rights, overseas sales rights, and DVD sales rights, creating difficulties for buyers.

Urgent need for improved distribution
The unreasonable inflation in sales prices that has arisen from a zeal for short-term profits should stop. By systematizing in the middle to long term a database for copyright holders of drama-related elements like the soundtrack and video clips, we should raise awareness of copyright. Efficacy of sales should also be improved by unifying paths to drama rights acquisition.

Improving program quality and creating secondary markets
In the short term, there is a need to overhaul the system in which dramas have become standardized through repetitive production patterns and excessive reliance on star power. In the long term, we must support quality content through,

---

[2] *Super Rookie* was reported to have been contracted at $110,000 per episode and *Princess Hours* at $150,000.

for example, the creation of a storyline database. In order to encourage stable and sustainable distribution methods rather than the current method of package exports, we must consider overseas ventures such as investment in Japanese broadcast corporations or bloc purchases. Furthermore, attempts should be made to establish Japanese affiliates to manage business related to DVDs, OSTs, and merchandising.

Taiwan

Utilizing Hallyu in Taiwan as a bridge to the Chinese diaspora
Taiwan's ability to serve as a testing ground for entry into the markets of China and Hong Kong and a stepping stone into the Chinese diaspora in Southeast Asia (through Taiwanese-dubbed programming) makes it a strategic location. As the Taiwanese government is making a large-scale investment in digital content to foster its domestic broadcast market between 2005 and 2010, the future entry of Korean content is expected to encounter difficulties.

Need to establish a Korean drama channel
The Taiwanese broadcast market relies on paid channels. Three channels already specialize in Japanese dramas and, of course, China and Hong Kong have their own paid channels. If Korea were to open a niche channel for dramas, exorbitant sales prices brought about by excessive competition among distribution companies may be brought down. Such an initiative should facilitate stable scheduling of Korean dramas, making *Hallyu* in Taiwan sustainable. SBS is currently working on a Korean drama channel with Taiwan's GTV, which will launch in 2007.

Other Destinations

Status and prospects
Although awareness of Korean broadcast material is growing in the Middle East, the region is still a new market requiring a proactive development strategy. In 2005, KBS's *Winter Sonata* and *Autumn Tales* became popular in Egypt when shown on ERTU Channel 2. *Jewel in the Palace* then aired in Egypt in February 2006. Although the broadcast of Korean content is being pushed forward within the whole Arab region via satellite, we are also currently seeking to widen possibilities for dramas and documentaries in cooperation with local broadcasters, in such places as Egypt (ERTU), Lebanon (LBC, Future TV), Jordan (JRTC), and Qatar (QTV).

In the case of Eastern Europe and the CIS, the success of South American *telenovelas* can serve as a useful model. Korean broadcast material needs such an entry strategy and must find a way to follow the success of *telenovelas* in these markets. We should broaden awareness of Korean media and culture in these regions through documentaries and feature-length films in addition to dramas.

Bold investment to develop new markets
Korean cultural content has not yet been presented to the Arab world, Eastern Europe, or the CIS, regions that are primarily composed of developing nations, and thus expectations for short-term profits are low. Program sales occur slowly and in isolation. As entry into these regions appears to require bold initial

investment, thorough market analysis and robust understanding of local distribution structures and systems are necessary to minimize losses during market entry. Afterward, it is advised that we promote, as a long-term strategy, awareness of Korean culture, and follow this up with active marketing.

2.1.3.   2009 Broadcast Video Content: Strategies and Policies for Propagation

Reference: "Strategies and Policies for Propagating the Korean Wave: Broadcast Video Content," Kwon Ho-young & Kim Young-su, KOCCA Research Report: 09–01, KOCCA, August 2009, pp. xi–xxvi.

A.   Research directions and trends in broadcast video content imports/exports

Research directions

Export of Korean broadcast content declined after 2006, and as the ratio of exports to Chinese-speaking areas fell sharply, the skewing of exports to Japan intensified, with a heavy dependency on dramas. In addition, since the release of *Winter Sonata* in 2004 and *Jewel in the Palace* in 2005, the East Asian market has not had a product that has met with sensational acclaim. Accordingly, the Korean Wave, once centered on broadcasting, is considered to be waning. Even domestic interest in *Hallyu* is shrinking. This study thus focuses on recommendations for expanding broadcast content.

Numerous studies discuss *Hallyu* and Korean broadcast exports. Existing research focuses on the current state of broadcast media exports; policy recommendations for the longevity and growth of *Hallyu* have been secondary. This study focuses therefore on strategies and recommendations for the sustainability and expansion of *Hallyu*.

Directions in broadcast video content imports/exports

Export of Korean broadcast content increased sharply after the 1998 release of *What Is Love?* and its popularity in China. Although annual market growth averaged 38.4% per year between 1999 and 2005, after 2006 growth slowed to an average of 11.9%. Meanwhile, the volume of content imported in 2008 decreased relative to 1994. In 2002, Korea experienced its first trade surplus for broadcast content, a surplus that then grew sharply.

Examination of content by genre reveals that Korea primarily exports dramas and imports films. Dramas occupy an overwhelming share of exports, and this proportion has risen steadily. Given that dramas are generally sold to East Asia and there is difficulty with sales to Europe and the US, Korean dramas face obstacles in becoming a global product. The proportion of animations and documentaries, with their low cultural discount, needs to be increased in foreign sales.

As can be seen in Table 2–11, East Asia is the main export destination, and the US is the main source of imports. In 2001, Chinese-speaking countries accounted for 50% of exports, and Japan 10%; however, by 2008 the proportion of exports to the Sinophone world had contracted to 14.8%, while Japan was receiving 68.7% of exports.

Table 2–9.   Volume and growth of broadcast video content imports/exports

Amount (Unit: $1,000)			Growth (%)		
Year	Exports	Imports	Year	Exports	Imports
1994	5,690	19,861	1994–1998	7.7	–6.4
1998	7,756	15,386	1999–2005	38.4	–2.8
2005	113,726	12,657	2006–2008	11.9	–32.3
2008	162,565	4,810	1994–2005	23.8	–10.1

Table 2–10.   Broadcast video content by genre

Year	Drama	Documentary	Animation	Film	Variety Show	Music	Other
Proportion of Exports (%)							
2001	64.3	2.7	19.8	0.0	3.2	0.7	9.3
2008	91.8	0.8	4.6	0.2	1.1	0.8	0.7
Proportion of Imports (%)							
2001	6.3	10.8	13.8	66.3	0.2	0.1	2.5
2008	8.5	7.9	7.1	69.4	0.3	0.3	6.5

Table 2–11.   Broadcast video content imports/exports by destination

Proportion of Exports (%)						
Year	China, Taiwan, Hong Kong	Japan	Singapore, Vietnam	Germany, UK, Italy	US	Other
2001	49.7	9.7	10.7	8.8	0.9	20.2
2008	14.8	68.7	2.1	0	4.8	9.6

Proportion of Imports (%)						
Year	US	UK	Japan	China, Taiwan, Hong Kong	Germany, Italy, France, Australia	Other
2001	66.2	7.8	11.4	5.3	6.0	3.3
2008	60.6	7.1	13.5	6.0	3.4	9.4

Criticism of *Hallyu*

Hallyu describes the booming interest in Korean popular culture in East Asia that began in the late 1990s, led by music and dramas. After 2006, when China and Taiwan began to restrict Korean drama imports, the Korean Wave receded in the Chinese-speaking world. The volume of broadcast exports has, however, increased since 2006 as exports to Japan spiked. Although total export revenue is on the rise, market growth has slowed dramatically, as no notable attention-grabbing dramas have been released since 2004's *Winter Sonata* and 2005's *Jewel in the Palace*, giving rise to criticism that *Hallyu* is in decline.

The primary reason for the decline in exports to China is that the Chinese government, viewing *Hallyu* as a threat, has enforced regulations. Drama exports to Taiwan and Hong Kong have declined as well, partly due to restrictions, but also as a result of the steep price of Korean dramas, as well as their recycled narratives. Conversely, although export to Japan is increasing, the shrinking number of Japanese broadcasters that offer Korean programming, along with diminishing demand for Korean drama DVD rentals and sales due to an economic downturn, has become a concern. The increase in foreign sales beyond Chinese-speaking areas and Japan remains a relatively insignificant proportion of total exports.

B.   *Structural problems and strategic directions for broadcast video content exports*

Structural problems in broadcast video content exports

Let us begin with a look at broadcast content production. Firstly, given the relatively small size of Korea's economy and population compared to the US or Japan, budgets are small. Korea also has fewer opportunities for external funding in the form of advertising; smaller budgets increase the likelihood that programming will be of lower quality. Secondly, from 2005, the proportion of fees going to casting and writing has skyrocketed. Such fees now comprise some 70% of the total budget, and funds for other necessary aspects of drama production lag. This rapid rise in fees for the cast and screenplay finds its roots in the practice of outsourcing to independent production companies. Third, as trendy dramas are the mainstay of productions, themes and content are becoming stale. Fourth, production companies have become complacent in their routine of primarily targeting the domestic market, and the drive to produce noteworthy material of global quality is weak.

If we turn to distribution and marketing, we find concerns with, and aversion towards, the unidirectional entry of Korean content into overseas markets. In China, this has taken the form of restrictions on Korean imports. Vietnam has also tightened regulations on the import of foreign content as a result of *Hallyu*, and policies to strengthen domestic production have been implemented. Secondly, with the sharp increase in the price of Korean content, Taiwan and China have begun initiatives to stimulate domestic production. The Philippines and Thailand have also engaged in selective purchasing given the rising price of Korean programming.

Domestic support for the sustainment of *Hallyu* is lacking. In the past, Korean broadcast policy has focused on developing a balance among different forms of media and strengthening their beneficial role in society, rather than global competitiveness and market expansion. As *Hallyu* has seen stagnation and decline as a result of regulations abroad, broadcast policy organizations have not worked adequately toward solutions on a national level.

Directions in broadcast video content export strategy

The following production strategies could be adopted: First, in order to improve programming quality, a shift must occur from reliance on "hastily written scripts" (*jjokdaebon*) to those that are fully developed and completed. Second, to foster globalization, international co-productions and productions on location abroad should be encouraged. Third, we need to establish a model that aims for a global, rather than domestic, market. Fourth, marketing and product placement (PPL) for Korean companies entering overseas markets should be organically linked with production. Fifth, casting and writer's fees must match the Korean context.

Distribution strategy recommendations are as follows: First, Korean terrestrial broadcasters themselves must broaden their approach and act as global companies. Second, continuous export of Korean content must be ensured, and niche TV channels for Korean programming, or a suite of channels (channel blocs), must be created. Third, synergy should be created through linking broadcast content and merchandising of Korean consumer products. Fourth, in order to open new markets, we must cultivate a long-term appreciation for Korean content. Fifth, Korea's involvement in and entry into trade fairs must encompass not only large events such as MIP-TV, but also smaller ones around the world. Sixth, the broadcast content industry must be understood as based on personal networks; it would therefore be wise to limit shuffling of industry personnel from position to position.

The following policy strategies may also be implemented: First, broadcast export should incorporate mid-to-long-term planning. Second, broadcast policy must be restructured with an emphasis on economic competitiveness. Third, to pioneer new markets, we should expand initiatives that support "reformatting." Fourth, a single government organization responsible for broadcast export policy would be more effective.

C.   Support policies for broadcast exports

From the mid-1990s, the MCST took an interest in the export of broadcast content and supported it via subsidies for attendance at trade shows. In December 1998, the Video Content Export Support Center was formed within the Korea International Broadcasting Foundation (Arirang TV) to foster export systematically. In 2001, the Korea Independent Productions Association opened its "Director School" to promote foreign sales through educating production and distribution personnel. In 2002, the international trade show Broadcast Worldwide (BCWW) was established in Korea, and from 2003, the Korea Broadcasting Institute promoted participation in trade fairs. In 2006, the Video Content Export Support Center was transferred from the Korea International Broadcasting Foundation to the Korea Broadcasting Institute.

Since 2005, the Korea Communications Commission has supported export through showcase events, and KOFICE, founded in 2003, has been purchasing overseas programming for domestic distribution in an effort to curtail negative reactions to *Hallyu*. In 2006, Busan and Gwangju each founded their own international film and broadcast trade shows.

Since 2009, KOCCA, which has now subsumed the Korea Broadcasting Institute, has been in charge of sales of broadcast content abroad, while the

Table 2–12.   Organizations involved in broadcast content support policy

Duty	Organization(s)
Support for reformatting export programming	Korea Creative Content Agency (KOCCA)
Support for attendance at overseas film and broadcast trade shows	KOCCA, Korean IT International Cooperation Agency
Support for hosting international film and broadcast trade shows	KOCCA, Busan Metropolitan City, Gwangju Metropolitan City, Korea Trade-Investment Promotion Agency
Showcase events	KOCCA
Support for new market entry	KOCCA, KOFICE
Support for international co-productions	KOCCA, Korean IT International Cooperation Agency
Development of broadcast content distribution personnel	Director School under the Korea Independent Productions Association
Support for overseas Korean-language broadcasting	Korea Communications Commission

Korean IT International Cooperation Agency has handled industry showcases and initiated support for co-productions. KOTRA opened the first Korean Media and Content Market in 2009.

D.   *Suggestions for improving export promotion policy*

Strategies for expanding export destinations

Export of broadcast content has focused on East Asia; recently, the proportion of exports to Japan has risen markedly, accounting for 69% of the total in 2008. From the perspective of those in charge, focusing on destinations where sales are successful may seem a wise strategy. However, to expand export of broadcast material and increase positive overseas response to *Hallyu* and Korean soft power, the target destinations must be diversified.

In order for such diversification to occur, content producers must first promote marketers and agencies and build networks in target countries; the MCST must strengthen its support policy; and the Ministry of Foreign Affairs and the Ministry of Knowledge Economy must cooperate closely with affiliated organizations. Let us now briefly discuss some suggestions for improving export expansion policy.

Companies involved in broadcast production have evaluated KOCCA's "Export Programming Reformatting Support Initiative" positively, and demand has been increasing. Additionally, businesses are requesting support for subtitling and dubbing in languages other than English for export to a wide variety of destinations, or requesting funds for the reformatting of high-quality export programming. However, budgets for such projects are shrinking. Considering the positive appraisal and feedback, more funding should be allocated to this scheme.

With KOCCA's "Support for Entry into New Markets Initiative," Korean broadcast content is offered free of charge for broadcast to countries outside of East Asia. This initiative is designed to improve awareness of Korean television in areas beyond the usual market for *Hallyu*, leading to further interest in Korean content and promoting further purchase. It has demonstrated visible success. Recently, KOFICE has been engaged in an almost identical initiative. To systematize distribution and increase efficiency, all such initiatives should be overseen by KOCCA.

Improving support for international broadcast content trade fairs and expos

Support for international trade fairs covers both the staging of fairs in Korea and attendance of overseas expos. Firstly, here are suggestions for improvements to domestic trade fairs: in addition to Korea's BCWW, which first took place in 2001, Busan and Gwangju initiated the Busan Content Market (BCM) and Asia Content & Entertainment (ACE) Fair, respectively, in 2006; in 2009 the first Korea Media and Content Market was held in Seoul. However, concern exists over the proliferation of domestic trade fairs. It would be advisable for just one or two trade fairs to be held in Korea. Secondly, an appropriate proportion of exhibition-to-consulting should take place at these fairs. Thirdly, there must be a shift in focus from showcasing Korean content to supporting exchanges of content from around the world.

Currently the government partially subsidizes Korean international business trade fairs. Given the limited budgets, numerous overseas fairs, and the number of companies that wish to attend, support must be selective. However, we must maximize efficiency by strengthening support of independent production companies and channel providers, which are less fiscally robust than terrestrial broadcasters, as well as strategically selecting which fairs to attend.

Strategies to expand the market through international joint productions

International co-productions are one means of obviating the current issue with the monodirectional transfer of Korean content. However, communication-related fees run high in international co-productions given differences in production style, language, and culture. Mutual trust is therefore essential. Also problematic is that Korea's national brand might not be as enhanced by co-productions. To overcome these difficulties, both companies must first outline their respective roles clearly. Second, because of cultural differences, documentary co-productions may work better than dramas. Third, joint productions should involve organizations that hold the public's trust or those that have the backing of related organizations in their respective countries. Fourth, policy changes on an institutional level are needed in tax systems and subsidies. On the other hand, since 2009, the Korea IT International Cooperation Agency has engaged in international co-productions, and its work would be more efficient if combined with that of KOCCA.

Strategies for genre expansion

Dramas' proportion of exports hit a staggering 91.1% in 2008. Given that dramas experience a "cultural discount" outside of Asia, especially in European and

North American markets, export is difficult. Accordingly, to export broadcast content, genres that experience fewer cross-cultural barriers, such as documentaries and animations, should see substantial growth.

Although KOCCA is working on distributing documentaries abroad, the scale of such endeavors is strikingly small. First and foremost, quality documentaries and works of animation must be produced domestically and, in time, policies to support foreign sales in these genres must be strengthened.

Coordination and cooperation between *Hallyu* support organizations

Although KOCCA is the main supporter of broadcast content export, other organizations are doing their part to stimulate foreign sales. As the endeavors undertaken by these organizations are nearly identical, consolidation would be wise. For programs that do not overlap, efficiency should be increased by creating systems in which close cooperation becomes possible.

Programs that should be consolidated with those of KOCCA include: (1) KOFICE's Korean Broadcast Video Content Overseas Distribution Project, and (2) the Korean IT International Cooperation Agency's Overseas Exposition Attendance Support Project and Overseas Co-production Support Project. In addition, the domestic broadcast video trade fairs (BCWW, BCM, ACE Fair, and Korea Media and Content Market) should be either consolidated into one event or differentiated from each other.

E. A new vision for broadcast content export support

Promoting Korean broadcasts in Chinese-speaking regions

Although *Hallyu* originated in the Sinophone world and the phenomenon, with drama at its core, was strongest in this region, it is also here that the strongest headwinds have been met. Directly after the success of 2005's *Jewel in the Palace*, representatives within broadcast and entertainment circles began to perceive anti-*Hallyu* sentiments in China. In 2006, the Chinese government restricted import of Korean broadcast content through programming review regulations. As soon as the Korean Wave washed upon Taiwan's shores, the country's own actors and producers began to show animosity towards the phenomenon and in 2006 took action to block the broadcast of foreign dramas during prime time.

In order to overcome current anti-*Hallyu* feelings, domestic experts prescribe a need for expansion of bilateral exchange, as opposed to unidirectional export, and rejection of the narrow focus on profits. However, such recommendations are more easily prescribed than put into practice. In order to get *Hallyu* back on its feet, the current Chinese restrictions need to be eased. In order to accomplish this goal, efforts on the part of Korea are necessary. Concrete suggestions to this end include the following:

First, we must seek the Chinese government's understanding regarding inequalities in the cultural content trade relationship between Korea and China. While in Korea we are not currently in a position to wholly support UNESCO's "Convention on the Diversity of Cultural Expressions," we can seek a mutual, reasonable understanding on *Hallyu* with China. Second, we must point out misinterpretations of *Hallyu* and Korea that occur in the Chinese media. Third, in an effort to advance Chinese understanding of Korea, there is a need for broad government efforts between organizations such as Korean Cultural Centers in China, public relations offices, commercial attachés, and educational centers. Fourth, the public and non-governmental organizations in China should be educated about Korea. Maintaining and supporting Chinese exchange students in Korea and strengthening social services for Korean-Chinese in Korea may help with these efforts. Fifth, misunderstandings and adverse perceptions that arise in Korean and Chinese online forums require correction. We may offer youths in both countries opportunities to understand one another by supporting the operation of joint homepages, for example.

Suggestions and strategies for the development of documentary exports: A look at *Ancient Tea Route*

Given dramas' overwhelming share of exports, broadcast export genres desperately need diversification. Aside from dramas, documentaries are a promising genre for export. The KBS documentary *Ancient Tea Route* (*Chamagodo*) was first sold in 2007 and by September 2008 had been exported to 19 countries, effectively demonstrating the export potential of Korean documentaries.

Production for *Ancient Tea Route* began in 2006 with a budget of ₩10 billion, and it was planned as the first installment of KBS's large-scale series *Insight Asia*. Planning for the documentary involved preliminary collection of material by three producers over a number of months. Production itself required over 2 years, with 3 teams shooting over 16 months. As the project was shot in HD with simultaneous sound recording, high-quality video and sound became available. Post-production demanded intense labor as well.

The conclusion to be drawn from *Ancient Tea Route* is simple: well-made content with a high degree of economic competitiveness sells well. Documentaries have an advantage in that there is almost no cultural discount involved in their distribution. In a context in which our domestic producers envy BBC and NHK documentary crews, *Ancient Tea Route* allowed us to catch up with leaders in this field and boosted Korean confidence.

The experience of distributing *Ancient Tea Route* has made it clear that the following efforts are necessary to expand documentary exports: in the international broadcast market, success can depend on personal contacts. As such, the expertise of distribution professionals should be recognized, and their ability to maintain relationships in the mid-to-long term should be nurtured. Also, we must consider introducing the BBC's content marketing system, in which personnel with production experience serve as marketers. These content marketers constantly monitor the international market, creating content that can compete internationally.

Current state and future directions of Korean drama presales

Competition in drama production has overheated, resulting in skyrocketing fees for actors and writers. As such, production fees themselves have skyrocketed. However, the production budgets provided by broadcasters and sponsorships from advertisers have either remained the same or diminished. The fees that production companies received from broadcasters in 2005 stood at approximately 70% of actual production costs; currently this figure stands somewhere above the

50% mark. For this reason, production companies have grown more interested in expanding overseas sales; dramas can be sold for a higher price during the production stage than after completion.

For example, after *The Legend* was sold in Japan in 2007 during its planning stages, *Le Grand Chef, Beethoven Virus, NEXUS: The Kingdom of Winds*, and *The Painter of the Wind* were presold in 2008, as were *Boys over Flowers, Style*, and *Cain and Abel* in 2009. Presales generally take place with Japan and are gradually beginning to occur with Taiwan, Singapore, and the Middle East as well.

Above all else, in order to secure drama copyrights and promote presales that involve ancillary products, content quality must be improved. In other words, we must build a production environment in which "sure-fire content" can aim for the global market. We should develop strong source materials and train producers to become savvy in international business. Through such methods, new *Hallyu* stars may be discovered, and *Hallyu* itself may become sustainable.

Invigorating format sales

Format sales are an alternative to content export. Format licensing constitutes a means of overcoming cultural barriers, and, as reality television has grown in popularity, such transactions have become more common. From the buyer's point of view, formats that have proven themselves abroad can be imported more cheaply than finished products, with the added bonus that production know-how can be acquired in the process.

Currently, format sales are led by a few companies, including Endemol and Freemantle Media. In order to realize format transactions, these companies emphasize the fact that one should first produce successful programs. Companies that sell formats examine carefully how a particular product has been made and sold and work to increase efficiency and profitability.

There is indeed an opportunity to sell formats abroad. Although not a typi-cal format export, *High School Quiz* (*Janghak Quiz*) has been popular in China for 10 years. In Vietnam, a show based on the script for *Soonpoong Clinic* has become popular. Other successful format sales include KBS's *Golden Bell Chal-lenge* and *A Chat with Beauties*. SBS's *Truth Game, Good Sunday*, and *Full House* have been exported as well. Several other programs are also under nego-tiation for format sale.

If Korea is to advance into the format market, we must strengthen our production capabilities. Doing so will require cultivating able producers and focusing not solely on production but on systematization. In order to nurture producers and systematic production, co-productions with overseas busi-nesses should be considered, as well as producer exchange programs with foreign companies.

F.   *Expanding export through production improvements*

Broadcast content export and independent production companies

There is little consensus about the benefits and drawbacks of outsourcing drama production to independent companies. Although policies encouraging indepen-dent production have led to an increase in the number of such businesses, most operate on a small scale. Primarily, documentaries and variety shows were handled by independents after the introduction of policy encouraging the practice in the 1990s. Beginning in the 2000s, even dramas were produced more often by independents than by corporate broadcasters. The revenue of companies that specialize in such productions can range from ₩8 billion to ₩40 billion; these companies generally operate at a loss.

Due to the lack of economic competitiveness, broadcast content is unique in being distributed via numerous routes. Terrestrial broadcast programming is distinct in being distributed via various media simultaneously, rather than successively over time. Domestically, second-round distribution paths for terrestrial broadcasters include cable TV, video-on-demand, and, to some extent, DVD production. As export represents only a fraction of broadcast sales revenue, it used to have no major pathways to speak of. However, as production costs rise but earnings from sales and endorsements do not, the importance of foreign sales is increasing. Currently some programs secure much of their production budgets through presales. One can also see that dramas produced by independent companies have been sold more than those produced by broadcast companies, because miniseries, with their shorter 10 to 20 episode format, comprise a large proportion of drama exports and are mainly produced by independent production companies.

To alleviate production problems, the following actions are necessary: First, to ensure that programs with high ratings reap more revenue from advertising, the means by which advertising prices are set must change. Second, we must switch to a system in which initial broadcast rights for programming produced by independent companies are purchased by terrestrial broadcasters. Third, we must establish fair and systematic transaction methods for copyright.

Invigorating product placement and exporting broadcast content

Although PPL is an effective means of advertising, concerns exist that overuse may lead to overly commercial programming. Although allowed in most countries, PPL is banned in Korea, though the government has signaled that the practice will soon be permitted. When PPL becomes legal, we may expect that export of related products will increase markedly.

Furthermore, although currently banned domestically, PPL is sometimes inserted into dramas sold abroad. In *Lovers in Prague* and *My Girl*, Pantech products were inserted into scenes via computer graphics and have been exported to Hong Kong and Indonesia. On the other hand, once PPL is allowed, Korean products will receive greater exposure in dramas. As the current surreptitious means of product placement are replaced by systematic agent management, drama producers will be able to attract sponsors smoothly.

Improving production structure

Currently, the majority of Korean independent production companies are strikingly small, and their incomes and expenditures are low as well. We should increase the scale of these businesses and systematize business administration through the inducement of mergers. As the spate of small-scale production companies is leading to destabilization of the market, the system of supervision must be revised so that terrestrial broadcasters do not take advantage of smaller independent companies. Penalties against corrupt practices such as false disclosure or stock manipulation by independent companies should be strengthened, and transparency in the flow of funds in broadcast production should increase. After increasing the size of production companies, we must open the domestic market to foreign competition and foster competition between domestic and overseas companies to increase the capability of domestic companies. Also, in order to boost the international savvy of producers and directors, we must offer them the chance to attend overseas events such as trade fairs. Finally, they should also have opportunities to join the entourage of presidential trips overseas and other international events to meet high-ranking officials and interact with other members of the broadcast industry.

G. Conclusion

Hallyu has immense potential for positive influence abroad in addition to its export revenues. However, the mainstay of the Korean Wave, broadcast exports, currently needs attention. In order for export to expand, it is not enough to introduce one or two new strategies and policy steps. Only through investing continuous effort and funding into source development, cultivating outstanding production staff and directors, enlarging production companies, improving domestic transaction practices, developing distributors, and pioneering new markets, will expansion be possible. If *Hallyu* is to grow, industry leaders must take a more long-term perspective, pushing goals forward with rational strategies; the government and related organizations must establish systematic support with a similar mindset.

2.1.4.   2011 Content Industry Trends: Korean Dramas in Japan

Reference: "Related Information Contents: *Hallyu*," *Content Industry Trends of 2011*, KOCCA, 2012, pp. 431–438, 442–443.

A.   Status of Korean dramas in Japan

(pp. 431–438)

Korean dramas' third boom

The number of younger fans has increased with the arrival of K-pop stars. The earlier fan base for *Winter Sonata* of women in their fifties and sixties, the demographic that still leads *Hallyu* drama rentals, expanded to men in their fifties with the success of *Jewel in the Palace* and *Jumong*, which screened in Japan in 2007. In the past couple of years, a new trend has emerged whereby younger generations are recognizing Korean shows as a form of viable entertainment. Recently, the age of fans has dropped. The 2010 hit *You're Beautiful*, which targeted those in their twenties, also saw popularity among teenage girls and women in their thirties.

Expansion of *Hallyu* drama fandom to the youth

One factor that led to the expansion of the Korean Wave to younger fans involved a new avenue for watching dramas: terrestrial broadcasters. For example, from

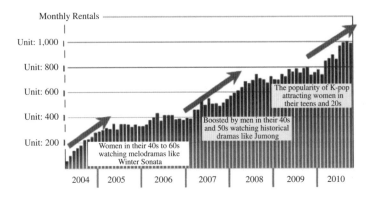

Figure 2–9.   Trends in Korean drama rentals and viewership (2004–2010)

January 2010, Fuji Television instituted the regular Korean drama slot *Hallyu α*. Also, beginning in April 2010, the Tokyo Broadcasting System (TBS) aired the Korean drama *Iris* during prime time. They also created the "Hallyu Select" hour (mornings from 10:00–11:00) and have been airing Korean dramas regularly ever since. Although program times differ, the original target audience was women aged 35–49. However, with the arrival of summer vacation, viewership among teens and women in the 20–34 age bracket increased.

Matsuzaki Yoko of Fuji Television's production department, responsible for *Hallyu α*, stated, "Although we hadn't planned it, viewership among teens reached 20%. Further examination of the figures revealed that kindergarteners were watching shows with their mothers, increasing dual-generation viewership." Ochiai Asaha, who is in charge of the Asia division of TSUTAYA, Japan's top video rental outlet, opined that, "Viewership among young people rose suddenly with the launch of *Hallyu α*. K-pop fans apparently have interest in Korean dramas as well."

TSUTAYA annual rental figures show a revival of Korean drama

According to figures released in May 2011 by the Culture Convenience Club (CCC), which operates TSUTAYA, Korean dramas have seen revitalization and broken past records. CCC attributes this rejuvenation to increasing viewership among women in their teens and twenties. Between January and May, the Korean dramas ranked #1 and #2 in the charts were *Sungkyunkwan Scandal* and *You're Beautiful*, respectively.

Yuchun of JYJ fame, star of *Sungkyunkwan Scandal*

Sungkyunkwan Scandal (full-length edition), which featured JYJ's Yuchun in the lead role, set a record for rentals within the first five days of its release. According to TSUTAYA, this figure represents a 230% increase over the 2010 hit Korean drama *You're Beautiful, Volume 1*, which starred Jang Keun-suk.

The growth of Korean dramas after terrestrial broadcasting

Fuji TV's *Hallyu α* is broadcast during the afternoon from Monday to Friday. Dramas such as *Magnificent Legacy*, *You're Beautiful*, and *Playful Kiss* placed in

Table 2–13.   TSUTAYA's Korean drama top 10 list for the
first half of 2011 (January 1 through June 30)

Ranking	Title
1	*You're Beautiful*
2	*Pasta*
3	*Sungkyunkwan Scandal*
4	*Playful Kiss*
5	*The Slave Hunters*
6	*Temptation of an Angel*
7	*My Fair Lady*
8	*Brilliant Legacy*
9	*Mary Stayed Out All Night*
10	*You're Beautiful (deluxe version)*

the Top 10 for most popular dramas on *Hallyu* α and ranked highly in TSUTA-YA's rentals. Programs with high ratings on "Hallyu Select" (broadcast on TBS, Monday through Friday, from 10:05 am) include *Mary Stayed Out All Night, My Fair Lady, Temptation of an Angel*, and *Pasta*. These shows also ranked highly in rentals, indicating that fans who began watching Korean dramas through terrestrial broadcasts started using retail services as well.

B.   Reasons for the popularity of Korean dramas

Popularity of love stories in Japan

Maeda Atsuko of the TBS production company responsible for "Hallyu Select" noted that, "Programs with love relationships as a core element have the highest ratings….Romantic comedies and 'over-the-top' (*makjang*) dramas that contain strong love stories have been popular." Korean drama itself has little appeal among general viewers of network television, so viewers are likely to decide whether to watch by considering "The casting and so on, of course, and then finally the content." Dubbing is also necessary. In this morning time slot the audience has a strong tendency to watch while engaged in other activities. An online questionnaire found that "although fans favor subtitles, the overwhelming majority of potential viewers prefer dubbed programming." Even if a program is unusually compelling and engaging, without a name actor or a title that lends itself to recognition as a Korean equivalent of *Oshin*, the popular Japanese tearjerker, as *King of Baking, Kim Takgu* was, then hit status is difficult.

Slump in Japanese dramas

Although Korean dramas remain popular overall, true hits are few. Nonetheless, fees for broadcast rights have risen sharply over last year. Yet Japanese broadcasters and distributors remain bullish on the expansion of Korean drama. One reason for this is a decline in Japanese dramas themselves. Before Fuji TV and TBS began their *Hallyu* broadcast hours, Japanese miniseries were frequently rebroadcast. TSUTAYA's Ochiai noted that, "Korean producers understand the Japanese consumer, and attractive young actors or K-pop artists are increasingly cast in dramas." The Korean drama industry is currently in an interesting state of flux as the market is expanding its existing base to include younger fans who enjoy K-pop.

C.   Latest trends in Hallyu dramas

Emergence of a gap between Korean and Japanese popular dramas

Melodramas like *Winter Sonata* and romantic comedies like *The 1st Shop of Coffee Prince*, a pioneering work in which the heroine cross-dressed as a male, are popular in Japan. Recently, morning soap operas such as *Temptation of Wife*, in which two women in love with one man join forces to plot revenge against him, have also garnered popularity. The majority of programs with high network viewership have been love stories. *You're Beautiful* and *Mary Stayed Out All Night*, which did not do especially well in Korea, garnered high ratings in Japan. *Master of Study*, however, a drama that takes place in a cram school and achieved top ratings in Korea, struggled on Japanese TV. Such examples demonstrate an emerging gap between what is popular in each country.

The popularity of family and historical dramas in Korea

Korean rankings for 2010 drama viewership reveal the rise of this clear split between programs popular in Korea and Japan. The three most popular programs in Korea were *King of Baking, Kim Takgu*, considered a "national drama"; *Dong Yi*, a historical drama; and the variety show *Happy Sunday*; in all of which romance played a minimal role. *A Fine, Windy Day* at #7 and *Life Is Beautiful* at #8 were both family dramas. Unlike in Japan, a drama series in Korea is broadcast twice weekly, and dramas comprise a high percentage of television programming. Rather than love stories that target a particular segment of society, shows that the whole family can watch while relaxing together achieve greater popularity and the highest ratings. Recently broadcast programs that reached a 50% viewership threshold in Korea include *Jewel in the Palace* (2003–2004), *My Lovely Sam Soon* (2005), and *Jumong* (2006–2007).

Unlike Japan, sitcoms offer a gateway for new faces

Though uncommon in Japan, sitcoms are widely produced in Korea. Given the recent trend of targeting the Asian market, including Japan, K-pop stars make frequent cameos in dramas and are often cast in them. This recognition of K-pop star power in drama production will likely continue.

D.   The next generation of Hallyu stars

New stars ride the coattails of *Winter Sonata*'s Bae Yong-joon and Choi Ji-woo

According to a survey conducted among 300 Japanese women aged 15–59 who enjoy Korean entertainment, *Winter Sonata* actors Bae Yong-joon and

Choi Ji-woo, who also appear in television advertising in Japan, remain most recognizable even among those who are not Korean Wave fans. Following Bae among actors are *Iris's* Lee Byung-hun and Jang Keun-suk, who rocketed to fame after *You're Beautiful*. Jang also appears in commercials in Japan and tops surveys of popularity. FT Island's Lee Hong-gi, TVXQ's Chang Min, and SS501's Kim Hyun-joong, who have debuted as actors in Japan, are also predicted to become stars. In second place among actresses is Yoon Son-ha, also well-known in Japan. Kim Tae-hee, set to star in the Japanese miniseries *99 Days with Me and a Star* in October, comes third. These three "most recognizable" actresses held similarly high rankings for "popularity." In addition, such actors as Park Min-young from *Sungkyunkwan Scandal* have also recently appeared in the charts.

Jang Keun-suk, popular for role in *You're Beautiful*

The popularity of Jang Keun-suk, currently one of *Hallyu*'s hottest celebrities, seems to be soaring to the level of Bae Yong-joon, whose fame is almost unassailable. A distinguishing factor, however, is the age of their fans. Whereas Bae's fan base is comprised primarily of women in their fifties and sixties, Jang's fans range from secondary school girls to women in their fifties. In many instances, older women attend fan gatherings with their daughters. Songs performed by Jang that featured in the drama are also gaining popularity. In April 2011, Jang's debut CD *Let Me Cry* sold more than 100,000 copies.

Focus of the generational shift in *Hallyu* Stars: SS501's Kim Hyun-joong

High expectations rest on SS501's Kim Hyun-joong, a new pretty boy on the scene. Active in both K-pop and dramas, Kim has the necessary qualities to maximize a fan base. In the Korean version of *Boys over Flowers*, the character that Kim played, Yoon Ji-hoo, was a hit with women. Kim now stars in *Playful Kiss* as a petulant genius, and the show is garnering popularity. The leader of SS501, Kim has acquired the nickname "Little Bae Yong-joon" because of his attractive appearance and soft smile.

Next generation actresses

Industry insiders regard Kim Tae-hee as a top contender to join the next generation of *Hallyu* stars. Having signed deals with the agency that manages Japanese celebrities such as Horikita Maki, Kim became active in Japan. She has graced the cover of fashion magazine *25ans*, and received wide exposure from her role in *Iris*, which was broadcast in prime time. *My Princess* screened on Fuji TV's *Hallyu α*. Starting in October, Kim is slated to play the female lead in *99 Days with Me and a Star*, alongside Nishijima Hidetoshi, well-known in Korea for the film *Sayonara Itsuka*. Park Min-young of 2011's most talked about drama, *Sungkyunkwan Scandal*, and Han Hyo-joo of *Dong Yi*, which rode the wave of historical programs like *Jewel in the Palace* and *Yi San* and was similarly well received, are drawing attention for their joint activities. Much is also expected of Yoona of Girls' Generation, Miss-A's Suji, who appeared on *Dream High*, and Eun-jeong of T-ARA, who was a child star.

Popularity of Korean dramas is rising again, boosted by K-pop

Korean dramas are being branded throughout Asia along with the popularity of K-pop. Although Western dramas continue to do well, in 10 Asian locales other than Taipei and Hong Kong, Korean dramas are more popular than those from Japan. In particular, popularity is rising in Bangkok, Ho Chi Minh City, and Manila. In ASEAN nation cities, K-pop is more popular than J-pop, a trend evidently reflected in dramas.

With increase in popularity, Korean actors increasingly appear in Japanese dramas

Choi Ji-woo, who become popular with *Winter Sonata*, and Takeuchi Yukawa appeared together in the miniseries *Rondo* (TBS). Most recently, the Korean novel *Gashigogi* was adapted as *Good Life, Thank You, Goodbye, Dad*, which featured Jung Woo-sung. Projects with roots in Korea that employ Korean actors are becoming more frequent. K-pop idols are also appearing more and more in Japanese dramas. FT Island's Lee Hong-gi had his first leading role in *Muscle Girl*, an evening drama broadcast in April 2011. Lee plays a young Korean man seeking his mother. He winds up living with female professional wrestlers and falls in love. L of INFINITE is currently starring in *Ji-woo: Special Crimes Investigation* (Fridays at 23:15, Tereya). He plays a murderer with a mysterious past.

E.   Hallyu in Japan and subsidiary businesses: Introduction

Popularity of Korean products in various sectors

Since 2010, *Hallyu* has seen a resurgence. Korean dramas, along with K-pop, have been experiencing popularity among young people and the fan base is growing. Korean foods and beverages are being launched one after another in Japan, and Korean products of various sorts are becoming popular. In addition to the core fan base of women 50 and older, popularity is growing among women from their teens to their forties. In July 2011, Takaoka Souseke criticized Fuji TV's "*Hallyu* bias" in his *Twitter* feed, inciting public criticism. He later was dropped from NTV's show *QP*. Hence, the attention of many in Japan was drawn again to *Hallyu*, and awareness was renewed. All in all, the weekly broadcast of Korean shows totals more than 90 hours (according to general programming in October).

Korean dramas: Expanding viewership greatly at low cost

Fuji TV attributes the sharp rise in Korean dramas to the dictum "High Demand = Viewership." Last January, Fuji TV began showing Korean dramas on *Hallyu α*. Last year, average viewership for Korean dramas hovered around 5%, but after broadcast of *You're Beautiful*, starring Jang Keun-suk, which took #1 for its time slot, this figure increased to 7%. Before *Hallyu α*, Japanese dramas rebroadcast in that slot achieved ratings of 2–3%. As programs at this time compete for rating variances of decimal points, a 2–3% rise is quite substantial (rating figures come from research for the Kanto region).

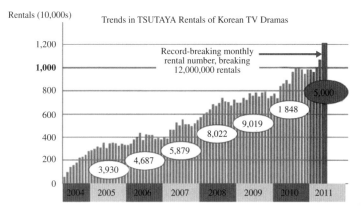

Figure 2–10. **Trends in TSUTAYA rentals of Korean TV dramas in numbers (Unit: 10,000 rentals)**
Source: (Monthly rentals of Korean dramas based on a Culture Convenience Club Company, Ltd. Survey)

Table 2–14. **Terrestrial (including BS) *Hallyu* drama broadcast times**

Medium	Broadcast Company	Approximate Hours	Total
Terrestrial Broadcasters	NHK	1 hr	93 hrs 40 min
	TBS	6 hrs 50 min	
	TV Tokyo	1 hr 50 min	
	Fuji TV	13 hrs 50 min	
Broadcasting Satellite (BS)	NHK BS Premium	2 hrs	
	BS NiTele	20 hrs 10 min	
	BS Asahi	21 hrs 50 min	
	BS-TBS	6 hrs 20 min	
	BS Japan	11 hrs 30 min	
	BS Fuji	8 hrs 20 min	

(Source: Mid-September survey)

The primary reason that each broadcaster, including BS, prefers *Hallyu* dramas is cost. Production costs for a single episode of a Japanese drama generally reach more than ¥10 million. A program that ended its initial run and is broadcast three more times in its first three years can cost up to half of production expenses for the broadcaster. As such, Korean dramas are seen as products that maintain price competitiveness while increasing viewership. High ratings on television mean that Korean dramas can generate profit through subsequent DVD rentals.

F.   Ancillary markets for Hallyu dramas

Overheating competition in *Hallyu* drama sales

(pp. 442–443)

A look at the composition of TSUTAYA's *Hallyu* drama rentals reveals that hits such as *You're Beautiful* have been increasing in popularity among viewers in their thirties and forties. Given the dearth of content, many companies are competing for *Hallyu* dramas and prices are rising quickly. "Around 2004, one episode cost a few thousand dollars. Now some cost over $100,000," noted one industry insider. Hit programs may generate great profits; however, risks increase accordingly.

Trend of investment growth for co-production enterprises

As the price of Korean dramas rises, joint ventures that invest in purchase are growing more active. Korean dramas are sold to video content companies, advertising affiliates, and television broadcasters. Several broadcasters release and advertise DVDs of Korean dramas. As companies aim for a market that has become vastly larger, purchase of new Korean dramas is common. CCC, Japan's largest DVD rental chain, which runs TSUTAYA, began purchasing *Hallyu* dramas last year. As sales are facilitated by the parent company, TSUTAYA has established a monopoly over certain series' rentals. *You're Beautiful* was CCC's first exclusive Korean import. Recently, film distribution companies have also entered the drama market. Sony Pictures Entertainment and Sony Entertainment have together joined the *Hallyu* drama distribution enterprise.

Change in Korean production landscape as Japanese demand evolves

High demand for Korean dramas is causing changes in Korean production. *Hallyu* dramas based on Japanese manga and books have increased significantly. In Korea, however, many screenwriters have strong reservations about this trend; therefore, such productions are not as common as in Japan. Even so, production companies are increasingly setting their sights on entry into the Japanese market

Table 2–15.   Instances of DVD and production sales by title

Program	Broadcaster in Japan	Production Year
1ˢᵗ Shop of Coffee Prince	TV Tokyo	2007
My Sweet Seoul	TV Aichi	2008
Boys over Flowers	TBS	2009
Magnificent Legacy	Fuji TV	2009
Mary Stayed Out All Night	TBS	2010
Big Thing	Fuji TV	2010

and looking at programming based on a Japanese original as a useful method for achieving this goal. Cognizant of the penetration of K-pop, many companies are casting more K-pop idols in their shows; content that reflects these demands is increasing. For example, Korean production company Group 8 collaborated with Japanese video content agency SPO from the planning stages of the Korean version of *Boys over Flowers* and *Playful Kiss*.

Increasing investment from Japanese companies

Recently, more Japanese businesses have invested in Korean productions. This year, dramas *Bad Boy* and *Mary Stayed Out All Night* were co-created by a Korean company and the Japanese video producer Asia Content Center, Inc. (ACC). NHK also coproduced *Bad Boy*. Whereas the Korean partner was responsible for the production of *Bad Boy*, *Mary Stayed Out All Night* made use of networks established during *Bad Boy*. ACC secured the rights to the original Korean graphic novel *Mary Stayed Out All Night* and handled the casting, which brought more exposure to Jang Keun-suk. "Generally only broadcast and DVD rights can be procured in the purchase of already completed dramas; however, event planning, merchandise, books, and music all fall within the purview of joint productions, and they can be transferred overseas," stated ACC's Teguchi Takaomi. In July, ACC opened a fund to support content enterprises with one goal being drama co-productions with Korean media companies. Investment stood at ₩30.5 billion (approximately ¥2.3 billion), half of which was supported by Korean governmental organizations. In Japan, in addition to ACC, TBS TV and Pony Canyon invested in this fund. Such participation from the planning stages shows a desire to create content that meets Japanese viewer demand.

2.1.5.   Korean Dramas' Entry into the Latin American Market

Reference: *US Content Industry Trends: Korean Dramas' Entry into the Latin American Market*, KOCCA US Office, November 8, 2013, pp. 2–11.

A.   Introduction

Although it has been over 10 years since the first Korean drama was broadcast in Latin America, serious entry into the market only began 3 to 4 years ago. The main destinations for Korean drama exports include Ecuador, Peru, Panama, and Puerto Rico; distribution to Paraguay, Venezuela, Bolivia, Chile, and Brazil has recently gained momentum. Numerous Korean drama fan sites also exist in these countries; for example, users on *Hallyu* fan sites are especially engaged in Panama, attending Korean Wave-related events, Korean broadcast showcases, and the like. On these sites not only is information about locally broadcast Korean dramas readily available but, in the case of Panama, information about new programs is uploaded before broadcast for members to share. Korean dramas enjoy popularity in most of Latin America, aside from Argentina and Brazil, where few are broadcast. Currently, KBS has a broadcast agreement with one corporation in Brazil. MBC released the documentary *Tears of the Amazon* and the drama *Boys over Flowers* in Argentina.

Table 2–16.   **Korean dramas broadcast in Latin America**

Country	Title
Mexico	*All About Eve, Star in My Heart, Jewel in the Palace, Winter Sonata, Four Sisters, Boys over Flowers, My Fair Lady*
Honduras	*Jewel in the Palace, Stairway to Heaven, Autumn in My Heart, My Fair Lady*
Colombia	*Stairway to Heaven, Jewel in the Palace, Secret Garden, A Thousand Days' Promise*
Chile	*Stairway to Heaven, The Greatest Love, Pasta, Dream High, Secret Garden*
Peru	*Jewel in the Palace, Stairway to Heaven, 1ˢᵗ Shop of Coffee Prince, All About Eve, Star in My Heart, Queen of Housewives, Princess Hours, Phoenix, Cinderella Man, Queen of Reversals, Flames of Desire, The Greatest Love, The Moon Embracing the Sun, Pasta, Autumn in My Heart, Winter Sonata, My Fair Lady, Dream High, Boys over Flowers, Manny, Full House*
Panama	*Jewel in the Palace, Princess Hours, My Lovely Sam Soon, Boys over Flowers, Phoenix, 1ˢᵗ Shop of Coffee Prince, Star in My Heart, Pasta, Cinderella Man, The Greatest Love, Autumn in My Heart, Winter Sonata, My Fair Lady, Dream High, Secret Garden, Stairway to Heaven*
Puerto Rico	*Jewel in the Palace, Phoenix, Queen of Housewives, My Lovely Sam Soon, Princess Hours, 1ˢᵗ Shop of Coffee Prince, All About Eve, Star in My Heart, Damo, Queen of Reversals, Cinderella Man, The Greatest Love, The Moon Embracing the Sun, Pasta, Secret Garden, Winter Sonata*
Ecuador	*Jewel in the Palace, Damo, My Husband's Woman, Stairway to Heaven, Phoenix, Princess Hours, Queen of Housewives, Jewel in the Palace, My Lovely Sam Soon, 1ˢᵗ Shop of Coffee Prince, All About Eve, Coffee Prince, Phoenix, Queen of Reversals, Cinderella Man, The Greatest Love, Flames of Desire, The Moon Embracing the Sun, Autumn in My Heart, Winter Sonata, My Fair lady, Dream High, Secret Garden, Manny*
Bolivia	*Jewel in the Palace, Stairway to Heaven, 1ˢᵗ Shop of Coffee Prince, Jewel in the Palace, My Lovely Sam Soon, Secret Garden*
Venezuela	*Jewel in the Palace, Stairway to Heaven, 1ˢᵗ Shop of Coffee Prince, Autumn in My Heart, Winter Sonata, Damo, All about Eve, Star in My Heart, Manny*
Paraguay	*Jewel in the Palace, 1ˢᵗ Shop of Coffee Prince, Star in My Heart, Princess Hours, Autumn in My Heart, Winter Sonata, My Fair Lady*
Cuba	*Queen of Housewives, My Fair Lady, Secret Garden*
Costa Rica	*Jewel in the Palace, Stairway to Heaven, Queen of Housewives*
Guatemala	*Jewel in the Palace, Autumn in My Heart, Winter Sonata, My Fair Lady*

(Continued)

Table 2–16. *(Continued).*

Country	Title
El Salvador	*Jewel in the Palace, Autumn in My Heart, Winter Sonata, My Fair Lady*
Uruguay	*Stairway to Heaven*
Dominica	*Autumn in My Heart, Winter Sonata, My Fair Lady*
Nicaragua	*Jewel in the Palace, My Fair Lady, Queen of Housewives*
Cameroon [sic][1]	*Jewel in the Palace*
Argentina	*Boys over Flowers*

[1] This error was introduced into the original source by drawing from a governmental publication in which Cameroon was the first African country listed after Latin American nations. [editors]

B. Status of Korean drama marketing

SBS currently distributes dramas in Latin America via the US-based network Telemundo International. Thus distributor, which is on par with subsidiaries of Hispanic broadcast networks in the US, has also begun to distribute Korean dramas in Latin America. It provides Korean content to MundoFox in the US and RCN in Colombia. MundoFox is a joint venture between the Fox Broadcasting Company and Colombian broadcaster RCN, which, via its Hispanic channel in the US, recently aired the Korean drama *Stairway to Heaven*. Despite having been broadcast in the unfavorable time slot of 1 o'clock in the afternoon, the program was well received among Hispanic viewers in the US. One viewer even created a 10-minute video heralding the drama and uploaded it to *YouTube*.

In addition, MundoFox is advertising *Stairway to Heaven* on *YouTube* and looking into broadcasting further Korean dramas. MBC sent its dramas to Chile and Panama with sponsorship from Daewoo Electronics and LG, respectively, and, except for some free content sponsored by the Korean government, is directly selling the majority of dramas in Latin America. As of this writing, 13 dramas and 3 documentaries have been dubbed into Spanish and are being sold in various countries. In the US, San Francisco-based terrestrial network and cable channel Cosmovision broadcast *All about Eve* and *Star in My Heart*, both of which received a positive response. KBS has recently become the first Korean network to sell a drama in Brazil; the program is slated for broadcast soon.

C. Reception from Latin American viewers

Korean dramas are similar to *telenovelas* ("television novels," or dramatic series broadcast in Spain, Portugal, and Latin America) in that their plots are convoluted and intertwined; however, Korean shows differ in their non-violent, family-friendly content that highlights familial affection and respect for elders. Whereas *telenovelas* often feature a character who dies only to reappear months later or the occurrence of unrealistic events in the course of a divorce, Korean dramas center on conservative values or on the protagonists' pure, heartwarming love stories and thus carry a clean-cut image in Latin America. Moreover, in Korean dramas, aside from storylines akin to those of fairy tales, elements such as handsome actors, beautiful actresses, and original soundtracks attract audience attention. Korea's family-friendly content appeals to Latin American viewers.

In Paraguay, after the broadcast of *The 1ˢᵗ Shop of Coffee Prince* and *Princess Hours*, for example, the soundtracks also recorded high sales. Currently more than 100 *telenovelas* are broadcast in Latin America each week; also, import and broadcast of US dramas has continued for a number of years. The smaller number of episodes per series and fast-paced plot development of Korean dramas are other aspects preferred by Latin American viewers. In fact, Mexican broadcaster Televisa has, under the influence of Korean dramas, begun to produce dramas of fewer than 50 episodes. More than 60 *Hallyu* fan clubs are active in Peru, and *Korea Special*, a weekly *Hallyu* program, is broadcast in Panama. In Chile, most viewers are in their teens or twenties and enjoy both dramas and K-pop. The audience in Paraguay has a wide age range but is predominantly composed of women. In Puerto Rico and Ecuador, broadcast representatives, in line with high viewer demand for Korean dramas and frequent requests for DVD sales, are seeking DVD production and supply. Broadcast corporation websites are receiving requests for video-on-demand services as well. Recently in Colombia, RCN replaced several Korean dramas with those from Mexico but, after viewer complaints, is considering reintroducing the Korean shows.

Members of *Hallyu* fan clubs hold Korean drama screenings and K-pop contests at their regular meetings; combined events are also held with members from countries around the region such as Argentina, Peru, Chile, and Panama. An impressive 70% of housewives aged 40–70 in Peru state having watched Korean dramas, and at least two corporations are competing in the broadcast of popular Korean dramas. A *Facebook* survey of Korean drama fans by country revealed that thousands, if not tens of thousands, count themselves as *Hallyu* fans. Among the 884,466 fans who "liked" the page of the drama *City Hunter* on *Facebook*, 7 of the top 16 countries represented are in Latin America. Dozens of Korean drama and K-pop fan clubs exist on *Facebook*. Peru alone has more than 10 active groups, including Asia Zone and Mundo Asianik.

D. Ratings trends for Korean dramas

Last year Red Guarani in Paraguay broadcast *My Fair Lady*, which received the second highest ratings of any program broadcast by that station. In Panama, Korean dramas are broadcast during prime time at 8:00 or 9:00 p.m.; viewership increased 12% over the previous year. Although in Peru program ratings average about 2%, Korean dramas typically exceed 6%. In Ecuador, the drama *Damo* received the second highest audience ratings in the country. Korean dramas are regularly broadcast at 6:00 p.m. and, as people aged 11–25 account for 46% of viewers, young people comprise the main audience demographic. In Figure 2–11, the first column represents total viewing households; next, viewers 18 and up; then, women; and lastly, men.

Table 2–17. *City Hunter* fan statistics by country (from *Facebook*)

Rank	Country	Number of Fans	Percentage (%)
1	Philippines	207,802	23.50%
2	Indonesia	167,336	18.90%
3	Malaysia	55,830	6.3%
4	Vietnam	54,021	6.1%
5	Peru	46,197	5.2%
6	Mexico	34,690	3.9%
7	Thailand	26,796	3%
8	Turkey	26,008	2.9%
9	US	23,506	2.7%
10	Korea	16,807	1.9%
11	Ecuador	13,999	1.6%
12	Colombia	12,940	1.5%
13	India	9,988	1.1%
14	Chile	9,698	1.1%
15	Argentina	9,121	1%
16	Venezuela	8,004	0.9%

E. Analysis and conclusion

Although Korean programming has only been sold in Latin America for a few years, it is broadly popular. Countries in which major networks do not broadcast Korean dramas are limited more or less to Brazil and Argentina. As the Korean government and related organizations have in the past distributed programming in Latin America free of charge, major broadcast corporations have yet to pay for Korean content licenses. In Mexico, one of the three main markets in Latin America, Mexiquense TV broadcasts Korean dramas; however, Televisa and Azteca, two other important networks, have yet to do so. Nonetheless, numerous Korean dramas are being purchased for remake, and Azteca has commenced partnerships to purchase Korean dramas. In Latin America, dubbed content is preferred, except in countries with higher levels of education like Argentina. High rates of illiteracy mean that viewers in many countries, accustomed to dubbing, are reluctant to read subtitles.

On the other hand, as K-pop fans grow in number and viewers are enchanted by Korean dramas, desire to hear the actors' actual voices is growing. This trend is even more prevalent among young viewers who watch dramas online. Although conservative broadcasters still request dubbed programming rather than subtitled content, as Internet use becomes more common in Latin America, it would seem that subtitling, more economically competitive, might target younger viewers more effectively and offer more content to a greater number of countries.

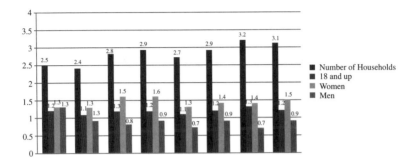

Figure 2–11.   Programming Korean dramas: Viewer ratings

Currently digital piracy is a serious problem in Latin America. The illegal IPTV service TV Pad, which quickly spread in the United States, is also spreading quickly in Latin America, a situation that calls for close observation. In the United States, Chinese and Korean broadcasters have initiated litigation against TV Pad and made use of government options to crack down on illegal activity. In addition, illegal streaming services operate openly in Latin America; however, as Korean dramas have yet to be offered there via legal video-on-demand sites, enforcement is even more challenging. Of course, *Viki* and *Dramafever* offer such services legally; however, programming must enter via mainstream Latin American sites similar to the United States' *Hulu* or *Netflix*, which have gained entry into Brazil.

In North America, Korean broadcasters are seeing steady success with dramas. It appears necessary to proactively follow the growth of new media by expanding activity to Latin America. In order to target young audiences, K-pop and Korean dramas must be marketed through this demographic segment's preferred communication media, social networking sites, and mobile services. Although many households remain without computers in Latin America, the majority of youths own mobile devices. As such, we should consider marketing via mobile devices and, eventually, video-on-demand enterprises.

2.2.   FILM

Beginning in the late 1990s, the Korean film industry saw spectacular growth, and Korea is now frequently touted as one of the few countries in the world where domestic features triumph over Hollywood blockbusters. Increasing production budgets enabled movies to appeal to sophisticated audience tastes. At the same time, the extent of capital investment also created a virtual necessity to expand markets, making the film sector's participation in the Korean Wave essential to the industry's ability to thrive. As the documents in this section demonstrate, demand for Korean films surged in the early to mid-2000s in East and Southeast Asia. Elsewhere, however, Korean cinema is generally viewed as part of world cinema and is screened in art-house theatres or at film festivals. Films from Korea have largely become known for their artistic and, indeed, often "extreme" and exotic qualities.

Document 2.2.1, "Film and the Korean Wave: Status and Policies for Promotion," is one of the first major report and policy pieces on film export from KOFIC. Written at the peak of the Korean Wave's film successes in Asia, it assesses the industry's achievements and contemplates its future. The document surveys seven target destinations from Japan to Singapore and also offers an interesting glance back to Korean movie exports in the 1960s. For some countries, it provides a useful complete list of film releases with dates, distributors, and box office revenues between the years 2003 and 2005. The document argues that in most regions the popularity of Korean dramas has had a positive trickle-down effect on films, especially works featuring *Hallyu* stars. In general, Korean romantic comedies and horror films perform well in Asia, and Document 2.2.1 provides illuminating speculation on why particular films succeeded or failed at the box office in particular destinations.

Although "Film and the Korean Wave: Status and Policies for Promotion" ends with optimistic projections, the industry's future has not always turned out as brightly as hoped, as can be seen from Document 2.2.2, "'K-Movies' as a Growth Engine for *Hallyu*," which considers film exports in 2014. Though international distribution prices rose, returns did not grow as expected; Korean films came to be seen as a bad investment, and in 2009, Korean film export experienced its nadir. The business is slowly picking up, and this document suggests potential strategies for industry recovery. Celebrated Korean directors are making forays into Hollywood, while Korean independent and art films continue to appear at international festivals. Co-productions in Asia are gathering momentum with the backing of such media conglomerates as CJ E&M, which is making headlines for capital investments and international ventures. However, few Asian co-produced films have broken even in the market so far, and questions remain over whether the Korean film industry can find sustainable success in Asia and beyond.

2.2.1.   Film and the Korean Wave: Status and Policies for Promotion

Reference: *Film and the Korean Wave: Status and Policies for Promotion*, Park Hee-seong and Nam Gyeong-hee, KOFIC Research Report 2006–1, KOFIC, 2006, pp. 1–6, 22–28, 52–60, 68–75, 87–97, 106–111, 120–123, 132–134, 137–139.

A.   Summary

(pp. 1–6)

Objective

Following *A Study on the Entry of Korean Films into the Asia-Pacific Region*, published by KOFIC in 2003, this report takes an objective look at *Hallyu* in the film sector in major Asian countries through analyses and summary and aims to provide information that may be helpful in the expansion and stabilization of *Hallyu*.

Subject

The subject of this research is *Hallyu* in the film sector in major Asian nations, including Japan, China, Hong Kong, Taiwan, Thailand, Vietnam, and Singapore.

Research purposes

To assess the role of the film sector in *Hallyu* in each region and, with it, the possibility of cooperation with other nations' cultural industries, and to increase understanding of local cultural industries more generally.

   To examine the status of the film industry as a whole and the standing of Korean films in each region in order to determine their prospects and establish strategies for the film industry in different destinations.

Research method

Examination of bibliographic records of books, magazines, websites, and publications from relevant organizations, and interviews with industry professionals. Data discrepancies among sources were reconciled by selecting more reliable sources in consultation with researchers and comparing levels of accuracy. Interviews and estimates were used to compensate for a lack of reliable statistics in most target regions.

Background and status of film *Hallyu*

Until the late 1990s, few South Korean films were screened overseas, and those that were did not do well. The earliest successes came with the releases of *Christmas in August* and *Shiri* in Hong Kong in 1999, followed by *Shiri* in Japan in 2000. In 2002, *My Sassy Girl* drew large audiences throughout Asia, including China, Taiwan, Thailand, Hong Kong, and Singapore. After that, Korean movies began to attract audiences in the Asian market across multiple genres, including melodrama and horror. *April Snow* and *A Moment to Remember* were hits throughout the region in 2005, and Korean films continue to garner considerable attention in Asia.

   The popularity of Korean films in the region in the 2000s is generally attributed to the quality of the finished products, their diverse genres and stories, the presence of subject matters and themes familiar to Asians, and their casting of attractive performers. Oft-cited merits include superior quality for their price and displays of modernity that coexist with traditional Asian sensibilities. A dearth of low-cost content to replace Hollywood movies in Asia, due in part to the decline of Hong Kong cinema and a lack of diversity among films from Japan, has also worked in favor of Korean films.

Korea's film brand has clearly become well-known throughout Asia. However, impact varies greatly by region, and the degree of acceptance of Korean movies depends on local infrastructure and the maturity of markets. To affirm the existence of a Korean Wave in the film sector in a given location, two conditions must be met: first, Korean movies must be screened regularly; and second, a significant audience for these films must be maintained. By such criteria, *Hallyu* cannot be considered to have taken root in the film sector but merely to have passed the initial entry phase.

Prospects for *Hallyu* and measures for invigoration

–   Continuously develop excellent, diverse content, taking a lesson from the history of Hong Kong and Japanese films.
–   It is necessary to understand the production strengths of each Asian nation and increase cooperation and co-production.
–   Choose direct distribution in conjunction with local agents to control the release schedule for Korean films, acquire accurate information on local markets, and conduct sophisticated marketing campaigns.
–   Increase promotion through local media to create a favorable environment for Korean movies.
–   Operate sites that can introduce Korean films in order to build a stable audience and secure a positive brand image.
–   *Hallyu* in film ultimately aims to invigorate the Asian market in general and boost awareness of Korean culture. Efforts to promote *Hallyu* will facilitate exchange and consensus between Korea and other Asian nations.

B. Japan

(pp. 22–38)

Largest export market for Korean film

In recent years, South Korea has seen a rise in not only the number of films exported to Japan, but also the value of distribution rights. Between 1995 and 2005, Korea's total film exports increased a whopping 360-fold, from $208,680 to $75.9 million. In the same period, the average film price grew 27-fold, from $13,900 to $376,200.[3]

The growth of the Korean film industry overseas is helped greatly by export to Japan. Of total film export royalties of $30.9 million in 2003, Japan accounted for 44.8%, or $13.8 million, showing a 107% increase from the previous year. Japan accounted for 69.3% of the total export value of $58.2 million in 2004 ($40.4 million). In 2005, 79.4% of total export revenues were from Japan, a figure that has been rising consistently and significantly. Amidst such growth,

---

[3] The low average film price relative to export amount is due to the greater number of films being exported. According to Japanese film magazine *Kinema Junpo*, Japan imported and released 19 South Korean films in 2002 and 26 in 2003, increasing the average price per film from $343,900 to $423,100.

Table 2-18. *Hallyu status by destination*

Destination	Film Market Characteristics	Hallyu Status	Development of *Hallyu* in the Film Sector	Current Statsus of Film Hallyu	Successful Films	Issues/Strategies
Japan	– The second largest market in the world – Theaters: ¥200 billion; Video: ¥300 billion	– Since the success of *Winter Sonata* in 2003, the Korean Wave has been led by TV dramas featuring *Hallyu* stars – *Hallyu* is being utilized actively to overcome the slump in Japanese cultural industries	– *Shiri* was successful in 1999, but *Hallyu* was not yet established as a trend – Films featuring *Hallyu* stars like Bae Yong-joon began to draw attention – Audiences for Korean films became diverse and releases grew in number – Korea's dependence on export to Japan increased	– Trend towards attracting audiences through film quality rather than star power (e.g., *A Moment to Remember*)	– *Shiri* (2000) – *My Sassy Girl* (2003) – *Windstruck* (2003) – *A Moment to Remember* (2005) – *April Snow* (2005)	– Content diversification – Continuous distribution – Broaden audience – Pioneer new markets and develop business models customized for the Japanese market
Hong Kong	– A film industry with heavy reliance on overseas markets – Decline of local film industry from mid-1990s – Search for breakthroughs as a hub for entry into Chinese market	– *Hallyu* began with films – Drama *Hallyu* began with broadcast of *Jewel in the Palace* in 2005	– Few films received attention in 2000–2001, after success of *Shiri* in 1999 – In 2002–2003, some 20 Korean movies were released and achieved popularity	– Popularity of Korean movies dwindled in 2004–2005, with few Korean films becoming hits – Hong Kong continues to premiere 1–2 Korean titles monthly	– *Shiri* (1999) – *My Sassy Girl* (2002) – *My Wife Is a Gangster* (2002) – *Classic* (2003) – *Windstruck* (2005)	– Continuous supply of diverse content – Efforts to brand actors – Facilitate co-production – Attempt worldwide releases

China	– Closed film industry structure under planned economy caused downturn in local film market – Policies for opening markets have been accelerating since 2000 – The national film industry began to grow between 2004 and 2005	– Around 1998, *Hallyu* surfaced in various sectors, including TV dramas and music – Due to a policy limiting film imports, Korean movies have had few opportunities for entry	– In 2002, *My Sassy Girl*, introduced through pirated DVDs, became a big hit – Korean films are very popular among the general public	– Korean films maintain popularity equal to US films in the illegal DVD market – Official market entry via theater release, broadcasting through movie channels, etc., have been rare and not borne fruit	– *My Sassy Girl* (2002, pirated copy) – *Windstruck* (2004)	– Seek partnerships and co-production – Secure direct export routes and worldwide release – Pioneer sales venues other than theaters – Apply pressure to increase crackdown on pirated DVDs – Build political infrastructure
Taiwan	– The film industry is depressed due to cable television and other factors – Hollywood films occupy over 95% of the market; domestic films, under 2%	– Since *Fireworks* became a hit in 2000, Korean TV dramas have aired continuously and spearheaded *Hallyu* – *Hallyu* has occurred in popular music and games	Films featuring TV drama stars, including *Friend* (2001) and *Joint Security Area* (2002), flopped – In 2002, however, the success of *My Sassy Girl* and *The Way Home* showed the potential of Korean movies – *A Tale of Two Sisters*, *Phone*, and other horror films have done well	– Hopes for success increased the number of film releases, but few have performed well at the box office – Film is the only Korean cultural industry in a slump – *Hallyu* consumers, consisting mostly of middle-aged women, are not attending theaters for Korean films in large numbers – Non-Hollywood movies suffer from difficult market entry	– *My Sassy Girl* (2002) – *The Way Home* (2002) – *A Tale of Two Sisters* (2003) – *Phone* (2003)	– Support for direct distribution and marketing – Attempt longer theater runs, considering the characteristics of each film – Nurture a fan base for Korean movies

(Continued)

Table 2–18. (*Continued*).

Destina-tion	Film Market Characteristics	*Hallyu* Status	Development of *Hallyu* in the Film Sector	Current Statsus of Film Hallyu	Successful Films	Issues/Strategies
Thailand	– The share of domestic films grew significantly from 2000 – Annual box office revenue around ₩100 billion – Largest market in the region excluding Japan and Chinese-speaking countries	– TV dramas, including *All About Eve* and *Autumn in My Heart*, became popular in 2000. They have been followed by a steady stream of Korean TV dramas, including *Full House* and *Jewel in the Palace*	– After the release of *Il Mare* in 2001 and *My Sassy Girl* in 2002, interest in Korean movies rose. – Korean films are being released regularly	– Since the downturn in 2004, few films have been successful – Low-key romantic movies tend to be popular – A remake of *The Letter* was produced	– *Il Mare* (2001) – *My Sassy Girl* (2002)	– Encourage technology cooperation and on-location shooting exchange – Introduce films from diverse genres – Develop subsidiary products, such as games based on movies and character merchandise – Increase promotions, including celebrity branding

Vietnam	– The movie industry is relatively small, and has not escaped completely from a state-controlled system	– *Hallyu* has been led by TV dramas, such as *Medical Brothers*, *Model*, *Autumn in My Heart*, and *All In*	– Helped by the popularity of TV dramas, the number of Korean movies released increased after 2000 – In 2000, *The Letter* became the first Korean movie released in Vietnam. Since then several others, including *Love Wind Love Song* and *Tie a Yellow Ribbon*, have been released – *My Sassy Girl* has been the most successful Korean film	– After Hollywood, Korean films have the largest number of releases – Romantic comedy is the most popular genre – Distribution is challenged by pirated copies	– *Tie a Yellow Ribbon* (2001) – *My Sassy Girl* (2001)	– Develop customized cultural products for the market – Provide a steady supply of content – Celebrity branding
Singapore	– Market size is around ₩84 billion – Because the black market is small, the legal video market is relatively large – Indian films are released in significant numbers	– *Hallyu* began with films – After the success of *Shiri* in 2001, *Bichunmoo*, *Il Mare*, and others were well received – *Hallyu* spread from films to TV dramas. – *Fireworks*, *Autumn in My Heart*, and others became popular, leading to an increase in the broadcast of Korean dramas – Recently, dramas such as *Jewel in the Palace* have been leading *Hallyu*	– The success of *Shiri*, *Joint Security Area*, and *My Sassy Girl* in 2001 confirmed the wide appeal of Korean films – *Wishing Stairs* was a major hit in 2003	– *Hallyu* has dwindled since 2004 – *April Snow* and others had weak showings – Pirated DVDs of Korean films flowing into Singapore from Hong Kong and China are having a serious impact	– *Shiri* (2001) – *My Sassy Girl* (2001) – *Wishing Stairs* (2003)	– Seek co-production and attract investment – Utilize celebrity branding and strategic marketing – Secure profit from DVD and secondary markets

Table 2–19.   Change in export of Korean films, 2000–2005 (Unit: $)

Year	2000	2001	2002	2003	2004	2005
Exports	7,053,745	11,249,573	14,952,089	30,979,000	58,284,600	75,994,580
Annual Growth Rate	18%	59%	33%	107%	88%	30%
Average Export Price	185,625	110,289	112,422	188,896	300,436	376,211

(Source: KOFIC, *2005 Report on South Korean Film Exports*)

films have been sold before completion based on their directors and casts, even if they are not celebrities. Buyers began showing interest in Korean films that had achieved domestic popularity. Such international sales have also opened doors for non-commercial films that can be classified as art cinema. In other words, opportunities are expanding for Korean films of various genres in Japan.

In 2004, Japan's share in Korea's film exports increased 191% from 2003. During this period, the growing influence of *Hallyu,* created by the popularity of Korean dramas, affected film distribution, and films featuring popular Korean actors were sold for strikingly high royalties. In addition, with more films distributed in Japan simply as a result of having been produced in Korea, the number of films exported also increased, together with royalties earned.

The pre-*Hallyu* period in the film sector[4]

The total number of Korean films sold to Japan remained in the single digits in the 1990s. Over 10 films were exported upon entering the new millennium, and 33 films were exported in 2004. This figure has continued to grow rapidly, and 20 films were exported in the first half of 2005 alone. Between 330 and 340 films are released annually in Japanese theaters. Of these, the share of Korean films remained at 3–4% throughout the early 2000s, but in 2004 Korea accounted for approximately 10% of all films released in Japan. This can be attributed to *Hallyu* and the resulting popularity of Korean films, changes in the distribution structure within Japan, and the repeated failure of major Hollywood titles to become box office hits. The introduction of Korean films into Japan before 2004, when the *Hallyu* boom carried over from dramas into films, can be largely divided into three phases:

Phase 1 (Liberation-1990s)

In 1962 *Seong Chunhyang* became the first South Korean film to be released in Japan after Korea's liberation. From the 1980s, Korean films began to be introduced in large numbers. In the 1990s, films by directors Lee Jang-ho, Bae Chang-ho, Im Kwon-taek, Chung Ji-Young, and others were well received. In 1994, Im

---

[4] Interview with Kakeo Yoshio, reporter for *Kinema Junpo.*

Table 2–20.   Export of Korean films by region, 2003–2005 (Unit: $)

Region	Exports 2003	Share	2004	Share	2005	Share
Asia	19,024,000	61.4%	45,327,500	77.8%	66,143,686	87.0%
North America	4,486,000	14.5%	2,900,000	5.0%	2,014,500	2.7%
South America	82,500	0.2%	141,500	0.2%	235,600	0.3%
Europe	5,724,000	18.5%	8,245,250	14.1%	7,315,970	9.6%
Oceania	30,000	0.1%	152,850	0.3%	147,830	0.2%
Africa	0	0.0%	0	0.0%	35,320	0.0%
Other	1,632,500	5.3%	1,517,500	2.6%	101,674	0.1%
Total	30,979,000	100%	58,284,600	100%	75,994,580	100%

(Source: KOFIC, *2004 Report on South Korean Film Exports, 2005 Report on South Korean Film Exports*)

Table 2–21.   Export of Korean films to eight major countries, 2003–2005 (Unit: $)

Country	Exports 2003	Share	2004	Share	2005	Share
Japan	13,893,000	44.8%	40,401,000	69.3%	60,322,686	79.4%
US	4,486,000	14.5%	2,361,000	4.0%	2,014,500	2.7%
France	709,000	2.3%	2,084,000	3.6%	1,504,820	2.0%
Thailand	1,448,500	4.7%	1,771,500	3.0%	1,520,000	2.0%
Germany	1,908,500	6.2%	1,558,000	2.7%	1,237,250	1.6%
Taiwan	906,500	2.9%	1,069,000	1.8%	997,000	1.3%
China	805,500	2.6%	206,000	0.4%	530,500	0.7%
Hong Kong	834,500	2.7%	702,000	1.2%	1,145,500	1.5%
Other	5,987,500	19.3%	8,132,100	14.0%	6,722,324	8.8%
Total	30,979,000	100%	58,284,600	100%	75,994,580	100%

(Source: KOFIC, *2004 Report on South Korean Film Exports, 2005 Report on South Korean Film Exports*)

Kwon-taek's *Sopyonje* was released in a single theater to positive reviews,[5] after which one to three Korean movies, mostly art-house films, were released in Japan each year. Korean films began to show signs of growth, but such growth was an insignificant antecedent to the popularity that they enjoy today.

---

[5] Park H. et al. (2003), *Studies on the Expansion of Korean Film in the Asia-Pacific Region*, KOFIC, p. 43.

Table 2–22.　Share of Korean films among films released in japan

Year	Korean Films Released	Total Films Released	Share of Korean Films
2000	14	362	3.8%
2001	13	349	4.2%
2002	10	347	3.4%
2003	14	335	4.7%
2004	33	339	10.0%
2005	20	N/A	N/A

(Source: Reports from late February issue of *Kinema Junpo* annually, 2000–2004)

Phase 2 (2000–2003)
Interest in South Korean film spiked with the release of *Christmas in August* in June 1999. This led to the successive release of such films as *Shiri, Girls' Night Out, The Quiet Family, Whispering Corridors,* and *Joint Security Area,* all of which were well received. *Shiri*'s success was unprecedented, and its box office record remained unbroken until recently. Though limited to film aficionados, this new interest contributed to raising awareness of Korean cinema and proving its potential for success in Japan. Although most Korean films were released in a single theater by an independent distributor and targeted a small number of enthusiasts, this period revealed a market potential for Korean films and led to opportunities for further distribution.

Shiri cannot be omitted from any discussion of Korean films in Japan. As the first Korean film to arouse general interest, it fueled awareness that Korea produces not only art films but also commercial hits. Even before the *Hallyu* boom, *Shiri* raked in a record-breaking profit of ¥1.85 billion, remaining the top-grossing Korean film in Japan until recently, when *Windstruck* surpassed it. The success of *Shiri* is notable in that the box office record can be attributed to movie fans interested in the film itself rather than its stars. Factors contributing to *Shiri*'s achievement include its subject matter, as the Japanese take great interest in North-South Korea issues, the popularity of the action film genre, and the theme of tragic love, also popular in Japan. The film sold in Japan for a record price of $1.3 million, and attracted some 1.4 million viewers, grossing ¥1.85 billion at the box office.

On November 3, 2001, *Joint Security Area,* which also centers on the relationship between the two Koreas, was given wide release via the long-established Japanese theater chain Hibiya Scalaza. Following successfully in *Shiri*'s footsteps, *Joint Security Area* was the year's 25th highest-grossing foreign film in Japan, attracting some 900,000 viewers and earning approximately ¥1.2 billion. These box office successes led to the further release of Korean films like *Volcano High School, Friend,* and *Double Agent* by relatively large theater chains.

My Sassy Girl was initially released in 2 theaters in Tokyo on January 25, 2003, and eventually expanded to 70 theaters, attracting over 300,000 viewers and grossing ¥500 million at the box office. The accomplishment of *My Sassy*

Girl is noteworthy in that the film initially had a limited release that then grew. *My Sassy Girl* had a positive impact in increasing name recognition for its lead actress, Gianna Jun, which in turn became a factor in the success of *Windstruck*. *My Sassy Girl* also achieved respectable DVD sales.

My Sassy Girl was also notable because it elicited a positive response from not only movie buffs but also a young, general audience. This was an unprecedented triumph for a romantic comedy, a genre widely believed to be a difficult sell in overseas markets, and even more so for one lying outside the new wave of tearjerkers and horror movies popular in Japan.

While the films mentioned above are highly commercial, *Peppermint Candy* has strong artistic qualities. The film was released in Japan in 2000 using the typical channels of distributors specializing in Japanese art cinema. After clearly setting out the target audience, the film was promoted for about eight months, as art films are typically given lengthy promotion in Japan. Just 3 prints of the film circulated between 23 theaters across the country.[6]

Hallyu in the film sector from 2004 to today

Increased screening of South Korean films
Over 30 South Korean films were released in Japan in 2004, and over 20 in the first half of 2005. This increase reflects active sales and a positive atmosphere for Korean films, which led to a rush to release films that had been stockpiled in anticipation of a favorable climate. The jump also partly arose from the paid screening of 22 films at the *Hallyu Cinema Festival*.

South Korean films as a substitute for Hollywood
Some in Japan believe that from the point of view of large distributors, Korean cinema has content that can replace Hollywood films, which, though expensive to import, have been experiencing successive failures.[7] In fact, many Hollywood films were unable to turn a profit over the last two years. *Van Helsing* cost approximately ¥1.5 billion in licensing fees, and ¥1 to 1.5 billion to market, but the results were far from ideal. *The Aviator* likewise cost around ¥2.5 billion for purchase and promotion. Theaters were booked in blocks for nine weeks but the film failed to attract a sufficient audience. As similar situations continued, companies began replacing Hollywood films, often with Korean films, which are esteemed for their low cost compared to Hollywood films, high production values, and qualities that make them accessible to Japanese audiences. Recently, Korean films have increased in value, with the growing popularity of actors adding celebrity attraction as a further asset.

Changes in distribution
Traditionally, theaters have held sway over the Japanese film industry, and three major companies—Toho, Shochiku, and Toei—have dominated the market in an oligopoly of distribution and screening networks, although this structure has begun to change recently with the advent of multiplex theaters. Now that multiplexes account for over 60% of screens in Japan, screening opportunities have

---

[6] Lee E. et al. (2001), *Japanese Film Industry White Paper*, KOFIC, p. 169.
[7] Interview with Kakeo Yoshio.

opened up for films distributed by companies other than the three major players. This phenomenon works in favor of Korean films, most of which are imported through small- and medium-scale distributors.[8] In the case of small-scale distribution or screenings in a single theater, a company might start screenings in any theater available, even if the theater is not large or highly regarded,[9] since there are now increased opportunities to expand to multiplexes if a film becomes popular through word of mouth.

Case studies
After 2004, as the Korean Wave reached the film sector, the popularity of TV dramas had a key influence. *Winter Sonata* initiated *Hallyu* in Japan, and *My Sassy Girl* played a major role in changing the image of Korean cinema. As *Hallyu* became prominent in film, releases relied heavily on the draw of the cast, and the Korean Wave shifted its focus significantly from the film itself to its actors, who are now the crucial factor for success.

Only one South Korean film was released in Japan in 1996, but this number grew to 14 in 2000, 13 in 2001, 10 in 2002, and 14 in 2003. In 2004, a total of 33 South Korean films were released. The boost in sales resulted from the popularity of Korean TV dramas, which in turn increased awareness of Korean culture and celebrities. As demand for Korean films soared, companies rushed to distribute Korean films that they had already purchased. Of some 30 Korean films released in 2004, 10 were released in Tokyo in June and July. In just the first half of 2005, 20 Korean films were released.

Of the 12 films in Table 2–24, 6 were released successfully in or after 2004, when *Hallyu* became prominent in Japan. The data suggests that cast has a significant impact on box office success. With the exception of *Shiri*, released in 2000, and *Joint Security Area*, released in 2001, name recognition for the cast and directors of past hits were key marketing points, as with *My Sassy Girl* and *Windstruck*, both directed by Kwak Jae-young and featuring Gianna Jun. The success of *Windstruck* followed that of *My Sassy Girl*, which grossed ¥490 million, making it the 12th highest film on the list, just below *Silmido*.

Phone is exceptional. This horror film's use of the cell phone, familiar to the younger generation, is considered to have played a role in its success. Considering Japan's longstanding preference for the horror genre, the favorable reception of *Phone* is encouraging for Korean horror films.

A Moment to Remember appealed to Japanese tastes for melodrama. The movie's origin in a Japanese TV drama increased the film's accessibility to the local audience. Featuring actress Son Ye-jin from *April Snow*, *A Moment to Remember* became the highest-grossing Korean film in Japan despite the absence of a popular male *Hallyu* star. Its success suggests that while the spread of *Hallyu*

---

[8] Films may be roughly understood as "large-scale" if released in major theater chains (Toho, Toei, and Shochiku), "medium-scale" if screened at 50–100 theaters across the country, including the three major Tokyo theaters and multiplexes, and "small-scale" if screened in a single theatre. Recently, expansion to about 100 screens has become possible based on box office results. Several hits have appeared among medium-scale films distributed through small theater chains. Many changes are occurring in Japan's distribution system (Lee E., 2005).

[9] Films typically experience a long promotional period in Japan. Under the block booking system, theaters have a year's worth of movies lined up, but many recently released Korean films have not followed this practice (interview with Kakeo Yoshio).

Table 2–23. Korean films released in Japan in 2004 and in the first half of 2005

Title	Distributor	Release Date
If You Were Me	Kino Kinema	Jan. 15, 2005
Sympathy for Mr. Vengeance		Feb. 05, 2005
The President's Barber	New Select	Feb. 11, 2005
Romance of Their Own	Cine Qua Non	Mar. 19, 2005
Make It Big	IMX	Mar. 19, 2005
Bungee Jumping of Their Own	IMX	Mar. 19, 2005
Sword in the Moon	Fine Films	Mar. 19, 2005
Samaritan Girl	Happinet Pictures	Mar. 26, 2005
Spider Forest	Movie-Eye	Apr. 09, 2005
Please Teach Me English	Art Port	Apr. 16, 2005
Bunshinsaba	Buena Vista	Apr. 23, 2005
A Bittersweet Life	Pony Canyon, Nippon Herald	Apr. 23, 2005
Wonderful Days	Gainax	Apr. 23, 2005
The Scarlet Letter	Cine Qua Non	May 14, 2005
Three Extremes		May 14, 2005
My Brother	Universal Pictures Japan	May 28, 2005
Too Beautiful to Lie	Happinet Pictures	May 28, 2005
My Mother, the Mermaid	Presido	May 28, 2005
My Little Bride	SPO	June 18, 2005
Marathon	Cine Qua Non	July 02, 2005
Classic	Klock Worx Co., Media Suits	Jan. 24, 2004
Turning Gate	Bitters End	Jan. 31, 2004
Happy End	Gaga	Jan. 31, 2004
The Record	Bio-Tide	Jan. 31, 2004
Oasis	Cine Qua Non	Feb. 07, 2004
Cry Woman	Miracle Voice, Bitters End	Feb. 28, 2004
Bad Guy	SPO	Feb. 28, 2004
Memories of Murder	Cine Qua Non	Mar. 2004
Addiction	SPO	Apr. 24, 2004
Three	Kadokawa	Apr. 24, 2004
My Wife Is a Gangster	Shochiku, NAC	May 08, 2004
Untold Scandal	Cine Qua Non	May 22, 2004
Silmido	Toei	June 05, 2004
The Uninvited	Toshiba Entertainment	June 05, 2004
A Good Lawyer's Wife	Gaga	June 12, 2004

(Continued)

Table 2–23. *(Continued).*

Title	Distributor	Release Date
Take Care of My Cat	Pony Canyon	June 26, 2004
Taegukgi	UIP	June 26, 2004
Nightmare	Shochiku	July 03, 2004
Lovers' Concerto	Libero, Taki Corporation	July 17, 2004
A Tale of Two Sisters	Comstock	July 24, 2004
Wishing Stairs	Toshiba Entertainment	Aug. 07, 2004
Yesterday	Gaga	Sep. 04, 2004
The Scent of Love	Bitters End	Oct. 16, 2004
Spring, Summer, Fall, Winter... and Spring	SPO	2004
Over the Rainbow	Taki Corporation	Nov. 06, 2004
Oldboy	Toshiba Entertainment	Nov. 06, 2004
Tube	Shochiku	Nov. 06, 2004
Digital Short Films by Three Filmmakers 2004	Uplink	Nov. 20, 2004
Au Revoir, UFO	Taki Corporation	Nov. 27, 2004
Everybody Has Secrets	Toshiba Entertainment	Nov. 27, 2004
Windstruck	Warner Bros.	Dec. 11, 2004
Chihwaseon	Espace Sarou	Dec. 18, 2004

(Source: www.seochon.net)

and a handful of actors have helped Korean films enter Japan more broadly, content ultimately has a greater impact than cast.

Universal Pictures purchased *April Snow* in a pre-order deal for $8 million. This sale was sufficient to cover 90% of the film's production cost. The high distribution price was influenced heavily by Bae Yong-joon's name recognition, and was further aided by anticipation of another melodrama by the audience who appreciated Bae Yong-joon's charisma in *Winter Sonata.*[10]

Following the customary practice of long, meticulous promotion by Japanese distributors,[11] *April Snow* underwent a half-year marketing campaign, including a visit to Japan by Bae Yong-joon. On September 17, 2005, the film was released

---

[10] Interview with Son Min-kyung, Manager of Overseas Distribution, Show East Co.

[11] In Japan, much time is allocated to promotion, which is often detailed and extensive. Japanese companies frequently request preview (*seonje*) material, which is seldom the case in Korea. Hence, a simultaneous worldwide release entails significant challenges in scheduling and providing the material appropriate for the scale of the release. Even though pirated copies have little impact in Japan, unlike in other Asian markets, simultaneous release of a movie in Korea and Japan can be advantageous for promoting films featuring well-known actors. Nonetheless, Korean production companies can struggle with deadlines and preparing appropriate preview material while trying to complete the film for a simultaneous release.

Table 2–24.   Top 12 Korean films released in Japan by box office revenue

	Title	Release Year	Box Office Revenue in ¥100 Million	Distributor (Number of Screens)	Marketing Focus
1	A Moment to Remember	2005	30*	Gaga (308)	Genre; based on a Japanese TV drama
2	April Snow	2005	28*	UIP (434)	Bae Yong-joon
3	Windstruck	2003	21	Warner (320)	Genre; Kwak Jae-young, Gianna Jun
4	Shiri	2000	18.5	Cine Qua Non/ Toshiba (180)	Action
5	Taegukgi	2004	15	UIP (303)	Action blockbuster; Jang Dong-gun, Won Bin
6	Joint Security Area	2001	11.5	Cine Qua Non/ Toshiba (235)	North and South Korea; Action
7	Phone	2003	8.8	BV (288)	Horror
8	Untold Scandal	2004	8	Cine Qua Non (117)	Bae Yong-joon
9	Everybody Has Secrets	2004	7.5	UIP (160)	Lee Byung-hun, Choi Ji-woo
10	A Bittersweet Life	2005	6.5	Herald (120)	Action; Lee Byung-hun
11	Silmido	2004	5.5	Toei (228)	Action blockbuster; true story
12	My Sassy Girl	2003	4.9	Toshiba (85)	Genre; Kwak Jae-young, Gianna Jun

* Projected box office revenue; still screening at time of data collection.
(Source: Data from in-house research by Lee E. et al. (2005))

on 434 screens, the widest ever circulation of a Korean film in Japan. The film attracted 180,000 viewers in only 12 days, breaking the record for highest gross of a Korean film in such a period. *April Snow* is expected to top the box office record of *Windstruck*, with an anticipated profit of about ¥2.8 billion from theater distribution. *April Snow* was screened in theaters using 435 prints, 118 of which were dubbed.

Untold Scandal was released on 115 screens in May 2004, attracting 28,600 viewers on opening day. Over its first weekend, the film attracted an audience of around 47,000, bringing in ¥67 million at the box office. *Untold*

Scandal recorded a final gross revenue of approximately ¥900 million, a decent showing, but the general consensus is that the figure did not meet expectations, given local fan adoration of Bae Yong-joon. The result can be attributed to the assumption that middle-aged women who flocked to the theaters expecting Bae's image from *Winter Sonata* found the change unsettling, and that the costume genre was unable to evoke a strong response. This interpretation suggests that preserving the images of actors on whom *Hallyu* depends is crucial to continuing the Korean film boom. Simply featuring a popular actor does not guarantee success.[12]

Everybody Has Secrets starred Lee Byung-hun, another key *Hallyu* actor like Bae Yong-joon. In the first week after its release in December 2004, the film ranked #4 at the box office and earned approximately ¥100 million over its first weekend. In total, *Everybody Has Secrets* had an audience of about 700,000, grossing approximately ¥900 million. At the 2004 Tokyo International Film Festival, tickets sold out within some two minutes of going on sale. On an online auction site, tickets sold for as much as ¥200,000 (the original price tag was ¥1,500).[13] Tickets included the opportunity to see Lee Byung-hun and Choi Ji-woo, the lead actress of *Winter Sonata*, in person. This appearance attracted not only the general festival audience, but also many of the housewives and female fan groups who have been driving the *Hallyu* boom. In addition to films, Lee Byung-hun has been promoted in music videos, OSTs, and other positively received video clips.

Windstruck, distributed in Japan on a large scale (302 screens), became the highest-grossing Korean film to date.[14] Released on December 11, 2004, the movie was viewed by 166,083 people, earning ¥234.2 million. Over the six weeks it screened, the film grossed ¥1,825 million, just shy of ¥2 billion, and broke the box office record previously held by *Shiri*.[15] Factors that led to its success include the director Kwak Jae-yong, whose earlier film had confirmed his ability to create hits in Japan, and actress Gianna Jun, the lead in *My Sassy Girl*, whose audience returned as expected.[16] Notably, audiences for *Windstruck* were mainly composed of young people, especially couples in their teens and twenties, and did not include the older women who have been at the center of *Hallyu*. Although *Windstruck* features Jun, it lacks an established *Hallyu* actor popular in Japan, and therefore the fact that it surpassed *Shiri* is especially encouraging.

Taegukgi was also sold before completion of the film. It attracted its buyer for many reasons: it was directed by Kang Je-gyu immediately following *Shiri*; it features two of the "Four Heavenly Kings of Korea," as they are termed in Japan (Bae Yong-joon, Lee Byung-hun, Jang Dong-gun, and Won Bin); it deals with the conflict between the two Koreas, a topic of great interest in Japan; it has a tragic plot, to which many Japanese are partial; and conditions seemed favorable for its large-scale distribution in multiplex cinemas. The sale was concluded two years

[12] *Untold Scandal* was certainly a box office success, but heightened expectations for a film featuring Bae Yong-joon likely spurred understated assessments of its box office performance.
[13] Akiko Matsumaru, reporter for P3 Entertainment. October 14, 2004.
[14] A release on over 300 screens is very difficult to manage for an average-sized company.
[15] www.tojapan.co.kr.
[16] Akiko Matsumaru, reporter for P3 Entertainment. December 17, 2004.

before the film was completed, and *Taegukgi* became the first Korean movie sold before completion. Universal Pictures, who bought the rights, is a major distributor that deals mostly with films that are widely released, and considered the film's potential for broad appeal essential. *Taegukgi* was thus released in 295 theaters across Japan in 2004. In its first weekend, the film attracted 130,000 viewers and earned approximately ¥1.5 billion.

Silmido was handled by Toei, one of the three major distributors in Japan. Unlike most Korean films, typically released on a small scale and screened in smaller theaters, *Silmido* was released simultaneously on 228 screens across Japan.[17] Thanks to promotion by this major distributor and active support from a Korean counterpart, *Silmido* was in circulation from June 5 to July 9 in 2004 and recorded ¥550 million at the box office. It ranked #9 in gross earnings among South Korean films released in Japan,[18] an impressive showing for a movie without a *Hallyu* star as its lead. *Marathon* was released amidst this celebrity-centered environment. As it featured no star actor, speculation about how the film might fare was keen. Imported by Cine Qua Non and distributed by Shochiku, *Marathon* was released on 128 screens, grossing approximately ¥288 million. Although this figure cannot be considered poor, neither is it especially high, considering marketing costs. The film's lackluster reception appears to have resulted from insufficient time allocated to promotion and obstacles during the cast's publicity visits to Japan.

The box office success of select Korean films released in or after 2004 was made possible by changes in distribution. Instead of starting small and expanding screens gradually, more films are now released simultaneously in over 300 theaters across Japan. This shift in exhibition for Korean films has been made possible in part because major distributors have stepped in.[19]

C. Hong Kong

(pp. 52–60)

Characteristics

The Korean Wave in film has passed beyond the introduction phase in Hong Kong; Korean cinema already swept through the country in 2002 and 2003. However, it has not yet reached the established stage. Having gradually increased their presence since the mid-1990s, Korean films are being steadily introduced, and the number of films released in Hong Kong represents a sizeable market. While distribution fees are rising, box office hits have been rare, which has led to a slowdown in Korea's film exports to Hong Kong.

Despite the sensation caused by *Jewel in the Palace*, which recorded viewership rates of nearly 50%, Korea's exports to Hong Kong in key categories of *Hallyu*—film, television, and music—decreased 15.3% from the previous

---

[17] Compared to Hollywood films released on over 500 screens, this would be considered a medium-scale release.

[18] At the time of writing, the film was playing in select theaters. Akiko Matsumaru, reporter for P3 Entertainment. July 16, 2004.

[19] See interview with Kakeo Yoshio. Some films that fit this description include *Windstruck* (Warner Bros.), *Taegukgi* (UIP), and *Phone* (Buena Vista).

Table 2–25.   Korean films released in Hong Kong, 1996–2005

Year	Number of Films Released	Box Office Revenue (HK$)	Market Share
2005	10 (first half)		
2004	14	21,497,024	2.3%
2003	18	22,483,809	2.6%
2002	22	42,270,556	4.9%
2001	17	16,413,340	1.6%
2000	3	5,649,231	0.6%
1999	2	6,786,075	0.8%
1998	0	N/A	
1997	0	N/A	
1996	1	1,027,310	
Total	87	94,630,321	

(Source: System Administrator, Korean Movies (韓國映畫) website (http://www.krmdb.com))

year.[20] The response to Korean films and *Hallyu* in Hong Kong appears different from Japan and Southeast Asia. While *Hallyu* in the latter began with TV dramas and Korean Wave celebrities, and then spread to other *Hallyu* media, Korean dramas did not create a sensation in Hong Kong. Rather, the Korean Wave for film began in the mid-1990s, and surged a few years later with the releases of *Shiri* and *Christmas in August*. Korean films pioneered the Hong Kong market without a boost from other media. After establishing a presence in the market, they enjoyed an apparent boom with the success of *My Sassy Girl* in 2002. However, a downturn followed in 2003, and distributors began to approach Korean films with caution.

Korean films saw rapid growth in Hong Kong after the success of *Shiri* and *Christmas in August* in 1999. In 2001, 17 Korean films were released, grossing HK$16.4 million, a 1.6% share of the Hong Kong film market. In 2002, 22 Korean films were released, with a record-breaking market share of 4.9%, and box office revenue of HK$42.2 million. This high figure largely resulted from the success of *My Sassy Girl*, which set a milestone for Korean films, grossing over HK$10 million, and remains the best-selling Korean film in Hong Kong.

Korean films have been showing signs of exhausting the Hong Kong market. Many factors are involved in this, including a lack of circulation time in the market due to the excessive inflow of videos/DVDs as well as theater releases; a decrease in novelty value; insufficient promotional effort and strategy resulting from oversupply; distribution without consideration of quality or marketability; and recession in the Hong Kong domestic film industry.

---

[20] *Dong-A Ilbo*, June 4, 2005. http:// www.donga.com/fbin/output?sfrm=4&n=200506040080.

Development

1996: Introduction
South Korean films in Hong Kong were first introduced with *The Gingko Bed* in November 1996. However, the film did not attract significant attention, and no further Korean films were released in 1997 and 1998.

1999: Surge in release of South Korean films
In 1999, *Christmas in August* screened at the Hong Kong Arts Centre to a positive response. Edko released the film formally at a commercial theater, opening up opportunities for Korean films. The potential of South Korean films in Hong Kong was confirmed when *Shiri* earned HK$6 million.

2000–2002: Korean film box office success
Once Korean films' potential in the Hong Kong market had been successfully proven, releases soared. In 2001, 17 films in various genres, including horror, melodrama, and comedy were released. Edko's careful promotion efforts and dubbing by star actor Stephen Chow made *The Foul King* successful. Although comedies generally do not do well overseas, the film grossed HK$5.3 million. The melodrama *Il Mare* grossed HK$2 million, and the horror films *Nightmare* and *The Record* respectively grossed HK$1.5 million and HK$1.2 million. *Tell Me Something* earned over HK$5 million. Several films that attracted little attention in Korea were successful in Hong Kong, including *The Isle*, which had a HK$1 million box office take, and *La Belle*, which grossed HK$1.6 million. The unexpected success of *The Isle* indicates the diverse interests of the Hong Kong audience and the market potential of art films.

The sudden boom in Korean films in Hong Kong in 2001 was followed by the further release of 22 diverse films in 2002. *My Sassy Girl*, which grossed HK$10 million, became the biggest hit to date. *My Wife Is a Gangster* also fared exceptionally well, earning nearly HK$10 million. The film had wide appeal as the gangster genre is broadly popular in Hong Kong. *Three* and *The Way Home* were also successful, respectively grossing HK$7.4 million and HK$4 million. The market share of Korean films rose to 4.0% in 2002. However, comedies (*Hi! Dharma!*, *Just Do It!*, and *My Boss, My Hero*) and martial arts action movies (*Volcano High School* and *Warrior*) performed below expectations, presumably because of differing senses of humor, difficulties for comedies in overseas markets, and martial arts movies' lack of appeal to the Hong Kong audience, who are all too familiar with the genre. The political thrillers *Joint Security Area* and *Phantom: The Submarine* also had little success. While the combination of romance and action made *Shiri* popular, the psychological and lyrical narrative of *Joint Security Area* seems not to have resonated with the Hong Kong audience. Moreover, audience size there is greatly affected by pirated VCDs and DVDs, which are distributed immediately after theater and DVD release in Korea. Thus, many potential Hong Kong viewers have already seen a movie by the time it appears in theaters.

2003: Expansion of market base
In 2003, the growth of Korean films in Hong Kong became stunted. Distributors shifted from unconditional to more cautious purchases. The number of films

released dropped to 18, with a market share of only 2.6%. After 1999, demand for Korean products grew with recognition of their market potential, and their sales price naturally rose. However, in light of the increase in price and films released, box office hits were few. Nevertheless, Korean films have secured marketability in Hong Kong. Consistent demand, if not box office success, may be expected, as they have become familiar locally and established a firm base audience.

Melodramas were the most successful Korean films distributed in Hong Kong in 2003. *The Classic, Lover's Concerto*, and *Crazy First Love* brought in box office revenues of HK$5.4 million, HK$3.4 million, and HK$2.9 million, respectively. On the other hand, horror films *Phone, A Tale of Two Sisters*, and *The Uninvited* had low earnings despite success in Korea and high expectations for the genre. *Marrying the Mafia, Sex Is Zero*, and other comedies successful in Korea also did poorly in Hong Kong.

2004–2005: Bracing for a leap
In 2004 and 2005, a diverse selection of Korean films continued to be introduced in Hong Kong. With the exception of *Windstruck*, which grossed HK$8 million, numbers have not been promising. *Taegukgi* and *Silmido* performed below expectations, and most others earned less than HK$1 million.

Although this steady introduction of Korean films is positive, it will be difficult for Korean films to establish a stable long-term presence in Hong Kong if the recession lasts. New strategies and opportunities are urgent if Korean films are to make a leap in the Hong Kong market.

Windstruck was released on June 3, 2004, and screened until July 15. Grossing HK$8.02 million, the film placed 28th in the year's box office rankings. *Taegukgi* was shown from July 22 to August 18, earning HK$3 million in total and ranking 85th in 2004. *Untold Scandal*, ranked 111th, screened from March 25 to April 21, earning HK$1.47 million, while *Oldboy*, ranked 117th, screened from October 14 to December 1 and grossed HK$1.28 million. *Silmido*, ranked 197th, earned HK$93,000 in about two weeks, from September 2 to September 15. *Into the Mirror*, ranked 223rd, screened from May 13 to May 27 and grossed HK$23,000.

A Moment to Remember, a smash in Japan, was the biggest Korean hit in Hong Kong in 2005. Released in 27 theaters, the film grossed HK$3.01 million. *April Snow*, highly anticipated and distributed simultaneously in 8 Asian countries, was released in 27 theaters on September 15, 2005, and earned HK$1.82 million. *Sympathy for Lady Vengeance*, directed by Park Chan-wook, who rose to prominence after his award at the Cannes Film Festival for *Oldboy*, was released in Hong Kong along with *Mapado* on October 13. *Sympathy for Lady Vengeance* was released in 28 theaters, a record for a Korean film, and grossed HK$2.13 million.

D. China

(pp. 68–75)

The Korean Wave has truly progressed in China with respect to film. Although not enjoyed as widely as Korean TV dramas, it is difficult to find anyone between 20 and 40 years of age who has not been exposed to South Korean films. In addition

Table 2–26.   Korean films released in Hong Kong in 2004 and 2005

Title	Release Date	Revenue (HK$)	Distributor
H	Jan. 06, 2005	20,785	Intercontinental
Over the Rainbow	Jan. 06, 2005	57,025	Edko
Addicted	Jan. 02, 2005	27,824	Edko
Phone	Jan. 16, 2005	1,130,000[1]	
2009: Lost Memories	Jan. 24, 2005	13,340	EVA
My Brother	Apr. 15, 2005	258,739	Edko
3-Iron	May 05, 2005	79,477	Golden Scene
When I Turned Nine	May 05, 2005	136,336	Lark Films
Romance of Their Own	May 26, 2005	126,871	Edko
A Moment to Remember	June 02, 2005	3,016,924	Lark Films
Marathon	July 21, 2005	1,518,698	Golden Scene
Little Brother	N/A	Scheduled	
The Ghost	Sept. 01, 2005	1,076,022	Panasia
April Snow	Sept. 15, 2005	1,828,729	Golden Scene
Sympathy for Lady Vengeance	Oct. 13, 2005	2,133,668	Panorama
Crying Fist	Oct. 13, 2005	5,545	Universe
The Red Shoes	Oct. 13, 2005	682,344	Panasia
Innocent Steps	Nov. 10, 2005	1,762,286*	Edko
Mapado	Nov. 24, 2005	2,407,944*	Panasia
Everybody Has Secrets	Dec. 01, 2005	356,852*	Panasia
Memories of Murder	Mar. 4, 2004	587,001	Edko
Untold Scandal	Mar. 25, 2004	1,473,418	Edko
Into the Mirror	May 13, 2004	23,664	Lark Films
Samaritan Girl	May 13, 2004	126,627	Golden Scene
Windstruck	June 03, 2004	8,022,061	Edko
Taegukgi	July 22, 2004	3,005,952	Lark Films
Face	Aug. 26, 2004	782,306	Pan Asia
Silmido	Sept. 02, 2004	93,385	Universe
Three Extremes	Sept. 02, 2004	803,421	Ko Film
Oldboy	Oct. 01, 2004	1,282,042	Edko
My Little Bride	Nov. 04, 2004	2,294,039	Edko
Love So Divine	Nov. 03, 2004	1,968,414	Edko
Again	Dec. 02, 2004	1,034,694	Newport

(Source: Ryan Lo and Gary Mak (Managers, Edko Cinematheque))
Note: All figures are as of December 15, 2005. Revenue for films still playing in theaters is marked with an asterisk (*).
[1] Revenue collected in the first four days of release only.

Table 2–27.   Introduction of South Korean films in China

Year	1998	2002	2003	2004	2005
Theater	Release of films featuring TV drama stars		Nationwide release	• Release through revenue-sharing quota slot	• Lull
DVD	Popular in DVD black market				
Major Films	*Marriage Story, Tie a Yellow Ribbon*	*My Sassy Girl*	*Warrior*	*The Classic, Windstruck*	*April Snow*

to broad viewership, they are well regarded. Many Chinese viewers admit that Korean films have changed their perceptions of Korea, and Koreans working in China's cultural industries often observe this point to be true, which suggests that Chinese consumption of Korean films has reached a stable level. Among imported films, Korean films are second only to those from the US. Distribution of Korean films is, in fact, more active in China than in any other country.

One problem, however, is that the Korean Wave of film in China is largely propagated in the illegal DVD market (盗版). Therefore, both theater releases and DVD markets should be taken into account. China imposes a strict import quota of around 50 foreign films a year, making official theater release extremely difficult. Because of the limited number of theater releases and expensive tickets, pirated DVDs, cheap and diverse, have become the predominant means of movie consumption.

Recently, several Korean films have been released in theaters, attracting attention, but none has achieved a significant result. Ultimately, the Korean Wave for film in China is limited to the illegal DVD market.

Theater releases[21]

Films featuring TV drama stars
Korean films have a relatively short history in China. The first noteworthy release was *Marriage Story*, which screened in and around Shanghai in 1998. Its star, Choi Min-soo, had played Daebal in the TV drama *What Is Love?*, which enjoyed great popularity in China in 1997. Choi's role was an important factor in the import and release of *Marriage Story*. The introduction of Korean films came on the heels of popular TV dramas. Most Korean films released in China in the late 1990s featured drama stars. *Tie a Yellow Ribbon* and *First Kiss* starred Ahn Jae-wook, who rose to fame as one of the first *Hallyu* celebrities through his role in *Star in My Heart*. Jang Dong-gun and Kim Hee-sun, who received attention as two of the most attractive stars from South Korea, played the leads in *Repechage*.

---

[21] Park H. et al. (2003), pp. 107–112, is the main reference for sections i, ii, and iii. The same reference was used for the revenue earned by each film and the distribution process.

Co-productions: Bichunmoo and Warrior

The 2000s marked the beginning of Korean and Chinese co-productions. *Bichunmoo*, starring Kim Hee-sun, was released on a small scale in the Shanghai area, with reasonable box office earnings of RMB 1.6 million. *Bichunmoo* was heralded as a "joint production" (合拍) between a Korean company and Shanghai Film Studio, which invested in the film by offering equipment support in exchange for Chinese distribution rights. As joint productions are treated as domestic features, their release is not affected by the import quota.

Warrior was a co-production between a Korean company and Beijing Film Studio, which took the form of an "assisted production" (協拍), wherein Beijing Film Studio provided labor for location shooting for a fee, but did not gain rights to the final product. Still, Chinese participation simplified the import and release of the film.

Warrior was released on January 10, 2003, on 160 screens in 6 major cities around China, grossing RMB 7.24 million. Although *Warrior* was not allotted a revenue-sharing quota slot, it has significance as the first nationwide release of a Korean film. Unfortunately, the release was not well timed, following on the heels of *Hero*, an unprecedented box office hit. Moreover, the Chinese release of *Warrior* came 16 months after the film's release in Korea in September 2001. Since pirated copies had already circulated, *Warrior* was not perceived as a new release.

Revenue-sharing: The Classic

There are two types of quota slots for films imported by China: revenue-sharing (*bunjangje*) and flat-fee (*maedanje*). Revenue-sharing slots are set at 20 films per year, most of which are Hollywood blockbusters, widely released and given extensive promotion. Lump-sum license fees are paid to the distributor of flat-fee films at the time of purchase. Available slots for flat-fee films are roughly half of those produced domestically in the previous year. Most flat-fee films have relatively low budgets and are released on a small scale.

The Classic, the first South Korean film allotted a revenue-sharing slot, was released in six major cities around China on September 6, 2003. The film was imported through Edko, its Hong Kong distributor. Leading cast members, including Jo Seung-woo and Son Ye-jin, visited China to promote the film, but its gross was only RMB 3 million, lowest among the 20 foreign films allotted revenue-sharing quota slots in 2003.[22]

Films starring Hallyu Stars: Windstruck and April Snow

The years 2004 and 2005 saw several sizeable releases of Korean films featuring *Hallyu* stars popular in China and other Asian countries. *Windstruck* was released on June 5, 2004, in over 30 cities and featured Gianna Jun, who emerged as a star in China through her role in *My Sassy Girl*. The film screened for about two weeks,[23] and earned RMB 8 million at the box office. In 2005, *April Snow*, starring Bae Yong-joon, was released, grossing roughly RMB 5 million.

---

[22] The highest-grossing film among those allotted revenue-sharing quota slots in 2003 was *Harry Potter and the Chamber of Secrets*, which earned RMB 52 million. Chinese Film News, Dec. 4, 2003. Cited from Park H. et al. (2003).

[23] Research by Lee Y., Chinese Office of KOFIC.

Expectations were high for films featuring *Hallyu* stars, but the less than satisfactory results suggest that a celebrity or two is not enough to attract a large audience. In May 2005, *The Romantic President* and *Tube* screened for about a week each to box office revenues of less than RMB 1 million. *Crying Fist*, released in July of 2005, grossed roughly RMB 1 million.

Factors in poor theater earnings
No more than two or three South Korean films are released in Chinese theaters each year, and only one might be released on a large scale. No Korean film has been allotted a revenue-sharing quota slot since *The Classic*. Korean films are only making their first steps into the market, thus there exists no true Korean Wave of film in China.

Several factors explain this poor showing. Above all, Korean films have not been proactively imported. Many obstacles to import exist in China beside quotas. Because China lacks a rating system, only films appropriate for all ages can be imported. Few Korean films meet this criterion. In addition, films of a political nature, those dealing with relations between the two Koreas, and gangster movies do not meet censorship criteria. Due to a downturn in China's theater market, films approved for revenue-sharing slots tend to be very commercial, high-grossing films featuring A-list stars. However, such films produced in Korea mostly fail to meet the aforementioned censorship criteria.

Another factor is that import sales are not usually arranged directly between Korea and China. In many cases, Korean companies include the rights to distribute a film in China when they make deals with companies in Hong Kong or Singapore. Indirect import leads to a late release, after much of the potential audience has already viewed the movie on pirated DVDs. This causes poor box office performance, which in turn has a negative impact on other imports, creating a vicious cycle.

The biggest problem, however, is China's outmoded film import and release systems. Korean films will have great potential in the market if China enforces a rating system, relaxes censorship, lowers ticket prices, and roots out pirated copies.

Korean films in the illegal DVD market
A boom for Korean films in China began with *My Sassy Girl*. The film appealed to the Chinese audience, and pirated DVDs appeared in early 2002. Roughly 10 million copies were sold, though accurate statistics are unavailable. Factors in the popularity of *My Sassy Girl* included its urban love story, uncommon in Chinese films; the fresh and compelling lead characters; and the appealing soundtrack and setting.

At present, the number of Korean films that do not appear in China's illegal DVD market is negligible, even counting short films. In the past, many pirated DVDs originated from poor quality camcorder footage shot in theaters. Of late, however, most are transferred directly from Korean DVDs. Illegal but high-quality copies of *My Wife Is a Gangster 2* were sold even before the official DVD release in Korea, after a master copy was presumably stolen and smuggled into China.

In 2005, director Kang Je-kyu was invited to a Korean film festival in Beijing. Kang expressed surprise that many Chinese knew of him even though his work had never been released in China. Numerous audience members had seen his films *Shiri* and *Taegukgi* on illegal DVDs. Likewise, many Korean dramas that have not been aired have also become popular through pirated DVDs. *Hallyu* arose as Korean media products began to dominate China's illegal DVD market and made a deep impression on the public.

E. Taiwan

Development

(pp. 87–97)

Introductory phase: Whispering Corridors (1999)
Few South Korean films were screened in Taiwan until the late 1990s, when Korean films began to attract attention in international markets and Korean dramas became popular throughout Asia. In 1998, the first Korean film of the decade was released in Taiwan with *Their Last Love Affair*, which earned a mere NTD 58,000 in Taipei. In 1999, five Korean films were released, including *Whispering Corridors* and *Shiri*. The box office earnings of *Shiri* fell far below expectations, as it grossed only around NTD 4.8 million in Taipei.[24]

Whispering Corridors exemplifies the context of opportunities and demand that led to the import and release of Korean films in Taiwan, where Japanese content continues to be very influential. After the horror film *Ring* grew popular in 1998, sparking a Japanese film boom, 15 further films from Japan were released that year, and 21 in 1999. Key factors that led to the release of *Whispering Corridors* included its low cost compared to Japanese films, its quality, and the assumption that a horror film with a school setting could take advantage of existing fandom for Japanese cinema and attract attention.[25] The financial crisis in Asia in 1997 and the great earthquake in Taiwan in 1999 took a toll on Taiwan's cultural industry. Taiwan then began to take interest in Korean media products, which were less expensive than those from Japan.

Influence of drama stars: Friend (2001) and Joint Security Area (2002)
Korean films initially had difficulty getting a foot in the door of the Taiwanese film industry and met with little success. No Korean film was released in 2000. From 2000, however, *Fireworks* and other Korean dramas became extremely popular, leading to the import of Korean films featuring drama stars. The import of *Friend* despite its high price was only possible because lead Jang Dong-gun had risen in popularity through his roles in *Model* and other dramas. *Friend* was imported by a major Taiwanese distributor, Spring International, and released in Warner Village Cinemas, the largest chain in Taiwan, but the film ended up failing at the box office. *Joint Security Area*'s female lead, Lee Young-ae, the most popular Korean actress in Taiwan, played a key role in the film's release in early 2002. The result, however, fell far short of expectations. Many more Korean

---

[24] Park H. et al. (2001), *Chinese Film Industry White Paper I*, KOFIC, p. 324.
[25] Due to the Taiwanese audience's fondness for horror, Korean horror films continue to see steady release. While Hollywood films occupy the majority of the Taiwanese market, Asian horror films tend to have greater box office success.

films imported with similarly high hopes because of their featured stars failed in succession.[26]

In Korea, many actors star in both TV dramas and films. Although Asian celebrities are thought to have a relatively strong impact throughout the region, celebrities other than Hollywood stars, or at least Korean stars, seem to have little impact at the box office in Taiwan.

Also notable is that films dealing with relations between North and South Korea, such as *Shiri, Joint Security Area, Silmido,* and *Taegukgi,* have not been successful. One might expect that cross-Strait tensions would give such films appeal in Taiwan, but the Taiwanese appear to be generally individualistic and indifferent to the political history of other nations. These films do not attract Taiwanese viewers, who are not as sensitive to North Korean threats as the Japanese audience.

Box office hits: My Sassy Girl and The Way Home (2002)
The Taiwanese market was long cool toward Korean films. In 2002, however, two Korean films reaped NTD 10 million in box office revenue for the first time. These films, *The Way Home* and *My Sassy Girl,* struck a chord with the Taiwanese audience, even though they are neither blockbusters, nor uniquely Korean, nor horror films, which are generally popular, nor films that starred well-known actors at the time.

That the film's importer, Group Power Workshop (群體), convinced Gianna Jun and Cha Tae-hyun to visit Taiwan likely played a role in the success of *My Sassy Girl,* but word of mouth is thought to have been decisive. The film had already been successful in Hong Kong and enjoyed tremendous popularity when pirated DVDs of the film reached mainland China. Many Taiwanese had presumably watched illegal copies of the film. Still, a spate of positive reviews appeared online, attracting many to the theater even if they had already seen the movie.[27]

Various factors led to the Taiwanese success of *My Sassy Girl.*[28] First of all, the film has a fresh plot uncommon in Hollywood or Taiwanese films, and while it does not contain the explicit content of Hollywood, its romantic aspects offer sentiments familiar to audiences across Asia. The contrast between the "sassy" female lead and her mild male counterpart is comical at first, but the revelation of the scars she carries because of her innocent love eventually moves the audience. The attractive leads, beautiful images, and excellent soundtrack combined to appeal to the Taiwanese audience.

Spring International, the importer of *The Way Home,* chose a low-price policy, dropping tickets from the usual ₩7,000–8,000 to about ₩5,000, and its marketing strategies, which included premier events for teachers, were quite successful. This universal tale of love between a grandmother and grandson appealed

---

[26] A case in point is the poor performance of *Oh! Happy Day* in 2003. This film was released following the popularity of the drama *Successful Story of a Bright Girl.*

[27] Park H. et al. (2003), p. 171.

[28] *My Sassy Girl* was adored in China, Hong Kong, Thailand, Japan, and much of Asia. If *Christmas in August* laid the groundwork for a Korean Wave in the film sector, *Shiri* announced its real emergence. *My Sassy Girl* then demonstrated the true potential of Korean films.

to Taiwanese audiences.[29] The success of *My Sassy Girl* and *The Way Home* suggest that what the Taiwanese expect from and are moved by in Korean films are lyricism and a certain uniqueness.

Horror films: A Tale of Two Sisters and Phone (2003)
In contrast to 2002, the two Korean movies that performed well at the box office in Taiwan in 2003 were horror films. *A Tale of Two Sisters* was distributed by FOX, a US direct distributor, and released in 11 theaters, a relatively large-scale release for a non-Hollywood film. The film grossed over NTD 10 million. *Phone*, distributed by Buena Vista, enjoyed a relatively high box office gross of NTD 7.89 million. In 2004, Buena Vista distributed *Bunshinsaba*, which broke the record for the highest-grossing Korean film in Taiwan.

Although these figures suggest new possibilities for Korean horror films, they reflect a commercial strategy by a US company to distribute non-Hollywood horror films to capitalize on Taiwanese interest. Such success may therefore be only temporary. In other words, distributor strategy may have played the pivotal role, not the films themselves.

Status of Korean films

Since Taiwan began importing Korean films, 2 to 3 titles had been introduced each year on average, but in 2004, 28 South Korean films were released in Taiwan, showing an explosive threefold increase over the previous year. In terms of total films released, Korea is now the second largest source after the US. However, the details behind this figure render it less impressive.

Silmido and *Taegukgi*, smash hits in Korea, did poorly in Taiwan. *Windstruck* and *Untold Scandal*, featuring popular stars, fared better than other Korean films, but still fell below expectations. Except for *Spring, Summer, Fall, Winter... and Spring*, directed by Kim Ki-duk, all films that have grossed over NTD 1 million, including *Acacia, Into the Mirror, Face*, and *The Ghost*, are of the horror genre.

As of September, 13 Korean films had been released in Taiwan, but other than *Oldboy*, which grossed NTD 10 million, none were hits. Even after Lee Byung-hun's promotional visit, *A Bittersweet Life* grossed a mere NTD 70,000. *My Brother* and *Everybody Has Secrets* earned NTD 300,000 and NTD 270,000, respectively. *April Snow* enjoyed higher revenue than most in its opening week at NTD 1.1 million,[30] but its total also fell below expectations. Several horror films, including *The Red Shoes* and *The Doll Master*, as well as films in other genres, such as *A Family*, were released in 2005. Director Kim Ki-duk's *3-Iron* achieved unusually high earnings after star Lee Seung-yeon's controversial photo shoot, which drew on comfort women imagery, and a prize at the Venice International Film Festival attracted interest to the film.

Japan ranked fourth in films released in 2004 with 20, just below France in the Taiwanese film market. Japanese films also performed much more impressively than those from Korea. The highest-grossing Japanese film, *Quill*, recorded

---

[29] Park H. et al. (2003), pp. 171–172.
[30] Report by Lim Jung-gui, Taiwan correspondent, Asia Cultural Exchange Foundation

Table 2-28.   Korean films released in Taiwan, 1998–2002 (Taipei)[1]

Year	English Title	Local Title	Release Date	Box Office Revenue (NTD)	Distributor
1998	*Their Last Love Affair*	最後一次偷情	06.13	58,640	Crown Films (向洋)
1999	*Whispering Corridors*	死亡教室	09.17	385,185	Spring International (春暉)
	Shiri	魚	11.12	4,387,890	Long Shong Pictures (龍祥)
	If the Sun Rises in the West	如果太陽從西邊出來	11.12	60,990	Spring International
	Soul Guardians	退魔錄	11.20	945,000	Scholar Films (學者)
	An Affair	情事	12.11	60,350	Spring International
Total	5			5,839,415	
2000	None				
2001	*Nightmare*	靈魘	05.05	152,040	Ying Tai Films (英太)
	Friend	朋友	10.06	944,460	Spring International
	Il Mare	觸不到的戀人	11.03	487,940	Spring International
Total	3			1,584,440	
2002	*Tell Me Something*	殘酷線索	01.04	497,970	Mata Films (邁拓)
	My Sassy Girl	我的野蠻女友	06.21	11,012,890	Group Power Workshop (群體)
	Joint Security Area	共同警戒區	07.05	772,125	Distributor
	Whispering Corridors (re-release)	死亡教室	07.19	21,430	Spring International
	An Affair (re-release)	情事	08.17	12,000	Spring International
	My Wife Is a Gangster	我的老婆是老大	08.30	1,576,830	Long Shong Pictures
	The Way Home	有你真好	10.04	10,012,100	Spring International
	Hi! Dharma!	我的朋友好野蠻	10.10	94,380	Long Shong Pictures
Total	8 (including two re-releases)			23,999,725	

(Source: Chinese Taipei Film Archive (1999 & 2000), *Taiwan Cinema Yearbook*)
[1] Generally speaking, Taipei accounts for about 70% of all box office revenue in Taiwan. In the case of Korean and other Asian films, the figure is closer to 80%.

Table 2-29.   Korean films released in Taiwan in 2003 (Taipei)

English Title	Local Title	Release Date	Box Office Revenue (NTD)	Distributor
Phone	鬼鈴	05.02	8,016,335	Buena Vista
Black Honeymoon	身魂旅行	06.07	49,140	Sanben (三本)
White Valentine	白鴿情書	06.07	31,800	Sanben
Lovers' Concerto	向左愛向右愛	06.20	833,790	Group Power Workshop (群體)
Volcano High School	火山高校	08.01	34,190	CMC (中藝)
Oh! Happy Day	張耐立OH! HAPPY DAY	08.04	4,371,350	Mata Films (邁拓)
A Tale of Two Sisters	鬼魅	08.15	11,241,570	FOX
Addicted	中毒	08.16	91,720	Full Jong Int. (福鐘)
Teacher Kim Bong-du	老師你好	09.19	1,017,685	Yin Hui (銀暉)
Jail Breakers	逃回藍獄	10.24	120,025	Peng Chi (朋馳)
Sex Is Zero	色卽是空	10.31	1,033,075	Long Shong Pictures (龍祥)
H	分屍	10.31	140,740	Group Power Workshop
Crazy First Love	我的野蠻初戀	10.31	873,730	Yin Hui
Whispering Corridors 3: Wishing Stairs	斷魂梯	11.14	3,272,845	Hong Jun
The Uninvited	四人餐桌	12.26	509,120	Group Power Workshop
Total	15		31,637,115	

(Source: Government Information Office, *2004 Cinema Yearbook*, pp. 84–88)

Table 2–30. Korean films released in Taiwan in 2004 (Taipei)

English Title	Local Title	Release Date	Box Office Revenue (NTD)	Distributor
Marrying the Mafia	黑道千金逼我嫁	02.06	140,920	Peng Chi (朋馳)
The Romantic President	總統要出嫁	02.13	421,100	Long Shong Pictures (龍祥)
Acacia	千年鬼寶寶	02.27	2,010,635	Scholar Films (學者)
Wonderful Days	晴空戰士	02.27	38,200	CMC (中藝)
2009: Lost Memories	決戰異次元	03.05	60,755	Full Jong Int. (福鐘)
Untold Scandal	醜聞	03.06	4,364,335	Da Fa (大發)
The Classic	緣起不滅	03.19	295,720	Group Power Workshop (群體)
Silmido	實尾島風雲	04.02	1,448,560	Scholar Films
Warrior	武士	04.02	457,440	Long Shong Pictures
My Wife Is a Gangster 2	我的老婆是老大2	04.09	392,405	Long Shong Pictures
Desire	慾望男情	04.24	143,360	Hua Zhan (華展)
Into the Mirror	鬼鏡	04.30	2,745,910	Long Shong Pictures
The Legend of Evil Lake	妖魅湖	04.30	231,285	Scholar Films
Whispering Corridors 2: Memento Mori	鬼戀人	05.22	46,020	Qian Jing (前景)
Spring, Summer, Fall, Winter... and Spring	春去春又來	05.28	1,185,720	Hua Zhan
Taegukgi	太極旗生死兄弟	07.09	3,169,235	Long Shong Pictures
Ardor	密愛	07.23	475,480	Hua Zhan

(Continued)

Table 2–30. (*Continued*).

English Title	Local Title	Release Date	Box Office Revenue (NTD)	Distributor
100 Days with Mr. Arrogant	綁架愛情100天	08.06	110,630	Hong Jun (砬書)
Windstruck	我的野蠻女友2蠻風再現	08.27	3,278,555	Long Shong Pictures
Face	鬼變臉	08.27	1,858,110	Hong Jun
Arahan	阿羅漢	09.10	69,775	Hong Jun
Bunshinsaba	筆仙	09.10	7,897,900	Buena Vista
Samaritan Girl	援交天使	09.24	573,970	Hua Zhan
My Little Bride	幼齒老婆Oh My God!	10.08	225,665	Long Shong Pictures
The Ghost	靈	11.12	1,391,770	Long Shong Pictures
The Coast Guard	海岸線	11.26	154,480	Hua Zhan
Fighter in the Wind	追風武士	12.03	77,410	Hong Jun
Oseam	五歲的心願	12.24	237,180	Swallow Wings Films (海釀)
Total	28		33,502,525	

(Source: 2004 Film Market Review (電影市場總覽), http://taiwancinema.com/ct.asp?xItem = 52457&ctNode = 168)

Table 2–31.   Changes in the share of Korean films in the Taiwanese market

Year	Total Box Office Revenue (NTD)	Box Office Revenue of Korean Films (NTD)	Market Share
2004	2,585,401,980	33,502,525	1.30%
2003	2,002,908,513	31,637,115	1.58%
2002	2,391,532,905	23,999,725	1.00%
2001	2,284,737,140	1,584,440	0.07%

Source: 2004 Film Market Review (電影市場總覽), http://taiwancinema.com/
ct.asp?xItem = 52457&ctNode = 168.

Table 2–32.   Number of films released, box office revenue, and share of
Taiwanese market by country

Country	Number of Films	Share	Box Office Revenue (NTD)	Share
US	120	52.63%	2,069,559,230	80.04%
South Korea	28	12.28%	33,502,525	1.29%
France	21	9.21%	40,595,895	1.57%
Japan	18	7.89%	88,704,765	3.43%
Germany	5	2.19%	50,908,665	1.96%
Italy	4	1.75%	157,880	0.00%
UK	3	1.31%	917,290	0.03%
Sweden	2	0.87%	1,632,955	0.06%
India	1	0.43%	979,925	0.04%

revenue of NTD 40.66 million, fourth among films released in Taiwan for the
year. The total box office revenue of Japanese films was NTD 89.29 million, 2.7
times higher than the NTD 33.5 million earned by Korean films.

These financial results are related to signs detected from around 2003 of an
incipient cult following for Korean films. Korean films appear to be sought by
a small audience that wants something different from Hollywood films, rather
than by a wide spectrum of viewers. The possibility of Korean blockbusters
prospering is faint at present, considering that they have to compete with Hollywood films.

F.   Thailand

(pp. 106–111)

Development

As in most destinations, the popularity of Korean dramas sparked *Hallyu* in Thailand. Film, however, is not faring as well. Distribution of Korean films began
in earnest around 2000, and Thai awareness of Korean cinema is substantial.

Although approximately 40% of Bangkok's population has been exposed to Korean films, reception has experienced a downturn since 2004.[31]

In Thailand, Hollywood and Thai films form the mainstream. Among films from elsewhere in Asia, Hong Kong action movies have enjoyed the steadiest audience. After the Hong Kong industry slumped in the mid-1990s, however, its films did not meet with strong response in Thailand, except for those starring Jackie Chan, and Korean films began to take their place. Korean films entered the Thai market in a concerted way from the early 2000s. A total of 5 Korean titles were released in 2001, followed by 18 in 2002, 23 in 2003, and 25 in 2004, although these figures refer only to theatrical releases. Including titles distributed directly on video, 20 were released in 2001, 52 in 2002, and 37 in 2003. Growing demand for Korean films has caused the average price tag of distribution rights to jump from roughly $250,000 in 2002 to $920,000 in 2003. In 2004, the figure increased 22% from 2003.

Initially, various Korean films, including *My Sassy Girl, Volcano High School, The Classic, My Tutor Friend,* and *A Tale of Two Sisters* were exported to Thailand for between $30,000 and $70,000. Export prices have gradually risen over the years. *Arahan* sold for $100,000, *Volcano High School* for THB 10 million, *A Tale of Two Sisters* for THB 11 million, and *Windstruck* for THB 15 million.[32] The rise in the price of film rights is making Thai companies increasingly careful when purchasing Korean films, because of the growing burden of securing a profit after release, and several cases of loss.

While the largest Hollywood films are released in 100–200 theaters, Korean films get medium-scale exposure or less, being released in around 40 theaters. They generally attract young, urban audiences who appreciate the films' entertainment value.

My Sassy Girl set a box office record for Korean films, grossing THB 16–18 million, approximately $500,000. Considering that no other Korean film has yet surpassed this figure, local distributors appear to carry a heavy burden, as they often spend around THB 10 million on film rights and promotion.[33]

Case studies

A variety of factors account for the appeal of Korean films in Thailand. First, the Thai audience, also in the Asian cultural sphere, has no aversion to Korean content. Second, Korean films have replaced highly commercial Hong Kong films, but do not lag behind them or the films of any country in terms of commercial (entertainment) value. Third, Korean actors are attractive and act well. Finally, Korean films generally have high production values and are known for the quality of their technical aspects and compelling screenplays.

---

[31] Interview with Nantakwang Sirasunton. Recently, few Korean films have had box office success, and their excessive import is making it difficult to stagger releases appropriately. The influence of *Hallyu* has caused the price of Korean film rights to skyrocket, and Thai distributors are slowing their purchases.

[32] Interview with Anont Asvanund.

[33] Even for Sahamonkol, a company with stable funding, in order for a Korean film to make a profit in the Thai market distribution rights and promotion costs together should not exceed more than $50,000 (interview with Gilbert Lim).

Table 2–33. Distribution contracts for Korean films in
Thailand, 2001–2005

Year	Number of Contracts	Amount ($)
2005	48	1,520,000
2004	56	1,771,500
2003	37	1,448,500
2002	52	722,500
2001	20	249,000

(Sources: Park H. et al. (2003), p. 187; KOFIC, *2005 South Korean Film
Exports*)

Interestingly, the Korean film genre most popular among the Thai audience
is melodrama, not action, comedy, or horror. Melodramas produced in Thailand
are few and generally of lesser quality. Therefore, the Thai audience has readily
accepted Korea's stylish, emotional melodramas. Moreover, Korean melodramas
have been able to target a niche market because they convey Asian sentiments not
reproduced by Hollywood.

Melodramas: Il Mare and My Sassy Girl
Released in October 2001, *Il Mare* led to the subsequent box office success of
Korean films. After *Il Mare* aroused Thai interest in Korean melodramas, *One Fine
Spring Day* and *Wanee & Junah* were released. *One Fine Spring Day* screened in
only one theater, but was well received considering the limited scale.[34]

My Sassy Girl, which proved the market potential of Korean films throughout Asia and sparked their boom, has been the most successful Korean film in
Thailand. Released there in May 2002 in 34 theaters, it earned a profit of approximately $500,000. As elsewhere in Asia, *My Sassy Girl* paved the way for other
films. Gianna Jun, who first achieved recognition in Thailand through *Il Mare*,
became highly recognized after *My Sassy Girl,* which was also a video market
smash. Some 5,000 DVDs were sold, along with 19,000 VCDs, which accounted
for 40% of the film's revenue. *My Sassy Girl* did not incur high promotional costs,
even though its marketing strategies, including the targeting of urban students,[35]
were vital to its success.

Action films: Volcano High School and My Wife Is a Gangster
The action film *Volcano High School* was released in August 2002 to high expectations. It grossed $200,000 at the box office and slightly more in video and VCD
sales. The audience consisted mainly of young people. Active promotion, including TV commercials, bolstered the film, effectively showcasing its unique plot
and cinematography.

---

[34] Park H. et al. (2003), p. 192.
[35] Ibid., p. 193. Most South Korean films, especially romantic comedies, employ a word-of-mouth
marketing strategy for a target audience. *My Sassy Girl* utilized such a strategy as well as advertising
through media such as television and radio. The film's promotional strategies included playing the
soundtrack frequently on radio programs.

My Wife Is a Gangster was released on a relatively large scale, in over 20 theaters, in September 2002. Success was anticipated for the film, which blends comedy and action, but results fell below expectations.

Horror films: A Tale of Two Sisters
A Tale of Two Sisters was released on 25 screens in August 2002. Because horror films typically do well in Thailand, success was anticipated, but results did not meet expectations here either. The generally accepted explanation is that the audience sought the light entertainment of a conventional ghost film, but the plot was based on a classic Korean tale and was inaccessible to many in the Thai audience. The relatively complex narrative is also assumed to have been a stumbling block.

Political thrillers: Shiri, Joint Security Area, and Double Agent
Shiri, which was successful in Japan and Hong Kong, the two major Asian film markets, did not meet with noteworthy response in Thailand. General audiences were not familiar with the political and historical backdrop of the film, which hindered appreciation. *Joint Security Area* is thought to have done poorly for the same reason. *Double Agent* was released directly on video to ease the burden of promotion necessary for a theatrical run.[36] Thai audiences also favor comedy. Bolstered by the popularity of melodramas, Korean film *The Classic* and the Thai remake of *The Letter* were well received.

G. Vietnam

(pp. 120–123)
Boosted by the popularity of dramas, many Korean films have been introduced in Vietnam. Notable films released in the 2000s include *The Letter, Love Wind Love Song,* and *Tie a Yellow Ribbon.* Since 2001, around 10 titles have been imported annually. *My Sassy Girl* was sold for approximately $10,000, a much higher price than films previously sold to Vietnam. In 2002, nine titles were imported for a total of around $85,000, showing a great increase in the average price of distribution rights over 2001, when nine films totaled $56,000. *Tie a Yellow Ribbon* met with significant success, attracting an audience of 100,000. Korea's most successful film, *My Sassy Girl,* set a record with 150,000 viewers.[37]

As films in Vietnam are generally consumed as entertainment, a film's fundamental role is to provide pleasure. Vietnam does not have a rating system, so films must be appropriate for all ages. Films with violent or explicit content or that are too political or frightening cannot enter the Vietnamese market. The local audience prefers family-oriented films that appeal to all ages, such as romantic comedies and genres that invite laughter and tears while providing enjoyment.[38] Rampant piracy of material and underdeveloped technology hinder formation of

---

[36] Interview with Songpol Wingkon, Nontanund Entertainment Co., Ltd.
[37] Lee H. (2002), p. 96.
[38] As evidence of such tastes, *My Little Bride* was found to be the most loved Korean film in Vietnam. See Asia Cultural Exchange Foundation, "Research on Measures to Boost *Hallyu* through Analysis of the Current Status of *Hallyu*," Feb. 22, 2005.

Table 2–34.   Distribution contracts for Korean films in
Vietnam, 2001–2005

Year	Number of Films	Amount ($)
2005	8	72,000
2004	6	51,000
2003	7	43,000
2002	9	85,000
2001	9	56,000

(Sources: Park Hee-sung et al. (2003), p. 207; KOFIC, *South
Korean Film Exports in 2005*)

a market for Korean films.[39] Goodfellas, a company founded with 90% Korean
capital, works proactively as a direct distributor to introduce Korean films and
build multiplex theaters in major cities.

Vietnam's open-door economic policy and *Hallyu*, which began with the
popularity of Korean dramas, have had a significant impact on the distribution of
Korean films. Rights to nine films were sold to Vietnam in 2001 and 2002, but the
difference in total sales was significant due to the rise in the price of film rights.
The number of contracts dropped slightly in 2003 and 2004, but the drop in average revenue was insignificant.

In 2000, *The Letter* became the first South Korean film to be released in
Vietnam. In March of that year, *Love Wind Love Song* was also released. Featuring Jang Dong-gun, who had starred in the successful drama *Medical Brothers*,
the film was well received. *Tie a Yellow Ribbon* was released in Hanoi's 900-
seat Tangtan Theater. The movie screened for about 90 days from March 1 and
proved the popular appeal of Korean films. Although *My Sassy Girl*, released on
December 5, 2001, broke the box office record for a Korean film, it did not spark
a Korean film boom as anticipated. Since then, a steady stream of Korean films
have been introduced in Vietnam, but none has met with a significant response.
The recently released *A Moment to Remember* appears to be gaining traction in
the market, as is *My Little Bride*.

H.   Singapore

(pp. 132–134)

After *Shiri*, a string of Korean films, including *Bichunmoo* and *Il Mare*, were
released, increasing awareness of Korean films and giving them popular appeal.
Only 18 Korean films were exported to Singapore in 2001, but this figure more
than doubled in 2002, when 43 titles were exported. The figure dropped to 26 in
2003 and 25 in 2004.

In 2002, the revenue from the sale of 43 films totaled SGD 435,600. The
number of titles dropped in 2003, but the negligible change in total revenue is

---

[39] Vietnam's state-run film studios own printing facilities with superior systems, but their high prices
drive Vietnamese filmmakers to make prints in Thailand. See Bae Yang-su, *Vietnam Business Trip
Report*, 2005.

Table 2–35. Korean film distribution contracts in Vietnam, 2001–2005

Year	Title	Company	Scope
2005	*Innocent Steps*	BHD	All rights
	Daisy	Vietnam Media	All rights
	The Beast and the Beauty	BHD	All rights
	April Snow	BHD	All rights
	She's on Duty	BHD	All rights
	Duelist	BHD	All rights
	My Boyfriend Is Type B	Cine Net	All rights
	My Girl and I	Vietnam Media	All rights
2004	*Spin Kick*	Cine Net	Theatrical
	Someone Special	Cine Net	Theatrical
	Arahan	Cine Net	Theatrical
	My Little Bride	BHD	MG
	Please Teach Me English	BHD	All rights
	Mr. Handy	Cine Net	Theatrical
2003	*Out of Justice*	CK Corporation	All rights
	Marrying the Mafia	CK Corporation	All rights
	Madeleine	CK Corporation	All rights
	The Classic	CK Corporation	All rights
	My Tutor Friend	CK Corporation	All rights
	My Wife Is a Gangster 2	CK Corporation	All rights
	The Romantic President	CK Corporation	Including Thailand and China
2002	*Break Out*	Cine net	All rights
	Libera Me	Goodfellas	All rights
	Warrior	Chang Kyung	All rights
	Surprise	Cine Net	All rights
	Over the Rainbow	Fafilm International	All rights
	Chihwaseon	Cine Net	All rights
	Guns & Talks	Cine Net	All rights
	Volcano High School	Cine Net	All rights
	Who Are You?	Lee In-sik	All rights

(Continued)

Table 2–35. *(Continued).*

Year	Title	Company	Scope
	Art Museum by the Zoo	CK Corporation	All rights
	Bichunmoo	Goodfellas	All rights
	Last Present	Goodfellas	All rights
	Kick the Moon	Goodfellas	All rights
2001	Father	Lee In-sik	All rights
	My Sassy Girl	Goodfellas	All rights
	Love Bakery	Lee In-sik	All rights
	Calla	Chung Kyung	All rights
	A Day	Goodfellas	All rights

(Sources: Park Hee-sung et al. (2003), p. 207; KOFIC, *South Korean Film Exports in 2005*)

Table 2–36.   Korean film distribution contracts in Singapore, 2001–2005

Year	Number of Titles	Box Office Revenue ($)
2005	30	739,000 (including bundled sales of rights in Malaysia and Singapore)
2004	25	326,500
2003	26	424,500
2002	43	435,500
2001	18	174,900

(Source: Park Hee-sung et al. (2003), p. 198)

attributed to the rise in the value of film rights due to the increased local appeal of Korean films, international recognition of their quality, and the influence of popular actors and TV dramas.

My Sassy Girl was released on 12 screens and played for roughly 7 weeks. The film grossed SGD 300,000 at the box office and had excellent results in video and VCD sales. *Wishing Stairs*, released in November 2003, broke the box office record for a Korean film, grossing SGD 377,000 in only 11 days from November 13 to November 23. It surpassed *My Sassy Girl*'s record of SGD 295,000, earned in 49 days, and *Marrying the Mafia*'s SGD 222,000, earned in 42 days. In the third week of November 2003, *Wishing Stairs* ranked second at the Singaporean box office, after *Matrix 3: Revolution*.

Most Korean films are released on two or three screens. While *Marriage Is a Crazy Thing* and *Hi! Dharma!* were released in 2 theaters, both *My Sassy Girl* and *Marrying the Mafia* were released on 10 screens, a relatively large scale.[40]

---

[40] Jackie Chan movies, popular in Singapore, are released on as many as 55 screens.

Table 2–37.   Korean films released in Singapore, 2001–2003

Title	Date of Release/ Screening Period	Number of Screens	Audience (approx.)	Box Office Revenue ($)
Shiri	2001	7	N/A	N/A
Joint Security Area	2001		N/A	N/A
My Sassy Girl	7 weeks	12	18,000	295,411
Marrying the Mafia		10	13,000	222,586
Happy End		2	8,000–9,000	N/A
The Isle		2	8,000–9,000	N/A
Marriage Is a Crazy Thing		2	6,000	N/A
Ardor		2	6,000	N/A
Summer Time		1	9,000	N/A
Hi! Dharma!	June 2002, 3 weeks	2	N/A	N/A
My Wife Is a Gangster	9 weeks	2	15,000	250,000
Wishing Stairs	November 2003	About 10	N/A	377,299

(Source: Park Hee-sung et al. (2003), p. 203)

Good results were anticipated for Korean films released in 2005, including *April Snow*, but their box office take is reported to have been relatively poor.

I.   Conclusion: Prospects of Korean films

(pp. 137–139)

In order for Korean films to ensure sustainability as part of an ongoing wave they need to take a lesson from Hong Kong and Japanese films, which faded after a boom in Asia through the 1980s and 1990s. Much effort is necessary to cast light on the strengths of Korean films. Creation of quality content must be continuous, and acceptance of Korean films must be fostered by understanding each target destination in detail. Regional strategies and prospects have been explained in the body of this report. The points below consider the prospects of Korean films in Asia as a whole.

Co-production among Asian nations

Co-production should be promoted actively with an understanding of each nation's strengths and will need to move beyond simple human resource exchanges and seek measures to establish firm local roots, such as by forming partner companies.

Direct, simultaneous distribution

In order to stabilize the supply and demand of Korean films, it is necessary to consider more direct methods of distribution in select areas, possibly by liaising with local distributors. Doing so will allow control of film distribution periods and access to accurate local market information.

Marketing strategies by region

Romantic melodrama and horror are generally popular in Asia. Strategies based on detailed information for each destination must be established to concentrate on promoting competitive genres.

Support for media promotion

Interested parties must increase promotion of Korean films. Media attempting to cover Korean films in Asian countries often face difficulties arising from a lack of resources. Effectively providing information and images of the movies to the press and hosting junkets for journalists are among many potential marketing strategies.

Preparing access routes

In each export region, organizations such as Korean Cultural Centers must prepare access routes to help instill deeper understanding of Korean films. *Hallyu* must not remain confined to the pursuit of commercial and industrial profits. By providing opportunities to view films from the past, offering easy access to movie information, and opening avenues for discussion, Korean cinema can help the world recognize Korea as a culturally rich nation.

Ultimately, a boom in Korean cinema must aim to invigorate the overall Asian film market and increase awareness of Korean culture. Efforts made to guide films in this direction will increase exchange across the region and help form bonds of solidarity within Asia.

2.2.2.   "K-Movies" as a Growth Engine for *Hallyu*

Reference: "Shared Imaginings & Stories for the Global Village: 'K-Movies' as a Growth Engine," *Herald Economy*, Lee Hyeong-seok, January 24, 2014.

Film revenue at standstill despite 10 years of *Hallyu*
New breakthroughs with manpower and tech expertise with visual effects, stunts localized, globalized co-productions with big-name stars: *Stoker, Snowpiercer* – milestones in film exports

The year 2003, widely regarded as "Year One" for the *Hallyu* phenomenon, saw Korean movie exports yield $30.97 million. In 2005, the peak year for the Korean Wave, figures reached $75.99 million. By 2012, however, those numbers had fallen drastically to $20.17 million. After 10 years, exports of Korean films are flatlining, or considering the amount of time that has passed, posting negative growth. What happened?

In 2005, Korean movies benefited enormously from the Korean Wave, a trend sparked by TV dramas such as *Winter Sonata*. In fact, *April Snow*, starring the drama's protagonist Bae Yong-joon, was sold to Japan for a record-breaking $7,000,000. Truly, 2005 was a golden year for Korean films. But this glory was short-lived. Just one year later, exports fell by one-third to a paltry $24.51 million. It was hardly surprising that this "K-movie" bubble burst, as receipts were too poor to merit the films' high price tags. The slump continued until 2009, when figures dipped below the $10 million mark before rebounding to $20 million in 2012.

Although over the last decade Korean films have consistently been invited to international festivals and even garnered awards, and several Korean film directors and actors have ventured into Hollywood, exports have slowed to a crawl—primarily because they have been limited to the sale of films themselves. New strategies can combat this trend.

A. *Exporting manpower and technology*

Last year, Korean movies achieved record earnings domestically and set new export milestones. Korean directors successfully debuted with English-language movies in Hollywood and internationally: Park Chan-wook with *Stoker,* Kim Ji-woon with *The Last Stand,* and Bong Joon-ho with *Snowpiercer.* Lee Byung-hun also performed in two Hollywood movies last year.

Film exports have hit a dead end, but technology and production expertise have surfaced as products that can be sold at a profit. KOFIC has looked into film-related services including visual effects (computer graphics, 3D, digital color grading, and special effects makeup), martial arts choreography, stunts, sound mixing, and location shooting and reported that 14 Korean companies together won such contracts overseas worth $17.64 million last year. In 2010, revenue from technical services was higher, at $28.63 million, and in 2011, the figure was roughly $19.04 million. On average, revenue held steady near the $20 million mark. Figures dropped in 2011–2013 because skills and manpower had to be redirected to the domestic market, as many more Korean films were made during those years. Currently, the largest film-producing countries in size and number of released titles in the world are the US (40.6%) and China (29.1%). If Korean companies and personnel can be mustered to meet demand, services will offer the most potential for growth.

B. *Co-productions based on storyline and imagination*

The biggest issue in selling films is overcoming cultural and language barriers. An alternative way to increase exports is to localize and globalize using Korean manpower, technology, and planning expertise. By making use of experienced Korean directors, the production know-how of film crews, the technical capabilities of production companies, and visual, sound, and special effects expertise, Korea can bring "universal imagination" to the cinema, in English or other languages. A good example is Bong Joon-ho's *Snowpiercer,* based on a French graphic novel series, shot in English, starring Korean and Hollywood actors, and backed by Korean investment. *A Wedding Invitation,* which opened in China last year to become the country's eight highest-grossing romantic comedy ever (RMB 191.9 million), is another example. *A Wedding Invitation* was developed by CJ E&M, directed by Oh Ki-hwan (*Last Present, The Art of Seduction*), and starred Chinese actors Bai Baihe and Eddie Peng. The film was released in China by the country's largest public distributor CFG. Korea and China supplied 50% apiece of the production cost, essentially allowing each country to call the movie its own. *A Wedding Invitation* became both the highest-grossing Korean movie and Korea-China joint venture film in China.

C.   The US and China, destinations for K-movies

Diversifying export destinations is an urgent challenge for Korean cinema. In 2003, Japan was the largest recipient of outbound Korean films, receiving 44.8% of the total share of K-movie exports. In 2005, this figure jumped to 79.4%. Even in 2012, Japan remained a huge market for Korean movies, taking in 48% of total exports. The US has not been as welcoming a destination, with only 12.8% in 2003, and 11.5% in 2012. Exports to China have also stayed flat, hovering between 2.6% and 4.1% for 10 years. Although the US and China are the biggest film markets in the world, they represent the most formidable challenges for Korean-made completed films—all the more reason to support a new global strategy that harnesses Korean manpower, technology, and imagination to target these two markets.

CJ E&M has been the most active in its pursuit of the American and Chinese markets. The company has partnered with US producers to release Korea-US joint venture English-language movies this year, including *Make Your Move* starring BoA and the animated *Dino Time* and *Final Recipe*. In China, CJ is masterminding three Korea-China joint venture films (Jang Yun-hyeon's *Pyeongando,* Park Gwang-hyun's *The Fist,* and Park Gwang-chun's *Love and Lingerie*) with a production scheme similar to *A Wedding Invitation*

2.3. MUSIC

While this sourcebook has emphasized government policy reports and industry data thus far, the next two subsections on music and celebrity dip into journalistic and anecdotal discourses on the Korean Wave in order to broaden the picture presented. The two subsections share thematic links in foregrounding the role of noteworthy individuals in the success of *Hallyu*.

Document 2.3.1, "K-Pop Drives Resurgence of the Korean Wave," discusses the recent rise of K-pop. Rather than using language borrowed from digital technology (e.g., *"Hallyu* 1.0") as a way to highlight the role that K-pop played in reigniting interest in Korean cultural products, it speaks of *shinhallyu,* a "New" Korean Wave. The piece also pays more attention to the singers than the songs they perform, signaling the Korean music industry's dependency on idols. Analyzing the Chinese and Japanese music markets and industry practices, it suggests ways for creating "killer content" (*kireo contencheu*) that cannot miss in the target market. Despite this phrase's colloquial flavor in English, it frequently appears in *Hallyu* strategy and policy guides as a quasi-technical term.

Document 2.3.2, "The Three Emperors of K-Pop," draws on the classic Chinese historical novel *Romance of the Three Kingdoms* to characterize and compare the three most successful K-pop conglomerates: SM Entertainment, JYP Entertainment, and YG Entertainment. This document, culled from a monthly current events magazine, compares the epic battles and intrigues of ancient China to the struggle for dominance among these three corporations. While casual in tone, the article offers a fresh perspective on K-pop, as seen from the side of star production. The piece also appraises the strengths and weaknesses in the business and marketing strategies of the ruling triumvirate of the Korean music world. Particularly interesting is the information on auditioning methods, trainee periods, and differing preferences for idol types.

Even though controversy over the practices of Korea's talent management companies spills beyond the music industry, as teenage idol groups are most frequently caught up in disputes we have excerpted here a discussion of the less savory side of the Korean Wave and its potential for corporate exploitation. Taken together, the first two pieces in this subsection make a strong case for an overhaul of talent management by putting in place transparent business models, strict guidelines for best practice, and revisions of contract law.

The informative and appropriately technical "Revitalizing the Talent Management Industry" (Document 2.3.3) assesses how stars are currently groomed and promoted in Korea. While the full original compares Japanese talent agencies with their Korean counterparts, often to the detriment of the latter, we have excerpted sections that focus specifically on Korea. The document's legalistic language makes it difficult in parts, but it provides an insider view on key issues at stake in the talent management industry, given scandals over exclusive (often termed "slave") contracts. The sober consideration of talent management strategies in, for example, Table 2–53 on page 199, "Status of Talent Management Companies," illuminates the volatile nature of an industry in which corporations involve themselves in risky business ventures with significant expenditure in the hope of high returns. The document provides a useful perspective on why feuds frequently arise between management and labor, a categorization regularly obscured by the notion that the laborers have the potential to become stars. Document 2.3.4, "The World of Idols: Jumping through Endless Hoops," first appeared in *Shin Dong-A*, Korea's oldest monthly magazine. It reviews the strenuous process through which idol stars are born, arguing that what may appear glamorous to outsiders often brings little profit to the performers themselves. The piece contains snippets from interviews with industry insiders who tell of teenagers giving up not only school but also their families and social lives to endure the hardships of a trainee period, which can last up to eight years, for the coveted goal of debuting. Most enlightening here is the detailed account of idol group TVXQ's schedule, which requires demanding foreign travel funded at the band's own expense, and further highlights the potentially exploitative nature of K-pop and its global ambitions.

2.3.1.   K-Pop Drives Resurgence of the Korean Wave

Reference: "K-Pop Drives Resurgence of the Korean Wave: Status and Challenges," Byeon Mi-young, KOCCA Focus, No. 31, March 15, 2011, pp. 4–22.

A.   Evolution of Hallyu and the status of neo-Hallyu

Hallyu began in China in 1997 with the drama *What Is Love?* and has since evolved in three phases. In the initial phase of *Hallyu*, from 1997 to the early 2000s, Korean content first impressed itself on overseas consumers. The liberal social environment and self-expression showcased in the drama *What Is Love?* were refreshing to Chinese viewers, who had not encountered such content before. In the late 1990s, the popularity of Korea's TV dramas was followed by its music, with dance music at the center, in China, Taiwan, and elsewhere. In China, the youth flocked to concerts by H.O.T. and other Korean artists, and radio programs introducing Korean popular music appeared.

Table 2–38.   Phases of *Hallyu*'s evolution

Characteristics	Phase 1	Phase 2	Phase 3
Keyword	Formation	Expansion	Diversification
Period	1997-early 2000s	Mid-2000s	Late 2000s-today
Key Fields	TV dramas, music	TV dramas, music, films, games	Music, TV dramas, games, films, animation, licensed characters, food, Korean language
Key Target Destinations	China, Taiwan, Vietnam	China, Japan, Taiwan, Southeast Asia	China, Japan, Taiwan, Southeast Asia, Central Asia, Africa, US
Representative Content	*What Is Love?* H.O.T.	*Winter Sonata, Jewel in the Palace*	K-pop, idol groups, online games

(Source: Ko J. (2009), *Hallyu: Beyond Asia and into the World*, KOFICE)

During the second phase of *Hallyu*, from the early to mid-2000s, TV dramas achieved wide recognition. In 2002 and 2003, Korean dramas and popular music grew popular in Southeast Asia, China, and other regions, but did not create as large a sensation as in the first phase of *Hallyu*. *Winter Sonata* became a smash hit in Japan, creating a *Hallyu* boom there. The drama excited nostalgia among middle-aged Japanese women and caused a frenzy over actor Bae Yong-joon. The drama also contributed to changing Japanese perceptions of Korea from a war-torn nation to a stylish and romantic land. After *Winter Sonata*, *Jewel in the Palace* played a key role in disseminating *Hallyu* globally. *Winter Sonata* enjoyed great popularity in Japan, but *Jewel in the Palace* spread to 62 countries, including China, Hong Kong, and countries in Southeast Asia, Central Asia, Africa, and Eastern Europe. The show played a significant role in demonstrating the quality of Korean dramas and transforming *Hallyu* into a global phenomenon. *Jewel in the Palace* had a positive effect not only on other dramas, but also on diplomatic relations and the globalization of Korean food.

While the second phase of *Hallyu* can be considered the heyday of Korean dramas, music and other content sectors also enjoyed success. BoA topped Japan's Oricon chart on numerous occasions. TVXQ became popular in Japan, China, and elsewhere. Rain proved himself an international star through overseas concerts. South Korea's globally competitive online games gave life to a "digital *Hallyu*" through high market shares in Taiwan and China. Such games achieved dominance in China and Southeast Asia, areas that became staging posts for the wider spread of a digital Korean Wave.

The third phase of *Hallyu* began in the mid-2000s and continues today, with a new boom led by K-pop and idol groups. During this phase the Korean Wave expanded into Central Asia, Africa, the US, and elsewhere. Since the mid-2000s, the significant rise in the price of Korean content has led to strong opposition from foreign importers, and various governments have begun enforcing anti-*Hallyu* policies in order to protect their own cultures and curb excessive penetration of Korean products. Consumers in importer countries have also begun to demonstrate anti-*Hallyu* sentiment, thus slowing the boom in major importers like China and Japan. *Hallyu* has grown again in Central Asia and other regions. While until the mid-2000s the Korean Wave had been centered on TV dramas, since the late 2000s, the phenomenon has centered on K-pop, led by idol groups, and come to be designated "neo-*Hallyu*."

Neo-*Hallyu* (*shinhallyu*), led by K-pop, has an expanded fan base, including teens and those in their twenties, a demographic group familiar with the digital environment. K-pop kick-started this new surge of the Korean Wave in Southeast Asia. Artists such as TVXQ, SHINee, Girls' Generation, and Rain gained popularity and instigated a boom for Korean idols there ahead of Japan. Idol group 2PM's Thai member Nichkhun is an example of a foreign national joining a Korean idol group and boosting K-pop in another land.

Neo-*Hallyu*, which began in Southeast Asia, peaked in Japan, with all-female groups like Girls' Generation and KARA at the forefront. These groups caused a sensation among Japanese women, who imitated their dances, cosmetic styles, and fashions. In 2010, music placed highest among the categories of KOFICE's

Table 2–39.   2010 Korean wave index by category

	Music	Games	Television	Films
Index (Base year 2009 = 100)	107	101	100	94

(Source: Ko J. (2010), "Calculation of the Korean Wave Index and *Hallyu*'s Economic Effect," KOFICE)

Table 2–40.   Changes in the size of Korea's content industry

Measure	2005	2006	2007	2008	2009	Annual Growth Rate ('08–'09)	Annual Growth Rate ('05–'09)
Sales (₩ One Trillion)	57.3	62.8	64.4	66.0	69.0	4.5%	4.8%
Exports ($100 Million)	13.0	13.7	19.4	23.4	26.0	11.4%	18.9%

(Source: MCST, *2010 Content Industry Statistics*)

Korean Wave Index,[41] reflecting the popularity of K-pop. Music is truly leading the third phase of *Hallyu*. In 2010, music topped the index at 107 points, followed by games (101 points)[42] and television (100). Films performed poorly, scoring only 94 points. Setting the base year of 2009 at 100, the 2010 index thus shows that music and games gained in popularity, while films dropped and television remained steady.[43]

Statistics for Korea's exports show a rapid increase for the music industry. Content exports doubled in four years from $1.3 billion in 2005 to $2.6 billion in 2009. Despite the small size of the music industry, its growth is exceptional (90% growth in 2009 over the previous year). This growth is attributed to the popularity of idol groups, who are leading the new surge of the Korean Wave in Southeast Asia and Japan.

Japan is the largest export destination for the Korean music industry. In 2009, exports to Japan totaled $21.63 million, 69.2% of all music exports. Exports to Southeast Asia in 2009 reached $6.41 million, a significant increase of 149.6% from 2008.

This new surge in the Korean Wave suggests the possibility of continuation. Neo-*Hallyu* has dispelled concerns that *Hallyu* might not bounce back after its recent recession. Led by K-pop, the new Korean Wave is spreading through social media beyond Asia to every corner of the world, including the US, Europe, and South America. Various industries, including TV, music, and games have led *Hallyu* in different periods. TV dramas drove the Korean Wave in the mid-1990s, followed by music in the late 1990s, dramas and films in the mid-2000s, and K-pop and games in the late 2000s. The key destinations have shifted over time,

---

[41] Calculated by combining quantitative indicators (consumption – statistics) and qualitative indicators (desirability – survey).

[42] While game exports are increasing significantly, this sector does not score highly in the Korean Wave Index because of the industry's small overall impact on *Hallyu*.

[43] This figure was influenced by a reduction in foreign currency imports caused by the global economic recession in 2009.

Table 2–41.   Changes in Korea's content exports (Units: $1,000,000, %)

Industry	Export Amount					Growth Rate ('08–'09)
	2005	2006	2007	2008	2009	
Music	22.3	16.7	13.9	16.5	31.3	89.7
Games	564.7	672.0	781.0	1,093.9	1,240.9	13.4
Television	123.5	147.7	162.6	180.2	183.6	1.9

(Sources: MCST (2010), *Content Industry Statistics*; Ministry of Knowledge Economy (2010), *Annual Report of Import and Export Trends*; KOCCA (2010), *Import and Export Status of Broadcasting Content*)

Table 2–42.   Korea's music industry exports by destination (Units: $1,000, %)

	Export Amount					Share	Growth Rate ('08–'09)
	2005	2006	2007	2008	2009		
China	–	850	1,665	1,844	2,369	7.6	28.5
Japan	801	14,309	9,431	11,215	21,638	69.2	92.9
Southeast Asia	–	621	2,061	2,569	6,411	20.5	149.6
North America	–	49	306	346	351	1.1	1.4
Europe	1,600	549	217	296	299	1.0	1.0
Other	30	288	205	198	201	0.6	1.5
Unclassified	19,847	–	–	–	–	–	
Total			13,885	15,468	31,269	100	89.9

(Source: KOCCA (2010), *2010 Music Industry White Paper*)

from China and Southeast Asia in the 1990s to Southeast Asia in the early 2000s, and from Japan in the mid-2000s to Central, West, and Southeast Asia and Japan in the latter part of the decade.

B.   Current status of K-pop by country

China

K-pop is enjoying steady popularity in China. An impressive 7 K-pop tunes ranked among the top 10 songs from Korea and Japan on *Baidu* (百度), China's largest portal site, in February 2011.

K-pop fandom in China centers on idol stars. Preference is based not on individual songs, but particular singers. Multiple songs on albums from Super Junior, Rain, Girls' Generation, and Big Bang chart simultaneously on Korean and Japanese portal sites. Reasons for the success of Korean idol stars include the quality of their music, their excellent singing, and their polished performances. The popularity of Korean idols has led to copycat Chinese groups whose names, concepts, and choreography evoke Korean bands.

Table 2–43.   *Baidu* ranking (Feb. 11, 2011)

Rank	Title	Artist	Rank	Title	Artist
1	That Man	Hyun Bin	16	Rock U	KARA
2	Good Day	IU	17	Virgin Road	Hamasaki Ayumi
3	Love Song	Hamasaki Ayumi	18	Back It Up	Jewelry
4	Keep Your Head Down	TVXQ	19	Get Ready	JYJ
5	W	JYJ	20	Mission	JYJ
6	Kiss	Ito Yuna	21	Long Way	JYJ
7	Remember	Kat-tun	22	Beginner	AKB48
8	Because of You	B2ST	23	Supa Luv	Teen Top
9	Scent of a Woman	SeeYa	24	Thank You (ありがとう)	Ohashi Takuya
10	Here I Am	4Men	25	Precious	Ito Yuna
11	Moon	Hamasaki Ayumi	26	Do it Again	Hamasaki Ayumi
12	Loveless	Yamashita Tomohisa	27	I Want to Protect You (守ってあげたい)	Ito Yuna
13	Lost	Benylan	28	Rumor	TVXQ
14	Turn Around	Joo	29	Pierrot	JYJ
15	Ayyy Girl	JYJ	30	With You Always (いつだって君に)	JYJ

Japan

The focus of K-pop fervor is moving from male to female idol groups. Previously centered on such male groups as TVXQ, SS501, Big Bang, and Supernova, popularity is shifting to girl groups, including 4Minute, 2 NE1, KARA, and Girls' Generation. Teens and those in their twenties form the major consumer base of K-pop. It is notable that consumption of Korean products, which centered on middle-aged consumers, has changed. Artists imitating K-pop idols have appeared in Japan. Japanese girl group strategies emphasize K-pop style and choreography.

The popularity of Korean girl groups is attributed to the freshness fans perceive in "complete package" (*wanseonghyeong*) idols. The Japanese and Korean pop music markets differ as follows: performers are divided into idol and artist categories in Japan, and audience expectations differ for the two. While outstanding voices and performances are sought from artists, fans seek familiarity, entertainment, and positive images from idols. Japanese talent agencies produce idols who are not extraordinarily attractive, but rather slightly above average in appearance, and whose singing techniques are not

Table 2–44. Comparison of K-pop and J-pop idol groups

Characteristics	Girls' Generation and KARA	AKB48
Idol style	"Complete package" idols	Developing idols ("incomplete" idols)
Major fan base	Female	Male
Visual image	Cool	Cute
Attraction	Vocal skills, dance, and performance Attractive idols with all-around skills	Audience feels as though it is nurturing the band, and cheers for its members. The band appeals to parental instincts.
Fans' perception of idols	Mystical elements	Idols fans want to meet

(Source: KOCCA (2011), *Japanese Content Industry Trends*, No. 9.)

fully honed. In contrast, Korea's idol industry has increasingly nurtured skilled idols who can compete in the domestic market. Korean idols debut after professional training with not only outstanding dance and singing skills, but also foreign language ability, including English and Japanese. They are thoroughly polished before debut in Japan.[44] The appearance of fully trained, "complete package" idols from Korea offered novelty for the Japanese audience, which had tired of regurgitated concepts.

TV programs related to K-pop dramatically grew in number. The introduction of K-pop on music programs and variety shows on terrestrial and satellite networks increased, as well as production of independent K-pop programs and the appearance of K-pop artists on various shows. NHK News, for example, reported on the Girls' Generation Tokyo concert in real-time as headline news (Aug. 25, 2010). Girls' Generation appeared on *Music Station*, a popular show on TV Asahi. *Kantame POP*, *Music Japan*, and other various in-house productions on K-pop aired on Fuji TV Two.[45]

Taiwan

Successful K-pop artists include Super Junior, SS501, Girls' Generation, Rain, and BoA. Market entry through popular TV drama OSTs has a high success rate. SS501, who recorded the OST for *Boys over Flowers*, put on a concert in Taiwan in October 2009 as part of their Asia tour. The group swept the Taiwanese market, selling out the venue's 12,000 seats. SS501 was selected as Best Group at the 2009 Yahoo! Asia Buzz Awards, held at the Hong Kong Convention Center in December. Group leader Kim Hyun-joong was voted by Internet users as Asia's Top Buzz Male Artist and Taiwan's Top Buzz Korean Artist. On April 18, 2010, Girls' Generation fans organized a unique event on a street in the Ximending neighborhood of Taipei, dancing to the band's hit "Oh!" A crowd of

---

[44] Sisa IN, November 17, 2010.
[45] KOCCA (2010), *Japanese Content Industry Trends*.

Table 2–45.   Timeline of entry of K-pop artists into Japan

BoA	*Listen to My Heart*, BoA's 2002 debut Japanese album, ranked #1 on the Oricon chart (one million copies sold). Received six Gold Artist Awards at the Japan Best Hit Pop Music Awards between 2002 and 2008.
TVXQ	Set the record for most #1 singles by any artist in a single year on the Oricon Chart in 2008. #1 overall in the Live DVD category of the Oricon Chart in 2009 (first for an artist from elsewhere in Asia).
	Ranked #1 on the Oricon chart six consecutive times from 2006 to 2009.
	₩130 billion in album sales in 2010.
Girls' Generation	"Genie," the group's first single in 2010, sold 45,000 copies within a week of release (sales record for a debut single album by a foreign female artist). "Gee" reached #2 on the weekly Oricon Singles Chart (highest position for an overseas female band in 30 years).
KARA	Debut album *Girls Talk* sold 250,000 copies. Received a Platinum Award from the Japan Record Association. Ranked #1 for bestselling album and DVD by a new artist on the Oricon chart (₩18 billion). *KARA BEST CLIP* topped the chart for DVDs overall (first time for an overseas female artist).

(Sources: Oricon chart and various Korean reports)

Table 2–46.   Top-selling DVDs of foreign artists in Japan

Record-Set Date	Artist	Title	Release Date
April 14, 2003	The Beatles	The Beatles Anthology (special price at initial release)	March 31, 2003
June 23, 2003	Led Zeppelin	Led Zeppelin DVD	June 11, 2003
October 12, 2009	TVXQ	4th Live Tour 2009 "The Secret Code" Final in Tokyo Dome	September 30, 2009
March 29, 2010	TVXQ	TVXQ Video Clip Collection: The One	March 17, 2010
October 11, 2010	TVXQ	Tohoshinki History in Japan Special	September 29, 2010
September 20, 2010	JYJ	Thanksgiving Live in Dome	September 8, 2010
December 6, 2010	Michael Jackson	Michael Jackson VISION	November 24, 2010
March 7, 2011	KARA	KARA Best Clips	February 23, 2011

(Source: KOCCA (2011), *Japanese Content Industry Trends*. No. 9.)

roughly 600 gathered. Girls' Generation held a successful concert on October 17, 2010, filling 12,000 seats at the Taipei Arena. Online reservation servers were crashed when tickets went on sale, even though Girls' Generation had not yet officially debuted in Taiwan (August 2010). K-pop artists have topped rankings on Taiwanese pop music and audio websites. In January 2009, "Rainism" by Rain, "Eat You Up" by BoA, and "MIROTIC" by TVXQ ranked highly among Japanese and Korean pop songs in Taiwan. In December 2009, songs by Super Junior, SS501, Girls' Generation, and SHINee placed in the top 10 in Taiwan. Super Junior held first place on the Korea-Japan Chart of Taiwanese music site KKBOX for 30 consecutive weeks as of Nov. 2009. The group was invited to the Golden Melody Awards, a major event in Taiwan, and praised highly.

There is, however, a backlash to the high popularity of K-pop. A Taiwanese TV show libeled Girls' Generation, falsely accusing the group of giving sexual favors. Nonetheless, anti-*Hallyu* sentiment receives little attention in the Taiwanese media. Instead, overreaction in Korea to provocative remarks has been criticized for aggravating the issue.

Vietnam

K-pop is passionately consumed by teens and twenty-somethings; artists enjoy high recognition and popularity. Korean celebrities such as 2 AM, CNBLUE, After School, Big Bang, Girls' Generation, and Lee Hyori, and their song titles are recognized by most young Vietnamese. K-pop success is typically determined by the performance of OSTs from TV dramas and films and artists' profiles. A strong Korean influence can be observed in the Vietnamese market, with frequent imitation of Korean artists and collaboration with Korean companies. The local music industry's market potential is small relative to the popularity of Korean content. Vietnam's pop music market is marginal, with illegal copies accounting for over 90% of music distributed. Hence, K-pop companies are not making special efforts to enter Vietnam. On October 18, 2009, Girls' Generation performed at a concert commemorating the 17th anniversary of the establishment of bilateral diplomatic relations between Korea and Vietnam. Korean artists have not yet held any solo concerts in Vietnam.

Thailand

K-pop has surpassed J-pop in popularity; Korean albums have the highest sales of overseas releases and account for 50–60% of foreign album sales. Thailand's record industry has annual sales of THB 20 billion (₩730 billion). Of this amount, 17.5%, or THB 3.5 billion (₩128 billion), is estimated to derive from K-pop (based on 2010 figures). An album by 2PM topped the chart for foreign artists from January to September 2009. K-pop is popular among Thai youths, and the Internet allows them to access it. Korean artists have become role models, and Thai teens imitate their fashions. Shinzong Cover Super Junior (www.shinzong.co.cc) is an example of the many emerging cover dance groups.[46] Interest in K-pop is sparking interest in Korean dramas and variety shows. Factors for

---

[46] While the term "cover" traditionally refers to remakes of songs, the recent cover phenomenon involves imitating fashion and choreography as well.

K-pop's popularity are the attractive appearance, addictive songs, and powerful choreography of male performers.

US, Europe, and South America

K-pop is in its early stages in the American and European markets. Although Korean content is not widespread enough in the US and Europe to allow us to speak of a Korean Wave as in Asia, Korean cultural products, particularly films, music, and games, are enjoying growing recognition, and a fan base is being established. K-pop got a foot in the door in the US, the largest content market in the world. Girls' Generation, KARA, Rain, Wonder Girls, BoA, 2 NE1, and Big Bang, among other artists, are active in the US. Wonder Girls' "Nobody" placed 76th on the Billboard Hot 100 singles chart in 2009. The group plans to release its first EP in the US in 2011.[47] In September 2009, Epik High's 6th album, *[e]*, placed in the top 100 on the iTunes US Hip-Hop and Rap chart, a first for an Asian group. The SM Town Live Concert, held in September 2010 at the Staples Center in Los Angeles, built a foundation for future concerts in the US. In March 2011, Big Bang's 4th mini-album reached #7 on the Billboard Heatseekers Albums chart, which rates the sales of up-and-coming artists, and placed at #3 on the World Albums chart. The album placed in the top 10 on the overall albums chart on iTunes in the US, Canada, New Zealand, Australia, and Finland.

K-pop's spread in Europe occurred via *YouTube* and other social media rather than through local promotion. On January 3, 2011, a show titled *Un oeil sur la planète* (An Eye on the Planet)[48] on France 2, a French public national television channel, featured *Hallyu* and the status of Korean idol stars in the Asian music market. Belgium's public TV program *Sans Chichis* introduced K-pop as a new fan passion that has spread across Belgium as well as the US and Japan. In January 2011, TVXQ's new song, "Keep Your Head Down," ranked #4 on the United World Chart of German website *Media Traffic*, which tracks global album sales.

K-pop stars are emerging as idols for Brazilian teens. In January 2011, *Leitura Dinamica*, an entertainment program on Brazil's Rede TV, introduced K-pop artists and music videos by genre. The show claimed that K-pop came to Brazil via the US, that its increasing popularity cannot be ignored, and that Korean artists have become idols for Brazilian teens without ever doing a live performance.[49] A similar phenomenon has been observed in Mexico and Peru. In Peru, fans of Korean idol groups, including SHINee, B2ST, and U-KISS, have active websites and offline meetings.

C.   Factors in K-pop's overseas competitiveness

Localization strategies target global market from planning stage

Groups are formed to target foreign markets, receiving systematic training in music and dance. They enter the market as a highly competitive "complete

---

[47] EP (extended play) albums: this format falls between a mini-album and a full-length album, and includes a half dozen songs.

[48] A comprehensive show, well received by French intellectuals and overseas media, which airs in various Francophone countries, including Canada, Belgium, and Switzerland.

[49] According to a survey of 2,826 teens residing in Brasília at the end of 2010, the most popular K-pop artist was Super Junior (KOFICE).

package." Entry into overseas markets began in the late 1990s, and this decade of accumulated *Hallyu* experience aids strategic preparation. Quick adaptation is made possible by learning foreign languages and dance moves, choreography, and stage manners specific to target countries, thereby diminishing cultural barriers. BoA's Japan debut followed thorough research on the local market. Her dance music targeted early teens, the consumer group with the highest growth potential. Idol groups with local members help secure fans. Nichkhun of 2PM is from Thailand, Sandara Park of 2 NE1 grew up in the Philippines, Jia and Fei of Miss A are from China, and Victoria and Amber of F(x) are ethnic Chinese. Idol groups have been successful in the home countries of foreign members.

SM Entertainment earned over ₩68.23 billion in the first three quarters of 2010, which was more than the company's total 2009 sales of ₩61.79 billion. During this period, overseas revenue reached ₩39.3 billion (63% of the total), a 182% increase from ₩13.9 billion the previous year.

Robust system for fostering idols with strong foundations

Korean talent agencies form idol groups in a phased system of audition, training, production, and promotion. This system allows for the speedy production of quality content. A stable supply is established through a system managing every aspect from training to overseas debuts. The idol training and globalization strategies of Korean agencies are attracting international attention. Representatives of SM, JYP, and other large agencies have been invited to speak about the Asian entertainment industry at prestigious university venues, including Harvard Business School.

Competitiveness of K-pop and its stars

K-pop demonstrates chic and structured musicianship. Its unique style derives from absorbing hip-hop, R&B, and electronic dance music from Britain and the US and infusing them with an Asian sensibility. This style has penetrated North America and Europe, as well as Asia. A significant number of K-pop producers have roots in American pop music: Teddie (YG; producer for 2 NE1 and Big Bang), Kenzie (SM; composer for Girls' Generation, TVXQ, F(x), and BoA), Kim Young-hoo (SM; lyrics and music for TVXQ, SHINee, and BoA), and Park Jin-young (JYP; producer for Wonder Girls, Rain, 2PM, and 2 AM). These are a few examples of the many composers and producers trained overseas who entered the popular music market in the 2000s, devoting themselves to Korean interpretations of American pop.[50] "While based on American pop, which is characterized by strong bass and mid-range beats, the music of Korean idols has become influential by adding diverse rhythms, vocals, and choreography." (Ishihara Shin, Executive Producer, Variety Show Department, Japan NHK). With solid vocal skills, K-pop stars showcase unique charm with powerful, stylish dancing, visual effects, artistic talent, and fashion. Some recent idol groups are concentrating on genres other than dance and hip-hop, such as rock (e.g., CNBLUE and FT Island) and ballads (e.g., 2 AM).

---

[50] Jung T. (2010), "SERI Management Note," Samsung Economic Research Institute.

D. Digital distribution and marketing of K-pop

Social media platforms including *YouTube*, *Twitter*, and *Facebook* have been used for distribution and marketing. Securing distribution networks is crucial for content entry overseas; before the late 2000s, primarily local networks were used. For example, Japanese company AVEX was in charge of distribution and promotion for BoA.

YouTube and other social media have allowed K-pop to spread beyond Asia to the US, Europe, the Middle East, and South America and be consumed without any time lag after release in Korea. In the era of neo-*Hallyu*, which took off in the late 2000s, local distribution networks of Korean companies and distribution and promotion through social media have been extremely effective. SM Japan is cooperating with a subsidiary of Universal Japan to expand entry for its entertainers, such as Girls' Generation. *YouTube*'s introduction of a subtitling service in 2008 and a voice-to-subtitle service in 2009 has helped overcome language barriers and worked in favor of K-pop. Overseas entry is attempted after confirming a group's potential through *YouTube* promotion and other methods. 2PM uploaded a teaser video for the title track of the group's latest album on their *YouTube* channel. Reaction has been explosive, with over a million views. The group's Japanese debut album will be released in April 2011. GD & TOP, a Big Bang subgroup formed by members G-Dragon and T.O.P., was the first Asian ensemble to showcase a debut album live on *YouTube*. The event attracted 390,000 real-time viewers.

Korean talent management companies SM Entertainment, JYP Entertainment, and YG Entertainment (hereafter SM, JYP, and YG) were quick to open official *YouTube* channels and use them to market their artists. SM's *YouTube* channel opened in 2006 and had 6.11 million total channel views, 244 million total upload views, and 170,000 subscribers as of early November 2010. The video for "Gee" by Girls' Generation was viewed over 40 million times (Thailand 12.3%, US 12%, Japan 9%, Europe 8%), and Super Junior's "Sorry Sorry" had nearly

Table 2–47.   Export methods used by the Korean music industry (Unit: %)

Export Method	Entry Path	2007	2008	2009	Change from Previous Year
Direct Export	Participation in overseas exhibitions and events	1.5	3.2	3.4	0.2
	Contact with foreign distributors	75.7	66.5	62.1	–4.4
	Online overseas sales	7.9	8.1	9.6	1.5
	Overseas corporations	1.6	2.8	4.5	1.7
Indirect Export	Domestic agents	2.3	3.6	4.1	0.5
	Overseas agents	11.0	15.8	16.3	0.5
	Total	100.0	100.0	100.0	–

(Source: KOCCA (2010), *2010 Music Industry White Paper*)

22 million views. JYP opened its *YouTube* channel in 2008. As of November 2010, the channel had 1.2 million channel views, 28.7 million total upload views, and 620,000 subscribers. Channel views and total upload views for the *YouTube* channels of Wonder Girls and 2PM exceeded those of JYP, their management company. YG opened its *YouTube* channel in 2008. By November 2010, the channel had 3.9 million channel views, 194 million total upload views, and 160,000 subscribers. 2 NE1's "Clap Your Hands" was the most viewed video globally on the day of its release, with over 470,000 hits (most viewed in South Korea, Japan, Taiwan, Hong Kong, Australia, Canada, and the UK).

K-Pop Video Views on *YouTube*: SM, YG, and JYP, the Three Major Talent Agencies

800 million views in 229 [sic] countries worldwide:
Asia (566.27 million) > North America (123.47 million) > Europe (55.37 million) > South America (20.58 million) > Middle East (15.19 million) > Oceania (10.73 million)
The increasing view counts in the US deserve note:
Japan (113.54 million views) > Thailand (99.51 million views) > US (94.87 million views)

Diversified fan bases in different destinations:
K-pop videos were viewed over 300,000 times in several countries in the Middle East, including Egypt (630,000 views) and Kuwait (414,000 views). K-pop was also viewed many times elsewhere, including such locales as Montenegro (22,000 views) and New Caledonia (14,000 views).

E.   Increasing global status of Korea and rapid growth of Asia's pop culture market

The increased economic status and desirability of Korea has spurred global interest in its culture, which in turn has had a positive effect on the dissemination of *Hallyu* in Southeast Asia, Central Asia, and other regions that admire Korea's economic growth. Korea now enjoys an image as a technology powerhouse (e.g., Samsung Electronics), outstanding performer in global sports (Kim Yuna, Park Tae-hwan, Park Ji-sung), and host of the G-20 Summit. The rapid growth of Asia's pop culture market has led to increased consumption of Korean content and reduced the intensity of competition with other nations' popular cultures, thereby fostering the spread of *Hallyu*. The growth of Asia's pop culture market, in which *Hallyu* has occupied a pre-eminent position, is expected to continue.

F.   Challenges and issues

Unreasonable contract practices and unfair profit sharing

Korean talent management companies are growing rapidly through vertical integration, corporate expansion, financial investment, globalization of star training

Table 2–48.   Global content industry outlook (2009–2014)

Market	2009 (p)	2010	2011	2012	2013	2014	Annual Growth Rate ('09–'14)
Global Market ($)	1.322 trillion	1.357 trillion	1.416 trillion	1.498 trillion	1.589 trillion	1.690 trillion	5.0%
Asia ($)	348.1 billion	365.6 billion	388.2 billion	414.5 billion	443.8 billion	474.9 billion	6.4%

(Source: PricewaterhouseCoopers (2010), *Global Entertainment and Media Outlook: 2010–2014*)

Table 2–49.   Global status of the Korean music industry and future prospects

Size of the Music Industry ($1,000,000)							
2009				2014 (est.)			
World	26,372	Asia	8,419	World	26,965	Asia	10,384
Korea	275	Korea	275	Korea	490	Korea	490
Share	1.0%	Share	3.3%	Share	1.8%	Share	4.7%
Ranking	9	Ranking	3	Ranking	6	Ranking	3

Note: Based on PwC statistics; the figures refer to domestic (consumer) market size and may differ from figures reported in domestic music industry statistics.
(Source: Ibid)

and content production, and boosted distribution and circulation.[51] Nonetheless, such issues as unreasonable contracts and unfair profit sharing are not being resolved. If these issues persist, they will attract negative publicity and damage the credibility of K-pop.

Group breakups from disputes with management over profit sharing

Many groups, from H.O.T. to TVXQ to KARA, have experienced issues with management. An anonymous music industry source claimed, "Conflicts arising in the management process over profit sharing have accumulated." One speaker at a national policy seminar stated, "Contracts between talent management companies and singers are personal service contracts, and the government must propose a standard contract that prohibits excessive media appearance requirements and exploitation of labor, and provides appropriate compensation."[52]

Lack of globally competitive major music enterprises

Korean music companies, small compared to major overseas corporations, have a lower threshold for entering the global market. Despite the glamorous appearance

---

[51] Korean talent management companies carry out the functions of both management (spotting and managing talent) and agencies (securing business).

[52] Jung G. (2011), "Policy Measures in the Culture and Tourism Sectors for a Fair Society," March 2011, National Policy Seminar.

of *Hallyu*, Korean companies' sales lag far behind their overseas counterparts due to the small domestic market and the prevalence of illegal downloading. Korea lacks large music enterprises that can provide financial and human resources to effectively secure networks and carry out business overseas.

Imbalance of profitable export destinations and music genres

As Table 13 shows, profits are heavily concentrated in Japan. The Korean music industry's exports to Japan account for about 70% of the total, as, except for Japan, other music markets are small and illegal downloading is rampant. K-pop is only beginning its entry into the US and European markets. K-pop consists of mostly dance music; Korean rock and R&B have had little impact on the foreign market. Such a genre imbalance is also an issue. Even though dance music seems to be our globally competitive genre for now, long-term development of other types of music should be encouraged.

Illegal downloading

It is difficult to achieve profitability in the Chinese and Southeast Asian markets due to illegal downloading. There overall sales are low despite wide interest in K-pop. As a result, events and concerts have been used to earn revenue. Piracy is an issue inside Korea as well, and weak enforcement has had an impact. Although the music industry has contracted because of a lack of profitability, mobile and other paid digital downloads are slowly increasing.

Anti-*Hallyu* sentiment

The resurgence of the Korean Wave has also sparked a resurgence of anti-*Hallyu* sentiment, which originated in more broad anti-Korean feelings. Angered by the disqualification of a Taiwanese taekwondo competitor at the 2010 Asian Games, one Taiwanese newsreader said that even if Girls' Generation were to apologize, the offense was not pardonable. Anti-*Hallyu* remarks, which rarely occur abroad, often receive disproportionate coverage in Korea's domestic media. This coverage extends the life-span of the remarks and potentially leads to a vicious cycle that inflames tensions as such reports are in turn picked up by foreign media. Many people learn about negative feelings towards the Korean Wave through these reports, causing the situation to deteriorate.

Table 2–50.   Music export destinations (2009) (Units: $1,000, %)

	Japan	Northeast and Southeast Asia	China (incl. Hong Kong)	North America	Europe	Other	Total
Music Exports	21,638	6,411	2,369	351	299	201	31,269
Share	69.2	20.5	7.6	1.1	1.0	0.8	100.0

(Source: KOCCA (2010), *Music Industry White Paper*)

G. *Future tasks*

Production of "sure-fire content" and emergence of global K-pop stars

Universally appealing "sure-fire content" gave birth to *Hallyu*, and K-pop needs content that can generate global hits. Since the influence of individual K-pop hits is not as lasting as that of TV dramas, successful songs must be continually released for solid artist branding. The Korean music industry must develop international stars as well as competitive content to leap into the global market. Stars are linked with content: quality content creates stars, and vice versa. Entrenchment of this virtuous cycle can lead to global stars. As singers have the greatest potential to become stars, the popularity of Korean music and film in the US could give rise to global *Hallyu* celebrities.

Preparing a transparent and fair contract system

Stable growth for this new surge of *Hallyu* in the global market requires the construction of transparent contractual systems acceptable by international standards and the stabilization of the talent management industry's star production processes. Cooperation between the private and public sectors is necessary to induce and improve constructive and fair practices. In July 2009, the Fair Trade Commission (FTC) announced and recommended the use of the "Standard Contract for Artists of Popular Culture." Reasonable improvements to this contract are necessary.

Differentiated localization by target market

Entry strategies should consider local consumer preferences and differentiation from competitors. Girls' Generation chose "Genie," not "Gee," as its debut song in Japan upon deciding that "Genie" would most effectively impress Japanese fans by inscribing a distinctive image in contrast to girl groups in Japan. Partnering with strong local distribution networks or opening new distribution channels is important. We should understand local management, contract, and profit sharing systems and apply them by utilizing local personnel.

Entry into the US, the world's largest content market

The US content market's enormous size and symbolic status make success there a shortcut for global entry. The US market is composed of exclusive inner circles; thorough strategies are necessary to overcome this hurdle. Key networks should be established in Hollywood, including with Korean-American and other Asian counterparts. Strong networks can be achieved through social media, which provide direct exposure and deliver information to relevant industries and foreign media that have the public's attention. For example, in 2008, influential entertainment industry blogger Perez Hilton shared the music video for "Nobody" by Wonder Girls, praising it highly. His blog entry led to the group signing a contract with CAA, the largest talent agency in the US, and laid the foundation for their entry into the American market. Epik High used the group's website *Map the Soul* to meet overseas fans and sell audio files. After happening upon a 2 NE1 music video, will.i.am, producer and leader of globally renowned group the Black Eyed Peas, proposed collaboration on an album targeting American and global audiences.

Cooperation with corporations and governments to protect intellectual property

Asian nations must prepare globally oriented institutional strategies to protect copyright. Strong laws and institutions appropriate for digital environments must be put in place, along with education and promotion efforts to increase awareness of copyright protection. New profit models must be developed in order to deal with intellectual property issues.

2.3.2. The Three Emperors of K-Pop

Reference: "The Three Emperors of K-Pop," *Monthly Jungang*, Baek Seung-ah, December 2011, pp. 106–111.

A.   The records of the three Hallyu kingdoms: innovators in the music industry, foreign marketing strategies, and everything in between

A recent British newspaper headline read, "London Is Going K-Pop Crazy." The trend extends beyond the UK. The younger generation in Latin American countries such as Peru and Mexico, as well as in France, Germany, and other parts of Europe, is being mesmerized by the novel appeal of K-pop. What is it about K-pop that entices them? Japanese critics praise K-pop performers as "idols who've evolved into artists." Credit is due to the talent agencies that groom idol stars and plan their careers. Herewith is an in-depth report on SM, JYP, and YG Entertainment, the three talent agencies pushing the boundaries of the Korean Wave.

"Ring ding dong, ring ding dong, ring diggy ding diggy, ding." The familiar tune echoes across Red Square in Moscow. Over 200 young men and women flock to the center of the square and get in formation. What on Earth is going on?

At the end of September, a flash mob for the idol group SHINee in Red Square was shown on MBC-TV's *K-Pop Road Show 40120*. A flash mob is an event in which people prearrange via social media to gather and perform in public. It is not every day that you see a large-scale dance performance set to foreign songs in Red Square, the centuries-old symbol of power in Russia and the site of countless historic events. The members of SHINee were moved to tears by the sight that unfolded before them. The moment offered proof that the Korean Wave has spread across Asia and reached Europe.

K-pop isn't a fleeting trend. It is well established as a unique genre that has captivated young music fans all over the world. At least a dozen K-pop idol groups—Girls' Generation, Super Junior, SHINee, Wonder Girls, 2PM, 2 NE1, Big Bang, and KARA—enjoy great popularity abroad.

K-pop is a hot topic among the foreign media as well. The BBC and the French press have featured articles about K-pop's conquest of Europe. The articles focused on the strategies of Korean talent agencies and the singular grooming process of idol stars. One article's analysis held that "the precise calculations of talent agencies" lie at the root of K-pop fever.

The major Korean talent agencies have indeed been a prime force driving neo-*Hallyu* through K-pop. SM Entertainment, JYP Entertainment, and YG Entertainment (hereafter SM, JYP, and YG), led by Lee Soo-man, Park Jin-young, and Yang Hyun-suk, respectively, have produced numerous idol stars and are referred to these days as the "*Hallyu* triumvirate." Far surpassing other agencies in size and strategizing, each company has a clearly defined style that mirrors the personality of its CEO.

Aspects of SM, JYP, and YG have much in common with the states of Wei, Shu, and Wu, whose histories are detailed in the *Records of the Three Kingdoms.* Let's now have a closer look at the inner workings of these three *Hallyu* empires.

B.   SM—Wei state: Strongest army, best strategy

"No American teen pop group has been this productive even at the height of its popularity. This success is significant enough for a Korean group to be coveted by an American reality program, or any other TV show or major talent agency." A local review of the SM Town Live World Tour at Madison Square Garden praised the performance that took place on October 23. A *New York Times* reporter who attended this concert, which featured Girls' Generation, Super Junior, TVXQ, SHINee, and F(x), wrote a rave review with thorough analyses of the appeal of each group. An impressive 15,000 people flocked to the concert, which ran for over 3 and a half hours. Fans from all over the US sang along to the songs and cheered in Korean, to the stars' surprised delight. The power of SM, which had proved its magnitude in spreading K-pop across Europe, had now reached across the Atlantic to the US.

SM without a doubt sits in the eye of the K-pop storm. Lee Soo-man (60) evokes Cao, the Wei general who ruled a state with over 10 million subjects and 1 million soldiers, and brought order back to the land with his meritocratic promotion policy. Like Wei, which boasted the greatest military power and most effective diplomatic strategies, SM is ahead of JYP and YG in recruiting talent and tackling foreign markets.

Above all, Lee Soo-man has had an illustrious career as an "idol groomer" without equal. Since the end of the 1990s with H.O.T. and SES, the original Korean idol groups, SM has taken talented performers and put them through rigorous training to produce stars. Lee was also the first to come up with the concept of the "trainee period." The average trainee period of SM performers is around five years. Sooyoung, Jessica, and Hyoyeon of Girls' Generation each spent seven years as trainees.

SM holds open auditions every Saturday in Korea and regular international auditions in the US, China, and Thailand, which Lee Soo-man attends as a judge. The "K-Pop Global Audition," held in Almaty, Kazakhstan on July 11, attracted 1,600 aspirants from within the country as well as neighboring nations like Russia and Kyrgyzstan.

Those who pass the auditions receive individualized vocal, dance, and acting training, as well as Japanese or Chinese language classes. The trainees regularly perform concerts in which their progress is evaluated. SM ensures that its trainees meet adequate academic standards: those with substandard grades are dropped regardless of their artistic talent. Debut opportunities only come for those who have successfully worked through all parts of the trainee program. Currently 30 trainees at SM are working towards their dreams.

SM prefers attractive young men and women. Choosing conventional good looks over individual character, SM prepares a concept for a new idol group and slots trainees in. Idol groups typically consist of members with distinctive yet complementary qualities: the "ace" who sets the image of the group (Yoona, in the case of Girls' Generation), the vocalist who sets the musical standard (Taeyeon), and the innocent youngest member (Seohyeon).

To assume that SM sacrifices musical standards for pretty faces, however, is a serious misjudgment. SM seeks a high standard in both. Music critic Lee Mun-won has said, "Surprisingly, SM produces the best singers of the agencies. For instance, the members of TVXQ, who can handle all genres including hip-hop, ballad, and even classical, are as talented as the vocalists who appear on *I Am a Singer*."

SM's strategies for expanding into foreign markets also seem unparalleled. In the late 1990s when Korean singers rarely had careers abroad, SM carved out a space in Japan for SES, then later BoA and TVXQ. In 2001, SM founded SM Japan, a subsidiary based there, to pave the way for its expansion. In cooperation with the large Japanese agency AVEX, which employs such big-name stars as Namie Amuro, SM increased the visibility of its own singers. Using the same strategy, it founded SM USA in 2008, and SM-True, with the Thai telecommunications company True, in August.

Collaborating with well-known foreign songwriters has also been a key SM strategy. For the last few years, SM has been buying songs written by composers from Norway, Denmark, and elsewhere in Europe. Popular Girls' Generation songs "Genie," "Run Devil Run," and "Hoot" all received the European touch. "Genie" was written by DSign Music, a songwriting group based in Norway, and "Run Devil Run" is the work of British composer Alex James. SHINee's "Juliet," F(x)'s "Hot Summer," BoA's "Hurricane Venus," and Super Junior's "Miracle U" were all written by foreign songwriters.

"The Girls' Generation song 'Genie' incorporates melodic, prototypically European trance (a genre of electronic music characterized by repetitive rhythms)," said Lee Mun-won. "But it surpasses conventional Europop in its stylishness. SM's strategy of rearranging foreign songs seems to have met a positive response in Europe."

"The Boys," the most recent Girls' Generation song to sweep the charts, is the brainchild of Teddy Riley, producer for the late Michael Jackson. SM seems to be moving away from European stylings and opting for a more American sound to increase accessibility. The third album by Girls' Generation will be distributed internationally through Interscope Records, a Universal Music Group (UMG) subsidiary. But Girls' Generation has no immediate plans to enter the American market. The plan for now is to focus on Korea and Asia, and then slowly expand to the US. "It's a wise move on SM's part to pave its way to the international stage by employing a 'glocal' strategy rather than going global right away," says pop culture critic Jeong Deok-hyun. "Whether it's about nurturing talent or marketing tactics, SM is a Goliath, far surpassing all other agencies."

C. JYP—Shu State: The strict Park Jin-young kingdom

"When Park Jin-young stumbles, so does JYP," popular music experts say half-jokingly about JYP. Park Jin-young (40), CEO, producer, and composer, is involved in every aspect of all JYP artists' work. The "Park Jin-young Army" would be a more fitting name for the JYP stable, where everything from recruitment to album production and styling revolves around Park.

"Tell Me," Wonder Girls' song with the catchy disco melody that swept the charts four years ago, was written, choreographed, and produced by Park. Its retro choreography, which was wildly popular among all demographics in Korea from children to office workers and soldiers, has a notorious origin. Park Jin-young was in the US working on a record and could not be present for the meeting to set the choreography for "Tell Me." So he came up with some moves on the spot and sent a video file to Korea. The clip of Park dancing the original "Tell Me" dance in shorts and a tank top circulated widely on the Internet. The anecdote speaks to the strict Park Jin-young autocracy at the agency.

Park's hands-on style is reminiscent of Zhuge Liang, the chancellor of Shu who controlled every detail of every plan, from the military to the diplomatic sphere. Just as Zhuge Liang had nothing in his sights for seven years besides the northern expeditions, so is JYP intent on breaking into the US market.

JYP's strategy for foreign expansion is simple enough. Although 2PM and 2AM entered the Japanese market recently, JYP has never been interested in Japan. The US has been JYP's one and only goal. Wonder Girls, who enjoyed massive popularity in Korea since their debut, chose the US as their first foreign market in 2009. Most Korean artists go through the Asian markets of Japan and China before attempting the US, but Wonder Girls skipped this step. Their strategy initially seemed to have succeeded. In their first year in the US they entered the Billboard charts with "Nobody," and toured the country with the Jonas Brothers.

However, it now appears that Wonder Girls gained little from their time in the US. As Teddy Riley so bluntly put it, "Wonder Girls are flops in America." What they accomplished in the US falls short of success. Jeong Deok-hyun says, "JYP is following a strategy that is too global for an era of glocalization. JYP's strategy is to re-establish his artists' domestic prestige through the glamour of their 'entry into the US market.'"

JYP's musical style largely draws on retro black music from the 1970s. Sensational, feminist lyrics are Park's trademark and unique to his artists. JYP artists are often not conventionally attractive but have memorable personalities. When recruiting talent, a unique look is ranked above a pretty face. But Park doesn't have a set list of criteria—all depends on his instincts.

JYP holds open auditions every first and third Sunday of the month. A development team for new talent runs a tight ship from audition to training, and all trainees receive at least two years of intensive coaching from Park himself. Only those who survive these two grueling years go on to become JYP artists. The examples of Sunye from Wonder Girls and Jo Kwon from 2 AM, who both spent eight years as trainees, attest to the challenges of the JYP stable.

Meanwhile, Wonder Girls released their second album on November 7, after a hiatus of a year and a half. The title song "Be My Baby" was written and composed by Park, but the album generated a buzz long before its release thanks to Wonder Girls' collaboration with Jonte, Beyoncé's choreographer, and Johnny Wujek, Katy Perry's stylist. Early next year, *Wonder Girls at the Apollo*, a TV movie produced by Nick Cannon, Mariah Carey's husband, will air. Given JYP's "Westward Ho!" expedition, one can't help but be curious what will come of Wonder Girls' ongoing efforts to establish themselves in the American market.

D.   YG—Wu State, blazing its own trail

From singers Big Mama and Gummy to idol groups 2 NE1 and Big Bang, YG artists are recognized for their talent. Agency head Yang Hyun-suk (42) is a former member of Seo Taiji and Boys, the group that pioneered hip-hop in Korea. The "YG" stands for Yang-gun, his nickname during his days with Seo Taiji. After the group disbanded in 1996, Yang founded "Hyun Productions" to discover and train new singers; the company was renamed "YG" in 1998.

True to his musical origins, Yang continued to train hip-hop artists through YG. Hip-hop is a genre that originates in the African-American youth culture of 1970s New York. Embracing ideals of freedom and improvisation, hip-hop is characterized in large part by rap and break dancing. These days, new forms of hip-hop have incorporated acoustic sounds.

Like hip-hop, YG suggests a general atmosphere of freedom. YG artists pursue their own artistic visions without being restricted by trends, a feature that has earned YG a reputation as a maverick.

YG's behavior can be likened to Wu State, which did not take part in the war between Wei and Shu over who would receive the torch of power from the Han Dynasty. Instead, Wu cultivated its own culture based on fertile land and plentiful resources. YG and Wu State are similar in that the latter dedicated itself to settling the vast unclaimed territories to the south rather than fighting over the northern territories as Wei and Shu did.

YG artists are not as attractive as the artists of the other two agencies, to the extent that some say, "You shouldn't look too good if you want to become a YG trainee." YG idol groups do not follow the conventional idol formula of a pretty or handsome look. The reputation for talent is boosted in that YG takes advantage of a general prejudice that good looks excuse lack of talent. In other words, the YG strategy is to find untapped markets by thinking outside the box. The ethos is well represented by 2NE1, a girl group known for talent superior to other girl groups and its large female fan base.

YG does not hold regular open auditions. Instead, the talent development team sifts through demo tapes and videos. Recently, YG opened an audition site for user-created content to cast a wider net. The first round of evaluations takes two to five weeks. Applicants who pass the first round go through scrutiny of their talent and a screen test; those who make it through a second round get an interview, which is the third stage before becoming a trainee. Currently 32 artists are training at YG, 2 of whom (Kang Seung-yun, 18, and Kim Eun-bi, 19) made the top 11 of the survival audition show "Superstar K2" last year.

YG started breaking into foreign markets late in the game. It would be accurate to say that YG has concentrated on Korea rather than venturing overseas.

Jeong Deok-hyeon points out, "Instead of following the currents of popular music, YG artists are more inclined to develop their own style and broaden their territory organically." A few years ago, however, YG also began to focus on expanding in Japan, where Big Bang, a five-member all-male hip-hop group, was introduced in 2009. YG founded a new agency in July called "YGEX" with the Japanese talent agency AVEX. With YGEX as a platform, 2NE1 also entered the Japanese market in September.

The two groups have been well received in Japan. Big Bang's first single reached #3 on the weekly Oricon Singles Chart, a leading Japanese music chart, and the album went on to sell between 30,000 and 40,000 copies. Recently 2NE1's debut mini-album reached #1 on Oricon two days after its release. The success of 2NE1 in Japan is particularly notable given that hip-hop is not as popular in Japan as in Korea.

YG's penchant for specialization is also reflected in 2NE1's Japan debut. Whereas most Korean artists debut there with a mini-album that contains one or two tracks, 2NE1 debuted with an official album of five songs. There is little doubt that YG took into account the improbability of fans shelling out a lot for an album by a relatively unknown artist. "They must have predicted that using the same tactics as Girls' Generation or KARA, who are already popular in Japan, wouldn't help with a non-mainstream genre like hip-hop," says music critic Lee Mun-won. "YG appears to have found a strategy that discouraged the comparison." YG characteristically does not compromise on musical style, and targets niche markets and avoids shortcuts even in foreign territories.

Befitting the expression the "Records of the Three *Hallyu* Kingdoms," SM, JYP, and YG each have their own personality, concepts, and strategies, but are united in contributing to the foundation of a love of K-pop and their role in leading K-pop into the future.

While some foreign media outlets have argued that these agencies employ inhumane trainee programs to mold idol groups into perfect products, K-pop as we know it would not have been possible without these systematic programs and meticulous strategies. I look forward to the new strategies and concepts they will come up with to keep the Korean Wave surging onward.

2.3.3.   Revitalizing the Talent Management Industry

Reference: *Talent Agency Registration System and Revitalization of Talent Management Industry: A Comparative Analysis of Korea and Japan*, Baek Seung-hyuk, KOCCA Focus: 2012–7, No. 55, July 10, 2012, pp. 5–22.

A.   Context

Talent management companies as key player in content production

The four main elements in the content production and distribution system are producers, distributors, talent management companies, and entertainers. From early in the new millennium, talent management companies, with their exclusively managed entertainers, began to have a significant influence over the casting and production of broadcast content, films, variety shows, and concerts. The role of managers and talent management companies, which in the past was limited to overseeing entertainers' schedules and private affairs, has become more segmented and specialized. Their role now includes public relations, image management, conclusion of contracts, and securing copyright. Therefore, there has been a shift in the main players in the talent management industry from small outfits to expert companies. The introduction of digital technology has opened a new multichannel, multimedia era. Talent management plays an important role in forming strategies and systems to brand and expose entertainers in various platforms.

Talent management companies leading *Hallyu*

With increased demand for *Hallyu* content, enterprises in other industries are watching the success of entertainment companies with interest. Conditions for industrial growth are becoming increasingly favorable for talent management companies to take a leading role in driving *Hallyu*. K-pop by idol groups TVXQ, SHINee, Girls' Generation, 2AM, and Big Bang created and managed by SM, JYP, YG, and other large talent management companies has sparked a new boom in *Hallyu* centered on Southeast Asia. TV dramas such as *Iris* and *You Are My Destiny*, which feature members of idol groups, have also played a major role in spreading *Hallyu*. The status of talent management companies has been elevated through their strategy of training idols as "total entertainers" who cross genres, and media channels' desire to exploit idols' celebrity power.

Talent management: A definition

In general, the terms "management" and "entertainment" are used in combination when discussing talent agencies and their business in Korea. Academic discussions do not offer a universal definition of talent management. According to Kim Y. (2009) and Lee S. (2009), however, talent management forms part of the cultural industry and involves the production and overall management of activities that bring mass entertainment. The talent management industry includes individuals and groups that plan, manage, and maintain entertainers' acting appearances, album productions, and product endorsements with the intention of generating a profit. Talent management businesses engage in entertainer training, content production, public relations, management of celebrities, etc. Talent management systems were created to reduce transaction costs and maximize the efficiency of the value chain. By reducing the overall cost of planning, information gathering, management, and production, these systems facilitate the overall operation of the cultural industries (Park S., 2007).

Agencies

Agencies act as brokers between producers (broadcasters and production companies) and entertainers, and oversee the negotiation of casting and contracts. After the signing of a contract, an agency takes on the role of ensuring its fulfillment, protecting the entertainer's legal rights, and negotiating product endorsements and events. In the US, the functions of management and agency are separated, and management companies and agencies do not train entertainers. Agencies are not legally allowed to own a production company or engage in production. Unlike talent management companies, individuals and groups are required to obtain legal licensing to form agencies, which are then categorized under the rubric of employment agencies by the Employment Security Act. In Korea, only modeling agencies that place models for advertisements and events require licenses, while most talent management companies and agencies operate without a license or authorization, as their business type is registered as a "service" and falls under the category of "entertainment agency" or "talent management" (Jang G., 2011).

Necessity of knowledge of industry structure and enforcement of policy measures for continuous growth of talent management industry

The talent management industry gives impetus to the creation and development of content. Without a continuous and abundant supply of content creators and performers (entertainers), not only does ongoing development of the content industry become difficult, but opportunities for development, discovery, and commercialization of new content are also lost. Then the potential added value to related industries is nullified, which makes slow growth difficult to overcome. The development of related industries depends on the quantity of goods and services produced and supplied. In the case of the content industry, producers and performers are crucial in determining growth. Therefore, talent management companies, which aid development of content producers and performers as well as plan and create new outlets, have become and will continue to serve as an important structural basis for healthy industry growth.

B.   Evolution and structure of the talent management industry

From personal to corporate management

Talent management in Korea began in the 1960s with managers for singers. This personal management system continued to expand and was adopted by movie actors in the 1970s and TV actors in the 1980s. The system was not compli-cated, and personal management companies operated on a small scale and varied little from a standard structure that consisted of a president, director, and (road) manager.

Talent management enterprises began to develop in the mid-1990s with investment from large corporations such as Daewoo Group, SaeHan Media, Cheil Jedang (CJ), and Hanbo Group. Digital Media, an affiliate company of SaeHan Media, founded a subsidiary talent management company, Star Search, in 1994, heralding the rise of management enterprises. Daewoo Group began a management business focusing on fostering aspiring actors under the production company Cine 2000, which was fully funded by Daewoo.[53] From the 2000s, mergers and acquisitions of small management compa-nies and an influx of capital led to more extensive and sophisticated corporate structures, giving rise to large, comprehensive companies. Idol management companies founded by ex-entertainers have emerged and developed into indus-try leaders. SidusHQ (currently IHQ), a large talent management company, was

---

[53] Kim G. (1996), "Cultural War among Large Corporations, Part 6: All Eyes on the Growth Potential of 'Star Systems,'" *Dong-A Ilbo*. Feb. 27, 1996.

Table 2–51. Estimate of talent management companies in Korea

Specializes in Singers	Specializes in Actors	Manages both Singers and Actors	Total
245	86	59	390

(Source: KOCCA (2010), "Fact-finding Survey on South Korea's Entertainment Industry")

formed through the merger of the successful venture firm Locus, production company Uno Film, talent management agency EBM, and online movie theater Web Cinema. The merger proved successful, and the company soon listed its stock. SM Entertainment, founded in 1995 by singer Lee Soo-man, was listed on the KOSDAQ trading board of the Korea Exchange in April 2004. Following this achievement, the company began to show rapid growth. JYP Entertainment and YG Entertainment, founded by Park Jin-young (1996) and Yang Hyun-suk (1998), respectively, emerged as worthy rivals of SM Entertainment, and both have demonstrated continuous high growth.

According to business reports for the first quarter of 2012, disclosed on the Financial Supervisory Service Data Analysis, Retrieval and Transfer (FSS DART) system, SM Entertainment reported estimated sales of ₩38.5 billion, a 198.71% increase year on year, and higher than the sales of JYP Entertainment and YG Entertainment combined. In that period, total revenue for YG Entertainment was around ₩17.9 billion, and that of JYP Entertainment was ₩1.1billion.[54]

An estimated 1,000 talent management companies are known to be active in South Korea. According to the "Fact-finding Survey on South Korea's Entertainment Industry" published by KOCCA in 2010, as of the second half of 2009, 245 talent management companies specialized in singers, 86 specialized in actors, and 59 managed both singers and actors.

According to a press release from the MCST (2012),[55] the Corea Entertainment Management Association and the Korea Entertainment Producer's Association have identified approximately 500 talent management companies. The actual number of active companies, however, is estimated to be around 1,000. Small- and medium-sized talent management companies are frequently established and liquidated, as this type of business does not require licensing. In order to establish a company, one must receive a business license. This can be achieved by simply registering each place of business at the tax office with local jurisdiction, in accordance with Article 5 of the Value-Added Tax Act.[56] Because of this easy registration process and frequent changes of company names, the exact number of companies is difficult to ascertain.

---

[54] Total sales of JYP Entertainment are relatively low because JYP Creative, a subsidiary of JYP Entertainment, is unlisted and its sales are, therefore, not included in the total (Lee H., 2012).

[55] MCST (2012), "Thorough Investigation of Talent Agencies to be Executed with Introduction of Agency and Manager Registration System" [Press Release].

[56] Article 2 of the Value-Added Tax Act stipulates that an "entrepreneur," a person who independently supplies goods or services on a business basis, whether commercial or not, is liable for value-added tax. The purpose of business registration is to manage entrepreneurs who are liable for tax payment through a government registry.

Industry size and revenue

The total revenue of talent management companies traded on KOSDAQ is about ₩450 billion. Among the 304 member companies of the Korea Entertainment Producer's Association and the 184 member companies of the Corea Entertainment Management Association, 8 talent management companies are publicly traded on KOSDAQ, including SM Entertainment, YG Entertainment, JYP Entertainment, LOEN Entertainment, and Pan Entertainment. Only two listed talent management companies, LOEN Entertainment and SM Entertainment, reported revenue of over ₩100 billion. Total revenue of all talent management companies listed on KOSDAQ is estimated at ₩450 billion. This figure is lower than Kyobo Book Centre's total revenue of ₩544.1 billion in 2011.[57] The revenue of IHQ is lower than LOEN Entertainment, SM Entertainment, and YG Entertainment, but IHQ is the only talent management company listed on the securities market. IHQ reported revenue of ₩48.3 billion in 2011. Of the 500 member companies of talent management industry associations, only a few are listed on the stock exchange, which implies that most talent management companies in Korea are small and that their assets and financial stability are undervalued.[58]

C. Types of talent management companies

Talent management system based on scouting established entertainers

This is a system for managing influential and established entertainers scouted by experienced producers. It involves producers with extensive experience in the entertainment industry and investment of capital by large corporations. Contracts are entered upon with popular, established entertainers, who are assigned professional managers. With investment from SaeHan Media, Star Search pioneered management enterprises in the mid-1990s. The company established contracts with 23 popular and established entertainers, such as Shin Eun-kyung, Yeom Jung-ah, Kang Moon-young, Kim Hye-ri, Choi Soo-ji, and Woo Hee-jin, which displayed their prowess as a total talent management company. IHQ, the parent corporation of large talent management company SidusHQ, has exclusive contracts with around 60 celebrities, including Kim Su-ro, Jang Hyuk, Jo In-sung, Park Jae-bum, Cha Tae-hyun, and Han Ye-seul. The company relies on a corps of celebrities with established popularity derived from their image and talent.

Talent management system based on investment in talent search and production

The talent management system centers on strategies for creating idols. Former entertainers utilize knowhow from their industry experience to determine investment direction and shape would-be performers discovered through auditions into complete entertainers. Since SM Entertainment's discovery and nurturing of BoA, JYP Entertainment, YG Entertainment, and most large talent management companies have introduced an audition and training system, which they continue to develop.

---

[57] Kyobo Book Centre Audit Report, FSS DART System.
[58] YG Entertainment, even with a strong lineup of top idol singers, was disqualified from listing in 2010. After a second application, the company was listed on KOSDAQ in 2011.

Table 2–52.   Revenue of KOSDAQ-listed talent management companies

No.	Talent Management Company	Revenue in 2011 (₩1 billion)
1	LOEN Entertainment	167.2
2	SM Entertainment	109.9
3	Wellmade STARM	21.4
4	Yedang Company	5.7
5	YG Entertainment	78.1
6	JYP Entertainment	9.9
7	KeyEast	26.1
8	Pan Entertainment	31.7
Total		450.0

(Sources: KRX KIND System and the FSS DART System)

Table 2–53.   Status of talent management companies

Survey Item	Result
Time in business under current ownership	5.5 years (mean)
Number of companies managed by company's representative in past decade	2.45 companies (mean)
Business areas	Talent search (29%), actor training (27%), agency fees including casting (19%), subsidiary rights including portrait rights (11%), entertainment academy (3%), album production (3%), other (6%)
Number of salaried employees	10.95 (mean)
Number of casual employees	2.41 (mean)
Total employees	12.36 persons (mean)
% of companies engaged in both management and agency work	89%
Sales ratio of management business to agency business	79:21
Number of entertainers currently under contract	11.41 persons (mean)
Breakdown of entertainers by category	Actors (83%), MCs (7%), models (4%), non-adult actors (3%), comedians (2%), other (2%)
Number of shareholders among entertainers currently under contract	1.89 persons (mean)
Share of largest shareholding entertainer	33.92% (mean)

(Source: KOCCA (2010), "Fact-finding Survey on South Korea's Entertainment Industry")

Table 2–54.   IHQ sales composition (Unit: ₩1,000,000)

Category	First Quarter of 2012 Revenue	%	2011 Revenue	%	2010 Revenue	%
Management	6,186	46.2%	17,751	36.8%	16,754	41.2%
Albums	23	0.2%	159	0.3%	416	1.1%
TV Performances	4,452	33.3%	9,997	20.1%	1,841	4.8%
Variety Shows	718	5.4%	3,970	8.2%	3,086	8.1%
Digital Content	1,452	10.8%	13,661	28.3%	14,162	37.0%
Content (concerts)	364	2.6%	2,070	4.3%	2,194	5.7%
Entertainment Academy	168	1.3%	640	1.3%	710	1.9%
Other	23	0.2%	52	0.7%	99	0.2%
Total	13,386	100.0	48,300	100.0	39,262	100.0

(Source: FSS DART System)

Table 2–55.   Pros and cons of talent management system based on scouting established entertainers

Pros	Cons
Exposure is possible immediately after scouting.	Difficult to maintain continuity of contract between company and entertainer.
Entertainers' influence can be maintained.	Difficult to provide sustainable and stable training and embrace new challenges after setbacks.
Low investment in development.	High dependency on entertainers.
Entertainers have more freedom to act independently.	High possibility of disputes between entertainers and managers.
Opportunities for success through drive and passion can be found.	

(Source: Korea Entertainment Industry Association (2007), "Forum Document 2")

This system involves strict post-debut star management and production. Recently, talent management companies have come to practice comprehensive handling of stars, wherein discovery and nurturing of talent are followed by strict post-debut management of image, training, marketing, etc. The system includes strategic personal branding of idol groups' lead singers along with increasing recognition and popularity of the group as a whole, and carefully planned post-debut management coverage, including additional training camps, etc. (Lee M., 2011). The sales composition data disclosed through the FSS DART System for JYP and YG Entertainment show that star management businesses relying on the marketability of well-rounded entertainers accounted for over 70% of the companies' sales.

Table 2-56. JYP entertainment sales composition (Unit ₩1,000,000)

Year	Sales Category	Revenue	%
First Half of 2012	Commodities	0	0%
	Records	143	13.3%
	Management	877	81.6%
	Online Music	45	4.2%
	Other[1]	10	0.9%
	Total	1,075	100.0%
2011	Commodities	19	0.2%
	Records	228	2.3%
	Management	4,253	42.9%
	Online Music	859	8.7%
	Other	4,564	46%
	Total	9,923	100.0%

[1] "Other" includes subsidiary sales through merchandising and licensing of dramas and movies, publishing, brand management, etc.
(Source: FSS DART System)

Table 2-57. YG entertainment sales composition (Unit ₩1,000,000)

Year	Sales Category	Revenue	%
First Half of 2012	Albums/Audio	4,338	24.3%
	Product endorsements	3,190	17.8%
	Concert performances	3,164	17.7%
	Other	7,183	40.2%
	Total	17,875	100.0%
2011	Albums/Audio	20,371	25.8%
	Product endorsements	11,933	15.3%
	Concert performances	17,425	22.3%
	Other	28,391	36.3%
	Total	78,121	100.0%

(Source: FSS DART System)

D. Outcomes

Creating idol stars with multiple talents and skills through training

Recently idols have been branching into genres outside their specialization by capitalizing on their skills in their primary field and their visual appeal. K-pop stars are not only acting in TV dramas but also featuring in other genres, including motion pictures, variety shows, and musical theater.

Table 2–58.   Pros and cons of management system based on investment in talent search and production

Pros	Cons
Entertainer's chance of stardom increases with brand of management company.	Contracts may extend over a long period.
Increased feasibility of market entry at home and abroad.	Overzealous fandom might arise among youth.
Managing entertainers' activities through strategic teams can increase economic benefits for company and diversify business models strategically.	Contribution to spread of a celebrity-oriented mentality.

(Source: Korea Entertainment Industry Association (2007), "Forum Document 2")

JYJ member Kim Junsu starred in the Korean production of the Austrian musical *Mozart!* at the Sejong Center for the Performing Arts in 2010; tickets sold out. Kyuhyun of Super Junior and Sunny of Girls' Generation played in the musical *Catch Me if You Can* and received positive reviews.

Hallyu has increased the number of tourists visiting Korea to attend concerts featuring idols, thereby pushing up the value of derivative *Hallyu* products. According to statistics from the Korea Tourism Organization, roughly 9.8 million foreign nationals visited South Korea in 2011, an 11.3% increase from the previous year. Between 2010 and 2011, tourism from countries in which *Hallyu* is influential increased significantly: Japanese visitors increased from 3.02 million to 3.29 million, Chinese from 1.86 million to 2.22 million, and Taiwanese from 400,000 to 420,000.

"The 2011 Fact-finding Survey on Foreign Tourists," published by the MCST in 2012, surveyed visitors from Japan, China, Taiwan, and Singapore on their reasons for visiting Korea and the major activities they participated in.[59] "Visiting drama or movie filming locations/fan meetings" and "concerts, folk events" ranked among the top 10.[60] The results showed minor variation between male and female tourists.

Expanding *Hallyu* content through global management

After the rise of such actors as Bae Yong-joon, Choi Ji-woo, and Ryu Si-won, *Hallyu* seemed to subside until star management systems trained and produced idols that were able to imbue *Hallyu* with new life. The global spread of *Hallyu* is expected to contribute greatly to elevating Korea's rank on the National Brand Competitiveness Index, benefiting the nation. More and more K-pop stars are being featured in Japanese TV dramas. TVXQ's Hero Jaejoong and Micky

---

[59] This analysis is based on foreign tourists who responded that their main purpose for travel to Korea was leisure/relaxation/vacation, healthcare and treatment, religion and pilgrimage, or shopping.

[60] According to an annual survey of Japanese tourists, between 2007 and 2010 more people came to visit drama or movie locations or attend fan meetings than for recreation. In 2011, the percentage of those who came to visit locations or fan meetings (11.1%) was only slightly lower than those who came for general recreation (11.5%) (MCST, 2012).

Table 2–59. Idol star expansion into new genres

| Case | Strategy | |
	Fan Base Formation (Strategic Branding)	One Source Multi Use (Strengthening Content)
TVXQ	Micky Yoochun: KBS Drama – *Sungkyunkwan Scandal*	Xiah Junsu: Musical – *Mozart!* U-Know Yunho: Musical – *Goong* TVXQ: Photo Album – "The Prince in Prague" **(Content)**
Bug Bang	Daesung: SBS Variety Show – *Family Outing*	T.O.P: TV Drama – *Iris*, Film – *71: Into the Fire* G-Dragon: MBC Variety Show – *Infinite Challenge*
Girls' Generation	Yoona: KBS Drama – *You Are My Destiny*	Sunny: Musical – *Catch Me if You Can* Yuri and Tiffany: MBC Music Program – *Show! Music Core*
Super Junior	Choi Si-won: SBS Drama – *Oh! My Lady*	Kyuhyun: Musical – *Catch Me if You Can* Heechul: KBS Drama – *Sharp*, SBS Drama *Bad Family* Kangin: Film – *Hello, Schoolgirl* Shindong: SBS Variety Show – *Strong Heart*
CNBLUE	Jung Yong-hwa: SBS Drama – *You're Beautiful*	Kang Min-hyuk: KBS Drama – *My Husband Got a Family* Lee Jong-hyun: Film – *Acoustic*

Table 2–60. Korea's cosmetic exports to China by year (Unit: $1,000)

Year	2006	2007	2008	2009	2010	2011	2012 (June)
Value	85,099	101,354	108,503	127,057	336,795	217,027	92,039

(Source: Korea Customs Service (2012), "Import and Export Trade Statistics")

Yoochun appeared on Fuji TV, playing, respectively, the lead in *Hard to Say I Love You/Sunao ni* Narenakute and a supporting role in *Beautiful Love*. The group KARA was featured in *URAKARA*, a TV drama on TV Tokyo. Satellite TV channel BS Japan added *Music Bank*, produced by KBS, to its regular programming, and BS Asahi added Korean dramas *Marrying the Mafia*, *Golden Fish*, and *Sign*.

The global spread of *Hallyu* has increased interest in Korean consumer goods and services, leading to an increase in exports for industries connected to *Hallyu* on the value chain. With the exception of 2011, Korean export of cosmetics to China has increased steadily since the passion for Korean TV dramas and K-pop first appeared there. This increase is attributed to exposure to the fashion and make-up styles of Korean stars.

E.   Issues for talent management companies and measures for improvement

Lack of specialization in management systems

Korea's talent management systems can be divided into three types: those integrating management and agency work; those that combine management with talent search and training; and those that integrate management and content production. Such systems by their very nature do not specialize, for they encompass multiple business areas simultaneously. Currently, most Korean management companies operate an apprenticeship system. The majority of companies offer personal management for only one to three entertainers, and are not equipped to build an organized, systematic, and specialized management system.

According to a study by Chang Y. (2010),[61] a talent manager's responsibilities can be divided into 7 categories, which are further divided into 14 tasks. Under these 14 tasks are a total of 110 jobs, which include those of both managers and agents. The seven categories of a talent manager's responsibilities are: planning, production, public relations, marketing, administration, management, and other. The 14 detailed tasks are: talent search and development, planning, album production, filming and on-site tasks, PR, online fan club management, data collection, marketing, contracts, clerical work, schedule and road management, personal management of entertainers, assistance in entertainer activities, and human relations.

Advanced talent management systems cannot form under such a comprehensive management structure without specialization. In countries with highly developed management systems, such as the US and Japan, in order to become an agent or manager at a well-known company or agency that provides exclusive services to celebrity entertainers and athletes, one must not only have expert knowledge of the field but also compete fiercely to receive specialized training from the organization. In the US, the functions of management and agency are separate. The agent training programs of the "Big Three" agencies, WMA, CAA, and ICM, are known for their stiff competition. In 2004, the acceptance rate for a training program at a major talent agency was 1 in 30, compared to 1 in 9 for Harvard Law School, 1 in 4 for Columbia University's Graduate School of Journalism, and 1 in 4 for Stanford Graduate School of Business.[62] Actress Yoon Son-ha rose to fame in Japan during the early days of *Hallyu*. Yoon's former manager, who oversaw her every activity, was a Japanese man who had graduated from the prestigious Waseda University and had expert knowledge of management.

Increasing disputes due to an imbalance between supply and demand

While interest in the Korean content industry, centering on K-pop and dramas, has risen steadily at home and abroad, disputes involving talent management companies have also increased since the mid- to late 1990s due to a power imbalance

---

[61] Chang Y. (2010), "A Preliminary Study of Job Performance in Entertainment Management," *Journal of Secretarial Sciences*, The Korean Association of Secretarial Studies.

[62] Bae K. (2005), "Becoming an Agent to a Star is a Greater Feat than Entering Harvard Law School." *MyDaily*, January 25, 2005. Retrieved from http://www.mydaily.co.kr.

Table 2–61. Talent management companies by number of entertainers managed

Contracted Entertainers	Number of Companies	Percentage (%)
0	106	22
1–3	174	36
4–10	172	35
11 or more	36	7
Total	488	100

resulting from a mismatch of supply (entertainers) and demand (management).[63] Despite investigations by the government and the FTC and efforts at self-reform on the part of the talent management industry, remnants of a feudal mentality continue to manifest themselves in criminal cases.

First, issues surround would-be entertainers and trainees. TV producers' acceptance of bribes in exchange for TV appearances by particular entertainers, illegal and fraudulent practices on the part of talent management companies, and sexual harassment of aspirants and trainees are growing social problems. The entertainment industry is plagued by predators taking advantage of the weak: a pop music composer raped a teen after selecting her as a dancer in a music video (1996), a talent management company CEO repeatedly assaulted and took bribes from would-be entertainers (2002), and the CEO of another management company raped an aspiring entertainer and took nude photos of her (2011). The range of assaults and criminal targets is widening.[64]

Secondly, unfair agreements in exclusive management contracts have become a source of problems. Endless disputes have arisen over contracts that give management companies exclusive rights to the activities of entertainers, with mandatory clauses on performances, profit sharing arrangements, privacy rights, etc. Talent management companies make long-term investments in trainees with the hope of the artists' future success. In 2009, TVXQ filed suit against SM Entertainment over their 13-year exclusive contract period and unfair profit sharing. In 2011, singer Younha initiated proceedings against her management company, Lion Media, over unfair profit distribution and invasion of privacy. Actress Kim Hyun-joo is currently in the midst of a legal dispute with her management, The H Entertainment, regarding the deposit on a TV drama deal.[65] Legal disputes over excessive penalties for breach of contract are common after termination of exclusive management contracts as a result of a deliberate violation by entertainers.

Thirdly, there is an issue of limiting the principle of contractual freedom. An entertainer and a talent management company enter into a contract of their own

---

[63] Experts estimate that one million students from primary to high school aspire to become entertainers. Some place the number as high as two million, citing the increase in audition programs by broadcasting companies from 2011. (Kim Go Geum Pyung, May 2012)

[64] Kim Go G. (2012), "Lives of Two Million Would-be Entertainers in the 'Dark Hands' of Shameless Agencies." *Munhwa Ilbo*, April. 20.

[65] Jung E. (2011), "What Can Be Done about the Endless Disputes between Entertainers and Exclusive Management Companies?" *Segye Ilbo*, July 18.

volition, in accordance with the principle of contractual freedom.[66] However, further limits must be placed on the freedom of contract, in order to eliminate unreasonable terms.

- Limiting the principle of contractual freedom: various laws address the principle of contractual freedom by restricting contract methods that exploit a disadvantaged party. The Business Affairs of Licensed Real Estate Agents and Report of Real Estate Transactions Act, the Housing Lease Protection Act, and the Labor Standards Act are examples of legal measures to limit the principle of contractual freedom in order to promote equality between contracting parties.[67]
- Standard contracts: many unfair provisions have been found in the contracts of small- and medium-sized talent management companies as well as those of large companies that give them an advantage over entertainers.[68] Limiting the principle of contractual freedom by introducing standard contracts will help further public welfare, order, and standards of decency. The exclusive contract proposed by JYP Entertainment was approved by the FTC as meeting standard contract criteria. There have been many similar self-regulating efforts in the industry, but the overall situation remains largely unchanged. Adoption of the standard contract published and recommended by the FTC is not mandatory, and its application in the market is wanting. Legal regulations will be necessary to spread fair rules and contract methods throughout the market.

Measures for advancement of the talent management industry

The entertainment industry has been leading the Korean Wave. Since the mid- to late 1990s, however, when the commercial structure of talent management businesses took shape, illegal and fraudulent practices have plagued the industry. Continued growth will require increased transparency and accountability of talent management companies. In order for Korea to foster a professional talent management industry that can systematically facilitate advancement of the entertainment industry, the market must first address unregulated companies run by nonprofessionals unfit to operate them and increase transparency and accountability in the industry.

A joint governmental-civil response system should be formed to investigate talent management companies thoroughly, introduce registration of companies and managers, operate a complaint report center, reinforce education, etc.

---

[66] Freedom of contract refers to the freedom to decide whether to form a contract, the type of contract to form and with whom. It includes the right not to form a contract, meaning that one should not be coerced into an undesired contract. It is derived from the general freedom of action implied in the right to pursue happiness in Article 10 of the Constitution. (Korean Constitutional Court Report, 89Hun-Ma204, June 3, 1991).

[67] Article 103 of the Civil Act (Juristic Acts Contrary to Social Order) stipulates that "a juristic act which has for its object such matters as are contrary to good morals and other social order shall be null and void." Article 104 of the Civil Act (Unfair Juristic Acts) stipulates that "a juristic act that has conspicuously lost fairness through strained circumstances, rashness, or inexperience of the parties shall be null and void."

[68] Seo K. (2010), "Exclusive Management Contract of 291 Entertainers Ordered for Correction," *Joongang Daily*, June 25.

> **Exclusive Management Contracts**
> **Seoul High Court Decision 2004 Na78754: Scope of Exclusive Representation**
> **by Talent Management Companies**
> An exclusive management contract with an entertainer stipulates that the management company or manager provide services related to negotiating contract terms for appearances and fees, managing performance schedules and public relations, and that the contracted entertainer does not perform independently or through a third party outside the contracted management company or manager. The purpose of most entertainment contracts is to secure the provision of personal services by the entertainer. Even if a manager has an exclusive management contract with an entertainer, concluding a contract for the provision of services without the entertainer's consent, and obliging the entertainer under the exclusive contract, violates the personal liberty and liberty of conscience of the entertainer, and therefore should not be allowed.

In Phase One, companies engaged in businesses such as album planning and production, talent training, and management would be surveyed and analyzed to obtain such data as basic information, main business areas, employees, and exclusively managed entertainers (May 2012). In Phase 2, talent management companies for actors would be thoroughly investigated (first half of 2013). An annual fact-finding survey would help build a database of the talent management industry to facilitate verification of information.

Through the introduction of a registration system for managers and companies, personnel and material requirements will be strengthened to prevent the social problems caused by small, inexperienced talent management companies and managers.[69] The system will increase requirements for companies with assets greater than a set monetary value and level of infrastructure, and build a database of detailed information about management companies' and managers' status. Through the proposed Act on Supporting the Popular Culture and Art Industry, those who violate the Act on the Punishment of Acts of Arranging Sexual Traffic, the Act on Regulation of Amusement Businesses Affecting Public Morals, or the Juvenile Protection Act will be barred from operating or engaging in management businesses. Violations after registration will result in strong sanctions, including suspension of businesses and cancelation of licenses.

The Support Center for Popular Culture Artists under KOCCA (opened on May 12, 2011) works together with a related association to provide ongoing monitoring and legal consultation services. Professional education programs for employees of talent management companies, rookie actors and singers, and aspiring pop artists increase their understanding of the popular culture and art industry (e.g., service contracts) and help them develop a grounding as entertainers.

---

[69] A bill supporting the popular culture industry is currently being developed, but a clear outline for management company and manager registration and for reporting, registering, and licensing businesses has not been established or publicized. In December 2010, Assemblywoman Na Kyung-won presented a bill to support the development of the industry, but it was abrogated with the expiration of her term of office. Clause 3 of this bill stipulated registration and operation of popular culture and talent agencies.

Table 2–62.   Unfair contracts reviewed by the Fair Trade Commission for corrective measures

Date	Target Company	Unfair Provisions	Corrective Measure
July 18, 2002	(Ltd.) 12 talent agencies (Digital SUDA, etc.)	• Requiring excessive indemnity • Requiring biased exclusivity	Corrective recommendation
July 19, 2002	Six record companies (Hyesung Media Tech, etc.)	• Requiring approval of president of the Korea Entertainment Producer's Association for exclusive management contract to take effect • Ruling out or limiting claims for damages without probable cause • Allowing the management company to circumvent public summons procedures in cancelling the contract	Corrective recommendation
June 14, 2004	Power M Co., Ltd.	• Excessive invasion of privacy • Excessive penalties for breach of contract • Coerced PR activities and performances	Corrective recommendation
Sept. 19, 2006	Lee Byung-hui case	• Indefinite period of exclusive contract • Allowing transfer of contract rights	Corrective recommendation
Nov. 20, 2008	10 large talent agencies	• Coerced PR activities and unpaid performances • Excessive invasion of privacy • Allowing talent agency to unilaterally authorize and direct client activities • Allowing talent agency to claim all profit from client activities after the company gives notice of cancellation of contract • Allowing transfer of contract rights to a third party without consent of other party to contract	Corrective order
June 8, 2009	20 small- and medium-sized talent agencies (Star Empire Co., Ltd., etc.)	• Excessive invasion of privacy • Permitting infringement on freedom of occupation • Coerced PR activities and unpaid performances, including events hosted by the company • Allowing transfer of contractual rights to a third party without consent of other party to contract	Voluntary correction, under the condition that the investigated company adopts the Fair Trade Commission's standard exclusive talent management contract by July 20, 2009

(Source: Fair Trade Commission)

The effects of measures to improve the talent management industry are not likely to manifest in the short term. However, dissemination of information and legal regulations are expected to increase transparency and competitiveness in the industry over time. Verification of companies' integrity by an advisory panel will enable trust-based management, and an industry database of corporate structures, operation policies, managerial duties, and so on will help reduce problems like unfair contracts and sexual exploitation. However, the barrier to market entry will be raised with the introduction of the registration system.

Establishing and revising standard contracts to create a fair trade environment in the entertainment industry

Compared to the growth of the entertainment industry, as seen in the recent global spread of *Hallyu*, the creative environment and systems for the protection of the rights of entertainers, including singers and actors, remain underdeveloped. Measures are needed to address fundamental problems in the overall production process, including last-minute delivery of scripts (*jjokdaebon*), all-night shootings, and missed payments. Standard contracts should be established and revised to offer specific guidelines for producers, entertainers, and broadcasters. These should include detailed provisions on the conditions, rights, and duties of contracting parties with regard to media appearances, production, and performance of concerts and events.

Standard contracts should be established and revised and entertainers should be educated on contract terms in order to address issues arising from the related industries' lack of sophistication and the imbalance of bargaining power between contracting parties. A taskforce will be formed to review different fields of the entertainment industry in order to establish practical and realistic standard contracts for the popular culture and art industry within the year, while taking into account subtle differences among genres and entertainers. The Standard Exclusive Management Contract, established in 2009 primarily for singers and actors, will be thoroughly revised in order to reflect changes in the entertainment market and industry. Humanities education and counseling will be provided to the entertainers through the Support Center for Popular Culture Artists operated by KOCCA.

These measures are expected to help establish a creative environment for the production of quality content by protecting the rights of established entertainers and production staff, eliminating unfair trade practices, improving labor conditions, and preventing aspiring and rookie entertainers from being exploited at the start of their careers.

2.3.4. The World of Idols: Jumping through Endless Hoops

Reference: "The World of Idols: Jumping through Endless Hoops: After the Audition Come Grueling Rehearsals and Slave Contracts," *Shin Dong-A*, Song Hwa-sun, March 2011, No. 618, pp. 141–146.

"Is this how you repay us after all we've invested in you?" – Talent Agencies
"We want fair compensation for our work." – Entertainers

Following popular idol group TVXQ, KARA is now also engaged in legal wrangling with its management. The two groups have spoken out against the unfairness of their contracts and the distribution of profits during the height of their popularity in Japan, and each has split among its members three to two on the issue. Sources in the pop industry predict that because Korean idols go through a lengthy training period before debut, these disputes will continue to arise.

No one can deny that this trainee system, unique to Korea, is a primary reason behind the new surge in *Hallyu*. The five members of TVXQ dance in perfect sync down to their fingertips and boast flawless vocal talent. The sight of five slender, beautiful women dancing impeccably choreographed "booty moves" while singing live made KARA famous in Japan. Behind this level of perfection that Japanese idols can only dream of lie enormous agency investments as well as entertainers who hone their craft through grueling practice.

"In the past, many entertainers would just be 'discovered' by casting directors, and this would lead to their debut. Seong Yuri from FinKL, a first generation idol group, became a singer after being scouted by a talent agent at a school art contest. That would be unthinkable these days. Thousands of applicants turn up every time a large agency holds open auditions." "A," who worked as a manager at a major agency since the mid-90s and recently opened his own company, says, "After trainees pass the audition, their path to debut is so demanding that they nickname it the 'Entertainment Service Examination.'"

"A" is not exaggerating. The 1.34 million applicants for the audition show *Superstar K2* on cable channel Mnet reveals just how many in Korea aspire to stardom. "Kids Who Dream of the Stars," a website where aspiring entertainers swap audition information, has 780,000 members. Many of them take vocal and dance lessons in preparation for auditions. Their first goal is to become a trainee at a large agency like SM, JYP, or YG Entertainment. Success does not come easily even if an applicant has talent. According to JYP Entertainment, singer Lim Jeong-hee failed twice before passing on her third attempt as her tenacity was appreciated. When CL, a member of YG girl group 2 NE1, was not given the opportunity to audition, she waited outside the offices of agency head Yang Hyeonseok. After several days, she managed to pass her demo tape to him in person and finally became a trainee.

A.   *"Kids Who Give Up on Studying"*

Becoming a trainee means embarking upon life as an entertainer-in-training. These prospective stars receive personalized instruction in singing, dancing, acting, and foreign languages in order to become an idol. Trainees in middle or high school must attend two to three classes several days a week, before going through an internal evaluation to be selected for debut. Not all trainees become singers, which is why this is when the real competition begins.

"Everyone works so hard," says "B," a former trainee who dropped out and now gives vocal lessons. "So many kids skip afternoon classes at school to practice. They practice all day. If you bring a letter from the management, the school counts practice as 'field study' and lets you out early. But when you become a trainee, your teachers and friends start to think of you as having given up on academic subjects. Some trainees basically live in the practice rooms on week-ends and school vacations."

B. Empty adolescence

The trainees practice as though their lives depend on it because good scores are necessary on their endless evaluations. On average, only about half the trainees manage to debut. SM periodically holds trainee concerts to keep track of their progress. YG also has a meticulous evaluation system that involves, for example, foreign language tests every two weeks. Those who stand out during these evaluations can debut within two to three years, whereas those who don't must continue to endure the interminable, challenging life of a trainee.

The average trainee period for the members of Girls' Generation was five years, but Sooyoung, Jessica, and Hyoyeon each spent seven years as trainees. As competition among idol groups has intensified, standards have risen and trainee periods grown longer. Rumors circulated before the debut of JYP's boy band 2PM that the agency was training a group that could pull off singing live even while doing cartwheels.

At large agencies, as soon as trainees sign up they are given time cards to record their comings and goings, which become tokens of their passion and dedi-cation. "Sunye of Wonder Girls didn't miss a single rehearsal in the seven years she was a trainee from starting while in elementary school," says a JYP staff member. "Her commitment was highly praised during her evaluations." Taeyang of YG's boy band Big Bang once fell ill as a trainee and was sent to the hospital, but as soon as they removed his IV drip, he went back to rehearsing.

It's no surprise that some trainees quit school altogether to focus on their careers. Popular idol group high school dropouts include Seungri and Taeyang of Big Bang, Hero Jaejoong of TVXQ, and Sohee of Wonder Girls. 2NE1 member Minzy did not even start high school. Experts find this trend worrying. Hwang Sangmin, a professor of psychology at Yonsei University, notes that, "Trainees who have not had the benefit of standard education among peers may experience anxiety and pain in their adult lives."

C. The snare of the exclusive contract

Stress also plagues the daily lives of trainees. In the YG practice rooms hangs the motto, "Before you become a performer, become a human being." SM trainees are supposed to greet everyone around the company building enthusiastically no matter who they are. Trainees, whose every move counts towards their evalua-tions and who must endlessly compete under circumstances with no way out, have a single-minded goal: to complete the program as soon as possible and debut. Jo Kwon, who trained for eight years at JYP before debuting with 2AM, once said in a TV interview, "I don't have any memories of adolescence. I hope no one ever has to train as long as I did."

In the meantime, as trainees go through these strenuous years, the agen-cies invest in them so that they can grow from "unpolished talent" into "*Hallyu* stars." Agencies provide all lessons, food, and upkeep costs, and trainees who pass evaluations and prepare to debut in a pop group are provided room and board. "C," who managed a popular girl group at a large agency, says, "The major companies pay for plastic surgery. If trainees or entertainers want a procedure done, they pay for it themselves, but agencies usually pay if they recommend it." Agencies also take responsibility for finding a concept for the group and lyricists, composers, choreographers, stylists, and managers and for making all members distinctive by giving them a "role." "An idol group is actually a product created in the agency's vision," says C.

Kim Gwang-su, head of Core Contents Media, the agency managing the quintet Five Girls, says "This part of the process costs an unimaginable amount." According to Kim, monthly costs for Five Girls during training totaled ₩18 million a month, including 1.4 million for rent, 5 million for lessons, 2 million for car maintenance and transport, 2 million for food, and 1 million for medical expenses. Right before their debut, the agency also had to shell out for music video shooting, costumes, composers, a recording studio, etc. If the group doesn't catch on, the agency still must foot these bills.

During this period of uncertainty, idol group members sign exclusive contracts. Xiah Junsu of TVXQ was chosen as a trainee at SM in elementary school. In 2000, when he was in middle school, he signed an exclusive contract, according to which he was to work for SM for 10 years upon debut. If he voided his contract, he would have to repay triple the investment received and twice the projected profit he would have earned in the remainder of the 10 years. Lim Sang-hyeok, an attorney with the firm Shin & Kim, who is representing Xiah in his suit against SM, says, "The contract was later extended to 13 years, which would have taken him through his entire shelf life as a boy idol star. The penalties are unreasonable too. Yet how can trainees say no when they're dependent on the agency and desperate for debut?" As evident with TVXQ, such contracts can lead to disputes when idol groups become successful.

Another problem in TVXQ's contract was the stipulation that "during the contract period, the contracting party must diligently carry out decisions made by SM." Because TVXQ did not have the right to refuse work, they were forced to follow demanding schedules, such as traveling back and forth to Japan in a single day. Jeong Hae-im, the head of "People against Unfair SM Contracts," claims, "According to TVXQ fans, the group traveled the equivalent of 6 and a half times around the earth in the 68 months since their debut. Based in Korea and Japan, they also toured China, Taiwan, and over the whole of Asia; they had less than two weeks off per year."

D.   Sustainable business

Trainee frustrations regarding profit distribution began to grow. According to TVXQ's contract, each member receives 12% of revenues after deducting all operating expenses, including transportation, rent, food, backup dancers' wages, salaries for makeup artists, production coordinator salary, manager and road manager salaries, basic living expenses, and training fees. From what remains, 40% goes to the agency and the rest is divided among the five members.

A source in the entertainment industry who chose to remain anonymous says, "I understand that the members complained about paying for their flights when they were doing more shows abroad." In other words, with going back and

Table 2–63. 2008 end of year schedule for TVXQ

Dec. 27, 2008	TVXQ leave Korea
Dec. 28, 2008	Record Japanese television show
Dec. 28, 2008	Photo shoot for Japanese magazine
Dec. 28, 2008	Return to Korea
Dec. 28–29, 2008	Rehearsal for SBS Music Festival
Dec. 29, 2008	Leave Korea
Dec. 29, 2008	Practice for Arena Tour in Japan
Dec. 29, 2008	Photo shoot for Japanese magazine
Dec. 29, 2008	Return to Korea
Dec. 29, 2008	Perform at SBS Music Festival
Dec. 30, 2008	Leave Korea
Dec. 30, 2008	Japanese magazine photo shoot
Dec. 30, 2008	Attend Japanese Records Award
Dec. 30, 2008	Red and White Music Competition Rehearsal
Dec. 30, 2008	Music Japan Rehearsal
Dec. 31, 2008	Music Japan Recording
Dec. 31, 2008	Red and White Music Competition
Dec. 31, 2008–Jan. 1, 2009	5-1/2-hour New Year's Eve premium live show (p.m. 11:40–a.m. 5:00)
Jan. 1, 2009	Early morning Japanese radio show
Jan. 1, 2009	Return to Korea
Jan. 1, 2009	Meeting to discuss concerts in Korea
Jan. 2, 2009	Leave Korea

forth to Japan and China for TV appearances, the members may actually have lost money from their grueling schedules. Group members once said in an interview, "When we go from Japan to Korea or vice-versa, we have to flip a switch. Not only are the languages different, of course, but the studios, the songs we sing, and our choreography is also completely different." It is possible to become disgruntled with a schedule that is so physically demanding and time-consuming and yet yields little profit. According to "C," "SM has a lot to gain when TVXQ appears on TV. Singers who debuted more recently can be introduced alongside TVXQ and get good PR. But the members may have believed that the company was exploiting them."

Heard we finally made it big overseas. Made money beyond our dreams.
I walked on clouds all the way to work on payday. But the bill said
₩40 million in the red. Thought I saw wrong, checked again, and all of
it disappeared into expenses.
Expenses, shit.

So go the lyrics to "Song without a Title, Part 1," released by JYJ, the three members of TVXQ who filed a lawsuit against SM Entertainment. Members of KARA also sued their agency over profit distribution, saying, "'Lupin' was a major hit last year, but all we got on average was ₩140,000." They also highlighted the problematic aspects of a contract that prevents them from refusing work by mentioning an incident where "one member was forced to perform with a back injury." The agency's response to both situations has been to say, "We invest a great deal to turn trainees into stars, and contracts are signed under mutual agreement. Backing out just because the group has become famous is unfair." Some say that to come up with a fundamental solution to idol group contract disputes, the system itself must change. Tak Hyeon-min, an affiliate professor at Sungkonghoe University, says, "It's important to fix unfair clauses in the contracts, but as a long-term solution, we need to create an environment where someone can become a star without going through a big agency."

Also, many argue for the necessity of legal protection so that idols can be treated with respect as individuals rather than as commodities, and so that young trainees can receive an education, make friends, and live as their peers do. According to California law, school-age minors, defined as those seven and older, cannot work for more than eight hours a day, and three out of eight hours must be devoted to study. Labor laws in the UK state that entertainers under 16 cannot be on set for more than 9 and a half hours per day. As Kim Dong-min, a teacher at Hanlim Multi Arts High School, insists, "A system that makes teens sacrifice everything to become performers is unsustainable. We have to create a system that allows teenagers, who are at the center of the entertainment industry these days, to achieve a balance between work and school so they can have a good life after they retire from performing."

2.4. CELEBRITY

The increasing penetration of media into daily life around the world has also increased the spread of commercial systems to market celebrities. It is not a coincidence that the rise in new media platforms that has made the global propagation of Korean popular culture possible has also gone hand in hand with a burgeoning awareness and exploitation of Korean star potential. Strict mechanisms operate to create a star image suitable for a market, which is followed by an intense effort to sustain and manage that success. This section explores a number of issues involving *Hallyu* celebrities, including the system of star production; the management of public profiles; the realities of life as an entertainer; and fandom and community formation. Underpinning these issues are the challenges and opportunities that Korean performers face when venturing into a foreign market. Given the highly charged and nationalistic nature of *Hallyu* business and discourse, celebrities' situations become precarious and politicized as they represent Korea to the wider world. The fraught histories that haunt post-colonial Asia in particular both foster and obstruct the Korean Wave.

An oft-quoted hypothesis for the ascendancy of Korean popular culture in the larger Asian region in contrast to Japan is that Korea lacks the political baggage and the deep-seated feelings of resentment aroused by its neighbor's actions in the first half of the 20th century (see Document 1.1.2). At the same time, lingering rancor between Korea and Japan can create barriers to acceptance of Korean products in Japan. The political relationships that South Korea has developed with China, Vietnam, Cambodia, and other neighbors similarly affect how its popular culture is regarded and can lead to situations where incidents covered—or even in large part manufactured—by the media cause spikes in animosity before becoming forgotten again.

Document 2.4.1, "Yonsama Madness Unveiled," offers an early report on the Japanese craze over Bae Yong-joon when *Winter Sonata* became a major hit there. The piece details the frequently relayed anecdote of Bae's arrival at Narita Airport and his popularity with middle-aged women. Bae led the platform for future *Hallyu* stars and deserves special attention for both this reason and his crucial role in the development of South Korean-Japanese relations in the 21st century. Bae has walked a diplomatic tightrope, spreading a positive image of Korea to Japanese fans while studiously avoiding gaffes.

Celebrities, as important agents in driving the Korean Wave, are often placed in uncomfortable positions in which the need to maintain goodwill in target destinations toward their products clashes with an equal need to uphold Korean nationalist credentials. Document 2.4.2, "Lead Us Not into Temptation: Entertainment and Politics," reports how in the 2005–2006 period, heightened attention to the territorial dispute over Dokdo/Takeshima trapped many *Hallyu* celebrities. Bae faced the dilemma keenly, as did many others, including foreign stars visiting Korea. This document also discusses singer and artist Jo Young-nam, a well-known *agent provocateur* in Korea, who caused public outcry with his visit to Yasukuni Shrine and the publication of his book *Taking a Risk with a Pro-Japan Declaration* (*Majajugeul gagorosseun chinil seoneon*).

The next four documents consider case studies of distinctive *Hallyu* stars. Korean singer and actress Jang Nara is the subject of Document 2.4.3, "Jang Nara, Empress of *Hallyu*, Crisscrosses China." This in-depth interview focuses on Jang's fledgling career in Korea's huge neighbor. With diplomacy and mature candor, she recounts her travails in building a career on Chinese television. Like Bae, Jang represents early *Hallyu* stardom. Her personal history intertwines with the larger imperatives of serving as a vessel for popular understandings and aspirations for the Korea-China relationship. While Korean media discourse sometimes suggests that the Chinese cultural market is readily penetrable, eager to consume all things Korean, Jang's struggle for acceptance provides a window into the efforts necessary to form a stable fan base overseas and adapt to new markets.

Document 2.4.4, "The Reality of Idol Star Debuts in the US," echoes issues covered earlier (see 2.3.2 and 2.3.4 on the talent management industry) in revealing the challenges Wonder Girls encountered in the American music market. Leaving behind a successful career in Korea in 2009, JYP's top girl group battled and ultimately failed to build a career in the greener—or at least more extensive—pastures of the US. Their story bespeaks the vagaries of *Hallyu* and, perhaps, the hubris of JYP's Park Jin-young, all the while highlighting the Korean obsession with American recognition. Entry into the Billboard music charts, however modest, becomes a resounding marker of achievement.

In recent years, *Hallyu* has witnessed one remarkable success that confounds expectations of the requirements for the international penetration of Korean cultural products. With "Gangnam Style," PSY experienced a global triumph that was as unprecedented as it was unanticipated. As this book goes to press in 2015, PSY remains the most globally recognized Korean celebrity as a result of his hit music video. The immense viral sensation spawned an enormous number of articles and reports inside and outside Korea. PSY largely encountered a smooth path in his rise to mega-stardom despite, or perhaps even in part because of, an *enfant terrible* persona that was paradoxically endearing and notably distanced him from manufactured idols. In Document 2.4.5, "PSY: One-Hit Wonder or First of Many K-Pop Hits?" Im Jin-mo, a renowned pop music critic, attempts an analysis of PSY's success. Unlike other articles on PSY, which chart the stages of his commercial success or offer laudatory assessments of the qualities of "Gangnam Style" that made it a hit, Im argues that PSY's global reach was made possible because American music industry insiders and celebrities opened avenues. Although Im may make some questionable generalizations based on anxieties over what he clearly perceives as Korea's neocolonial relationship with the US, the piece's publication in the prominent magazine *Weekly Chosun* indicates the level of media interest and speculation in unraveling what led to the remarkable success of "Gangnam Style."

This section ends with a discussion of one of *Hallyu*'s unsung heroes: Document 2.4.6, "The Pororo Syndrome: *Hallyu*'s Brightest Star," tells of the animated penguin who has been spearheading the licensed character industry. Though this sourcebook does not discuss at length the cultural and economic impact of popular Korean characters, such as Pucca, Pororo's fame suggests that the reach of *Hallyu*'s ambition extends even to toddlers. We therefore end this section with a brief tribute to the charming avian adventurer.

2.4.1.   Yonsama Madness Unveiled

Reference: "Yonsama Madness Unveiled," *Weekly Chosun*, Choi Heub, Dec. 9, 2004.
No. 1832, pp. 50–52.

A.   *Bae's seven secrets of popularity*

- Always maintain a smile
- Refer to fans as family, and interact with them attentively
- Treat fans earnestly and without guile
- Maintain Prince Charming image
- Avoid slips of the tongue
- Project a cultured image
- Behave humbly, shed tears, apologize for mistakes

B.   *"Darling, what's so great about Yonsama?"*

So runs the copy on a product catalogue for a Japanese telecommunications corporation. The accompanying image depicts models dressed to resemble Bae Yong-joon. Most Japanese fans of Bae Yong-joon—or Yonsama as he is called in Japan—are happily married. They do not hide their adoration of Yonsama from their husbands, but rather join them on *Winter Sonata* tours to Korea and appear at fan meetings with children in tow. Their first impulse if they see Yonsama in person would be to phone their spouses. "Honey, honey, I saw Yonsama for real! I feel overwhelmed." Their husbands reply, "Wonderful! Are you happy now?"

To women who have devoted their entire lives to being good wives and mothers, and have now found Yonsama to obsess over, husbands can offer no more objection than to ask with a bitter smile, "What's so great about Yonsama?" On the one hand, husbands appreciate that something is giving their wives such happiness, but on the other, they wonder what they lack so desperately that Yonsama arouses such passion. Thus, *Winter Sonata* swept Japan, leaving Koreans curious about the phenomenon and the Japanese re-examining themselves. Yonsama himself, the center of this excitement, paid an official visit to Japan on November 25, after a "lengthy" absence of seven months.

"The Korean Air flight with Yonsama on board touched down at 1:34 p.m." The announcement creates a commotion among the 5,000 fans gathered at Narita International Airport. Cheers come from all directions. Two private TV stations are at the airport to broadcast Bae's arrival—not a show or an interview, but the arrival—live. It is not news channel NHK that is present, but private stations, for whom ratings are all.

TV Asahi broadcast the event for over two hours, and Nippon TV was "lucky enough" to start coverage just as Bae touched down and to open the program with his arrival. The show's hosts grinned from ear to ear, saying, "It's almost as if Yonsama has flown in to be on our show." TBS sent a helicopter for the occasion and followed Yonsama from the airport to his hotel. Even as they were airing other programs, a window at the bottom of the screen played a live feed of the vehicle escorting Yonsama.

Haneda Airport was brought to a standstill when Bae last visited in April. Thrown into a panic by unprecedented traffic, the airport administrators begged the star to use Narita Airport on his next visit. Narita, located a 90-minute commuter rail ride from downtown Tokyo, was flooded with fans who had come to greet Bae from Tokyo and cities several hundred kilometers away around Japan. Over 100 additional police officers were dispatched. Another 100 security guards were hired from private companies, on top of the usual 100 hired for extra help, totaling 300 reinforcements to deal with Bae's arrival.

In an attempt to avoid creating chaos, Yonsama did not reveal his flight or hotel information, but his fans had been tracking him since Incheon. News that he had boarded a Korean Air flight departing just after 10 a.m. spread like wildfire through international phone calls, television, and plain word of mouth.

Fans had begun their vigil at Narita from 10 p.m. the previous night. The airport does not open until 5 a.m., but fans slept outside with giant banners that read, "Welcome home," "Welcome," and "I love you," and brought posters bearing his picture. Some 98% of the welcome party were female fans between the ages of 20 and 80. An estimated 3,500 to 5,000 people gathered at the airport that day. Even the lower estimate would make the greeting party the largest in the history of Narita. According to the Japanese media, the record had been held by Daniel Radcliffe from the *Harry Potter* series, an unprecedented hit in Japan, who drew a crowd of 3,000 last December. Parties of 1,000 greeted David Beckham, upon whom "Beckham-sama" status was bestowed during the 2002 World Cup, as well as Leonardo di Caprio in 2000 and Michael Jackson in 1987. Brad Pitt drew somewhere between 500 and 1,000, and Tom Cruise about 700. In light of these numbers, the crowds of 2,000 that came to see Jang Dong-gun and Won Bin were also very notable.

But the huge turnout at the airport was merely the tip of the iceberg of the Yonsama phenomenon. Those who had given up on going to Narita were waiting at hotels. Bae had not announced where he would stay, so fans camped out at several hotels. Certain hotels were ruled out based on the live broadcast of Bae Yong-joon en route to the hotel, and this information was swiftly communicated within the fan networks by cell phone. The scene was like something out of a James Bond movie. Some zealous fans booked rooms at three different hotels, saying, "I'm just happy we're in the same place."

Each restaurant that Bae visited last April was hopping again. The owner of a pork *shabu shabu* establishment at which Bae had eaten set the table where Bae had sat with the same food he'd ordered and displayed it to members of the Japanese media who arrived for an interview. "People come from all over Japan and even from Southeast Asia to eat where Yonsama sat. Often they just sit and weep," said the owner.

Television programs read into every gesture Bae made. One show host laughed, "There are lots of actors in Japan too. Japanese actors, you gotta try harder." The program's panel watched as Bae smiled continuously at his fans and offered praise. "He treats fans very thoughtfully and refers to them as 'family.' That is a real strength of Korean actors." The Japanese media noted that Bae's thoughtfulness came naturally, not as a calculated gesture.

The popularity of many foreign stars has dwindled after visits to Japan. The Russian female duo t.A.T.u., who had been very popular in Japan last year, canceled a concert and made rude remarks that caused Japanese fan interest to vanish instantly.

But Bae has earned points with each Japan visit. In television interviews, he maintained his Prince Charming image, avoided gaffes, and was well-mannered. Some said, "The Japanese don't have much access to the details of his personal life because he's Korean, but once dirt gets outs, his popularity will wane." So far, however, he has grown more popular with each interview and each passing day.

An unfortunate accident occurred on November 26, when a thousand fans blocked access to Tokyo's New Otani Hotel, where Bae Yong-joon had stayed the previous night. Bae planned to sneak out the back entrance. His agency had initially planned a surprise fan meeting with those who had gathered and promised that if they remained quiet and orderly, Bae would be able to leave through a particular exit and meet them on his way out. The fans kept their promise and waited calmly. However, hotel administrators later informed them that Bae had left through a different entrance out of concern for their safety. The fans, therefore, were about to disperse when Bae's car appeared at the front entrance. A window rolled down and Bae was seen waving from inside. The fans rushed the vehicle, causing a scuffle that lasted 10 minutes and injured 10 people.

Bae and his staff responded to the incident immediately and thoughtfully, almost as if they had envisioned something of the sort might occur. Bae held a press conference that very day and apologized, "I was too selfish. I thought that there wouldn't be any trouble. I am very sorry that members of my family were injured." The ribbon-cutting ceremony at the photo exhibit was canceled, as were some other events scheduled that day. Thanks to an interview in which Bae shed a few tears, fans stopped blaming the accident on his change of plans. They defended "Poor Yonsama" and implored him not to be angry with Japan. Bae moved to a different hotel, but the fans found out right away. About 100 turned up at his new accommodation.

Of course, the photo exhibit that opened on November 27 was a smashing success. Held at Roppongi Hills, a rising posh venue in Tokyo, the exhibit welcomed 4,000 visitors on its first day. Even though it was made clear that Bae would not be making an appearance due to the previous day's incident, tickets for the day sold out an hour before the exhibit opened. Roppongi Hills set a maximum capacity for each time slot, imposing a limit on daily visitors, who were admitted on a first-come, first-served basis and had to wait their turn. An hour before the exhibit opened, a queue of some 5,000 people stretched for a kilometer. Those at the front of the queue had been waiting since six in the morning the day before the exhibit opened and spent the night in sleeping bags. Those unable to buy a ticket said they were happy simply to be breathing the same Tokyo air as Yonsama as they turned to leave.

The Japanese media reported enormous enthusiasm from the fans inside and outside the exhibit. Stories circulated of many fans who wept upon seeing the pictures. A total of 4,000 visitors arrived the first day and 6,000 on the second. The entrance fee of ¥1,500 led to ¥15 million in ticket sales. Merchandise sales were not reported. The general opinion is that the prints exhibited would sell at astronomical prices if put up for auction.

Bae Yong-joon mania is different from other manias that Japan has seen. Although all "Four Heavenly Kings of *Hallyu*"—Bae, Lee Byung-hun, Jang Dong-gun, and Won Bin—are virtually worshiped in Japan, according to Japanese media reports, Bae's popularity is of a different order and is unprecedented.

When Bae's fans express how they feel, they do not say "He's handsome" or "I like him." Their sentiments are closer to gratitude. This awe has granted him the highest honorific, "-sama," rarely bestowed upon anyone outside the Japanese royal family. In a Japanese survey on foreign relations in 2003, South Korea (55%) was the second most well-liked country, after the US (78%), followed by Australia and New Zealand (54.8%), the EU (51%), and China (48%). It is also third from the bottom on the list of "least likable countries," with the US being the least likable and Australia and New Zealand being the second least likable. Thanks to *Hallyu*, experts predict that Korea's likability in Japan will rise this year, since the demographic that has fallen in love with Bae, women over 30, have traditionally been the same demographic that has expressed the greatest dislike for Korea. If their opinions on Korea change, "the Bae effect" will have a magnitude that can have an impact upon Korea-Japan bilateral relations.

Yonsama has fans among those over 60 as well. Many have reported that *Winter Sonata* restored their resolve at a point in life when the parents they were nursing had passed away and they had become despondent. On talk shows, we often see elderly couples bowing their heads in gratitude to the hosts for making a show about *Winter Sonata*. The economic effect *Hallyu* exerts in Japan is surely far from negligible.

Products advertised by Bae have seen increases in sales of between 20–30%. Next to Japanese fans who display such genuine gratitude for Bae's existence, Koreans seem heartless for even calculating profit margins. So brightly and meaningfully does the Yonsama phenomenon blaze in Japan.

2.4.2.   Lead Us Not into Temptation: Entertainment and Politics

Reference: "Lead Us Not into Temptation," *Weekly Dong-A*, Kim Min-gyeong, No. 484, May 10, 2005, pp. 56–57.

Mounting tensions between Japan and Korea force entertainers to answer sensitive questions. Anti-fans overreact to ambiguously phrased responses.

"What's your opinion on the Dokdo Island controversy?" "J," who works for a film company, had been dreading this moment. His company had discussed the matter before the press conference and concluded, based on the responses of a few reporters they had queried, that no one would ask such a young actor about Japan-Korea relations, which had nothing to do with the film. But one journalist did put such a question to Yagira Yuya, the 15-year-old star of the Japanese film *Nobody Knows*. "J" did not interpret the question but averted crisis by pleading, "The actor is too young to be familiar with the Dokdo issue."

Jo Young-nam has also taken some flack as a result of rumors that he had paid his respects at a Japanese shrine. Jo and Yagira are not the only celebrities caught in the crossfire of the Japan-Korea diplomatic conflict, a quandary whose solution even experts cannot agree upon. Journalists have sprung this question on many entertainers, however, as though it is their problem to fix.

Popular *Hallyu* star Bae Yong-joon also received a Dokdo question on the set of his new film, *April Snow*. His response ("It's a shame") was deemed controversial by journalists and anti-fans who harassed him in order to clarify what he meant. He later stated on his website, "Dokdo is South Korean territory," a declaration that made headlines as if the International Court of Justice had delivered the verdict. When pressed, Bae's manager said that addressing the issue of Bae and Dokdo was burdensome and declined further comment.

A.   Dokdo trumps film discussion

"In the Korean film business, we refer to it as the *April Snow* Incident," said one entertainment company staffer. "Inviting journalists and fans to the set was a major undertaking that involved a lot of preparation over a long period. But the day turned out to be all about Dokdo. Based on comments about Dokdo made on the set, online discussion boards were flooded with comments boycotting or supporting a film that we were still shooting. The staff decided we needed to be extra careful about the issue."

Because of this incident, the host of the press screening of *A Bittersweet Life* asked that comments and questions be kept to the film. This point was stressed because many Japanese journalists were present. The film features *Hallyu* star Lee Byung-hun and had been sold in Japan in advance at a high price.

But director Kim Ji-woon jumped the gun. "In any case, Dokdo is Korean territory," he said, almost as if tearing off a Band-Aid. Kim likewise stated during an interview with *Sankei Shimbun*, "Japan must strive to be a great nation ethically as well as economically." The interviewer had not even prompted him.

According to reports, Lee Byung-hun, the lead in *A Bittersweet Life*, refused to make the ceremonial first pitch for the Yomiuri Giants or appear on the popular Japanese TV show *SMAPxSMAP* due to a strong belief that "Dokdo belongs to Korea." However, Lee insisted such rumors were false, emphasizing that he "never made any statements about Japan." Rather, he "turned down the offers because they would not have helped publicize the film."

The manager of one Korean Wave star said that both the star and staff are scrupulous about everything they do and say when it comes to Japan-Korea relations. "No matter what we do, the focus always ends up being Japan-Korea problems. Journalists from all sorts of media follow us around and put us on the spot. It has us on edge."

"Korean actors can hardly afford to speak ill of Japan while promoting a movie there," said Suchida Maki, a Japanese reporter who writes about Korean film. "And yet they're anxious that what they say in Japan may be interpreted as 'pro-Japanese' in Korea. It's Koreans who prod them about Japan-Korea relations. If you ask Japanese to refrain from doing something, they tend to obey. In Japan, entertainers rarely comment on politics or social problems, and when they do, the media does not blow it into a big story since entertainers are not experts in those fields. I understand that these are sensitive issues because Japanese politicians continue to say offensive things and Dokdo carries deep meaning for Koreans. But I do think it's unfair for the press to turn every comment entertainers make into a controversy, knowing full well how people in Korea react."

B.   Watching every word about Japan

Moviegoers and netizens expect an unambiguous "Dokdo is Korean territory!" from *Hallyu* stars and were relentless in their demands that Jo Young-nam be banned from TV despite explanations from both Jo and *Sankei Shimbun*. By contrast, organizations like the Party for Dokdo Protection or the Institute for Research on Collaborationist Activities, which criticize pro-Japanese activities in Korea and offensive remarks from Japanese politicians about Korea, are indifferent towards celebrity comments.

"It's true that what entertainers say carries a lot of weight in Korea," says Kim Byeong-gu, the publicity manager at the Party for Dokdo Protection. "But entertainers don't have a lasting impact." One staff member from the Institute for Research on Collaborationist Activities who wished to remain anonymous said, "The larger problem is not rash remarks from celebrities, but the discourse of colonial modernity that permeates the educated classes. The incident with Mr. Jo seems like an unfortunate misunderstanding."

Of course, the majority agrees with Kim Sam-ung, director of the Independence Hall of Korea, that "Mr. Jo's high opinion of Japan seems to come from romantic, naïve impressions. Even as an entertainer, it's unwise to get on the bad side of your fellow countrymen." In an age where theories that all art reflects social and economic contexts are persuasive and the myth of the genius of artists and entertainers is considered a fallacy, commentary on politics and society is part of the professional lives of artists and entertainers.

Unfortunately, statements from artists in Korea from the Japanese occupation to military rule in the 1980s were often used as little more than propaganda. This history has resulted in entertainers' downplaying the value of their own words and acquiring a reputation as untrustworthy. Recently, however, young artists' political commentary and unorthodox behavior have met with popular empathy because their opinions come from a place of some logic and sincerity, in spite of their romantic and emotional nature. It is pointless, therefore, to ambush entertainers with questions whose expected answer is obvious, such as, "Which country does Dokdo belong to?" Cruel questions and answers with no lasting consequences offer nothing more than instant gratification.

Jo Young-nam's concern about the *Sankei Shimbun* incident should be given serious consideration: "In Korea we have had heated debate about the misinformed reports of Japanese right-wing media when we could have taken charge and made a formal complaint. I'm concerned that once again we have played into their hands."

2.4.3.　Jang Nara, Empress of *Hallyu*, Crisscrosses China

Reference:　"Jang Nara, Empress of *Hallyu*, Crisscrosses China," *Shin Dong-A*, Choi Ho-yeol, No. 566, November 2006, pp. 385–396.

It's been two years since Jang Nara, the beloved actress known for playing cute, carefree characters rose to fame with *Successful Story of a Bright Girl*. Her triumph in the face of difficulties and rise to the top of the Chinese entertainment industry are truly like that of the proverbial crab that skitters this way and that but eventually makes its way across vast lands.

The strong winds of *Hallyu* have abated. Resentment and anxiety over the Korean Wave have been developing in China and Japan. However, one *Hallyu* entertainer has established herself firmly in China: singer and actress Jang Nara.

Jang shot to stardom through her portrayal of the title character of the TV drama *Successful Story of a Bright Girl* (2002), becoming adored by fans as both singer and actress. Using this success as a stepping stone, Jang moved to China in September 2004 to pursue a career. In the two years since, she has focused her time and energy on projects in China, appearing in just one drama in Korea.

Last year, Jang won numerous awards in China: "Asia's Best Female Singer" at the Asian-Pacific Music Chart Awards and "Most Popular Singer" at the China Golden Disc Music Awards. Her Chinese TV drama, *My Bratty Princess/Diao man gong zhu*, enjoyed great popularity. The Chinese press has bestowed the honorific *tianhou* (empress) upon her. The equivalent of "*-sama*" in Japanese, the term is only given to those at the very top of their field.

Recently, Jang's father, Ju Hoseong, published a book about his daughter's career in China and the realities of *Hallyu* there. The book's title *Jang Nara Crisscrosses the World* (*Jang Nara Hoenghaengcheonha*) comes from the image of a crab that crawls haphazardly but in the end travels across continents. It is an analogy for Jang Nara's success as a Korean Wave star in China in spite of the stomach problems, eye infection, and exhaustion she has suffered, in addition to her fear of flying.

I met up with Jang in Cheongdam-dong in Seoul at Mou, a coffee shop with a dream-like Moroccan interior design. Jang was still as adorable as ever, but seemed to have matured in two years. "I finished shooting *Good Morning Shanghai* in China and got back to Korea a couple of days ago. I have to be in Hong Kong tomorrow for the recording of the TV drama soundtrack and the music video. Then I return to Beijing to start recording a new album."

Jang said she spent her three-day visit home in meetings with composers, producers, and others, working on her album. "When I come for a visit, I barely have enough time to pack things I'm bringing back to China with me. I hardly ever get to see close friends or colleagues. I can only get two to three days off at a time." Her words confirm her tight schedule in China. According to Jang, her fifth album will be released in November at the earliest. Her fourth album came out in spring 2004, which will make this her first album in two and a half years.

A. Spreading the image of Warmhearted Hallyu

Jang debuted in China with *Silver Love Story* (*Yinse nianhua*), a TV series that first aired in September 2004, but she'd long been planning on expanding her work to China.

"Initially I had Japan in mind when I was preparing for my debut. Japan was a popular next step for entertainers back then. But it wasn't my cup of tea. After my debut, I did concerts in Taiwan and China a few times for fan clubs there, and it felt like a good fit. So I started preparing for China."

Most *Hallyu* stars work mainly in Korea and go to China or Japan for short promotional tours or concerts. Jang, likewise, did not at first plan to invest all her energy in China. "It was more fun than I thought, and I started to get ambitious."

She went to China prepared. She focused on conveying to the Chinese audience that she was there for the long haul, not just another visiting foreign entertainer. She donated all her profits from *Silver Love Story* to charity, giving the public the impression that the Korean Wave had a heart. Similarly, she was introduced at a music show with other debuting Chinese singers when her first Chinese album, *Yizhang*, was released, which suggested that she wasn't a special guest but a singer working in China. Like other Chinese singers, she traveled the whole country, holding concerts at over 30 venues.

"In Korea, all the TV stations are in Seoul and they broadcast throughout the country, so the only thing you need for visibility is to be on TV. But that isn't the case in China. Just because you're on TV in Beijing and Shanghai doesn't mean you're known around China. When my first album came out, we held a press conference at the Great Hall of the People with reporters from all over the country, but when I went to Guangzhou in Guangdong a month later, my fans didn't even know that my new album had been released. China is vast, and each area has its own independent information networks. The only way to do publicity is to go to each region to appear on local TV stations and hold concerts."

Jang was able to sense just how popular she'd become when her second album, *Erzhang*, was released. She had to escape from the hordes that flocked to see her at an album signing by having window bars removed with an acetylene torch.

Q: Do you feel you're at the top of your field in China?

A: Not at the top, no. There are so many entertainers in China. I still have a long way to go. I think I'll have to speak Chinese like a native first. It was the same thing in Korea. Even when I had a lot of fans, I was still a baby compared to veteran colleagues.

Q: What entails real success in China?

A: There's a program called *New Year's Gala* (*Chun jie wan hui*) on CCTV1 on Chinese New Year, their biggest holiday. Only the real cream of the crop appears. It's difficult even for top Chinese stars from Taiwan and Malaysia to get a spot on the show, which has unbelievable ratings. Everybody in China watches. Even people who are playing with firecrackers all through the holiday take a break to go home and watch. I'll know I've made it in China if I make it on that show.

Q: You must have been lonely early on in China.

A: I didn't have friends to hang out with or places to go on days when I didn't have work, so I watched the shows I was on when I was in Korea. I was embarrassingly bad in so many of them. I didn't realize it at the time, but I'd been lazy. I did everything half-heartedly—acting happy, talking, laughing... I think I was always making excuses for myself. I was always too tired or sick. I didn't see it when I was in Korea, but my shortcomings became all too evident to me once I had some distance. It was embarrassing how naïve I was. I think I'd do much better if I could do it over.

Q: Have you made friends in Chinese entertainment?

A: I bawled my eyes out after our last shoot for *My Bratty Princess*. I've kept in touch with the cast and crew, and meet up with them when they're in the area. We couldn't help but grow really close because even though people go home at the end of a shoot in Korea, it's impossible to do that in China because shooting locations are so far away. You work and live together 24/7 for several weeks, so you get plenty of opportunities to chat. In Chinese, the green room is called *huazhuangshi*, which sounds a lot like *hwajangsil*, or "bathroom" in Korean. (Laughs) We'd get together in the "bathroom" for dumplings and beer after shoots. Also, maybe because it's a socialist country, everyone relates as equals. People are chummy with one another, from the director to the youngest crew member.

Q: What was the greatest difficulty for you?

A: One thing that was hard but also fun was traveling to lots of different places. China is huge and you need to travel by air, but I have a fear of flying. Once when I had to travel from Beijing to Shanghai, I went by train. Even on a bullet train the trip took 12 hours. I was exhausted by the time I arrived. Traveling is stressful, but meeting lots of different people and trying local delicacies was fun.

Jang has also had unfortunate experiences. Once she eagerly went to help at a Korea-China cultural exchange event that turned out to be a store opening:

"I couldn't bring myself to endorse it, so I asked the reporters for their understanding and canceled the event. But one local paper ran a story claiming that because I demanded RMB 250,000, the store had to call off the press conference, based only on what the event organizers told them. What's even more outrageous is that almost the second this article appeared on the Internet, the same story came out online in Korean news. And then the Chinese media quoted the Korean media and turned it into a big story. I had such a hard time clearing things up. The Chinese reporters who were present at the event had to back me." Similar incidents happened quite often. Some articles reported such stories as "Jang's lip-sync earns scorn from Chinese fans" or "Jang turns up drunk at a shoot."

"Sometimes, stories in the Chinese media make me proud and happy. But these stories never make it to Korea. But negative stories are always all over the news, even when I've done nothing wrong. And the stories come up so fast it's hard to believe someone isn't tipping off the press. I've been really surprised. I guess the only solution is to watch myself. Making a lot of money isn't important to me. If I behave poorly just to make money, what will the Chinese think of Korean stars? I pay close attention to how I behave so that when Korean entertainers go to work there, people will think 'Jang Nara was great to work with. Koreans are nice folk.'"

Q: Since the topic of money has come up, can I ask how much you make on your TV shows?

A: I think about fairness in terms of what other actors are making. Whether China or Korea, it's nice to get paid well, but if you're paid far above what is appropriate, it drives a wedge between you and your fans as well as other actors. Especially with TV dramas, you know they're on a tight budget, and if you ask for higher pay, you're cutting into that budget. But I think people who do period dramas should get paid a little more. Period drama is hard work.

Q: Do you ever worry about being forgotten by Korean fans?

A: I'm satisfied as long as my work is engaging, and I give my all to it. If I start worrying about popularity or ratings, that would consume me. I've seen a lot of entertainers ruined because they got greedy. Some developed weird personalities. In the two years I've worked in China, I've come to realize just how complacent and short-sighted I'd been, and I've gained a different sense of accomplishment from how I felt when I debuted. I want to do my job well so that the Chinese audience will think Korean stars are worth what they're paid.

When there is tension between Korea and Japan, Koreans tend to want the Japanese to confess the error of their ways. A rift in Korea-China relations has grown since last year. The Northeast Project controversy, the Chinese lead fish scandal, the garlic crisis, and the kimchi wars all represent rising tension between the two countries. Do Chinese reporters ever put her in a difficult position by asking her about these issues?

"They don't ask me about political issues because they think I'm too young. What they're most curious about is whether I'll get myself a Chinese boyfriend, since I'm not seeing anyone right now."

B.   Hallyu and cultural invasion

Anti-*Hallyu* sentiment plays a role in tensions between Korea and China. Some go so far as to call the Korean Wave a "cultural invasion," and China has threatened to limit airtime for Korean shows if Korea does not import shows from China in return.

Q: Is anti-*Hallyu* feeling noticeable in China?

A: Honestly, no. Everyone I meet has been very kind to me. To tell you the truth, not all of China is swept up by *Hallyu*. Many people are into Korean products, and since the country's population is huge, it seems very significant to Koreans. Compared to the influence of other countries like Japan, the Korean Wave is more noticeable. I think it's important to think about what "exchange" means. When goods move between countries, it's called trade; when pop culture moves from one country another, it's called exchange. I think what we "exchange" is not profit but our understanding and respect for others. It seems to me as if we've been chasing money and gotten caught up in a false sense of superiority that has led to underestimating foreign audiences. These kinds of mistakes may have made the Chinese misunderstand us and feel offended. The Korean press likes to use phrases like "conquering China" or "invasion" when describing the success of *Hallyu*. Koreans might feel good about it, but it's no surprise if the Chinese are unhappy to hear that kind of language.

Q: I sometimes come across questionable accounts of *Hallyu*'s success in China. For example, I read about new pop groups that are not very well known in Korea holding concerts at 50,000-seat venues to great success. Is *Hallyu* really that intense?

A: If I answer this question honestly, I'll probably get a lot of hate mail (laughs). It's extremely difficult for a foreign singer to put on a successful concert in China. Even ethnic Chinese from Taiwan and elsewhere often cancel Shanghai concerts. There are concerts at several levels of venues in China, from small theaters that seat 500 to larger theaters for 3,000, sports stadiums for 20,000, and mega-concerts for 50,000. Top stars who've been working in

China for at least 10 years can fill 20,000 seats for a solo concert. It's hard to get people to buy tickets. There's a difference between popularity and visibility. Just because people have heard of you doesn't mean they'll pay to see you perform. Many Korean singers plan concerts in China based on their visibility and then cancel because they can't sell tickets. I know of one concert that was canceled due to "weather conditions," but the weather was actually great that day.

C. Playing psychopaths and middle-aged women

As the daughter of stage actor Ju Ho-seong and TV actress Yi Gyeong-ok, Jang dreamed of becoming an entertainer since she could speak. In the ninth grade, she declared her heartfelt wish to go into entertainment, but her father was very much against the idea. "You won't physically mature as a woman until high school. It won't be too late if you start then," he said. A year later, she had a serious talk with her father. "I'm in high school now," was all she had to say.

But becoming an entertainer was no easy task. She trained in acting, dance, and singing with her father, who turned out to be a very strict teacher, but opportunities did not come knocking. After inquiries at many talent agencies and many unsuccessful auditions, she persevered and was finally able to make a solo album four years later as a college sophomore.

"I often got discouraged, but I kept at it. Singing and performing was all I knew. The tears I shed before my debut could fill a bathtub." Maybe those experiences spawned her first release, "Burying My Face in Tears," but the song only met with a lukewarm response.

She began to receive attention with the MBC sitcom *New Nonstop*. Now able to draw on the reputation she had built on the show, the songs she put out afterwards were a great success and won her a Best New Female Artist award that year. The following year, she found adoration as she played a cheerful young woman in *Successful Story of a Bright Girl*. Fans, tired of scandals involving actresses, fell in love with Jang's pure, innocent image. Since then, her films and TV shows have proven her a decent actress, and her commitment to live performances has earned her a reputation as a talented singer. Her cheerful persona resonated with the Chinese audience as well. Both *My Bratty Princess* and the new TV show *Good Morning Shanghai* captured Jang's characteristic image.

Q: Some say you always play the same roles.
A: I don't want to be typecast either. I'd like to try different things, but when people encounter a striking image, they expect to see it each time. But I'm not worried. I'm confident I'll get to play other roles. I plan to reveal different sides of myself in the future.

Q: Are there any roles you're especially interested in?
A: Well, I want to play unconventional characters. I'm most interested in playing a lesbian. A psychopath would be a fun role too. I also can't wait to play middle-aged women and mothers.

Q: That could be interpreted as a wish to get married soon.
A: I don't know about that. It'd be nice to get married soon, but in reality, it's not easy. It's hard enough for two people who've lived independently to make a

life together, but on top of that, marriage isn't just a union of two people but of two families. I don't think it will be easy.

Q: It sounds like you're too busy to date.

A: That's not true. If I wanted to date, I could. When you can't be together, you can always call. But I haven't met anyone I could be with long-term yet.

Q: Who manages your money?

A: My mother. I have no idea how much I have.

Q: You're also famous for being a philanthropist. Was this your idea?

A: Before I debuted, my mother said that if I became famous, I should share with those in need. My father agreed, and I do too.

Q: Around March 2005, you estimated on your website that you had donated ₩1.9 billion up to that point. I understand you've given away quite a lot of money since. How much have you given so far?

A: I don't like to calculate these things. It's embarrassing. If someone had asked me to take ₩1.9 billion out of my bank account for charity, I wouldn't have been able to do it. It's not easy for anyone to give away money that they already have. So I donate what I earn right away when I shoot commercials or get paid for event appearances. That way, I'm doing volunteer work as I'm making ads and participating in events.

D. *Sending milk and sanitary pads to North Korea*

Since giving away all her earnings from *Successful Story of a Bright Girl* for North Korean children, Jang has supported North Koreans in need. At the end of 2003, she shot milk and feminine hygiene product commercials and used the proceeds to send ₩500 million worth of supplies to North Korea, and received her fee for a Chinese clothing company commercial in the form of winter jackets. She's sending half the jackets to North Korea and half to underprivileged Chinese.

"Economic problems in North Korea have gotten so serious that there is a shortage of sanitary pads, which is leading to poor hygiene. I'm a woman, so I can relate. Men don't understand—it's easy to become ill when hygiene is not taken care of. I felt sympathy as a woman. There are mountains of these products at supermarkets in South Korea, so I figured, why not send some north? What really broke my heart, though, was that infants in North Korea weren't able to eat properly."

Q: Did you shoot the commercials to send baby formula and sanitary pads to North Korea?

A: Fortunately, with both the menstrual pad and formula manufacturers, my demands and theirs lined up. I'm also grateful that they sent far more formula and pads than what my fee was worth.

Q: You're quite sympathetic to North Koreans. You must have been unnerved by the recent nuclear test.

A: All I know is singing and acting. I don't know much about politics. My only hope is that politicians—in both North and South Korea—look after the average citizens. So I hope the nuclear test issue gets resolved soon too.

When asked about her future plans, she said that once her album is released she plans to perform in Korea and appear in a TV drama early next year. After two years of concentrating on China, she now plans to divide her time evenly between China and Korea, which seems to indicate that her Chinese career has reached a level of stability.

2.4.4. The Reality of Idol Star Debuts in the US: The Case of Wonder Girls

Reference: "The Reality of Idol Star Debuts in the US: Wonder Girls," *Shin Dong-A*, Ko Gyu-dae, No. 606, March 2010, pp. 396–403.

Beneath the Glamorous Veneer Lies a Track Record of Failure and Scars from Insurmountable Challenges

Sunmi of Wonder Girls suddenly announced her departure from the all-female idol group that had been known for its success in the US. Though conveying an image of success, including having been the first Korean singers to reach the Billboard chart, battle scars are now becoming more apparent than glory won. BoA and SE7EN, who announced their US debuts before Wonder Girls, have made little progress and are now planning comebacks in Korea and Japan. Why did they go to the US, and why are they returning to Korea?

In the middle of Wonder Girls' episode of "The Knee-Drop Guru," a segment on MBC TV's show *Golden Fishery* that aired in November 2009, an abrupt pause occurred immediately after Park Jin-young, the CEO of JYP Entertainment stated, "The members of Wonder Girls all agreed that entering the US market was the next step for them as they were peaking." After a few seconds of silence, Yeeun said that they couldn't refuse Park's offer only three years into their careers. At the end of January 2010, not long after the episode aired, JYP Entertainment announced Sunmi's departure from the group and her wishes to "return to her everyday life and resume her career after entering college."

Sunmi's resignation came as a shock, especially since it came when Wonder Girls were holding concerts all over the US and actively pursuing a career abroad. Through her agency, Sunmi said, "Touring 50 cities in the US for the past year has been a wonderful, valuable experience," but she admitted doubts as to whether she could "continue to live this kind of life."

Since Sunmi's departure, fans have examined Wonder Girls' episode of "The Knee-Drop Guru" with renewed interest. The expressions of the group members, especially that of Yeeun as she made her loaded comment and the brief silence that followed Park's assurance that the members agreed to the US debut, have led fans to suspect that Wonder Girls may not have responded with equal enthusiasm to JYP's decision. In the same interview, Sunmi confessed, "It was so lonely [in the US]. I didn't know how I could adjust." If the "forced overseas debut" theory holds, a talent management company pushed idol stars, young and sensitive, to change their environment, leave family and friends behind, and debut in the US, even if it meant battling loneliness. How did this happen?

A.   *Opportunity for fame and fortune*

The most obvious motivation is money. DSP Entertainment, the agency that orchestrated the Japan debuts of SS501 and KARA, explains, "Going abroad is the only option." The Korean market is small, profit margins are limited, and the record industry is in recession. To maximize profits from idol groups that agencies have spent a fortune grooming and training, heading overseas is the sole answer. The US is regarded as the top destination for international recognition and profit maximization.

The US stage also takes stars one step closer to ranking among the "world's best." Those who succeed in the US receive global attention and become "international stars." Because star status in the US maximizes exposure around the world, if an artist sells one record in the US, five more can be expected to sell elsewhere. International stars generally sell a million records in the US and five million globally.

Secondary markets are also enormous in the US. Touring the US is tantamount to a world tour. On their US tour, Wonder Girls opened for the Jonas Brothers, who drew 50,000 fans per concert. Digital audio, DVDs, and endorsements also bring in profits. Top artists in the US can gross ₩1 trillion in sales per year. Korean agencies cannot walk away from such dreams. No wonder they become obsessed with breaking free from dwindling opportunities for profits in Korea and expand to Japan, China, and the US.

From the management company's perspective, the success of one artist or group can catapult its reputation to that of a leader in Asia. This possibility is too enticing to abandon. Now that TVXQ and BoA have succeeded in Japan, groundless hopes are spreading among producers at SM Entertainment, YG Entertainment, and JYP Entertainment that such success can be replicated in the US. Thus far, SM has sent BoA, YG has sent SE7EN, and JYP has sent Rain and Wonder Girls to the US after testing them in Japan and the greater Asian market.

B.   *Disappointing report card*

So have Korean artists who "conquered" the US raised profits that live up to the rumors? In reality, no. Even Wonder Girls with their business model, recognized as the most successful to date, did not break even in the US. The high initial investment required for marketing and settling down abroad is to blame. BoA and SE7EN reportedly lost more money than Wonder Girls. Only Rain, who worked as both a singer and actor, turned a profit.

SE7EN announced his intention to debut in the US in 2008, at the height of his career in Korea. Lil' Kim, who sang "Lady Marmalade" with Christina Aguilera, Maya, and Pink for the soundtrack to *Moulin Rouge*, featured in SE7EN's first American single, "Girls," which drew popular attention. The song was composed by producer/composer Rodney "Darkchild" Jerkins, who wrote Michael Jackson's "You Rock My World" and "Déjà Vu" for Beyoncé and Jay-Z. But in spite of this notable support, the single went largely unnoticed. SE7EN returned to Korea at the end of last year and is working on an album for release early this year.

BoA's career in the US also seems to have hit a wall. She released her debut US single "Eat You Up" last March after many years of preparation, but nothing has come of it. Once the most popular singer in Japan, BoA is now in her mid-twenties, too old for an innocent young girl image, but she has been unable to bring a sexy concept to life.

The bruises BoA and SE7EN received go far deeper than their unsuccessful careers in the US. They wasted prime years and forfeited profits that they could have made in Korea and Asia. According to industry insiders, the opportunity cost amounts to over ₩10 billion. BoA, in fact, made ₩100 billion in sales each year in Japan, but had to stop her activity in Asia after she announced her intention to try to break into the US.

C. *Huge opportunity costs*

Some artists who had been considered rising stars in Korean pop music have been forgotten since their attempts at careers in the US. G-Soul, a JYP artist, entered the trainee program the same year as Sunye of Wonder Girls. Once a "pop music prodigy," he has been living in the US for six years now and has made little progress. He is still preparing to debut and take the US and international market by storm. Last year witnessed the return of Min, another artist who had been preparing to debut with G-Soul.

The case of singer Lim Jeong-hee is heartbreaking. Once a promising new female singer known from her busking as a "diva of the streets," she suddenly announced her intention to make a career in the US. JYP, of course, was the one to oversee this plan.

Lim got off to a great start, and in September 2007 signed an album contract with American hip-hop artist Big Boi from Outkast. Big Boi was the featured rap artist for the title song of her album "Madly in Love" and appeared in the music video. Lim came tantalizingly close to a breakthrough. She returned to Korea last year and has been keeping a low profile since. It is not difficult to imagine her sense of disappointment. Wonder Girls, who can relate all too well, have spoken of their anxiety because they had nothing on their schedule for the first two months in the US.

Experts believe the factor that most contributes to Korean artists' failure in the US is a sloppy approach. "You can tell by the way Korean producers are preoccupied with networking with American producers," said one insider. "JYP claims to have connections in the mainstream American music industry, but [given his failures to date] you have to question whether his connections can guarantee success."

Depending on a reliable fan base of Asian heritage rather than targeting mainstream American music fans is also viewed as problematic. One singer has been touted as having "made it in the US," but in reality, the singer's concerts were filled with Korean-American and other Asian-American fans.

Lack of proficiency in English is another obstacle. The struggles Rain and SE7EN had with English in their early years in the US are well-known. No matter how hard Sunye of Wonder Girls trains, she will not pull off an accent that sounds natural to Americans. Some say the reason JYP put Hyelim into Wonder Girls the moment Sunmi left is precisely because Hyelim is fluent in four languages, including English and Mandarin.

Another roadblock to success for Korean artists is the yawning gap between how stars are made in Asia and in the US. Korean idols are products of corporate grooming, discovered by agencies at a young age and trained for years until ready for debut. In the US, however, artists start out on small stages and make their way to larger venues. Lady Gaga, a popular American singer, advised Korean artists that they should start at local clubs if they want to break into the American market.

D.   *Wonder Girls, halfway to success*

Learning from the mistakes of Korean artists before them, Wonder Girls seem to have had a better approach to facing the challenges of the American market. Unlike SE7EN and BoA, who embarked on their US journeys with extravagant concerts and events booked, only to peter out, Wonder Girls accompanied the Jonas Brothers on tour as the opening act. In the 3rd week of October last year, a Wonder Girls song reached #76 on the Billboard "Hot 100" singles chart, a clear indication that their plans for a soft landing had worked, as it was the first time in 30 years that an Asian artist had reached the Billboard chart following Kyu Sakamoto in 1963, Pink Lady in 1979, and Yellow Magic Orchestra in 1980.

Wonder Girls also made themselves known in the American market by appearing on TV programs like *The Wendy Williams Show* and the prime time *So You Think You Can Dance*. They have had the most success of any Korean artist to date in the US, but rumors circulate that they have had to endure great hardships in the process. Top Korean stars are stooping to hanging around concert venues in order to make their names known.

Wonder Girls have also had to resort to novel ways to boost album sales. JYP made an agreement with a popular brand of children's apparel and sold Wonder Girls CDs at clothing stores rather than record stores. JYP says they were targeting the tween demographic (ages 8–14), which is less biased against people of color, but the group members were "deeply shocked and mortified" by this promotion. Even though the members added that the experience made them stronger, these ordeals have supported speculation that Sunmi's decision to leave was related to pressures to debut in the US and these upsetting promotion strategies.

E.   *Debuting in the US with American capital, and through Americans*

A growing argument suggests that Korean idol stars' attempts to crack the US market need a fundamental overhaul; for example, by taking advantage of the interest the three major American record corporations—Columbia, Sony, and Universal–has in Korean idols.

UMG has been the most enthusiastic of the three, investing in Cube Entertainment, which represents 4Minute and BEAST, and announcing a strategic partnership. With UMG taking charge of licensing and publishing, 4Minute's mini-album *For Muzik* was released simultaneously in nine countries in Asia. UMG also announced plans to groom an artist who, depending on the success of *For Muzik*, would debut in the US without being introduced in Asia first. UMG president Max Hall said that he had been following the dynamic development of the Korean music industry with keen interest and saw its potential in the global market. "We're happy to use Universal Music's powerful marketing strategies and networks to introduce Cube artists to the world," said Hall. Sony has also announced plans to establish a subsidiary in Korea.

Large American corporations are taking an interest in Korean idols because they are "groomed talents" who have been trained for between 2 to 10 years in dance, music, and acting. If record companies with international renown back them, Korean idol stars have a real chance of making it in the US market.

Another interesting strategy that Korean agencies have implemented is grooming American artists for the US market. U-KISS, who released the song "Manmanhani," was formed with the international market in mind. Kevin and Eli, the two American members, are fluent in English and Mandarin, and Alexander, the Chinese member, was born in Hong Kong, raised in Macau and Singapore, and speaks English, Mandarin, Portuguese, Japanese, Spanish, and French. According to the management, they will "begin their career in Korea and overseas simultaneously, rather than establishing a base in Korea before heading abroad." JYP also announced plans to "recruit and train a Korean-American or a Korean resident in America and fluent in English to debut in the US."

Many Korean idol groups these days include members from countries like Thailand or China. These members enjoy massive popularity in their country of origin, and so by extension do their groups. SM Entertainment's Super Junior benefitted from its Chinese member Hankyung, and 2PM were invited to perform for the Thai Imperial Court thanks to Thai member Nichkhun. Thai fans have embraced the group as their own. Following this trend, Baby V.O.X. recently welcomed a Thai member through auditions. "Foreign members can facilitate entry into foreign markets," said Yun Deung-nyong, head of DR Music, a company that represents Baby V.O.X. Such strategies are now being applied to the American market.

"Making it in the US means making it on the international stage," said Jeong Wook, CEO of JYP Entertainment. "It's an opportunity that all artists and agencies dream of. JYP will continue to strive for that goal." Perhaps we will have a new notch to add to the history of Korean idols abroad when these strategies bear real fruit.

2.4.5. PSY: One-Hit Wonder or First of Many K-Pop Hits?

Reference: "PSY: One-Hit Wonder or First of Many K-Pop Hits?" *Shin Dong-A*, Im Jin-mo, November 2012, No. 638, pp. 400–405.

A. *The secret behind the PSY Craze: One-hit wonder, or first of many K-pop hits?*

Popular singer PSY's "Gangnam Style" is a smash hit all over the world. Logging over 400 million hits on *YouTube* and taking the #2 spot on the Billboard chart, "Gangnam Style" is the hottest pop item this year. Experts say "Gangnam Style," with its simple but fun "horse dance" and an addictive tune that has captivated fans around the world, may have raised the value of Gangnam—the Beverly Hills of Korea—and Korea as a brand. But that's not all: everything PSY does is making the front page; everything he touches turns to gold. PSY mania is spreading like wildfire in the global market.

The gusts of PSY's "Gangnam Style" have been stirring up dizzying waves for the past month. Seoul used ₩400 million in emergency funds for a free PSY concert to be held at Seoul City Plaza on October 4; public transportation will run for an extra hour that day, a special measure only granted for national holidays and events, or for crises like blizzards. Having subway trains run an extra hour to accommodate a concert is genuinely unprecedented. This is just one of many perks of making it all the way to #2 on Billboard, which once sounded like something that only happened to those from far-off lands.

The music industry has also been blown away by PSY's Billboard conquest. Even experts are flabbergasted that a Korean singer has reached #2 not on Oricon, but the prestigious Billboard chart, with a song *in Korean*. "How is this happening?" is all they can ask. While acknowledging PSY's hard work and talent, experts admit his success would not have been possible without incredible luck.

B.   *B-grade image draws fans by the millions*

Musically, it is less surprising that this song wound up an international hit. The song takes prototypical dance music, a potential catalyst of mass hysteria and excitement, and mixes it with trance electronica, which is trendy these days. Overdoing trance can come across as vulgar and too much restraint can make it dull, but PSY's talent allows "Gangnam Style" to walk a fine line between the two.

The shuffle rhythm in the song offers a subtle nod to "Party Rock Anthem" by LMFAO, the electronica duo who have gone to #1 on Billboard, and so the rhythm of "Gangnam Style" likely did not come across as too foreign or unfamiliar to foreign audiences. Had "Gangnam Style" been either too different from current trends or too Korean, its appeal would not have been as immediate.

Domestically, the lyrics did the trick. Some say "Gangnam Style" is the most amusing and lighthearted song to paint a portrait of a man and a woman since Byun Jin-sub's "Wish List," released in 1989. Lines like "A girl whose heart gets hotter when night comes"; "A guy whose heart explodes when night comes"; "A girl who lets her hair down at the right moment"; and "A guy who has bulging ideals rather than muscles," provide a special kick. It's hard not to get those catchy phrases stuck in your head.

The name of the song itself accounts for much of its wild popularity. On top of catchy lyrics and fun dance moves, the endlessly adaptable title—Taereung Style, New York Style, Masan Style, Pervert Style—boosted its relentlessly spreading popularity. The song had the elements for a runaway hit.

The message of the song, lying just below the surface, is not to be overlooked either. In the music video, PSY is decked out in suit and shades, but seems a little soft in the head and looks ridiculous as he does his horse dance. He appears uncouth. At a press conference held upon his return to Korea, PSY said, "Americans say I remind them of the comical, quirky character, Austin Powers." In other words, his image is that of a jester. PSY says he's a B-rate artist, a supporting actor who can barely scratch the top 20. But this man has convinced the world that Gangnam is the Beverly Hills of Korea. Honestly, he must be joking.

This irony creates the fun of the song and has helped spawn its immense popularity. It would have been obnoxious if someone handsome, say, Jang Dong-gun or Kang Dong-won, had become the face of Gangnam and put forth an image of traditional elegance. The popularity of "Gangnam Style" reflects an explosion of affection for the second-rate: the sidekick or underdog. PSY functions as an unlikely hero who offers a subtle jab at a society dominated by worship of the posh and arrogant, ruled by the number ones, the 1%, those who have it all.

C. Popularity of K-pop lays the foundation

Some have been hesitant about attributing PSY's Billboard success to the spread of K-pop. They insist that his accomplishment is isolated and personal, and that it is a stretch to see it as representing a global leap for Korean popular culture or new opportunities for K-pop.

PSY himself in an interview with *Time* said, "I'm just an entertainer. I don't want to represent my country like an athlete." His discomfort with being called a "global superstar" rather than an "international artist" can be understood in this context. The media portrayal of the success of "Gangnam Style" as demonstrating global recognition of the value of Korean popular culture and PSY as the pride and glory of Korea understandably makes him feel pressured.

Since the broadcast of a special feature called "K-Pop Goes Global," there has been something unnatural about the way media in Asia, Europe, South America, and even *Time* have treated PSY mania as unrelated to K-pop. PSY undeniably owes his success in part to K-pop stars such as Rain, Wonder Girls, and Girls' Generation, who've been knocking on the door to the American music industry for the last seven to eight years: the knocking of those who came before him left it wide open for PSY.

Still, PSY entered the American market by a completely different route— he was virtually summoned to the US. Some even say, "PSY was forced to go abroad, while other K-pop stars had to work hard to get there." The phenomenon gathered steam when CNN chose "Gangnam Style" as a "Must-See Video." Thanks to the warm reception that the video won among such celebrities as international pop star Katy Perry, who posted a shout-out to PSY on social media, PSY wound up with a record deal with Island Def Jam, a high-end recording company that has produced Justin Bieber.

The popularity of "Gangnam Style" did not move from Korea to the US, but skyrocketed when Americans picked it up. In other words, a Korean song did not conquer the US: rather, American fans took up a worthy Korean song. Instead of being won over by the success of "Gangnam Style" overseas, the US music business chose "Gangnam Style" to promote elsewhere. That PSY attended Berklee College of Music and is comfortable with English was a bonus for both PSY and the US industry.

It goes without saying that the song's potential to elicit a positive response worldwide lay behind this choice. A product like "Gangnam Style," backed by US marketing resources, has overwhelming commercial power. It has been widely marketable, and American interests are profiting enormously from it. What does it matter if the singer is Korean or Thai when billions can be made internationally? Exoticizing "oriental" culture and imposing an "othering" gaze are things of the past. Xenophobia no longer sells.

D. Expert marketing of the US music industry

The dissolution of white supremacy can be observed in Major League Baseball as well. Baseball teams have been overflowing with Asian and Latino players. As the LA Dodgers scouted Park Chan-ho and Manchester United took Park Ji-sung, the American music industry asked for PSY, or more specifically, "Gangnam Style." It's no surprise that "Gangnam Style" evoked memories of Los Del Rio's "Macarena" (1995) for more than a few people.

"Macarena," sung by 2 middle-aged men from Spain, spent 14 weeks at the top of the Billboard chart supported by deliberate US music industry choices. Both "Macarena" and "Gangnam Style" are fun dance songs that followed similar routes to success. It doesn't matter if the singer is American, Spanish, or Korean when the US puts its marketing resources to work to distribute a product and turn a profit.

Similarly, the success of KARA, the most popular Korean girl group in Japan and the only one to have performed at Tokyo Dome, means profits for Japan, not Korea. To put it crudely, the group's singers are mere faces that allow Japanese capital to churn out profits. The nationality of the entertainer does not matter. Of course, PSY will make money and YG will take its share, but only the basic fee that US labels are obligated to pay. It is the US music industry that will reap huge profits.

If it weren't for commercial decisions made in the US, "Gangnam Style" would not have become a runaway smash. Therefore, contrary to what people in Korea might wish, it won't be easy for other K-pop artists, including PSY himself, to produce another Billboard hit like "Gangnam Style." The US responded to "Gangnam Style" because it was a fun song with potential to become an international hit, not because of their faith in PSY, K-pop artists in general, or even the K-pop genre.

After the unprecedented international sensation of "Macarena," Los Del Rio never had a second hit, and the success of "Macarena" did not pave the way to international stardom for other Spanish artists either. "Macarena," not Los Del Rio, was the product that met market demands. It is wishful or nationalistic thinking to equate the success of "Gangnam Style" with opportunities for K-pop. PSY himself will work hard to produce a piece that tops "Gangnam Style," but those in the music industry, including the artist himself, understand that replicating his success won't be easy.

E.   Back-to-back hits will be no simple matter

The UK-based *Financial Times* ran a column about PSY that included the following:

> The phenomenal success of 'Gangnam Style,' a video by Korean rap artist PSY... is a quirky (and rather catchy) indication of South Korea's rising fortunes. The dance video gently sends up the nouveau riche, plastic-surgery-enhanced lifestyle that has been made possible by an economic transformation so extraordinary it is known as 'the miracle on the Han River.' ... [In an economic model] skewed towards a privileged elite... more Koreans feel poor, overworked and weighed down by social pressures.[70]

---

[70] David P. (2012), "South Korea Wallows in Existential Angst," *Financial Times*, September 26.

A jester is poking fun at a world dominated by the elite. The magnetism of "Gangnam Style" can be attributed to this counterpunch that accompanies the enjoyable song and dance. Since PSY debuted in 2002 with "Bird," and on to his songs "Champion," "Paradise," "Entertainer," and "Right Now," he has always danced passionately, as if he's on fire. People experience a liberating catharsis as they watch a jester devoted to his art. It seems society no longer values that sort of passion and devotion.

For the first time in a long while, an energizing pop song that nods to the underdog has captivated the global community. Just as we experience pathos while enjoying the slapstick and wordplay of a jester, we get a small thrill from the mockery behind the effervescent dancing of "Gangnam Style." As if that weren't enough, Korea has been handed the booty of international success, or, in PSY's words, an added bonus. My interpretation may well be steeped in nationalism, but I do not tire of hearing that "Gangnam Style" will go down in history as another triumph for Korean culture.

2.4.6.   The Pororo Syndrome: *Hallyu*'s Brightest Star

Reference: "The Pororo Syndrome: *Hallyu*'s Brightest Star," *Dong-A Ilbo*, Lee Sae-saem, April 30, 2011.

A.   Nicknames such as "President Pororo" and "the Good Lord Pororo" reflect current trends, as exports of the show have spread to 110 countries

"Please put in a scene where Pororo is eating Korean food," read one petition uploaded to portal site *Daum*. By the afternoon of April 29, more than 3,200 people had signed the petition. The petition arose because "there are so many scenes in which the characters bake cookies that our children only want sweets. Pororo is such an icon. Please put in scenes where he eats Korean food so that our kids imitate him."

Pororo the Little Penguin, first broadcast on EBS in 2003, has come to be called "The Kids' President," transcending mere fame to become a social sensation and veritable royalty. Pororo fandom has exploded, and the little penguin is now referred to by such nicknames as "President Pororo," "the Good Lord Pororo," and "Pororomme" (a combination of "Pororo" and *homme fatale*). Iconix Entertainment, Pororo's production company, announced in relation to the petition that, "A level of responsibility comes with Pororo's popularity, and so we intend to make a public service video showing Pororo eating Korean food."

Pororo the Little Penguin is set in a perennially snow-covered Arctic. The protagonist, a penguin that wears flight goggles and an aviator hat, is joined on the show by such characters as baby dinosaur Crong and Loopy, a little beaver. In addition to domestic sales of related character products and DVDs, the program is popular abroad. Of course, these "*Hallyu* stars" have become popular in Asian countries already accustomed to Korean content, but they have now also been exported to 110 countries, and appear on France's terrestrial broadcaster TF1 and Al Jazeera.

"President Pororo" is slated to make an appearance at the Lotus Lantern Festival for Buddha's Birthday on May 7. The lantern to be created and displayed is an image of a young monk of the Hanmaum Seon Center grasping the hand of Pororo. The center announced, "We want to make Buddhism accessible and friendly to children and toddlers, so we made a lantern with Pororo."

Netizens' comments on Pororo have been collected in a "Pororo Confessional Series," which is spreading online. The series includes such testimonials as, "I bought a Pororo computer and my child mastered Korean in a month"; "If you give children Pororo bandages when they get shots, the tears stop right away"; and "Only when Pororo is on can we have some peace and quiet at home. Seriously, he deserves the Nobel Peace Prize." Tributes in other forms are appearing as well, such as the "Pororo Hero Series" with portraits and videos of Pororo depicted as notable figures such as Admiral Yi Sun-shin and King Sejong, or without his signature flight goggles as "Pororo without Glasses."

Thanks to this popularity, 80% of the 4 million stamps printed with the image of Pororo, roughly 3.2 million, sold in just 9 days at the beginning of the year. In the same period, a series of 10 notable figure skaters, including Kim Yuna, sold only 35% of the total 5.5 million stamps, prompting some to refer to the incident as "the humiliation of Yuna."

The Iconix Entertainment producer in charge of *Pororo the Little Penguin*, Kim Ji-young, explained, "Since Pororo is intended to be the same age as four or five year olds, we put material into the episodes that they can relate to. Children really enjoy these stories that involve what they've seen and experienced, or things that could happen around them."

PART 3

International Reception

Much of this final section, which focuses on the international reception of the Korean Wave, is taken from *Hallyu Forever: The World Is Hallyu Style*, a book published in 2012 by KOFICE. Established in 2003 as the Asia Cultural Exchange Foundation, this non-profit organization changed its name in 2006. Although under the auspices of the MCST, KOFICE differs from governmental institutes and agencies working on *Hallyu* in that it focuses on promoting academic research on cultural trends and puts less emphasis on industry-directed policy guides and strategic plans. KOFICE has hosted major international fora, established a network of foreign correspondents, and published five volumes in the *Hallyu Forever* series, the most recent of which is excerpted here. The content, focus, and tone of the *Hallyu Forever* books differ from documents from KOFIC or KOCCA. Rather than focusing on certain genres or industries, these volumes discuss target regions and countries and provide a historical overview of Korean cultural exports, underscoring their reception and cultural impact.

Included in this section, together with excerpts from *Hallyu Forever*, are articles and blog posts describing the Korean Wave from the outside. These personal, everyday encounters and experiences provide a counterpoint to official discourse on *Hallyu*. A total of seven major target destinations are discussed: China, Japan, Southeast Asia, the Americas, Europe, Central Asia, and the Middle East.

Document 3.1.1, "*Hallyu* Forever: Chinese-Speaking Regions," discusses the origin of the word *Hallyu* in detail. Examining popular culture flows from Korea to Sinophone areas in their early days, the document charts a burgeoning history of the Korean Wave. While making essentialist speculations about the nature of *Hallyu*, it also takes into account political realities inside the Asian region, especially diplomatic tensions between South Korea and Taiwan, to paint a picture of the Korean Wave's political and economic context.

Document 3.1.2 derives from *OhMyNews*, Korea's foremost civilian-led, participatory Internet news site. Established in 2000, many non-professional journalists have contributed opinions and reports to the website. The document carries the provocative title "Do the Chinese Hate *Jewel in the Palace*?" and discusses Korean media reaction to surveys that show Chinese animosity toward Korea. Observing the continued warm reception of Korean dramas by mainland fans amidst tension between South Korea and China over cultural exports and the protection of national industries, the author criticizes the media's tendencies to feed online feuds.

Subsection 3.2, focusing on Japan, contains three documents. An excerpt from *Hallyu Forever* recapitulates and adds further depth to the success stories that appeared earlier in this volume by offering a pre-history of *Hallyu* in the 70s and 80s Japanese music scene. The piece further engages with the term neo-*Hallyu* and gives an account of the broader secondary markets that the

Korean Wave opened. Document 3.2.2, "A Firsthand Account of *Hallyu* Fever in Japan," typifies *OhMyNews* articles in blending personal experiences and observations with semi-professional reportage. Its Korean author is a wife and mother living in Tokyo who observes how *Hallyu* has helped her forge warmer everyday relationships with Japanese peers. Document 3.2.3, also written by an *OhMyNews* contributor, reports from Shin-Okubo, a Tokyo neighborhood with a concentration of Korean shops and restaurants. The author speculates on a lull in *Hallyu* in 2012, as suggested by the title "Tokyo: Where Have All the *Hallyu* Fans Gone?" and asks whether the respite is temporary or signals the phenomenon's end.

Subsection 3.3 deals with Southeast Asia, a region where *Hallyu* has been particularly strong. The excerpt from *Hallyu Forever* (Document 3.3.1) offers a comprehensive view of eight ASEAN nations (Thailand, Malaysia, Indonesia, Vietnam, the Philippines, Singapore, Myanmar, and Cambodia) and discusses not only popular culture but also exports of Korean manufactured goods. Document 3.3.2, "*Hallyu* Grips Phnom Penh," written by a Korean tourist who stumbles upon an enthusiastic K-pop dance class on the streets of Cambodia's capital, neatly echoes the report on a similar phenomenon in the *Hallyu Forever* excerpt (p. 289).

Vietnamese women have formed a significant portion of marriage migrants into Korea. Document 3.3.3, "A Vietnamese Bride's Country Diary," speaks from the perspective of a migrant who loves Korean dramas. A fan before she came to Korea, she continues to enjoy dramas on her new flat-screen TV with her young son while her husband is at work. The article links *Hallyu* to the rise in women from elsewhere seeking Korean husbands, suggesting that many immigrate to Korea in the hope of living out in some modest way the fantasies portrayed on TV screens.

Hallyu promotional efforts have gone hand in hand with efforts to promote the Korean language and its script, as seen in Document 1.1.3 on Korean Cultural Centers and the inauguration of King Sejong Institutes. The small city of Bau Bau, located in Indonesia's Southeast Sulawesi, and its regional language Bahasa Cia-Cia, spoken by a local ethnic group, made headlines in Korea in 2009 when it was reported that the Cia-Cia, who did not have a standardized way of writing their language, had adopted *hangeul* as their script. Document 3.3.4, "The Truth behind *Hangeul* and the Cia-Cia," discusses how the phrase "official adoption of *hangeul*" that came to circulate was misleading and had the potential to create diplomatic strain between Korea and Indonesia by undermining Indonesian central authority. A mix of nationalism, overenthusiastic journalism, and popular linguistic misunderstanding created a small-scale debacle. The document goes on to re-examine the controversy in 2012; government and corporate sponsorship of *hangeul* education in the area has declined, while a project launched by a few enthusiastic Korean linguists continues to cause confusion.

Subsection 3.4, focusing on the Americas, begins with further excerpts from *Hallyu Forever* and contains an extended report on the success of PSY's "Gangnam Style" in the US. Document 3.4.2, written in 2006, reports how "The Korean Wave Laps American Shores," and details how Asian-Americans led the introduction of Korean cultural products in the US. The piece makes for an interesting comparison with Document 3.4.3, "New Year's Party for Those Who Make

Hallyu Shine: A Mexican Fan Event." Composed by a Korean expat and focusing on a Korea-themed party in Mexico City, the piece hints at curiously lackluster support from the Korean Embassy and local Korean Cultural Center. Although Document 1.1.3 spoke optimistically of the role of such cultural centers, this report calls into question how well some cater to the demands of *Hallyu* fans.

The *Hallyu Forever* book begins its discussion of Europe with Korean movies rather than K-pop or dramas (Document 3.5.1). Indeed, as seen in the *2012 Broadcast Content White Paper* (Document 2.1.1), Korean dramas and K-pop, with the exception of "Gangnam Style," have had little impact on the European market at large. Interestingly, however, Europe is touted as the prime destination for Korean *manhwa*, and artistic Korean graphic novels that target an adult readership have been particularly popular in France and Belgium (p. 332–333).

Document 3.5.2, "President Park Meets *Hallyu* Fans as First Official French Event," tells of an interesting cultural diplomacy initiative. In revealing the emphasis given to *Hallyu* in building the bilateral relationship between France and South Korea, the document gives ample indication of how the Park Geun-hye Administration has attempted to follow in the footsteps of previous governments and appropriate *Hallyu* to further its agenda. Document 3.5.3, "A Korean Culture Club Opens in Lithuanian Capital," by way of contrast, reports the grassroots-led opening of a Korean Culture Club at a university in Lithuania. Our excerpts from *Hallyu Forever* then consider three countries in Central Asia (Kazakhstan, Uzbekistan, and Mongolia) in Subsection 3.6, and then move briefly to the Middle East in Subsection 3.7.

This sourcebook's final document, "Myeongdong 'Cosmetics Road' Today," brings the discussion back to Korea and considers the international spread of Korean popular culture bringing visitors to the country. The piece focuses on a must-visit site for *Hallyu* fans, where the reach of *Hallyu* may perhaps be felt most acutely within Korea. In this expensive plot of land in Myeongdong in downtown Seoul, Korean cosmetics companies compete to attract customers from Japan, China, and beyond. Thanks to *Hallyu*, inbound tourism has surged. The question is: Should we consider this situation another part of *Hallyu*, or rather a result of its impact? Korea is indeed experiencing cultural and social changes; aside from the opportunities for monetary gain, *Hallyu* offers Koreans an opportunity to re-examine their understanding of culture and the nation's global standing.

Each country and region in this section has accepted and explored the Korean Wave in its own distinct way. Similarly, Korea is also coming to terms with the aspirations, pride, and responsibilities that accompany *Hallyu*. Despite its hyperbole, the title *Hallyu Forever: The World Is Hallyu Style* underscores the successes of a nation that has long thirsted for recognition on the world stage.

3.1. CHINA

3.1.1. *Hallyu* Forever: Chinese-Speaking Regions

Reference: *Hallyu Forever: The World Is Hallyu Style*, Ko Jeong-min et al., KOFICE
Hallyu Series V, 2012, pp. 74–108.

A. *Hallyu in Mainland China*

Spread of *Hallyu*

In China, the Korean Wave has been driven largely by TV dramas and dance music. Dramas in particular have been widely popular across all generations and contributed to the early development of *Hallyu*. In 1993, the year after South Korea and China established diplomatic relations, a Korean drama, *Jealousy*, was first broadcast across mainland China, albeit to little fanfare. In 1997, China's main network, CCTV1, broadcast *What Is Love?*, thus ushering in the Korean Wave. *What Is Love?* enjoyed ratings of 4.2%, an impossibly high percentage at the time. It became the second most watched show from outside China ever to that point and gained a nationwide following. Viewer demand caused the network to rebroadcast the series, a rare practice for an import. When *All about Eve* and *Autumn Tales,* purchased by China's cable TV and shown in 1999, also became massive hits, the popularity of Korean TV dramas soared.

Since then, Korean dramas have maintained their appeal, becoming mainstream to the point that the terrestrial network ATV began featuring Korean dramas in its prime time lineup. In 2002, the year the FIFA World Cup was held in Korea, 67 Korean drama series were shown across China to great popularity. Of these, *Autumn Tales,* which had already achieved success through cable, was broadcast simultaneously on 21 channels across the country. Other dramas, such as *Again and Again, Miss Mermaid,* and *The Last Empress,* despite being shown after 11 p.m., also enjoyed ratings of over 10% and overwhelmed competition from other imported dramas.[1]

A total of 107 Korean dramas were broadcast in 2004 alone, causing *Hallyu* to pick up speed. The phenomenon reached its peak in China in 2005, when *Jewel in the Palace* was shown across the country by Hunan TV. However, a backlash against Korean products also developed. Hong Kong actor Jackie Chan and Chinese actor Zhang Guoli led the movement by bringing awareness to what they considered a worrisome trend. Their actions encouraged many Chinese TV and film personalities to make anti-*Hallyu* arguments more explicitly. Voices cried out for a check against the reckless spread of Korean pop culture within Chinese society. Even the Chinese government was gripped with fear that the Korean Wave was encroaching upon local culture; the government scrutinized Korean dramas closely and limited the amount of Korean broadcasting in order to control drama imports. The popularity of Korean dramas waned following this series of developments.

---

[1] In a survey conducted by CCTV on China's imported TV dramas, 71% of participants responded that *Miss Mermaid* was their favorite, and 28% responded *The Last Empress,* bringing Korean dramas to the top of the list.

However, the surge in those with Internet and smartphone access has allowed Korean dramas to maintain a strong following. Although unresolved copyright issues still pose a difficult challenge in monetizing viewership, most major portal sites in China offer Korean drama channels and free streams of Korean television from past and present. Chinese fans can watch their favorite dramas and entertainment shows over the Internet within a day or two of their broadcast in Korea, complete with Chinese subtitles. *Youku Tudou*, China's biggest online video website, and numerous other Chinese sites similar to *YouTube*, have acquired the rights to several Korean dramas and offer them to Chinese viewers simultaneously with broadcast in Korea.

Korean dance music has also strongly contributed to the growth of *Hallyu* in China. In fact, it was Kim Yun-ho, the CEO of WoojeonSoft, who first used the term *Hallyu* in China. Kim was responsible for creating and producing *Seoul Music Library* in March for a Beijing FM radio station. Soon after, Chinese artists began recording covers of Korean songs for the first time. Clon's dance tune "Kungtari Shabara" was covered by Sun Yue and released under a Chinese title in 1998. This remake was a huge hit. Thereafter, Sunnan, the most popular male musician in China at the time, covered Shin Seung-hun's "I Believe," which caused interest in Korean pop music to explode. Many famous Chinese artists either translated Korean songs or recorded covers, making them more familiar to Chinese listeners.

In May 1998, the first Korean studio album was officially released in China. This was a 10-song album by H.O.T., with the single "Happiness" as the featured title track, and it was distributed by the largest record label in China at the time. Within a month of its release, the album had sold over 50,000 copies. In February 2000, H.O.T. performed a hugely successful concert at the Beijing's Workers Stadium, and "Happiness" became a catalyst in popularizing Korean dance music across China. H.O.T.'s success was followed by such acts as Clon, NRG, Shinhwa, Lee Jung-hyun, Jang Nara, Younha, Baby V.O.X, Yoo Seung-jun, Goofy, Rain, TVXQ, and Wonder Girls. The Chinese music scene, which had until then largely only experienced ballads from Hong Kong and Taiwan, fully embraced the fast beats, energetic moves, and loud fashions of these Korean dance acts. Younger audiences in their teens and twenties were drawn to Korean dance music. Indeed, this phenomenon gave rise to the neologism *ha-hanzu* (哈韓族), referring to Chinese youth crazy for Korean music.

While in its early days *Hallyu* was spread by TV dramas and reinforced by dance music, neo-*Hallyu* was spawned by K-pop. In particular, Korean idol groups have surfaced as cultural icons in China and led a resurgence of the Korean Wave. Unlike dramas, which experienced ups and downs in popularity, K-pop has been consistently popular, putting to rest the view that *Hallyu* will turn out to be a temporary fad. On the contrary, one can readily sense that Chinese interest in K-pop is growing wider and deeper. A case in point is the Korea Week Special Concert featuring Super Junior, Girls' Generation, BoA, Kangta, and f(x), held at the Shanghai Expo on the evening of May 30, 2010, the last day of Korea Week. Fans in their late teens and early twenties traveled from across China the day before the concert and waited all night in line to buy tickets. Those who failed in getting tickets protested tearfully outside the venue.

As with dramas, the Korean Wave in K-pop has grown even further online in China. Of the top 10 fan club websites compiled by China's largest search engine *Sina* (www.sina.com), nearly half are dedicated to *Hallyu* stars. Most began as subscriber communities for fans to share the schedules of favorite stars and other information. "Gangnam Style," which recently became an enormous hit in the US and Europe, was also an Internet sensation in China. On November 11, 2012, the single reached the number 1 spot on the Top 500 chart of *Baidu*.

The Chinese aren't as feverish about Korean music as they were in the past; rather, they now view it as mainstream. Almost every day traditional media outlets also offer the latest news on Korean idol groups. Moreover, new stars are attracting popularity as well.

Movies have also contributed to the Korean Wave. In 1998, *Wedding Story* became the first Korean film to be released in China. Initially films weren't as popular as TV dramas; however, *My Sassy Girl,* released in Korea in 2001, became a runaway hit in China when it debuted there the following year. As the movie opened around the same time the drama *Autumn Tales* was first broadcast, it did enormously well. *My Sassy Girl* brought in revenues of RMB 10 million despite a surfeit of pirated copies. Furthermore, over four million DVD copies of the film were sold in 2002 alone; given the number of illegal copies in the market, actual circulation is estimated in the tens of millions.

Publications have added to the growth of *Hallyu* as well. Copyright sales of Korean books began in earnest in the 2000s. These early copyright sales, driven largely by fiction, shot to 240 in 2005 but then stagnated for the next 3 years. The figures began to increase again after 2009. According to data released by the Korea-China Publication Seminar held on August 30, 2012, over 1,400 Korean books, including works of literature and practical self-help books, have been translated and published annually since 2009. These numbers place Korea fifth in outbound copyright to China, behind the US, UK, Taiwan, and Japan. Korean books sell for less than Japanese books, while boasting superior design and content. According to the Korean Publishing Research Institute, 49.2% of Korea's total exports of copyright sales from 2009 to 2011 went to China. The Chinese market is clearly very important to the Korean publishing industry.

Ever since Kim Jeong-hyeon's novel *Father* became a hit in China in the late 1990s, Korean fiction has consistently performed well. Kim Ha-in's 2002 novel *Scent of Chrysanthemums* sold no fewer than two million copies and topped many bestseller lists; the book was also adapted for the theater and inspired a popular song. Choi In-ho's *Sangdo, Merchant of Joseon* sold over 400,000 copies in 2003, and Guiyeoni's *The Guy Was Cool* topped several Chinese fiction charts, ultimately selling over 1 million copies. Lee U-hyeok's fantasy series *The Soul Guardian* sold hundreds of thousands of copies in China. Following the popularity of Korean TV dramas, novelizations such as *Full House, My Lovely Sam Soon, Lovers in Paris,* and *Jewel in the Palace* became hugely successful in 2005, even beating out *Brothers*, a new release by one of China's most popular writers, Yu Hua. However, the sales of Korean novels tapered off after 2005, until 2010, when Shin Kyung-sook's *Please Look after Mom* captured the imagination of Chinese readers once more.

The latest phenomenon has seen the attention formerly given to fiction shifting to non-fiction, including self-help books and books on business and finance.

Nam In-suk's 2007 *A Woman's Life Is Determined in Her Twenties* has remained popular for five years, and many estimate the book to have sold over two million copies. Kim Nan-do's *Youth Hurts* was published in February 2012; it went on to sell 500,000 copies. By July, the book had remained at the top of the best-seller list for 16 weeks running. The China Communist Youth League, which has spawned some of China's most renowned leaders and opinion-makers, including President Hu Jintao, selected *Youth Hurts* as a recommended book.

Go Deuk-seong's *30 Years in Retirement without Worrying about Money* was published in China in April 2010. In its first year, the book made it to the top of the bestseller list in the finance category and to 15th on the overall list in 2011. In two years, the book sold over 500,000 copies in China, overtaking its sales in Korea. According to the explanation offered by a Korean publisher, Chinese and Korean readers share concerns about their life post-retirement in the midst of skyrocketing real estate prices and household debt and are therefore turning to self-help books. As one Chinese publisher notes, Korea's trendy dramas and idol groups have turned the attention of Chinese readers to health and beauty concerns. Korean popular culture has changed the game for China's book market, which was formerly dominated by practical guides for success and psychology books.

Children's literature and educational books targeting preschoolers and elementary schoolchildren have also risen in popularity, testifying to the zeal for education in China. Previously, educational books such as *Aesop Theater, Eyewitness Science,* and the *Talmud,* were very popular. Korean educational books have enjoyed staggering sales in the Chinese market. In 2007, the *Survival* series sold over one million copies. The rights to the 80-volume *manhwa* series *Why?* have already been sold to a Chinese publisher. Other such series, like *Confidence-boosting Basic Science, Counting Rocks Math,* the storybook *The Hen that Left the Yard,* the picture-book *Sex Education with Parents,* and *My Wannabe Makeup,* a how-to book for young girls interested in make-up application, have all been consistently popular.

Due to China's one-child policy, Chinese families have fewer offspring than in the past and more resources to invest in their education. This situation has caused the local children's book market to expand rapidly. In 2011 there were 220 million children aged 14 and under in China, and the book market targeting them was valued at RMB 5.64 billion (₩1 trillion), 14.2% of total book publication, which is valued at RMB 40 billion (₩7.147 trillion). As Chinese parents are willing to indulge their "little emperors," book series with over 10 volumes sell well there. Economic development has improved quality of life for many Chinese, and they have become increasingly interested in top children's books from the US, Europe, and Korea. The market has also grown due to the efforts of the publishing industry. Despite the increase in sales, however, growth doesn't always translate directly into income, as book prices are controlled by the state. Therefore, publishers have scrambled to increase sales and make ends meet.

Online games likewise play an important role in the Korean Wave in China. The influence of *Hallyu* has drawn many Chinese fans to Korean games, and China, along with Japan, is now Korea's largest market for online and mobile games. WeMade's *The Legend of Mir* made up 65% of the Chinese online gaming market in 2002, and Korean online games at one point were the most popular in China, with the Chinese market practically monopolized by Korea. Although Korean games no longer enjoy such a high market share, games such as *Crossfire* and *Dungeon & Fighter* continue to top the Chinese online gaming market. In September 2011, *Crossfire* broke *Dungeon & Fighter*'s record for the highest number of users simultaneously connected to a game (2.6 million). In March 2012, it broke its own record and brought in 3.5 million users to the platform simultaneously. This remains the record not only in China but worldwide.

According to *Baidu*, several Korean games ranked in the top 10 online games in China as of November 18, 2012: *Crossfire* in 1st place, *Dungeon & Fighter* in 2nd, and *Legendary* at 10th. *Dragon Nest,* which ranked eighth, remained Korean until 2012, when Actoz Soft was bought by China's Shanda. The top 20 list contains more Korean games such as *Maple Story, KartRider,* and *Battlefield;* and the top 30 includes *Blade and Soul, Aion,* and *Audition Dance Battle.*[2]

In 2011, 38.2% of all Korean game exports went to China, 27.4% to Japan, 18% to Southeast Asia, 7.6% to North America, and 6.4% to Europe. China had a clear lead. The gaming industry makes up 53.6%, or more than half, of all Korean content exports. Its growth rate over the past three years has also been on the rise. Gaming is truly propping up content-related exports.[3]

However, aside from a few Korean gaming companies, most companies are struggling in the Chinese market. The Chinese government is cracking down in order to protect its local industry, and many Chinese companies are violating Korean copyrights. The quality of Chinese games has also improved. These challenges have driven down the high market share that Korea once held. China's online gaming industry has been experiencing double-digit growth every year, and in 2008, it surpassed Korea to become the world's largest market. Chinese companies with high-quality games now in fact export to Korea.

Behind *Hallyu*'s rise

The late 1990s, when *Hallyu* first took root in China, coincided with the rapid capitalization of the Chinese market following Deng Xiaoping's 1992 southern tour, during which he vigorously reaffirmed China's economic reforms and market openness. Subsequent reforms and resulting social changes enabled *Hallyu* to carve out a portion of China's cultural industry.

Experiencing a better quality of life, Chinese consumers became more demanding, expressing a quiet discontent that was quickly sensed by the government. However, the government believed that increased import of Western and Japanese products would subordinate the local cultural industry. Concerned as well that Western democratic notions of pluralism would threaten socialist state ideology, China only grudgingly accepted Western and Japanese cultural imports and limited their scope.

In this way, the Chinese government attempted to protect its local cultural industries at least until they had matured enough to compete against Western and Japanese products and the regime became more confident in its stability. Around this time South Korea and China established diplomatic ties; Korean products emerged as a potential solution to China's problem and were gradually accepted.

---

[2] "China's Online Game Rankings," *Baidu,* http://top.baidu.com/buzz.php?p=mmogame.
[3] KOCCA (2012), *2012 Gaming Industry White Paper.*

The Chinese government wanted to further open its market through the power of reforms and globalization, but also wished to protect its socialist ideology, cultural identity, and cultural industries. It viewed Korean culture, a reinterpretation of Western and Japanese cultures filtered through the lens of Confucianism, as a lesser threat to political stability and social unity.

Hallyu succeeded because it brought together a blend of influences while maintaining a unique edge. Korean dramas and movies aren't merely Westernized products fed to Korean audiences. Rather, they successfully, and with sophistication, merge East Asian traditional culture with Western narratives and tropes. In this way, Korea has achieved a sense of intimacy with Chinese viewers. K-pop songs, for example, combine globalized Western pop music and its Japanese cousin with Korean elements that are easy for Chinese audiences to swallow. In this way, K-pop has created its own unique style. Because Korea was able to rapidly absorb the popular music and choreography of the West, mix it with East Asian elements, and put it all in a sophisticated package, K-pop succeeded across China, Japan, Southeast Asia, and beyond to the Middle East and South America, going so far west as to reach the US and Europe.

Another selling point for *Hallyu* was that, because Korea had experienced industrialization and urbanization one step ahead of China, the lifestyles of Koreans shown on TV and in the movies were realistically approximate to what Chinese viewers themselves knew. The Chinese public, undergoing the turbulent social changes that came from rapid industrialization and adoption of a capitalist market economy, were drawn to Korea's dramas, movies, and fiction that dealt with themes such as individual success, family disintegration, and feelings of isolation and loneliness, as the experiences of characters on TV and in novels were similar to what many Chinese were going through or were likely to see in the future. The proximity that the Chinese public felt to Korean pop culture allowed *Hallyu* to spread easily across China, and weakened any backlash or initial resistance. By allowing the expansion of *Hallyu* to satisfy the cultural demands of the youth, the Chinese government used it as a mechanism to sanitize the dominant elements of modernity.

Furthermore, the success of *Hallyu* gave the Chinese government a model for its own cultural industries. To that end, China embraced *Hallyu* and even benchmarked the phenomenon. Another factor in this success was that Korean cultural products were of a higher quality than local products but still more affordable than those from the West or Japan.

Hallyu resistance and regulation

Coinciding with *Hallyu*'s sweep across China were outbreaks of an anti-*Hallyu* backlash that came from an unfolding sense of crisis and resistance that changed how the public interpreted and viewed the Korean Wave. Early on, *Hallyu* was not seen as especially threatening to China's economy or politics, and China considered benchmarking the Korean Wave to grow its cultural industries. However, as *Hallyu* experienced wild growth and became more widespread across the land, many voiced concerns over cultural imperialism, with *Hallyu* overwhelming the local market. These concerns led to a change in attitudes.

China was trying to harness the hard power derived from its economic development to grow its soft power in order to become a true superpower. Because

Hallyu was increasingly viewed as a threat to China's cultural marketplace and identity, it no longer served as a viable model for Chinese aspirations. This change in thinking provoked a rise in protectionism. The public started to display resistance to *Hallyu* while the government instituted measures to regulate the trend. The state also began to invest heavily in developing and growing its own popular culture products to replace demand for Korean and Western pop culture.

The Communist Party originally interpreted the concept of culture within the socialist tradition; that is, it saw culture as a political tool for educating the masses as it propagated and promoted the superiority of its regime. Now the party sees culture as an industry, a high-value-added product, and a symbol of its national standing. The Chinese government has determined that its popular culture, which lags far behind China's economic development, will be a decisive element in its struggle with the US for global influence. The government has revealed its ambition to treat its cultural industries as being of strategic importance and use soft power to become a global superpower. In the end, the rise of *Hallyu* has been critical to the formulation of this new policy.

The spread of *Hallyu* and the local backlash against it both derived from the government's response to and conception of this trend. When the Chinese government started to perceive Korean cultural products as a threat, it enforced strict institutional and non-institutional regulations, such as giving preferential treatment to local companies and offerings, and investing heavily in growing and promoting its cultural industries. These actions added fuel to the public's anti-*Hallyu* reactions and gradually led to nationalistic anti-Korean sentiments spreading through Chinese society.

The current rise of nationalism in China stems from increased confidence based on economic development, a sense of cultural superiority, Sinocentric pride, and feelings of victimhood in relation to former imperialist powers. This complex nationalism has also contributed to the spread of anti-*Hallyu* and anti-Korean sentiment.

In the midst of a weakening socialist identity, the Chinese Communist Party either turns a blind eye to this movement or quietly supports it in order to slow radical democratization, strengthen party control, curb secessionist movements, and achieve regime stability and social unity. The post-80s and post-90s generations who grew up studying under the strongly nationalistic curriculum introduced after 1991 unleash particularly vehement opinions online. This phenomenon has played a decisive role in checking *Hallyu*.

B.   Hallyu in Taiwan

Hallyu has had a longer history in Taiwan than on the Chinese mainland. Korean singer Jang Ho-cheol released two hits in Mandarin while studying in Taiwan in 1988. Up until 1998, Jang released two or three songs every year that all became hits. In particular, his 1990 "*Bei feng du he*" (北風渡河) and 1996 "*Hao nan ren*" (好男人) were wildly successful across all generations, and even now are beloved by many Taiwanese. His album sales are officially estimated at 20 million. Considering how popular pirated versions were across Taiwan when his career was at its peak, the figure surely is higher. He commands the kind of love and devotion that Cho Yong-pil has in Korea, and his reputation among Taiwanese fans has endured.

Jiang Yu Heng, an ethnic Chinese raised in Korea (*hwagyo*), was among the first to render Korean songs into Chinese and in fact released more translated cover versions than anyone else in Taiwan. Some of the more popular Korean songs he translated into Mandarin include Noksekjidae's "I Will Love You," Lee Mun-se's "She Is Nothing but Laughter," Park Sang-min's "Farewell to Arms," Seo Yu-seok's "Solo Arirang," and Kim Jong-hwan's "Reason for Living." His Chinese rendition of Kim Hyeon-sik's "My Love Next to Me" was hugely popular and still has many devoted fans.

Taiwan's market is receptive not only to Korean pop music, but to foreign culture in general. Taiwan was variously colonized by Spain, the Netherlands, and Japan, which left it adept at assimilating outside cultures within its borders. Although Taiwan was a Japanese colony for 50 long years, much longer than Korea, anti-Japanese sentiment isn't as strong. Rather, Taiwan has consistently turned to Japanese pop culture to fill its needs. One could say that Japan's colonial assimilation policies were relatively more successful in Taiwan than in countries like Korea. This phenomenon is the single biggest difference between Taiwan and China.

For that reason, Japan had a strong presence in Taiwan even before *Hallyu*, unlike on the Chinese mainland. In particular, Japanese music reigned in the mainstream Taiwanese music scene in the 1980s. Korean pop culture was introduced in the midst of this situation as a mix of Japanese, Western, and Korean elements and thus felt familiar to Taiwanese while at the same time maintaining distinctiveness. Taiwan had long been home to numerous cultural influences, given its colonial experiences. When Korea's soft ballads and upbeat dance music came to Taiwan's shores, they were immediately embraced. The gentle sensitivity and raw, powerful image that Korean pop culture became known for set it apart from Japan and had great appeal for Taiwanese listeners.

However, the establishment of diplomatic relations in 1992 between South Korea and China effectively severed Korea's ties to Taiwan. Following this development, anti-Korean sentiment reared its ugly head.[4] After the eradication of official diplomatic channels between South Korea and Taiwan, the Taiwanese public grew disappointed over the split and succumbed to anti-Korean sentiment and an acceptance of all things Western and Japanese. This delayed the spread of *Hallyu* in Taiwan.

Kim Wan-seon turned the tide. By early 1994, she had become a household name in Korea as its number one dance artist. She entered the Taiwanese market under the name Jin Yuanxuan. Her debut Chinese language album *The First Touch* became wildly popular and sold 100,000 copies. Her second album, released the following year, sold 500,000 copies, making her the most popular female artist in Taiwan and the first *Hallyu* dance star in a Chinese-speaking region. In 1997, one of her albums stayed at number 1 on the charts for 10 consecutive weeks. In September of that year, the duo Clon released a "Best of" album in Korean and then debuted with it in Taiwan, selling over 500,000 copies. These events led to

---

[4] Taiwan, which was a permanent member of the UN Security Council until 1971, was forcibly removed from the United Nations following China's accession. Although the Republic of China was then effectively isolated from the international community, South Korea continued to acknowledge it as the sole legitimate Chinese government; however, in 1992 the government changed its position and recognized the People's Republic of China instead.

a boom in Korean language education and laid the groundwork for Korean dance music to succeed in Taiwan.

That same year, the term *Hallyu* (韓流), a homonym of the Chinese word *Hallyu* (寒流, "cold wave"), was first introduced by the Taiwanese press to refer to this "fierce onslaught of a foreign culture." Not only did Korean pop music enjoy explosive popularity at the time, but the fall in the value of the Korean won due to the monetary crisis of 1997 also allowed low-cost products from Korea to flood Taiwan. The term *Hallyu* was also used to describe the shock that this wave of Korean products and culture brought to the Taiwanese market.

Korean dance music became even more popular in the 1990s when Taiwanese artists translated Korean songs into Chinese. In 1998, singer Yuki Hsu covered Clon's "City Escape" in Chinese, and this single became a huge hit. This song was followed by the release of the original Clon album in Taiwan, which was adored by many fans. Yuki Hsu also covered such Korean songs as Diva's "Why Are You Calling Me," FinKL's "I Can't Cry" and "Call Me," Yoo Seung-jun's "Please," Turbo's "Creating Memories," Roo'ra's "Prayer," and others.

Tarcy Su became popular for her Chinese-language version of JuJu Club's "I Am Me." Karen Mok, Alex To, Winnie, and other artists also did Chinese covers of Korean songs. These Korean songs translated into Chinese contributed significantly to the popularity of Korean dance music in Taiwan and meant that acts that followed such as H.O.T., S.E.S., Rain, BoA, SS501, Super Junior, TVXQ, and Shinhwa had a solid foundation on which to grow their fame through dance music. In the case of T's "Every Day," the Chinese version "May I Love You" was more popular in Taiwan than the original, which allowed T to follow up this success with a strong debut in Taiwan.

From the late 1990s, *Hallyu* in Taiwan was led primarily by dance music and TV dramas. The melodrama *Autumn Tales* was a huge success in 2000 and was followed by the success of such dramas as *The Last Empress, Miss Mermaid, Damo,* and *Full House.* Korean TV dramas slowly took over the 8 p.m. prime time slot. *Jewel in the Palace,* broadcast in Taiwan in 2004, brought in the highest ratings to date for a Korean TV drama, at 6.22%. This drama singlehandedly brought *Hallyu* to the status it enjoys today in Taiwan and went on to have immense reverberations through not only sales of DVDs, VCDs, and OSTs, but also the book upon which the drama was based, *manhwa* about royal Korean cuisine, and *Jewel in the Palace* games, etc.

The phenomenal popularity of *Winter Sonata* and *Jewel in the Palace* led to an influx of Taiwanese tourists on themed sightseeing tours in Korea that included trips to locations where the dramas were filmed. In March 2005, 12 years after the dissolution of Korea-Taiwan diplomatic ties, their national airlines bilaterally resumed regular flight routes. In 2006, Taiwan established its first channel for Korean TV programs, GTV Channel K, which broadened the scope of Korean broadcasting to areas such as drama, celebrity news, entertainment, and cooking shows. The continuation of *Hallyu* and sustained interest in the goods and styles displayed on Korean TV dramas resulted in growing demand for Korean clothes, dolls, and accessories.

Nonetheless, the meteoric rise of *Hallyu* in Taiwan also inspired anti-Korean sentiment. Taiwanese actors and TV producers were explicit in their hostility towards *Hallyu.* Some 200 members of the local film and TV actors' guild once held a street protest and claimed that imports of Korean dramas were taking away their right to livelihood and work. These protests in turn upset Korean netizens and led to online clashes between Korean and Taiwanese Internet users. Eventually, in 2006, measures were put in place that banned Taiwanese networks from broadcasting imported TV shows during prime time. This resentment towards Korean products threatened to extinguish *Hallyu* in Taiwan, but the fire was sparked again in 2007 with the drama *Hwang Jin Yi*. That same year, *The Legend* was sold to Taiwan at a cost reported to be the highest in the country's television history and broadcast by Taiwan's public network at 8 p.m. in a prime time slot. Despite lingering anti-*Hallyu* sentiment and regulations, *Hallyu* has remained strong in Taiwan ever since.

At the Guangzhou Asian Games in 2010, the disqualification of Taiwanese taekwondo athlete Judy Yang in her match led to an intense spike in anti-*Hallyu* sentiment in Taiwan. The public even called for a boycott of Korean television programs. Advertisers pulled their ads from shows and Korean celebrity concerts in Taiwan were canceled. Despite all this, however, *Hallyu* still maintains a strong local presence.

In 2011, when Korean dramas became popular once more, 19 politicians from the Taiwanese ruling and opposition parties argued that Korean shows were taking over the 3 major Taiwanese drama channels—GTV, Eastern Television, and Videoland. They proposed an amendment to the Act on Cable, Radio, and TV Broadcasting[5] to strengthen regulation of Korean dramas. As on the Chinese mainland, Taiwanese authorities attempted to amend laws to protect local programs and culture. However, the public did not support the amendment and the bill died in the legislature.

Before Korean programs arrived, Japanese dramas commanded the largest following in Taiwan. However, as the years passed, the characteristic quirkiness of Japanese shows grew too strong for Taiwanese viewers. Around this time, Korean pop culture was introduced with its unique interpretation of Western pop culture processed in a way that appealed to East Asian tastes. Korea's cultural elements, which brought the past together with the present in a familiar yet fresh style, won over the Taiwanese.

Korean melodramas, typically structured around the theme of innocent love, became popular in Taiwan, which also opened up the latter's book market. In 2001, the year after *Autumn Tales* drew huge crowds in Taiwan, Oh Su-yeon released a novelization of the drama that sold 200,000 copies. The novel that inspired *Jewel in the Palace* also shot to number 1 on the bestseller list in 2004 and sold over 200,000 copies. Many other novels that spurred drama spinoffs became popular in Taiwan, the most recent examples being *The Lives*

---

[5] The revision of the Act on Cable, Radio, and TV Broadcasting mandated an increased quota for Taiwanese local dramas, from 20% to 40%. Taiwanese authorities were attempting to control an influx of non-Taiwanese dramas that included not only Korean but Chinese and Japanese dramas. Lin Su Fun, the Democratic Progressive Party legislator who led the movement for this revision, said, "The revision's main purpose is to control the broadcast of Korean, Chinese, and Japanese programs that are overwhelming our Taiwanese TV channels." Ryuo Su Rei of the Nationalist Party, who helped to draft the bill, added, "Low-cost Korean dramas are flooding the market. We must nurture local dramas." He was extremely cautious about Korean dramas. *Dong-A Ilbo*, January 11, 2011; *My Daily*, January 12, 2011.

of Sungkyunkwan Students, which served as the basis of the 2011 drama *Sung-kyunkwan Scandal,* and the novel that inspired the drama *Personal Taste.* Taiwan's interest in Korean publications extends not only to *Hallyu* novels but also to non-fiction, including language textbooks and books on child-care. Fantasy novels are also popular: in 2005, Jeon Min-hui's *Children of the Lune* became a number 1 bestseller, and Lee Yeong-do's *Dragon Raja* sold over 300,000 copies, landing it on the bestseller list in 2008. The *Survival* series sold over 800,000 copies in Taiwan in 2008, making it a best-selling children's book. Other educational books such as the *Distant Land, Faraway Land* and *Why?* series also became hugely popular. Jeong Da-yeon's *Hot Body Diet* was one of the most popular Korean non-fiction books in Taiwan in 2012.

According to the Korean Publishing Research Institute, 208 contracts were signed for the sale of copyrights to Taiwan between 2009 and 2010, making Taiwan the 4th largest market for Korean copyright sales after China, Thailand, and Indonesia. Korean publications are prospering in Taiwan because they have moved away from heavy themes such as the Korean War, the democratization movement, and other local social challenges, to deal with lighter topics. Taiwanese readers can relate to personal and everyday life stories in Korean publications, as the two countries share similar experiences of economic development and democratization. At the same time, the publications also contain uniquely Korean features that add fresh, interesting elements for Taiwanese readers.

Korean movies, however, are having difficulty gaining traction, as Hollywood remains an absolute force in Taiwan's theaters. Movies released in Taiwan are primarily imported rather than locally produced. American movies occupy nearly half of all screens, which gives Hollywood control of the market. A total of 28 Korean movies were exported in 2004 as Korean TV dramas were faring remarkably well, but these films flopped at the box office. Since then, the number of exported films has fallen, and Korean movies are not a leading *Hallyu* product in Taiwan.

The story is different with online games, however, which have benefited from the Korean Wave that began with dance music and dramas. In 2000, NCSOFT's *Lineage* debuted in Taiwan and became the first Korean online game to go overseas. *Lineage* remained popular for a long time, leading the trend of Korean games in Taiwan. Many Korean casual games grew in popularity in Taiwan. In 2004 in particular, the year of Korean dramas' strong showing, Taiwan's largest gaming company, Gamania, conducted a survey at over 200 Internet cafes in downtown Taipei and discovered that such Korean online games as *Lineage, Lineage 2, Ragnarok, SEAL Online,* and *The Legend of Mir* were enjoying immense popularity.[6]

In March 2012, Kunlun Korea's *Legend of Emperors* (*Tian zi kou qi;* 天子传奇) saw 450,000 Taiwanese players log in simultaneously to the platform. Currently, 7 of the 10 most popular online games in Taiwan are Korean, and Korea occupies over 60% of the market share, while locally produced games only make up 30%.

[6] *Sports Seoul,* April 6, 2004.

C. Hallyu in Hong Kong

Hong Kong has historically been an *entrepot* and center of economic exchange between East and West. Because of its location, Hong Kong served as a cross-roads where the two met and, sometimes, collided. Hong Kong's popular culture was especially welcoming to the foreign and itself represents a fusion of Western and Chinese cultures. Because of these characteristics, Hong Kong has embraced Korean pop culture as well. The popularity of Korean dramas and music is show-ing no signs of slowing down there, and Hong Kong's youth are mesmerized by the cultural and sartorial styles of Korean singers and actors on the small and silver screens. Many diehard fans copy the fashions of Korean stars.

Korean dramas are very popular in Hong Kong. In 1997, Hong Kong's Phoenix TV, which broadcasts across China, aired *Star in My Heart,* which introduced *Hallyu* to the Sinosphere. In 1999, Hong Kong cable TV aired *All about Eve* and *Autumn Tales*, which helped *Hallyu* further grow in popularity and spread across Hong Kong. *Autumn Tales* in particular was re-run for a few years after 2001 and served as an especially strong element in boosting *Hallyu* in Hong Kong. The terrestrial network ATV screened Korean dramas regularly in its prime time slot.

The single biggest contributor to the Korean Wave in Hong Kong was *Jewel in the Palace.* Broadcast by the popular network TVB in 2005, *Jewel in the Palace* had an average viewership of 2.35 million people for all episodes. Over 3 million people, or more than 50% of the entire Hong Kong population, tuned in to watch the finale, smashing the record set by *The Emperor's Daughter,* which had been the most viewed program since television was first introduced to Hong Kong.

The explosive success of *Jewel in the Palace* worried many local broad-casters and entertainers, including Jackie Chan, who ignited the first wave of anti-*Hallyu* sentiment. In an interview with the Chinese media, he insisted that the local entertainment industry unite against *Hallyu*, which was threatening to monopolize the market. Chinese actor Zhang Guoli repeated these urgings, which led to a rise in anti-*Hallyu* sentiment in China, Taiwan, Hong Kong, and other Chinese-speaking areas against the phenomenal popularity of Korean cul-tural products.

Nevertheless, manifestations of anti-*Hallyu* sentiment in Hong Kong dif-fered strikingly from those on the mainland in their level of severity and duration. Although an anti-*Hallyu* movement posed a significant threat to Korean products for a time, dramas remained popular. In 2012, TVB, Hong Kong's largest terres-trial channel, broadcast six Korean dramas on weekends and two on weekdays. ATV also aired two Korean offerings on weekends and one on weekdays. Watch-ing Korean dramas has undeniably become an established and regular part of the lives of many in Hong Kong.

Gourmet, from 2009, was almost as popular as *Jewel in the Palace*, and it led to more attention being paid to Korean food. Old episodes of *Gourmet* were being shown at 7 a.m. on nioTV as of November 2012, and the series remains popular. *Sungkyunkwan Scandal*, broadcast by TVB in early 2012, did especially well with women in their twenties and thirties. *Oh! My Lady,* which aired in 2010, was also given a prime time slot and watched by viewers of all generations.

It ran again in 2012. ATV aired *Kingdom of the Winds* at 9:45 p.m., and it became the only imported drama to be given that slot, known to attract high viewership.

Korean films have screened regularly in Hong Kong since 1999, but despite generally positive response, they haven't been as popular as TV dramas. However, such films as *Shiri*, *JSA*, and *Silmido* dramatically changed how the Hong Kong population viewed Korean movies. After their introduction, local audiences responded more favorably to Korean films in a variety of genres. In 2002, *My Sassy Girl* reached number one at the Hong Kong box office. *Hwang Jin Yi* and *King and the Clown* also became big hits. The most talked-about Korean movie in 2012 was *The Thieves*; that it starred Gianna Jun of *My Sassy Girl* and was shot in Hong Kong was enough to capture local media attention, and the film opened at number one.

Many Hong Kong singers performed Cantonese versions of Korean pop songs, much as singers performed Mandarin ones in Taiwan. Jacky Cheung and Andy Lau both sang local versions of Korean songs. Jacky Cheung performed tunes by JYP and Rich, while Andy Lau covered JTL's "A Better Day." Sammi Cheng released several albums with covers of Lee Jung-hyun's material. The translated songs of these local stars allowed Korean pop music to enter the Hong Kong market.

Fans played a major role in popularizing Korean products in Hong Kong. Countless websites are dedicated to Korean celebrities; in fact, there is even a fan website with a considerable following dedicated to H.O.T., a group that disbanded years ago and has become something of a legend. H.O.T.'s former member Kangta has his own fan site. Idol groups such as Big Bang and Wonder Girls were very popular in Hong Kong in 2012, and Girls' Generation remains highly successful.

Fans recently began uploading screenshots of Korean singers appearing on Korean TV, a phenomenon occurring not only in Hong Kong but also in China, Taiwan, and most regions where *Hallyu* has a presence. The convergence of cultural and infrastructure technologies has made possible the success of this neo-*Hallyu*. Koreans, with their ubiquitous high-speed Internet, can bring their creativity to bear on existing elements, thus creating fresh new content for digital delivery the world over.

D.   *Success and failure of Hallyu in Chinese-speaking countries*

Although politics remain rooted in socialism in China, development has transformed the nation into one of the world's biggest economies. For *Hallyu* to succeed there it is necessary to understand the mixed feelings of pride and inferiority felt by the Chinese. The Chinese maintain a sense of superiority and elitism that stems from a Sinocentric worldview, but also carry a sense of victimization over what they suffered at the hands of Western imperialistic powers after the Opium Wars. The values China has molded itself upon and through which it views the world continue to influence its attitude towards the introduction of outside cultures.

China aims to develop its cultural industry intensively on the back of its gigantic economy in order to grow its soft power and ultimately win back its past glory. Nevertheless, the nation tends to view the spread of foreign, more advanced cultures within its borders as cultural invasion and market encroachment. In keeping with this context, the government offers unstinting support to local cultural industries while tightly controlling distribution of foreign products in China. China cracks down on Korean products mainly because it regards *Hallyu* as competition. Early on, the Korean Wave was accepted by China because it was anticipated that material from Korea would be more palatable than existing options. When Korean products became so popular that they began threatening China's cultural sovereignty and its cultural market, however, the state initiated a crackdown, and the resulting mood gave rise to anti-*Hallyu* sentiment. Strict regulations curbed the growth of *Hallyu*. As long as the Chinese state views *Hallyu* as a menace to Chinese identity and cultural industries, it will not relent. In other words, China will open its doors only when it feels confident that its cultural industries have become competitive.

Korea should thus change its approach to the Chinese market. Recently, more attention has been paid to Korea-China co-productions. Joint productions can fend off charges that Korea is invading China and circumvent government regulation, while still continuing Korean presence in China. Co-production can come in the form of resource collaboration, where capital is invested by both parties, or assembling the cast or crew from Korea and China. The first co-produced drama was *Well-matched Families* (*Men dang hu dui*; 門當戶對), which aired in 2004. Starring Korean actress Im Gyeong-ok and a Chinese male lead, it was shot in Beijing and Seoul. The drama, produced with a Chinese script, encouraged exchange between Korea and China but wasn't a hit with Chinese viewers.

Ever since the quota for Korean TV and movies shrank and imports were banned from prime time, Korean producers have scrambled to collaborate. Content produced by the two countries has been packaged as made in China, which theoretically allows it freer distribution across the country. The Chinese government has welcomed this new gesture as it creates content through mutual cooperation rather than relying on Korean imports.

The 2004 drama *Beijing My Love* co-produced by KBS and a Chinese network starred a famous Korean and Chinese cast and was aired in China. However, a dull storyline and uninspired acting ruined its chances for success. Unsurprisingly, it only achieved single-digit ratings. That same year, MBC worked with China to co-produce *Good Morning Shanghai,* starring Jang Nara, which did not even air in Korea. The broadcast of this drama was not well received in China either.

The 24-episode drama *Bichunmoo*, the first Korean series to be completely finished before broadcast began, was aired in 2005 and featured a massive scale and gorgeous visuals. Based on Kim Hye-rin's bestselling *manhwa* series of the same name, the scenes were shot in China over eight months, but the drama failed to capture viewers from either country. The drama's joint production made it foreign to Chinese viewers, while the Chinese locations and actors left the Korean audience nonplussed. Because numerous performers from both countries appeared, voice actors had to be brought in to dub some dialogue, which diluted the actors' personalities.

In 2008, the drama *First Love* was shot entirely in the Yanbian Korean Autonomous Prefecture. From inception, *First Love* involved leading Korean experts in production, writing, photography, and lighting, who attempted to distinguish this drama from other contemporary dramas in China. In 2010, the drama aired on Korean cable and China's CCTV to a lukewarm reception. The 20-episode fantasy melodrama *Qin Shi Huang Love,* co-produced by Korea's Modu Production and China's Shandong network, starred leading actors from Korea and China, but also flopped.

Thanks to the widespread popularity of *Hallyu,* Korea-China film co-productions enjoyed a heyday in 2005. Korean actress Kim Hee-sun, affectionately known to the Chinese as a "dragon's daughter," the highest compliment that can be paid to an actress, starred in *The Myth* with superstar Jackie Chan. *Seven Swords,* released that same year, featured top Chinese actors along with Korean actress Kim So-yeon. *The Promise* starred Korea's Jang Dong-gun. These three films broke records and sold out seats all across China. However, despite the star casts, they did poorly at the Korean box office because they were squarely marketed to Chinese audiences and were essentially Chinese movies with a few *Hallyu* stars tossed in. Their lack of success suggests that if co-productions try simply to ride on the coattails of *Hallyu* or rely too heavily on a handful of celebrities, they will fail to impress the audience. The lukewarm reception they met with was an obvious result of an attempt to win a free ride via *Hallyu.*

Korea-China co-productions can, in either TV or movie formats, offer a novel way to overcome anti-Korean sentiment and government regulation in China while allowing *Hallyu* to continue. Because the results are neither completely Korean nor Chinese, they can appeal to Chinese viewers and lay the groundwork for future pan-Asian co-productions that might compete with US productions that draw on greater capital.

However, most Korea-China co-productions released so far have only superficially brought together a few cast and crew members without focusing on coherent, smooth storylines. Accordingly, in attempting to ingratiate themselves with Chinese and Korean audiences, the productions have not done well with viewers and have come across as awkward and unnatural. A lack of chemistry between crewmembers and constant revisions to the scripts to satisfy China's censorship laws have also damaged overall production quality.

If a drama or film begins with high-quality material, it may still seem fresh to audiences even with the awkwardness that comes from tweaks made to get it approved by Chinese authorities. To the extent that a production retains the tight plotting and bouncy rhythm of Korean dramas and movies, changes can be made if they highlight unique cultural elements of Korea that appeal to Chinese viewers. In doing so, the production can offer the fresh and the familiar to both audiences.

Korea-China documentary co-productions, which have been on the rise, provide interesting case studies. Documentary co-production between KBS and CCTV, the public broadcasters of each nation, marked the beginning of such exchanges. China's *Ancient Palaces* and *The Rise of Great Nations,* and Korea's *Noodle Road* were broadcast in both countries. In 2011, *Noodle Road* had a second run in China, followed by *Amur River: Exploration of Northeast Asia's Ecosystem.* The Chinese documentary *China on the Tip of the Tongue* aired in Korea. All these documentaries were widely watched. Moreover, in a situation where Chinese authorities have been strengthening regulation on TV imports to respond to the anti-*Hallyu* backlash, these exchanges build trust and understanding between the terrestrial networks of each nation.

Based on such trust and understanding, KBS and CCTV collaborated between August 2011 and September 2012 to produce *The Hans of Wangjing, People of New*

China, The Miracle on the Han River, and *1.3 Billion Racers,* all of which traced the development of both countries in order to commemorate the 20th anniversary of their establishment of diplomatic ties. The major media outlets in China received these efforts positively. The documentary *1.3 Billion Racers,* which portrays the lives of early Chinese emigrants, the everyday lives of contemporary Chinese, and the dealings of Chinese companies in Africa and South America from the point of view of Koreans, was broadcast in prime time by CCTV in September 2012, with reruns during the October holiday season. These co-productions represented meaningful work done to sustain *Hallyu* in China's massive market of 1.3 billion potential consumers. The work was also positive in that the documentaries involved exporting production systems rather than actors or content.[7]

The decisive factor that caused a downturn for *Hallyu* after its successes in China was the perception that it was invading China's cultural industries and the anti-Korean sentiment and government crackdown that resulted. However, the hard work of many *Hallyu* stars who had debuted in China and were working to overcome these strict regulations gave Korean products a presence in China. These stars took lead roles in Chinese dramas and Korea-China co-productions and helped curb both regulations against *Hallyu* and anti-Korean sentiment and fostered the sustainable growth of the Korean Wave.

In particular, Jang Nara, Jang Seo-hui, and Chu Ja-hyeon took up long-term residence in China. By earning the affection of Chinese viewers, they contributed heavily to the expansion of *Hallyu*. The work of these Korean stars in China helped enhance the image that the Chinese public had of Korea, Korean pop culture, and its stars. In the end, their work went beyond what can be calculated in economic terms alone.

Chinese audiences are most actively accepting of *Hallyu* online, where popular Korean dramas are offered almost in real-time to Chinese viewers, complete with subtitles for free. Some shows and movies released long ago can also be streamed online. Occasionally, drama-related merchandise based on a particular Korean TV character has debuted in China before introduction in Korea. While some *Hallyu* websites operate under official licensing agreements signed with Korean producers, many others are run illegally by individuals or companies. Although such sites constitute clear copyright violations, it is nearly impossible to prevent these practices in China.

Such copyright problems pose a serious challenge, but the Internet has undeniably enabled the spread of *Hallyu*, even transforming modes of distribution. In the past, Korean dramas or movies that had reached a sufficient level of popularity in Korea were sold to China, but currently Korean products are offered almost simultaneously in the two countries. *Youku* and *Tudou*, Chinese versions of *YouTube*, and *Weibo*, China's equivalent of *Twitter*, as well as other SNS platforms have become key channels for *Hallyu* to reach a larger audience. This is obviously true of K-pop as well.

As of December 5, 2012, PSY's "Gangnam Style" stood at number one on the music download charts of the top three Chinese portal websites: *Sohu, Baidu,* and *Sina.com*. Its success occurred without any local promotion whatsoever; the song gained popularity through word of mouth and fans logging on to view the

---

[7] KOCCA (2012), *China's Content Industry Trends*, KOCCA China Office, October 31.

music video online. Kim Jeong-hoon's album was also translated into Chinese around the same time, and his singles "Without You" and "White Winter" followed directly behind "Gangnam Style" on *Sina.com*'s Korean and Japanese pop chart. The Internet clearly serves as an effective means for providing and distributing information.

The Internet is also making a substantial contribution to the spread of *Hallyu* through the many fan websites dedicated to Korean stars. In December 2012, *Sina.com*, which owns *Weibo*, conducted an online survey to choose the "*Weibo* King," the year's most popular star. Although several Korean actors and singers were on the list, Jang Keun-suk outdid all contenders, including many famous Chinese stars. Lee Min-ho, Lee Da-hae, Lee Jun-ki, Victoria and Amber of f(x), Kim Hui-cheol and Choi Si-won of Super Junior, and Kim Hyeon-jung were also on the list. PSY, whose "Gangnam Style" became a global sensation and who is also very popular in China, shot to the top of the contenders less than a month after he opened a *Weibo* account. To the extent that the level of feedback and number of followers on *Weibo* offer a barometer of a celebrity's fame, these votes serve as a key indicator for taking stock of *Hallyu* stars.[8]

The communication of so many *Hallyu* stars with Chinese fans through platforms like *Weibo* means that *Hallyu* remains steady in China. Digital media have lowered the entry barrier for *Hallyu* stars. It is imperative therefore to better understand the characteristics of the digital era in order to enter the Chinese market through more diverse routes.

3.1.2.   Do the Chinese Hate *Jewel in the Palace?*

Reference: "The Chinese Hate *Jewel in the Palace?* The Error of Judging the Korea-China Relationship from Minor Distaste," *OhMyNews*, Jo Chang-wan (chogaci), January 17, 2008.

Last month's Amazon China bestseller rankings: #3 and #4 are Don't Laugh! I'm an English Book! *and #8 is* A Woman's Life Is Determined in Her Twenties. *Kim Hye-ja's book has been advancing rapidly in the last week.*

Chinese interest in Korea is rising again. As of January 16, 4 Korean releases rank among the top 10 books at China's largest online bookstore, and interest in study abroad in Korea and the Korean alphabet is on the rise. Still, as some journalists' and scholars' anti-Korean sentiments make their way to Korea, we are witnessing worrisome misunderstandings that Chinese society at large is opposed to the Korean Wave.

(…)

Chinese students are also showing strong interest in study abroad in Korea. According to the Ministry of Education & Human Resources Development, Chinese students in Korea have increased approximately 50% per year, from around 5,600 students in 2003 to 8,600 in 2004 and 12,300 in 2005. In 2006, the figured exceeded 20,000, and growth is continuing. Chinese preference for Korea can be attributed to the effects of more than a decade of *Hallyu*.

---

[8] "Jang Keun-suk Tops List as China's Weibo King," *Sports Seoul*, December 5, 2012.

This fervor also transferred to *hangeul* itself quite a while ago. The Korean Cultural Center in China has been running a Korean language course for 10 years. Classes fill quickly once registration opens, and many foreign language institutes in China have started Korean courses. Moreover, although previously only 2 or 3 universities offered Korean majors, the number is now approaching 100.

Interest in *hangeul* is also reflected in a passion for the Korean script in fashion. In China, one can now readily find t-shirts and handbags with Korean lettering, showing that the Korean Wave has expanded even to our alphabet.

A.   Antagonistic reports on Hallyu and Korean media rehashing

Nonetheless, because of surveys demonstrating anti-*Hallyu* sentiment, journalists who publish those surveys, and Korean journalists who unreflectively relay their reports, negative sentiment towards China is growing in Korea.

Last year, around December 10, Korean media outlets reported on a Chinese survey under such titles as "In China, South Korea Tops Least Favorite Countries" (*NEWSis*) and "South Korea Regarded as Even Worse than Japan" (*Chosun Ilbo*). These reports stated that the most disliked countries in China were South Korea followed by Japan, and that the most liked countries, in order, were Pakistan, Japan, and Russia.

Last year was the 70th anniversary of the Nanjing Massacre, and since general animosity between Korea and China had been relatively low compared to the historical hostility between China and Japan, these surveys were sufficient to incite negative feelings in Koreans. That the articles' source, *The International Herald Leader*, fell under the jurisdiction of China's official Xinhua News Agency made the report more shocking. However, the first to release the report was the conservative Japanese newspaper *Sankei Shimbun*. The inflammatory report was published on the afternoon of the 10th by *NEWSis*, who cited *Sankei Shimbun*. The following morning the online version of the *Chosun Ilbo* cited a correspondent in Beijing, rather than *Sankei Shimbun*.

Following these events, and based on these articles, other media outlets began publishing stories about Korea's image in China. As the articles appeared on portal sites, Korean netizens' animosity towards China grew.

Nonetheless, from this reporter's perspective, these articles seemed unreliable, in that they were based on a public opinion survey determined to ferret out ill will. The entire survey included only eight questions, such as "Is there a neighboring country you would not like to travel to? If so, why?" Possible responses included such reasons as territorial disputes, which significantly influenced negative opinions of Korea. In addition, the text conveying the survey results mentioned issues like hostility to *Hallyu* or territorial disputes. International relationships were compared with such statements as "the more one learns about Korea, the more precarious the China-Korea relationship seems," while describing Chinese attitudes towards Japan as "a complicated love-hate relationship," further highlighting impressions of Chinese antipathy towards Korea.

It is unfortunate that the Korean media spread unfiltered content from *The International Herald Leader* without considering its context or examining the story in a level-headed way.

B.   *Images of anti-Hallyu sentiment in a story on "most disliked dramas"*

The problem in coverage does not end here; Korean journalists continue to report on aversion to Korean products as if it were the norm in China. Just a few days ago, reports circulated in Korea that Chinese netizens had selected *Jewel in the Palace* as their "most disliked drama," on the basis of a poll conducted by *China Youth Daily*, the bulletin of the Communist Youth League of China. The poll was conducted from the beginning of the year on portal sites such as *Sina.com* and *Yahoo*.

China Youth Daily noted that the prize for "the most disliked drama broadcast in 2007" would be the "*Gochujang*/Korean Hot Pepper Paste Award." If one notes that Chinese tend not to eat *gochujang*, it is clear that the prize targets Korea.

In this survey of 60 dramas, *Jewel in the Palace* was listed 4th among the options to choose from, and received 80,000 responses (6.64%), which made it "the most disliked drama." As the survey result made its way back to Korea, belief in a strong anti-Korean sentiment in China spread. Likewise, as reports made such surveys seem the norm, hostility towards China increased in Korea.

However, one question is whether such survey results suggest that dislike of Korean material is the norm. Only five dramas received a response of more than 6% in this survey; aside from *Jewel in the Palace*, the other four were Chinese.

In addition, the four dramas on the list of options before *Jewel in the Palace* all received more than 5% of votes, making it difficult to say, based on this survey alone, that the majority of Chinese dislike *Jewel in the Palace*. From this journalist's perspective, that *Jewel in the Palace* topped the survey is not a sign of overall aversion towards Korean dramas, but of a complicated relationship with Korea.

If we stop thoughtlessly conveying the results of such surveys, which do not present the Chinese context in detail, we could alleviate both anti-Chinese feelings in Korea and anti-Korean feelings in China. In fact, in the comment sections of these articles negative remarks, in place of rational discussion, run rampant.

Of course, voices in China warning against Korean influence exist, to be sure; however, such voices are not the whole story. In order to foster friendship between our two countries we must be pragmatic and refute the slanders of official Chinese media, even if doing so requires action by our government.

3.2. JAPAN

3.2.1. *Hallyu* Forever: Japan

Reference: *Hallyu Forever: The World Is Hallyu Style*, Ko Jeong-min et al., KOFICE *Hallyu* Series V, 2012, pp. 152–165, 190–203.

A. *Hallyu in Japan: The beginning*[9] (pp. 152–165)

Beginning

Korean popular culture was introduced to Japan long before the term "*Hallyu*" came into being. Korean music in particular was very well received. Cho Yong-pil performed in Japan for over 10 years, until he decided not to pursue a career in the country any further. Gye Eun-suk appeared at the NHK Red and White Song Battle (*Kōhaku*) seven years in a row from 1988 to 1994, and Kim Yeon-ja also had success in the Japanese market from 1988.

While these performances failed to coalesce as a single overarching genre or trend and merely wound up as individual performances given by isolated artists, more and more Korean dramas and films began to be shown across Japan after the 1988 Seoul Olympics, which opened the floodgates for Korean popular culture. Korean dramas were brought into Japan in earnest from 1996. In that year, multi-channel CS digital satellite broadcasting was introduced in Japan, which established such Korean-language channels as KNTV and K-ch. These channels offered not only dramas but also documentaries, news, variety shows, and music programs. Korean dramas also began to be broadcast by Japanese terrestrial channels free to all viewers in 1996. In October of that year, TVQ broadcast the dramas *Jealousy, Pilot,* and *Fabulous Day* around Kyushu. Although these shows all did well in the region, their popularity did not extend to the rest of Japan. Nonetheless, these forays suggested that Korean dramas might succeed in the Japanese market.[10]

Expansion

The 2002 Korea-Japan World Cup laid a foundation upon which Korean popular culture could build a stronger presence in Japan. Japanese terrestrial channels began producing shows on Korea and broadcasting Korean dramas leading up to, and continuing slightly beyond, 2002, shedding a favorable light on Korea. Thanks to these public networks, Korean society and cultural content were on wide display to Japanese viewers, which led to a more positive opinion of Korea spreading among the populace. This introduction to Korea did not confine itself to offering information on the country, but extended to movies, TV, music, books, games, and other cultural content.

Shiri was the first Korean film to capture the attention of the Japanese in earnest. In 1999, the film was sold to Japan for $1.3 million, the highest sum paid for a Korean movie up to that time. *Shiri* brought in 1.3 million viewers in 2000 and had revenues of ¥1.85 billion. It ranked #21 at the Japanese box office that

---

[9] Based on Chae J. (2005), "A Study of *Hallyu* Consumers in Japan with a Focus on the Consumption Patterns of Loyal Fans & Average Consumers."

[10] Kim Y. (2005), "Stocktaking and Forecasting Korean Drama Programming in Japan," *Broadcasting Trends and Analysis,* KOCCA.

Table 3–1.   Activities of Korean artists in Japan pre-*Hallyu*

1982	Cho Yong-pil performs to commemorate the 30th anniversary of Nippon Cultural Broadcasting
1985	Gye Eun-suk wins Best New Artist at the All Japan Request Awards
1986	Gye Eun-suk wins grand prize at Japan Record Awards
1987	Cho Yong-pil becomes first foreigner to appear at NHK's Red and White Song Battle
1988	Gye Eun-suk is named top artist at All Japan Request Awards
	Kim Yeon-ja debuts in Japan with "Land of the Morning Calm," the closing song of the 1988 Olympics
	Gye Eun-suk appears at NHK's Red and White Song Battle
1989	Kim Yeon-ja appears at NHK's Red and White Song Battle
	Gye Eun-suk appears at NHK's Red and White Song Battle
1990	Gye Eun-suk appears at NHK's Red and White Song Battle
1991	Gye Eun-suk appears at NHK's Red and White Song Battle
1992	Gye Eun-suk appears at NHK's Red and White Song Battle
1993	Gye Eun-suk appears at NHK's Red and White Song Battle
1994	Gye Eun-suk appears at NHK's Red and White Song Battle
	Kim Yeon-ja appears at NHK's Red and White Song Battle
2001	Kim Yeon-ja appears at NHK's Red and White Song Battle

(Source: Japan Prime Minister's Office (2012), *2012 Intellectual Property for Innovation Plan*)

year and provided a stepping stone for *Hallyu*. Thereafter, the release of such films as *JSA* (2001), *My Sassy Girl* (2003), *Taegukgi* (2004), and *Silmido* (2004) drove the Korean Wave in Japan.

Korea-Japan drama co-productions such as *Friends* (2002), *The Afternoon after the Rain* (2002), and *The Sound of Stars* (2004) were broadcast by TBS and Fuji TV across Japan from 2002 to 2004. Won Bin, who played the lead in *Friends,* became hugely popular with the youth market and helped pave the way for a Korean Wave in drama.

The popularity of Korean music began with BoA, who typified the synergy brought about by masterful Japanese planning strategies paired with Korean content. BoA debuted at #17 on the Oricon chart in May 2001 with *ID: Peace B* under the label of "new artist" rather than "Korean artist." She went on to perform at the NHK Red and White Song Battle each year between 2002 and 2004 and succeeded in winning popularity and recognition in Japan. BoA continued to work in both countries and contributed to building friendly ties between the two. By acting as a Korean cultural ambassador to Japan, she too helped smooth the path for *Hallyu*.

The *Hallyu* boom

Despite the introduction of diverse Korean content to Japan, what allowed *Hallyu* to boom and even become a social phenomenon was NHK's broadcast of the

Table 3–2.   Korean popular culture products in the expansion stage

Period	Product	Genre
January 2000	*Shiri*	Film
May 2001	*JSA*	Film
May 2001	BoA's debut	Music
February 2002	*Friends*	Korea-Japan Co-production/ MBC and TBS
October 2002	*All About Eve*	Drama
November 2002	*The Afternoon After the Rain*	Korea-Japan Co-production/ MBC and Fuji TV
December 2002	BoA appears at NHK's Red and White Song Battle	Music
January 2003	*My Sassy Girl*	Film
January 2003	*Sound of Stars*	Korea-Japan Co-production/ MBC and Fuji TV
December 2003	BoA appears at NHK's Red and White Song Battle	Music
January 2004	*Sound of Stars*	Korea-Japan Co-production/ MBC and Fuji TV

drama *Winter Sonata.* The term *Hallyu* appeared in Japanese discourse around this time, and after *Winter Sonata,* Korean dramas enjoyed significantly enhanced status.

Along with the drama itself, Bae Yong-joon, the actor who played the series' protagonist, spearheaded the *Hallyu* boom. His brand power could be felt in such coinages as "Yonsama," "Yonfluenza," and "Yongel coefficient." Not only did *Winter Sonata* become a hit in its own right, but the sale of related merchandise, such as DVDs, novels, scripts, OST albums, and so on, also became enormously popular, creating *Winter Sonata* fever and offering a firm foothold for the export of Korean cultural content.

The *Hallyu* boom affected the export of Korean TV programs to Japan. Before the boom, that is, between 2001 and 2003, *Hallyu* was in its infancy and expansion stages. However, from 2004, *Hallyu* exports increased dramatically, doubling those of the year before.

In the first half of 2005, over $30 million worth of Korean movies was purchased by Japan, a 38.3% increase from the same period of the previous year, when 36 Korean films were sold at an average price of $620,000. In 2005, the same number of films was sold, but the average had risen to $860,000.[11]

Korean music sales also proceeded apace. The CD and DVD market grew ninefold between 2003 and 2004, from ¥2 billion to ¥18.4 billion (13.6 billion

[11] KOFIC (2005), *First Half of 2005 Korean Film Exports.*

for DVDs, 4.8 billion for CDs).[12] Changes also occurred in the composition of the singers who had a presence in Japan: along with established figures like Kim Yeon-ja and BoA, stars such as Ryu Si-won, Park Yong-ha, and Lee Byung-hun, who sang songs that were included in the soundtracks of dramas they starred in, launched successful music careers in Japan.

Stagnation

When the *Winter Sonata* craze died down, media critics and scholars expressed opinions that *Hallyu* had ended, or at least gone into hibernation. However, even in periods with significant social controversies, Korean popular culture consistently resonated with Japanese fans. In fact, consumers of Korean cultural content increased in number. In 2010, before the new boom in *Hallyu* that began with the debut of KARA in Japan, a survey asking residents of the Tokyo area about *Hallyu* showed that 44.9% of respondents became fans of Korean dramas after *Winter Sonata*, testifying to the immense impact of the show.[13] However, a higher percentage (49.4%) responded that they became fans after 2006, which shows that Korean dramas have remained popular even after *Winter Sonata*. In other words, while *Winter Sonata* got a foot in the door for Korean products in Japan, many new consumers of Korean dramas appeared later.

In music, TVXQ's popularity was initially unrivaled. The band released its debut Japanese single in April 2005. In 2008, TVXQ achieved its first number one on the Oricon Weekly Singles Chart. The group has placed consistently in the top spots since. TVXQ's popularity is important not only in and of itself, but in its role as a bridge in Japan for other acts, such as KARA and Girls' Generation. Many say that if TVXQ hadn't disbanded, the history of K-pop in Japan would have been different. Their break up was unfortunate for Korean popular music.

"Neo-*Hallyu*"

Korean content, which had been quietly and consistently popular in Japan without the aid of any dramatic event, was transformed in 2010 with the K-Pop boom. On August 11, KARA staged a "guerilla" concert at Shibuya109 in the center of Tokyo. Thousands of fans rushed to see the group, forcing the organizers to call off the unannounced show within just three minutes. This event signaled the resurgence of *Hallyu*, led by K-pop. On November 24 of the same year, KARA released its first Japanese studio album, *Girl's Talk*. The band became the third Korean act to sell over one million copies of a release, following BoA and TVXQ. By the end of November 2011, over two million copies had sold. KARA's so-called "booty dance" became popular on Japanese entertainment TV, which led to a frenzy over the group, and the girls were featured in a number of advertisements. Girls' Generation is now doing extremely well in Japan on the

[12] KOTRA (2005), *Hallyu in Northeast Asia & Marketing Measures.*
[13] Chae J. (2005), "A Study of *Hallyu* Consumers in Japan with a Focus on the Consumption Patterns of Loyal Fans & Average Consumers."

heels of KARA's achievements; many boy bands, following in the footsteps of TVXQ, have found success in Japan as well.

B.   *Hallyu today*

Broadcasting

In the past, Japanese fans of *Hallyu* were typically depicted as middle-aged women who loved to watch Korean soap operas, but after 2010, the average age of *Hallyu* fans in Japan dropped. In 2010, dramas such as *Brilliant Legacy* and *You Are So Handsome,* which targeted the younger demographic, became hugely popular. Jang Keun-suk took over the throne once held by Bae Yong-joon in a generational shift for *Hallyu* stars.

Since *You Are So Handsome,* and continuing into 2012, Korean dramas, especially romantic comedies or dramas about K-pop, have targeted young female viewers. The cable-channel drama *We Need Romance* also benefited from this trend and enjoyed a rating high of 4.6%, all the while gaining in popularity among younger viewers.

Programs on K-pop also greatly increased. CS broadcast 166 K-pop titles on 16 channels in June 2012, a 2.3-fold increase over the previous year. BS also continued to introduce Korea's latest music charts and broadcast information programs on Korean celebrities and entertainment. Likewise, terrestrial channel TokyoMXTV now offers infotainment involving Korean celebrities through its *Hallyu Fondue* program.

K-pop

K-pop grew in popularity in Japan after 2010, leading to an increase in export volume. The Japanese market is particularly significant as it is responsible for 80% of total Korean music exports. An increase in exports usually corresponds to a further increase in the number of K-pop businesses in Japan. In 2009, K-pop's share of revenue (singles, albums, and DVDs) in the Japanese music market was 3% (¥10.6 billion), but in 2011, this percentage shot up to 7.8% (¥24.5 billion).

As of 2012, the popularity of K-pop has reached a fever pitch. Following the success of girl groups like KARA and Girls' Generation in 2010, boy bands such as 2PM, CNBlue, FT Island, BEAST, and SHINee have become better known. Currently, K-pop trends in Japan include both male and female idol groups. K-pop artists are typically based in Korea, but an increasing number of acts work exclusively in Japan. KARA, Girls' Generation, and other Korean idol groups won Japanese Gold Disk awards in 2011 and 2012, a testament to the popularity of K-pop there.

The growing presence of the Korean music industry in Japan has increased attention to large-scale performances and arena tours planned by record labels or TV networks. In 2011, SM Town organized a family concert, followed by arena tours from Girls' Generation, 2PM, and Jang Keun-suk. In 2012, Big Bang had an arena tour, which was followed by a YG Entertainment family concert, a Super Junior Tokyo Dome concert, a SHINee arena tour, and a TVXQ live tour. In 2013, KARA became the first female performers to confirm a show at Tokyo Dome. These large-scale performances will continue in 2013.

Table 3–3.   Korean drama programming on BS/CS channels

	2005.12	2007.8	2008.3	2009.8	2010.10	2011.8	2012.3	2012.7
BS		8 channels, 12 dramas	8 channels, 14 dramas	9 channels, 33 dramas	9 channels, 39 dramas	8 channels, 31 dramas	9 channels, 42 dramas	8 channels, 41 dramas
CS	10 channels, 45 dramas	12 channels, 100 dramas	20 channels, 112 dramas	25 channels, 136 dramas	17 channels, 160 dramas	18 channels, 162 dramas	16 channels, 167 dramas	15 channels, 179 dramas

(Source: KOCCA (2012), *The Content Industry Trends in Japan*)

Table 3–4.   2011 Japan Gold Disk Awards: Awards for Korean artists

Title	Korean Artist
New Artist of the Year (Domestic)	Girls' Generation
New Artist of the Year (International)	KARA
Best Five New Artist (Domestic)	Girls' Generation
Best Five New Artist (International)	KARA
Best Five Album	TVXQ
Best Music Video	TVXQ

(Source: Recording Industry Association of Japan. http://www.riaj.or.jp/e/data/gdisc/2012.html)

Table 3–5.   Top five total sales by artist, 2011

Rank	Artist	Sales (Unit: ¥1)
1	AKB48	16.2 billion
2	Arashi	15.4 billion
3	EXILE	5.6 billion
4	KARA	4.9 billion
5	Girls' Generation	4.0 billion

(Sources: KOCCA (2012), *The Content Industry Trends in Japan*; Oricon http://www.oricon.co.jp)

Table 3–6.   2012 Japan Gold Disk Awards: Awards for Korean artists

Title	Korean Artist
Best Asian Artist	KARA
New Artist of the Year	2PM
Best Three New Artists (Asia)	Jang Keun-suk, BEAST, 2PM
Best *Enka/Kayokyoku* New Artist	Park Hyeon-bin
Album of the Year	Girls' Generation
Best Three Albums of the Year (Asia)	Girls' Generation, TVXQ, KARA
Song of the Year by Download	KARA
Best Five Songs by Download	KARA
Best Music Video	KARA

(Source: Recording Industry Association of Japan. http://www.riaj.or.jp/e/data/gdisc/2012.html)

One might think that *Hallyu* is struggling amidst such issues as the Dokdo-Takeshima conflict, but in light of the numerous examples to the contrary above, it appears that *Hallyu* is still going strong.[14]

---

[14] KOCCA (2012), *The Content Industry Trends in Japan*.

Table 3–7.   Korean artists in top 100 list of CD singles sales, 2011

Rank	Artist	Song Title
16	TVXQ	*Why? (Keep Your Head Down)*
25	KARA	*Go Go Sama!*
26	KARA	*Jet Coaster Love*
29	Jang Keun-suk	*Let Me Cry*
41	TVXQ	*Superstar*
46	Girls' Generation	*Mr. Taxi/Run Devil Run*
54	TVXQ	*Winter – Winter Rose / Duet – Winter version*
65	KARA	*Winter Magic*
66	SHINee	*Replay – You Are My Everything*
84	2PM	*Ultra Love*
85	Super Junior	*Mr. Simple*
91	2PM	*I'm Your Man*
96	CNBLUE	*In My Head*
97	T-ARA	*Bo Peep Bo Peep*

(Source: Oricon. http://www.oricon.co.jp)

Table 3–8.   Korean artists in top 100 list of CD album sales, 2011

Rank	Artist	Album Title
5	Girls' Generation	*GIRLS' GENERATION*
7	KARA	*Super Girl*
20	TVXQ	*TONE*
22	KARA	*Girl's Talk*
42	Girls' Generation	*HOOT +6*
63	Big Bang	*BIG BANG 2*
71	KARA	*KARA, Best of 2007–2010*
87	BEAST	*So Beast*
92	SHINee	*The First*
95	Girls' Generation	*The Boys*

(Source: Oricon. http://www.oricon.co.jp)

Table 3–9.   Korean artists in top 50 list of DVD sales, 2011

Rank	Artist	DVD Title
5	KARA	*Best Clips*
32	Girls' Generation	*New Beginning of Girls' Generation*

(Source: Oricon. http://www.oricon.co.jp)

Table 3–10. Korean artists in the top 50 list of CD single sales in
first half of 2011

Rank	Artist	Song Title
18	Super Junior	*Opera*
23	TVXQ	*STILL*
25	KARA	*Speed Talk/Girls Power*
29	2PM	*Beautiful*
31	Kim Hyeon-jung	*Kiss Kiss/Lucky Guy*
44	Super Junior Dong-hae & Eun-hyeok	*Oppa, Oppa*
50	CNBLUE	*Where You Are*

(Source: Oricon. http://www.oricon.co.jp)

Table 3–11 Korean artists in top 50 list of CD album
sales, first half of 2012

Rank	Artist	Song Title
7	KARA	*Super Girl*
11	Girls' Generation	*Girls' Generation*
26	Big Bang	*Alive*
28	Jang Keun-suk	*Just Crazy*

(Source: Oricon. http://www.oricon.co.jp)

Table 3–12 Korean artists in top 50 list of DVD sales, first half of 2012

Rank	Artist	DVD Title
4	Girls' Generation	*Girls' Generation First Tour of Japan*
9	KARA	*KARA BEST CLIPS 2 & SHOWS*
30	Big Bang	*BIG BANG PRESENTS "LOVE & HOPE TOUR 2011"*
41	SHINee	*SHINee The 1st Concert in Japan "SHINee World"*

(Source: Oricon. http://www.oricon.co.jp)

C. Successes and failures of Hallyu in Japan (pp. 190–203)

Generational shift with *You Are Beautiful*

You Are Beautiful is a 16-episode miniseries produced and then broadcast by SBS between October 7 and November 26, 2009, in Korea. The script was written by a popular duo, sisters Hong Jeong-eun and Hong Mi-ran. The show's ratings were not remarkable in Korea, however, averaging roughly 10%, and it struggled to compete with *Iris,* which starred such A-listers as Lee Byung-hun and Kim Tae-hee and captured an average 30% viewership.[15]

Nonetheless, its soundtrack album sold 20,000 copies within a week of release in October 2009, and a second OST released the following month sold 30,000 copies. The drama's DVD sold 7,000 copies after it went on sale in 2010,[16] figures that indicate the show had built a small but diehard fan base.

Although *You Are Beautiful* only drew a few loyal fans in Korea, the series became a phenomenal hit in Japan. After broadcast by KNTV in 2010, it was later reintroduced during the Fuji TV Hallyu Alpha Summer Festival, and then had three additional seasons of reruns. In Japan, its ratings peaked at 6.9%,[17] but it was shown in the slower afternoon hours between 3 to 4 p.m.; had it been broadcast during prime time, this 6.9% would equate to some 10%. *Iris,* on the other hand, which had far surpassed its competition in Korea, reached only 8% in Japan despite being broadcast on Wednesday nights.[18]

The popularity of *You Are Beautiful* becomes obvious when one looks at the DVD rental market. The drama conquered the TSUTAYA Asia weekly and monthly charts for TV and DVDs from August 2010 to August 2011, occupying the top eight spots. It topped the *Hallyu* drama category on both the TSUTAYA 2010 and 2011 yearly charts.[19]

All 4,000 tickets to a Shibuya meet-the-stars fan gathering with Jang Keun-suk and Park Shin-hye, the show's leads, sold out in less than 5 minutes.[20] By May 2011, the drama was even being screened in 60 theaters across Japan as a limited release.[21]

In 2011, TBS produced a Japanese version of *You Are Beautiful*, entitled ㅤ (*Ikemen desu ne*), which had average viewership ratings of 9.5%.[22] Jang Keun-suk made a guest appearance in the eighth episode. This Japanese remake was also very popular; its DVD sold 32,000 copies in the first week of release, which took it to #3 on Oricon's overall DVD sales chart and #1 for dramas.[23] According to TBS public data, it recorded the highest DVD sales from April 2011 to March 2012 in Japan.[24]

With *You Are Beautiful*, Jang Keun-suk established a name for himself, becoming the new, post-Yonsama face of *Hallyu* in Japan. He then made his music debut in April 2011, with the release of the single "Let Me Cry,"[25] which sold 120,000 copies in its first week and shot to the top of the Oricon Singles Chart, the first time that a male solo artist's debut had done so since Masahiko

---

[15] TNS Media Korea, http://www.tnms.tv.

[16] SBS *You Are So Handsome* Press Release Bulletin Board. http://wizard2.sbs.co.kr/w3/template/tpl_iframetype.jsp?vVodId=V0000339966&vProgId=1000553&vMenuId=1011332&no=232.

[17] Fuji TV, http://www.fujitv.co.jp/fujitv/news/pub_2011/110426-077.html.

[18] Video Research Ltd., http://www.videor.co.jp.

[19] TSUTAYA, http://www.tsutaya.co.jp.

[20] *Chosun Ilbo* (2010), http://thestar.chosun.com/site/data/html_dir/2010/08/05/2010080500559.html.

[21] *Chosun Ilbo* (2010), http://news.chosun.com/site/data/html_dir/2011/04/19/2011041900871.html.

[22] Video Research Ltd., http://www.videor.co.jp.

[23] *Dong-A Ilbo* (2011), http://sports.donga.com/3/all/20111214/42596614/1.

[24] TBS, http://www.tbs.co.jp.

[25] *Mail Business Daily* (2011), http://star.mk.co.kr/new/view.php?mc=ST&no=267648&year=2011.

Kondo 30 years previous, and certainly the first time that a non-Japanese artist had achieved such a level of fame.[26]

That same year, Jang performed at 5 arenas in 3 Japanese cities and set a record, selling 60,000 tickets in 5 minutes.[27] At the request of fans who had been unable to purchase tickets, Jang performed an encore concert at Tokyo Dome in November 2011.[28] Building on this popularity, in May 2012 he released his first studio album *Just Crazy*, which reached the top of the Oricon chart during its first week.[29] Recently, Jang has been appearing on such famous Japanese TV variety shows as *Sanma no Manma* and *Tetsuko's Room,* as well as music programs like *Music Japan* and *Hey! Hey! Hey!*[30] A full-page ad that featured Jang on page eight of the *Asahi Shinbun* to promote the release of his first studio album was given heavy coverage by the Japanese media. In October, its creators received an award from the Japan Newspaper Publishers and Editors Association for innovation.[31] Jang's influence in Japan has been growing by the day.

However, his subsequent endeavors, such as the drama *Mary Stayed Out All Night* and the film *You Are My Pet*, unfortunately have not fared as well. The drama *Love Rain* received a great deal of attention from Japanese fans as it was broadcast in Korea for starring Jang and Yuna of Girls' Generation, but it also did poorly, despite heavy publicity involving appearances by many *Hallyu* stars. This example makes it apparent that while celebrities like Jang are undoubtedly important for the *Hallyu* market in Japan, success will not come without sufficiently strong content.

KARA in Japan

The girl group KARA debuted on March 29, 2007, under the management label DSP Media. Its initial four members were Park Gyu-ri, Han Seung-yeon, Kim Seong-hee, and Nicole, but in June 2008, Kim left the group and two others, Goo Ha-ra and Kang Ji-young, joined and KARA proceeded as a five-member team. In Korea, KARA had become a mainstay through such hits as "Pretty Girl" (2008), "Honey" (2008), "Mister" (2009), "Lupin" (2010), and "Jumping" (2010).

KARA first became a hit in Japan thanks to popular comedian Gekidan Hitori, who is well-known locally for his fun, cheerful image and wields considerable influence among the youth. When he began professing his love for KARA on Japanese TV, even talking about the girls on the popular program *Arashi's Homework,*[32] the group became known. His interest led to increased attention to not only KARA but also Girls' Generation and other Korean girl groups, creat-

[26] ORICON, http://www.oricon.co.jp/prof/artist/403223.

[27] *Asia Today* (2011), http://www.asiatoday.co.kr/news/view.asp?seq=532251.

[28] *Korea Economic Daily* (2011), http://economy.hankooki.com/lpage/sports/201109/e20110929120 102120390.htm.

[29] *Joongang Daily* (2012), http://article.joinsmsn.com/news/article/article.asp?total_id=8386423&cl oc=olinkIarticleIdefault.

[30] *Maeil Business Daily* (2012), http://star.mt.co.kr/view/stview.php?no=2012062809024621373&ty pe=1&outlink=1.

[31] *Chosun Ilbo* (2012), http://thestar.chosun.com/site/data/html_dir?2012/10/23/2012102300862. html.

[32] *News EN* (2009), http://www.newsen.com/news_view.php&uid=200911231803211002.

ing a base for them in the Japanese market. KARA's "booty dance" for "Mister" became a huge hit on Japanese TV and was often parodied by celebrities. Renowned actor and member of the group SMAP Takuya Kimura performed the dance on the program *Ocha no Mizu Hakase*,[33] and celebrities parodied it during the December 29, 2010, broadcast of variety show *Waratte Iitomo Special.*

Famous child actor Mana Ashida is also recognized as a KARA fan. In a two-hour special before the last episode of the Fuji TV hit *Marumo's Rules,* KARA threw a surprise birthday party for Mana, who later even danced with the group on stage at the Fuji TV FNS Music Festival held at the Tokyo Grand Prince Hotel on December 7, 2011.

KARA's popularity is also evident in animation, Japan's traditional stronghold: The Asahi TV series *Doraemon,* one of Japan's most well-known, featured an episode in which Nobita's friend Gian showcased the "booty dance" while wearing an outfit similar to what KARA wore during the video for "Mister."

KARA had an official showcase debut in Japan on February 7, 2010. Very little marketing effort was made before the showcase and no albums were released. Most of their audience was composed of Japanese fans who had heard of KARA from their performances in Korea. The girls then planned a 30-minute guerilla concert on August 11 at Shibuya109 in downtown Tokyo to celebrate their new album. However, a throng of 3,000 screaming fans showed up and organizers shut down the performance after 3 minutes because of safety concerns. "Mister" was promoted widely; the music video was shown on 8 massive LCD screens in Shibuya, while the song played as background music in over 1,800 convenience stores. Their CD album cover was exhibited as well.[34]

On November 24, 2010, KARA released their official Japanese album debut *Girl's Talk*, which sold 100,000 copies in its first week and shot to #2 on the weekly Oricon Album Chart. In total, the album sold over 500,000 copies. On November 23, 2011, KARA released their second studio album *Super Girl,* which sold 270,000 copies and went to the top of the weekly Oricon Album Chart. KARA became the third Korean act after BoA and TVXQ to sell one million records, and by the end of November 2011, they had sold over two million copies.

After signing a contract with Universal Sigma, a subsidiary of Universal Music Japan, KARA released the compilation album *Special Premium Box.* With that release, they entered at #7 on Oricon's daily chart. At a Tokyo press conference to promote their new album, the girls announced "Mister" as the lead single and had a fan club launch at Minato Mirai Hall in Yokohama. They released the Japanese version of "Mister" as their debut single and with pre-sales of their album took over the #1, #2, and #3 spots.[35] The band performed this version of "Mister" for the first time in Asia on the Mariwood segment of Nippon TV's *Sukkiri.* "Mister" ranked 5th on the Oricon Daily Chart and 1st on the music video chart on iTunes Japan.[36]

---

[33] *Asia Today* (2010), http://www.asiatoday.co.kr/news/view.asp?seq=419218.
[34] *Sports World* (2010), http://sportsworldi.segye.com/Articles/EntCulture/Article.asp?aid=2010081 2003095&subctg1=10&subctg2=00.
[35] *TV Daily-Nate News* (2010), http://news.nate.com/view/20100811n20585.
[36] *TV Daily-Nate News* (2010), http://news.nate.com/view/20100811n22912.

With their Japanese debut single reaching #5 on the weekly Oricon Singles Chart, KARA became the first Asian female group and the first non-Japanese female group in 30 years to reach the top 10.[37]

KARA BEST 2007–2010, released on September 29, also reached #2 on the weekly Oricon Album Chart, making KARA the first Korean girl group to enter the top 10. The release holds the record for any Korean language album in Japan and is by far the most impressive accomplishment of all artists who debuted in Japan in 2010. With its unusually large following, KARA is now a leading Hallyu icon in Japan.

In November 2010, KARA was hired as the face of AU by KDDI, one of Japan's three major telecommunications service providers, and in December, they appeared in the TBS drama URAKARA. In January 2011, they became the spokespersons for the beauty care company TBC, and in June, they appeared in ads for LG Electronics' Optimus cell phones in Japan. In July, they were featured in an ad for Daesang Chungjungone's red vinegar drink, helping boost the drink's sales to ₩50 billion in 2011, a 35.7-fold increase over the previous year's ₩1.4 billion. Sales exploded in the second half of the year and totaled ₩47 billion from July to December alone. According to Nikkei's POS data, since the second week of September the 500 ml version of the beverage has enjoyed the top share in Japan's vinegar drink market, valued at approximately ₩250 billion.[38]

Apparently, KARA's success has arisen because Japanese listeners are more drawn to cute and adorable females than cool, chic ones. KARA's members Kang Ji-young and Goo Ha-ra became popular as fans compared them to actress Nozomi Sasaki and singer Namie Amuro, respectively. They are frequently named as celebrities whose facial features are most desirable in surveys. In a Nikkei Entertainment 2012 survey asking teens to vote for the most popular celebrities, KARA ranked #6 after Arashi, highest for any Hallyu star.[39]

SM entertainment's overseas strategy

Korea's leading music management company, SM Entertainment, has done phenomenally well in Japan. BoA successfully tested the Japanese market for SM, and TVXQ solidified the standing of Korean artists. With Girls' Generation, SM's efforts to penetrate the Japanese market paid off in a dramatic way. On November 4, 2011, SM president Kim Young-min was interviewed on the popular Japanese entertainment program Friday Super Prime on FBS TV and discussed SM's Japan strategy. The interview helps to understand the label's overseas strategy. Below is a summary of the main points:

Thorough training
Groups on the SM label undergo an extensive and thorough grooming process. Once a band's "concept" or direction has been decided upon, members spend an average of five years in training to learn songs, choreography, and foreign languages relevant to their image and strategy. The equivalent of roughly

[37] TV Daily-Nate News (2010), http://news.nate.com/view/20100817n05259.
[38] Dong-A Ilbo (2012), http://economy.donga.com/total/3/01/20120410/45411487/1.
[39] Joongang Ilbo (2012), http://japanese.joins.com/article/340/155340.html.

¥200 million is invested during this period. Despite the staggering costs, SM's highest priority lies in discovering and training new talent, which is why it holds auditions worldwide and spends between ¥200–400 million a year on auditions and training costs alone.

The reasoning behind SM's thorough training system is that as the Korean market is small, SM has little choice but to expand globally, and it becomes important to train its artists to display foreign language skills immediately upon debut. On average, training lasts from three to five years. In TVXQ's case, the members trained for seven years. Annually, 300,000 hopefuls audition for spots; among them, fewer than 100 become eligible for final training.

Importantly, would-be artists are educated in moral and ethical values, and it is crucial to teach trainees to honor appropriate principles. When they become celebrities, they often come across situations in which their judgment can be challenged, and so SM prepares them for those moments in a variety of ways, including having them live together in a dorm.

Localization

Before an artist debuts overseas, the styles of the destination country are incorporated into the artist's look and music. For example, the Japanese version of the music video for the Girls' Generation single "Gee" differs from the Korean version, as the members localized their look, from hair and clothes to dance choreography. SM opened an office in Japan to better understand Japanese trends and conducted its own marketing research. The results have been helpful in styling Korean idols to suit Japan. Currently, over half the staffers at SM Entertainment speak a foreign language, and they contribute significantly to forming localization strategies. The groups themselves have members who speak a variety of languages to better promote *Hallyu* in other countries. SM has been working on ways to respond to the Japanese media environment in which TV exposure plays a determining role in an artist's success.

Use of the Internet

SM uses an online marketing strategy to disseminate information about its artists. It takes advantage of *YouTube*, the largest video sharing platform in the world, to distribute clips of SM artists digitally. SM's marketing strategy rests on predicting the demands of each country by looking at hit counts for particular videos. Girls' Generation was already familiar in Japan before their official debut, having become widely known to fans through *YouTube*. With this online fan base, Girls' Generation brought in 20,000 spectators to their debut performance, which further generated interest among local media and led naturally to more press coverage. In today's media environment, users can access global content through smartphones and websites like *YouTube*. SM makes use of these platforms for its marketing needs, despite unresolved challenges such as copyright infringement.

SM's future strategy

SM Entertainment hopes that the Asian market as a whole will grow in the future, not simply a few select areas like Korea or Japan. If Asia itself can reach the size of the US market, with no national distinctions such as "K-pop" or "J-pop," then it will become the world's largest and greatest market for music. Once talented producers make good music that does well in Asia, it will be recognized as the world's best. Asia's entertainment labels will compete among themselves, and SM's music will go global, moving beyond the current notion of *Hallyu*. SM is planning for that eventuality by training talented artists who can create an "SM Entertainment Wave."

D.   Hallyu stars and advertising (pp. 208–220)

In the popular culture industries, celebrities' star power is measured by the number of advertising campaigns they have under their belt and the paycheck they command per ad. It's easy to determine the popularity of *Hallyu* stars in Japan by examining their endorsements.

According to 2012 rankings of endorsement deals published in the Japanese magazine *Woman's Own*, Jang Keun-suk came fourth on the list for male stars, and KARA was third for females. TVXQ placed 7th, and Girls' Generation occupied the 12th slot. These figures demonstrate the popularity of Korean stars in Japan.

Jang Keun-suk enjoyed a reported ¥120 million per endorsement in 2011, but when he came under fire for demanding too much, he scaled back his asking fee to ¥80 million per campaign in 2012. After this adjustment, he signed deals with four additional companies, bringing him even more profit.

E.   Hallyu and Makgeolli

Exports of the Korean traditional rice liquor *makgeolli* have increased 11-fold since 1995. At that time, total sales stood at a meager $1.74 million. Export

Table 3–13.   Ranking in endorsement deals in Japan

Male Stars: Rank	Name	2011 (Unit: ¥10,000)	2012 (Unit: ¥10,000)
1	Arashi	15,000	15,000
2	SMAP	12,000	12,000
3	Ishikawa Ryo	8,000–12,000	8,000–10,000
4	**Jang Keun-suk**	**12,000**	**8,000**
5	Exile	5,000	5,000
	Darvish Yu	5,000	5,000
Female Stars: Rank	**Name**	**2011**	**2012**
1	AKB48	5,000	5,000
2	Sawa Homare	?	3,000 + 2,000 in a team
3	**KARA**	**4,000**	**4,000–5,000+**
4	Denda Mao	5,000	4,000
5	Shinohara Ryoko	4,000	4,000

(Source: *Women's Own* (2012), "2012 CF Guara Ranking")

Table 3–14.   Advertisements featuring *Hallyu* stars

Star	Korean Brand	Japanese Brand
Bae Yong-joon	Lotte Duty Free, Hotel (2004–2006) Hyundai Motors (2005–2006, two ads each year) The Face Shop (2008–2009) Korea Tourism Organization (2009–2010) Korea Ginseng (2012)	Ootsuka Pharmaceutical Oronamin C (2004) Lotte F&B Flavono Gum Almond Chocolate (2004–2005) SONY Handycam (2004) SONY Cybershot (2004) KDDI (2004) Daihatsu Motors Mira (2005) Japanese Coca-Cola Seven Acha (2005) Pizza-LA (2005–2006) Lotte Chocolate & Gum (2006) Megane Ichiba eyewear (2007–2008) Secom (2006–2007)
Choi Ji-woo	Korea-Japan Eco Campaign (2008) Lotte Duty Free (2011)	Obagi Cosmetics (2004) La Parler Aesthetics (2005) Lotte Xylitol (2007) Katana Golf (2005) Formal Klein (2006) Asuku (2010) HIS (2011) VanaH Water (2009–2012) Arrow Slots (2011) Shiseido Korea (2012)
BoA	Cf. Appearance at the summit dinner for President Roh Moo-hyun and Prime Minister Koizumi	Lotte Air-Le Chocolate (2011) Kirin Afternoon Tea (2001) Lotte Macadamia Chocolate (2002) Japan National Tourism Organization spokesmodel (2002) Honda Fair (2003) Calpis Drink (2003) Skechers (2003–2004) Toshiba Au KDDI (2003–2004) Kose Fasio Cosmetics (2004–2007) Wired Watches (2004–2005) Lotte Arte Chocolate (2004) Lipton Leaf In (2005) NIKE (2006) Toshiba Au KDDI (2007–2008) Mod's Hair Shampoo (2008) Asahi Mintia (2009) Audio-Technica (2008–2012)
Lee Byung-hun	Korea Tourism Organization (2004) LG Japan cellphones (2010)	NEC cellphones (2005) Toyota (2008) Dove Shampoo (2010)

(Continued)

Table 3–14. *(Continued).*

Star	Korean Brand	Japanese Brand
Gwon Sang-wu	The Face Shop Japan commercial (2005)	Ventuno F-Cure Shampoo (2005) Kanbi Vinegar (2005) Morinaga Milk (2006)
Won Bin	Jinro Japan Hite D (2011)	IT Forval (2005)
Jang Dong-geon	Jinro Soju's Chamisul Japan commercial (2006)	OZIO Cosmetics (2005)
TVXQ	Missha Asia (2012) Samsung Shilla Duty Free (2006)	Suzuki Chevrolet MW (2008) Ootsuka Pharmaceutical Oronamin C (2009) Menard Fall Festival (2009) Frente Pinky (2009) Seven & I (2011) Nissen (2011) Glico Ice Cream (2012) Medical Shine (2012)
Kim Hyeon-jung	Lotte Duty Free (2011–2012)	AEON (2011–2012) Slim Beauty House Coolish Fact
Girls' Generation		E-ma Candy (2011) Morinaga Lipton (2011) Seven Eleven Fair (2011)
KARA	Chungjungone Vinegar Drink (2011–2012) Chungjungone Corn Silk Drink (2012)	TBC Commercial Song (2011) Dariya Co. Palty CM Song (2011–2012) Family Mart (Chicken Song) (2011) Ootsuka Pharmaceutical Soikara (2012) Rohto Pharmaceutical C-Cube Eye Drops (2012) Karaoke DAMCommercial Song (2012)
Jang Keun-suk	Lotte Duty Free (2011) Lotte Charlotte (2011)	Lotte Santori Seoul Makgeolli (2011–2012) TBC (2011) Shufoo (2011) Lawson (2011) ACUO (2011) Japan qiip Android App (2012)
Kim Tae-hee	Iriver Japan (2006)	Sougen Bicha (2006) Rohto Pharmaceutical Yikigo Kochi (2012)
Big Bang	Visit Korea (2012) Sudden Attack Characters (Japanese CM) (2010) Lotte Duty Free (2009)	Yamaha TTX Motorbike's Thailand music video (2012)

destinations have also become more diversified, now including about 30 countries,[40] such as Japan, the US, China, and Taiwan. Because of the widespread popularity of Korean dramas and K-pop, interest in and demand for Korean food and drink have grown, with Japan contributing heavily to this trend.

Exports of *makgeolli* increased dramatically after 2008, largely due to the promotion strategy for *makgeolli* in the Japanese market, where it was touted as a healthy drink for modern, sophisticated young women. This was not the image *makgeolli* had in Korea, but as a result, *makgeolli* in Japan was branded as an expensive wine, sold in pretty glass bottles and stocked in department stores and major retail chains. It was also popular as a mixer in dozens of cocktails. In 2010, Jinro and Lotte Liquor saw their *makgeolli* sales explode in Japan, which has become Korea's largest partner in the liquor trade. In fact, Japan made up 90.9% of total *makgeolli* exports by volume in 2011. Although this share had fallen by August 2012 to 86.3%, followed by the US at 5.6% and China 4.3%,[41] it remains by far the largest overseas market for the product.

In 2011, Lotte Liquor tapped Jang Keun-suk to be the face of its product Seoul Makgeolli, as he was the most popular Korean celebrity in Japan at the time. Through this decision, Lotte's exports doubled its 2010 goal.[42] In July 2011, the drink was chosen as one of the hit products of the first half of the year by the Japanese retail magazine *Nikkei Marketing Journal.*[43] *Hallyu* celebrity marketing has had a huge impact on *makgeolli* exports. The above tactics with localization and diversification of the product portfolio allowed the *makgeolli* market to grow and expand its customer base.

According to the "Recent Major Liquor Export-Import Trends Report" published by the Korea Customs Service in September 2012, although *makgeolli* exports increased ninefold from $6 million in 2009 to $54 million in 2011, exports decreased 22% in August 2012 compared to August of the previous year. *Makgeolli* exports grew in volume from 7 million liters in 2009 to 41 million liters in 2011, representing almost a sixfold increase, but these figures dropped 22 million liters in 2012, a 24% decrease [sic]. The market suffered in 2012 from a downturn in Korea-Japan relations stemming from political issues such as the territorial dispute surrounding Dokdo and President Lee Myung-bak's demand for an apology from the Emperor of Japan.

F.   Hallyu and the Korean language

The Korean Wave in Japan has carried over to language study. The National Institute for International Education's Test of Proficiency in Korean (TOPIK), has witnessed a substantial rise in applicants since the test was launched in 1997. In 1997, only 1,529 Japanese took the test. However, the first decade of the new century saw phenomenal growth and the test had to be offered twice a year beginning in 2008 to meet demand. In 2011, 12,913 Japanese applied for the test,[44] an 8.5-fold increase over 1997.

---

[40] KOFICE (2012), *Hallyu Story,* Vol. 2.

[41] Korea Customs Service (2012), *Recent Liquor Exports.*

[42] *Chosun Ilbo* (2012), http://biz.chosun.com/site/data/html_dir/2012/03/07/2012030702934.html.

[43] Korea International Trade Association Tokyo Office (2011), *Trends in the Japanese Liquor Market.*

[44] Korea Foundation for Education, http://www.kref.or.jp/contents_shu_nouryok.html.

NHK has aired Korean language programming since 1984 and broadcasts foreign language education programming in a variety of languages that also includes English, Chinese, and French. Textbook sales for these programs testify to a particular language's popularity. Interest in Korean began to grow in the 2000s, much as TOPIK has reflected. In 1994, only 80,000 textbooks were sold,[45] but this number grew to 200,000 in 2004, the year *Winter Sonata* took Japan by storm. In 2008, 220,000 books were sold,[46] an upward trend that is holding steady. On the other hand, sales of textbooks for European languages such as French and German, which were originally much more popular than Korean, have decreased by half.

In 2002, Korean was included as an official foreign language subject for Japan's National Center Test for University Admissions, equivalent to the SAT. Korean was the fifth language to be included, after English, German, French, and Chinese. More and more Japanese high schools have been incorporating Korean in their curricula. According to statistics compiled by the Japanese Ministry of Education, Culture, Sports, Science and Technology, in 1993 only 42 high schools in Japan had Korean in their curricula, but by 2009, the number of schools had multiplied by a factor of 10 to 420.[47]

The Japanese are demonstrating sustained interest in Korean. Learning a foreign language can serve as an important tool in deepening interest in a particular country. In that respect, the boom in the study of Korean is quite encouraging. Japanese interest in the Korean language came from infatuation with Korean pop culture, and study of Korean will broaden interest in Korea. Eventually, this process will establish a virtuous cycle for Korean culture and language. Japanese fans are not simply enjoying Korean pop culture as a fad; they want to better understand Korean culture in and of itself.

G. Outlook for Hallyu in Japan

Although some anti-*Hallyu* sentiment surfaced early on, it did not necessarily reflect mainstream Japan. However, on a program in August 2011, the Japanese actor Sousuke Takaoka remarked that he "turns off the TV when a Korean show is playing." He went on to say that he doesn't watch Channel 8 (Fuji TV) and sometimes wonders if this network is in fact Korean. These remarks added fuel to the anti-*Hallyu* fire. Protestors began demonstrating near Fuji TV's offices, shouting slogans such as "No More *Hallyu!*" Nevertheless, Japan's mainstream media did not devote much coverage to the anti-*Hallyu* movement, and fans stayed faithful, believing that politics and culture are separate.

Anti-*Hallyu* sentiment was also triggered in August 2012 after President Lee Myung-bak visited Dokdo and made remarks about the Emperor of Japan. In the past, Japanese fans of *Hallyu* have faithfully maintained the Korean Wave in spite of numerous political clashes between the two countries. However, this latest contention over Dokdo has become more than a diplomatic and political

---

[45] Hideki N. & Hitoshi N. (2005), "Korean Language Education in Japan," *Korean Language Education Theory 3.*

[46] Kobayashi A. (2009), "*Hallyu* Wave," *Nikkei Plus 1, Japan Nikkei Shinbun.*

[47] Ministry of Education, Culture, Sports, Science and Technology (2010), *International Exchange for High School Students Over 20 Years.*

concern; it is also having an impact on cultural exchange between Korea and Japan.

At least on the surface, Japan's fondness for Korean idol groups appeared steady in 2012. CNBLUE topped the Oricon daily chart on the day it released its first Japanese major studio album. On September 26, Girls' Generation made it to #1 with a single and DVD/Blu-ray disc. KARA released a single on October 17 that also went to #1 on the Oricon charts.

Many in Japan argue that politics and entertainment have no bearing on each other and that Japan should take the high road. Entertainment critic Hiruma has remarked, "Politics and entertainment are fundamentally separate. Fans of *Hallyu* should remain fans. Only now are Korea and Japan engaging in close cultural exchange. I think Japan should respond generously on this issue."

On September 4, an editorial in the *Yomiuri Shinbun* furthered this argument, "It's up to individuals to consider the relationship between politics and culture, but in fact, they have nothing to do with each other. Once any country lumps the two together, it will lag behind. Instead, the more pop culture exchanges we have, a field relevant to the average citizen, the more they can help solve troubling political issues. Popular culture knows no borders. Japanese culture and the Korean Wave must overcome political barriers and continue to flow to and fro freely, like the tide."

However, despite the expression of such hopes by Japanese consumers and intellectuals, the market has witnessed unusual behavior. Koichi Akaza, the president of BS Nittele, announced he was indefinitely postponing the airing of *A Man Called God* and *Crime Squad,* as they both star Song Il-guk, a Korean actor who attracted attention in Japan when he swam to the disputed island of Dokdo. Koichi feared that Japanese viewers would not take kindly to programs in which Song starred. At a press conference on October 7, 2012, Akaza announced that his channel would cut the number of Korean programs down from four daily. Fuji TV declared at a meeting the same month that while it would revisit its decisions based on a program's merit, it "has no plans to broadcast Korean dramas for the time being." By the end of 2012, Nippon TV, TV Asahi, and TBS also had decided to scale back Korean programming and appearances by K-pop artists.

Following President Lee Myung-bak's 2012 comments on Dokdo, the Japanese women's magazine *Woman Seven* surveyed 100 female *Hallyu* fans ranging in age from their twenties to their sixties and asked how they felt about the rise of anti-Korean sentiment in Japan. Of the respondents, 71% replied that they believed politics and entertainment were not related, and that they would continue as fans. In fact, 12% remarked that they would become advocates for the Korean Wave to help improve bilateral relations. However, 10% of the respondents, generally those in their twenties or thirties, answered that they were thinking of giving up interest in *Hallyu* altogether, which shows that to an extent politics influences consumption of Korean popular culture.

PSY, though a global sensation, is conspicuously less popular in Japan. Many analysts have interpreted this point as a manifestation of festering political tension between Korea and Japan. *Time* magazine reported that "Gangnam Style" lacks popularity only in Japan because of diplomatic tension over Dokdo. Gohari Susumu, a distinguished Korean studies professor at Shizuoka University, argued that another reason PSY wasn't popular in Japan was that he doesn't have the look and style that Japanese fans seek in a *Hallyu* star. However, Gohari went on to say that he believes bilateral political tensions have played a role as well.[48] In August and September 2012, when PSY was at the height of his popularity in the US and elsewhere, the Japanese media instead focused on deteriorating relations with Korea. Coverage of Korean pop culture or PSY was almost non-existent. Gohari argued that had "Gangnam Style" surfaced at another time, the press would likely have given daily coverage to the song's viral success. Japanese channels only began reporting on PSY after October 3, long after the song had reached #2 on the US Billboard Chart and #1 in the UK.

Although Japanese consumers and intellectuals are trying to separate politics and culture, if Japanese society itself continues to swing to the right, average consumers will also be influenced by anti-*Hallyu* sentiment. Worse still would be a decrease in appearances by K-pop artists or Korean television programming, including public networks. The role of public TV is immensely important in spreading awareness of popular culture. If the Japanese media cut back on *Hallyu* programming because of social trends, the Korean Wave will suffer long-lasting effects. The wisdom of both countries must be combined so that Korean and Japanese fans are not compelled to interrupt consumption practices that they enjoy.

3.2.2.   A Firsthand Account of *Hallyu* Fever in Japan

Reference: "A Firsthand Account of *Hallyu* Fever in Japan," *OhMyNews*, Lim Mi-ok, January 9, 2005.

Hmm, where did Hallyu come from? Time will tell whether it is something temporary that will end up blowing away like the wind. I am a Korean housewife living in Japan, and you can feel the impact of *Hallyu*. This pleases me and puts me in high spirits.

Around four o'clock this afternoon, I went to a neighborhood beauty parlor to get my hair done. I was thumbing through a magazine, surrendering my head to the salon manager (*dancho*), who looks like the popular Japanese celebrity Nakai from the boy band SMAP. "Interest in Korea is huge these days, isn't it?" the manager, also the head stylist of the salon, asked with interest. I wanted to grin and say, "Yes!" But I have learned a Japanese-style response from six years of living in Japan. "Hmm…We'll see…" I gave a vague answer, tilting my head with an ambiguous smile.

Sure enough, he responded, "Right?" The manager was pleased. He followed up with another question, "In America people say, 'Happy New Year,' and here we say '*Shinnen akemashite omedeto gozaimasu.*' Do you have a New Year's greeting in Korea?"

"Of course. We say, 'Saehae bok mani badeuseyo.'"
"I didn't understand a thing you said."
"Repeat after me. It's not that difficult. 'Sae-hae bok ma-ni ba-deu-se-yo.'"

---

[48] *Chosun Ilbo* (2012), http://news.chosun.com/site/data/html_dir/2012/10/08/2012100801097.html.

I'd gone to the salon to get a trim but ended up giving a Korean lesson. It's certainly positive that more and more Japanese are becoming interested in Korea and our language because of *Hallyu*. I was pleased by the encounter, as well as my new hairstyle, and gladly paid the ¥3,500 for the service.

On my way back, I stopped at the drugstore to buy toilet paper (Japan has chain drugstores that sell prescription drugs, over-the-counter meds, and household goods). Because my eyesight is bad, I often don't recognize people I know unless they are very close. A woman with a child greeted me as if she knew me, but I ignored her, unsure whether she was addressing me. She kept approaching, and I thought she was coming to grab the hair dye I was picking up.

When she got close, I realized it was the mother of Yoshino, a boy in the same class as my second child last year. "Ah... Good evening!" I quickly greeted her, a little embarrassed.

After shopping, I was standing next to the traffic lights at a small intersection, waiting for my child to return from piano class, when someone walking past bowed and beamed at me. It was none other than Yoshino's mom again. I thought, "No way! Could that stuck-up woman really be that nice?"

Yoshino's mother was notorious among us mothers for being arrogant. Until then, we'd only ever greeted each other formally, even if we met each other at school.

Actually, most Japanese housewives around me have become kinder and more polite, and have begun to approach me with twinkling eyes.

Japanese men, though, are starkly different from their wives. They know about the media's breathless reports about *Hallyu* but don't seem to care.

For three days at the end of last year, under the direction of the Korea Tourism Organization's Tokyo Branch, two researchers surveyed about 200 Japanese men and women in Ginza. They showed people a scene from a commercial promoting tourism in Korea (Japan edition) produced by the Korea Tourism Organization and featuring Korean stars Choi Ji-woo and Lee Byung-hun. They then asked them several questions, including whether their perception of Korea had changed as a result of watching the commercial, and how they rated the desirability of Korea and the featured actors.

Japanese women between 30 and 70 happily volunteered. On the other hand, men in their 40s and 50s were not cooperative. The researchers tried very hard to fill the quota for male respondents in their 40s, who they needed many more of. "If you participate in the survey, we'll give you a mouse pad with pictures of Choi Ji-woo and Lee Byung-hun and other gifts. Wouldn't your wife like these gifts?" Hearing this offer, one man in his forties stopped his hurried steps. Though indifferent to the Korean Wave himself, he must have been unable to ignore his wife's devotion to *Hallyu*. After the survey, looking at the gifts he had received, a faint smile appeared on the man's face, as though he was picturing how happy his wife would be.

Eager fans of *Hallyu* should neither be scorned nor treated as a mere corps of middle-aged women. Behind each one lies a platoon of other supporters.

At the very least, *Hallyu* is undoubtedly bringing warmth to many Koreans residing in Japan. I sincerely hope that this heat will melt the hard feelings of history and offer an opportunity to build a system of cooperation between South Korea and Japan in which both participate equally.

3.2.3. Tokyo: Where Have All the *Hallyu* Fans Gone?

Reference: "Tokyo: Where Have All the *Hallyu* Fans Gone?" *OhMyNews*, Lee Seon-pil (thebasis3), September 7, 2012.

A. A visit to Shin-Okubo Street, center of the Korean wave:
Was Hallyu a bubble?

It's been a year since I visited Tokyo. Last November I went to Shin-Okubo Street, a popular neighborhood for Korean exchange students to live in. Recently, *Hallyu* stars such as Song Il-guk have seen their activities in Japan stifled or postponed indefinitely, and I wanted to reexamine the situation.

On September 3 and 4, I walked the streets of Tokyo, including Shin-Okubo. From Shinjuku to the luxurious shops of Roppongi, I could see occasional ads for Korean celebrities. Shin-Okubo in particular has a high concentration of shops devoted to the Korean Wave. At first glance, it seemed tranquil.

Recently, an entertainment industry insider noted that one of his company's actors had signed a contract in Japan but that the actor's promotional activities had been put off for the time being. The source also admitted to sensing a cooling of interest in Korean pop culture. The anti-*Hallyu* sentiment that once seemed a blip on the radar has now become quite palpable.

B. The Dokdo issue: "We're really feeling its effects."

As I tried to retrace my steps from last year's trip to Shibuya and Shin-Okubo, I was discomfited by the changes. Shin-Okubo was quiet. My previous visit was on a similar afternoon, and although the shops have become more numerous, they seemed to have fewer patrons.

I met a vendor selling streetç snacks like *hotteok* and *ddeokbokgi*. In between his busy calls in Japanese to "Try a Korean pancake! They're delicious!" I asked if he'd noticed a change recently. "There are definitely fewer Japanese people walking the street now," he said. "I can't be sure, but whether people are conscious of it or not, political issues like Dokdo have led to some resentment about Korea." He turned back to a passerby.

I went to a Korean grocery, the kind of supermarket you could find in any of our neighborhoods. In one corner of the store, soft tofu stew was available for sampling, and quite a few people were browsing.

"I can sense what's going on with our customers," said a Korean employee running the display. "Something does seem to be up because of issues like Dokdo. There's plenty of news and discussion on TV about Korea." He added that the overall tone had changed as well. According to him, patronage at his store had shrunk in recent months by roughly 30%.

C. "We're definitely seeing a slump, but they don't hate Korea!
It's just a phase."

Arguments can also be found against such negative assessments. Kim Chang-hyeon, who works at a shop near Shin-Okubo Station, said, "There's been a drop in customers lately, but it might be because summer vacation for students is over."

Kim added, "People think that *Hallyu* will make a comeback. I think it's difficult to say that the Dokdo issue has put an end to the Korean Wave."

If so, I wondered what this recent decline in sales meant. I managed to get a frank answer. Kim noted that sales were down 50% from last year. When asked whether this was a widespread trend, he said, "Since the start of the year all stores that sell products related to the Korean Wave have experienced a drop. I don't think it's an anti-Korea thing so much as a bursting of the *Hallyu* bubble."

Kim added, "Super Junior and Big Bang are still the most popular. As far as actors go, Jang Keun-suk continues to be big and Park Si-hoo has really gotten popular here." The situation may have become rougher, but Korean stars remain stars, or so Kim noted, based on the more popular items in the store.

From my trip to Japan, I'd say that although the influence of anti-Korean sentiment is being felt, it is not strong. Of course, signs remain, such as the weekly rallies conservative groups hold in front of the Korean Embassy every Wednesday. Nonetheless, given that such events occur, those involved with Korean pop culture have to keep up content quality and prepare for the future and to broaden the base from Japan to other countries.

3.3.   SOUTHEAST ASIA

3.3.1.   *Hallyu* Forever: Southeast Asia

Reference: *Hallyu Forever: The World Is Hallyu Style*, Ko Jeong-min et al., KOFICE
Hallyu Series V, 2012, pp. 254–274, 293–296.

(pp. 254–274)

A.   *Hallyu in Southeast Asia*

In the early 2000s, *Hallyu* was driven largely by TV dramas, but recently it has spread, primarily through music and online games, and is expanding beyond Taiwan, Japan, and China to Southeast Asia, and across the world.

Southeast Asia, in particular the ASEAN countries, is extremely important to Korea economically and represents a key export destination for *Hallyu*. Thailand is the largest recipient of Korean content exports in Southeast Asia. Following the growth of the Wimax and mobile TV markets in countries like Indonesia and Vietnam, demand for Korean content has risen consistently.

Thailand

Thai troops came to South Korea to fight during the Korean War, and since then the two countries have maintained close ties. The Thai people have a good impression of Korea; they see it as the land of *Arirang* and of ginseng, as a role model for its Saemaul movement and rapid economic development, and as the successful host of the 1986 Asian Games, the 1988 Olympics, and the 2002 World Cup. Thailand was thus ripe for the spread of the Korean Wave. Korea first gained a foothold in Thailand in the mid-1980s, a period during which Korean FDI to the country started increasing and Korean tourists began to travel there in large numbers. These processes led to a Korean language boom, with several Thai universities offering classes. Even though the country lagged slightly behind destinations such as China, Taiwan, Hong Kong, and Singapore in receiving actual content imports, the Korean Wave in Thailand did not start late. Nevertheless, not many Koreans realized that *Hallyu* was growing in Thailand.

Before the Seoul Olympics, few Thais knew anything about Korea. *Hallyu* began in earnest in 2002 when Thailand's iTV broadcast the drama *Autumn Tales*. A handful of Korean dramas aired on Thai television before 2002, but for the most part the Thai people knew little of Korea and Korean culture. However, the success of *Autumn Tales,* later reinforced by the popularity of *My Sassy Girl,* paved the way for *Hallyu* to take root in Thailand. Korean dramas and movies began to find a loyal fan base. *Hallyu* grew stronger thanks to the release of albums by such artists as Baby V.O.X, SE7EN, and Rain, which led to the launch of fan clubs across the country. More Thais began to take an interest in Korean online games and foods, which in turn led to growing popularity for Korean language classes.

According to data from 2004 analyzed by the Korea Tourism Organization, the growth of *Hallyu* in Thailand led to an increase in Thai tourists to Korea. *Hallyu* also contributed to shaping a positive image of Korea. In fact, while visitors to Korean from Japan, the US, and Hong Kong decreased in 2011, Thai tourists increased by 5.7%. *Hallyu* greatly improved what had been a less than spectacular image for Korea, and there was a measurable growth in appreciation for Korean products such as cell phones, home appliances, cosmetics, and stationery.

Many Korean artists and celebrities have visited Thailand, and Korean dramas are currently doing phenomenally well. There were even appearances by the K-pop artist NS Yunji and dance team Black Queen at New I-Mobile Stadium in Thailand during the country's largest national festival, Songkran, held from April 13 to 15.

In 2011, Thai director Prachya Pinkaew, famous in Korea for his *Ong Bak* series, produced a taekwondo movie called *The Kick*. It starred actress Jeeja Yanin Vismitanada, who is best known for having performed the challenging action sequences in *Chocolate,* similar to the action-packed *Ong Bak,* without a stunt double. *The Kick* also featured the comedy stylings of popular actor Mum.

The Kick was funded by Korea's CJ Venture Investment and Thailand's Bangkok Film Studio. A total of 70% of the film's dialogue is in Korean. Set in Bangkok, this movie focuses on Master Mun (Jo Jae-hyeon), a former medalist on the national taekwondo team who now runs a gym; his wife Yun (Yae Ji-won), proprietor of a Korean restaurant; and their son Tae-yang (Na Tae-ju) and daughter Tae-mi (Kim Gyeong-suk). The family has a run-in with a gang led by the charismatic Seok-du who are attempting to steal a legendary sword owned by the Thai Dynasty. The family fights the gang to retrieve the sword. In an effort to appeal to Thai moviegoers, the movie contains a lot of Thai humor. Unfortunately, though, having been shot in Korea, box office sales were below average.

Only You was another highly anticipated film that wound up faring poorly. It starred Han Hyo-ju, who played the lead in the 2011 TV hit *Dong Yi.* Unfortunately, the film suffered from a lack of publicity and was removed from theaters after just three weeks.

Six Korean movies were featured at the international film festival held in Hua Hin, the vacation spot for Thai royals: *Only You,* which opened the Busan International Film Festival in 2011, *Moby Dick, The Client, White, The Kick,* and *Ronin Pop,* starring Jeong Hui-cheol and Min U-gi and directed by Japanese filmmaker Keita Matsuda.

The festival was a star-studded event that included many world-renowned directors and actors. Also in attendance were So Ji-seop and Han Hyo-ju, whose appearances were covered by the local press.

Thai youth are infatuated with Korean pop culture, an interest that has branched out to fashion. Many Thai teens imitate the styles of Korean celebrities and purchase the cosmetics, accessories, and clothes they favor. Other Korean products such as cell phones and electronic appliances are equally popular. Many Thais think of Korea as a leading nation for technology.

Indonesia

K-pop has a strong fan base in Indonesia as well. Traffic came to a standstill when aficionados rushed to the booth outside Jakarta's Twin Plaza Hotel to purchase tickets to the Super Junior concerts held on April 28–29, 2012. A total of 12 fans fainted at the scene. All 17,000 tickets completely sold out by 3 p.m. on the day they went on sale, despite their high prices of between 500,000 to 1.7 million rupiah (roughly ₩60,000 to ₩200,000). Scalped tickets were selling for up to 4 million rupiah (roughly ₩500,000).

In the past, Korean companies invested in Indonesia to draw on cheap labor and to manufacture products for export. Most of the workforce was concentrated in the textile and footwear industries. Recently, however, thanks to the growth of the ASEAN market and a strong rupiah, Indonesians have been exercising greater purchasing power, starting in the big cities and extending throughout the country. Accordingly, and buoyed by the Korean Wave, the number of Korean companies entering Indonesia has risen markedly.

LG, Samsung, and other large corporations now have a local presence and work with over 100 small-to-mid-sized suppliers of parts and intermediate goods. Investment from such companies as POSCO and Hankook Tire is enabling many Korean SMEs to open offices in Indonesia as well. POSCO is building a steel mill near Banten, and Hankook Tire has offices in Cikarang. Many Korean companies have followed their lead and set up offices there.

In 2009, Lotte Mart bought 20 Indonesian Makro stores in order to enter the warehouse outlet market. As of 2012, Lotte Mart had 27 stores scattered throughout Indonesia. Lock&Lock, Glass Lock, and other consumer goods companies are also setting up operations in Indonesia, and in 2011, Korean chain stores like Lotteria and Tous Les Jours opened branches.

Vietnam

Truong Van Minh, head of programming at the Ho Chi Minh TV (HTV) network, has proposed that *Hallyu* began in Vietnam in 1997 when the drama *Calendula* aired during prime time on HTV's V7 channel. HTV has been managing the flow of the Korean Wave since its inception. From 1997 to early 2000, Korean dramas were introduced to Vietnam as part of an exchange program between networks in both countries. Since then, Korean companies have purchased advertising on Vietnamese channels, allowing major broadcasters and local terrestrial channels to feature regular Korean programming. Korean dramas made up 56% of all imported programs in 1998, and from 2000 to 2005, HTV aired Korean dramas between noon and 2 p.m. On the V7 channel, Korean shows made up 19.8% of all dramas broadcast. According to surveys, about 64% of young Vietnamese between the ages of 11 and 25 watch Korean dramas; networks are eager to broadcast them for strong ratings and advertising revenue. Vietnamese television has notably increased its share of Korean dramas.

Despite this increase, however, the share of Korean dramas in the TV lineup fell from 19.8% to 8.4% from 2005 to 2011. Reasons vary: viewers grew tired of the same storylines; many Vietnamese dramas were produced, replacing Korean ones; and public opinion turned against *Hallyu* and calls arose for the protection of Vietnamese traditional culture. As a result, HTV also reduced its import of Korean dramas.

Korean programs make up 70% of all foreign programs shown in Vietnam; as late as 2009, they occupied 10% of all programming. Entertainment shows

Table 3–15.   HTV and *Hallyu*'s development

Period	Characteristics of *Hallyu*
Phase 1 (Introduction)	From 1997 to early 2000, Korean dramas were introduced to Vietnamese viewers through Korea-Vietnam exchange programs involving networks from both countries. Moreover, Korean corporations offered sponsorships so that their dramas could air regularly on major networks and local terrestrial stations. By 1998, Korean dramas occupied 56% of all imported TV programs. They were subject to review by the Vietnam Culture Regulatory Commission.
Phase 2 (Maturity)	From 2000 to 2005, HTV showed Korean dramas between noon and 2 p.m. These dramas made up 19.8% of all dramas broadcast by HTV's V7 channel. Nearly 64% of residents aged 11 to 25 in Ho Chi Minh City said they enjoyed Korean dramas. Networks preferred Korean programs for their high ratings and advertising revenue. This period was the heyday for Korean dramas.
Phase 3	From 2005 to 2011, the proportion of Korean dramas in the TV lineup decreased from 19.8% to 8.4%.

such as *Golden Bell Challenge* and *Vitamin* are also popular. A total of 26 Korean dramas aired in Vietnam in 2011, of which 9 were shown on state-owned channel VTV, 6 on Hanoi Radio Television, 6 on HTV, and 5 on digital broadcasting.

K-pop is enjoying increased popularity with the help of online sites such as *360kpop.vn*, *2 sao.net*, *kenh14.vn*, *VCTV3*, and *Yan TV*. *Hallyu* is influencing the styles and consumption habits of Vietnam's urbanites and youth. Korean fashion, cosmetics, food, and consumer culture have been introduced and made Korean brands popular. Demand for Korean products has increased, leading to export opportunities for Korea in targeting the Vietnamese middle class.

Local demand for entertainment is growing, but without adequate infrastructure; even worse, the few movie theaters that exist in Vietnam are shrinking in number. Many Korean distributors have entered the Vietnamese film market to satisfy local needs. CGV opened a theater in Ho Chi Minh City's Megastar Crescent Mall in 2011 and now operates nine. CGV plans to open 24 theaters with 198 screens by 2016. Episodes of Korean TV programs exported to Vietnam totaled 2,076 in 2007, at a cost of $1.296 million. In 2010, the number decreased to 1,866, although revenue increased to $2.210 million.

When Vietnam lacked the means to import foreign forms of entertainment and TV programs, Korea offered its dramas at no cost except for the ability to show sponsor ads. As a result, Vietnamese viewers were able to enjoy Korean shows, and Korean companies benefited from product exposure. LG Household & Healthcare represents perhaps the most notable case. A survey of customers who visited their brick-and-mortar stores found that 94.2% were familiar with Korean dramas, music, and movies.

My Princess, starring Kim Tae-hee and Song Seung-heon, was broadcast on Vietnam's SCTV17 from mid-January 2012. Before the series aired, the cast

Table 3–16.   Korean program exports to Vietnam

	2007	2008	2009	2010
Amount ($1,000)	1,296	971	2,075	2,210
Number of Programs	2,076	1,099	2,607	1,866

visited Hanoi on January 7 for a press conference and fan meet-and-greet. Song also participated in a fundraising event hosted by the Vietnam Children's Fund at the National Convention Center and donated $50,000 to the cause. The KBS soap opera *The Way Home* was broadcast from March 27 on VTC9. The channel described the series as follows: "Starring Lee Sang-wu, Jang Shin-yeong, Yun Yeo-jeong, and Park Geun-hyeong, this drama explores the idea of 'home,' a place people long to return to."

Korea's EBS shot footage of the Mekong River for a special three-part feature in 2011. The show highlighted the beautiful scenery of the Mekong as it flows through several countries, and also took an ethnographic perspective in discussing the youth of Vietnam and their aspirations.

MBC collaborated with VTC, a Vietnamese multimedia group under the Ministry of Information and Telecommunications with businesses in broadcasting, communications, and the Internet, to launch a 24-hour channel in Vietnam. On April 17, 2012, the two parties signed an MOU on content partnership. Through this, MBC cornered a market that deals with content supply, drama production, *Hallyu* event planning, and sales of drama-related merchandise.

Korean companies are active in Vietnam. Keangnam Enterprises finished construction of the Landmark 72 building in September 2011, a massive project comprising a multi-purpose building and a couple of 48-story apartment towers. Keangnam invested $1.12 billion in the development, the largest of its kind built by a Korean company in Vietnam. Landmark 72's gross area spans 609,673 m², 1.3 times that of Dubai's Burj Khalifa, the tallest building in the world. At 72 stories, reaching 347 meters, this multi-purpose building is the tallest in Vietnam.

The observatory located on the uppermost floor of Landmark 72 is equipped with facilities that afford 360-degree views of Hanoi. A promotion booth, 5D theater, and digital experience center are also on the top floor. Landmark 72's commercial facilities include Parkson, Malaysia's largest retail chain, and Lotte Cinema. According to Keangnam Enterprises, "nearly 40,000 visitors come to Landmark 72 every day, and the project has created over 5,000 jobs."

Cambodia

In Cambodia, *Hallyu* has largely been driven by youth consumption of K-pop and Korean movies, which in turn has led to increased interest in Korean food and fashion. My TV, Sea TV, and other Cambodian channels offer Korean music videos and music programming. It is common to see people dancing to K-pop in the evening at Hun Sen Park and at Riverside. A dance instructor plays the music and teaches choreography. Locals pay a fee of 1,000 riel (about ₩300) to join the class. Because K-pop is so beloved, many locals already have the moves memorized. There are tribute bands for SHINee, Wonder Girls, and other Korean idol groups. The members of RHM, who style themselves after Wonder Girls, uploaded a video of their rendition of *Nobody* to *YouTube* and racked up over 500,000 hits. While some Cambodians profess embarrassment at such practices, many say they don't see a problem.

Because of low awareness of intellectual property rights in countries like Cambodia, issues over copyright infringement may erupt in the future. Popular K-pop songs have been translated into Cambodian and registered in local karaoke machines. Big Bang, Girls' Generation, and 2 NE1 are the most popular acts. In 2011, Son Dam-bi and After School visited Cambodia to perform and participate in volunteer activities.

Korean dramas are also doing exceedingly well. Almost every local station in Cambodia broadcasts Korean movies. *Full House* and *Jewel in the Palace,* two earlier *Hallyu* hits, achieved high ratings and became cultural mainstays. Most Korean dramas and entertainment programs such as *Running Man* are broadcast with subtitles. K-pop programs also enjoy wide popularity. Of the stations that show K-pop, My TV is second only to the public network CTN in ratings (14%).

Movies are also generating a great deal of interest, thanks to the popularity of *Hallyu* dramas. As TV actors like Lee Yeong-ae, Song Hye-gyo, Gwon Sang-wu, and Rain increasingly achieve popularity, films in which they star have been successful. More actors should follow in the future as K-drama broadcasts continue. Sorya Shopping Center, Cambodia's largest mall, has a huge section devoted to Korean movie and TV DVDs. Unfortunately, most are illegal copies. There are few theaters in Phnom Penh, and as yet, Korean movies have not opened on any screens. However, given demand for Korean movies among Cambodia's youth, openings are likely before long.

Korean animation is not as strong in Cambodia. The American cartoon *Tom and Jerry* is the most popular series. Character merchandise such as Angry Bird shirts and the like do well but aren't sold under official licenses. Cambodian children do not play computer games often; rather, they watch cartoons on TV, which explains their high ratings locally. This market may offer enormous opportunities for Korean animation producers in the future.

Internet connections are poor and few PCs exist outside Phnom Penh, where computers are only now becoming more common. As a result, Cambodian teenagers are not familiar with online games. However, nowadays members of Cambodia's own baby boom generation are using computers and smartphones more frequently. The gaming market shows potential for growth. *Audition*, an online dance battle game, recently became available in Cambodia, although it hasn't fared well. Vietnamese and Chinese games such as *Justice X War* and *Attack Online* do better, and Cambodians appear to prefer shooting games.

The market for Korean fashion, beauty, and medical services is growing in Cambodia. Korean dramas and movies have impressed Korean fashion upon the Cambodian youth. Vintage clothes from Korea, in particular, are popular with the young crowd. Beauty salons are opening across Cambodia to cater to richer clientele. Many women are interested in skin whitening products, but the price tag for sun creams can be intimidating. Nature Republic, a cosmetics retail chain, has begun servicing Cambodia and plans to open more stores.

Many Cambodians are becoming fans of Korean food. Several Korean restaurants in Phnom Penh cater to Korean expats and tourists, and they are second in number only to Chinese restaurants for foreign cuisine. Because of their relatively expensive prices, however, many locals find it difficult to frequent them. The Korean Food Festival, held in 2011, attracted more interest to Korean cuisine. Kimchi, *gimbap*, and *samgyeopsal* are the most popular dishes.

Tous Les Jours, a Korean franchise bakery chain, plans to enter Cambodia. Tourism still has much room for growth despite the interest of many Cambodians in Korea, as few families have the means to visit.

Myanmar

Myanmar, too, is caught up in *Hallyu*. *Autumn Tales,* which aired at the end of 2002, became hugely popular and ignited a fever for Korean dramas. Myanmar has two channels, MRTV and MWD, which together show four to five Korean dramas every week.

Celebrities such as Song Seung-heon, Lee Min-ho, Song Hye-gyo, Won Bin, Jang Dong-geon, Choi Ji-wu, Bae Yong-joon, and Chae Rim are immensely popular. Many fans are scrambling to learn the Korean language, which in turn is fueling interest in all Korean-made products. Although concerns exist that *Hallyu* might end abruptly, it would be safe to say that its popularity will continue for some time.

Korean investment in Myanmar began in 1990 when Daewoo Electronics built a home appliance factory in the country. This project was followed by further investment from Daewoo affiliates. Currently, there is a great deal of Korean investment in Myanmar's textile industry.

Esquire and Sunny Industrial Co. Ltd., both shoemakers, began manufacturing shoes in Myanmar in 2000 for export to Japan and elsewhere. However, clothing exports to the US have decreased in the wake of Myanmar's deteriorating economic conditions and US sanctions on the country. Many Korean garment factories have shut down and overall investment plummeted. Hyundai Corporation, CJ, and Daewoo Electronics left the market after 2002, and POSCO, which produces zinc plates in Myanmar, had to halt operations in 2005 and resume a year later.

Outside the garment and footwear industries, manufacturers with a presence in Myanmar include Daewoo Wood Co. (plywood), The One (furniture and pieces made from Japanese wisteria), Mercury Lace (PVC hose), Samgong Korea (rafts), Miwon (PVC pipes, plastic packaging filler), Yes Box (cartons), and UPI (plastic products) among others. Several smaller trading companies also work with Myanmar. Many of these, however, operate under the name of a Myanmar citizen and have not followed official FDI procedures. Companies interested in labor-intensive industries such as textiles and wig-making have surged, as well as those like forestry and fishing that can benefit from Myanmar's rich natural resources; likewise, several Korean companies have shown interest in the agricultural industry, including grains and biofuel crops, the service sector, and the real estate market.

B.   *Achievements of Hallyu*

90% of Vietnam's young workers in Dong Nai watch Korean dramas

In May 2012, Professor Mai Kim Chi of the Korean department at Ho Chi Minh University surveyed 400 residents of Dong Nai about Korea.[49] A total of 96.5% of the respondents said they knew of Korea. Of these, 89.5% said that they learned about Korea from *Hallyu* dramas, and of these respondents, 76.8% said they watch Korean programming regularly.

Young workers in particular, nearly 90%, watched Korean dramas often. Also, 80% of college students and 56% of high school students watch these shows frequently.

The favorite Korean drama was *Full House*; 93.3% of Korean drama viewers watched the show, and 68.2% of the show's audience said that they enjoyed it very much. *Full House* was followed by *Medical Brothers,* watched by 70.3% of the respondents. Of these, 48% said that they found the series very enjoyable. *Jewel in the Palace* and *Winter Sonata* were watched by 64.8% and 62.3% of respondents, respectively.

Over 10 Korean dramas are broadcast every day on Dong Nai's TV station. As of May 12, 2012, Dong Nai TV had *Love You a Thousand Times, Call of the Country, Sharp 3, Cinderella Man,* and *Myung Ga* in its programming lineup, while other channels were offering *High Kick, Chuno, Queen of Reversal, A Man Called God, The Princess' Man, You Are My Sunshine, Iris, Love Marriage,* and *You Are So Handsome.*

Korean dramas are especially popular in this region for their storylines and production values. Whereas Western shows are seen as too violent, Chinese dramas too over-the-top, and Hong Kong dramas clunky in their translations, Korean dramas appeal to average Vietnamese viewers who are able to identify readily with the traditional values they find there.

Of the 400 respondents in the survey, 72% said that they like Korean dramas for their attractive casts, while 52.3% said that they enjoy the stories. Different responses were given by respondents under and over 30, but the viewers shared cultural sensibilities.

Many fans want to copy the style of *Hallyu* celebrities. Young fans imitate the hairstyles, fashion, accessories, and makeup of stars such as Rain, Jang Dong-geon, Song Hye-gyo, Lee Yeong-ae, and Kim Nam-ju. In fact, some 55% of younger respondents said they want to emulate Jang Dong-geon's style.

Dong Nai stores selling Korean merchandise are popular mainly with the youth. A "Korea Street" arose organically in Long Binh Tan at the heart of Bien Hoa City. Clothing stores, cosmetics shops, and beauty salons line this street. Whereas many Vietnamese consumers once preferred Japanese and French beauty products, they now turn to Korean products. E'Zup, endorsed by actress

---

[49] Dong Nai is located in the center of an economic district in Vietnam's southeast region, about 30km from Ho Chi Minh City. Economically, socially, and culturally it is similar in scope to Ho Chi Minh City, with a population of 2.5 million. The district is dynamic, with 30 industrial complexes. Korean companies make up the largest share of these complexes, with 185 having established offices there. Koreans have hired 120,000 workers and form a majority of the foreigners living in Dong Nai, numbering 1,273.

Table 3–17.   Favorite *Hallyu* dramas in Dong Nai, Vietnam

Drama Titles	College Students (%)	High School Students (%)	Workers (%)	Misc. (%)
Full House	70	48	76	70
Jewel in the Palace	39	12	64	42
Sweet 18	43.5	44	37	36
Medical Brothers	39	46	76	62
Winter Sonata	52.5	20	43	42
Lovers in Paris	59	20	61	50

(Source: Mai Kim Chi (Korean Department at Ho Chi Minh University), Survey Results)

Table 3–18.   Possible reasons for preferring Korean
dramas in Dong Nai, Vietnam

Reason	Under 30 (%)	Over 30 (%)
Interesting Plot	62.50	52.88
Attractive Cast	80.74	47.12
Fashion Style	62.16	43.27

Table 3–19.   Favored *Hallyu* products and styles

	Under 30 (%)	Over 30 (%)
Fashion	82.77	46.15
Cosmetics	64.19	32.69
Actors' Hairstyles	48.99	9.62
Actresses' Hairstyles	73.31	24.04
Kimchi	58.56	11.54
Samsung Cell Phones	62.84	36.54
Cars	55.07	25.96

Kim Nam-ju, is the most popular brand. Korean makeup application styles are also widely popular. *Hallyu* not only influences Vietnamese consumption practices but also outlook and behavior.

Dan Tri, a Vietnamese news outlet, reported favorably on *Hallyu* in an April 5, 2012, story. The article described young Vietnamese who love Korean culture and went on to state that Korea is promoting itself effectively in the world through its culture. In January 2012, *Dan Tri* included a piece that noted that in the 21st century Korea draws inspiration from patriotism and nationalism in educating its youth and asked when Vietnam would have a pop culture that reflects such a spirit. The piece went on to suggest that in Korea important life goals are discussed in dramas and values are instilled in its youth, and queried what the older generations in Vietnam have done for the nation's young people.

Malaysian students want to study in Korea

Abdullah Zawawi Tahir of the Malaysian Embassy in Korea remarked on December 22, 2011, that a growing number of Malaysian students were coming to Korea to study engineering. He noted that bilateral exchange had expanded following various events and festivals held in 2010 to commemorate the 50th anniversary of the establishment of diplomatic ties between Korea and Malaysia. No fewer than 116 official visits to Korea have been organized by the governments thus far. In April 2011, the Malaysian Prime Minister visited Korea, followed by a visit from the King, who congratulated the two nations on this anniversary.

The success of *Hallyu* had an impact in Malaysia as elsewhere in Asia in 2012. Agriculture remains Malaysia's largest economic sector, but the country is industrializing and is eager to learn from Korea's successful model. In line with these efforts, Malaysia is expanding cooperation, especially in the field of education. In particular, the number of Malaysian students coming to study engineering has increased as a result of Korea's strength in science and technology.

A wave of Korean construction in Singaporean real estate

Korean companies have increasingly been awarded contracts to build urban landmarks around the world. Ssangyong Engineering and Construction built Marina Bay Sands in Singapore, which along with its Merlion sculpture (a mythical creature with the head of a lion and body of a mermaid) became a major landmark immediately following completion in 2010. The eastern tower rises at an angle reaching 52 degrees at its maximum until it meets the western tower at the 23rd story (70 meters high). The building is 57 stories tall, and on its top floor is located the boat-shaped Sky Park, complete with observatory, swimming pool, restaurant, and walking trail. The project involved an irregular design and complexities that confounded other leading contractors. For Ssangyong, the ₩900 billion contract was its largest overseas development project up to that point, and ultimately proved the skill of Korean construction.

Hallyu concerts in Cambodia

Cultural exchange with Cambodia began in earnest in April 2001, following the signing of a Korea-Cambodia agreement that led to growing contacts in the arts, education, and film. Korean groups and companies began to perform in Cambodia, and in September 2006, the 1st Korean Film Festival was held. At the 2nd Korean Film Festival, Baby V.O.X performed, along with acts from various genres. After a slowdown following the global financial crisis, the holding of concerts accelerated once more after 2010.

K-pop, delivered through channels like My TV and Sea TV that offer music videos and music programming, leads *Hallyu* in Cambodia. It is common to see

Table 3–20.   Bilateral performance exchanges with Cambodia

2001.12	Korean traditional art performance
2003.11	Korean traditional music performance (Southeast Asia tour)
2003.11	Heo Trio performance
2004.06	Angkor Wat exhibition performance (June 29-September 12, Seoul Museum of History)
2004.08	Cambodia's Royal Ballet performance in Korea (August 31-September 5)
2004.11	Incheon City Dance Company Korean traditional dance performance (Asia tour)
2006.09	1st Korea Film Festival
2006.12	Namwon National Folk Traditional Music Center performance (twice in Siem Reap, once in Phnom Penh)
2007.02	Gimhae City Gayageum Company performance
2007.08	Percussion group Gongmyeong performance celebrating the 10th anniversary of resumption of diplomatic ties
2007.10	2nd Korea Film Festival
2007.12	Baby V.O.X concert
2007.12	Gangneung Dano Festival Team participates in Cambodia Traditional Folk Dance Festival
2008.10	3rd Korea Film Festival (*The Romantic President, Barking Dogs Don't Bite, Best Chef, The Host*)
2008.11	Gyeonggi Province Traditional Dance Company performance
2009.11	4th Korea Film Festival
2010.04	2010 "Footsteps of Civilization" event, Jeongdong Theater Dance Company traditional performance
2010.10	Cambodia Rainbow Association hosts Korean musicians invitational concert (Cambodia, Awakening the World)
2010.11	Imsil Pilbong Farmers' Band performance
2010.11	Korea Food Trade Association hosts Korean Food Bazaar in Cambodia
2010.12	6th ICAPP traditional shaman performance "Land of Festivals"
2010.12	5th Korea Film Festival
2011.01	Beautiful Mind charity concerts at five schools in Phnom Penh and neighboring areas
2011.02	Cambodia Rainbow Association hosts Korean musicians invitational concert (Cambodia, Awakening the World II)

people dancing to K-pop at Hun Sen Park and at Riverside. Korean dramas are also widely popular. Nearly all local stations air Korean dramas.

In a survey asking Cambodian high school students which country they would like to visit, Korea and Japan were cited as the most desired destinations. The Korean dream is alive and well. An increase in cross-border marriages

Table 3–21. Inbound tourists from four countries with top growth rate (Unit: persons)

	2006	2010	Growth Rate
Thailand	72,278	217,739	178%
Vietnam	36,680	91,428	149%
China	740,201	1,708,561	131%
Indonesia	29,002	60,772	110%

(Source: Ministry of Justice Immigration Statistics)

Table 3–22. Level of favorable perception of Korea

	Major Countries (Rank)
High	**Indonesia** (1) Russia (2) **Thailand** (3) **Vietnam** (6) **Saudi Arabia** (7) **Egypt** (8) **Mexico** (10)
Medium	**Turkey** (12) India (14) South Africa (15) **Brazil** (16) **China** (18) Canada (19) Poland (20)
Low	US (22) Australia (23) **France** (24) UK (26) **Taiwan** (28) **Japan** (29) Italy (30)

(Source: Presidential Council on National Branding (2009), "2009 National & Industrial Brand Map for 31 Countries," December)
Note: Key destinations for Korean cultural products are in bold.

means that more Cambodian brides are traveling to Korea. Cambodians show heightened interest in Korea when one family member or more resides there. Korean travel agencies plan medical tourism excursions for Cambodians. Little to no anti-*Hallyu* sentiment exists in Cambodia.

C. Successes and failures of Hallyu in Southeast Asia (pp. 293–296)

K-pop is sweeping Southeast Asia thanks to neo-*Hallyu*, which has in turn led to a sharp increase in the export of Korean cosmetics, accessories, women's wear, cell phones, and specialty goods.

Korean tourism statistics over the past five years show that visitors from Southeast Asia increased after 2005, when *Hallyu* began taking these countries by storm; people from the region tend to have an extremely positive impression of Korea. Visitors from Thailand, Vietnam, China, and Indonesia in particular doubled.

Vietnam

When Korean dramas flooded the Vietnamese airwaves from 2000 to 2005, some viewers expressed concern over what they viewed as a "cultural invasion." Broadcasters subsequently adjusted their schedules. The government also tightened regulations. In early 2005, Vietnam's Ministry of Culture and Information ordered a 50% quota for Vietnamese dramas, and soon after, HTV began producing shows locally.

Truong Van Minh, the head of programming at HTV, stated that many viewers have tired of Korean drama plotlines and that Vietnamese dramas have been replacing them. He went on to remark that public opinion has begun calling for the protection of Vietnamese culture and opposition to foreign influence. He cited these factors as reasons for the decrease in Korean programming; in fact, HTV also cut back on its import of Korean dramas. For *Hallyu* to continue, it must extend its reach to other areas like technology, electronics, food, music, and sports. Although KBS and CJ Entertainment have established ties with Vietnamese partners by offering training and the like, Truong stressed the need for stronger collaboration with a clear purpose between Korean and Vietnamese TV networks and an increase in program import and export as well as co-productions.

Korean companies with capital, technology, and experience should proactively assess investment in Vietnam. With such investment, *Hallyu* can localize itself within Vietnam, which will both keep the essence of *Hallyu* alive and respect Vietnam's identity. As a result, *Hallyu* can grow and a sustainable win-win relationship for the two countries will eventuate

Myanmar

Despite governmental control, increased awareness of freedom and capitalism in Myanmar has been palpable and has been inspiring the younger generation to shed older traditions. Myanmar society is now eager to create wealth and engage in commercial activities. Satellite broadcasts and foreign dramas have rendered the youth more open in their thinking. Fewer wear the traditional *longyi*, and many cultural and business activities now resemble Western norms. Since the broadcast of *Autumn Tales* in 2002, at least four Korean dramas have been offered weekly on Myanmar television, which has led to an environment conducive to Korean investment.

Popularity of "Gangnam Style" in Southeast Asia

PSY's "Gangnam Style" has become immensely popular with fans around the world. According to a report by Jeong Gang-hyeon and Lee Hyeon for *Joongang Ilbo*, the song's video had recorded 100 million views on *YouTube* by September 3, 2012, drawing users from 220 countries. Of the total 100,155,923 views, Americans had watched the most (19,366,054 views), even more than Koreans (17,062,827 views). Next came Thailand (8,976,791) and Malaysia (6,791,181). "Gangnam Style" recorded fewer *YouTube* views in Japan (967,901/20th) and China (2,785/128th), although *Hallyu* is strong in both. This statistic is telling, as Japanese users watched the most K-pop videos on *YouTube* globally in 2011, with 423,683,759 views.

Lee Taek-gwang, a professor of Anglo-American literature and culture at Kyunghee University, reasoned, "Asian fans want to enjoy the sophistication of K-pop, but PSY broke the rules with a deliberately nonconformist, cheesy and vulgar look. This look, however, appealed to North American and European fans, who preferred the style PSY affected to a more sophisticated feel." PSY's popularity in Thailand and Malaysia was rather unexpected. As Lee states, "In some cases, countries hostile towards American culture prefer Korean pop culture. For these viewers, PSY's accessible look and humorous video lowered barriers to access."

3.3.2. *Hallyu* Grips Phnom Penh

Reference: "Vietnam/Cambodia 17-day trip: *Hallyu* Grips Phnom Penh," Wander Lust, Naver Blog, July 13, 2013.

I woke up early one morning and headed to Phnom Penh, a journey of roughly six to seven hours from Siem Reap. Sinh Cafe, my constant travel partner, is where I caught the bus. We arrived in Phnom Penh, had lunch, and then found a guesthouse.

<text omitted>

For dinner, I ate the noodles I'd had in Siem Reap yesterday. Street stalls line the park entrance. I decided to have a simple dinner there. Of course, MSG is apparently my favorite flavor. (Smiley face emoticon) After I ate, I was watching the crowd when I heard the sounds of a song. At first I thought the music was to accompany people doing light calisthenics like the Chinese do, and I went over for a look.

But all of a sudden I wondered, "Is that PSY's 'Gentleman'?!" About 30 people had perfectly memorized the choreography for "Gentleman," and it was amazing! (Smiley face emoticons) They weren't just moving to the beat, they were dancing exactly like in the video. At first I figured, "Okay, PSY is a superstar, so no wonder he is popular in Cambodia, too." But the next song was 4 minute's "What's Your Name?" Then came stuff like TEEN TOP's "The Girl with Long Hair," CL's "Bad Girl," followed by U-Kiss, Super Junior, Wonder Girls, and FX ... About 2/3 of the songs were Korean, and they were new ones too!!!

There were a lot of people watching, and some even started dancing along. The choreography was too hard for me to follow, but they were all dancing in sync, move by move. I was eating a snack and watching, and an "instructor" was showing the moves. Everyone was following this leader. It seemed like they danced this way every day. They were all dancing without even having to look at the instructor. The ones dancing along in back looked as if they were paying a fee for the "class," like to cover the cost of the streetlights.

Depending on who you ask, it's Cambodian youth culture. As I watched them dancing along to Korean songs I felt proud.

Later, when "Gangnam Style" played, even more people joined the crowd and danced. Of course I had to join! They all knew I was Korean and welcomed me warmly. Even though I'm a terrible dancer, I tried my best. LOL.

Maybe it was all the intense dancing and watching, but afterward I felt like having a snack of corn in sauce. I ate it with beer. Two hours later, they were still dancing. LOL. They were really something!

<text omitted>

I was totally surprised today seeing how Korean pop culture has taken over Phnom Penh. I'd seen *Hallyu* in places like Taiwan, China, and Thailand, but that day, I think seeing it in a much poorer country like Cambodia put a little spring in my step.

3.3.3. A Vietnamese Bride's Country Diary

Reference: "Vietnamese Bride Dinh Thi Nguyen's Country Diary: Happy to Be Able to Watch Any Korean TV Drama Any Time," *Weekly Chosun*, Kim Kyung-soo, No. 1954, May 14, 2007.

Why are Korean men so into sports? My husband is always jumping up from his seat when he watches games. I don't get what's so exciting. I'd rather watch a drama. Korean dramas capture what it's like to be a woman. They help a woman cry when she needs to, and to laugh when she's in a good mood.

Lots of Korean dramas are on Vietnamese TV. I called home recently and they told me *Jumong* is on these days. Not many houses in the Vietnamese countryside have TV, so four or five families get together to watch. Sometimes there's only one television in a village. The whole village might gather.

My family back home has no television or computer. Few families in the countryside in Vietnam have computers. I used to go to an Internet café in town to watch Korean dramas, which were available online. Time flew when I'd watch them. Internet places charge around 3,000 dong per hour, about ₩200, and that is a lot of money in the countryside. A family lives on roughly ₩100,000 a month. The cost of living is about ₩3,000 a day. Drama episodes are an hour long or so and cost around ₩200 per episode. Since a series has around 20 episodes, you need about ₩4,000 to see the whole thing. Only people with some money can watch dramas.

Jewel in the Palace was on Vietnamese TV many times. A lot of Vietnamese men will tell you that just watching Lee Young-ae puts them in a good mood. Vietnamese dramas don't have much variety and aren't very entertaining. In the past, the war was the subject of most dramas. These days, more dramas are about family and love. I was fond of *The River of Our Home* starring Cong Boong and *My Childhood Memories* starring Thuy Em. But Vietnamese dramas can't compete with Korean ones. If I watch one episode of a Korean drama, I feel like I have to see the next one.

Song Il-guk is becoming more popular in Vietnam these days, but Bae Yong-joon, from *First Love* and *Winter Sonata*, is the most popular by far. He's not as good-looking as my husband, though! Rain held a concert in Ho Chi Minh City not too long ago. He's popular too. Actors and singers from Korea are really good-looking. That's probably why Korean men are so popular in Vietnam.

A lot of the Vietnamese women who come to Korea as brides have been influenced by Korean dramas. They watch and develop fantasies about Korea. They think Korean guys must be good-looking and kind like the men in dramas. Many women marry Koreans for that reason, but sometimes they return home heartbroken after learning that their hopes were just fantasies. In the town where I grew up, girls dream of marrying Korean guys and living there. I don't think it's a good thing for people to create too grand a fantasy of Korea based on dramas. People have to understand reality. I've been lucky, and I'm satisfied with my life, but a few of my friends who came to Korea had trouble with their husbands and ended up returning to Vietnam with nothing to show for their trouble but scars.

I watched every single episode of *Witch Yoo Hee,* starring Han Ga-in, and *Hello, My Lady!* with Lee Da-hae. Han Ga-in is very pretty. These days I'm watching *High Kick.* It's very funny. The way the head of the family behaves is so bizarre. He's quite awkward, but that makes the show more interesting. I don't know how such a proper-looking man can act so silly. Sometimes I laugh so hard tears come from my eyes.

Actually, I think my husband is pleased that my Korean is getting better from watching dramas. I'm suspicious that he may have bought me a TV just so I could learn Korean. As I watch, I try hard to memorize the lines of the female leads, and then use them on my husband when he comes home from work. He's surprised a lot. Once I saw one give a big smile and say to a male character, "You've had a long day. You must have been eager to see me." This delighted him, and he hugged her tightly. When my husband came home, I said, "You've had a long day. You must have been eager to see me." My husband was very amused. Once when he came home from work I said "*Yeombyeonghal!*" ("Bloody hell!"). I was fooling around and didn't actually know what it meant, but my husband was shocked. He told me it wasn't a good thing to say. I hear phrases like "*Jaesu eopseo*" ("Jerk") and "*Jegiral!*" ("Dammit!") in dramas all the time. One by one, my husband is teaching me which phrases are inappropriate. But if they're inappropriate, why do the actors get these lines so often?

I like dramas so much. My husband subscribed to a TV service that lets me download any episode I want at any time. It's amazing. The TV screen is wonderfully big, and the face of the main character is larger than our baby. When my husband goes to work, I can pick whatever drama I want to watch. My days pass quickly when I watch dramas, cuddling my baby in my arms and eating snacks. Thank you, dear husband!

Din Thi Nguyen was born in 1988 in Haiphong, Vietnam and raised there. She met her husband, Kim Bo-sung, in 2006, at the age of 18, and now resides in Yangji-ri, Onam-eup, Namyangju City in Gyeonggi Province.

3.3.4.   The Truth behind *Hangeul* and the Cia-Cia?

Reference: "The Truth behind *Hangeul* and the Cia-Cia?" *Hankook Ilbo*, Kim Beom-su and Jeon Su-hyeon, October 18, 2012.

Kim Hye-seon, Director of the Korean Language Policy Division, MCST:
"The phrase 'adoption as the official script' is inaccurate... It can potentially create diplomatic friction."

Prof. Lee Ho-young, Dept. of Linguistics, Seoul National University:
"*Hangeul* is accepted as the script for writing the local indigenous language... Bahasa Indonesia is the sole official language."

On the 18th of this month, *Hankook Ilbo* ran a cover story on Korean textbooks containing incorrect information about the adoption of *hangeul* as the official script of the Cia-Cia ethnic group. That same day, the MCST held an official press briefing about the report. Kim Hye-seon, Director of the Korean Language Policy Division, pointed out that the phrase "official adoption" is inaccurate and may "potentially create diplomatic friction." Prof. Lee Ho-young of Seoul National University, who led the introduction of *hangeul* to the Cia-Cia, said in a telephone interview that the Hunmin

Jeongeum Society never used the term "official alphabet." Below is the truth of the "introduction of *hangeul* to the Cia-Cia," according to interviews with Ms. Kim and Prof. Lee.

Kim Hye-seon, Director of the Korean Language Policy Division, Ministry of Culture, Sports, and Tourism

Q: Has *hangeul* been adopted as the official script for Cia-Cia?

A: It is safe to say that *hangeul* is being taught, but to say "adopted" is inaccurate. The position of the Ministry of Foreign Affairs is that if the Korean media claim that the Cia-Cia have adopted our alphabet, Indonesia may find it a diplomatic issue, although Indonesia has not called it into question for fear of upsetting relations with South Korea.

Q: What is the official position of the Indonesian government?

A: They have expressed repeatedly that language, spoken and written, is an issue of national identity. Therefore, they stress that *hangeul* has not been officially adopted. Just as Korean, written in *hangeul*, is South Korea's official language, Indonesian law stipulates that "all ethnic languages should be transcribed in the Roman alphabet." While the Indonesian Embassy in Seoul has not filed an official complaint with us, this problem could turn into a diplomatic issue if it persists.

Q: What are some of the Indonesian government's concerns?

A: Indonesia is a multiethnic society, and unity is a crucial issue. The country is concerned that if one ethnic group begins using a different alphabet to form special ties with another country, others might follow suit.

Q: How was the introduction of *hangeul* possible under such circumstances?

A: When the Hunmin Jeongeum Society entered the town of Bau-Bau, it offered to establish a Korean language cultural center. This promise was not fulfilled, which ultimately led to the city severing its relationship with the society. Bau-Bau's internal politics played a role in this result. The end of this year also marks the end of the mayoral term. There are rumors that the current mayor will run for governor and his brother will run for mayor, which is what one Indonesian official was speaking of when he hinted at political motivations (in other words, that the mayor sought Korean support as a political base).

Q: Was the Korean government involved?

A: The government was not involved from the beginning. The government only established the Sejong Institute and dispatched employees to disseminate the Korean language.

Q: How about the situation in the Solomon Islands?

A: *Hangeul* is used as a script for indigenous languages that do not have their own alphabet, but an official script is stipulated by law. The pilot project on the Solomon Islands to teach *hangeul* was completely misrepresented by certain members of the Korean media, which reported that Korean had been "officially adopted as the mother tongue." Language and script need to be distinguished.

Prof. Lee Ho-young, Department of Linguistics, Seoul National University

Q: Is it true that *hangeul* was not adopted as the official script of the Cia-Cia?

A: From the initial stories in 2009, most of the Korean media reported that *hangeul* had been adopted as an "official script." We [the Hunmin Jeongeum Society] never used the term "official script." At the time, it was explained that we began "introducing and teaching *hangeul*." After the reports, we pointed out to reporters [that the articles were misleading]. The inaccuracy of the reports was discussed within the Society.

Q: Do you mean to say that the Cia-Cia people are not using *hangeul*?

A: The phrase "official script" is tendentious. The term, which media reports adopted, is rarely used. There is only an "official language" designated by law. Indonesia's official language is Bahasa Indonesia and nothing else. The Cia-Cia tribe chose *hangeul* as the script for their ethnic language. Using the term "ethnic script" would not have raised issues. Calling it the "official script" was problematic.

Q: The term "official script" was used in Korean textbooks...

A: It would have been responsible to correct this point from the get go.

Q: Did the Cia-Cia have no writing system of their own?

A: The Cia-Cia language has rarely been written down. A document mentions the language as being transcribed in Arabic script in the 15th and 16th centuries. The Roman alphabet was once used to record the names of people and festivals. Cia-Cia speakers have not documented their native tongue in writing.

Q: Can you elaborate on the MOU between Bau-Bau and the Hunmin Jeongeum Society for the dissemination of *hangeul*?

A: At the time of the MOU, the Hunmin Jeongeum Society asked if there were any potential issues, and Bau-Bau confirmed that there were none, perhaps because the parties involved were not familiar with the law. Thus, the MOU was signed. It turned out later that, in Indonesia, local authorities must seek approval from the central government before concluding an agreement with a foreign entity. The MOU needed to be established through the central government...

Q: Tell us about the Hunmin Jeongeum Society's current activities in Bau-Bau.

A: When the society began the project, the Wonam Cultural Foundation suggested that they would provide ₩450–700 million as an initial investment and then several million annually thereafter. We received ₩30–40 million initially, but the total received at the end of last year was only around ₩100 million. Increasing intervention from the Hunmin Jeongeum Society's chairman of the board, Lee Ki-nam, led me to believe that the project would not succeed, so I left the Society. (Bau-Bau has also severed its relationship with the Hunmin Jeongeum Society). Despite all this, *hangeul* is still being taught at three elementary schools in Bau-Bau for writing Cia-Cia. I am supporting the project independently at the moment.

3.4.   THE AMERICAS

3.4.1.   *Hallyu* Forever: The Americas

Reference: *Hallyu Forever: The World Is Hallyu Style*, Ko Jeong-min et al., KOFICE *Hallyu* Series V, 2012, pp. 378–415.

A.   *The early stages of Hallyu in the Americas*

The year 2012 will mark 109 years since the first Korean immigrants set sail for the US. In 1903, 102 weary, wide-eyed Koreans took their historic first steps on Hawaiian soil. Later generations of diasporic Koreans participated actively in shaping American society into its current form. *Hallyu* in the US first grew out of Korean-American communities, constituting roughly 2.5 million people (in Los Angeles, New York, etc.), which were instrumental in spreading Korean food (kimchi), traditional culture (*hanbok, pansori*), and Korean practices (Buddhism, taekwondo).

From the 1960s, Korean artists in the US included the world-renowned video artist Nam June Paik and the US-born violinist extraordinaire Jang Young-joo (Sarah Chang). Their work led more people to Korean pop culture and the arts. Recently, more Korean actors and musicians have begun working in Hollywood—the heart of the global entertainment industry. Increased export of Korean cultural content has popularized *Hallyu* across the US, although the phenomenon originated in Asia.

Americans now show great interest in Korean traditional culture, food, and pop culture. Korean food is touted as healthy and nutritious; these days, more customers are frequenting the 1,628 Korean restaurants in the US. Approximately 5 million Americans train at 22,600 taekwondo academies across the country, where they can learn about Korean values. Interest in Korean traditional culture has boosted sales of packaged tours like "temple stays."

In the late 1990s, *Hallyu* spread to Asian-Americans; from there, it made headway with mainstream American society. Many Korean-Americans now work in American television and cinema, and more Korean celebrities are entering Hollywood, which has contributed to a *Hallyu* boom in the US. Today, Korean film directors (Park Chan-wook, Kang Jae-gyu, Kim Ji-woon, Bong Joon-ho), actors (Kim Yun-jin, An Seong-ki, Lee Byung-hun), and performing artists (Rain) are represented by big US talent agencies such as CAA, William Morris Agency, ICM, and William Morris Endeavor.

PSY's "Gangnam Style" has recently become a *YouTube* sensation and the object of extensive coverage in the US media. His is the first real US success story for a Korean artist. Thus far, the American market has been a challenging frontier. However, the facts that the highest number of *YouTube* hits for "Gangnam Style" came from American viewers and that 40% of American fans of Korean dramas or K-pop are studying Korean indicate that Korean culture has gained ground in this influential market.

It has been 50 years since the first Koreans immigrated to Canada, a nation that is home to many other Asian peoples, in particular Chinese, Indian, and Vietnamese. Prime Minister of Canada Stephen Harper has stated, "Canada's Korean community is contributing to our rich and diverse culture. My government will spare no effort in supporting Korean-Canadians while honoring their traditions and heritage."

Jewel in the Palace and *Winter Sonata* set off a *Hallyu* boom in Canada, beginning in Vancouver and Toronto. In Toronto, hub of Canada's cultural industries, the initial spread of *Hallyu* among ethnic Chinese, the largest immigrant community in Canada, created a favorable environment for the Korean Wave. *Hallyu* vacation packages, triggered by the popularity of *Jewel in the Palace* and later shows like *All In,* evolved as location-specific, rather than program-specific, tours following the success of various dramas. For example, packages are now planned as destination tours to such locales as Jeju Island. In Canada, *Hallyu* began when Korean dramas were broadcast over the Chinese cable TV channel, but later expanded to fields like music and live performances (*Nanta, Jump, B-Boy*). Korean products are expected to remain strong among Chinese-Canadians. The Canadian reality TV star Shayne Orok recently made it to the final three on the Korean show *Star Audition: The Great Birth*, which suggests a level of K-pop penetration among Canadian teenagers. Asian communities in the US and Canada are contributing to the spread of *Hallyu* in their countries, as the phenomenon has outgrown its early stages to the point where it is now a veritable industry.

Meanwhile, the history of Korean immigration to Latin America (Brazil, Mexico, Chile, Argentina, Colombia, etc.) spans roughly 40 years. Early immigrants headed to these countries for economic reasons. Currently, immigrant communities consist of 1.5 and 2nd generation Koreans who have established themselves as leaders of the diaspora community. Brazil has the largest Korean community in Latin America. Korean professionals in Brazil are numerically strong and make significant contributions to society. Mexico has the longest history of Korean immigration in all of Latin America, and the form it has taken is unique. Chile was the first country in Latin America to recognize South Korea diplomatically and is also the bilateral partner in Korea's first free trade agreement. In Argentina, a number of Koreans work actively in the economy as well as other sectors of society, including politics. Argentina's Korean community is an example for others of how to best interact with mainstream society.

In South America, promotion of Korean cultural products started out as an initiative carefully planned by the Korean government. After the 2002 Korea-Japan World Cup, interest in Korean culture and language grew. In 2002, dramas like *All about Eve* and *Stars in My Heart* were broadcast in South America. K-pop has also been recently introduced, and K-pop cover contests are already very popular with the youth. Korean movies, dramas, and language are also widely appreciated by the public.

Brazil, which has accepted immigrants from Korea for 50 years, has some familiarity with our country, and all the more so as Korean corporations have been operating there since 1995. In the beginning, however, little to no interest was paid to Korean culture. Currently, roughly 80% of the 60,000 Koreans in Brazil live in São Paulo, the largest city in South America. Most work in the garment industry. Over 200 Korean companies, including Hyundai, Samsung, LG, and SK, have a presence in Brazil. Brazil's Korean community experienced its early years between 1960 and 1970, grew between 1980 and 2000, and since 2010 has become more established in Brazilian mainstream society. Brazil will take center stage globally when it hosts the FIFA World Cup in 2014 and the Olympics in 2016. In 2012, a taekwondo festival and games event was held, commemorating

42 years of taekwondo in Brazil. Over 1,250 athletes from 24 of the nation's states participated in the event, along with over 200 coaches and staff.

Recently, Korean products, including games, movies, animation, and character goods, have been growing in popularity; educational animation has done especially well. Various Korean cultural events have been held, such as the 6th Festival of Korean Culture, which was attended by over 20,000 Koreans, Brazilians, and immigrants of many ethnicities.

In Mexico, Korean dramas, music, movies (especially comedies), animation, and character goods are popular. Many dedicated fans have taken it upon themselves to learn Korean to enhance their enjoyment. In 2001, the dance game *Pump* was introduced, and in 2002, the drama *All about Eve* was broadcast on Mexican television, leading to growing interest in Korean culture. In Argentina, word has spread that Korean food is low in calories and healthy, having been cooked with ingredients that have been fermented. *Jewel in the Palace* was introduced in 2008 in Peru, followed by *Winter Sonata, Autumn Tales*, and *My Lovely Sam Soon*, which led to growing interest in Korea. The country now has an estimated 60 *Hallyu* fan clubs.

In 2003, actor An Jae-wook became phenomenally popular in South America. Recently, the dramas *Princess Hours* and *The 1st Shop of Coffee Prince* have been broadcast in this region; both star actress Yun Eun-hye, whose fame will likely skyrocket as a result. K-pop groups U-Kiss, JYJ, 4Minute, BEAST, G-Na, and ZE:A have performed in South America, ushering in the resurgence of the Korean Wave. Korean games also have a future in the Americas; a Korean "first-person shooter" game was launched in 20 countries in Latin America. Because South America has experienced explosive growth in its Internet and broadband rollout, and because Spanish is a shared language, foreign companies find it easier to localize products. Korean traditional food and beverages are also popular in the region.

Hallyu in Asia, Europe, and North America began with movies and television and moved on to K-pop. In Latin America, however, the phenomenon followed a different trajectory, with K-pop leading a trend that later led to movies, dramas, food, and the Korean language. *YouTube*, as a platform for music videos, has played a major role in the region in popularizing Korean culture.

According to a 2005 study, Koreans living in Latin America (Brazil, Mexico, Paraguay, and Argentina) had the highest degree of cultural acceptance for the food of their host countries, followed by dance/music, festivals, and national holidays. The younger the immigrants, the more open they were to accepting the adopted culture. These results imply that Korean immigrants serve as a bridge for bilateral exchange and an effective means of introducing Korean culture to local residents. If the Korean community can introduce more Korean food, music, and festivals, local interest in Korean culture will increase.

B. Hallyu after 2010

Hangeul: Korean language

TOPIK, a standardized Korean language exam, drew 2,274 applicants when it was administered for the first time in 1997. In 2012, over 19,000 people took the test, the highest number ever. According to the MCST, enrolments in Korean language classes at King Sejong Institute grew from 4,301 in 2009 to 6,016 in

2010 and to 9,348 in 2011. The total jumps to over 14,000 when students at the Korean Cultural Centers are accounted for. There are four King Sejong Institutes in the US (Los Angeles, New York, San Francisco, and Washington D.C.), one in Canada (Ottawa), two in Mexico, and one each in Peru, Colombia, Chile, Brazil, and Argentina.

41% of *Hallyu* Fans in the US "Learning Korean": Language Study Influencing Korean Food & Product Purchases

When the English-language *Hallyu* website www.soompi.com conducted a survey of 1,569 of its American readers about K-pop and Korean dramas, they found that 41% of respondents came to learn Korean through K-pop and Korean dramas. (*Herald Business Newspaper*, October 16, 2010)

*www.soompi.com was created by Joyce Kim, a second-generation Korean-American. Its membership base is 10% Korean, 50% Asian, and 35% Caucasian and African-American.

Hallyu has thus expanded to the realm of language. As more Korean companies hire local residents and gain an international profile, more and more foreigners are eager to learn *hangeul.*

The Korean Cultural Center in Los Angeles, which opened in 1980, runs a King Sejong Institute. A total of 75% of the earliest students were ethnically Korean, but as of February 2012, 74% were not of Korean descent. In beginner courses, the ratio rises to over 90%. The number of institutes is increasing, from 17 in 6 countries in 2009 to 23 in 12 countries in 2010, 60 in 31 countries in 2011, and 90 in 43 countries in 2012. The plan is to have 160 institutes by 2014 and 200 by 2016 to provide Korean language education to *Hallyu* fans, which will further expand the base for Korean cultural products.

More American primary and secondary schools are offering Korean as well. According to the SAT II Foundation for Korean Language and Culture in the US, 176 Korean language classes were offered in 55 schools nationwide to 4,391 students as of November 2004, an increase of 36 schools from the 19 that were offering Korean classes in 1997. The number of classes has also expanded to 176 classes in those 55 schools, and students have increased from 1,471 to 4,391. Southern California has the most schools with 34, followed by New York (10), Illinois and Washington (3 each), and Connecticut, Maryland, Michigan, New Jersey, and Virginia (1 each). High schools make up the largest share with 34 schools, followed by 10 middle schools, 7 elementary schools, and 4 schools of other types. If Korean becomes an advanced placement course, the number of classes offered at American high schools will likely double.

Although more Korean courses are now offered, they continue to lag behind Japanese (325), Chinese (228), and Spanish (17,060). The Foundation for Korean Language and Culture was established in 1997 in the US as a non-profit organization that works to have Korean included as an official foreign language in US curricula. Korean was the ninth minority language to be approved as an SAT II subject, and the third Asian language after Japanese and Chinese.

In 2012, a system was introduced to allow US middle and high school students to earn Korean course credits with their TOPIK test scores for the first time through an MOU signed between the National Institute for International Education and the Tacoma Board of Education. Korea's Ministry of Education has been promoting projects to include Korean in the curriculum of overseas primary and secondary schools since 1999. Due to these efforts, US schools with Korean in their curricula increased from 57 schools in 2009 to 71 schools in 2010 and 91 schools in 2011. When 10 public schools added Korean in 2011, it brought the total number of public schools to 60.

British Columbia in Canada included Korean in its high school curriculum in September 2006, making it an official language course along with English, French, Spanish, and others. Courses are offered to students from 9th to 12th grade. Brent Koot, the coordinator of the Korean program for the Delta District's Board of Education in Vancouver, has said the following:

> Koreans are very special to Canadian society. Nearly 100,000 live in Vancouver alone. Their potential is limitless. Including Korean as an official subject in the high school curriculum will be a stepping stone for Koreans to engage more closely with Canadian society and to contribute to the international community at large. Korea's very visible economic and cultural role in the era of globalization means that learning Korean will provide second generation Korean-Canadians as well as local Canadian students a necessary internationally competitive edge.

The Korean language has received attention in South America as well, due to the popularity of K-pop and Korean dramas. Brazil has a Korean school with primary and secondary school curricula approved by the Korean Ministry of Education. There are also 26 privately run Korean schools attended by a total of 1,500 students. There is a Korean department at the University of São Paulo, one of the leading universities in Latin America. A total of 302 people took the 24th TOPIK test hosted by the National Institute for International Education and administered by the Korean Education Center in São Paulo; 196 passed, a 65% success rate.

Because Argentina is an influential cultural leader in South America, it was designated as the Latin American site for the Korean Cultural Center in November 2006. More than 90 students take classes at this center's King Sejong Institute; over 70% of them are fans of K-pop and taekwondo. Argentina also has more than 15 online *Hallyu* fan websites with a total of nearly 4,000 members. Lee Jong-ryul, the director of the Korean Cultural Center, remarked in a media interview that, "Argentina, a nation where people of Italian and Spanish ancestry make up the majority of the population, is fiercely proud of its heritage. That Korean culture is so popular in a country that has a relatively low awareness of Asia is a testament to our influence."

Hallyu is clearly witnessing new possibilities in Latin America following its success in Asia, North America, and Europe. According to research conducted by the Ministry of Foreign Affairs through its embassies, 843 *Hallyu* fan clubs operated in 73 countries as of July 2012, with over 6.7 million members. By region Asia had the most fan club memberships (5.12 million members; 355

clubs), followed by North America (1.02 million; 25 clubs), Europe (350,000; 130 clubs), Latin America (180,000; 298 clubs), and Africa and the Middle East (20,000; 35 clubs).

K-food

Four Korean Dishes Make List of World's 50 Most Delicious Foods

(Kimchi 12th, Bulgogi 23rd, Bibimbap 40th, Galbi 41st)

CNN Go asked 35,000 online users to vote for the world's 50 most delicious foods. The winner was Indonesia's rendang and nasi goreng, followed by Japan's sushi and ramen; Thailand's tom yam kung, pad thai, and som tam; Hong Kong's dim sum; China's Peking duck; and Thailand's curry.

Kimchi was reported as one of the five healthiest foods in the world by an American magazine. It has since achieved wide popularity in mainstream US society. PBS produced a 13-part documentary titled *Kimchi Chronicles* to commemorate the Visit Korea Years from 2010 to 2012. The series aired across the US. More US grocery store chains now stock kimchi. The PBS cooking show *Cathlyn's Korean Kitchen* has been extended into its fourth season. Host Cathlyn Choi has explained that while second and third genera-tion Korean-Americans do represent a portion of the program's viewership, over 80% of the viewers are not ethnically Korean. Even New York mayor Michael Bloomberg reportedly frequents the Korean restaurant Kum Gang San in Flushing to satisfy his kimchi cravings. In these ways and more, kim-chi has contributed significantly to creating an image of Korean cuisine as healthy.

Americans see Korean food as traditional and unique as well as affordable and diverse. However, about 54% of survey respondents were not able to name a particular Korean dish, which shows that Korean food does not enjoy a high pro-file in America. There are over 10,000 Korean restaurants internationally, with 1,628 situated in the US. Of these, 41% are in California. Korean restaurants in the US can be classified into five categories: high-end *prix fixe* dining (e.g., Philkyungjae), high-end regular dining (e.g., Woolaeoak), mid-range single-menu dining (e.g., Bon Bibimbap), fast-food dining (e.g., Shin Dan Dong), and snack shops (e.g., Kimbap Cheonguk). Americans typically view Korean food as unique, diverse, healthy, and fortifying.

In December 2011, the Korean Food Foundation conducted a survey of 1,117 people living in New York, the globe's most trend-aware city. It asked them about their awareness of, impressions of, and willingness to buy Korean food. The results showed that impressions of Korean food had improved 9.9% in recent years. Awareness and willingness to buy Korean food had risen 4.3% and 5%, respectively. In the past, Korean food was seen only as a minority cuisine in the US and had little recognition value. In recent years, however, local media outlets such as New York's NBC affiliate, *The New York Times*,

The Wall Street Journal, and others have published over 600 stories with such titles as "Fine Dining Restaurant Jung Sik Offers Exquisite Korean Food" and reviews of the restaurant Danji, which earned a Michelin star. The succession of favorable local reports on the new flavors and possibilities of local Korean restaurants have in turn confirmed the possibility of the globalization of Korean food.

American chef Angelo Sosa, owner of Social Eatz, a popular New York hamburger joint, introduced a *bibimbap* burger to his menu, complete with Korean sauces such as *gochujang* (red pepper paste) and *dwoenjang* (soybean paste). It became so popular that it grew to account for 35% of the restaurant's total sales. The *bibimbap* burger became a hit not only in New York but also across the United States. In fact, it was voted the best American burger in 2011 at the Eater's Greatest Burger in America Contest and was featured on the popular TV program *Top Chef*. In this case, an American chef used a Korea-inspired recipe to capture the fancy of his customers. In April 2011, CJ opened its second Bibigo branch, a restaurant franchise that specializes in *bibimbap*, in Beverly Hills, California.

At the 28th Dallas Morning News and TexSom Wine Competition, one of the three biggest international wine competitions in the US, Kooksoondang's *makgeolli*, a fermented Korean rice liquor, received a medal for the third consecutive year. This *makgeolli* also won the bronze at the San Francisco International Wine Competition in 2010, making it the first Korean *makgeolli* brand to place at an international liquor competition. In 2011, it won a silver medal at the New York International Wine Competition. Kooksoondang's *makgeolli* has sold 250,000 boxes ($4.5 million) since 2010 when it was introduced to the American market. Kooksoondang cites the smooth taste of its *makgeolli* and its richness in organic lactic acid bacteria as reasons for its success.

Of the 21 countries in Latin America, 10 have Korean restaurants, with 58 in Brazil, 45 in Argentina, and 7 each in Chile and Peru, bringing the total to 132. Korean cuisine is gaining in popularity as more people recognize it as healthy food. Korean restaurants are generally located in capital cities or metropolitan areas; all 58 of Brazil's Korean restaurants are in São Paulo. In 2008, Argentina hosted a night of Korean traditional food and culture that introduced Korean food as a healthy alternative to Argentinian cuisine, which is heavily dependent on beef. Over 1,200 participants gathered at the event. With the growing popularity of K-pop in Latin America, more Korean restaurants, as well as Korean language schools, have opened in this part of the world.

A total of 41,000 Chinese restaurants and 11,000 Japanese restaurants operate in the United States. These popular ethnic restaurants typically provide hybrid, localized offerings of foreign cuisines. Sometimes restaurants have worked together as an industry to change the image that US consumers have of their food. In this way, they have attempted to strategically position their brand and image in the US market. Mexican food in particular is widely enjoyed across the US, thanks to its large Mexican population and the simple deliciousness of its food. Of the Hispanic population in the US, 60% are Mexican. Roughly 20% of the 13 million workers in the restaurant industry in the US are Mexican.

Music: K-pop

> World is Transfixed by K-Pop: From Idol Groups to Chubby PSY
> "K-pop, along with mobile phones and IT, becomes a leading symbol of Korea" (CNBC, July 17, 2012)
> "Gangnam Style has taken over the US" (Billboard, September 27, 2012)
> "PSY ranked 39th among the 49 most influential men of 2012" (askmen.com, October 10, 2012)

Korean recording artists who entered the US music market include solo acts (Rain, BoA, SE7EN, Im Jeong-hui), groups (Wonder Girls, Girls' Generation, 2 NE1, Big Bang), and producer/artists who specialize in rap, reggae, and hip-hop (JYP, Stony Skunk, PSY). Korean artists and management companies have invested immense effort into breaking into the US market, and with a growing acceptance of Asian musicians, the prospects for Korean music and artists have improved.

Singaporean news website *asiaone.com* designated Rain as "Asia's Justin Timberlake" and BoA as "Asia's Britney Spears," and called Wonder Girls "Korea's retro-styled pop sensation." Rain became the first Asian artist to perform at New York's Madison Square Garden. BoA, for her part, released a digital single in the US titled "Eat You Up" in 2008 through SM USA. This single went to #2 on the US iTunes dance music chart and #8 on the Billboard Hot Dance/Club Play chart. With their hit "Nobody," Wonder Girls reached #76 on the Billboard Hot 100 and performed as the opening act 48 times for the Jonas Brothers on their North American tour. The girls even appeared on Wendy Williams' syndicated talk show. In May 2010, their *Different Tears* album rose to #21 on the Billboard Heatseekers Album chart, a Billboard spinoff that ranks new artists. On October 5, 2012, Wonder Girls became the first Korean act to perform a solo show on I Heart Radio, the largest Internet radio platform in the US. This performance was broadcast live across the country through 70 major radio stations' websites. Korean idol groups are thus expanding their presence through *YouTube* and concerts in major American cities.

On March 12, 2011, Big Bang reached #7 on the Heatseekers Album chart and #3 on the World Album chart. Over 24,000 spectators came to their Alive Galaxy Tour 2012, and the band completed the most successful tour of the Americas for a K-pop act yet, with the last leg of the concert held in Peru. Jay Park's first studio album, *New Breed,* went to #4 on Billboard's World Album chart, and Ailee won 2011's Best Performance Video on a-Tunes, a site devoted to Asian-American music. From 2010, SM Entertainment staged concerts featuring its artists (TVXQ, Girls' Generation, Super Junior, SHINee, f(x), and BoA) in locations such as Los Angeles, New York, and Anaheim. The splinter group Girls' Generation-TTS released the album *Twinkle,* which got to #126 on the Billboard 200. Billboard, a definitive voice in the US music industry, launched a K-pop chart in 2011 to provide its own rankings of Korean music.

Girl group 2 NE1, cited by the US rock band Redd Kross as a talented up-and-coming young ensemble, held the first leg of their first global tour—the New

Evolution Tour—at New Jersey's Prudential Center before 7,000 fans. The Prudential Center has served as a concert venue for world-class acts like Lady Gaga, Bon Jovi, the Eagles, and Sting. 2 NE1 successfully completed their first solo concert less than a year after winning the title of best new band in 2011 on MTV IGGY. They wrapped up their US tour at the Nokia Theater in Los Angeles and visited *Facebook* headquarters to appear on a live interview show on "Facebook Live" and meet fans.

PSY's "Gangnam Style" was uploaded to *YouTube* on July 15, 2012. As of November 22, 2012, it had received over one billion hits. The video is the most watched in the world, and achieved this staggering record in a mere 160 days. During the 11-day inclusive period from September 20 to September 30 alone, 2,468 videos related to "Gangnam Style" were uploaded to *YouTube*, which themselves together drew an additional 1,128,155,683 hits. Of these, 1,227 videos were parodies and 742 were covers or flash mob videos. More specifically, 624 were parodies made by Korean users and 603 by international users, while 98 were covers by Korean fans and 161 covers by overseas fans; 342 were flash mob videos, and 396 were TV broadcasts or other related videos. The US uploaded the most parodies and flash mob videos. This derivative content from around the world has drawn over 600 million hits and 6 times more views than the Korean user-generated content. All this offers strong evidence that "Gangnam Style" has spread beyond the US to become a worldwide phenomenon, watched and loved by fans across the globe.

After "Gangnam Style" became a *YouTube* sensation, American media outlets such as CNN, the *LA Times,* ABC, and *The Wall Street Journal* featured articles on the video and artist, and on August 15, 2012, *Time* magazine featured PSY in its cover story. On July 1, 2012, CNBC, one of three major terrestrial networks in the US, featured a special report titled "Move Over, Bieber—Korean Pop Music Goes Global." In the report, it described how K-pop had infused Korean elements into the established genres of American pop, hip-hop, R&B, and European electronic music. ABC reported that "'Gangnam Style' is surprisingly popular across the US and is spawning numerous parodies." The UK's *Daily Mail* also reported online that "this chubby Korean rapper has become more popular than Justin Bieber." *Forbes* described PSY as a fun, charismatic star with easy, catchy dance moves and readily translatable lyrics that everyone can sing along to.

After "Gangnam Style" became the next "Macarena" sensation, PSY signed a deal with Justin Bieber's management company to establish a solid presence in the US market. "Gangnam Style" was featured not only on the MTV Video Music Awards, but also on the *Ellen DeGeneres Show*, the *NBC Today Show*, *Saturday Night Live*, *Jimmy Kimmel Live*, the MTV European Music Awards, the American Music Awards, and a host of other popular US TV programs.

A Billboard magazine cover story described "Gangnam Style" as having "invaded the US" and stressed that PSY came prepared for the fame. "Gangnam Style" debuted at #64 on September 13, 2012, on the Billboard Hot 100 chart and one week later had shot to #11. The following week, it catapulted to #2, where it stayed for seven consecutive weeks. "Gangnam Style" was the first Korean language pop song to make the Billboard Top 100. PSY has done something that no Asian artist had done before. "Gangnam Style" also landed on the Billboard Digital Songs chart, the Billboard Social 50 chart, and the Billboard On-Demand

Table 3–23.   "Gangnam Style" on the world's music charts

2012 Weekly Chart	Top Rank	2012 Weekly Chart	Top Rank
Australia (ARIA)	1	US Rap Songs (Billboard)	1
Austria (O3 Austria Top 40)	1	Mexico (Monitor Latino)	1
Belgium (Ultratop 50 Flanders)	1	Switzerland (Schweizer Hitparade)	1
Canada (Canadian Hot 100)	1	Sweden (Sverigetopplistan)	2
Czech Republic (IFPI)	1	Poland (Top 5 Video Airplay)	2
Denmark (Tracklisten)	1	US Billboard Hot 100	2
Europe (Euro Digital Songs)	1	Belgium (Ultratop 40 Wallonia)	3
Finland (Suomen Viralinen Lista)	1	Iceland (Tonlist)	3
France (SNEP)	1	Ireland (IRMA)	2
Germany (Media Control AG)	1	Spain (PROMUSICAE)	3
Greece Digital Songs (Billboard)	1	Italy (FIMI)	4
Honduras (Honduras Top 50)	1	Russia (2M)	6
Israel (Media Forest)	1	Colombia (National-Report)	6
Lebanon (Lebanese Top 20)	1	Slovakia (IFPI)	9
Luxembourg (Billboard)	1	US Hot Dance Club Songs (Billboard)	6
Mexican Airplay Chart (Billboard)	1	US Pop Songs (Billboard)	10
Netherlands (Single Top 100)	1	Japan (Billboard Japan Hot 100)	20
New Zealand (RIANZ)	1	Hungary (Radios Top 40)	8
Norway (VG-lista)	1	US Latin Songs (Billboard)	14
Portugal Digital Songs (Billboard)	1	US Adult Pop Songs (Billboard)	34
Scotland (Official Charts Company)	1	Venezuela Top 100 (Record Report)	49
UK Singles (Official Charts Company)	1	Romania (Romanian Top 100)	60

(Source: Wikipedia)

Songs chart. It also topped the Billboard K-Pop Hot 100 chart, reached #6 on the Billboard Dance/Club Play Songs chart, and #12 on the Billboard Radio chart.

"Gangnam Style" made it to #1 in 37 of the 52 countries with an iTunes music video chart. As of this writing, it had reached #2 or #3 in an additional eight countries. Wikipedia also has a page devoted to "Gangnam Style," explaining the song's concept and the larger phenomenon. According to Wikipedia, "Gangnam Style" has achieved a #1 ranking in over 20 countries, including the UK, Finland, Denmark, New Zealand, and Canada.

The United Cube Concert, the first K-pop concert in South America, featured the bands BEAST, 4Minute, and G-Na, and was held in 2011 in Brazil. The daily newspaper *Estado de S. Paulo* reported that "K-pop enjoys a popularity that is overtaking world pop." REDE TV, which introduced K-pop to Brazil, reported on the 4,000 fans who flocked to the concert. In March 2012, JYJ became the first Korean band to tour Santiago, Chile and Lima, Peru. Chile's influential channel Mega News and the publication *La Tercera* described JYJ as popular not only in Asia but across the world. Their description ran in an article under the headline, "First South American Concert by Korean Artist." Over 6,000 fans stampeded to the Lima concert, and the local newspaper *El Comercio* reported that the popularity of JYJ rivaled Britney Spears.

A K-pop competition has been hosted for the last three years in Latin America; in fact, K-pop is now part of its regional popular culture. A total of 281 participants came to the first competition in 2010, and 407 came in 2011. In 2012, the number dropped to 339 once Mexico had its own Korean Cultural Center. While K-pop is popular in Brazil, Korean hip-hop by artists such as Tiger JK and Yun Mi-rae also has a large following.

Clarin, the newspaper with the highest circulation in Argentina, recently featured a four-page spread on the "K-Pop Wave in Argentina," while news channel C5 N described K-pop as a "trend that has conquered the world." *Hallyu Chingu,* a leading online community devoted to the Korean Wave, was formed in Argentina; in Brazil as well, *Hallyu* clubs are growing fast. After the first ever Brazilian K-pop flash mob gathered in downtown São Paulo, effort was put into publishing a magazine on Korean concerts, movies, history, food, and language. K-Pop Argentina, a K-pop fan club, regularly organizes flash mobs involving around 300 to 400 fans in downtown Buenos Aires.

That PSY's "Gangnam Style" made it to #14 on the Billboard Latin Airplay chart shows that the song has received radio and TV airplay usually reserved for Mexican and Latin rhythms.

Movies

In the 2000s, Korean movies enjoyed a boom in the US market with films that were either planned for wide release in major theaters, or produced for the independent market. Examples of the former include *D-War* (2007), *Warrior's Way* (2010), and *The Last Godfather* (2011); examples of the latter include *Never Forever* (2007), *American Zombie* (2008), and *West 32nd* (2007).

Chinese (and Hong Kong) films make up the bulk of Asian movies that have achieved box office success in the US, with *Crouching Tiger, Hidden Dragon* the only movie to draw revenues over $100 million. In fact, 15 of the 20 most popular Asian films in the US have been Chinese. Korean films *D-War* and *Warrior's Way*

Table 3–24. "Gangnam Style" in the US

July 15	PSY releases official music video for "Gangnam Style" on his *YouTube* channel
August 3	Major US media outlets cover the video, beginning with CNN and the *LA Times*
August 15	US weekly magazine *Time* features "Gangnam Style"
August 21	"Gangnam Style" lands on top of the US iTunes music video chart
August 22	PSY's appears on VH1's *Big Morning Buzz Live*
August 27	"Gangnam Style" lands at #65 on the US iTunes Realtime Top Songs chart
August 31	"Gangnam Style" makes it to #1 on the Billboard Social Chart 50
September 1	"Gangnam Style" becomes the most watched K-pop music video on *YouTube* (record formerly held by Girls' Generation's GEE)
September 4	PSY signs deal with Scooter Braun, Justin Bieber's manager
September 4	"Gangnam Style" receives 100 million *YouTube* hits (first ever for a Korean artist)
September 6	PSY makes an appearance at the MTV Music Video Awards 2012 (MTV's annual awards ceremony, equivalent to the Grammy Awards or the Academy Awards for the youth, with approximately 6.13 million viewers)
September 7	ABC's *Nightline* reports on "Gangnam Style"
September 10	PSY appears on NBC's *The Ellen DeGeneres Show* (with reappearance on September 19)
September 10	PSY appears on KIIS FM Radio's *On Air with Ryan Seacrest*
September 12	ABC's *Good Morning America* releases special report "Gangnam Style's Flash Mobs" (*Good Morning America* is a news program broadcast live from a studio in New York's Times Square)
September 13	"Gangnam Style" debuts at #64 on the Billboard Hot 100 (the first Korean song to make it to the Hot 100, which considers all of Billboard's singles charts)
September 14	PSY appears on NBC's *Today Live Show*
September 15	"Gangnam Style" lands at #1 on the iTunes chart, a first for K-pop
September 15	PSY appears on NPR
September 15	PSY appears on NBC's *Saturday Night Live*
September 15	PSY appears on NBC's *Extra* (entertainment info program)
September 17	PSY appears on E!'s *Chelsea Lately* (late night talk show)
September 18	"Gangnam Style" surpasses 200 million views on *YouTube*
September 20	*Harvard Business Review* analyzes brand marketing, citing "Gangnam Style" as a case study
September 21	"Gangnam Style" lands at #11 on the Billboard Hot 100
September 21	PSY appears on the iHeart Radio Music Festival

(Continued)

Table 3–24. *(Continued).*

September 24	*Time* puts "Gangnam Style" on the cover
September 27	"Gangnam Style" lands at #2 on Billboard Hot 100
September 30	"Gangnam Style" surpasses 300 million views on *YouTube* 76 days after its release (world record for shortest time this milestone was achieved)
October 1	"Gangnam Style" reaches #1 on UK Singles Chart: First Asian artist to achieve this record six weeks after "Gangnam Style" entered the charts
October 2	PSY appears on ABC's *Jimmy Kimmel Live* (live performance on this popular talk show)
October 3	"Gangnam Style" keeps #2 spot for 2 weeks in a row on Billboard Top 100
October 4	"Gangnam Style" enters *YouTube*'s Most Viewed Videos Top 10 list
October 7	"Gangnam Style" surpasses 400 million hits on *YouTube* (number 9 on the list of most searched videos)
October 11	"Gangnam Style" reaches #1 on China's *Baidu* Chart 100
October 12	"Gangnam Style" holds #2 spot on Billboard Hot 100 for 3 weeks
October 12	"Gangnam Style" lands at #1 on Billboard Rap Songs chart
October 23	"Gangnam Style" holds #2 spot on Billboard Hot 100 for 5 weeks
Late October	"Gangnam Style" reaches #1 on the iTunes music video chart in 37 out of 52 countries
November 2	"Gangnam Style" passes 600 million hits on *YouTube* (second most watched video ever)
November 7	"Gangnam Style" holds #2 spot on Billboard Hot 100 for 7 weeks
November 9	"Gangnam Style" receives the highest number of "likes" for a *YouTube* video with 5 million "likes" (makes Guinness Book of World Records for most "liked" video)
November 11	"Gangnam Style" surpasses 700 million views on *YouTube*
November 12	"Gangnam Style" receives best video award at the MTV European Music Awards 2012
November 14	"Gangnam Style" lands at #5 on the US Billboard Hot 100
November 15	"Gangnam Style" receives 2012 New Media Award at the 40th American Music Awards
November 24	"Gangnam Style" surpasses 800 million views on *YouTube*
November 30	"Gangnam Style" receives Song of the Year award and Best Music Video award at MAMA 2012
December 2	"Gangnam Style" surpasses 900 million views on *YouTube*
December 10	PSY gives special performance at the White House for President Obama
December 22	"Gangnam Style" surpasses one billion views on *YouTube* (most searched video ever on *YouTube*)

Table 3–25.   "Gangnam Style" in South America

August 29	"Gangnam Style" is featured in Argentina's largest daily, *Clarin*
August 30	Argentina's terrestrial network TV Telefe's entertainment program *AM* features "Gangnam Style" (the show's average ratings of 7–8% surged to 10.5% when "Gangnam Style" was played)
September 6	"Gangnam Style" reaches #1 on the Chile iTunes music video chart
September 12	Mexican daily *El Universal* reports on "Gangnam Style"
September 15	"Gangnam Style" reaches #1 on Brazil's iTunes downloads chart
September 17	*Excelsior*, a Mexican daily, reports on "Gangnam Style"
September 20	Mexican daily *Reforma* carries coverage on the "Gangnam Style" craze in the US and an introduction to PSY for Mexican readers
September 21	"Gangnam Style" reaches #1 on Mexico's iTunes downloads chart
September 23	Brazil's newspaper *Folha de S. Paulo* reports on PSY
September 24	"Gangnam Style" reaches #1 on Mexico's Alpha Radio chart
September 25	Brazilian newspaper *O Estado de S. Paulo* introduces "Gangnam Style" and Gangnam district
September 25	"Gangnam Style" reaches #1 on the iTunes chart of 15 Latin American countries including Argentina, Chile, Colombia, and Costa Rica
November 2	Argentina's largest newspaper, *Clarin*, features the "horse dance"

also made the list. Over 20 Korean movies have been sold to the US; on average 4 are distributed through US theaters annually. Marketing for these Korean films centers primarily on the director, i.e., on names such as Kim Ki-duk, Hong Sang-soo, Park Chan-wook, and Bong Joon-ho. The films include art-house movies and genre flicks. Korean films are distributed primarily by LA CGV, with Lotte also seeking to open a theater in the US, which will allow for broader screening of Korean releases.

Several Korean movies have enjoyed a general release in the US, such as *D-War* and *Warrior's Way*. *D-War*, produced and distributed for the US market in 2007, opened widely across theaters. It currently ranks at the top in box office sales for a Korean film. *Warrior's Way,* Jang Dong-gun's Hollywood debut, which opened in December 2010, was shown across 1,622 screens and ranks second. Most Korean movies have been screened under limited release and distributed primarily by independents such as Tartan Films, Kino International, Sony Pictures Classics, and IFC Films in 10 or fewer theaters. Korean movies are typically shown on a small number of screens at first, and scaled up if audience response is positive. Korean art-house movies that achieve success typically do so using this method, such as the classic example of Kim Ki-duk's *Spring, Summer, Fall, Winter... and Spring*. First opening on 6 screens, it later went on to be played in 74 theatres across America and generated revenues of $2.3 million. *Oldboy* also opened on a mere 5 screens initially, but in its fifth week expanded to 28 screens.

Another noteworthy point to consider is the US release of such films as *Tae-gukgi, Typhoon,* and *The Host. Taegukgi*, a local take on *Saving Private Ryan,* was a box office smash in Korea. Audiences were drawn to the blockbuster epic of war and the superior film technology displayed. In the US, it secured 29 screens upon its first week of release, which was rather large for a Korean film. However, its box office receipts were a meager $1.11 million. *Typhoon* also started out on 24 screens in its first week but only grossed $130,000. *The Host* opened on 71 screens in its first week but achieved a paltry box office gross of $2.2 million. Anticipation had been high for the film given its production values, genre, critical acclaim, and the high praise for director Bong Joon-ho, but the results were lackluster. Director Shim Hyeong-rae's second foray into Hollywood, *The Last Godfather,* managed three weeks on 58 screens but only made $164,000, leaving it outside the top 10 Korean films in the US.

CJ USA, owned by Korea's CJ E&M, opened a CGV theater in L.A.'s Koreatown to have a direct distribution venue and allow a larger selection of movies to enter the US market in the future. Movies shown there include *71: Into the Fire*, *Moss, The Man from Nowhere, Quiz King, A Better Tomorrow, Who Are You?, Don't Cry for Me Sudan, Warrior's Way, Bad Deal, Recipe, Finding Mr. Kim, Two Women, The Housemaid,* and *Hello Ghost.* Specific long-term promotion and marketing plans will be put in place to target the Korean community in the US, while also appealing to local moviegoers.

Hollywood has begun to view the Korean film market, which grew rapidly in the first years of the new millennium, as a source for remakes. Beginning with 1999's *Tell Me Something,* films of the early 2000s such as *My Wife Is a Gangster, Marrying the Mafia,* and *Hi! Dharma!* led to a boom in potential Hollywood remakes. This trend decreased slightly in the mid-2000s, only to pick up again with *The Host, The Chaser,* and *The Good, The Bad, The Weird.* Rights to over 30 Korean movies have been sold to Hollywood. A leading example is *Il Mare,* which was turned into *Lake House,* starring Keanu Reeves and Sandra Bullock. With this top-star billing, the movie recorded $52 million at the box office but $3.5 billion in video rental sales. *Into the Mirror* served as the inspiration for *Mirrors* (2008), and *A Tale of Two Sisters* spawned *The Uninvited* (2009). *My Sassy Girl* (Korean) led to a US version under the same title, and the film *Addicted* inspired *Possession* (2008).

Korean actors are venturing into Hollywood. Jeong Ji-hun (Rain) starred in *Speed Racer* (2008) and *The Ninja Assassin* (2009), while Lee Byung-hun had co-star billing in *G.I. Joe 1* and *2.* Gianna Jun became the first Korean actress to land a leading role in an international film with *Blood* (2009), a vampire action flick inspired by a popular Japanese anime series. Bae Doona also debuted in Hollywood with *Cloud Atlas* (2012), produced by the Wachowski siblings and starring Tom Hanks, Hugh Grant, and Halle Berry.

Directors are also attempting to break into Hollywood: Park Chan-wook directed *Stoker* and Bong Joon-ho recently shot *Snowpiercer.* The best year for Korean movies in the US was 2011, when 18 films were shown in American theaters. With many Korean films set to be remade by Hollywood, more will debut in the US market and local audiences will likely see more Korean movies and more appearances by Korean actors.

TV: Korean dramas

In 1988, KBFD-TV, Hawaii's first terrestrial Asian programming TV network, was launched, offering Korean dramas complete with subtitles to Hawaiian

Table 3–26.   Top 20 Korean films in the US by box office revenue (2004–2010)[1]

Rank	Title	Distributor	Year of Release	Number of Screens	Revenue ($)
1	*D-War*	Freestyle Releasing	2007	2,277	10,977,721
2	*Warrior's Way*	Relativity Media	2010	1,622	5,666,340
3	*Spring, Summer, Fall, Winter... and Spring*	Sony Pictures Classics	2004	74	2,380,788
4	*The Host*	Magnolia Pictures	2007	116	2,201,923
5	*Taegukgi*	IDP	2004	29	1,110,186
6	*Oldboy*	Tartan Films	2005	28	707,481
7	*Mother*	Magnolia Pictures	2010	38	551,509
8	*Tokyo!*	Liberation Entertainment	2009	18	351,059
9	*Haeundae*	JS Media	2009	–	344,024
10	*Thirst*	Focus Features	2009	17	318,574
11	*3-Iron*	Sony Pictures Classics	2005	31	241,914
12	*Sympathy for Lady Vengeance*	Tartan Films	2006	15	211,667
13	*The Last Godfather*	Roadside	2011	58	164,247
14	*Into the Fire*	Independent	2010	20	159,335
15	*Typhoon*	Paramount Classics	2006	24	139,059
16	*The Good, the Bad, the Weird*	IFC Films	2010	15	128,486
17	*Three... Extremes*	Lionsgate	2005	19	77,502
18	*A Tale of Two Sisters*	Tartan Films	2004	9	72,541
19	*Untold Scandal*	King International	2004	8	63,332
20	*Treeless Mountain*	Oscilloscope Pictures	2009	---	60,336

[1] Excluding animated films and documentaries; inclusive of 2011's *The Last Godfather.*

viewers. In 1991, the satellite channel TAN went into service across North and Central America, allowing viewers in Canada and Mexico to access Korean dramas. KBFD-TV sold its channel to DirectTV in August 2010. Currently, the three major terrestrial networks in Korea, along with a number of other channel operators, offer Korean programming on US terrestrial and cable channels.

Table 3–27. Purchase of remake rights for Korean films

Year	Film	Buyer	Remake
1999	*Tell Me Something*	Fox 2000 Pictures	
2000	*Il Mare*	Warner Brothers	*Lake House* (2006)
2000	*JSA*	David Franzoni	
2001	*My Wife Is a Gangster*	Miramax	
2001	*My Sassy Girl*	Dreamworks	*My Sassy Girl* (2008 DVD release)
2002	*Marrying the Mafia*	Warner Brothers	
2002	*Jail Breakers*	Miramax	
2002	*Addicted*	Vertigo Entertainment	*Possession* (2009)
2002	*Phone*	Maverick Entertainment	Co-production with Imprint (deal signed in 2009)
2003	*My Teacher, Mr. Kim*	Miramax	
2003	*Oldboy*	Universal Pictures	
2003	*A Tale of Two Sisters*	Dreamworks	*Anna and Alex: A Tale of Two Sisters* (2009)
2003	*Into the Mirror*	New Regency	*Mirrors* (2008)
2004	*Dead Friend*	Dimension Films	
2006	*The Host*	Universal Pictures	
2008	*The Chaser*	Warner Brothers	
2008	*Seven Days*	Summit Entertainment	
2008	*Die Bad*	Universal	

Korean drama viewers in the Americas had largely been limited to diaspora Koreans, but dramas have recently gained in popularity among Japanese and Chinese immigrants as well as Hispanics and in mainstream America. In California, especially Los Angeles, Korean programming can be viewed via satellite or cable TV. DVD stores have also served as excellent intermediaries in distributing Korean culture.

DramaFever, an online video site that streams Korean dramas with English subtitles, has nearly two million visitors per month. Viewers break down roughly as 28% Asian and 72% non-Asian (Caucasian 53%, African-American 10%, and Hispanic 6%). *DramaFever* will soon be available on iTunes and will debut in Latin America with Spanish subtitles. The largest joint online cable TV network in the US, *Hulu*, has attracted investment from NBC, FOX, and Disney-ABC. *Hulu* includes Korean drama as one of its 25 genres, offering 54 shows in this category. CJ E&M makes use of the *Hulu* platform to offer its dramas on *Global Mnet.com*. Although Korean dramas have their own distinct cultural code, they appeal widely to Asian-Americans and are picking up viewers more broadly in America. *Mvibo.com* also offers Korean TV programming with English subtitles for viewers in the US, Canada, and other Anglophone countries.

With more Korean actors cast in American programs, overall awareness of Korean performers has increased in US television. Actress Kim Yun-jin co-starred in all seasons of ABC's flagship program *Lost*, which was broadcast in 220 countries and consistently topped ratings. Daniel Dae Kim and Grace Park co-starred in *Hawaii Five-O*, an investigative series set in Hawaii. Korean-American actor Tim Kang was recently cast in *The Mentalist*, a series that after one season overcame *CSI* to become America's most popular crime drama.

A total of 9 Korean programs won awards in 10 categories at the 2012 45th Worldfest-Houston International Independent Film & Video Festival, including *Infinite Challenge, Queen Seondeok,* and *Royal Family*. Worldfest-Houston is the longest-running independent film festival and third longest-running film festival in North America after those in San Francisco and New York. Korean programs won many awards at the 2012 New York TV Festival, an international event with participation from over 400 TV institutions, including the UK's BBC Worldwide and CBS, Canada's CBC, Germany's ZDF, and Japan's NHK.

Close to 94.4% of all foreign programs broadcast in Korea come from North America; however, only 1.8% of Korea's total TV exports go to North America. As of 2011, Korean export sales to the US stood at $2.8 million and at $130,000 for Latin America.

Korean dramas have been very popular in Latin America; in 2002, the Mexican public broadcaster Mexiquense rescheduled *Stars in My Heart* and *All about Eve* to prime time. Other dramas, such as *Winter Sonata* (2005), *Autumn Tales* (2007), *My Lovely Sam Soon* (2008), and *Jewel in the Palace* (2009) were also shown across the region, and many fans eagerly took up Korean to better appreciate Korean programming.

At the 2011 Korean TV Content Showcase held in three South American countries (Brazil, Peru, and Colombia), Korean dramas earned $90,000 in export revenue. Peru's Panamerica TV bought the rights to *The Greatest Love* and *Flame of Desire,* while Panama's SERTV bought *Jewel in the Palace* and *Princess Hours*. The documentary *Um Hong Gil Goes to Sea* was sold to Globosat, the satellite arm of Globo, one of Brazil's three major broadcasters. Panama's SERTV recently broadcast *The 1st Shop of Coffee Prince*, and Paraguay's Red Guarani showed *Princess Hours,* which led to a boom in interest in Yun Eun-hye, the actress who played the lead in both series.

Korean dramas are successful in Latin America because their themes are similar to those explored in *telenovelas*,[50] which make them emotionally accessible to Spanish-speaking viewers. *Telenovelas* are typically shown from 5 p.m. onward in Brazil, Mexico, and other Latin American countries.

Games

Korean game companies are active internationally, with overseas sales accounting for 75% of the total revenue of some manufacturers (WeMade Entertainment). With the free-to-play payment model gaining in popularity in the North American market, which developed primarily on the basis of PC and console

---

[50] The term *telenovelas* combines *tele-* from television and *novela* from the Spanish word for novel and refers to a genre of serials popular in Latin America.

games, Korean games will likely do well with their massively multi-player online role playing game (MMORPG) platforms. In early 2012, NCSOFT began pre-sales of *Guild Wars 2*, which topped the US MMORPG charts. Nexon opened a US office in 2005 and invested $5 million in its SNG subsidiary to enter 104 countries around the world, including some in North and South America. Consequently, it drew 67% (₩800 billion) of its total revenue in 2011 from international markets. Neowiz Games also opened an office in the US and introduced *War of Angels* to the US market. CJ E&M's NetMarble is also planning to establish a US subsidiary, while NHN released its online game *Tera* in the US in 2011.

Korean game-makers are also entering the Latin American market. Despite its deficient Internet infrastructure, this market represents high potential for growth. Social and mobile games are particularly popular. Neowiz Games introduced *Crossfire* to 15 countries including Brazil, Argentina, and Mexico, and signed deals with 17 countries for *S4 League*. Eya Soft began supplying *Iris Online* to the North American market and is planning to expand service to Brazil, Mexico, Argentina, and Uruguay. KOG recently signed deals with 20 South American countries for *Fighters Club*. M Game sold *Knight Online* to Brazil, Nexon sold FPS *Combat Arms*, and Dragonfly sold *Special Force*. Hangame sold *Karos Online* around Latin America under publishing contracts.

Table 3–28. Searches for MMORPG games in the US on *MMORPG.com*
(September 18–October 2, 2012)

Rank	Game	Publisher	Genre	Distribution	Searches
1	*Guild Wars 2*	NCSOFT	Fantasy	Downloads/ CD sales	220,497
2	*Star Wars: The Old Republic*	LucasArts	Sci-Fi	CD sales	39,631
3	*The Secret World*	Funcom	Real Life	Downloads	34,419
4	*World of Warcraft: Mists of Pandaria*	Activision Blizzard	Fantasy	Downloads/ CD sales	32,780 *
5	*Darkfall: Unholy Wars*	Aventurine SA	Fantasy	Downloads	28,072
6	*World of Warcraft*	Activision Blizzard	Fantasy	Downloads/ CD sales	26,741
7	*Rift*	Tron Worlds	Fantasy	Downloads/ CD sales	23,698
8	*World of Warplanes*	Wargaming	Historical	Downloads	20,315
9	*MechWarrior Online*	Infinite Games	Sci-Fi	Downloads	16,983
10	*Vanguard: Saga of Heroes*	Sony	Fantasy	Downloads/ CD sales	13,840

(Source: MMORPG.com (2012))

Animation/Licensed Character Goods

Korean animated films produced for theatrical release have done extremely well in North America, with *Leafie, A Hen into the Wild* (2.2 million domestic viewers), *Speckles, the Tarbosaurus* (sold to 56 countries; Korean domestic audience of 1 million), and 2012's *Dino Time* opening on over 2,500 screens across the region.

The Legend of Korra, co-produced by Nickelodeon and the Korean animator Studio Mir, was broadcast on US television in April 2012 to 29 million viewers. Average viewership for each episode was three million. It drew the highest ratings of any animated show on Nickelodeon over the last three years; not only did it become the top cable network children's program, it also drew the highest weekly audience and ranked fourth overall among cable programs.

The Korean animated character Pucca was featured in a 20-part 3D TV series on the Toon Disney channel. Voozclub's Canimals were turned into an eponymous app for smartphones, and at one point, the application topped downloads on iTunes. At the LIMA Show, the world's largest character goods licensing expo, Voozclub signed deals worth $4 million for Canimals that included character licensing, merchandise exports, and video distribution. In 2007, Pucca was named one of the top five characters in Brazil, which even witnessed a Pucca fashion show. In Mexico, *Pucca* was broadcast as a TV animated series. RedRover's *The Nut Job* received an award for best short at the 3D Film Festival held in Hollywood. After signing deals with a major US distributor, the company confirmed plans to open in the US in 2012.

3.4.2.   The Korean Wave Laps American Shores

Reference: "The Korean Wave Laps American Shores," *Weekly Chosun*, Kim Hye-yeong, Oct. 23, 2006, No. 1926, pp. 172–174.

Japanese- and Chinese-Americans have fallen in love with Jewel in the Palace, Winter Sonata, Phoenix, *and other Korean TV dramas. Korean-American organizations declare 2006 "The Year of the Korean Wave" and prepare related events.*

Sean (20), a Japanese-American who lives near Los Angeles, had an unusual experience last summer: he stayed up all night watching the Korean drama *Full House*. "I found the DVD set at home one day. It was my younger brother's. He's into Korean celebrities. I had no expectations when I started watching, but it turned out to be pretty good. I completely lost track of time as I watched one episode after another, and before I knew it, the sun was coming up. I went to bed at 6 a.m. with my eyes bloodshot."

Sean was introduced to Korean pop culture by his Japanese mother. She, like many immigrants in the US, follows the news back in Japan through the Internet and has easier access to *Hallyu*. Sean's younger brother, Brian (18), has already become an avid Lee Hyori fan.

Sean had been indifferent towards Brian's obsession with Korean pop music until one day he happened upon *Full House* and became hooked. "I want to see more Korean dramas when I get the chance. I'm into exercising and sports, like soccer or track, and haven't really cared for TV. But Korean shows are good. I could relate to the characters because they're my age."

Even in the US, the most popular genre of Korean cultural products is dramas. The reception accorded *Jewel in the Palace,* which aired on a few cable channels between the end of last year and early this year, proved that an age of *Hallyu* has dawned in the US as well. The series was also picked up by public television station KMTP. Most Korean dramas had been broadcast on Chinese stations with Mandarin subtitles, but *Jewel in the Palace* became the first Korean program to air with English subtitles for an Anglophone viewership, Asian descent or otherwise. Korean dramas thus took a big step forward with American viewers.

When KMTP first aired trailers for *Jewel in the Palace* last November, many viewers responded enthusiastically. "I'd heard so much about the show from friends in China. I couldn't wait to see it," said Yvonne (49), a Chinese-American living in Virginia. She recalled how excited she was to watch *Jewel in the Palace* with her daughters, who were visiting for Christmas.

Enthusiasm for Korean products, first ignited by *Jewel in the Palace*, led to support for other shows such as *My Lovely Sam Soon, Sad Love Story,* and *Phoenix.* More genre diversity means a more diverse fan base. Viewership has since expanded from middle-aged housewives to teens and even men, who had previously been indifferent towards television dramas.

Jeffery Lee has also recently joined the ranks of *Hallyu* aficionados. A third-generation Chinese-American resident of Hawaii who does not speak Mandarin, he had no interest in Chinese dramas or film. One day, though, he chanced upon *Emperor of the Sea* while flipping through the cable channels and found himself more and more engaged with each episode. He is now waiting for a similar period drama.

With male viewers like Lee lending support, Korean drama videos now fill entire walls at video rental stores in Chinatowns across the US. Korean celebrity news is printed in Chinese newspapers for immigrants almost at the same time as it is printed in Korea. It is no longer surprising to see pictures of Korean celebrities in Chinese papers.

Japanese-Americans are just as dedicated to *Hallyu.* While Chinese-Americans favor historical dramas like *Emperor of the Sea,* Japanese-Americans prefer *Winter Sonata* and other contemporary dramas. Yonsama is a familiar name for Japanese-Americans, many of whom are under his spell.

Junko (36), who immigrated to the US 10 years ago, is ready to fly anywhere to see Bae Yong-joon if he visits the country. She also shows great interest in Hwang Shin-hye, who recently became very popular in Japan. She loves *gom-tang,* a Korean beef soup, and eats Korean food an average of once a week. Her American husband has also acquired a taste for Korean cuisine thanks to her.

One of the most notable results of the success of *Hallyu* in the US is heightened interest in the Korean language. Professor Koo Eun-hee, a Korean instructor at Adroit College in San Jose, now teaches Korean on KMTP TV using a curriculum she developed herself.

Koo's show teaches Korean through expressions that come up in *Jewel in the Palace.* It adds short lessons on the historical and cultural background of the series and serves as a good example of how the Korean Wave can spur greater interest in Korea.

"Many of my students have decided to learn Korean thanks to dramas. One Taiwanese-American professor who retired from UC Berkeley knows more about Korean dramas than I do. I nicknamed her 'Queen of Korean Drama.' Some students have already seen *Jumong* online, which hasn't even been broadcast in China yet."

Students love it when she invokes the names of Korean celebrities during class. "*Bieup* as in Lee *Byung*-hun. *Jieut* as in Bae Yong-*joon*." Among her students is an elderly couple who are big fans of Korean dramas. Upon occasion, the wife brightens the mood in class by playfully calling her husband *oppa*.

Another great change brought on in the US thanks to *Hallyu* is increased interested in Korean cuisine. Je Mi-gyeong, a news anchor at TKC TV, a New York-based Korean channel, said that New Yorkers' interest in Korean food became pronounced around the time *Jewel in the Palace* videos started appearing in stores on West 32nd Street in Manhattan, a neighborhood otherwise known as Koreatown.

"*Jewel in the Palace* was so popular, even here in New York. It goes without saying that Korean restaurants became much more popular too thanks to the show. Korean food drew large crowds at school functions as well. There's a festival at American schools called 'International Day' in which children bring food from their cultural backgrounds. More and more have been asking for *bulgogi*, *japchae*, and *gimbap* lately."

Hallyu has fostered Korean-American pride in Korea. Unlike first-generation or 1.5-generation Korean-Americans, second-generation Korean-Americans are often no different from other Americans in terms of language and values, despite their appearance. As a result, Korean dramas have been the domain of Korean mothers and Korean video stores while the children flipped through cable networks and immersed themselves in American culture. But a few years ago, things began to change. Once their friends of Chinese, Filipino, and Taiwanese descent at school began to watch Korean dramas, second-generation Korean-Americans became prouder of their heritage.

"Kids just started talking about Korean celebrities or dramas. My friend John, who's Filipino-American, told me about a Rain concert in Las Vegas that he was really excited about, and asked me if I wanted to go," said O Jin-seon, a sophomore at Palo Verde High School in Las Vegas. "He's watching *My Lovely Sam Soon* on cable on the Asian Channel. My friend Giselle's mom is from Taiwan and watches *Princess Hours*. Everyone loves it. Giselle's mom is crazy about Korean dramas. She has practically every DVD set."

The Korean Cultural Centers in New York and Los Angeles are also lending their support to *Hallyu*. The New York branch declared this year "The Year of *Hallyu*" and enthusiastically supported the New York Korean Film Festival and the Korean Film Festival at Harvard University. They also provided funding for Korean groups to perform at international venues, in an effort to create a *Hallyu* boom in performance and fine arts as well as television and film.

The Los Angeles branch opened its Korea Center on August 30 and is laying foundations to become an active ambassador of *Hallyu*. Korea Center LA provides access to the resources of the Korean Cultural Center, the Los Angeles office of the Korea Tourism Organization, and KOCCA. The first floor holds a Tourist Experience Gallery and a *Hallyu* Gallery where merchandise is displayed.

So far, regrettably, the work the Korean Cultural Center does has been limited to promoting Korean films through the Korean International Film Festival or

Korean film screenings and the like. In order for *Hallyu* enthusiasm instigated by the Asian-American community to spread to Anglo viewers as well, the Korean government will have to be more proactive in promoting Korean television dramas.

Some have also voiced concerns that *Hallyu* may wind up being promoted by other Asian-American communities. Rain's concert, which will take place at Caesar's Palace in Las Vegas this December, was in fact organized by ethnic Chinese. "The head of China marketing has been asking for help since last year to put together a Rain concert," said one Caesar's Palace insider. "We've been trying to schedule it for a long time and finally set the date for the Christmas holidays, peak season for Chinese tourists."

As Lunar New Year and Christmas are high season for Chinese tourism in Las Vegas, Caesar's Palace has invited celebrities from Hong Kong and Taiwan to perform at that point. This year, Rain will perform alongside them.

"Concerts from individual artists are also nice, but I want to put together a big event that really shows the power of Korea," said MGM Hotel's Korea marketing director Robert Min. "Rather than inviting a Korean singer to a Chinese show, I'd like to organize a concert for Korean singers and really market it as a showcase of Korean talent. I'm still figuring out the details, but I definitely want to make it work." Here's to hopes that the *Hallyu* flag will soon be flying high in the US.

3.4.3.   New Year's Party for Those Who Make *Hallyu* Shine: A Mexican Fan Event

Reference: "New Year's Party for Those Who Make *Hallyu* Shine: A Mexican Fan Event," *Dongpo Sinmun*, Im Yong-wi, December 20, 2006.

Kwon Sang-woo, Bae Yong-joon, Ahn Jae-wook, Kangta, and Jang Dong-gun are some of Korea's top stars. Gathered here are those who consider themselves ardent fans and send these stars unceasing devotion. Of course, these fans are all Mexican. Although most are fresh-faced youths, middle-aged and older fans also catch the eye, as do even younger boys and girls.

About five years ago *Hallyu* began making its way into Mexico, but not as a result of government efforts or overseas Korean organizations; even without the flames being fanned, enthusiasts have gathered, building projects out of love for the country and working to discover a new, special Korea.

Last weekend, at a party to see out the year held at a restaurant in the historic center of Mexico City, one could see the love these fans put into Korean pop culture. Seven fan clubs dedicated to Korea's top stars and Korea itself had come together, and although the event was nothing fancy, the fruitful, fun program made it, how should I put it, an event reminiscent of... "Korea Day."

Indeed, the event was paid for by what members could scrounge up. Two Korean newspapers supplied prizes for the song contest, and the Korean embassy's public affairs officer put in an appearance as well.

For these fans, the impressive spread that they scraped together for the festival was no simple feat. Believing that their event was small enough not to be a major burden, they sought out Korean sponsors, unsuccessfully. The Cultural Club of Koreans in Mexico, however, graciously fulfilled their request for a Korean percussion troupe, and two newspapers helped make the reservation for the huge, folksy, down-to-earth restaurant.

For a while rumors flew, telling of criticism of the embassy, of a reneging on a promise to "support the event in friendly cooperation," and of resentful remarks about the embassy's insincerity. Of course, given that these whisperings were only rumors, the fans tried to brush them off, but as the words passed from one *Hallyu* follower to another, the seeds of offense were sown.

I was aware that Public Affairs Officer Lee had shown care for and interest in the fan club members; I figured the comments in circulation were exaggerated rumors. Still, this gossip arose in the waning days of his tour of Mexico. Worried that the fan club members might be influenced by groundless rumors, the officer was asked to clarify a few issues. But his explanation at the event was vague, leaving questions unanswered.

In any case, the event itself left little to be desired; it was filled with content and looked wonderful. Although the food was not as lavish as one might expect of a traditional Korean spread, there was plenty for all in attendance. The *gimbap* they learned to make and stayed up all night preparing, although not a rival for what one might expect in Korea, was nonetheless a special item on the menu enjoyed by all.

The tables were strewn with puzzles and games of bingo, which created a festive air of competition. Performances of folk songs and dances from both Mexico and Korea made for an even more exciting event and led to the highlight of the evening, a Korean song contest. The magical spell cast by the fierce movements and local dances accompanied by fireworks and the infectious rhythms and melody of the Korean Cultural Club's *samulnori* troupe, its performance far more sophisticated than in the past, made for a dynamic event. The juxtaposition between the two stages captivated the roughly 200 fan club members in attendance.

Mexico is not just fascinated with Korea; there is a reverence for things from the East, with these fan clubs tracing histories back to interest in both Japan and China. Korean immigrants in Mexico envy the way Japanese and Chinese cultural centers have long reached out to and developed relations with such clubs. This writer attended a gathering of Mexican fans of Japanese popular music last spring in the expo hall of the Reforma Hotel.

Of course, from the outside the function seemed neither particularly lavish nor stately. Still, the Japanese Embassy and Cultural Center put genuine energy into "Discover Japan" experiences around the event, providing a sense of extensive effort. Mexican fan club members were taught skills like Go and flower arranging and had opportunities to experience traditional handicrafts, very simple decorations, and calligraphy. Participants were also exposed to advertising from some of Japan's most prominent corporations. This two-in-one effort, a seamless melding of both culture and business, should not be underestimated; I found myself admiring the organizers' work without even realizing it at first.

Yet, for some reason the pictures of top Korean stars on display in the restaurant for the event seemed tacky. Perhaps that is a lingering image that only I, a Korean, felt. Had I not heard that the Public Affairs Office had been "missing an important meeting at another organization and wasting time" there, maybe I would have been able to shake off that feeling.

3.5. EUROPE

3.5.1. *Hallyu* Forever: Europe

Reference: *Hallyu Forever: The World Is Hallyu Style*, Ko Jeong-min et al., KOFICE
               Hallyu Series V, 2012, pp. 474–501.

A. *Korean cultural exports*

The European market accounted for 7.8% of Korea's content industry exports
in 2006, 8.6% in 2007, and 10.2% in 2008, before decreasing to 8.9% in 2009
and 8.8% in 2010. Apparently, Korean cultural content has yet to achieve a firm
footing in Europe even though the continent makes up a significant share of the
world market. Fortunately, as Table 3–29 illustrates, exports to Europe are rising
overall. They were $202.33 million in 2009 but increased to $267.68 million in
2010. Profits from Korea's cultural trade with Europe increased from $11 million
in 2006 to $123 million in 2009.

In Europe, movies, *manhwa*, characters, and animation appear to be the most
popular Korean products. Europe receives 33.3% of the total share of Korean film
exports, which is relatively high. This figure is more meaningful when one considers that there have been no commercial film hits so far. Most films have been
introduced to Europe on the strength of a director's name, or have been art-house
shorts. Korean *manhwa* are also faring well; in 2010, they made $2.26 million,
making up 27.7% of all cultural product exports to Europe. However, the average
annual growth rate of Korean *manhwa* in this market over the 2008–2010 period
stands at only 18%, lower than Japan (57.4%), Southeast Asia (98.8%), and North
America (35.7%). Still, it is noteworthy that export destinations are diversifying.

The European market is very important for the character goods industry.
In 2010, character products sold to Europe totaled $59.66 million, or 21.6%
of total exports of licensed character goods, making Europe the second largest
market after North America (30.9%). Character goods sales to Europe have
consistently increased, from $50.44 million in 2008 to $51.34 million in 2009
and $59.69 million in 2010. The region accounts for $19.52 million, or 20.2%
of all outbound exports for the Korean animation industry, which makes the
European market second in size to North America here as well (54.2%). Animation sales to Europe have grown at an average annual rate of 25.6%, from
$12.39 million in 2009 to $16.50 million in 2009 and $19.53 million in 2010.
Sales to Europe, however, only account for 8.6% of Korea's total game exports.

Table 3–29.   **Korean cultural exports to Europe**

Category	2008	2009	2010
European Share of Total Exports	9.0%	8.9%	8.8%
Exports to Europe ($1,000)	202,327.0	217,449.1	267,680.6
Total Exports ($1,000)	2,245,962.6	2,430,748.4	3,048,979.9

(Source: KOCCA (2012), *Content Industry Statistics*)

Music sales drew $396,000 in 2010, a mere 0.5% of total cultural exports; however, average growth between 2008 and 2010 was 15.7%, which suggests future potential. This rate has been climbing since 2009, and in 2010, sales increased 32.4% on average from the previous year. Sales of European music to Korea in 2010 totaled $5.46 million, 52.8% of music industry imports.

B.   Hallyu in Europe by industry

Film

Korean movies have primarily been introduced to Europe through film festivals, which provide information on Korean directors, actors, and the works themselves. The most well-known Korean director in Europe is Kim Ki-duk, who in 2004 received both the Silver Lion at the Venice Film Festival for *3-Iron* and the Silver Bear at the Berlin International Film Festival for *Samaritan Girl*. In September 2012, his film *Pieta* garnered him the Golden Lion, the most prestigious honor, at the 69th Venice Film Festival. His entire filmography has been shown in the Czech Republic. Other renowned directors include Im Kwon-taek, whose *Chihwaseon* won him a Best Director Award at Cannes, and Park Chan-wook, who won the Grand Prize for *Oldboy*. In 2012, Kim Ki-young's *The Housemaid* opened in 14 theaters in France on August 14. Korean films have been invited to show or entered into competition at Poland's New Horizon International Film Festival, Spain's Sitges International Film Festival, the Venice International Film Festival, Germany's Fantasy Film Festival, the Hamburg Film Festival, and others.

These events serve as important venues for introducing Korean cinema to Europe. Table 3–31 shows a list of festivals in Europe beyond Cannes, Berlin, and Venice that have consistently shown Korean movies. The Vienna International Film Festival, for instance, features Korean films annually. The Amsterdam Film Festival also introduces Korean works, while the annual Seoul-Stockholm Film Festival showcases Korean feature films. Every autumn, Helsinki hosts an international film festival in which two to four works of Korean cinema are screened.

Eastern Europe also has film festivals and events that introduce Korean cinema. Following the 2003 screening of Kim Ki-duk's *Spring, Summer, Fall, Winter... and Spring* at the Era Nowe Horyzonty, a leading Polish film festival, Korean movies have consistently been shown in Poland. In 2004, Park Chan-wook's *Oldboy* was screened at the same festival, further highlighting Korean cinema. The International Warsaw Film Festival is also an important outlet, as is the Five Flavors Film Festival, which hosts a special Korean section each year. In 2010, this segment was titled *Smak Korei* ("Flavors of Korea"). It featured major works by five master directors (Im Kwon-taek, Lee Chang-dong, Park Chan-wook, Kim Ki-duk, and Bong Joon-ho) and screened not only in Warsaw but in Krakow and Poznan. In 2011, the section included a special exhibition of Hong Sang-soo's works as well as 12 other Korean films. The Off Plus Camera International Festival of Independent Cinema is another important medium that introduces Korean films together with the Busan International Film Festival.[51] The Korean embassy in Hungary organizes an annual film festival, and a separate

---

[51] Choi S. (2012), *Study on the Acceptance of Korean Pop Culture in Finland*.

Table 3–30.   Sales of Korean exports in Europe by category (Units: %, $1,000)

Category	Film	*Manhwa*	Characters	Animation	Games	Publishing	TV	Knowledge and Information	Music
Export Share to Europe	33.3%	27.7%	21.6%	20.2%	8.6%	5.9%	1.8%	0.9%	0.5%
Cultural Content Exports to Europe	4,518.0	2,258.0	59,668.0	19,527.0	138,125.0	20,976.0	2,317.6	3,398.0	396.0
Total Cultural Content Exports	13,583.0	8,153.0	276,328.0	96,827.0	1,606,102.0	357,881.0	127,074.	363,282.0	83,262.0

(Source: KOCCA (2012), *Content Industry Statistics*)

Table 3–31.   **Recognitions for Korean cinema at European film festivals**

Cannes	Venice	Berlin
2011 Kim Ki-duk - *Arirang*; *Prix Un Certain Regard*	2012 Kim Ki-duk - *Pieta*; Golden Lion Jeon Gyu-hwan - *Weight*; Venice Days	2011 Park Chan-wook and Park Chan-gyeong - *Night Fishing*; Golden Bear
2011 Son Tae-gyeom - *Night Flight*; Cinefondation 3rd Place	2005 Park Chan-wook - *Sympathy for Lady Vengeance*; Cinema of the Future, Young Lion Award, Best Innovative Film Award	2011 Yang Hyo-ju - *Broken Night*; Silver Bear Jury Prize
2010 Lee Chang-dong - *Poetry*; Best Screenplay	2004 Kim Ki-duk - *3-Iron*; Little Golden Lion, FIPRESCI Best Film Award, SIGNIS Award	2010 Jang Ryul - *Tumen River*; winner Youth Jury Generation 14 Plus
2009 Park Chan-wook - *Thirst*; Jury Prize	2002 Lee Chang-dong - *Oasis*; FIPRESCI Award, Special Director's Award, SIGNIS Award, Best New Actress (Mun So-ri)	2009 Lee Suk-gyeok - *One Fine Day*; Netpac Award
2009 Hong Sang-soo - *Hahaha Prix*; *Un Certain Regard*	1987 Im Kwon-taek -*Surrogate Womb*; Best Actress (Kang Su-yeon)	2009 Kim So-yeong - *Treeless Mountain*; Berlin Prize of the Ecumenical Jury-Forum Award
2009 Jo Seong-hui - *Don't Step Out of the House*; Cinefondation Troisième Prix		2007 Park Chan-wook - *I'm a Cyborg, but That's Okay*; Alfred Bauer Award
2008 Park Jae-ok - *Stop*; Cinefondation Troisième Prix		2005 Shin Jae-in - *Disappearance of Shin Seong-il*; Berlin Zeitung Reader's Award
2007 Lee Chang-dong - *Secret Sunshine*; Best Actress (Jeon Do-yeon)		2005 Im Kwon-taek - *Chunhyang*; Honorary Golden Bear
2007 Hong Seong-hun - *A Meeting*; Cinefondation Troisième Prix		2005 Lee Yun-gi - *This Charming Girl*; Netpac Award
2004 Park Chan-wook - *Oldboy*; Grand Prize		2004 Kim Ki-duk - *Samaritan Girl*; Silver Bear, Best Director Award

(Continued)

áticas。,

Table 3–31. *(Continued).*

Cannes	Venice	Berlin
2002 Im Kwon-taek -*Chihwaseon*; Best Director		1994 Jang Seon-wu - *Hwaeomgyeong*; Alfred Bauer Award
		1962 Shin Sang-ok - *To the Last Day*; Special Award (Jeon Yeong-seon)
		1961 Kang Dae-jin - *Mabu*; Special Silver Bear

(Source: KOFIC (2012), KOBIZ Data Recompilation)

event is hosted by Korean movie buffs. Bulgaria also has numerous Korean film fan societies and Korean movie nights are held often in the capital Sofia. The 1989 work *Why Has Bodhi-Dharma Left for the East?* was the first Korean movie screened in Sweden. Following a lengthy hiatus, the Umeå Film Festival reintroduced Korean films in 1997. Kim Ki-duk's pieces were shown that year, and Park Chan-wook's *Sympathy for Lady Vengeance* was screened in 2005. From 2002, Swedish video distribution company Noble Entertainment offered a sample of Korean cinema, which helped form a fan base. These fans organized the Seoul-Stockholm Korean Film Festival in 2007. Thanks to such smaller, intimate events, Korean films became more accessible to the public. However, fans remain few and far between. They are typically native European, middle-class men whose existing interest in Asian cinema led them to Korean films.[52]

Korean cultural centers are making headway in introducing Korean movies to Europe. For example, the Korean Cultural Center in France hosted a film exhibition in 2012 (September 14-October 26), and the UK center screened *Crossroads of Youth* on August 2, 2012. The 7th London Korean Film Festival was held in November 2012, and it was so successful that tickets to the opening (*The Thieves*) and the closing (*Masquerade*) films sold out. The event also featured a K-pop movie section—the first for a festival.

More Europeans have become aware of Korean cinema because of increased offerings at festivals, events, and cultural exchange programs. However, better-known Korean films have mostly been promoted as works of a particular director, instead of being released commercially. Furthermore, Korean movie viewers tend to be a select group of dedicated fans, not the general public. A handful of Korean movies have been screened in commercial theaters, but none have achieved box office success. *Chihwaseon* has fared best so far, with 316,000 spectators. In the UK, *Mother* was shown in over 60 theaters in 2010, and *Poetry* opened in 7 indie film venues in Spain.

---

[52] Tobias H. (2012), "The Reception and Consumption of *Hallyu* in Sweden: Preliminary Findings and Reflections," *Korea Observer*, Vol. 43, No. 3, pp. 503-525.

In Poland, Gong Su-chang's *R-Point* (2005) and Kim Ji-woon's *The Good, the Bad, the Weird* (2009) both opened directly in theaters instead of taking the film festival route but failed to meet with financial success. Most commercial releases have gone straight to DVD instead of opening in theaters.

Manhwa, animation, and licensed character goods

Lee Hyeon-se's *Angel Dick* was the first Korean *manhwa* translated into French and was published in December 1996. Many have been translated and published since, but until the early 2000s, they did not constitute an individual brand and were perceived as a subcategory of anime, which included Asian graphic novels and Japanese manga more broadly.

Beginning in 2003, however, Korean *manhwa* became recognized as a separate category in Europe, different from Japanese manga, when the Angoulême International Comics Festival held a Korean *manhwa* exhibition. Thereafter, many French publishers began translating *manhwa*, which have featured at Angoulême every year since. From April 25–29, 2012, the Centre Pompidou hosted a special Korean subsection in its World Comics Exhibition. In 2005, Korea participated in the Frankfurt Book Fair as a partner and introduced more *manhwa*. Korean *manhwa* are actively promoted at festivals and expos in France and Germany, which function as hubs for the European market.

Europe is showing more interest in *manhwa* artists as well. Gwon Yun-ju's *To My Cat* received an award from France's National Society for the Protection of Animals. In 2008, Oh Yeong-jin's *Visiteur du Sud, Le Journal de Monsieur en Corée du Nord*, translated and published by FLBLB, was awarded the Prix Asie-ACBD by the Association des Critiques et Journalistes de Bande Dessinée at the France Japan Expo. Now creators are increasingly working directly with local publishers to sidestep Korean distributors in order to enter Europe. Publishers like France's Kana and Soleil not only translate works by Korean artists but also collaborate with them. In Germany as well, since 2003 EMA, Panini comics, and Tokyopop have published Korean material, which is held in high esteem in Europe for its artistic and commercial value. The active collaboration of European publishers with Korean graphic novelists suggests positive feedback in the region about the potential of *manhwa* artists.

On the other hand, Korean animation is much less well known in Europe than *manhwa* paperbacks, with the exception of *Pororo the Little Penguin*. Since the beginning, the makers of *Pororo* planned to market the show to European festivals. In February 2003, the animation featured at Italy's Cartoons on the Bay, and in April, it was shown at France's Annecy Festival. *Pororo* won a distribution contract with French terrestrial public network TF1 in 2004, later bringing in ratings of 47% in 2004 and 51.7% in 2005. In Europe, animations are typically short, produced for television, and offered as educational content for children, conditions amply fulfilled by *Pororo*, which targets infants and toddlers, unlike Japanese anime. *Pororo* became the first Korean animation broadcast on a public channel in Europe. In 2011, it also became the first Asian animated show broadcast on Nederland 3, the Dutch public TV network.

Leafie, a Hen into the Wild was shown on 70 screens in 17 cities across Italy beginning on April 20, 2012. On October 6, *The Airport Diary* won the grand prix in the kid's jury category at MIPJunior, one of the world's largest showcases for animated programming. *The Airport Diary* is a 3D animated series for toddlers that tells the story of Winky, an anthropomorphic plane who tackles various adventures at different airports. It is currently broadcast on the KBS2 channel. *Robocar Poli* is also broadcast across the UK and Belgium.

However, the limited popularity of *manhwa* and animation is not translating into business opportunities. Attempts to attract revenue from merchandising deals have been rare. Pucca is one character that has had success in Europe. The character is making inroads into the broader European and Latin American markets, using France as a launch pad. Pucca was launched in the UK and the Netherlands in 2003; in July of that year, merchandising deals were signed with Fox Kids Europe Properties. Pucca has also entered the fashion industry. In 2006, a licensing contract was signed with Benetton, the clothing manufacturer. In Europe, the main consumers of Pucca products are people in their teens and twenties.[53]

Publishing

Sales of publication copyrights to Europe have increased since 2005, but growth is slow. Publishers in France, who have long been infatuated with Japanese novels, are finally paying attention to Korean children's literature. In 2006, Kim Jin-gyeong's five-part story for children, *Cat School*, won the *Prix des Incorruptibles* in France. This award is given by French bookstores, and winners are based on votes cast for favorite children's book. In 2010, the international rights to Pyun Hye-young's debut novel *Ashes and Red* were sold to a French publisher.

Television

Korean television programs, including documentaries, debuted in Europe in 2004 and 2005 with *Emperor of the Sea* and *Jewel in the Palace*, respectively. The latter drew top ratings in Turkey in 2008. *Boys over Flowers* was also highly popular, with episodes subtitled in 20 languages offered to Europe within 3 days of broadcast in Korea. However, Korean dramas are not as popular in Western Europe as elsewhere around the globe. They are not broadcast on German, French, or UK networks, for example. In France, dramas are offered on Korean channels KBS World and Arirang TV as part of a basic satellite package. Fans typically watch the shows online.

Those who consume Korean drama in Western Europe tend to be diehard fans, comprised of women in their twenties to forties who also enjoy Japanese manga, anime, and dramas.[54] In Sweden, drama fans either purchase DVDs through *YesAsia* or stream them online. Fans also run blogs such as *Dramacrazy* and *MySoju*. In 2008, the KBS documentaries *Ancient Tea Route* and *Noodle Road* were shown in Europe and opened a new chapter in the history of documentary export.

---

[53] KOCCA, *2012 Character Goods Industry White Paper.*
[54] KOTRA (2012).

Table 3–32.   Outbound copyright exports to Europe
(figure in parenthesis = excluding *manhwa*) (Unit: volumes)

Category	2004	2005	2006	2007	2008
Fiction	4	16	8	8	5
Children's Books	2 (1)	3 (2)	12 (8)	15 (10)	22 (16)
Miscellaneous	2	8	15	7	1
Other Publications	6	28	36	30	28

(Sources: Korean Publishers Association (website); Ok Seong-su (2011), "Export Forecast and Strategy Analysis for the Content Industry Following FTA Ratification," Korea Culture and Tourism Institute)

In Eastern Europe, Korean dramas were shown in 2009 and 2010 and generated much interest. *Jewel in the Palace* was broadcast in Hungary in 2010, followed by the airing of period dramas such as *Queen Seondeok* and *Dong Yi* in prime time by state-owned channel M1. The Romanian network TVR1 also broadcast *Jewel in the Palace* in 2009 and went on to show *Queen Seondeok* and *Heo Jun* in 2010. Bucharest hosted the Korea TV Content Showcase in 2011, which was attended by KBS Media, MBC, and SBS Content. These events were successful for Korean programming, which was later included in Romania's network scheduling. In Bulgaria, *Love You a Thousand Times* and *Iris* were shown in 2011 and received generally positive feedback.

Games

The popularity of Korean games varies greatly across Europe; for example, they are big hits in Germany and Romania. Korean online games typically debut in Europe through distributors in Germany, where Korean products make up 70% of the online gaming market. GamesCom, Europe's largest gaming exhibition, sees active participation from Korean exporters. European online games have recently experienced dramatic growth, and more attention is being directed to Korean games, which have also been doing well in Turkey and Romania. Awareness is growing in such countries as the Netherlands, Switzerland, and Finland, but the trend is by no means significant.

K-pop

SM Entertainment's hosting of the SM Town Paris Concert at Le Zénith concert hall in Paris on June 10–11, 2011, signaled the onset of a *Hallyu* buzz in Europe. Before the concert, few Europeans had any awareness of the presence of K-pop.[55] Even so, tickets to the concert sold out within 15 minutes, and fans who were unable to purchase tickets participated in a flash mob demonstration in front of the Louvre and in other European cities. The flash mobs offered a visible confirmation of what were until then mere suppositions about the spread of Korean popular culture in Europe.

---

[55] France's *Le Monde* reported on June 4, 2006, that Korean popular culture has spread across Asia.

Table 3–33. Current export figures of broadcast content to Europe (2005–2010)
(Units: $1,000, %)

Category	2005	2006	2007	2008	2009	2010	Share of Total Korean Television Export Content (%)
France	–	20.0	17.9	3.0	34.0	38.0	0.03
UK	16.0	116.6	1.5	29.0	4.7	–	–
Germany	9.0	10.0	16.0	2.0	132.0	–	–
Italy	–	69.0	40.0	45.0	51.0	56.5	0.04
Spain	–	–	74.5	23.0	19.0	66.8	0.1
Hungary	–	1.0	54.6	82.0	6.0	53.4	0.04
Russia	–	–	61.0	133.0	18.0	1,536.4	1.2
Netherlands	–	–	–	–	1.7	–	–
Romania	–	–	–	–	–	459.0	0.4
Israel	–	–	48.5	37.0	–	–	–

(Source: MCST and KOCCA (2011), *Content Industry Statistics*)

The SM Town Paris Concert, an important turning point, captured press attention. On February 9, 2012, Girls' Generation appeared for approximately 28 seconds on *Le Grand Journal* on French cable channel Canal+. Super Junior held their first solo Paris concert on April 6, 2012. The Korean Cultural Center in Paris held a K-Pop Rising Star Contest, the main competition category for their K-Pop World Festival. A total of 10 teams participated. In Berlin, JYJ, a major Korean boy band, performed a solo show on November 7, 2011.

In September 2012, PSY's "Gangnam Style" swept not only the US but Europe as well. The video for this megahit song won an award at the MTV European Music Awards on November 11, 2012, in Frankfurt. According to the Official Chart Company, which tabulates album sales in the UK, "Gangnam Style" ranked first on the UK singles chart on September 30, 2012. Eastern Europe has a growing K-pop fan base. Although the numbers are not especially significant, fans are increasing thanks to the widespread use of *YouTube* and other digital media. Korean boy bands have many Hungarian and Romanian fans. In Sweden, consumers of K-pop turn to blogs, *YouTube*, fan sites, and iTunes for their K-pop fix. While fans were few in the first decade of the new millennium, by 2012 many in Sweden had embraced K-pop. In March of that year, SHINee's mini-album *Sherlock* shot to #6 on the Swedish iTunes list, and in June, 2 NE1's *I Love You* went to #20. Swedish fans demonstrate their love of K-pop by participating in K-pop flash mobs, cover dances, and concerts.

According to a 2012 KOTRA report, the popularity of Korean music in Europe varies by country. K-pop does relatively better in France, Belgium, Finland, Poland, Romania, and Bulgaria, but is not as well known in Germany, Sweden, Denmark, the Netherlands, Italy, Spain, the Czech Republic, or Slovakia. K-pop has even less of a following in the UK, Austria, Croatia, and Hungary.

Table 3–34.   K-pop concerts in Europe

Region	Date	Venue	Title	Host	Audience
Paris	2011.06.11–12	Le Zénith de Paris	SM Town Live in Paris	SM and MBC	14,000 (2 days)
Barcelona	2011.10.29	Poble Espanyol	JYJ European Tour	C-JeS Entertainment	3,000+
London	2011.11.03	Abbey Road Studio	SHINee in London	SM	800+
London	2011.12.05	O2 Brixton Academy	United Cube Concert Beautiful Show	Cube Entertainment	4,000+
Paris	2012.02.08	Bercy Stadium	K-Pop Festival Music Bank in Paris	KBS	10,000+
Berlin	2012.02.12	Columbia Halle	United Cube Concert Beautiful Show	Cube Entertainment	3,000+
Paris	2012.04.06	Le Zénith de Paris	Super Show 4 in Paris	SM	7,000+

While interest in K-pop is growing overall in Europe, it remains limited to small communities of dedicated fans.

C.   *Hallyu's success in Europe*

European festivals and exhibitions

Countless international festivals and exhibitions in Europe function as a marketplace for the world's cultural industries. They serve as important routes for Korean content to enter the European market. These events also offer opportunities for less experienced Korean content providers to implement effective marketing. The Korean cultural industries have participated in many such European events to promote their products and establish global networks.

Korean cinema and its directors were introduced to Europe through film festivals. Thanks to the increased opportunities for Korean filmmakers and their movies to win awards at these prestigious events, European interest in Korean cinema has grown enormously. Kim Ki-duk has won many awards, and Park Chan-wook's *Oldboy* won the *Grand Prix* at Cannes in 2004. Korean movies were recently introduced to Eastern Europe through festivals there as well. Korean *manhwa* providers are also making full use of the Angoulême International Comics Festival. The Frankfurt Book Fair, Bologna Children's Book Fair, and other international exhibitions have served as important means for Korean

Table 3–35.   Content industry festivals and exhibitions in Europe

Category	Time	Location	Title
Film	February	Berlin	Berlin International Film Festival
	May	Cannes	Cannes Film Festival
	August	Venice	Venice International Film Festival
	February	Oporto, Portugal	Fantasporto: Oporto International Film Festival
	April	Brussels	Brussels International Festival of Fantastic Film
	October	Cataluna, Spain	Sitges International Film Festival
Animation	April	Trebon, Czech Republic	AniFest International Festival of Animated Films
	May	Zagreb	Zagreb World Festival of Animated Films
	May	Baden-Württemberg	ITFS Stuttgart Festival of Animated Film
	June	Annecy, France	Annecy International Animated Film Festival
TV Broadcasting	April	Cannes	MIPTV
	September	Berlin	IFA Internationale Funkausstellung
	September	Amsterdam	IBC International Broadcasting Convention
Games	February	Nuremburg	Spiewarenmesse
	August	Köln	GC Gamescom
	October	Rome	SAPAR
	October	Essen	Internationale Spieltage SPIEL Friedhelm Merz Verlag
Music	January	Cannes	Midem
Publication	January	London	London Book Fair
	March	Bologna	Bologna Children's Book Fair
	October	Frankfurt	Frankfurt Book Fair
Manhwa	January	Angoulême, France	Angoulême International Comics Festival
	June	Lyon	Comic Festival in Lyon
	July	London	London Film and Comic Con
Character Goods	January	Harrogate, UK	Harrogate Toy Fair
	January	London	IBTHA, Briydh Toy & Hobby Association
	February	Nuremburg	Spielwarenmesse International Toy Fair

(Continued)

Table 3–35. *(Continued)*.

Category	Time	Location	Title
Advertising	June	Cannes	Cannes Lions (Emap Limited)
Information and Knowledge	July	London	eLearning Network Members' Showcase

(Source: MCST, *2010 Content Industry White Paper*)

publishers to enter the European market. These festivals and exhibitions bring awareness to Korean content, be it broadcasts, music, animation, or games.

Korean content providers' active participation in European events has been effective for promoting *Hallyu* in the region. The Korean government also provides support for Korean corporate attendance at these events and for the promotion of global marketing activities.

Spread of *Hallyu* through social media and the rise of active communities

With the development of new media, changes have occurred in how Korean culture is being introduced in Europe. Social media platforms such as *YouTube* and *Facebook* have served as key distribution channels, allowing Korean content providers to engage with consumers directly. *Hallyu* in Europe has to a large extent been fostered by fan efforts. For example, French teens have gone online since as far back as 2004 to watch dramas like *Full House*. In Europe, Korean dramas are not usually offered on traditional television outlets, so European fans struggle to access the programs they love. Within this context, *YouTube* and other social networking sites have greatly improved access to Korean dramas for European consumers.

K-pop also rose to prominence in Europe after 2008, when music fans in France and elsewhere in the region began to experience K-pop through *YouTube*, where the genre started trending, as well as on *Facebook* and other social media channels. These changes in the media environment allowed copyright holders to communicate with fans despite poorly supported on-the-ground PR activities and DVD sales distribution networks. In Europe, *Hallyu* has in fact grown without local promotional activities or album sales. K-pop spread especially rapidly in 2011 with Paris as its epicenter thanks to the influential role played by social media. PSY's "Gangnam Style," which became a phenomenon in 2012, was also introduced to Europe through *YouTube*.

Many consumers exposed to *Hallyu* through new media go on to participate in fan clubs. France's Korean Connection, founded on March 4, 2010, was one such non-profit club. In June 2011, it planned flash mobs to demand that SM hold concerts in Paris. By the time Korean Connection closed in July 2012, it had amassed over 10,000 fans on its *Facebook* page. In November 2011, the non-profit organization Kachi to Korea was formed to spread awareness of Korean culture. Kachi to Korea began as a group of friends who were taking language lessons at the Korean Cultural Center in France. It hosted "Kachi's Week," a K-pop festival, from April 10–15, 2012.

Fans of K-pop in the UK and Germany also enjoy the genre on social media and exchange information in online communities. On July 7, 2012, K-pop fan club So-Loved organized a *"Running Man"* event at Spandau Square in Berlin that imitated the Korean program of that name.

K-pop's popularity grew in Turkey from 2007 thanks to *YouTube*. Currently, Turkey contains 17 fan clubs with over 170,000 members who share pictures and videos, translate news articles, run fan community websites, and advocate for concerts. On November 26, 2011, Turkey's Korean Cultural Center hosted the 2011 K-Pop Contest and Night of K-Pop, and in February 2012, JYJ's Hero signed autographs at a meet-and-greet event in the country. On March 5, 2012, the club Kore Fans hosted a K-Pop Day at the Korean Cultural Center in Ankara.

This growth of *Hallyu* based on social media, which encourage active communication between both content creators and consumers as well as among fellow users, has expanded the phenomenon's base. However, the core group of *Hallyu* consumers remains limited to women in their teens and twenties.[56] Furthermore, *Hallyu* based in social media has yet to lead to monetization of ancillary goods and markets.

Increased European interest in Asian culture and special features of Korean content

In Europe, *Hallyu* arose from a combination of the local socio-cultural context and the characteristic elements of Korean content. Respect for cultural diversity and artistic value had a significant influence on the introduction of Korean shorts and art-house films to the region. In Europe, Korean material is recognized as co-existing with that of many other cultures, and the penetration level of *Hallyu* differs across the continent. Korean material is popular in Germany, France, and Poland, but less so in Greece, Denmark, Austria, and Italy.[57]

Lee S. (2012) explains K-pop fandom in Europe from the perspective of cultural hybridization and argues that the "Asianness" of Korean content has played a key role in the rise of *Hallyu*. Lee points to an article in the *Frankfurter Allgemeine Zeitung* that interprets the birth of Korean idol groups as a hybridized outcome of Confucianism and capitalist production methods, which also suggests that elements of Confucianism operate in the factors that led to European audiences' fascination with K-pop stars. European pop stars are less accessible to their fans and sit on pedestals, whereas K-pop idols have a younger look and are less intimidating to teenagers, with songs and choreography that appeal to the youth. Korean artists also communicate well with their fans via their websites. In research from 2012, KOTRA suggests that the influx of Asian and Middle Eastern immigrants into Europe has also played a role in the growth of *Hallyu*, as these diasporic fans have brought a love of Korean material to their adopted continent.

---

[56] "K-Pop Statistics in Germany," a *Facebook* page created by German fans, conducted a survey in February 2012 in which 1,041 respondents participated. Of these, an overwhelming majority (90.8%) were female. Teens comprised 71%, with 53.6% of respondents living in mid-to-small-sized cities and 42.4% in big cities.

[57] KOTRA, *2012 Research Report*.

Another perspective links *Hallyu* to East Asian pop culture consumption patterns. According to Hong S. (2011), who studies *Hallyu* in France, Western Europeans see the different genres of East Asian pop culture as pieces of a greater whole. According to Hong, East Asian anime, dramas, and movies based on manga brought manga fans to TV dramas; cross-media strategies that connected the drama, anime, and music industries later introduced these fans to Asian pop, including K-pop. For example, many French *Hallyu* fans in their twenties enjoyed Japanese pop before moving on to Korean pop.

Hallyu still has a weak presence in Sweden and other Nordic countries, where it would be a stretch to call the trend a "wave." However, sizeable fandom for Japanese pop culture exists there. Korean *manhwa* were introduced in Sweden in 2005 through the efforts of publishers, but remain categorized with Japanese manga. In Sweden, the consumption of East Asian pop culture is limited to Japanese manga, anime, and computer games. UppCon, which began in 2001, focuses on Japan, but did feature some Korean computer games, *manhwa*, and K-pop karaoke in 2012.

The aforementioned 2012 study conducted by KOTRA argues that European interest in, and acceptance of, Asian culture, and in particular youth interest in Japanese dramas, manga, and anime, now encompasses Korean dramas and K-pop. Increasing numbers of Europeans recognize that Korean content differs from Japanese content—for example, that *manhwa* are distinct from manga. Content producers are trying to distinguish themselves as well. Korean animators target the infant and toddler markets, which Japanese animation has left largely untouched.

The uniqueness of Korean content has been cited as a factor to explain its popularity in Europe. Ryu E. (2012) argues that the themes, sensitive yet strong male characters, and popular styles seen in Korean dramas appeal to French consumers. In explaining K-pop's rise, Son S. (2012) points to the following features: novelty (choreographed dancing as a group); openness (hybridization with Western commercial culture); restraint (Asian values such as family love and innocent love); and the friendliness of its stars (the seeming accessibility of *Hallyu* artists). In its 2012 study, KOTRA suggests that K-pop presents new, addictive melodies to European listeners, along with sophisticated beats, good-looking artists, and fresh choreography. The highly systematized artist recruitment, education, and training processes promoted by K-pop talent management companies have also been cited as factors in K-pop's success in Europe.

Increased attention from European media

European media have also shown greater interest in the growing *Hallyu* phenomenon. In the past, coverage of Korean pop culture was virtually non-existent. In this respect, *Hallyu* has played a positive role in introducing Korean culture in Europe. In 2006, the 120th anniversary of the establishment of diplomatic relations between Korea and France, in its June 4 edition *Le Monde* gave Korean pop culture's wildfire spread across Asia a passing mention. However, only in 2011, after the big K-pop concerts held in Paris, did the European press show eagerness to learn more about Korean culture. Coverage of K-pop by the European media has focused on: K-pop's move beyond Asia to Europe; K-pop's characteristics, artists, and talent management companies; the influence of *YouTube, Twitter,* and other social media, and the activities of K-pop fan clubs; the improvement in South Korea's national image as a result of K-pop; and the introduction of Korean culture.[58] Recently, European television and press have reported extensively on "Gangnam Style."[59]

French public broadcaster France 2TV discussed the influence of K-pop in Asia on its program *An Eye on the Planet.* On January 29, 2012, another public network, TF1 TV, analyzed K-pop on its *Sept à Huit* program under the title "Do You Know Super Junior?" On June 18, *Le Monde* carried a special report on the success of K-pop, citing developments in social media and the Internet, the single-sex girl and boy bands of Korea, and Korean government support as factors contributing to K-pop's success. The report also suggested that K-pop is establishing South Korea as dynamic and hip, improving the image of Korean companies. *The Financial Times'* story on February 10 about K-pop's forays into Europe points out a shift in Korean exports from manufacturing to the cultural sector. The article also notes how European fans access K-pop via social media like *Facebook* and *YouTube.* *The Independent* and *The Guardian* have also described K-pop's entry into the European market. BBC and KBS jointly produced a documentary on K-pop in 2012. *The Economist* reported on the two sides of Korea's pop music market in their August 18, 2012, edition: despite K-pop's global popularity, because the music is technically "borrowed" rather than purchased by listeners, profits from intellectual property rights remain low.

Le Monde and the BBC have been critical of Korean talent management agency training practices. An article in *Le Monde* on June 11, 2011, argued that K-pop is "the engineered product of music producers who have trained young boys and girls to sell their music overseas." On the 14th of that month, BBC critically examined the dark underbelly of K-pop success, particularly the unfair exclusive long-term contracts that many artists must sign for a shot at stardom.

Expansion of *Hallyu*-based cultural exchange programs

The rise of *Hallyu* has served as an opportunity for Europeans to learn about Korea and its culture. *Hallyu* consumers are showing interest in Korean language, culture, and the country itself, and discussing this interest with like-minded individuals in fan clubs. In 2012, the Korea Tourism Organization released a report entitled "Status of *Hallyu* in France & *Hallyu* Fans in France," which points out how French fans of *Hallyu* have experienced a change in their view of Korea

---

[58] The articles referred to in the text below include: *Financial Times* (December 14, 2011), "Talent Agencies Ride a Wave of K-Pop"; *The Independent* (June 30, 2012), "Observations: More Treats in Store for the UK's Korea-minded Pop Fans"; *The Independent* (August 7, 2011), "Korean Wave Stars Lapping on Europe's Shores"; *The Guardian* (December 15, 2011), "Bored by Cowell Pop? Try K-Pop"; *The Guardian* (April 20, 2011), "Behind the Music: What Is K-Pop and Why Are the Swedish Getting Involved?"; French public network TF1 TV's K-pop feature on *Sept à Huit* (January 2, 2012), "Korea, at the center of research on cultural industries."

[59] Recently (August 8, 2012), on the current events program *Le 19.45,* French channel M6TV introduced PSY's comic "horse dance" as an example of skilled choreography. A French daily cited PSY's silly, humorous choreography as a reason for his global success (August 18, 2012).

after exposure to K-pop. Of respondents in one survey, 66.3% answered that they "became interested in Korean culture," and 62.5% noted that they are "considering staying in Korea for an extended period of time." Furthermore, 41.2% said that they "are learning Korean," and 28.7% answered that they "want to work at a Korean company," all of which suggests that while *Hallyu* may still be in its early stages in Europe, it has had many repercussions.

In 2012 KOTRA released the "Report on *Hallyu* in Europe & Korea's National Brand: A Study on University Students in Italy, Hungary, Germany, France, and the UK," which also examined the ripple effects of *Hallyu*. According to data in this report, while *Hallyu* takes on different forms depending on the particular country in Europe, one commonality is that in every country it is growing. As a whole, *Hallyu* is having a positive impact on South Korea's national brand. The data also shows that the most common association with Korea for European youth is K-pop, over Seoul or the World Cup.

This spread of the Korean Wave in Europe has, moreover, yielded many international cultural exchange programs. Korean language programs and culture experience programs are increasingly offered across the continent. The Korean Cultural Center in the UK established a K-Pop Academy on February 25, 2012, with the first graduating class announced on May 29, and organized a Korean cultural event at the Thames Festival on September 8 and 9. The Korean Cultural Center in France has expanded its Korean language program. The center in Hungary, which opened in February 2012, and the one in Poland are also expanding their cultural programs. On April 3, 2012, the Korean Cultural Center in Budapest hosted a gathering celebrating Korean traditional music, and its Polish counterpart offered screenings of the popular drama *The 1st Shop of Coffee Prince* to the public. On September 8, 2012, the Korean Embassy in Poland, together with the Korean Cultural Center, hosted the "Feel Korea, Taste Korea, Buy Korea Festival," which afforded the public an opportunity to learn about Korean traditional music, K-pop, taekwondo, *hanbok,* and Korean food.

In 2011, Turkey opened the "Window on Korea" reference room in its national library, and in October, a Korean Cultural Center was established. Turkey designated 2012 as Visit Korea Year, and the Arts Council Korea collaborated with the Turkish Ministry of Culture and Tourism to host Korea Week in Ankara from October 13–22, 2012.

For the 100 days from June 1 to September 9 in the same year, the MCST hosted the All Eyes on Korea event at the South Bank Centre in London, around the time of the Olympics. The event introduced Korean art, performances, film, fashion, food, and literature to the public. Earlier in the year on May 17, KOCCA held a Korean music workshop, which was included in the Liverpool Sound City Festival. On September 22 and 23, the Hamburg Museum of Ethnology organized a Korean Cultural Festival, which featured shaman ritual demonstrations, K-pop dance contests, calligraphy workshops, and a *samulnori* (Korean traditional percussion) performance.

These cultural exchange programs will bring more people closer to Korea, offering expanded opportunities to experience its culture firsthand, and ultimately lay down an important foundation for *Hallyu.*

3.5.2. President Park Meets *Hallyu* Fans at First Official French Event

Reference: "Park Attends 'K-Drama Party'… Watches Performance by K-Pop Contest Winners, Greets *Hallyu* Fan Cub… Bids Them Bonjour," *News 1*, Jang Yong-seok, November 4, 2013.

President Park Geun-hye attended a "K-drama party" organized by members of a local *Hallyu* fan club, marking it as the first official event on her visit to France. President Park is now on the second day of her visit to France at the invitation of President François Hollande. She attended the K-drama party this afternoon at the Pierre Cardin Cultural Center in downtown Paris, where she listened to the title song for the MBC drama *The Moon Embracing the Sun*, sung by Deborah Civera, the winner of France's K-Pop Contest this year. The president also enjoyed a performance by Supreme Crew, contest runners-up.

President Park then attended a meeting with Sandrine-Sue Geslin, president of the organizing fan club Bonjour Corée, and the club's senior members. They shared views on *Hallyu* and cultural exchange between the two countries.

At the meeting, Park addressed the participants in French and remarked how happy she was to mutually take part in the occasion with the fans supporting the K-drama party. President Park further expressed her joy at "meeting so many Korean drama fans, after hearing about the surge of K-pop in Europe." She also noted, "French culture is beloved in Korea, and I myself enjoyed singing *chansons* as a child and love watching French films to this day."

Park added, "Sharing our culture is the first step we take in learning and understanding one another. Culture has an amazing power to bring strangers together. These days, the Internet and the media allow fans in France to access Korean songs and dramas almost as soon as they're shown in Korea. I hope ties between France and Korea can deepen through this power of culture."

According to the Blue House, Korean dramas can be watched in France on TV channels GongTV and KZTV, as well as via the online platform *Dramapassion* (http://www.dramapassion.com).

In response to a participant's question about whether she had favorite dramas, the President replied that she particularly enjoyed *Jewel in the Palace*. She added, "Like France, Korea has a rich culinary heritage, and this drama portrayed that very well for the world to see. I've heard that many tourists came to Korea for our food after the drama became popular."

When the fans were asked by the president what they found most interesting about Korean dramas, one responded, "K-dramas express so well Korean values, especially respect for elders, keeping one's manners, and establishing equality between men and women. We need those values in France, too, which is why I appreciate how they are represented in Korean dramas."

Over 500 members of Bonjour Corée attended the event, which was hosted by Adrien Lee (Lee June) of Arirang TV. The proceedings included performances by winners of the K-Pop Contest, screenings of the most popular Korean dramas as voted by Bonjour Corée's members, tips on singing soundtrack titles, and a Korean drama quiz.

Bonjour Corée is the successor to Korean Connection, a fan club credited with hosting the June 2011 Paris SM Concert together with SM Entertainment. The Blue House has explained that Bonjour Corée "is introducing not only K-pop, but various aspects of Korean culture to French society."

Blue House senior press secretary Lee Jeong-hyeon described the K-drama party as "an event planned by French fans and not organized by the government" and found it meaningful that "President Park visited the party herself to spend time with fans and speak to more people about our culture, which will ultimately facilitate 'cultural enrichment,' one of the four main policy initiatives of this administration."

3.5.3.   A Korean Culture Club Opens in Lithuanian Capital

Reference: "'Squeal!' Baltic Students Fall for South Korean Idols: A Korean Culture Club Opens in Lithuanian Capital," *OhMyNews*, Seo Jin-seok (perkunas), April 4, 2011.

Every country has its representative images. In the case of Japan, images of traditional culture such as geisha and samurai, innovative new technology, and animated films have captivated the world. China is famed for its manufacturing industry, founded on cheap labor. Since the 2008 Summer Olympics, China has been making concerted efforts to clear its name of alleged human rights violations and radically reform how it is perceived. Recent years have seen global efforts to improve national images, which directly affects policy. For example, the Japanese Ministry of Foreign Affairs appointed Doraemon, an iconic animated character, as the nation's cultural ambassador.

However, even if nation-states put forward cute, charming, wholesome images, the gulf between image and reality can disappoint. Students of Japan and China are often disenchanted by Japan's war crimes, hidden behind boasts of distinctive traditional culture and cute images, and by oppression of minority groups in China that is obscured by the nation's historic architecture and the grandeur of its natural landscapes. South Korea and Lithuania are similar in one aspect: foreigners attracted to these two countries by their representative national images have little danger of disappointment, because these images are not yet fully formed. By the same token, foreigners have less interest in the two.

A.   No official mutual interest between Lithuania and Korea

For years, Lithuania has invested foreign and domestic capital in a less-than-successful effort to present an image of "Brave Lithuania" around the world. Korea, too, has long worked hard at an image makeover, promoting selected images of a distinctive Korea, especially those of *hansik* (food), *hangeul* (alphabet), and *hanok* (architecture). These endeavors have failed to penetrate the three Baltic states at Europe's northern edge.

In October 2010, in celebration of Hangeul Day, the Korean Cultural Center from Poland hosted a cultural event in Kaunas, the second largest city in Lithuania. Titled "Korea Comes to Kaunas," this was the sole promotion hosted in the region by the Korean government, which has made little effort to imprint its image in Lithuania or its Baltic neighbors.

Although it may be too much to expect a positive image of Korea to be sown without a diplomatic office in Lithuania, interest in, and favorable impressions of, Korean culture are in fact spreading with remarkable speed among local youth.

B. Hallyu sweeps Lithuania

In December 2010, I reported on the Hallyu Club in Kaunas, a cultural organization formed by university students (Related article: "*Boys over Flowers* and Big Bang Overtake American Dramas and Pop Music").[60] The club held an event to celebrate its first anniversary in February 2011. Just over a month later, a tidal wave of Korean culture reached the capital of Lithuania. On April 2, another club focused on Korea, named Han-Vilnius, was established at Vilnius University. The university is one of the most prestigious in Lithuania and boasts a long history and exceptional programs.

A group of seven students studying Korean in the Department of Eastern Languages took the initiative in forming Han-Vilnius. Participants come not only from Vilnius University, but include people from such diverse backgrounds as high school students, office workers, and even the Lithuanian consul based in Sovetsk in Kaliningrad Oblast, Russia.

Club members settled upon the name after weeks of contemplation. The syllable *han* appears in words that represent South Korea: *hanguk* (the country itself), *hangugeo* (language), *hanbok* (dress), *hangeul* (alphabet), and the Han River. *Han* and Vilnius in combination lead to Han-Vilnius.

Questions were raised over the choice, however, and a heated debate followed among members on whether the name might also evoke the Han Chinese, the largest ethnic group in China, and whether the club's interests extended to North Korea, which undeniably shares Korean culture. On April 2, the founding members hosted an official ceremony to formally announce the meaning and purpose of the club and to christen it as "Han-Vilnius."

C. Club foundation ceremony draws a full house

Originally, the club members wanted to perform a *gosa*, a shaman ritual in which food is offered to the spirits to avoid misfortune and bring good luck. Such rituals are common in Korea before embarking on an important undertaking, but the plan did not eventuate due to difficulties in preparing the required tableware and food. Instead, the members took turns introducing aspects of Korean culture to lead the ceremony.

Without a proper website or official recognition from Vilnius University, Han-Vilnius lacked a means of promotion and instead relied on personal networks to advertise the event via *Facebook* and other social media.

Members did not know how many people would show up for the ceremony. By the time it began, however, the lecture room on the second floor of the Vilnius University Centre for Oriental Studies was packed with more than a hundred people. Scarcely a seat was empty. The students discussed such aspects of Korean culture as the alphabet, history, food, popular music, and films, and captivated the audience with compelling presentations.

---

[60] http://www.ohmynews.com/NWS_Web/view/at_pg.aspx?CNTN_CD=A0001486467.

D.   *Lithuanian students go wild for Korean idols*

As images of Korean idol groups 2PM, 2 AM, Girls' Generation, TVXQ, and SHINee appeared on the screen during the pop music presentation, the audience erupted in cheers, causing delays. The students leading the segment ran out of time before they could present everything they had prepared.

Lineta Gvazdauskaité, the President of Han-Vilnius and a philology major at Vilnius University, explained the foundation of Lithuania's second Korean culture club as follows: "The members who participated in the ceremony are friends I met at university. All of us are studying language, but we have interests in different facets of Korea, from films to music, politics, and society. The main reason I started the club was that I wanted to create a space for us to learn more about Korea and share our knowledge with others who are curious about the country."

Lineta says that South Korea had felt like a mysterious land covered in a veil, unlike elsewhere in East Asia. While local youth have become enamored of the country through online exposure to popular music, films, and dramas, no other outlet exists in Lithuania through which people can satisfy their curiosity about Korean culture or access information on it.

E.   *"One Day, I'll Watch Korean Dramas without Subtitles"*

Lineta, who decided to major in philology and harbored a dream of someday speaking all the world's languages, happened upon Korean dramas while contemplating study of a language that not many choose to learn. Lineta made a firm decision to pursue Korean, drawn by its unique, beautiful sounds, and by its similarities to the languages of neighboring Finland and Estonia, which she had studied.

Inka Miskittie, the Lithuanian consul in Sovetsk, said that she became a fan of Korean culture after chancing upon a Korean drama. She began learning Korean, determined to one day watch dramas without the help of subtitles. She added that many female members of the club started learning the language after becoming infatuated with Korean idol groups.

Passionate fans of Korean culture in Vilnius had previously been envious that Korea-related events were held only around Kaunas, which has a university with a Korean studies department. This discontent explains the explosive atmosphere at the foundation ceremony. Kim Yoo-myeong, president of the Korean Society in Lithuania, and other Koreans invited to the event, could not conceal their joy at the unexpected turnout.

F.   *Korean culture club founded in a building renovated with Japanese government funding*

Han-Vilnius is expected to face many challenges in the future. While the Kaunas Hallyu Club is supported by a university with a formal Korean studies program and has a space to hold events, Han-Vilnius receives no official support from Vilnius University, where Korean is offered only as part of a weekend program operated by the Centre for Oriental Studies, and is not recognized as part of the curriculum. For 15 years, the Vilnius University Centre for Oriental Studies has tried to add Korean classes formally without success.

In contrast, the Confucius Institute, run by the Chinese government for the global promotion of Chinese culture, has been officially inaugurated at the university. The lecture room where young fans of Korean culture gathered for the foundation ceremony is located in a Japanese studies building, newly renovated with a significant infusion of Japanese government funding. Considering these circumstances, news of the spread of Korean culture in Lithuania is not yet cause for unreserved celebration.

3.6.   CENTRAL ASIA

3.6.1.   *Hallyu* Forever: Central Asia

Reference: *Hallyu Forever: The World Is Hallyu Style*, Ko Jeong-min et al., KOFICE
Hallyu Series V, 2012, pp. 322–336, 352–355.

(pp. 322–336)

A.   *Kazakhstan*

After establishing diplomatic ties with both Koreas in 1992, Kazakhstan became
the most active of the six Central Asian countries (the former Soviet Republics
plus Mongolia) in exchanges with South Korea. In 2010, designated by Korea as
"Visit Kazakhstan Year," the mayor of Almaty was invited with a 160-member
delegation to Daegu. The delegates attended concerts, exhibitions, and fashion
shows. Representatives from Gyeonggi Province and Almaty also signed a sister
city agreement.

In turn, Kazakhstan designated 2011 as "Visit Korea Year" and organized
exhibitions, performances, and even taekwondo demonstrations to showcase Korea
and its dramas, movies, concerts, tourist attractions, and food. Many events were
held to deepen mutual understanding. Through such exchanges, *Hallyu* expanded
to areas like music, film, and food. Today, almost everyone in Kazakhstan is aware
of Korean electronic products, noodles, *bulgogi*, and *gimbap*. Familiarity with all
things Korean is widespread.

Dramas

Hallyu in Kazakhstan acquired far more influence than initially expected. The
trend began with TV dramas, which, together with movies, were introduced to
the country a few years ago. Now, viewers from their teens to their sixties enjoy
Korean dramas. The shows are popular because their plots incorporate elements
familiar to Kazakhs: respect for seniority and the elderly, the importance of family,
and filial piety (a value that was in danger of disappearing under Communist rule).
The year 2010 was the zenith for Korean dramas in Kazakhstan. Until then, only
state-owned networks aired Korean dramas, with Khabar, El Arna, and Kazakhstan
broadcasting them during prime time for years. After 2010, however, commercial
networks, seeing their popularity, also began offering Korean dramas, with some
even seeking material released five years earlier. This was a step forward, as in the
past, five of the most popular dramas, including *First Love, Autumn Tales,* and *All
In,* were broadcast in Kazakhstan free of charge as part of an exchange initiative.

New dramas shown in 2010 included *This Killing Love, Dong Yi,* and *The
Birth of the Rich*, and in 2011, *Marry Me, My Precious Child, Sungkyunkwan
Scandal, King of Baking Kim Takgu,* and *Kim Soo Ro.*

Music

On July 11, 2011, SM Entertainment held open-call auditions at the National Art
Academy in Almaty. SM believed nomads had latent vocal talent present in their
genes; furthermore, the company recognized that Eurasia is rich in resources and

thus has much potential for growth. Over 1,000 applicants from Kazakhstan as well as Russia, Uzbekistan, and beyond swarmed the venue. Outside, crowds of hopefuls awaited their turn. One girl admitted to flying four hours from Russia for the audition. Many came from Uzbekistan to demonstrate their singing and dancing abilities. Applicants were of various ethnicities, including Russians, East Asians, and various mixtures, and they performed everything from Korean to Kazakh pop and traditional songs. Many sang in Korean, which they had studied for the audition. The director of the Korean Cultural Center in Kazakhstan remarked, "As a result of *Hallyu*, we have over 1,000 people waiting to study Korean at our center, with 250 students currently enrolled."

As evidenced above, K-pop has a strong following in not only Japan and Southeast Asia, but also further afield in regions like Central Asia. Roughly a dozen *Hallyu* fan clubs of various sizes are active in Kazakhstan. Many fans practice the choreography of their favorite songs, participate in flash mobs, and copy the fashion of K-pop stars. This large fan base for K-pop began with the soundtracks that accompanied successful dramas. At the 1st Korean Pop Festival held in Almaty and sponsored by the Korean Cultural Center in Kazakhstan, most contestants sang songs from drama OSTs, such as "From the Beginning to Now" (*Winter Sonata),* "Love" (*Iris*), "It Hurts but It's Okay" (*Kim Soo Ro*), and "Him" (*King of Baking Kim Tak Goo*), all of which did well in Kazakhstan.

Film

Movie exchange with Kazakhstan is limited to free screenings of Korean films during Korea Film Week. This event is held biannually in Astana by the Korean Cultural Center. Films with historical subjects such as *Taegukgi* are popular in Central Asia, but have yet to match the success of dramas.

In June 2011, a Korea Film Festival was held at the Caesar Cinema in Almaty. Screenings included *Take-Off, Speedy Scandal, Beyond the Years,* and *For Eternal Hearts.* The festival inspired greater interest in Korean movies. The most well-known Korean director in Kazakhstan is Kim Ki-duk, of *Bad Man, Time,* and *Spring, Summer, Fall, Winter... and Spring* fame. Kim first came to prominence there when his work was introduced at the 2005 Eurasia International Film Festival. He has also appeared on Kazakhstan television several times, and served as Korea's spokesperson in front of other renowned directors and actors from Europe and Asia. Kazakhstan has demonstrated continuous affection for Kim, and in 2011, he was invited to serve as a judge in the international competition category at the 7th Eurasia International Film Festival.

Korean movies that have done well at international film festivals meet with great interest, regardless of box office receipts. Because Kazakhstan's film industry is looking for innovative ideas and is weak in musical films and comedies, it seeks inspiration from the fresh stories and stylized images of Korean cinema.

Korean language

Over its 30-year history, the Almaty Korean Education Center has witnessed an increase in locals who want to study Korean. Although Chinese language experienced an earlier boom in step with China's economic development, the Korean

Table 3–36.   Growth of students at Almaty Korean Education Center

Year	Number of Students
2009	441
2010, 1st Semester	639
2010, 2nd Semester	723
2011, 1st Semester	730
2011, 2nd Semester	827
2012, 1st Semester	844

(Source: KOFICE, *Hallyu Story*, Vol. 16)

dramas screened on television over the last decade have spawned a growing desire among people of all ages to study Korean culture and language. By the first semester of 2012, enrolments at the center had doubled from 441 in 2009 to 844 and ranged from elderly ethnic Koreans to younger students.

On September 3, an IT vocational program for ethnic Korean youth was launched in Kazakhstan. This program, supported by the Overseas Koreans Foundation, was first established a decade ago. Each year, roughly 25 local co-ethnics register. In 2012, students came from as far away as Bishkek, Kyrgyzstan. A total of 46 registered for the program, with 19 in the regular course, 12 in the advanced course, and 15 in a permanent course, which, in turn, shows the steady increase of interest in Korean language and culture.

Korean food

Korean food has become as popular as dramas and is widely found in both restaurants and local supermarkets. The five-star Hyatt Regency in Almaty hosts a Korean food festival once every two years. A professor at Abai Khan Kazakh State University noted, "It's difficult to find a Kazakh festival without Korean food involved somehow."[61] Although Kazakhstan borders China, Korean restaurants are more numerous than Chinese restaurants.

It is also easy to find Korean drinks, snacks, and ice cream in the supermarkets. The people of Kazakhstan consume an average of 12 kg of snack foods a year, on a scale that they almost become essential staples. Half of these snacks are imported. Orion's Choco Pie is one of the most popular treats, with revenues of approximately $600,000 annually.

B.   Uzbekistan

Hallyu in Uzbekistan has grown rapidly and has already entered the maturity stage.[62] Korean dramas are consistently popular, and free treatment offered by volunteer Korean doctors has also built a good reputation for the nation.

---

[61] KOTRA (2011), *Marketing Field Report*, November 29, Lee Jeong-gwan, Trade Officer in Almaty.
[62] KOTRA explains the development of *Hallyu* in five stages: "pre-entry - entry - recognition - growth - maturity."

Dramas

As in Kazakhstan, *Hallyu* in Uzbekistan began on TV. Most popular dramas shared a common historical theme detailing a past made painful by foreign occupation. Following the earliest *Hallyu* successes of *Jewel in the Palace* and *Jumong*, Uzbekistan's state-owned channel showed *Empress Chun Choo*, *King and I*, *Seodongyo*, and *The Last Empress* in 2010. *Queen Seondeok* was broadcast in 2011, and *Chuno*'s first episode aired in July 2012. Such period pieces enjoy great popularity in Uzbekistan. *Jewel in the Palace, Seodongyo, The Last Empress*, and *Winter Sonata* are rebroadcast at least once a year.

Uzbekistan's state-run networks—Uzbekistan, Yoshlar, and Tashkent—screen Korean period dramas in the evening hours for families to watch at home, as they appeal more broadly to all generations than contemporary dramas.

Films

Korean cinema is not yet widely known in Uzbekistan. Several films have been shown on TV, but none have opened in theaters. Uzbekistan still is not able to afford the rights to distribute Korean movies; thus, fans turn to illegal downloads or pirated CDs brought in from Russia. No laws are in place to crack down on copyright violations, so the circulation of pirated copies will likely continue.

Despite these limitations, efforts have been made to promote Korean film. For example, the Korean Embassy organized a film festival that allowed fans of Korean dramas and culture to watch movies for free. Films shown in 2011 included *Take-Off, Highway Star, Jeon Woo Chi*, and *A Barefoot Dream*. These movies, offered with Russian and Uzbek subtitles, have proven popular.

In 2012, Korean film festivals were held not only in the capital Tashkent but also in Jizak and Samarkand to commemorate the 20th anniversary of diplomatic ties between Korea and Uzbekistan. Nearly 1,500 fans crowded the opening

Table 3–37. Broadcast of Korean period dramas (2010)

Channel	Program	Hours	Period
Uzbekistan	*Jewel in the Palace;*	18:00–19:00	January-April
	My Sweet City;	20:00–22:30	April-April
	The Last Empress;	17:15–18:00	July-October
	King of Bread Kim Tak Goo	21:00–21:45	October-December
Yoshlar	*Yi San;*	21:10–22:00	January-May
	Queen Seondeok	22:00–22:40	May-August
Tashkent	*The Last Empress;*	21:10–22:00	April-July
	Seodongyo;	20:30–21:00	May-October
	Empress Chun Choo	21:00–21:40	September-December

(Source: KOFICE (2011), *Hallyu Trend Report*)

ceremony for the festival at the Navoi Theater in Tashkent. Vacant seats were scarce. Although *Hallyu* in Uzbekistan has not reached the point where Korean movies are released officially in theaters, film festival attendance has clearly increased.

Games

Korean online games, such as the highly popular *Lineage*, also do well in Uzbekistan. In fact, some fans go so far as to travel to Russia in search of *Lineage* game items or to acquire better skills in the game. *The Legend of Mir II,* officially released in Uzbekistan in 2009, is the only online game with a server in the country. Its makers promoted a localization strategy to encourage widespread use of the game and organized multiple competitions. This new approach to service and marketing enhanced the brand of Korean games and had an impact on Uzbekistan's gaming industry.

Korean language

TV drama fans regularly develop an interest in the Korean language, which leads to an increase in students of Korean. The Tashkent Korean Education Center, which supervised the 22nd TOPIK in Uzbekistan, reported that over 1,000 applicants came to take the test in February 2012. With more Korean companies operating in Uzbekistan, employment opportunities for Uzbek youth will likely grow; accordingly, more and more applicants are taking the test to work at a Korean company or study abroad in Korea.

Korean products

Korea is Uzbekistan's second largest trading partner behind Russia. After President Karimov's visit to Korea in the 1990s, and following the opening of a Daewoo Motors factory in Uzbekistan, bilateral trade increased significantly. In the 90s, 70% of all cars in Uzbekistan were manufactured by Daewoo. Korean electronic goods make up nearly 50% of the home appliance market, and 80% of the major home appliances.[63]

Uzbekistan has historically been most active with Russia in commerce. In 2011, it imported $2.29 billion from Russia, with Korea right behind at $1.49 billion. The Uzbek people see Korean products as "quality products that last a long time."[64]

The effect of *Hallyu* is felt in increased spending on not just Korean cultural products but virtually all Korean goods. According to a recent survey on Korea's national image, 54% of respondents stated that they learned about Korean culture through Korean dramas. Both male and female respondents had watched a significant amount of Korean television.[65]

---

[63] Korea Communications Commission (2008), "Establishing a Roadmap for the Spread of *Hallyu*."
[64] *Maeil Business Daily*, August 15, 2012, Kim S.
[65] Yun S. et al. (2010), "Korea's Brand Image in Central Asia," Korea Institute for International Economic Policy.

C. Mongolia

Dramas

Korean dramas are influential in Mongolia as well, with public networks taking turns to broadcast popular series. As elsewhere in Central Asia, Mongolians
enjoy family-oriented dramas. According to a survey conducted by a research
team at Mongolia's Press Institute, the drama with the highest ratings during
August 2010 was *Pink Lipstick*; in September, the crown went to *King of Baking
Kim Tak Goo*. Mongolian teens watch their favorite dramas on DVD. Prices are
relatively cheap at ₩3,000 each, so they are easy to find and purchase.

Networks compete to broadcast Korean dramas because of their popularity. Some channels so flooded the airwaves with Korean programs that several
viewers felt compelled to complain. After 2010, the broadcasters tried to find a
happy medium and began airing Russian, Chinese, American, and local dramas
as well. Due to the increase in Korean dramas, the Communications Regulatory
Commission of Mongolia limited television advertising. In an attempt to scale
back excessive commercials, no more than 15 minutes of advertisements were
allowed per hour.

As in China and Southeast Asian countries that sought to cut back on broadcasting of Korean dramas, networks were also required to fill 50% of their programming with local content.[66] Mongolian networks have also been diversifying
program sources to include Russian, Japanese, Chinese, and Hong Kong dramas.

Music

K-pop is spreading rapidly among Mongolian youth. Teenagers meet online and
organize fan clubs as elsewhere in Asia. Mongolian youths' affectation of the
styles of 2PM, 2 NE1, Big Bang, and Wonder Girls is similar to what one finds
in Korea. Unfortunately, albums by Korean artists are not yet sold officially in
Mongolia. As a result, it is difficult to tabulate statistics on profits or revenue.
Many Mongolians purchase Korean music through friends who travel to Korea or
online from such sites as *www.mglvideo.com* and *www.shared4.com*.

According to a rep from Hi-Fi Records, a Mongolian music store, Korean
music has many fans, but Hi-Fi doesn't carry releases by Korean artists because
they don't sell well. Most CDs brought in via Russia or China sell for roughly
10,000 tögrög (₩10,000), but the sales price for those from Korea is twice as
high.[67] A similar situation holds true in other industries. Mongolian distributors
tend not to purchase Korean movies either, because it is difficult to break even.

One Mongolian group has emulated Korean idol groups. In 2009, the five-
member Crush Bush was brought together with a style—clothes, songs, dances,
and so on—very evocative of Korean boy bands. It is difficult to quantify the
popularity of K-pop using Mongolian statistics or music charts, but the debut of
a band with a similar look and feel to Korean boy bands suggests the appeal of
K-pop in Mongolia.

---

[66] KOFICE (2011), *Hallyu Trend Report*.
[67] KOFICE (2010), Correspondence Report.

Table 3–38.   Korean programs broadcast by Mongolian networks in 2010

Channel	Program	Hours	Period
UBS-1	*Aeja's Sister Minja*	Mondays-Sundays 22:00	December 6– February 3
	Stairway to Heaven	Mondays-Sundays 22:00	February 4– February 25
	Winter Sonata (re-runs)	Mondays-Sundays 22:50	March 11–March 31
	My Wife Is Back	Mondays-Sundays 23:00, 11:00 (re-runs)	April 1–May 27
	Aquarius	Mondays-Fridays 22:10, 11:10	October 20– December 2
	King of Baking Kim Tak Goo	11:40, 22:00	October-November
UBS-2	*Terms of Endearment*	Mondays-Fridays 18:10	November 10– January 10
	Jang Gilsan	Mondays-Fridays 10:05	July 6–August 4
	Pink Lipstick	Mondays-Sundays 12:10, 23:00	May 29–August 26
UBS-3	*Jewel in the Palace*	Mondays-Fridays 10:40, 20:00	September 2–December
	Temptation of Wife	Mondays-Fridays 22:00	November 6-present
	Woman of the Sun	Mondays-Fridays 21:40	October–November
	Take Care of My Lady	Mondays-Sundays 23:00	September–October
	Temptation of an Angel	Mondays-Sundays 18:40	January 3–January 22
	Cinderella's Sister	Mondays-Sundays 09:30, 18:50	October 4–
	Kim Suro	Mondays-Sundays 09:30, 19:00	September 6–
	The Fugitive: Plan B	Mondays-Sundays 18:50	November 22–
TV-5–2	*Three Brothers*	Mondays-Sundays 09:30, 19:00	May 17–
TV 25–1	*Ambitious Times*	Mondays-Sundays 19:00	March 22–
	Iris	Mondays-Fridays 10:50	May 20–

(Continued)

Table 3–38. (*Continued*).

Channel	Program	Hours	Period
	Queen of Housewives	Mondays-Sundays 20:00	February 3–24
	Queen Seondeok	Mondays-Sundays 20:00	January 2–March 5
TV 25–2	*Who Are You*	Mondays-Sundays 17:45	February 7–25
	God of Study	Mondays-Sundays 17:45	March 20–
	Daejoyoung	Mondays-Fridays 23:00	November 22– January 28
B-TV	*Love You a Thousand Times*	Mondays-Sundays 20:00	March 24–
	Iris	Mondays-Sundays 18:10	March 20–
	Return of Iljimae	Mondays-Sundays 18:10, 10:40 (re-runs)	May 21–
	Marry Me	Mondays-Fridays 10:40, 18:10	December 7–
TV-9	*Hateful but Once Again*	09:00, 20:00	March–April
	Yeongaesomun	10:40, 18:10	March–May
	Janghwa Hongryeon		December 20– February 10
	Into the Storm	Mondays-Sundays 19:00	March 21–
	Jumong	15:50, 20:30	July–August
	Successful Story of a Bright Girl	Mondays-Fridays 11:20	September–October
	Sandglass	11:40, 19:00	August–September
TV-8	*1st Shop of Coffee Prince*	Mondays-Sundays 17:50, 10:30 (re-runs)	May 22–July
	First Love of a Royal Prince	Mondays-Fridays 18:00–19:05	July–August
	You Smile	Mondays-Fridays 18:00–19:05	August–September
	Personal Taste	Mondays-Fridays 18:00–19:05	June 8–August

(Continued)

Table 3–38. *(Continued).*

Channel	Program	Hours	Period
	White Tower	Mondays-Fridays 18:00–19:05	June 18-July
	My Man's Woman	Mondays-Fridays 18:00–19:05	June 15-August
	Yi San	Mondays-Fridays 18:00–19:05	October 4-November
	Cinderella	Mondays-Fridays 18:00–19:05	November
Magic MGTV	*Personal Taste*	23:10–00:20	March-April
	Smile Again	Mondays-Tuesdays 19:00, 09:10	May 20-July
Mongol TV	*Chuno*	22:00–23:10	July-August

(Source: KOFICE (2010), *Overseas Hallyu Trends*)

D.   Successes and failures of Hallyu in Central Asia (pp. 352–355)

Hallyu's success

Amongst Korean content, historical dramas enjoy the greatest popularity on Central Asian television, and they have established themselves as entertainment suitable for all ages. *Jewel in the Palace,* which aired in 2005, was so successful that many called 2005 the "Year of *Tanggem*" (the Uzbek pronunciation of the drama's title). The series had ratings of over 70% and requests were made to the state-owned networks for re-runs. *Tanggem* was also popular that year as a name for baby girls. *Jang Bogo, Jumong, The Immortal Admiral Yi Sun Shin, Seodongyo,* and *The Last Empress*, which followed *Jewel in the Palace*, were also embraced by Central Asian viewers. Children playing sword games in the streets often call each other "Jumong" or "Jang Bogo," from the names of characters in the series.

Along with *Jewel in the Palace, Jumong* and *Chuno* are television favorites in Central Asia. *Jumong*'s popularity in Kazakhstan is dizzying. First broadcast by Kazakhstan's TV & Radio from 2010 to 2011, viewers grew enamored of the drama and repeatedly asked for it to be rebroadcast. On May 5, 2011, over 5,000 fans rushed to see Song Il-guk and other Korean celebrities who came to a performance in Kazakhstan's capital Astana to celebrate Visit Korea Year, despite the fact that the venue only sat 3,000. Thanks to the broadcast of *Jumong* on Kazakhstan TV in 2009, Song Il-guk even became known as a "national hero." *Jumong* was screened as a rerun at viewer request and has far surpassed the popularity of Turkish dramas and Latin American *telenovelas*, which were originally preferred by Kazakhs.

This popularity might be due in part to the 100,000 ethnic Koreans living in Kazakhstan who watch the dramas produced in their ancestral homeland to learn about its history, culture, and mores.

Many fans of *Chuno* say that it has a different appeal from other Korean period dramas. Earlier dramas were rich in illustrations of the life of royals, whereas *Chuno* portrays the lives of commoners during the Joseon Dynasty. Its plot is dramatic and exciting, and its gripping images appeal to Central Asian viewers. Even the well-known Uzbek magazine *Bekajon*, which had avoided coverage of Korean dramas, featured an article on *Chuno,* testifying to its immense popularity.[68]

Central Asians are fanatical about Korean period dramas because the stories resonate. Viewers relate to the patriotic, loyal characters who strive valiantly to rescue their country and rejoice with them at their conclusion, as these series unfailingly have happy endings. Viewers from Uzbekistan, Kazakhstan, and other Central Asian countries can empathize, as their countries are newly independent states liberated merely 20 years ago, and their people have suffered numerous foreign invasions. The difficulties portrayed in the dramas recall what Central Asians suffered at the hands of Arab states, China, Turkey, and other neighbors. Central Asian viewers, reminded by watching Korea protect its culture of how they strived to protect their own, are attracted to these heroic tales and the sophistication of the images captured onscreen. They embrace the dramas passionately, as if they told their own stories.

Failure of *Hallyu*

Mini Karaoke, a karaoke bar that opened on a street in downtown Tashkent favored by the young, artsy crowd, ended up failing spectacularly despite the popularity of Korean dramas and their soundtracks. Having a group of people crowd a small room, regardless of gender, and sing loudly was not in keeping with Islamic tradition. Ultimately, the "karaoke culture" introduced by Korean residents of Uzbekistan carried a negative image that brought down Mini Karaoke.

---

[68] KOFICE (2012), *Uzbekistan Correspondent, 2012.*

3.7.   THE MIDDLE EAST

3.7.1.   *Hallyu* Forever: The Middle East

Reference: *Hallyu Forever: The World Is Hallyu Style*, Ko Jeong-min et al., KOFICE
Hallyu Series V, 2012, pp. 538–550.

A.   *Korean dramas*

Television dramas are at the forefront of the Korean Wave in the Middle East. The most recent example of the force of the Korean Wave in this region is the popularity of *Jewel in the Palace* in Iran. The show, which aired on the Islamic Republic of Iran Broadcasting's Channel 2 from October 2006 to October 2007, was a terrific hit with viewers. Ratings for the show hit a remarkable 90%, more than double the 30–40% average for the state-run network.

Jumong also exemplified the effects of *Hallyu* in the Middle East when it achieved ratings of 85%. The show first aired in Iran on December 9, 2008, and then was broadcast on Channel 3 of the state-run network every Tuesday evening at 8:30 under the title *Prince of the Legend*. The show, which initially screened in Korea from 2005 to 2006, centered on Jumong, the founder of the Goguryeo Kingdom. It achieved immense popularity upon debut and caused a sensation in Iran. In December 2009, an anonymous Iranian blogger contributed the following to *globalpost.com*, an English-language website where bloggers from around the world add posts about current events in their home countries:

> Family time in Iran has become Korean drama time. Frequent visits to family are a well-established tradition in Iranian society. Usually nights are spent sipping just-brewed tea and eating fresh fruit and salted nuts. This goes on for long hours into the night, especially in summer when children and university students are free from school schedules. Things have changed, however, since the national network started broadcasting the Korean drama *Jumong*. Now, in many homes after dinner, entire families race to huddle around the TV. Photos of the main characters grace everything from stationery to serving trays. Fans have set up blogs and forums to exchange news and discuss episodes.[69]

The tremendous success of *Jewel in the Palace* and *Jumong* in Iran was made possible by Ghassan, a specialty distributer based in Saudi Arabia. Ghassan spearheaded the Korean Wave among Arabic-speaking countries when it made a lump purchase of 16 MBC dramas—including *Yi San*, *Winter Bird*, and *Super Rookie*—and distributed them to 18 countries in the Middle East, including Saudi Arabia, Egypt, Lebanon, Iraq, Algeria, Bahrain, the UAE, and Jordan. Most notably, MBC Plus Media succeeded in selling *Joseon Scientific Investigation Unit, Byeolsungeom* to Iran and Saudi Arabia, which was the first time that a drama made by an independent production company and shown on a program provider channel was exported.

---

[69] http://www.globalpost.com/dispatch/middle-east/091216/iran-korea-tv.

SBS also sold distribution rights for over 30 popular shows, including *Lovers in Paris*, to the Dubai-based company Music Master for broadcast across the Middle East. KBS is expected to air the documentary *Ancient Tea Route* on Al Jazeera, and other documentaries, like *Yugo* and *Dojagi*, and cartoons, such as *Apple Candy Girl*, will be broadcast on MBC, the largest satellite network in the Middle East. SBS also recently made its first drama export to Iraq with the historical drama *Tree with Deep Roots*, which aired in 2011 to great popularity and earned lead actor Han Suk-kyu an award for his portrayal of King Sejong, inventor of the Korean alphabet. It is anticipated that the show will enjoy a similar reception in Iraq.

Currently, *Boys over Flowers* has begun airing on the Dubai channel MBC Drama under the Arabic title *Ayam Al Zuhour* and is receiving a positive response from *Hallyu* fans. Since September, it has been airing three times a day in the UAE—at 1 a.m., 9 a.m., and 5 p.m. Fans have been posting messages to the *Boys over Flowers'* website expressing gratitude to MBC for exporting the show. At the same time, complaints occasionally appear that the Arabic dubbing ruins the episodes. Because the dubbing uses Saudi Arabian dialect and slang, people in other Middle Eastern countries can be put off. Fans are calling for Standard Arabic to be used instead, or for subtitles to replace dubbing altogether. Standard Arabic is rarely used in conversation and appears primarily in mass media, such as news and books. However, with the increasing use of Standard Arabic dubbing of foreign films and television shows, people are growing more familiar with it and coming to prefer it.

Among Korean television stars, Kim Hyun-joong is receiving particular attention from fans in the Middle East. Fans share information about Kim, such as the fact that he's a wildly popular singer across Asia and a member of the boy band SS501, and post messages for him in Romanized Korean, peppered with terms like *oppa* and *saranghamnida*. Kim appears to have more fan exposure than other actors because he is also a singer and rapper. Episodes of *Boys over Flowers* are available any time through MBC's online TV service *shahid.net* for fans who miss the scheduled broadcasts.

Most Korean television shows airing in the Middle East are sold directly to local broadcasters, but as the influence of the Korean Wave grows in the region, Korean networks are creating channels targeting Arabic-speaking countries or adding shows to their regional programming. A particular example is the satellite network Korea TV, which has been broadcasting steadily since its launch in October 2008. Based in Cairo, it airs around the clock and provides its own subtitling of such shows as the MBC dramas *Young-Jae's Golden Days*, *What's Up Fox?*, *Lawyers*, and *One Fine Day*, and the SBS dramas *War of Money*, *Cannot Hate You*, and *Stairway to Heaven*. It also screens variety shows, such as MBC's *Infinite Challenge* and *We Got Married*.

Along with Korea TV, KBS World, KBS's overseas network, airs diverse entertainment programs in the Middle East. The shows, which include English subtitles below the Korean ones, have been well received by local viewers as well as Korean expats. Currently, KBS World is broadcast live simultaneously in 54 countries throughout Asia (except for Japan), Europe, and the Middle East. It is watched by approximately 140 million viewers in 34.7 million households.

B. Film

In 2011, the distribution company CJ E&M sold the film *Sector 7*, starring ·Ha Ji-won, to 46 countries around the world, from Europe to the Middle East, Africa, and all across Asia. The sales price of the movie broke records for a Korean film in Germany and the Middle East. It was shown in Iran, Saudi Arabia, Kuwait, Lebanon, and Palestine in the Middle East, and in Algeria, Egypt, and Ethiopia in Africa.

Festivals offer another opportunity to introduce Korean films locally. At the Abu Dhabi Film Festival, *Masquerade* was showcased to great applause. A startlingly large crowd packed the theater located in the Emirates Palace, Abu Dhabi's premier luxury hotel, well before the movie began. Director Choo Chang-min and lead actor Ryu Seung-ryong were present and took part in a brief but meaningful Q&A. One member of the audience asked whether the film was based on historical events. Choo answered, "It's a fictional story based on 15 days not recorded in historical documents." Another asked, "Has Lee Byung-hun always been that funny?" "Not really, but he tried." "What do you think of Abu Dhabi?" "I've never been to such a dazzling film festival. I look forward to coming back for the next one."

A Korean resident of Abu Dhabi, Kim Min-jae, said he was very impressed by the sight of the packed theater. "*Masquerade* was the first movie my fiancée and I saw together, so it holds a lot of personal meaning. I decided to see it again with friends here in Abu Dhabi, a land so far from home. I'd assumed that foreigners wouldn't feel the same emotions as we do, but when I heard their laughter fill the theater, I felt really happy and proud to be Korean." Kim complimented the film's smooth narrative flow from start to finish and its humor, which could be appreciated by all viewers regardless of nationality, and added a thank you to all involved in making the movie.

On the Abu Dhabi Film Festival's homepage, people posted comments praising the movie. Odel Al-Allaf, a festival attendee, wrote, "This movie was excellent. I was impressed by its handling of the subject and the mix of comedy and tragedy in a historical setting. The location, costumes, production design, cinematography, and acting were all superb. I'm not surprised it was such a hit in Korea."

The National, a leading local magazine, also selected *Joint Security Area* as a must-see film at the festival: "It's actually a bit of an oldie (2000) and was a huge hit in South Korea when it came out, but this is certainly something to see on the big screen if you haven't before. Explained through a series of flashbacks, the story follows an investigation into the deaths of two North Korean soldiers in the Demilitarized Zone between the two countries and the subsequent cover-up. Also, if you wanted an endorsement, Quentin Tarantino named it as one of his favorite films made since 1992."[70]

C. Music

Korean music is also causing tremors in the Middle East. As of January 2011, K-pop videos on *YouTube* had received 630,000 hits in Egypt, 410,000 hits in

---

[70] http://www.thenational.ae/arts-culture/film/what-to-watch-at-abu-dhabi-film-festival-2012-joint-security-area#ixzz2uyJt4cOd.

Kuwait, and an astonishing 10.3 million hits in Saudi Arabia. Up until recently, *Hallyu* in the Middle East had centered on television shows, but a new wave seems to have formed around K-pop. Saudi Arabia's 10 million-plus hits, the highest in the Middle East and 1/6th of South Korea's total hits, show that interest in K-pop has not been limited to a subset of hardcore fans.

According to a 2010 online survey of 26,122 people conducted by KBS World, approximately 40% chose Super Junior as their favorite band. TVXQ took second place, with ZE:A in third, Girls' Generation fourth, and 2PM fifth. Rain is also extremely popular in the Middle East. The May 19, 2011, edition of the tabloid *Gulf News* featured Rain on its front page: "As the South Korean artist gears up for a two-year break from the entertainment industry, his fans are confident he'll emerge from military service stronger."[71]

In addition to distributing K-pop online via such channels as *YouTube* and social networking sites, more K-pop stars are also traveling to the Middle East to publicize their music directly. The idol group ZE:A was the first to do so. They held a fan meeting-cum-concert in Dubai on April 22, 2012, followed by a thousand-seat showcase performance in Abu Dhabi. This event was their introduction to K-pop fans in the Middle East. The event was intended to follow up concerts held in Abu Dhabi the previous year by Seo In-young and Nine Muses, who are under the same management as ZE:A.

ZE:A landed in Dubai to great fanfare. At a time when K-pop fever has been spreading around the world, they took their first steps into the Middle East, the next big market for the Korean Wave. A representative from entertainment company Star Empire said, "Last year in Abu Dhabi, I attended the festival with Seo In-young and Nine Muses and witnessed K-pop fever with my own eyes." The representative added, "Interest in both girl groups and boy bands from Korea has grown. We were invited by local sponsors to produce the showcase." Korean idol stars have already been traveling to other parts of Asia, Europe, and South America. But given clothing restrictions for women in the Middle East, particular attention was paid to the Dubai fan meeting and showcase and how local fans would react to Nine Muses' wardrobe and performance on stage.

The Middle East has been no exception to the worldwide "Gangnam Style" craze. The song has received a record-breaking number of "likes" on *YouTube* and surpassed 700 million hits. It also held the #2 spot for three weeks straight on the world-famous Billboard charts; as of this writing, "Gangnam Style" was still going strong across Asia, North America, and Europe. Even more intriguing is the song's popularity in the Middle East and the infamously conservative Gulf states. PSY's tune has been playing nonstop on the radio and in clubs frequented by foreigners. The September 30 issue of *Gulf News* reported that "Gangnam Style" has opened the door for K-pop stars and listed other Korean artists together with PSY.

The Korean Wave is not new to the Middle East. Korean shows were being aired seven or eight years ago on KBS World and Arirang TV. The recent rise of K-pop has simply pushed *Hallyu* further.

The popularity of "Gangnam Style" has been mind-boggling. Young fans in the Middle East are crazy about Korea's unique brand of sugary romance, the

---

[71] http://gulfnews.com/arts-entertainment/celebrity/rain-set-to-take-a-break-1.809462.

tightly choreographed moves of Korean idol stars, and the easy-to-follow music. Korean TV shows are even being dubbed into Arabic now in the UAE.

Teenagers who once had no idea where Korea was now seek it out online and listen to Korean music. They are even showing an interest in the language and food and frequenting local Korean restaurants. But they're not stopping there. Eager to connect with Koreans, they are forming communities online with Korean teenagers and creating groups on social networking sites. International cultural exchange is proceeding apace among the youth. Korea, a smaller country that had attracted little attention until a few years ago, is now taking center stage at the global level.

Korean popular culture has become synonymous with Korea itself. People living thousands of kilometers away are checking out the country as a result of the Korean Wave. In addition, the ripple effects of the Korean Wave have gone beyond culture and are exerting significant force on the economy and diplomacy. The BBC reported that PSY's success has meant that Korea is developing as a country at the cultural vanguard. Nevertheless, given the many sensitive issues in the Middle East—religion, politics, culture, and so on—it is important that Korean Wave celebrities mind what they say and do, as the flames of the Korean Wave could just as easily flicker out as flare up.

D.   *Theater and cultural performances*

Few Korean plays have been performed in the Middle East because of numerous obstacles, from language barriers to lack of awareness of Korean theater. Official festivals have served as the venues for the few exceptions, such as the comedy troupe Ongals, or "Babbling Comedy," made up of comedians like Jo Su-won and Choi Gi-seop recruited by KBS and SBS. When Ongals was invited to perform at the Dubai Festival, the show sold out and drew much press attention. Jo Su-won, leader of Ongals, said, "I had no idea the audience would be so big. This just proves to me that the global language isn't English. It's laughter." Choi Gi-seop added, "After performing at the Edinburgh Fringe Festival two years in a row, I gained a lot of confidence and wanted to show that K-pop is not the only force behind *Hallyu*. Our comedy can also speak to people around the world."

Sungshin Women's University professor Seo Gyeong-deok, a public relations specialist who has been helping to promote Ongals abroad, said, "Our next stops are the Festival d'Avignon in France and the Montreal Comedy Festival in Canada, and we'll try to spread the word about Korean comedy."

Aside from these official events, other Korean cultural performances have been held in the Middle East. For example, a national university in Dubai hosted the creation of a "Korea street" with displays of Korean cosmetics, clothing with Korean script, and traditional Korean tea. The event was organized for a school festival by a Korean student group in order to promote Korean culture. Visitors were invited to sit and experience a traditional tea ceremony and try their hand at the *gayageum* stringed instrument.

Similar colorful events are held regularly at universities with the participation of Korean businesses in order to promote Korea. Curiosity about the country, which has mainly been generated through pop culture, particularly television and

K-pop, is expanding to all facets of Korean culture, and the scale of that interest is growing as the participation and effort of local fans increases each year.[72]

E. *Traditional Korean culture*

Taekwondo is the most popular traditional Korean activity in the Middle East. At the 2008 Beijing Olympics, 28-year-old Shaikha Maitha Bint Mohammad Bin Rashid Al Maktoum of the ruling family of Dubai participated in the women's taekwondo event in the 67 kg division. In order to be in medal contention, Al Maktoum received intense training in Korea, home of taekwondo. While there, she made news for contacting Hyun Bin's agency and requesting his autograph, describing herself as a devoted fan. At the time, *Winter Sonata*, *Jewel in the Palace*, *My Lovely Sam Soon*, and other Korean shows were very popular in Dubai.

Taekwondo is popular in Egypt as well. Already renowned as a form of self-defense, the martial art developed a reputation as good athletic exercise for sculpting one's body. As of 2007, taekwondo classes were being offered at 180 sports clubs around the country. In December 2007, the Embassy of the Republic of Korea in Egypt sponsored its third Ambassador's Cup taekwondo competition, with the participation of 600 athletes representing 34 clubs from around the country. It was the largest event of its kind since taekwondo was introduced to Egypt in the 1970s. Taekwondo is primarily concentrated in the metropolitan areas of Cairo, Alexandria, Tanta, Port Said, and Ismailia. The number of those who practice taekwondo is fewer than a thousand elsewhere in the country. More support from the government and athletic circles is needed if the sport is to continue to grow in popularity.

---

[72] http://news.kbs.co.kr/news/NewsView.do?SEARCH_NEWS_CODE=2467341&&source=http://news.kbs.co.kr/world/2012/04/25/2467341.html.

3.8.   *Hallyu* TOURISM

3.8.1.   Myeongdong "Cosmetics Road" Today

Reference: "Myeongdong 'Cosmetics Road' Today," *Weekly Chosun*, Kim Gyeong-min, November 21, 2011, No. 2182, pp. 66–69.

November 16, 4 p.m. A van emblazoned with a sign that reads "Foreign Tourists" in *kanji* stops at the entrance of Myeongdong-gil in Jung-gu, Seoul. Four Japanese women—Akino Yoko (32) and friends—get out. Akino holds a travel guide in her hand. They walk down Myeongdong-ro, which runs east to west through the heart of Myeongdong from Myeongdong Cathedral to Sogong-dong. Myeongdong's other main thoroughfare is Jungang-ro. Running perpendicular to Myeongdong-ro, the two intersect in the center of Myeongdong-ro, where Myeongdong Theater is located. Snippets of Japanese and Chinese are heard:

> "*Hai, douzo.*" (At your service)
> "*Mina-san mite kudasai!*" (Everyone, please look here)
> "*Huanying guanglin!*" (At your service)

Akino and her friends turn onto Jungang-ro. Cafes, shoe stores, boutiques, and accessory outlets line the street. Among the 50-odd stores on Jungang-ro are name-brand cosmetics shops. Life-size cutouts of *Hallyu* stars Jang Keun-suk and TVXQ advertise the shops. Sales clerks are soliciting customers outside the stores. In miniskirt uniforms despite the cold weather, the clerks enthusiastically call out to customers in Korean, Japanese, and Chinese.

First stop for Akino and her friends is Laneige, a shop for a Korean cosmetics brand. About 20 customers browse inside; apart from three or four, all of them are foreign. Akino does not speak a word of Korean, but this is not a problem. The staff addresses her in Japanese. "I was surprised to find that no matter what store in Myeongdong I went into, someone could explain the products to me in Japanese," said Akino.

Qin Lo (26), a Chinese tourist, similarly noted, "I went to six cosmetics stores in Myeongdong, and the staff at each one talked to me about the products in Chinese." Qin came to Korea on November 14 and planned to stay for four days. She had already purchased ₩300,000 worth of cosmetics. Her shopping bag contained nearly a dozen cosmetic items purchased at The Face Shop and Missha, as well as free facial mask packs and samples.

Cosmetics outlets have occupied Myeongdong's Jungang-ro. Laneige, The Face Shop, It's Skin, Nature Republic, Innisfree, The Body Shop, Missha, Baviphat, Holika Holika, Skin Food, Aritaum, Tony Moly, Etude House, The Saem, and Banila Co. line both sides as if the street were a gallery. According to *Chosun Weekly* research in Myeongdong conducted on November 15, of the 58 stores on Jungang-ro, including those under construction, 18 were devoted to cosmetics—almost 1/3.

To tourists, Jungang-ro is known as "Cosmetics Street." "The travel guide I read online before I came called this area 'Cosmetics Street'," said Madeline Kaye (38). "It's remarkable how many cosmetic shops there are here." Japanese tourists have dubbed Jungang-ro and the surrounding sections of Myeongdong-ro

with a high concentration of cosmetics stores "*kozumeroudo*," a word that combines "cosmetics" (*kozume*) and "road" (*roudo*).

The official address of *kozumeroudo* is Myeongdong 8-gil, Seoul. It stretches
for about 300 meters between Myeongdong Station on the number four line of
the Seoul Metro and Myeongdong Theater. From 500,000 to 1,000,000 visitors
come to Myeongdong every year, making it the most touristed spot in all of
Korea. As the majority of Myeongdong visitors stroll along this street, the exposure for stores on Cosmetics Street is enormous. Myeongdong real estate agents
refer to the street as "Golden Road."

The rent for ground-level stores in the area is exorbitant, ranging from ₩100
to 200 million per month for spaces between roughly 200 to 230 square meters.
The rent for the Nature Republic World Shop, a landmark on Cosmetics Street, is
₩150 million and required a ₩3.2 billion deposit. The price of the 169.3 square
meters of land the shop stands on reached ₩6.23 million per square meter in
2009, making it the property with the highest official assessed value in the nation.
"Rent is rising as brands compete for space," said one Myeongdong real estate
agent whose agency is simply named "Real Estate." "Monthly sales on Cosmetics Street reach upwards of ₩5 billion. Since cosmetics brands will rent out an
entire three-story building, landlords prefer them as tenants."

Brands have not disclosed revenue figures for their Cosmetics Street stores.
The public relations department at Amore Pacific, which has both a company-
managed store and a franchise outlet there, told *Chosun Weekly* that corporate
regulations prevented them from divulging individual stores' sales figures. Industry insiders offer estimates of ₩5–6 billion per month.

Cosmetics shops, however, do not make up a large part of Myeongdong as
a whole. According to Kim Seon-ah's 2010 study, "An Hourly Analysis of High-
traffic Areas in Myeongdong," 29% of the district's real estate is devoted to office
buildings. The 76 cosmetics stores make up only 2.8% of the total. Nonetheless,
most cosmetics stores are located at street level and are recognized as the liveli-
est businesses in Myeongdong. Furthermore, the ratio of those located on main
thoroughfares exceeds that of other types of business. "Jungang-ro, the central
commercial district in Myeongdong, has long been a golden goose," said Professor Lee Ho-byeong at Dankook University Graduate School of Real Estate and
Construction. "Stores on the ground floor have especially high visibility, even
compared to those on the second floor."

November 17, 10 a.m. Myeongdong is already bustling with foreign tourists.
On average about 10 customers can be seen browsing in each store. After lunch,
the customers flock in. By four in the afternoon, up to 50 customers crowd each
store. "Many people travel over weekends, so Friday through Sunday afternoon is
the busiest time of the week," said one staff member at Innisfree. "Even on weekdays, we have a constant stream of customers until 10 in the evening." The worker
also added, "The majority of our foreign customers used to be Japanese, but Chinese customers have been coming in greater numbers over the last two years.
These days, I'd say the ratio is half and half." Cosmetics industry insiders agree
that the Chinese now purchase more Korean cosmetics than the Japanese. Kim
Dae-su, a real estate broker based in Myeongdong, said, "Foreigners seem to be
propping up Myeongdong these days. I heard they account for 60–70% of sales."

According to a joint research project conducted in September by the Korea Chamber of Commerce and Industry (chairman, Son Gyeong-sik) and Hana Tour (president, Kwon Hee-seok) called "Shopping Patterns of Chinese and Japanese Tourists," cosmetics were the item Chinese tourists bought most frequently; 86.9% of Chinese tourists and 75.3% of Japanese tourists said they bought cosmetics. The Korea Chamber of Commerce and Industry reported, "As quality of life rises in China, cosmetics and other fashion products are becoming popular with visiting Chinese shoppers."

Diao Ling (34) stands in front of a cosmetics store in Myeongdong clutching three shopping bags containing beauty products she purchased for herself and friends back in China. "Korean cosmetics are multi-functional and less sticky than the ones we make," she said. "Besides, they're cheap [compared to prices in China], so I plan to buy as much as possible." Avery Ching (28) from Singapore said, "The tints of Korean cosmetics are very appealing. I have to go to a department store to get Korean products in Singapore, but they're at regular shops here and cheaper."

Hallyu also seems to play a major role in encouraging foreign customers to purchase cosmetics. Kim Hyo-jeong of Amore Pacific's public relations wing said, "As Korean dramas become more popular in China and Southeast Asia, women want to look like Song Hye-gyo, KARA, or Kim Hyun-jung. 'Flawless white skin' and 'sophisticated makeup' have become the ideal. In countries penetrated by *Hallyu*, the 'Made in Korea' label is held in very high regard."

"[Our competitors] draw foreign customers by offering CDs or posters of Korean celebrities with purchases," said one Tony Moly staff member who works at the Myeongdong branch. "Some *Hallyu* fans buy cosmetics to get these free gifts."

What are the most popular products among foreign customers? "Our products tend to do very well across the board, but customers ask for basic skin care products such as toner, lotion, and cleansing oil, rather than makeup," answered a clerk at The Face Shop. Choi Su-yeong at the Myeongdong Tourist Information Center said, "Tourists in their twenties and thirties generally look for the relatively cheap road shops like Laneige, Hanskin, and Missha, while those in their forties and fifties are after Sulwhasoo from Lotte Department Store."

Competition for foreign customers on Myeongdong's "Cosmetics Street" is fierce. "There's intense rivalry among stores to recruit staff who can speak Chinese and Japanese," said one employee. "Sometimes they scout clerks from other stores and try to lure them with a higher salary." Stores also offer limited edition products for tourists visiting Korea during the winter holiday season and put together special deals for Chinese customers who like to buy in bulk. In October, Nature Republic's Myeongdong branch hired 30 extra Mandarin-speaking employees to wait on Chinese travelers during their National Day holidays.

With its rising marketability, Myeongdong has lately been included in many Seoul itineraries as an attraction. "Many Japanese tourists enjoy DIY tours, so we've included Myeongdong in our Seoul itinerary for them," said Jeong Gi-yun of Hana Tour's public relations department. "There's no guided tour of Myeongdong, but many of our customers wish to shop there, so we typically plan half a day for it in our schedules." According to a Korean Chamber of Commerce and Industry report on shopping patterns of Chinese and Japanese tourists, Myeongdong is the top attraction in Seoul for Japanese, and second for Chinese.

The "Report on Foreign Tourists in Seoul, 2011," released by the city in September, notes that Myeongdong is the most popular tourist site for visitors, with 55.1% including it in a survey that allowed multiple responses. Next came Namdaemun Market (42.3%) and Insadong (39.9%). A Taiwanese visitor to Myeongdong noted, "Since Namsangol Hanok Village, Namdaemun, Myeongdong, and Insadong are near one another, I was able to visit them all in a single day." The report also revealed that cosmetic stores are becoming a new tourist attraction and that 26.5% of respondents said they wished to visit cosmetics stores in Seoul.

Change came to Myeongdong's Cosmetics Street on November 11. Uniqlo, an SPA brand (Specialty Retailer of Private Label Apparel, that is, a retailer that manufactures and supplies its own clothing lines) launched its Myeongdong branch at the southern end of Jungang-ro and thus became a new local landmark. This flagship store of 3,966 square meters, largest in Asia and second largest Uniqlo outlet in the world, symbolizes the brand's value. Other domestic and foreign SPA brands such as Zara, SPAO, and Forever 21 were introduced to Myeongdong from 2005, but the Uniqlo outlet is the first of such scale.

The morning of November 14. A small group of 20 gathers in front of this flagship outlet of Uniqlo and queues to enter 10 minutes before opening, at 11:30 a.m. Of this group, 70% are foreigners. According to Uniqlo's public relations team, "We took into consideration foreign demand when we chose Myeongdong, Korea's most famous shopping district, for our flagship store. SPA brands keep their prices broadly similar all over the world, but there may be price differences for individual items. Some foreign tourists come to shop here with that in mind." A staffer at Yangji Real Estate in Myeongdong said, "The large SPA brands and other noted clothing lines are changing the local flavor. Cosmetics stores still dominate, but the introduction of brand-name stores of different enterprises will ultimately create a synergy in sales figures."

Appendix

1. ENGLISH TITLES AND KOREAN EQUIVALENTS

1.1. Events and Organizations

English	Korean
Advisory Committee for the Promotion of Hallyu	한류문화진흥자문위원회
Broadcast Video Content Export Support Center	방송영상물 수출지원센터
Broadcast Worldwide	국제방송영상견본시인
Copyright Commission Officers	저작권 센터
Corea Entertainment Management Association	한국연예매니지먼트협회
Culture and Information Officers	문화홍보관
East Asia Investment/Export Consultation Fair	동아시아 투자수출 상담회
Export Gaming Publisher Invitational Consultation Fair	게임 퍼블리셔 초청 수출 상담회
Fair Trade Commission	공정거래위원회
Federation of Korean Industries	전국경제인연합회
Foundation for Korean Language and Culture	한국어진흥재단
Global Culture Industry Forum	글로벌 문화산업 포럼
Government Information Agency	국정홍보처
Hallyu Culture Promotion Taskforce	한류문화진흥단
Institute for Research on Collaborationist Activities	민족문제연구소
International Co-Production Support Taskforce	국제공동제작지원단
International Culture Communications Forum	국제문화소통포럼
Korean Association of Trade and Industry	한국국제통상학회
Korea Broadcast Industry Promotional Agency	한국방송영상산업진흥원
Korea Broadcasting Institute	한국방송영상산업진흥원
Korea Center for Cooperation	한국공동관
Korea Chamber of Commerce and Industry	대한상공회의소
Korea Communications Commission	방송통신위원회
Korea Culture and Tourism Institute	한국문화관광연구원
Korean Cultural Centers	한국문화원
Korea Customs Service	관세청
Korean Education Center	한국교육원

English	Korean
Korea Entertainment Producer's Association	한국연예제작자협회
Korea Entertainment System Industry Association	한국첨단게임산업협회
Korean Film Council	영화진흥위원회
Korean Food Foundation	한식재단
Korea Foundation for Asian Culture Exchange	아시아문화산업교류재단
Korea Foundation for International Culture Exchange	국제문화산업교류재단
Korean Game Industry Agency	한국게임산업진흥원
Korean Game Industry Development Institute	한국게임산업개발원
Korea Independent Productions Association	독립제작사협회
Korea International Broadcasting Foundation	국제방송교류재단
Korea IT International Cooperation Agency	정보통신국제협력진흥원
Korea Press Foundation	한국언론진흥재단
Korean Publishing Research Institute	한국출판연구소
Korea Tourism Organization	한국관광공사
Korea Trade-Investment Promotion Agency	대한무역투자진흥공사
Ministry of Culture and Tourism	문화관광부 (1998–2008)
Ministry of Culture, Sports and Tourism	문화체육관광부 (2008–)
Ministry of Education	교육부 (2013–)
Ministry of Education & Human Resources Development	교육인적자원부 (2001–2007)
Ministry of Education, Science and Technology	교육과학기술부 (2008–2013)
Ministry of Foreign Affairs	외교부 (2013–)
Ministry of Foreign Affairs and Trade	외교통상부 (1998–2013)
Ministry of Knowledge Economy	지식경제부
National Institute for International Education	한국국제교육원
Overseas Copyright Promotion Center	해외저작권진흥센터
Overseas Copyright Protection Commission	해외저작권보호협의체
Overseas Koreans Foundation	재외동포재단
Presidential Advisory Council on Science and Technology	국가과학기술자문회의
Presidential Council on Intellectual Property	국가지식재산위원회
Presidential Council on National Branding	국가브랜드위원회
Party for Dokdo Protection	독도수호대
Prime Minister's Office	국무총리실
Public Affairs Officer	공보관
Support Center for Popular Culture Artists	대중문화예술인 지원센터
Video Content Export Support Center	영상물 수출지원센터
World Intellectual Property Organization	세계지식재산기구

1.2. Schemes, Systems, and Legislations

English	Korean
Korean Culture at Your Doorstep	찾아가는 문화원
Act on Education Support, etc., for Overseas Koreans	재외국민교육지원 등에 관한 법률
Act on Press Arbitration	언론중재법
Act on the Punishment of Acts of Arranging Sexual Traffic	성매매알선 등 행위의 처벌에 관한 법률
Act on Regulation of Amusement Businesses Affecting Public Morals	풍속 영업의 규제에 관한 법률
Act on Supporting the Popular Culture and Art Industry	대중문화예술산업 발전지원법
Asian Film Talent Internship	아시아 영화인력 초청 인턴십
Business Affairs of Licensed Real Estate Agents and Report of Real Estate Transactions Act	공인중개사의 업무 및 부동산 거래신고에 관한 법률
Cultural Content Industry Promotion Law	문화콘텐츠 진흥법
Content Export Information System	문화콘텐츠수출종합정보시스템
Enforcement Plan for the Promotion of the Content Industry	콘텐츠산업진흥 시행계획
Export Programming Reformatting Support Initiative	수출용 프로그램 재제작 지원 사업
Extended Collective Licensing System	확대된 집중허락제도
Financial Supervisory Service Data Analysis, Retrieval and Transfer System	금융감독원 전자공시시스템
Framework Act on Intellectual Property	지식재산기본법
Framework Act on the Promotion of Cultural Industries	문화산업진흥기본법
Housing Lease Protection Act	주택임대차보호법
Illegal Copyrights Obstruction Program	온라인 불법복제물 자동 검색 및 증거수집 시스템
Juvenile Protection Act	청소년 보호법
Korean Broadcast Video Content Overseas Distribution Project	한국방송영상물의 해외 보급 사업
Korean Film Academy Association Asian Scholarship Program	한국영화아카데미 아시아 장학 프로그램
Labor Standards Act	근로기준법
Master Plan for the Promotion of the Content Industry	콘텐츠산업진흥 기본계획
National Assembly of Korea	국회
Newspaper Act	신문법
One Center, One Trademark Program	1문화원 1대표사업
Overseas Co-production Support Project	해외공동제작 지원 사업
Overseas Copyright Protection Commission	해외저작권보호협의체
Overseas Exposition Attendance Support Project	해외 전시회 참가지원 사업

English	Korean
Presidential Council on Intellectual Property	국가지식재산위원회
Program Provider	방송채널 사용 사업자
Proposals for Budget and Fund Management	예산안 및 기금운용계획안
Standard Contract for Artists of Popular Culture	대중문화예술인 표준계약서
Support for Entry into New Markets Initiative	신규 시장 진출 지원
Talent Agency Registration System	연예기획사 등록제
Telecommunications Business Act	전기통신사업법
Value-Added Tax Act	부가가치세법

2. REFERENCES

Baek, Gang-nyeong (2004), "Korea Conquers Gaming World," *Weekly Chosun*, March 11, No. 1794, p. 35.

Baek, Seung-ah (2011), "The Three Emperors of K-Pop," *Monthly Jungang*, December, pp. 106–111.

Baek, Seung-hyuk (2012), *Talent Agency Registration System and Revitalization of Talent Management Industry: A Comparative Analysis of Korea and Japan*, KOCCA Focus: 2012–7, No. 55, July 10.

Byeon, Mi-young (2011), "K-Pop Drives Resurgence of the Korean Wave: Status and Challenges," KOCCA Focus: 2011–03, No. 31, March 15.

Choi, Heub (2004), "Yonsama Madness Unveiled," *Weekly Chosun*, Dec. 9, No. 1832, pp. 50–52.

Choi, Ho-yeol (2006), "Jang Nara, Empress of *Hallyu*, Crisscrosses China," *Shin Dong-A*, November, No. 566, pp. 385–396.

Government Information Agency (2013), *Korea: A Cultural Stronghold*, 10th Volume from *National Administration White Paper of President Lee Myung-bak's Government* (2008–2013).

Im, Jin-mo (2012), "PSY: One-Hit Wonder or First of Many K-Pop Hits?" *Shin Dong-A*, November, No. 638, pp. 400–405.

Im, Yong-wi (2006), "New Year's Party for Those Who Make *Hallyu* Shine: A Mexican Fan Event," *Dongpo Sinmun*, December 20. http://www.dongponews.net/news/article View.html?idxno = 9142.

Jang, Yong-seok (2013), "Park Attends 'K-Drama Party'… Watches Performance by K-Pop Contest Winners, Greets Hallyu Fan Cub… Bids Them Bonjour," *News 1*, November 4. http://news1.kr/articles/1389821.

Jo, Chang-wan (2008), "The Chinese Hate *Jewel in the Palace*?: The Error of Judging the Korea-China Relationship from Minor Distaste," *OhMyNews*, January 17. http://www.ohmynews.com/NWS_Web/view/at_pg.aspx?CNTN_CD = A0000814406.

Kim, Beom-su and Jeon Su-hyeon (2012), "The Truth behind *Hangeul* and the Cia-Cia?" *Hankook Ilbo*, October 18. http://news.hankooki.com/lpage/culture/201210/h2012101821405886330.htm.

Kim, Gyeong-min (2011), "Myeongdong 'Cosmetics Road' Today," *Weekly Chosun*, November 21, No. 2182, pp. 66–69.

Kim, Hye-yeong (2006), "The Korean Wave Laps American Shores," *Weekly Chosun*, Oct. 23, 2006, No. 1926, pp. 172–174.

Kim, Kyung-soo (2007), "Vietnamese Bride Dinh Thi Nguyen's Country Diary: Happy to Be Able to Watch Any Korean TV Drama Any Time," *Weekly Chosun*, May 14, No. 1954. http://weekly1.chosun.com/site/data/html_dir/2007/05/11/2007051100345.html.

Kim, Min-gyeong (2005), "Lead Us Not into Temptation," *Weekly Dong-A*, Kim Min-gyeong, May 10, No. 484, pp. 56–57.

Ko, Gyu-dae (2010), "The Reality of Idol Star Debuts in the US: Wonder Girls," *Shin Dong-A*, March, No. 606, pp. 396–403.

Ko, Jeong-min et al. (2012), *Hallyu Forever: The World Is Hallyu Style*, KOFICE *Hallyu Series V*.

KOCCA (2012), "Related Information Contents: *Hallyu*," *Content Industry Trends of 2011*.

KOCCA (2013), *US Content Industry Trends: Korean Dramas' Entry into the Latin American Market*, KOCCA US Office, November 8.

Kwon, Ho-young and Kim Young-su (2009), *Strategies and Policies for Propagating the Korean Wave: Broadcast Video Content*, KOCCA Research Report: 09–01, August.

Lee, Hyeong-seok (2014), "Shared Imaginings & Stories for the Global Village: 'K-Movies' as a Growth Engine," *Herald Economy*, January 24. http://news.heraldcorp.com/view.php?ud = 20140123000747&md = 20140124113457_AT.

Lee, Sae-saem (2011), "The Pororo Syndrome: *Hallyu*'s Brightest Star," *Dong-A Ilbo*, April 30. http://news.donga.com/3/all/20110430/36820969/1.

Lee, Seon-pil (2012), "Tokyo: Where Have All the *Hallyu* Fans Gone?" *OhMy News*, September 7. http://star.ohmynews.com/NWS_Web/OhmyStar/at_pg.aspx?CNTN_CD = A0001775960.

Lim, Mi-ok (2005), "A Firsthand Account of Hallyu Fever in Japan," *OhMyNews*, January 9. http://news.naver.com/main/read.nhn?mode = LSD&mid = sec&sid1 = 103&oid = 047&aid = 0000056289.

Ministry of Culture and Tourism (2006), *2006 Cultural Industry White Paper*.

Ministry of Culture, Sports and Tourism (2012), *2011 Cultural Content Industry White Paper*.

Ministry of Culture, Sports and Tourism (2013), *Hallyu White Paper*.

Park, Hee-seong and Nam Gyeong-hee (2006), *Film and the Korean Wave: Status and Policies for Promotion*, KOFIC Research Report 2006–1, Korean Film Council.

Seo, Jin-seok (2011), "'Squeal!' Baltic Students Fall for South Korean Idols: A Korean Culture Club Opens in Lithuanian Capital," *OhMyNews*, April 4. http://www.ohmynews.com/nws_web/view/at_pg.aspx?CNTN_CD = A0001546702.

Song, Hwa-sun (2011), "The World of Idols: Jumping Through Endless Hoops," *Shin Dong-A*, March, No. 618, pp. 396–403.

Wander Lust (2013), "Vietnam/Cambodia 17-day trip: *Hallyu* Grips Phnom Penh," Naver Blog, July 13. http://blog.naver.com/cmonkey1/120195218010.

Yun, Jae-sik (2007), *Initiatives to Overcome the 2007 Broadcast Hallyu Crisis*, KBI Focus 07–01, No. 21, Korean Broadcasting Institute, January 2.